What happens when a prestigious text of one period is read and re-used in a different, much later world? What can we learn from the annotations accumulated by a single manuscript as it moved among new institutions and readerships? In this study Christopher Baswell takes as his model Virgil's ancient epic poem *The Aeneid,* and the many kinds of appeal it held for the culture of the Middle Ages. He examines a series of Latin manuscripts of the text which were copied in twelfth-century England but re-used and re-annotated for three centuries, and shows how their users approached the epic in significantly varied ways. He then charts the epic narrative as it moves from the Latin of the original to the vernaculars of the *Roman d'Eneas* and Chaucer's *House of Fame* and *Legend of Good Women,* showing how medieval vernacular poets used Virgil's prestige to lay their own claim to poetic and even political authority.

CAMBRIDGE STUDIES IN MEDIEVAL LITERATURE 24

VIRGIL IN MEDIEVAL ENGLAND

This series of critical books seeks to cover the whole area of literature written
in the major medieval languages – the main European vernaculars, and
medieval Latin and Greek – during the period *c.* 1100–1500. Its chief aim is
to publish and stimulate fresh scholarship and criticism on medieval literature,
special emphasis being placed on understanding major works of poetry, prose
and drama in relation to the contemporary culture and learning which
fostered them.

Recent titles in the series
11 *Rhetoric, Hermeneutics and Translation in the Middle Ages: Academic traditions and
vernacular texts,* by Rita Copeland
12 *The Arthurian Romances of Chrétien de Troyes: Once and future fictions,* by Donald
Maddox
13 *Richard Rolle and the Invention of Authority,* by Nicholas Watson
14 *Dreaming in the Middle Ages,* by Steven F. Kruger
15 *Chaucer and the Tradition of the 'Roman Antique',* by Barbara Nolan
16 *The 'Romance of the Rose' and its Medieval Readers: Interpretation, reception,
manuscript transmission,* by Sylvia Huot
17 *Women and Literature in Britain, 1150–1500,* edited by Carol M. Meale
18 *Ideas and Forms of Tragedy from Aristotle to the Middle Ages,* by Henry Ansgar
Kelly
19 *The Making of Textual Culture: Grammatica and literary theory, 350–1100,* by
Martin Irvine
20 *Narrative Authority, and Power: The medieval exemplum and the Chaucerian tradition,*
by Larry Scanlon
21 *Medieval Dutch Literature in its European Context,* edited by Erik Kooper
22 *Dante and the Mystical Tradition: Bernard of Clairvaux in the 'Commedia,'* by
Steven Botterill
23 *Heresy and Literacy, 1000–1530,* edited by Peter Biller and Anne Hudson

VIRGIL IN MEDIEVAL ENGLAND

Figuring the Aeneid *from the twelfth century to Chaucer*

CHRISTOPHER BASWELL

Associate Professor of English
Barnard College, New York

CAMBRIDGE
UNIVERSITY PRESS

Barnard

PA
6825
.B38
1995
C1

Published by the Press Syndicate of the University of Cambridge
The Pitt Building, Trumpington Street, Cambridge, CB2 1RP
40 West 20th Street, New York, NY 10011–4211, USA
10 Stamford Road, Oakleigh, Melbourne 3166, Australia

© Cambridge University Press 1995

First published 1995

Printed in Great Britain at the University Press, Cambridge

A catalogue record for this book is available from the British Library

Library of Congress cataloguing in publication data
Baswell, Christopher
Virgil in medieval England: figuring the *Aeneid* from the twelfth
century to Chaucer / Christopher Baswell.
p. cm. – (Cambridge studies in medieval literature; 24)
Includes bibliographical references and indexes.
ISBN 0 521 46294 0 (hardback)
1. Virgil. Aeneis. 2. Manuscripts, Latin (Medieval and modern) – England – History.
3. Chaucer, Geoffrey, d. 1400 – Knowledge – Literature. 4. Epic poetry, Latin – Criticism,
Textual. 5. England – Intellectual life – 1066–1485. 6. English poetry – Roman influences.
7. Virgil – Appreciation – England. 8. Rome – In literature. 9. Rhetoric, Medieval. 10. Virgil –
Influence. I. Title. II. Series.
PA6825.B38   1995
873′.01 – dc20 94–12708 CIP

ISBN 0 521 46294 0 hardback

In memory of Kevin Echart

Contents

List of illustrations   Page xi
Preface   xiii
List of abbreviations   xvi
List of conventions   xix

Introduction   Manuscripts and their contexts   1
    1: Manuscripts and their contexts   5
    2: Three dominant visions of the *Aeneid*   9

1   *Auctor* to *Auctoritas:* Modes of access to Virgil in medieval
   England   15
    1: Authority and challenge: the context of redactions   17
    2: The visual context   21
    3: Textual access: manuscripts and beyond   30
    4: The persistence of Virgil in England   36

2   Pedagogical exegesis of Virgil in medieval England: Oxford,
   All Souls College 82   41
    1: Production, ownership, and history of All Souls 82   41
    2: Servius and the continuity of pedagogical exegesis   47
    3: The twelfth–century annotations: difference eroded   53
    4: "Anselm of Laon" and Servian tradition in the High Middle Ages   63
    5: Reconstructing difference in the later annotations   68
    6: Pedagogical exegesis, medieval and renaissance   80

3   Spiritual allegory, platonizing cosmology, and the Boethian
   Aeneid in medieval England: Cambridge, Peterhouse College,
   158   84
    1: Exegesis and its formats: from *glosae* to *commentum*   86
    2: Late Antique Virgilianism and medieval modes of allegorical
      interpretation   91
    3: The emergence of allegory   101
    4: Fabulizing Virgil: integumental reading and the power of the
      exegete   108

5: "Bernard" and Boethian reading of the *Aeneid*   120
6: Peterhouse 158 and classicism in High Medieval England   130

4   Moral allegory and the *Aeneid* in the time of Chaucer:
    London, BL Additional 27304   136
    1: "Platonizing" versus "moralizing" exegetics   136
    2: The early marginalia   139
    3: Commentary III, Norwich, and the Peasants' Revolt   143
    4: Pedagogical annotation in the Norwich Commentary   146
    5: Ethical example and Christian allegory in the Norwich
       Commentary   151
    6: The Norwich commentator as reader   159
    7: The Latin Virgilianisms of medieval England   164

5   The romance *Aeneid*   168
    1: Lavine at her book   168
    2: The clerk at his book   173
    3: Containing Dido   184
    4: History at the center: empire in the *Eneas*   200
    5: Lavine and containment through metonymy   210

6   Writing the reading of Virgil: Chaucerian authorities in the
    House of Fame and the *Legend of Good Women*   220
    1: Aeneas and Geffrey as hermeneutic heroes   223
    2: Decentering authority in *House of Fame* I   230
    3: Allegorical Virgilianism in *House of Fame* II and III   236
    4: Geffrey in the circles of narrative, cosmos, and hermeneutics 244
    5: Authority: tyranny versus dialogue in the Prologue to the
       Legend of Good Women   249
    6: The temptation of authority in the "Legend of Dido"   255

Conclusion   Envoi, to the Renaissance: Books of Aeneas and
              of Dido   270

Appendices   285
    I   Manuscripts of Virgil written or owned in England during the
        Middle Ages   285
    II Doubtful, rejected, and ghost manuscripts   309
    III Glosses to Boethius at *Aeneid* 6.719 in Oxford, All Souls 82 311
    IV The *Aeneid*–accessus of "Anselm of Laon"   313

Notes   315
Select bibliography   410
Index of manuscripts   423
Index of names and selected subjects   425

Illustrations

1   Paris, Bibliothèque Nationale, fr. 60, fo. 148 *recto* (*Roman
    d'Eneas*)   *page* 27
2   Oxford, All Souls College 82, fo. 36 *recto*, opening of *Aeneid*   43
3a Cambridge, Peterhouse College 158, fo. 42 *verso*   88
3b Cambridge, Peterhouse College 158, fo. 43 *recto*   89
4   Cambridge, Peterhouse College 158, fo. 167 *verso*–169 *recto*   90
5   London, British Library, Additional 27304, fo. 5 *recto*   140
6   Oxford, Bodleian Library, printed book Wood 106, *verso* of
    wrapper and frontispiece   284

Preface

This book has been the object of so much kind interest and of so much generous help that it ought really to have a corporate author on the title page. My obligations to institutions, fellow scholars, and long–suffering friends are many, so many indeed that I am certain to forget some in the names that follow. To any unacknowledged helpers I add my apologies to my thanks.

Time and travel for initial research and writing came from a Fulbright–Hays Scholarship to Oxford and the Warburg Institute, and later from the American Philosophical Society, the American Council of Learned Societies, and a Special Assistant Professor Leave from Barnard College. Manuscript collections across Europe made their holdings available to me, and coped cheerfully with the special complications posed by a researcher who moves about in a wheelchair. All except one.

Three great teachers introduced me to classical and medieval studies: Marcia Colish, Nathan Greenberg, and Robert Longsworth. Their instruction and example have had a direct impact on the book I now publish, two decades after their tutelage. Three graduate professors were equally important as I began thinking about the role of classicism in medieval culture: Alice Miskimin, Marie Borroff, and Thomas Greene. The latter two directed the doctoral dissertation on which the present book is in part based.

Other scholars have provided help and encouragement as the book took shape, and did so out of no greater obligation than friendship and good will. Individual chapters and sections have been read, and always improved, by Elizabeth Archibald, John Boswell, Virginia Brown, Abigail Freedman, M. Victoria Guerin, James Hankins, Ralph Hexter, Mary Louise Lord, Sandra Pierson Prior, M. Alison Stones, and Marjorie Curry Woods. My colleagues at Barnard College have all shown warm interest in my work; Anne Prescott and Ruth Kivette lent their learning to several chapters; and Celeste Schenck and William Sharpe have been unflagging in their willingness to read and listen.

Many friends in and out of the academy have taken on the even more grueling tasks of simple encouragement and patience, especially April Bernard, Ann Birstein, Catherine Doty, Candyce Golis, Peter Holliday, Daniel Kiefer, and Jane Sarnoff. Judy Karasik and the late W. Duncan Stalker brought their skills as professional editors, as well as scholars, to various parts of the book, and did their best to make me be a writer.

Alastair Minnis offered enthusiastic encouragement when this book was only beginning to take shape. Katharina Brett, at Cambridge University Press, has been a skilled and patient editor. Above all, I am in the debt of Winthrop Wetherbee, who has read practically every word in the book, some in several revises, and who brought his vast learning, his critical eye, and his great kindness to every stage in its progress. Penelope Reed Doob has shown equal goodness as the book made its slow way out of the labyrinth of research and revision. Scholars like these prove to me how humane the academic study of the humanities can be.

Two major books appear too late for substantial inclusion in the chapters that follow. Barbara Nolan, *Chaucer and the Tradition of the Roman Antique* (Cambridge: Cambridge University Press, 1992), complements and enriches my study in several ways. Nolan includes the full Trojan and Theban narratives that are the background to my Virgilian focus; and she addresses their versions by Boccaccio, so crucial to the fourteenth century in England. My writing was completed before her book reached me, but I have been able to add footnote references to lead my readers to relevant parts of her important work. Marilynn Desmond's *Reading Dido: Textuality and the Medieval "Aeneid"* (University of Minnesota Press), announced but not yet in print as this book goes to press, will make a significant addition to current work on the subject.

Finally, I am enormously grateful to the National Humanities Center, which offered me shelter, encouragement, incomparable bibliographic services, and the company of great minds during the final preparation of this manuscript and its production as a book.

A book that stays with its author as long as this carries an inevitable burden of loss. I wish I could still express directly my obligations to scholars and to friends no longer alive: Richard W. Hunt, Neil R. Ker, T. Julian Brown, W. Duncan Stalker, and especially to the dedicatee.

Kevin Echart was a wonderful intellectual companion in the years during which I began research on medieval Virgilianism. It is a shame that a drunk driver stopped him from reading this book that he so greatly helped; it is a matter of endless sadness, and anger, that Kevin's many friends and colleagues can never read the books he would have written himself.

Abbreviations

AL	*Anthologia Latina*, eds. Francis Buechler and Alexander Riese, I.1 and I.2 (Leipzig: Teubner, 1894, 1906; repr. Amsterdam: Hakkert, 1964).
"Allegorization"	Christopher Baswell, "The Medieval Allegorization of the 'Aeneid': MS Cambridge, Peterhouse 158," *Traditio* 41 (1985): 181–237.
Allessio	Gian Carlo Allessio, "Tradizione manoscritta," in the article "Medioevo," *Enciclopedia Virgiliana*, general ed. Francesco della Corte (Rome: Istituto della Enciclopedia Italiana, 1987), III, pp. 432–43.
Baehrens	Emil Baehrens, *Poetae Latini Minores* (Leipzig: Teubner, 1882), IV.
Bayer	"Vergil–Viten," ed. Karl Bayer, in *Vergil Landleben*, ed. Johannes and Maria Götte (Munich: Heimeran, 1977), pp. 211–421, 654–764.
Comparetti	Domenico Comparetti, *Vergil in the Middle Ages*, trans. E. F. M. Benecke (London: Swan Sonnenschein, 1895).
Courcelle I	Pierre Courcelle, *Lecteurs païens et lecteurs chrétiens de l'Énéide*, I: *Les témoignages littéraires*, Mémoires de l'Académie des inscriptions et belles-lettres, Nouvelle série 4 (Paris: Institut de France, 1984).
Courcelle II	Pierre Courcelle and Jeanne Courcelle, *Lecteurs païens et lecteurs chrétiens de l'Énéide*, II: *Les manuscrits illustrés de l'Énéide du Xe au XVe siècle*, Mémoires de l'Académie des inscriptions et belles-lettres, Nouvelle série 4 (Paris: Institut de France, 1984).
Emden, *BRUC*	A. B. Emden, *A Biographical Register of the University*

	of Cambridge to 1500 (Cambridge University Press, 1963).
Emden, *BRUO*	A. B. Emden, *A Biographical Register of the University of Oxford to A.D. 1500* (Oxford University Press, 1957–59).
Enciclopedia I, II, III, IV,V1,V2	*Enciclopedia Virgiliana*, general ed. Francesco della Corte (Rome: Istituto della Enciclopedia Virgiliana), I (1984), II (1985), III (1987), IV (1988), V part 1 (1990), V part 2 (1991).
English Friars	Beryl Smalley, *English Friars and Antiquity in the Early Fourteenth Century* (Oxford: Basil Blackwell, 1960).
Hexter	Ralph J. Hexter, *Ovid and Medieval Schooling. Studies in Medieval School Commentaries on Ovid's "Ars Amatoria," "Epistulae ex Ponto," and "Epistulae Heroidum,"* Münchener Beiträge zur Mediävistik und Renaissance-Forschung 38 (Munich: Arbeo–Gesellschaft, 1986).
Jones and Jones	*The Commentary on the First Six Books of the "Aeneid" Commonly Attributed to Bernard Silvestris*, ed. Julian Ward Jones and Elizabeth Frances Jones (Lincoln, Nebr.: University of Nebraska Press, 1977).
Lectures	*Lectures médiévales de Virgile*, Collection de l'école fraņaise de Rome 80 (Rome: École fraņaise de Rome, 1985).
MCLBV	Elisabeth Pellegrin, Jeaninne Fohlen, *et al.*, *Les manuscrits classiques latins de la Bibliothèque Vaticane* (Paris: Éditions du CNRS, 1975–82), I, II, III.1 and III.2.
Munk Olsen	Birger Munk Olsen, *L'Étude des auteurs classiques latins aux XIe et XIIe sicles*, II: *Catalogue des manuscrits classiques latins copiés du IXe au XII siècle: Livius-Vitruvius* (Paris: Éditions du CNRS, 1985).
Murgia	Charles Murgia, *Prolegomena to Servius 5: The Manuscripts* (Berkeley, Calif.: University of California Press, 1975).
Niermeyer	J. F. Niermeyer, *Mediae Latinitatis lexicon minus* (Leiden: Brill, 1984).
Pattie	T. S. Pattie, "Latin Manuscripts of Virgil in the

	British Library," Appendix 1 in R. D. Williams and T. S. Pattie, *Virgil: His Poetry through the Ages* (London: British Library, 1982), pp. 125–38.
Présence	*Présence de Virgile: Actes du Colloque des 9, 11, et 12 Décembre 1976*, ed. R. Chevallier, *Caesarodunum* XIII bis, Numéro spécial (Paris: Les Belles lettres, 1978).
Suerbaum	Werner Suerbaum, "Hundert–Jahre Vergil–For-schung: Eine systematische Arbeits–bibliographie mit besonderer Berüchsichtigung der Aeneis," in *Aufstieg und Niedergang der Römischen Welt*, part 2, gen. eds. H. Temporini and W. Haase; XXXII.1, ed. W. Haase (Berlin and New York: De Gruyter, 1981), part F, "Nachleben und Nachwirkung," pp. 284–358.
T&T	*Texts and Transmission: A Survey of the Latin Classics*, ed. L. D. Reynolds (Oxford: Clarendon Press, 1983).
Thilo/Hagen	*Servii Grammatici qui feruntur in Vergilii carmina commentarii*, ed. Georg Thilo and Hermann Hagen, 3 vols. (Leipzig: Teubner, 1881–84; repr. Hildesheim: Georg Olms, 1961).
Vitae	*Vitae Vergilianae*, ed. Iacobus Brummer (Leipzig: Teubner, 1912).
Walther	Hans Walther, *Initia carminum ac versuum medii aevi posterioris latinorum. Alphabetisches Verzeichnis der Versanfänge mittellateinischer Dichtungen* (2nd ed., Göttingen: Vandenhoeck & Ruprecht, 1969).

All quotations of Virgil are taken from the edition of R. A. B. Mynors (Oxford: Clarendon, 1986) unless otherwise noted. Translations are from *The Aeneid of Virgil*, trans. Allen Mandelbaum (New York: Bantam, 1980) unless otherwise noted.

Conventions

In quotations from unpublished Latin sources:

< >   identifies editorial addition

[ ]   identifies editorial exclusion, explanation, or reference

\ /   identifies text inserted in the manuscript original

( )   identifies expansion of an abbreviation; most abbreviations are expanded silently

(...) identifies illegible letters

Proper names will be spelled as in the language under discussion, unless this will cause undue confusion: Aeneas in Virgil's Latin, for instance, but Eneas in Chaucer.

Manuscripts and their contexts

From the moment of its writing, Virgil's *Aeneid* has evoked a ceaseless dialogue in western culture. His epic records a preeminent story of racial movement and imperial foundation in the Mediterranean, from Troy to Rome. From that story, be it considered myth or history, dynasties and empires across Europe and the New World have drawn their models, their genealogies, their justifications for two millennia. But this only begins the impact of Virgil and of his epic. Patronized by the Emperor Augustus, Virgil was quickly revered as a master of Latin style in a culture where elegant Latinity was a gateway to political power. The classroom study of Virgil elucidated, and often generated, a density of recondite learning within the *Aeneid* that only expanded as the centuries passed. Virgil's story, his style, and his learning all become part of the dialogue – sometimes the debate – that at once enacts, challenges, and extends his prestige in later European civilization.

This is a book about books, about manuscripts of Virgil and particularly their margins as a crucial site of cultural contest and cultural recreation. In turn, it is a book about vernacular retellings of the *Aeneid* that are the products and extensions of these readerly dialogues in the Virgilian margin. My investigation centers on a particularly rich era in this ongoing dialogue: the high and later Middle Ages in Anglo-Norman and English culture. This period and place begin with the emergence of a new European empire in the reign of Henry II, explicitly connected by genealogy and emulation to the people of the *Aeneid*; and it ends with a new language, English, challenging the prestige and power of Latin, and doing so in subtle contest with Virgil, as later chapters will show. Many of the book's arguments are applicable, moreover, to Virgilian reading and redaction across Europe; and I will claim, in a closing "Envoi," that the Virgilian debate of the Middle Ages extends its terms to vernacular writers of the English Renaissance.

1

As an epic narrator, a model of Latin style, a master of obscure learning, even as an adept of religious arcana, Virgil was uncontested from late antiquity onward. What did become a matter of contest was which of these qualities should predominate in any reading and interpretation of the *Aeneid*. Connected to this variable emphasis within the learned tradition was the variety of audiences laying claim to Virgil's cultural prestige, his approbation of empire, and the power of his language. These audiences compete within and across periods: clerics or laymen, men or women, aristocrats or townspeople. Manuscripts of the *Aeneid* record the moment and setting of their creation, of course, but equally important, their marginal annotations and other added material record their use across centuries and the modes or classes of readership the manuscripts encountered in their own cultural journeys. Vernacular retellings in turn inherit the themes and, to some extent, the qualities of dialogue inherent in the Latin marginalia; more importantly, they mark the movement of Virgilian prestige into new, less Latinate hands.

Beyond the dense record of its manuscript margins and the explosive moment of crossing into the vernacular, Virgil's *Aeneid* was part of two other kinds of ongoing contest, both of which need to be considered at the outset. First, any pagan writer, but especially a pagan writer who dealt with the gods, had to be the object of ambivalence in a Christian world. This ambivalence was only the more intense in regard to Virgil because of his stylistic prestige in what remained a Latin culture. Second, whatever his eloquence, Virgil told lies, about the gods and about history. Even while its cultural and linguistic cachet remained undimmed, there grew up around the *Aeneid* a constellation of counter-traditions, some dealing with its paganism, and others offering alternate stories of Troy and Rome. Chapter 1 surveys some of these counter-traditions, as they at once contest and thereby acknowledge the authority of Virgil. From this perspective, these alternate approaches are themselves marginal contests.

The ambivalent rejection and reverence of the *Aeneid* so deeply ramify Christian Latin culture that they defy survey. Two opening anecdotes, though, may suggest the range of reaction. Both stories typify points of ambivalent reverence toward the figure of Virgil in their time – points that stand constantly, though in the distance, behind the multiple English Virgilianisms explored in the following chapters.

The first story is from the twelfth century, and comes not from

England, but from its Norman milieu, in a manuscript originally from the monastery of Aulne in Belgium.[1] The manuscript contains a miscellaneous collection of monastic texts, among them the cautionary tale of two clerks, great friends and dangerously eager in the study of pagan literature. One dies, and as he had promised on his deathbed, returns as a spirit – "a cinder-like shadow" – to visit his friend. The dead man explains that he is in hell because, although he had confessed and taken the eucharist before his death, he had done so unwillingly. The surviving master is singularly unsympathetic. Instead, he wants to know if his dead friend has met Virgil. He has: "Alas! Wretch that I am, I see and know him and he is with me in suffering, because I always frivolously lingered with him among his tales of nonsense."[2] The survivor is delighted with this news, and insists that his friend go back to Virgil and ask what was meant in two particular verses. The spirit agrees. But in leaving he places a single drop of his sweat on his friend's brow, to give some infinitesimal sense of the pains of hell. This burns through to the survivor's very bones; he is in agony. Finally the spirit returns and tells him to wash the wound in holy water.

But the master asked what Virgil had answered, to which the dead man responded, "When I asked him about what you had imposed on me, Virgil said, 'How stupid you and your questions are!' And know this for certain: unless you renounce the tales of the *auctores* and the frivolities of the liberal arts, and cling fast to evangelical truth, sooner than you hope you will endure with him the ruin of eternal perdition."[3]

The surviving master is restored by the holy water, and duly renounces the world.

Leclercq, who discovered and edited this story, speaks of its twofold injunction: to stop reading the poets and to enter the religious life. But the text contains an arresting irony. For the apparition is based in some detail on an episode in the very text it rejects: *Aeneid* 2, when the dead Hector appears to his comrade Aeneas and warns him to flee the burning of Troy (2.268–97). Hector too appears in a dark and frightening aspect. Like the monastic spirit, Hector's first sound is a great sigh. Both apparitions end by warning the living men to flee from the certain death (and fire) of their present circumstances, and to save themselves by embracing their deity. The monk must cling to evangelical truth; Aeneas must seize the Trojan gods as the partners and protectors of his fate. And in a less exact way, practically any report of a descent to hell must bring Virgil to a medieval reader's mind.

This seems an almost perfect example of Virgil's profound but vexatious hold over the medieval Christian imagination. An explicit rejection of pagan literary interests is inextricably bound, by language and associations, to a famous Virgilian episode. Whatever their theoretical hostility to the moral impact of pagan literature, medieval writers of Latin are tied to its greatest antique exponent, and their literary imagination inescapably draws from him. Trying to dismiss Virgil in Latin is, almost unavoidably, like trying to use words to enjoin silence.[4]

The second Virgilian anecdote comes from England, in a passage from the early thirteenth-century *Ars Poetica* by Gervase of Melkley.[5] Gervase is speaking about the rhetorical figure *antonomasia*, the use of an epithet in place of a proper noun. "This usage must always denote a certain preeminence, as in this case: one says 'The Apostle,' that is to say, Paul; 'The Poet,' that is to say, Virgil."[6] This brief, apparently casual reference is intriguing for its collocation of Virgil and St. Paul, two preeminent models of eloquence named here in the context of teaching the simpler mechanics of that eloquence. Gervase's reference, further, evokes the context of rhetorical and poetic pedagogy which we will encounter repeatedly in the annotation of Virgil throughout the Middle Ages.

The medieval connection of scriptural and Roman authors is not merely rhetorical, however. The same association elsewhere recalls a profound uncertainty as to whether Virgil is not just an instance of imitable verbal power, but also a source of historical truth. In the allegorical vision which opens the fourteenth-century *Scalacronica* by Sir Thomas Gray of Heaton, Sir Thomas dreams of a ladder whose uprights rise from two books. A Sibyl explains to him that one is the Bible, the other is the Troy story, and that the ladder's steps are the eras of history.[7] Yet this passage, like Gervase's reference, is symptomatic of implicit and widespread tensions in the reception of the *Aeneid*, between the continued evocative power of Virgil's pagan narrative ("*the* poet," and the leading secular historian of Sir Thomas's Troy) on the one hand, and on the other hand efforts to use the language taught through Virgil as a transparent medium and methodology in the service of Christian rhetoric.

Virgil's book – whether it is the central object of basic classroom study, of monkish fascination, or the foundation text for the worldly empires of Sir Thomas Gray's history – remains an almost irresistible model. Interpretation, imitation, alteration, and even rejection of that book are inevitably carried out in its own terms and often in the setting of its own stories. Whether acknowledging Virgil's centrality or challenging his truth and his faith, medieval writers repeatedly if unwillingly and even unconsciously find themselves writing in his margins. It is to such margins, literal and metaphorical, that this book addresses itself.

Two other books of Virgil, his *Eclogues* and *Georgics*, are left aside in what follows. While frequently accompanying the *Aeneid* in manuscripts of his works, the *Eclogues* and *Georgics* were less read than the *Aeneid* in medieval England.[8] The *Eclogues* did have a vital tradition, but were most actively read and annotated in collections and situations separate from the epic of Rome.[9] The *Georgics*, while not a rare text, were still less frequently read; indeed even in complete manuscripts of Virgil, the pages containing the *Georgics* remain the cleanest and least damaged, a testimony to their relative neglect.[10] For all their prestige and importance, neither of the earlier works had the topical appeal or the combination of stylistic model and ethnic history, that medieval European readers encountered in the *Aeneid*.

MANUSCRIPTS AND THEIR CONTEXTS

Especially in the examination of Latin tradition, but also when the book turns to vernacular retellings of the *Aeneid*, I will approach my material largely through its manuscripts – the specific codex with its many signs and inscriptions beyond the original central text, and with its own archeology resulting, often, from centuries of changing use. Indeed, I will argue that the challenge of the book itself comes to rival the Trojan narrative as a model for heroic vision and action in the later medieval Virgil.

A study of medieval English Virgilianism through its manuscripts can help us suspend certain assumptions about textuality and its boundaries, and in particular, our tendency to distinguish between the book (the concrete, historical, local manifestation of a work of literature) and its text (that abstract, finally theoretical phenomenon in which we imagine an author's original words, even an author's "intention"). This kind of distinction had only a limited role in the intellectual activities of medieval readers.[11] In fact, a conjunction of book and text – or at least an unstable frontier between them – is suggested by the tendency among medieval translators to include not only the "primary" text, but also parts of its surrounding commentaries. For instance, in the *Roman d'Eneas*, the translator seems to be responding to a widely found marginal note in his decision to tell the story of the Judgment of Paris.[12] We will return in chapter 5 to other codicological influences on the structure and detail of this romance. Much better known is the example of Chaucer, whose *Boece* unites Latin text and gloss, as well as French.[13] This absorption of framing materials into the translation – the insistent centripetal movement of the margins toward the center – suggests the extent to which textuality in the Middle Ages has vague and fluid limits, only beginning with the *auctor*'s words, and not necessarily ending even with the book itself.[14]

At the same time, by concentrating on manuscripts, with all their texts and other signs, as central transmitters of medieval Virgilianism, it should be easier to acknowledge the many agents beyond authorial intention that participate in the production of meaning. In a codicological setting where text and commentary form a functional whole, an original text is inevitably extended at each stage of annotation to include the intentions of its readers. As the *Pearl*-Poet says, it is the book which speaks: "The bok as I herde say..."[15] In such a phrase, the implied source of meaning resides in the concrete if ever-shifting phenomenon, the *codex*, far more than in some absent, personal *auctor*, or his originally intended text.

In the tradition of school introductions (*accessus*) to the works of Virgil, authorial intention is indeed regularly mentioned, but it is most often biographical rather than literary or ethical. In the most important allegorical commentary of the Middle Ages, Virgil is said to have praised Aeneas's acts "so that he might earn the favor of Augustus."[16] The same commentator says that Virgil also "taught the truth of philosophy,"[17] but the problem of intentional meaning is left behind when the allegorical interpretation actually begins.[18]

Even more important, an approach through the manuscripts, and using the resources of codicology, will encourage a recovery of the medieval *Aeneid* not as a monolithic entity, but as a series of historical phenomena, individual concrete events whose meanings are indeed conditioned by the language of the text, but simultaneously by an elaborate matrix of annotative and sometimes visual reinscription on the page. This in turn reflects the shifting institutional and historical situation of the book. Medieval schoolbooks record not just the efforts of their original scribes, but also those of ensuing generations of reader/writers who inscribe their own difficulties and responses – and those of their masters – between the lines and in the margins. These books, with their multiplying layers of annotation, become new and altered wholes to be encountered or resisted by yet another generation of reader/writers, until the codex wears out or is put aside in favor of a fresher copy or alternate tradition of exegesis.

But the readerly experience produced by the more heavily annotated medieval codices is not always one of comfortable acceptance. The redactor of the *Roman d'Eneas* selects with self-conscious wit from the learned material that accompanied twelfth-century study of the *Aeneid*. Readers of the late Middle Ages and early Renaissance sometimes reject the encrustation of annotations in the most overt fashion, by erasing some of them.[19] Other readers respond with real anguish to the excess of multiple and at times conflicting senses that so intimately, even inextricably, accumulate around the *auctores*. Both Chaucer and Douglas will claim to escape these conflicting, even excessive senses, and offer instead what Chaucer calls a "naked text." But as we will see, this claim is subverted in the shifting responses of Chaucer's narrator. And in Douglas the text is presented nakedly only by being framed with Prologues as multiple and varied as anything in the codicological tradition.

Through such an approach, then, taking account where possible of the changing historical and institutional setting of these manuscripts, we can see them as potential sites of contest between conflicting readerly groups, preoccupations, and demands. Any text as central to cultural and political self-conception as was the medieval *Aeneid* will have competing claims laid upon it; and the contested control of the epic – a battle fought in the margins and redactions studied here – takes on implications that are themselves cultural and political. Different readerly settings will inscribe around the *Aeneid* conflicting models of imitation (allegorical and spiritual, historical and political) and conflicting narrative emphases (academic, moral, erotic, imperial, genealogical).

Manuscripts, the protean forms they present and the commentaries they bear, however, provide no instant or final key to the past of the past. They are not, and must not be misunderstood as, some irreducible datum; and however comforting such an idea may be to our positivist nostalgia, attention to them will not generate the true, direct, empirical "medieval reading of Virgil." Manuscripts too must be interpreted; some past reading must be inferred from them, and any such scholarly alchemy will deform the moment it seeks, even as it reconstitutes that moment. There are, moreover, many alternate manifestations, beyond manuscripts and the archeology of their inscribed readings, of the multiple medieval Virgilianisms I hope to describe in this book. The bulk of chapter 1 will suggest the variety and impact of the Virgils that can be said to exist even in the *absence* of full textual access: library records, anthologies, prose summaries, citations in school texts, illustrations. Manuscripts do provide the most intensive local record of specific acts of reading, then, but these in turn must be understood in the context of that yet greater range of ideas and materials allowed by the wide limits of medieval notions of literary and interpretive relevance.[20]

Chapters 2 through 4 focus on the progressive encrustation of marginalia and separate commentaries in just three richly annotated manuscripts originating in twelfth-century England. Each of these, I will argue, typifies a major strand – respectively pedagogical, allegorical, and moral – in the multiple approaches practiced upon the *Aeneid* in the high and later Middle Ages in England, and elsewhere in Europe. While these dominant approaches will best emerge from discussion of the manuscripts themselves, I begin (pp. 9–14) by sketching their broad outlines, and that of yet a further, "romance" claim on the *Aeneid* that emerges in the early vernacular redactions.

In these chapters I am interested in exactly those English manuscripts of Virgil which represent traditions of reading equally available to Chaucer and the more learned (if perhaps quite limited) sectors of his audience; for this reason, when I turn to Chaucer's two retellings of the story in chapter 6, I take rather little account of Dante and the Italians, clear though it be that Chaucer himself was a profound reader of the *Divine Comedy* and its Virgilianism. I will also try, however, to take some account in later chapters of the impingement of more accessible, contemporary forms of classical story, particularly in the vernacular.

The first of the tasks I have outlined above – that of establishing the specific contours of the medieval reading of the Latin *text* as it survives in specific manuscripts – is still in its early stages, for Virgil or any of the major Latin *auctores*, anywhere during the high and later Middle Ages. Textual critics of Virgil and Servius have not needed to look past the manuscripts of the Carolingian period.[21] Students of the Renaissance have only just begun the study of the Virgil manuscripts and commentaries of their own period.[22] Only the *Dantisti* have made significant use of medieval Virgil manuscripts as sources of literary context, and their studies have naturally been limited to Italian materials.[23]

We must begin, then, not with "the state of the question," but with the state of our ignorance. The difficulties of access to medieval acts of classical reading are great, and remain (as they will remain) incompletely resolved. Scholarship has only recently begun seriously undertaking to recover and use the medieval past's own ancient books. Most of the material, much of it genuinely important, is unedited, and the full contents of manuscripts more often than not remain unknown. Older catalogs and handlists are usually of little use in seeking out independent commentaries, and provide even less information about material in the margins surrounding classical texts.[24]

Who in the Middle Ages was reading classical Latin texts, which ones, when, and where? Until a very few years ago we did not really know, in any statistical sense, at all. The evidence was spotty and local, and in great part indirect, a question of echoes and literary references.[25] A tool as basic as a survey of surviving manuscripts, however, used cautiously, can provide some real answers ("cautiously," because the survival of a manuscript can suggest precisely that it *ceased* to be used, or at least was used less often and hence less destructively). Just such a survey has now appeared thanks to the Herculean labors of Birger Munk Olsen.[26] Simply by listing and dating surviving manuscripts of Latin classical authors through the end of the twelfth century, with a certain amount of bibliography and peripheral information added, Munk Olsen gives us for the first time a solid notion of what works were being copied at what times, and often he can tell us where, as well.[27] I make constant use of Munk Olsen and related surveys in the pages that follow, and I provide information on surviving English manuscripts of Virgil and continental manuscripts brought to England during the Middle Ages, in Appendix I.

THREE DOMINANT VISIONS OF THE *AENEID*

In the medieval manuscripts and redactions of the *Aeneid*, three major trends of interpretation can be distinguished. They merge, divide, and recross throughout the period, but their identities are sufficiently clear to be useful. I will be calling these streams of interpretation the allegorical, romance, and pedagogical visions of the *Aeneid*.

Our received understanding of classical tradition generally, and of Virgil specifically, in the high and later Middle Ages has derived to a great extent from generalizations based on a rich but incompletely studied range of materials.[28] This scholarly orthodoxy has tended to concentrate on two strands of medieval classicism, both of which could be called "domesticating" interpretations. First, work on the learned tradition has focussed on allegorical interpretations, either the spiritual and learned allegories characterized by the Virgil commentary associated with Bernard Silvestris and by another on the *Metamorphoses* by Arnulf of Orléans, or the later moralizing and ethical allegories of Pierre Bersuire and the *Ovide moralisé*.[29] In what follows, I will be describing this as the "allegorizing" vision.

This style of commentary bases itself loosely on the late-antique allegorization by Fulgentius, and interprets the books of the *Aeneid* as stages in the spiritual life of man. The shipwreck of Book One is birth, the hunting and sexual involvement of Book Four are voluptuous adolescence. The descent to hell of Book Six is the centerpiece of this interpretation, since it is here that man achieves spiritual adulthood, descending to an enlightened knowledge of creation below so that he may understand the Creator above. Such an adaptation of the epic to new values and preoccupations allows further development of the already well-established notion that Virgil had hidden vast funds of recondite learning in his text. In the allegorizations of the twelfth century, Aeneas's spiritual development was linked to a more specific educational progress in the liberal arts, capped by a sort of second birth in Book Six. Chapter 3 explores an English manuscript dominated by such an approach. Later developments in the tradition were influenced by the moralizing allegories around Ovid's *Metamorphoses*. Such allegorical annotation dealt with Virgil's epic by an analogous process of fragmentation, concentrating on brief episodes and interpreting them as signs of moral flaws or virtues, or moments in Christian history. Chapter 4 is devoted to a fourteenth-century commentary in this tradition.

Work in vernacular classicism and its accompanying illustrations has demonstrated how classical story in romances and universal histories shifts the imagined world of the antique past – costume, architecture, social codes – into the time and place of the medieval redactor, even (to varying extents) suppressing the apparatus of pagan divinity and mythology; I am calling this the "romance" vision of the *Aeneid*.[30] The "romance" vision is expressed primarily in a linked, though also evolving, sequence of vernacular redactions of the Dido-and-Aeneas story, with only occasional (though repeated) recourse to the Latin text and its commentaries for fresh matter or detail. The romance vision of

Virgil is essentially vernacular, not Latinate, although in chapter 5, along with the *Eneas*, I will discuss some Latin poems where its preoccupations also operate.

This tradition is inextricably connected to the popular vernacular histories produced from the twelfth century and through the Renaissance. Some versions are independent works, like the *Roman d'Eneas*; but this text is often found in manuscripts in the company of other *romans antiques* or the *Brut*, which implicitly renders it part of a continuing Anglo-Norman history. Such an insertion of the story into a wider project of English imperial history invites political imitation, and creates a justifying prehistory for the Angevin line and its empire. The *Eneas* contributed to the prose *Histoire ancienne jusqu'à César*, which in turn influenced a later independent work, the *Livre des Eneydes*.[31] The romance *Aeneid*, far more than in its Latin source, is the story of Aeneas and his women, or even the story of Aeneas's women to the exclusion of Aeneas. As I will argue later, it can be seen as the untold Latin *Aeneid*: a completion, but also a subversion of Virgil's narrative, tending to extend those very episodes, especially that of Dido, which for Virgil are the restraints keeping Aeneas from his fortune in Italy.

These two Virgilianisms – one learned and recondite, the other more popular and accessible – may seem very different. But they have in common a will to make Virgilian authority more immediately accessible and relevant to their contemporary world, be it spiritual or secular, moral or imperial. Both approaches, it could be argued, to some extent domesticate and thus subvert that very alterity, historical or linguistic, in which much of the *auctor*'s power resides, and in particular both traditions evade (by interpretation or suppression) those elements which, since patristic times, had seemed most threatening to a Christian readership – the gods and the miraculous.

This generalization is open to several kinds of qualification, though. In particular, I will argue that both these traditions do not always so much *subvert* the mystery of Virgil's historical, mythological, and geographical difference, as they *replace* it with alternate but still functional wonders. The *Eneas*, for instance, as Poirion has best pointed out, replaces the pagan *mirabilia* of the Latin *Aeneid* with scientific and architectural wonders.[32] And this insight could be applied to the allegories of the *Aeneid* in terms of their exploration of spiritual and moral mysteries.

While this long-established focus on the dual domestication of the classical past has real validity, it must, I think, be seen in the context of a third, far more widespread habit of reading, based in the schools, which approaches classical Latin texts grammatically and rhetorically, and attempts to read them in a fashion that in some ways acknowledges and restores their historical and religious difference, rather than effacing it. That is, these readings respect the verbal integrity and imitability of the texts, yet attempt to reconstruct, within restricted scholarly limits, their historical, social, and geographical difference. I will be calling this third and most widespread appproach the "pedagogical" vision of Virgil.

Classical allegoresis, we have tended to assume, is motivated by a need among medieval readers to adapt the works to their own times, to reread them exclusively in terms of their own, Christian ethos. This kind of assumption participates in the more general truism, now increasingly challenged, that the Middle Ages lacked a developed historical imagination.[33] But the commentaries I study in chapter 2, and the earlier layers of marginalia described in chapters 3 and 4, despite their often very elementary level, show a real effort to explain Virgil in terms of what they could reconstruct of his own world – verbal, historical, mythological, and political. These pedagogical annotations work through a sustained use of the universally available commentary of Servius, but import their own independent rhetorical analyses, and turn, especially in the later Middle Ages, to independent sources of information about the antique world.

The pedagogical vision is found largely in commentaries of the schools, though, and probably the lower schools; it represents only one context and level of Virgilian reading, though the most widespread, and is not necessarily inconsistent with the more sophisticated allegorical interpretations proposed in the same periods. Indeed, the medieval model of biblical reading in the schools, with its typical move from literal sense to allegorical interpretation, provides a context in which we can see the pedagogical and allegorical *Aeneids* as parts of a continuing clerical approach to ancient epic. But at the same time, both the inherited prestige and the literal narrative of the *Aeneid* lent themselves as models of secular power and imperial ambition far different from, if not immediately opposed to, clerical efforts to use the epic as a colorless training ground for Latin eloquence and an allegorized tale of spiritual education. What is the implication if a pedagogically annotated manuscript is read not by a monk, but by a prince? I will suggest that this may have been the case with the manuscript I study in chapter 2. Even in its own time, then, a single tradition of annotation can be the site of divergent, potentially conflicting, claims on the narrative.

These three approaches to the *Aeneid* descend in three largely separate textual traditions – independent allegorizing commentary, vernacular redaction, and school commentaries both marginal and independent. The three manuscripts I study in detail have been chosen for their qualities representative of two of these major visions of the *Aeneid*, pedagogical and allegorical. Chapter 2 examines an example of the pedagogical impulse, renewed by annotations added throughout the period. Chapters 3 and 4 both present monuments of Virgilian allegoresis in England; but chapter 3 studies a manuscript emphasizing spiritual and scientific allegory, while the manuscript treated in chapter 4 offers allegories strongly moral in tone and overtly Christian in detail.

My persistent concern throughout the book, however, will be with some places in the tradition where these various approaches to Virgil cross or interpenetrate, as when a learned text is illustrated by a miniaturist whose visualizations reflect the "domesticating" tendencies of the vernacular tradition, or when two layers of marginal commentary reflect pedagogical and allegorical interpretations, as we will see in chapters 3 and 4. Challenges to and transformations of the *Aeneid* are liveliest where the narrative jumps from Latin to the vernacular, as we will see in the later chapters. This history of accretion and adaptation produces a challenging readerly problem for the consumer of classical literature, if not initially, then later when the institutional setting and habits of readership alter. The examples I will describe localize the broader problem of a culture that has generated competing versions of a single authoritative figure or story.

Perhaps the liveliest challenge to received readings of the *Aeneid* is played out in the texts of the romance vision. Here we see twin new claims being laid upon the received readings of the epic. First, the narrative is secularized, by its historical domestication and by the absence of apparatus meant to teach Christian eloquence; a vernacular reader of secular story takes hold of Virgil. Second, however, the growing presence of women both as readers and characters suggests yet another claimant on ancient history as a model for contemporary power. I will approach the romance *Aeneid*, particularly the *Eneas* produced for the Anglo-Norman court, as a site of this dual contest.

Ultimately, and perhaps most interestingly, the traditions can intertwine and compete in the mind of broad-ranging readers like Chaucer or Douglas. In chapter 6 we will see how, in the *Legend of Dido* and the *House of Fame,* Chaucer wrestled with all three visions, turning them to ends at once comic and visionary, and re-enacting for his own age the ancient struggles of Aeneas now refigured in terms of the power of the book and the heroic challenge of readership. A brief "Envoi" turns to William Caxton and Christine de Pizan, and thence to Gavin Douglas, where we witness a translator at once attached to the medieval heritage of Virgilian interpretation, and yet aware of newer renaissance notions of the text. Douglas, as we will see, used traditional codicological format to produce a translation that responds to both traditions at once. The book closes with Edmund Spenser's exploitation of inherited Virgilianisms in his *Faerie Queene,* Book Three.

I have already pointed out that the book of Virgil – either his surviving manuscripts or full redactions such as the *Eneas* – is by no means the sole transmitter of medieval Virgilianism. Indeed, it is at the edges of the tradition, such as where the narrative jumps from Latin into vernacular, that new challenges to control the epic appear in boldest relief. I open my study, then, before turning to the dominant Latin books, with a survey of some of these alternate modes of access, and an overview of the history of Virgilianism in medieval England.

CHAPTER ONE

Auctor *to* auctoritas: *modes of access to Virgil in medieval England*

The approach to Virgil's *Aeneid* in medieval England outlined in the Introduction is intensive rather than extensive; it proposes to focus on dense sites of Virgilian reception, manifested in Latin manuscripts and in vernacular redactions that purport to supply Virgil's narrative. In this chapter, however, I want at least to acknowledge the existence of far broader contexts for, and means of access to, Virgil in the Middle Ages. For the manuscripts and redactions studied in later chapters should be seen only as particular centers within more diffuse radial fields of literary, artistic, and popular materials all of which provided some access to Virgil himself, his hero, and his narrative. Such materials include direct but limited textual contact, knowledge of *florilegia*, classroom lecture, illustration, vernacular translation, and popular legend, among yet other possibilities. The absorption of commentary into "text," discussed in the Introduction, is simply the most immediate manifestation of that process by which the fluid textuality of medieval readership is affected by this constellation of – at first glance – less relevant materials.

What is more, the manuscript, while it is *a* center for the medieval reception of Virgil, is not necessarily *the* center for every medieval reader. To an Anglo-Norman aristocrat, for example, the *Roman d'Eneas* might be the functional core of his or her Virgilianism, rather than an iconic but less readable Latin manuscript. It can even be argued that Virgil's influence was most powerful exactly at the points where he was moving away from (escaping, one might even say) his most "authentic" avatar, the transmitted Latin text. Certainly the most complexly achieved "Virgil" of the high Middle Ages, and one that was to have considerable ongoing influence in the secular realm, was not Latin, but rather the mid-twelfth-century vernacular *Roman d'Eneas*. That "Virgil" functioned both as political propaganda for the imperial

15

and dynastic ambitions of the Angevins, and as a model for courtly eroticism and feminine power in the vernacular romances.

These shifting modes and centers of reception, of course, are by no means an exclusively medieval condition of readership. They operate in the understanding of any *auctor*, ancient or modern, who becomes central to a civilization. This is especially true of a figure who enjoys both a popular and a learned reputation. The place of Shakespeare in the nineteenth century provides an instructive example: contemporary stagings, bowdlerizations, popular adaptations and biography, illustrations, and widely recognized but contextless quotations, all affected his reception and influence in both popular and learned contexts.

The example of Sigmund Freud, today, is even more suggestive. Some concept of Freudian thinking is virtually universal. Even the least educated can speak of an Oedipus complex or Freudian slip; but far more than that, one can have a fairly extensive (if popularized and not always accurate) notion of major Freudian concepts having never read a word by him, or knowing his actual writing only in short, translated passages. So dominant a figure, then, comes to us in multiple forms and versions, and through a great variety of media. And yet one can hardly say that Freud is "not known" by those who happen not to know him directly and textually; he is just differently known. And as a result of such dissemination, it is virtually impossible for any reader today to approach Freud's actual writings without carrying a great load of culturally imposed preconceptions about what will be found there. These presuppositions may or may not have any necessary relation to Freud's own "Freud," but they will nevertheless almost inevitably affect the reader's understanding of the original materials.

Just as the "real," textual Freud gave rise to epiphenomena-Freuds as he moved into the general cultural baggage and escaped his own text, so Virgil escaped *his* writings in the Middle Ages, and there arose manifold versions of "Virgil," and manifold versions of his works, which in turn came to precondition any reading of the prior Latin text. This process has only its most exaggerated instance in the popular legends of Virgil the magician and inventor of wonders, or Virgil the Christian prophet of the fourth Eclogue. The magnetic field of the medieval Virgil is particularly large. We have noted that his redactors incorporated commentary, but they also incorporated more distantly related material. The *Roman d'Eneas* includes extensive details from Ovid and from scientific and legendary material without, I think, compromising for medieval readers its validity as an access to Virgil.

Indeed, such treatment enhanced access: it widened the door to encompass a larger part of Virgil's contemporary reception, his field of signification.[1] But, as we will see, by the time a Chaucerian narrator "dreamed" the text of Virgil, he could no longer disentangle his response to Dido from the inherited pathos of the Ovidian version long engrafted into the tradition.

AUTHORITY AND CHALLENGE: THE CONTEXT OF REDACTIONS

Virgil acquired a tremendous degree of literary authority within his own lifetime: his work almost immediately became the object of reverential academic study and literary imitation.[2] His broader authority as a philosopher and master of all *scientia* is seen in commentaries as early as the fourth century.[3] In the sixth century the assumption of universal knowledge hidden in Virgil's text was systematically developed by Fulgentius (of whom more later).[4] At the same time, great religious authority was sometimes attributed to Virgil as a result of the Christian prophecy supposed to be contained in the fourth Eclogue.[5] Such a reputation led to his occasional adoption as a Christian prophet and his role in the prophet plays of medieval religious drama. This kind of learned authority also stands behind popular belief in Virgil as a tremendously powerful and resourceful magician, an inventor of wondrous devices and protector of certain cities.[6]

Virgil's texts of course shared in their author's weighty cultural authority and took on certain powers that had no direct relation to any sense of the author as a controlling intelligence. These independent powers of the text, virtually isolated from the author, can be seen in phenomena like the *sortes Virgilianae*. In the *sortes*, Virgil's words, shorn of context, are used as a tool of divination through the random choice of a passage that is then interpreted in terms of the inquirer's situation. Even more fascinating as a manifestation of the cultural authority of Virgil's texts are the Christianizing *centones*. These poems, built up by a mosaic-like compilation of lines and half-lines from Virgil, show the intensity with which his works were studied and absorbed in the early Christian centuries. At the same time, they provide perhaps the most extreme example of the adaptation of Virgil to Christian wisdom, and witness an implicit trust in the capacity of Virgil's language to signify all wisdom and all learning. The production of *centones* was apparently limited to the early centuries of the Christian era, but the greatest of them, the *cento* of Proba, continued to be widely copied and read throughout the Middle Ages.[7]

On the other hand, when we turn to the figure of Aeneas and to the narrative of the *Aeneid* itself, we encounter an area where Virgilian importance and authority are very much open to challenge. For there exists, beginning with the Homeric roots of the Aeneas-story, a far broader legendary context that came to be known in the Middle Ages as the "matter of Troy."[8] Within the great framework of the fall of Troy and the early history of Rome, later expanded to encompass the founding of several European nations, the *Aeneid*-story plays only a small if crucial role. And even this minor role as a quasi-historical source is depreciated by the existence, particularly strong in the Middle Ages, of a counter-tradition that claimed and received greater historical authority than that accorded the *Aeneid*. The counter-tradition was based on the early medieval pseudo-histories of Dares and Dictys, but it continued to be expanded and reinforced by multiple redactions of the Troy story throughout the Middle Ages, entering England particularly through the Latin version of Guido delle Colonne, which was repeatedly translated into Middle English.[9] Even certain Latin manuscripts of the *Aeneid* reflect this uncertainty about the historicity of Virgil, since they accompany his works with Dares's *De excidio Troiae*.[10]

This tradition differs most importantly from the story of the *Aeneid* in its version of the character and actions of Virgil's hero. In Dictys's *Journal of the Trojan War*, the Trojan nobility is depicted as murderous, lustful, lying, and deeply treacherous. Aeneas embodies all these sins, especially the last. His swaggering and boastfulness destroy an early chance for peace. Later, when the Trojans begin to lose battles and Hector is killed, Aeneas and Antenor plot to return Helen to the Greeks; when this is prevented, they decide to betray their own city. After the Greeks depart, Aeneas even turns on his fellow-traitor and tries to drive Antenor from Troy. Instead, he himself is put to flight. This, according to Dictys, is the real cause of Aeneas's departure from Troy and his foundation of another city. Dares the Phrygian's *Fall of Troy* also depicts Aeneas's treachery. Priam, during a council to consider a truce, angrily attacks Aeneas for having helped begin the war by aiding Paris in the abduction of Helen. Dares also shows Aeneas betraying his city along with Antenor, though in this version it is angry Greek leaders who make Aeneas flee.[11]

Even in these fundamental sources of the counter-tradition,

however, there are signs of inconsistency in the attitude toward Aeneas. Dictys, the more hostile of the two, says that after Achilles was murdered by Trojans in the temple of Apollo, Aeneas refused to go into battle because "he was a devout worshipper of Apollo and detested the crime ... committed against this god."[12] This may reflect the influence of Aeneas's Virgilian *pietas*. Dares, who claims to be a Trojan himself, is naturally less critical of that people and of Aeneas. In a series of character summaries he says that Aeneas was "eloquent, courteous, prudent, pious, and charming."[13] Dares shows Aeneas taking a prominent part in battles, and gives examples of his eloquence.

Throughout the Middle Ages, Dares and Dictys were generally thought to be more historically accurate than Virgil. A twelfth-century allegorist makes this explicit. Virgil, he says, tells the story of Aeneas and the Trojans, though "not always according to the historical truth which the Phrygian describes; but everywhere, so that he might enjoy the favor of Augustus Caesar, he praises Aeneas's deeds and flight by means of fictions."[14] The chronological impossibility of Dido and Aeneas ever having met was the subject of frequent note, although as Macrobius points out, Virgil's rhetoric gave the fable a currency that approached fact.

The beauty of his storytelling has been so powerful that everyone, aware of Dido's chastity, ... nonetheless overlooks the fable and, burying the knowledge of the truth deep in their minds, they prefer to have proclaimed as true what the sweetness of his feigning has caused to enter their human hearts.[15]

This admission of the problematic power of Virgil's rhetoric, and the gap it opens between historical knowledge and the pull of fictional emotion, will trouble redactors of the matter of Troy throughout the Middle Ages. Guido delle Colonne, in his Latin redaction of Benoît, will later criticize

the failure of the great authors, Virgil, Ovid, and Homer, who were very deficient in describing the truth about the fall of Troy, although they composed their works in exceedingly glorious style, whether they treated them according to the stories of the ancients or according to fables, and especially that highest of poets, Virgil, whom nothing obscures.[16]

As we will see, a similar tension informs Chaucer's versions of the Aeneas-and-Dido story, and some of the Prologues to Gavin Douglas's translation.

This does not mean, however, that the *Aeneid* was never used as a historical source. The early *Excidium Troiae*, for example, inserts a "simple yet not ignorant summary of the *Aeneid*" for the section of its story following the fall of Troy.[17] Even when presented in a fairly complete (if much expanded) redaction like the *Roman d'Eneas*, the text's manuscript context implicitly made Virgil's epic only part of a bigger story. Of the nine surviving manuscripts, two present the *Eneas* by itself; in the other seven it appears with the *Thèbes*, *Troie*, or *Brut* in various combinations and sequences.[18] The *Aeneid* was again used as a historical source, condensed into a passing section of a much larger work, and with its divine apparatus, its marvels, and Aeneas's descent to hell suppressed, in the enormously popular vernacular *Histoire ancienne jusqu'à César*, written in the first third of the thirteenth century, but recopied until the end of the fifteenth.[19] The *Aeneid* and its author, thus denuded, are rendered largely documentary witnesses.

In both the *Excidium Troiae* and in Guido, the use of the *Aeneid* strikes an oddly uncertain note. The *Excidium Troiae* uses Virgil's plot-line yet depicts Aeneas as a cynical cad. And in his first reference to the *Aeneid*, Guido quotes with apparent approval the Emperor Justinian's statement that Roman emperors would better be called *Heneades* than *Caesares*. This makes a peculiar and inconsistent parenthesis for, as we have seen, Guido elsewhere sticks to the counter-tradition, showing Aeneas as a bad counselor and a traitor. Even when accepted as historical material, then, the *Aeneid* plays a reduced, depreciated role, strangely at odds with the awesomely authoritative Virgil of the allegories, prophecies, and *centones*. Conversely, even the exemplary Aeneas, the Everyman we will witness in the allegorical commentaries and the ideal prince of the humanizing tradition, is surrounded by the troubling penumbra of the counter-tradition. This uncertain heroism is vividly reflected in Chaucer's *House of Fame*, as we will see, and in the notoriously ambiguous opening lines of *Sir Gawain and the Green Knight*.

This dark aspect of Aeneas becomes even more emphatic as a result of his treatment of Dido. The earlier quasi-historical materials make little of this episode. But the letter of Dido in Ovid's *Heroides* provides an early and continuing basis for sentimental and unconditional sympathy with the abandoned queen. Vernacular redactions extend this attention to the linked themes of erotics and death, as does a group of Latin school poems, widespread in anthologies, based on the sorrows of Dido. We will return to these when we study the *Roman d'Eneas* and Chaucer's versions of the story. At the same time, yet another historical tradition depicts Dido as a chaste queen, casting Virgil's veracity further into doubt.[20] This tradition goes back at least as far as Justin's *Epitome* of Trogus and is transmitted by many Christian apologists (Tertullian, Jerome), who use Dido as an example of widowed chastity. The *Histoire ancienne* combines both versions of her story.[21] Early Virgil commentators like Servius also make a point of the chronological impossibility of contact between Aeneas and Dido. Both the sentimental and historical approaches to Dido thus influence conflicting attitudes toward the *Aeneid* and its hero.

We can see, then, that a great part of the complexity of medieval Virgilianism descends from the tense dialectic between the verbal *auctoritas* of Virgil and the hostile (or at least conflicting) historical claims of the counter-tradition. The historical tradition, moreover, does not merely attack Virgil's hero, it also diminishes his authority; for even when it accepts Virgil's historicity, it reduces his text to a cyclic fragment without any inherent predominance over other parts of the narrative. Medieval Virgilianism thus swings between awed respect for the *Aeneid* as an almost inspired text, and casual dismissal of it as an unreliable or minor story. This tension informs all the traditions of Virgilian interpretation and redaction, and particularly the vernacular versions studied in chapters 5 and 6.

THE VISUAL CONTEXT

The counter-tradition discussed above provides the most widespread historical and narrative materials in the radial field of presupposition and indirect access surrounding the *Aeneid*, and preserves for us much of the evidence for the Middle Ages' appropriation of the Aeneas story to its own place and time. A much more limited corpus of illustrations, most of them linked to these popularized redactions, and a few in Latin manuscripts of Virgil himself, offer an equally important register of the contemporary (and contemporizing) visualization of the classical past. Much work remains to be done on the illustrations of the *Aeneid* and especially of its redactions, but a recent book by Pierre and Jeanne Courcelle, along with an earlier work by Hugo Buchthal, lead toward some preliminary conclusions.[22]

For the narrower concerns of this book, specifically Virgil in England, illustration has only a small role to play. There are comparatively few illustrated manuscripts of any of the classics between the late-antique Virgil manuscripts and the manuscripts of the early Renaissance.[23] Only a handful of surviving medieval Virgils are illustrated, and only one of these had any medieval presence in England: London, Lambeth Palace 471 (Appendix I, no. 15), a twelfth-century manuscript which I believe was copied in England. Even this manuscript, however, has only one illustration, at the opening of the *Eclogues*.

On the other hand, vernacular and popular Latin redactions containing the *Aeneid*-story, either as centerpiece or passing episode, are often richly illustrated, and many of these circulated in the Norman milieu that included England. Their depiction of the story of Aeneas has much to teach us about how later medieval readers were taught to visualize the classical heroes and their world. The *Roman d'Eneas* was illustrated, as was its German translation by Heinrich von Veldeke, the *Eneit*. Benoît's *Roman de Troie* and its Latin redaction by Guido delle Colonne have considerable traditions of illustration, though the latter is largely Italian. And the numerous vernacular Troy books and universal histories, especially the widely distributed *Histoire ancienne jusqu'à César*, frequently have miniatures which, if not always numerous, are all the more significant for the episodes they do choose to depict.

In the absence of antique models on which to base their representations of the stories, artists (or those instructing them) were free to choose for illustration episodes of particular appeal, and they had to formulate those episodes in terms of the visual models available to them.[24] This state of affairs could generate intriguing shifts in narrative emphasis (often of course prompted by the texts), and a radical transposition of classical event, either into a contemporary visual world or into the terms of established biblical illumination.

Buchthal's comments on the earliest surviving sequence of Benoît illustrations (*c.* 1264) suggest the extent to which classical story had been visually domesticated in manuscripts of these high medieval redactions:

The illustrations, just like Benoît's text, transform the Trojan War into an entirely medieval *ambiente*. Any sense of history or historical distance is conspicuously absent. They might equally well serve to illustrate some medieval *chanson de geste*: there is no visual connection with classical art at all. The miniatures are based on the text alone and depict the action in contemporary terms, without adhering to any pictorial tradition. Their iconographical relations are rather found in contemporary Bible illustrations, which must indeed have been used wholesale for the creation of this and other early secular cycles.[25]

Despite their disinterest in portraying the geographical and historical difference of the classical past, however, such manuscripts – and others that depict episodes from the Aeneas story – did enrich access to classical story for non-Latinate readers, or those whose Latinity did not extend to Virgil.

Indeed, illustration of vernacular versions is occasionally so systematic that it may have been for some beholders the *sole* means of access to Virgilian story. Such appears to have been the case in some manuscripts of the German *Eneit* of Heinrich von Veldeke. One manuscript of the early thirteenth century (Berlin, Staatsbibl., Germ. in-fol. 282) has seventy miniatures on folios interleaved among the seventy-seven extant folios of text.[26] So dense a sequence of illustrations, showing great attention to the expression of psychological state, almost tells the story without need for recourse to the accompanying text, rather like a present-day comic book.[27] This impression is strengthened by the presence of brief lines of simple dialogue or explanation that accompany each miniature.[28] The same phenomenon occurs in another, early fifteenth-century manuscript of the *Eneit*.[29] And a similar procedure is found in the explanatory captions in an early fifteenth-century manuscript of the *Trésor des hystoires*.[30] When Geoffrey Chaucer found himself dreaming an *Aeneid* in captioned pictures in the *House of Fame*, then, his experience was not without precedent.

Vernacular manuscripts with far less extensive illustration, and even Latin manuscripts of the *Aeneid* itself, practice a comparable domestication of the story, showing its heroes in contemporary garb and local place. A twelfth-century Austrian manuscript (Klosterneuburg 742) shows Aeneas, in a historiated initial A, as a mounted warrior wearing contemporary mail and helmet, despite the Virgilian narrative in which he only fights on foot. In the tempest of Book Five, he again wears mail, with a hooded Palinurus shown as an oarsman.[31]

The most overt instance of biblical models affecting the visualization of the *Aeneid* is found in a Paris manuscript of classical authors; produced in about the year 1200 (Paris, BN lat. 7936), it has been studied by François Avril.[32] In this beautifully executed sequence of miniatures, the *Aeneid* takes place within a contemporary world complexly depicted not only in costume, but also in architecture and domestic interiors. As in the Klosterneuburg manuscript, the first book of the epic begins here with a mail-clad Aeneas (seated this time) in the initial. More interestingly, however, a number of the episodes have illustrations clearly based on miniatures in contemporary Bibles and psalters. The drowning of Palinurus, for instance, resembles contemporary depictions of Jonah falling into the sea.[33] Most telling is the image of Jupiter and the council of the gods in Book Ten; here, Jupiter is modelled on images of God the Father, holding an orb in one hand and phylactery in the other.[34]

This effort to depict the gods, even in biblicized form, is rare among *Aeneid* manuscripts before the Renaissance. Others deal with the classical gods simply by suppressing them. An Italian *Aeneid* of the fourteenth century (Oxford, Bodleian Library, Canon. class. lat. 52) emphasizes human experience both in war and love: three of its historiated initials include Dido, and others show Pallas, Nisus and Euryalus, and Aeneas and Turnus. Only the initial to Book Six represents the supernatural, with Aeneas and the Sibyl at the entrance to the Underworld; and even here they are met by a figure with the trident and pointed ears of a medieval devil.[35] The vernacular redactions display the same tendency, both in text and illustrations. The splendid early fourteenth-century *Eneas* manuscript, Paris, BN fr. 60, again shows its characters in contemporary dress, and provides no illustrations of Eneas in hell, or any of the other mythographical details, even in the reduced state in which they appear in the *Eneas*. Like the *Aeneid* manuscript, BN lat. 7936, many of its episodes appear to be based on similar scenes in the *Bibles historiales*.[36]

Even in later *Aeneid* manuscripts, which begin once again to show many mythological episodes, the visualized world will remain contemporary, although inhabited by divinities, so identified by their nudity or some standard attribute. This is especially true outside of Italy.[37] The phenomenon points up the delicate and unresolved attitude toward the classical past depicted in most of these manuscripts. Using biblical models to help visualize ancient episodes, and particularly the ancient supernatural, is not the same as the conscious Christianization taking place in some contemporary allegorical commentaries. There are indeed occasional mild Christian details, especially at points of religious ritual, as for instance in the early fourteenth-century *Eneas* manuscript mentioned above, which includes a man in a bishop's mitre in the illustration of Lavinia's engagement to Eneas.[38] This is exceptional, however. Rather, the bulk of the contemporizing images place classical events in a kind of historical limbo, in the contemporary Christian world but not of that world.

In such a visual (and, in some redactions, textual) world, with the more foreign and unsettling elements minimized if not eliminated, sensitive and interesting responses to the *Aeneid* could nonetheless take place. These can be traced in patterns of visual imagery that record themes in the text with considerable nuance. For instance, Virgil suggests Dido's fevered excitement as the hunt approaches through vivid imagery of color: the gold and purple of her dress and her stallion's trappings at once figure her quickened eroticism and the blood and fire that will follow it at her suicide. In the Paris Virgil of about 1200 (BN lat. 7936), Dido is shown only once, wearing a golden crown and red dress.[39] Again, in the almost cartoon-like sequence of illustrations to the *Eneit* discussed above, a striking and exotic tree with curling branches and heart-shaped leaves appears at two points, at the first erotic union of Dido and Aeneas, and then when Ascanius slays Silvia's hart.[40] This visual link may parallel the imagery of the wounded deer that connects the two episodes in Virgil's version; a tree is mentioned in both episodes in von Veldeke's text.[41]

While visual patterns like these arguably record sensitive responses to local details of Virgilian imagery, they are also suggestive of broader shifts in readerly attention which challenge Virgil's primary emphasis on male heroism (be it that of Aeneas or Turnus) and the foundation of empire. The twelfth-century *Aeneid* manuscripts of Klosterneuburg and BN lat. 7936 do indeed focus on men and battle, illustrating Aeneas at the head of the work and ignoring Dido's suicide.[42] But when we turn to the fourteenth-century Italian manuscript mentioned above (Oxford, Bodleian Library, Canon. class. lat. 52), a different emphasis emerges. Of its twelve miniatures, three depict Dido (during Aeneas's tale, at her suicide, and her burial), a fourth shows the Sybil with Aeneas before the descent to the underworld, and a fifth is devoted to Camilla.[43] While the sequence of miniatures in this manuscript begins and ends with Aeneas (debarking at Carthage and killing Turnus), much of its central attention is devoted to women in the epic. In such a visualization, a new text is blossoming from within the *Aeneid*, or at the least, its thematic center shows signs of shifting. In the *Roman d'Eneas* and later vernacularizations, we will see a parallel shift in attention, a new urgency of feminine voice, and new efforts at establishing feminine power.

The third miniature of Dido in this Italian manuscript is the most interesting, for it represents an episode that does not actually occur in the *Aeneid*: the Carthaginians mourning over the corpse of their queen. This episode is, however, reported in the *Roman d'Eneas* and the *Histoire ancienne*, the latter of which circulated widely in Italy.[44] The miniature, moreover, is placed in the initial of Book Five, thus holding attention on the death of Dido rather than turning to the departing Trojans with which the *text* of Book Five opens. What appears to have happened, then, is a rare instance of the vernacular, "popularized" story moving back into a learned, Latin manuscript and affecting ("contesting" may not be too strong a term) its textual focus.

Not surprisingly, this foregrounding of women in illustrations of the Aeneas story is most prominent in the very vernacular manuscripts that pay vastly expanded textual attention to Dido, Camilla, and Lavinia, and especially in manuscripts of the *Eneas*. The very beautiful opening page of the early fourteenth-century *Eneas* already mentioned above (Paris, BN fr. 60; see plate 1) provides a telling instance. The upper two thirds of this page are filled by six miniatures distributed in two registers across three columns. These possess an extraordinary rhythm which again focusses attention on the story of Dido.[45] The burning of Troy in the upper left corner is answered by the flames that envelop Dido in the lower right; this is yet another occasion where illustrations privilege thematically powerful parallel images from the text. The upper right corner, showing Aeneas as he kneels before Dido, is balanced by the lower left where they sit on the same level, now lovers. The center column, top and bottom, shows Aeneas sailing away from cities – Troy above and Carthage below – but the two miniatures are tellingly similar, differing only in heraldic details: Aeneas fleeing from fire and death at each turn. The sequence of illustrated episodes then moves directly from the suicide of Dido to a double miniature, showing the engagement of Lavinia, and Amata sending a messenger to alert Turnus.[46] Although the six later miniatures (rather less carefully executed) turn to scenes of battle, the choice of inital images gives primary attention not to Virgil's hero but to Dido and Lavinia, the two central women of this vernacular redaction.[47]

Even more startling is a slightly earlier manuscript of the *Eneas* (Paris, BN fr. 784), which possesses only a single illustration, at the very beginning of the text.[48] A miniature shows Dido in a tower at the left, watching the departing ships of Eneas at the right; then, in the historiated initial Q that begins the text, Dido is shown committing suicide. The heroine's move to the beginning of the text suggests a codicological response to those Latin manuscripts (like Klosterneuburg 742 and BN lat. 7936) where Aeneas occupies the initial A at Book One, line 1. Just as the French redaction subverts the imperial and martial emphases of the epic with its extended treatment of women

Plate 1 Paris, Bibliothèque Nationale, fr. 60, fo. 148 *recto*, opening page of the *Roman d'Eneas*. The arrangement of episodes emphasizes imagery of fire and themes of political and erotic abandonment in the romance. In the center above and below, Eneas sails away from Troy and Carthage. In the upper left and lower right, women die among flames. Heraldic devices in the marginal roundels connect medieval aristocratic houses to the imperial aspect of the *Eneas* narrative. Published with permission.

and erotic psychology centering on Dido and the events of *Aeneid* Four, so a manuscript like this subverts the visual hierarchy of the Latin *Aeneids*. The French Dido replaces the Latin Aeneas as central character of the work.

The *Aeneid* is again mined for narrative material in the early thirteenth-century *Histoire ancienne*. While the *Histoire* suppresses pagan reference even more systematically than does the *Eneas*, it otherwise stays much closer to the Latin narrative and its emphasis on Aeneas. Here too, though, visual attention in some manuscripts tends to resist the text, and remains focussed instead on women. Manuscripts of the *Histoire* generally devote only a few miniatures to the section entitled "Histoire d'Énée," and sometimes only two, and they render aspects of the narrative that are rather a "History of Women around Aeneas."[49] Two manuscripts of about 1300, from Naples and France, depict only Dido's suicide and Camilla in battle; not a single male hero appears in the section devoted to Aeneas, except for the departing Trojans, who are visually much less important than Dido in her death throes.[50] A slightly earlier manuscript of the same work, also Neapolitan, has four miniatures in the Aeneas section, but again begins with Dido's suicide.[51] Whereas the Latin *Aeneid* manuscripts like Klosterneuburg 742 and BN lat. 7936 emphasize the hero who embodies virtues that will lead to his success, these particular vernacular manuscripts depict the two women who most signally challenge standard social roles. Camilla is a warrior, and Dido at once a ruler and a suicide. Women thus take over the story of Aeneas in this pictorial tradition, just as they threaten to subvert his social values and erotic destiny in the text.

This pattern of attention to women, although widespread, is by no means universal. A late fourteenth-century French manuscript of the *Histoire ancienne* (Paris, BN fr. 301), while it portrays both Dido's first greeting of Aeneas and her suicide, devotes far more of its twelve miniatures in the Aeneas section to the hero, his voyages and battles.[52] A roughly similar balance of attention is to be found in the early fifteenth-century Paris, Arsenal 5077.[53]

Not all illustrations, then, record resistant readings or reflect the influence of eroticizing redactions like the *Eneas*. Indeed, some manuscript illustrations participate, to different and usually limited extents, in the efforts that will later be described as the "pedagogical" vision of Virgil. That is, briefly, such illustrations attempt to alert the reader to the difference of Virgilian place and time, rather than effacing or ignoring that difference as do most of the manuscripts discussed above. The Berlin *Eneit* manuscript, mentioned earlier as a largely visual source of access to Virgil, regularly shows the pagan gods, though in human guise, and to some extent distinguishes Aeneas as a leader of ancient origin by his *chlaina* or *chlamys*, the pleated outer garment worn by military or state leaders.[54] The illustrations make no Christian references. And while events take place in recognizably contemporary settings, exotic animals register the geographical difference of Carthage.[55] The Sybil is shown sitting in oriental style.[56] There is even a caption with a rare reference to the historical difference of the moment of the narrative (though only to emphasize continuity) when a stretcher is made for the body of Pallas, "just as we still do today."[57]

In mid-fourteenth century illustrations of Guido delle Colonne, Buchthal finds a similar incipient attempt at imaginative distance, not historical but geographical:

For the most part the Greeks and Trojans no longer appear in the familiar medieval garb, but have savage features and sport long hair and flowing beards. They wear Eastern garb and varied, pointedly foreign headgear... Through this device the story is removed – not indeed in time but, perhaps even more remarkably, in place – from western Europe into a remote and exotic world. The Trojan War is now located in the mysterious East.[58]

This visual exoticism will continue as the medium for imaginative distance as late as the 1502 Strasbourg illustrated Virgil of Sebastian Brandt.

The medieval illustrated tradition of Virgil and of his vernacular versions thus provides us with insights not only into contemporary visualization of the classical past, but also a sense of the specific kinds of attention that were being paid to that past, particularly among less learned readers. Indeed, as the production of illustrations moved out of the learned clerical world that might have produced a manuscript like Klosterneuburg 742, and into a context of lay production, they record occasions where popular preoccupations entered into the learned Latin tradition, and contested its textual dominance. Such crossing points are indeed rare – vernacular and learned Virgilianism descend in generally independent materials – but nonetheless significant. For they suggest the kinds of strain that could occur when competing readerly interests came together either in the codicological record or in the mind of a reader who moved among languages and traditions. We will return to similar situations of mutually inconsistent readership in the multiple annotation of manuscripts treated in chapters 3 and 4, and in the Virgilian reading of Chaucer.

TEXTUAL ACCESS: MANUSCRIPTS AND BEYOND

The materials outlined in the two sections above give an idea of some of the radial fields of ideas and presuppositions surrounding the medieval *Aeneid*, and challenging the preoccupations of the central Latin text. Moreover, the cultural *auctoritas* attached to Virgil himself, the historical context and its counter-tradition, and the illustrations all show us ways in which the story and setting of the *Aeneid* could be grasped without, necessarily, any direct textual access to Virgil.[59] This brings us, however, to another crucial issue: the real extent of direct and detailed reading of the *Aeneid*, or other textual access to Virgil beyond direct and continuous reading, during the Middle Ages generally, and in England in particular.

The most obvious gauge of Virgilian reading is of course the evidence of surviving manuscripts. Munk Olsen's handlist of surviving classical manuscripts, which extends only to the close of the twelfth century, includes well over two hundred and fifty extant whole or fragmentary manuscripts of Virgil.[60] A list compiled by Gian Carlo Alessio, extending to the fifteenth century, numbers over a thousand, with a large majority however produced in Italy during the Renaissance.[61]

Scholars of Middle English literature have in the past expressed doubt about strong direct Virgilian influence in high and later medieval England, because so few manuscripts of English origin or medieval English provenance have previously been identified.[62] But in Appendix I, I identify over thirty-five Virgil manuscripts copied in England or brought there during the Middle Ages; three of these will receive detailed treatment in the chapters to follow. These manuscripts alone represent a significant tradition. Moreover, the numerous sets of marginal notes in many of them show that their role was even greater than their mere numbers would suggest. For the simple survival of a manuscript does not demonstrate its influence. Indeed, on the contrary, a great many fifteenth-century Italian Virgils are as innocent of thumbprints and annotations today as when they were written. Their vellum is crisp and white, their contents quite unread: renaissance coffee-table books.

On the other hand, much-used manuscripts could fall to pieces.

Their very wide influence is attested by no physical survival at all, or only by fragments or even single leaves rescued from bindings and other odd corners. (See Appendix I, nos. 1, 2, 4, 5, 6, 27, 32, 35, and 37.) Because of this, a thorough treatment of manuscript access to Virgil should also, ideally, include a study of his presence in medieval library catalogs. Here, systematic analysis must await further publication, as there exists as yet no full edition of surviving English medieval book lists. Meanwhile, studies are based on incomplete materials. Nonetheless, they too show that Virgil manuscripts were widely distributed in medieval England. In the thirteen surviving book lists from Anglo-Saxon libraries, Virgil is mentioned twice, at the beginning and toward the end of the period.[63] Alcuin's problematic book list includes "Maro Virgilius," and a late eleventh-century list, possibly from Worcester, includes the *Bucolics* and *Georgics*.[64] (The generally accepted insular transmission of Servius, too, suggests interest in Virgil in the pre-Carolingian period.) And a study of eleventh and twelfth century catalogs finds Virgil manuscripts also at Bury, Canterbury, Durham, Glastonbury, Lincoln, Reading, Rochester, and Whitby.[65]

It would be a great mistake, however, to limit our sense of medieval command of the *Aeneid* exclusively to the evidence of manuscripts and the records of manuscripts. We have already seen that a great radial field of legendary, storial, and visual material surrounds the *Aeneid*, providing alternate access and affecting interpretations. Similarly, one measure of the *Aeneid*'s huge cultural influence is expressed by the tremendous range of texts that contain echoes and explicit quotations of the epic; and these in turn provide, in different degrees, significant textual access to, and alternate voicings of, Virgil.

Once again, the more recent examples of Shakespeare and Freud provide useful comparisons. Whether silent or overt, literary references to Freud provide us with some information about his ideas, be that information right or wrong, simplistic or sophisticated. The same is true for Shakespeare. In the case of both authors, as well, their cultural *cachet* alerts our attention even to isolated quotations; they carry a cultural weightiness that would be lacking in quotations of a lesser analyst or playwright. Even scattered references and quotations will be attracted, as it were magnetically, around our imaginative grasp of a central figure like Freud, Shakespeare or, for earlier centuries, Virgil. So some account must be taken of the great range of textual access to Virgil outside his actual manuscripts.

Virgil's effect on the Latin language, ever since his entry as a curriculum text, is virtually immeasurable. It is so constant and so widespread that any study of it, except for very narrow fields, becomes almost hopelessly unwieldy. Fortunately, Suerbaum's bibliography gives us a fairly systematic conspectus of these narrower studies. His sections on *Nachleben* and *Nachwirkung* in late classical and medieval times comprise forty pages, and give dramatic proof of the influence and continuity of Virgilian reading.[66] Equally convincing though largely unanalytical is Pierre Courcelle's magisterial survey, *Lecteurs païens et lecteurs chrétiens de l'Énéide*, 1: *Les Témoignages littéraires* (Courcelle I). Courcelle's survey is most complete for the fathers and other Christian documents through about the sixth century.[67] For later periods, through the twelfth century and occasionally extending to Petrarch, he is necessarily less thorough and often inconsistent. What his citations do prove, though, is the extent to which Virgil penetrated the language and imaginations not only of the learned early fathers – Jerome, Lactantius, Augustine, Ambrose, Tertullian – but also Christian poets (Paulinus of Nola, Ausonius) and epitaph writers. Courcelle shows all these writers using citations from and comparisons to Virgil to describe events in their own times,[68] their personal fortunes,[69] their religious history,[70] and their moral worlds.[71] The patristic debate over the use of pagan texts centers on Virgil; but even where Virgil is explicitly rejected, his presence in the language and thought patterns of the Latin fathers and later writers is inescapable. Hagendahl's two books give the best summary of this influence.[72]

Many such echoes of Virgil, patristic and later, are of course covert, or even unconscious. Especially in well-educated writers, they can represent more or less conscious evocation of the *auctor*, or they may simply be appropriate and eloquent phrases plucked from the vast mnemonic baggage of late-antique education, which happens inevitably to be replete with Virgil. The question in such cases is, are these echoes present in a fashion that effectively transmits some access to Virgil, as Virgil, or has he entered the language so successfully as to become buried in it? For instance, is Henry of Huntingdon's quotation from *Aeneid* 2 (mentioned in note 68, above) a conscious reference to Virgil, or is he rather echoing Jerome's Letter to Heliodorus, or some other intermediary, unaware of the source? In some cases, the Virgilian identification of a brief, well-known phrase must have been lost at an early point. This is particularly true of phrases (which are legion) that lent themselves to use as truisms. But echoes that evoke well-known moments from the *Aeneid* and apply them to a similar later context, as

Henry of Huntingdon in fact does, are more likely (though not certain) to be consciously manipulated.

It is certain, however, that some major patristic works of extraordinarily wide diffusion make frequent and overt reference to Virgil, thereby transmitting considerable sections of his text and sometimes implying modes of interpretation. Augustine's *City of God* is perhaps the most famous instance, with frequent and explicit citations of the *Aeneid*, both positive and negative; but the implicit Virgilian structure and references of the *Confessions* would also have been apparent to many readers.[73]

A less problematic and more easily traceable textual access to Virgil outside his own manuscripts is to be found in a broad range of educational materials. The emphasis of the *trivium* in medieval education was always the teaching and employment of the Latin language. From the late-classical period onward, Virgil was among the most frequently mined sources for examples of elegant Latinity. At almost any period, and in almost any educational center of the Middle Ages, a student of grammar and rhetoric would gain an intimate knowledge of great swaths of Virgil's text, even barring any direct contact with Virgilian manuscripts. Ralph Hexter reports that a medieval student could have known over three thousand lines of Virgil just by studying major late-classical grammar texts that used him as a source of examples far more than they did any other classical writer.[74] Other teaching tools are equally important and sometimes provide considerable textual access to Virgil outside of his manuscripts. Glossaries often draw extensive vocabulary and accompanying examples from Virgilian texts.[75] Metrical treatises also depend, often preponderantly, on Virgil.[76] This range of material also has a tremendous impact on actual readings of the *Aeneid*. We will see its influence when we turn to a detailed consideration of marginalia in Virgil manuscripts and see the extent to which some commentators approach the *Aeneid* as a series of rhetorical tropes and figures.

Priscian's *Institutes*, for example, were at the center of medieval grammar studies. Priscian includes extensive quotations from Latin prose writers, and from Horace, Juvenal, Lucan, Ovid, Plautus, Statius, and Terence. But Virgil is by far the most quoted author throughout the *Institutes*. He was thus embedded in the single most important grammatical text of the Middle Ages.[77] In the other major text for grammatical study, Donatus's *Ars Grammatica*, Virgil again provides the vast majority of the examples cited.[78]

These late-classical grammars had few rivals during the early Middle Ages and through the end of the twelfth century. In these periods, too, Virgil himself was of course the object of much direct study at more advanced levels.[79] With the coming of the thirteenth century, however, and the new organization of higher education into specialized faculties at urban universities, interest in the reading of classical literature is generally thought to have gone into decline. This belief, as formulated by Paetow at the beginning of this century, continues to be influential.[80]

Paetow rightly points out that the arts course became highly technical, and that Donatus and Priscian, gravid with classical material, were less and less present in lists of required texts in the thirteenth and fourteenth centuries. They were replaced by more summary grammatical works, chiefly the *Doctrinale* of Alexander of Villedieu (appeared 1199), and the *Graecismus* of Eberhard of Bethune (appeared 1212). Universities in the south of France, like Orléans and Toulouse, seem to have been exceptions to this trend.[81]

These assumptions about classical interest in the later Middle Ages were early challenged by E. K. Rand in two suggestive articles whose ramifications have not been sufficiently explored. Rand makes the obvious but important observation that major vernacular writers of the thirteenth century, like Dante and Jean de Meun, show a superb and undiminished command of classical literature for which Paetow's generalizations fail to account. Rand also points to the classical interests of lesser Latin writers like John of Garland, Vincent of Beauvais, and Etienne de Bourbon. He cites thirteenth-century anthologies and collections of *accessus* in which classical writers play a prominent role. Most important, Rand shows how very much citation of classical texts there is to be found in Eberhard's *Graecismus*, the very grammatical text that, according to Paetow, is at the root of the decline of classicism in the thirteenth century.[82] The same can also be said of the other rising grammatical text of the later Middle Ages, Alexander's *Doctrinale*.[83] Even Paetow includes an appendix on "Survivals of the Classics, circa 1225–1325," though he clearly sees these as sporadic and archaic interests.

Research since Paetow and Rand, while it has not directly addressed the issues they raise, has nonetheless brought to light some of the conduits for the kind of continuing classicism argued by Rand. It is now clear that Paetow's emphasis on the institutional aspects of intellectual history is much too narrow a basis on which to judge interest in classical authors. The rising professionalism of the universities attracted only one part of the educated public, or only one part of their intellectual lives. It is outside the universities, or outside their institutional structure, that we can seek the classicism of the thirteenth and earlier fourteenth centuries.

Medieval *florilegia* provide one of the most important sources and manifestations of this continuing classicism. They have received intensive and fruitful study in recent years.[84] These anthologies are extremely varied in form and content, serving a wide range of uses, from sources of *exempla* to teaching tools. They were enormously popular and survive in over a thousand manuscripts. Most of them were assembled in the later half of the twelfth century, largely in France.[85] Rouse has recently shown that the two most important, the *Florilegium Angelicum* and the *Florilegium Gallicum*, are closely connected to the classical school of twelfth-century Orléans.[86] Despite their twelfth-century French origin, however, these texts were copied and studied all over Europe, including England, throughout the Middle Ages.

While he is not the most quoted author, Virgil occupies an honored place in the *florilegia*; the more sententious, 'quotable' authors like Claudian, Horace, Martial, and especially Ovid, are generally given more space.[87] There is an important exception to this in the metrical *florilegium* of Mico Centulensis, the *Opus Prosodiacum*, in which Virgil is quoted seventy-four times – more than twice as often as the next-most cited poet, Martial. At least one copy of this work, London, BL Burney 257, was at the Cistercian house of Thame in the thirteenth century.[88]

There are a number of other *florilegia*, compiled or copied in England, which testify to continued Virgilian interest there after the twelfth century. Oxford, Bodleian Library, Rawl. C.552 contains "flores auctorum." It was copied in England in the early thirteenth century, but continuing interest in its contents is proven by the early fourteenth-century hand that entered a table of contents on a flyleaf (now separately bound as Rawl. D.1230). The collection contains "proverbia" from Virgil and other classical poets as well as post-classical writers like Prudentius, Alan of Lille, Geoffrey of Vinsauf, and Matthew of Vendôme. Virgil begins the collection and is given more space than any of the others except Ovid. Selections from Virgil include forty lines from the *Eclogues* and eighty from the *Georgics*. There are over one hundred lines from the *Aeneid*. Their presentation is particularly interesting: at the beginning of the *Aeneid* selections, a long marginal note gives a prose summary of the plot. The reader, thus armed with the story, is provided with a sort of "Greatest Hits" version

of the epic – all those lines that the compiler considered, as he put it in
his introduction, "fulgidiores." These include the first four lines of
Book One, parts of Aeneas's famous speech "O socii" (1.198 ff.),
Dido's dignified speech of welcome to the shipwrecked Trojans ("non
ignara mali miseris succerrere disco," 1.630), the description of *Fama*
(4.174-77), and many other celebrated passages. The quotations, like
the prose summary, do not dwell on Dido's fury and final agony.[89]

The *florilegia* were thus an important, if limited, channel for access to
classical authors, including Virgil, in a period when these writers were
no longer at the center of institutional learning. But, just as important,
they show us textual sites from which the classical fragments, denuded
of context, could be domesticated and applied to interests often quite
foreign to their original sense.[90]

THE PERSISTENCE OF VIRGIL IN ENGLAND

In this widespread and continuous history of medieval interest in
Virgil, marked by wide varieties of access and of interpretation, the
British Isles play an ancient and distinguished role. The chapters that
follow will examine several significant episodes in the specific traditions
of British Virgilianism during the high and later Middle Ages. Before
proceeding to those representative episodes, however, it will be well to
cast a brief glance at the earlier history of British Virgilianism and the
evidence for its persistence.

Roman Britain went through a period of peace and prosperity in the
fourth century, when many other Roman colonies were declining into
disorder. Coins, tiles, and mosaics from the period make visual and
literary reference to episodes in the *Aeneid*. Remains of villas show that
this knowledge occurred in a setting of some luxury and culture. The
famous tiled floor at Low Ham in Somerset shows the story of Aeneas
and Dido.[91] Another, now known only in drawings, shows Aeneas and
the Golden Bough. Yet another mosaic, depicting the abduction of
Europa, has an inscription referring to the fury of Juno in *Aeneid*
One.[92] In later sub-Roman Britain, too, there are signs of continuing study of
grammar, in which Virgil was the preeminent example of propriety.[93]
Michael Lapidge has shown that the writing of Gildas shows training in
traditional grammar and rhetoric, and echoes of Virgil so dense as to
be not always conscious.[94]

The Germanic invasions ended the long sunset of Roman Britain,
and in the following centuries classical learning must have declined

steeply, even if England and Ireland indeed "succeeded in bypassing the Dark Ages."[95] With the revival of Christian learning in Ireland and England, however, there was a renewed need for some improved command of Latin. This involved grammatical studies, and their accompanying range of Virgilian reference.[96] But the search for knowledge of Latin, and command of exegetic technique, did not end with the basic works of grammar. There is a large body of evidence that considerable study and actual compilation of Virgilian commentaries was taking place in the seventh and eighth centuries in Ireland and in those island monasteries whence northern England was converted.[97]

The evidence is most certain in the surviving manuscripts themselves, many of which show "insular symptoms": signs of textual confusion in extant manuscripts, caused by the misunderstanding of peculiarly insular graphs or abbreviations in the exemplars. This evidence can be ambiguous, since scribes born into or trained in insular scribal technique worked on the Continent.[98] But the bulk of the evidence is convincing: the Servian tradition certainly passed through the British Isles. In the seventh century, Aldhelm uses Servius in his *De metris*, and the commentary may be listed in Alcuin's catalog of books at York, if that is the work to which its "Seruius" refers.[99] It has also been widely thought that "Servius auctus" (or "Servius Danielis," an expanded Servius, whose additional notes indirectly reflect the work of Aelius Donatus) was actually compiled by an Irish scholar.[100] Moreover, the earliest extant manuscript of Servius is written in the Anglo-Saxon minuscule of the first half of the eighth century, possibly from the southwest.[101] The confused mass of scholia on the *Eclogues* and *Georgics*, now preserved in various combinations as the "Filargyrian scholia," the *Scholia Bernensia*, and the *Brevis Expositio*, also appear to have passed through insular, probably Irish, exemplars.[102] The study of commentaries for their grammatical and historical information, however, is not the same as the study of classical texts themselves; and it has been suggested that Virgil and other Latin poets rode through the early British Middle Ages to some extent on the backs of their commentaries, rather than *vice versa*.[103] But it is clear, at the very least, that Virgilian citations in the grammars were registered as issuing from an important *auctor*, and were echoed by insular Latin poets.

Ireland and Irish foundations were not the only centers of Virgilian interest. The southwest of England had its own early Christian foundations and in the sixth century, as already noted, the historian Gildas uses Virgilian echoes in his *De excidio et conquestu Britanniae,* as in the seventh century does Aldhelm (who was first educated at Malmesbury) in his treatise on metrics and elsewhere.[104]

Hadrien and Theodore of Tarsus brought Roman books as well as the Roman calendar when they came to Canterbury in 668. Since Aldhelm also studied at Canterbury, it is possible that his classicism came through this channel as well. This and other evidence of learning in the eighth century south of the Humber gives the impression "of a far more 'literary,' perhaps also a less well-ordered culture than in the Northumbria of Bede and Alcuin."[105] Benedict Biscop did carry books to his northern foundation on his return from Rome in 669. But if Bede is typical, Virgil and other classical poets were not so eagerly studied there as in the south.[106]

Ireland and England seem to have exported much of their intellectual energy along with the books and missionaries they sent out to the Continent. The study of Virgil, as well as other Latin secular texts, may already have been quiescent when the Viking invasions began to wreak their havoc in the ninth century. Wales was spared much of this, and there was considerable copying of classical texts there after 800. Alfred turned to a Welshman, Asser, for help in his translation of Boethius, and Wales was a source of texts in the monastic revival under Dunstan in the tenth century.[107] It is from this period that we possess our earliest extant English manuscripts of Virgil, one a few surviving lines in pointed Anglo-Saxon minuscule (Appendix I, no. 2), and the other a splendid English Caroline minuscule *Aeneid* perhaps from Worcester (Appendix I, no. 3).

It is impossible to say at this point whether these and later Virgils were copied from newly imported exemplars or from the survivals of ancient libraries at York, Canterbury, or in the West Country. Dunstan himself, for example, whose classical interests are well established, spent a period of exile on the Continent in the 950's; on the other hand, he was raised near Glastonbury where there was constant contact with the ongoing classical studies of the Celtic fringe, and he also studied at Canterbury.[108]

There is considerable evidence for the importation of manuscripts in the tenth and eleventh centuries. No Virgils have been so identified, but other manuscripts passed through Canterbury and the West Country, where there were Virgil manuscripts by the twelfth century.[109] Exacting textual study of the surviving tenth-century manuscript and the twelfth-century Virgils might show whether they come from common or independent textual families, and whether any of these are significantly independent of continental traditions.

The Norman Conquest brought with it new scholars and a considerable influx of new manuscripts, particularly from Norman monasteries. The arrival of the Virgil commentary attributed to Anselm of Laon (discussed in chapter 2), of which we possess a late twelfth-century copy from Canterbury or Rochester (London, BL Additional 16380), is probably to be associated with the Conquest. The cultural connection of Britain and Normandy also opened England to the interests of the twelfth-century Renaissance. The largest group of the manuscripts listed in Appendix I date from this period. And while the twelfth century has been called the *aetas Ovidiana*,[110] Birger Munk Olsen's work has now shown that no such neat division responds to the actual history of manuscript production. From the twelfth century, there survive sixty-five manuscripts of the *Aeneid*, an equal number of Horace's *Satires*, and twenty-eight of the *Metamorphoses*.[111] Whatever Ovid's popularity, and it was very great, this does not suggest that Virgil had been eclipsed, nor yet Horace. In chapters 2 and 3, I will give detailed attention to two manuscripts originally written in the twelfth century. Ireland also participated in the Virgilian interests of the age, and the first half of the twelfth century saw a close adaptation of the *Aeneid* into Irish prose.[112]

England shared in the decline of institutional concentration on classical literature after the twelfth century. But the indirect sources of access to Virgil also functioned fully in England. Further, as I will show in chapter 3, there are signs that the classical interests of the twelfth-century Renaissance continued longer in parts of England than they did generally on the Continent. And while Oxford, like Paris, turned away from classical studies, classical authors were nonetheless read there as part of the study of grammar in the early fourteenth century.[113]

An important group of friars who lectured at Oxford and Cambridge from roughly 1280 to 1350 showed tremendous interest in classical literature, though predominantly in writers of sententious and historical prose.[114] But Virgil also had their attention. Robert Holcot allegorized the arming of Aeneas in his Oxford lectures on the twelve prophets in 1333–34.[115] Chapter 4 will present evidence that their interests can now be extended to the 1380's. And it was exactly in that time that Chaucer was at work on his vernacular treatments of the Aeneas-and-Dido story that we will study in chapter 6.

The direct study of Virgil in the late thirteenth and early fourteenth centuries is further demonstrated by a densely annotated *Eclogues* manuscript (Appendix I, no. 22). Other surviving Virgil manuscripts from the fourteenth century are witness to a rising interest in classical literature, before influence was felt from the Renaissance in Italy (Appendix I, nos. 23 and 24). Finally, this interest in Virgil resulted in the importation to England of Italian manuscripts during the fifteenth century (Appendix I, nos. 25 and 28).

Interest in Virgil and the classical past, moreover, was not limited to the clerical classes. The Trojan legend had expanded by the twelfth century to include the foundation of France and England by later Trojan fugitives. Brutus had "founded" England, and this had given rise to spurious genealogical claims with considerable political repercussions and cultural echoes.[116] The powerful Mortimers claimed descent from both Arthur and Brutus.[117] Humphrey de Bohun, Earl of Hereford and Essex (*c.* 1276–1322) named one of his sons Eneas.[118]

Altogether, then, the British Isles were the scene of a lively and widespread interest in Virgil, which continued with only rare interruptions from late classical times through the end of the Middle Ages, and of course beyond. Their greatest contribution to the Virgil tradition in the west was no doubt the transmission of the late-classical scholia. As the following chapters will show, however, England participated actively in the continental Virgilianisms of the high and later Middle Ages. More than that, it made original contributions of its own, not only in the form of commentaries to be studied in chapters 2 through 4, but also through the *Roman d'Eneas*, the synthetic genius of Chaucer's treatment of Virgil, and through Douglas's extraordinary translation.

CHAPTER TWO

Pedagogical exegesis of Virgil in medieval England: Oxford, All Souls College 82

This chapter examines, in considerable detail, a representative twelfth-century English school manuscript of Virgil, Oxford, All Souls College 82, as it was used and re-used across three centuries. By studying the manuscript's progressive annotation, and the varied institutional settings of that annotation, I will claim not only that a single broad approach to the *Aeneid* characterizes the manuscript in its own history, but also that in this, the manuscript is typical of the dominant medieval Virgilianism. Moreover, I want to show that this approach has links (through similarity of aim and direct verbal dependence) back to the late antique commentary of Servius, and forward to the school commentaries of the earlier Italian humanists.

I will be calling this tradition of exegesis, based in the lower schools but at certain points moving out of them, the "pedagogical" vision of Virgil. This pedagogical tradition focusses almost exclusively on the letter of the ancient text, and displays little concern either to judge or reject the beliefs of the past, or to domesticate them through allegoresis or more direct ethical applications. Instead, it often goes to some lengths to provide the kind of information that would help a reader apprehend not just the verbal detail of the text, but also its historical, political, mythological, and geographical setting: the difference of the past. I see in this manuscript, then, and in much (perhaps most) medieval Virgilianism, an effort to gain a sense of the past that places it in a continuum with the Virgilianism of late Antiquity and the Renaissance.

PRODUCTION, OWNERSHIP, AND HISTORY OF ALL SOULS 82

All Souls 82 is typical, in its general character and history, of a number of Virgil manuscripts used in the monasteries and schools of twelfth-century England.[1] The manuscript is distinguished, though, by the unusually high level of discipline displayed in its production, and by the consistent, well controlled small book-hand of its text (see plate 2).[2] Typical of the high medieval English Virgils, it is also among the finest of them. The manuscript's history is not unlike others, moving from a house of canons in the twelfth century to a university college in the fifteenth, but it is unusual in the extent and precision with which we can trace its movements and ownership. Indeed, its particular history may connect it with the education of Henry II, and thereby suggest a context of readership and a political implication for its historicizing exegesis quite different from the clerical schoolroom.

All Souls 82 (hereafter AS82) has the long, narrow shape widely shared by school manuscripts of classical verse in the period after the grand, squarish books of the Carolingian period. In format it has the usual simple frame, ruled in hard point with rare precision. Its forty-four lines per page, slightly more than usual, are also observed with a regularity not often found elsewhere. In part, of course, this consistency should be attributed not to a self-consciously disciplined scriptorium but to the presence of only a single scribe. Elsewhere, startling changes of format are often introduced by new hands within a single manuscript.[3]

The manuscript is practically a compendium of the spurious and related works which appear in medieval English Virgils.[4] The pseudo-Ovidian verses summarizing each book of the *Aeneid* are very common, but not often so complete. The introductory autobiographical verses "Ille ego ..." are also widely found, and their uncertain authenticity is often resolved, as here, by sticking them in an odd corner.[5] (Indeed, these lines may have been added by the hand designated below as annotator IA.) All the other pieces listed in the description can be found in other English manuscripts of Virgil, but in no other case in England are they all found together.

AS82 received three major layers of marginal annotation, added at fairly evenly spaced moments in its history. Significantly, and again typically, new layers of annotation do not ignore or reject the old, but rather supplement them, displaying at the same time important changes in interest, emphasis, and information. What links these three groups of notes, spread across three centuries, is their common pedagogical emphasis. Each annotator tried to make available to readers of the manuscript some range of information that would provide access to a sense of the *Aeneid* in terms of its own verbal, historical, and religious realities. These will be studied in detail below.

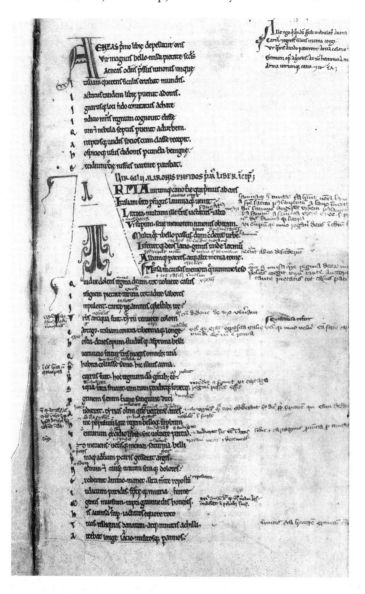

Plate 2 Oxford, All Souls College 82, fo. 36 *recto*, opening of *Aeneid*. The text of Book One is prefaced by a one-line and a ten-line summary of the book, here typically presented together. In the upper right corner are the pseudo-Virgilian "opening lines" of the *Aeneid*, their uncertain authority reflected in their position and size. The three major commentary hands in the manuscript are all visible on this page. Published with permission.

As is common in the English manuscripts, the format of marginalia is haphazard; the margins are not ruled and the notes usually lack lemmata and *signes de renvoi*. Text and notes are related only by juxtaposition, and even this is often imprecise. There are neither interlinear glosses nor marginal annotation to the *Eclogues* and *Georgics*.[6] This imbalance of attention is also reflected in the condition of the membrane, far more dirty and worn in the *Aeneid* than in the first booklet.

Surviving manuscripts of classical Latin poets from medieval England are generally silent about their early history. Most ecclesiastical libraries were disturbed or disbanded in the religious turmoil of the 1530's and 1540's; classical manuscripts were eagerly collected by English humanists and antiquarians, and often rebound, thus usually losing the flyleaves which frequently carry marks of earlier ownership. The fortunate preservation of the original flyleaves by a fifteenth-century binder, and the meticulous habits of an early All Souls librarian, however, allow us to associate AS82 with four of its medieval owners, and four interestingly varied intellectual contexts: one Magister Aluredus (modern "Alfred," possibly the tutor of Henry II), the Augustinian canons' Abbey of St. Mary at Cirencester, Henry Penwortham, and (in 1438) All Souls College.

A flyleaf inscription, "Liber Magistri Aluredi," allows us to associate the manuscript not just with the milieu of the schools, but perhaps with a particular if little-known teacher.[7] Identical inscriptions appear in two other extant manuscripts of the twelfth century, Oxford, Jesus College 26 (Ivo of Chartres's legal text, the *Panormia*) and Hereford Cathedral O.2.iv (Gilbert of Poitier's commentary on the Pauline Epistles).[8] The preeminent work of canon law before Gratian, and a very important and popular Bible commentary, thus were held in the same ownership as the great Roman poet. This nicely balanced if certainly fragmentary collection suggests a master of wide range, teaching the *trivium* but also moving through law and theology.

All three of these manuscripts have strong West Country connections.[9] Neil Ker thought their ownership inscriptions "probably . . . late twelfth century," and mentions a John Alured who was chaplain to the bishop of Hereford from 1200 to 1219 (though not identified as Magister).[10] By the end of the twelfth century, though, this group of books would probably have seemed rather out of date. Gilbert wrote his commentary about 1130 and it was in England by the 1140's, but while still read and copied at the end of the century, it had largely been superseded by the *"magna glosatura"* of Peter Lombard which started circulating in the 1160's.[11] Similarly, Ivo's *Panormia* was eclipsed as Gratian's *Decretum* (completed about 1140) began to circulate.

It may be reasonable then to look for a somewhat earlier Alfred, with links to western England, as the teacher who owned these manuscripts. Richard Hunt suggested as a candidate "the man who attested writs of Henry II, including one for Cirencester Abbey of c. 1155"; in all these he is identified as *magister*.[12] We can go further. At an uncertain period before 1179 an "Alfred, Canon of Cirencester" witnessed a charter granting land to St. Peter's Abbey, Gloucester.[13] An Aluredus was Abbot of another Augustinian house, at Haughmond in Shropshire, from about 1163 into the 1170's. Moreover, this Aluredus is identified in a Haughmond charter as having been a *nutricius* (mentor, tutor) of Henry.[14] Could these be the same man, and could AS82 have belonged to the tutor who gave the young Henry some of his education?

Here we skate on thin ice, but a believable picture does emerge from the documents. The Augustinians were a learned order, and Cirencester a distinguished abbey in these years.[15] A young but learned canon of Cirencester, with some connection to the wealthy and influential Benedictine house of St. Peter's Gloucester (ruled in the 1140's by Gilbert Foliot), could have been a reasonable candidate to teach Duke Henry, whose education was overseen by his uncle, Robert Earl of Gloucester. And a trusted tutor might well continue to move in and out of the young king's circle early in his reign, thus witnessing occasional charters; he might also help push through and witness a charter benefiting his old house at Cirencester. It would be a typical move, too, for such a man to be made abbot of another rising Augustinian abbey, Haughmond, in the Welsh border country where Angevin patronage enriched many religious houses.[16] And Master Alfred's early connection to Cirencester (if we are indeed speaking of the same person) could help explain why his Virgil manuscript ended up at that abbey.[17]

Certainly the three books owned by "Magister Aluredus" would have made a quite up-to-date collection in the 1150's, and their range – classical Latin epic, law, and *sacra pagina* – would well befit the education of a prince admired for his learning.[18] The West Country connections suit, too, since we know that some of Henry's education took place in Bristol. And these books would not be too ambitious for a young man who was also taught by towering figures like William of

Conches and Adelard of Bath.[19] Whether or not the owner of AS82 was indeed the Aluredus who was the prince's tutor, Henry did become a patron of intellectually connected houses, among them the Victorine priories of Bristol and Wigmore (whose prior was the great biblical scholar Andrew of St. Victor). Moreover, the later literary patronage associated with Henry's court (which we will examine in chapter 5) would center around the classical literature of empire and *translatio imperii*, and this reflects interest and real training in Latin classics.[20] As I will show in chapter 5, the *Roman d'Eneas* assumes and exploits a sophisticated grasp of classical Latin literature in at least part of its audience. A better-attested tutor of the prince, Pierre de Saintes, composed a Latin Troy poem that could serve as introduction to such study.[21]

The manuscript's third flyleaf carries another, later inscription, largely erased: "Liber ecclesie Sce Marie de <Cyrence>st<r>'."[22] The house of Augustinian canons at St. Mary's Cirencester was founded in 1131. It was well respected at the end of the century and ultimately became "the richest house of the order in England."[23] This early record of ownership thus places AS82 again squarely in the world of the schools, in cathedral and larger parish establishments, usually run by regular canons, in which the great flowering of *trivium*-study took place.[24] It was in these cathedral and parish schools that the classical Latin poets, Virgil among them, were read as part of the study of grammar and rhetoric, and it is apparently for such a context that the manuscript was provided with the interlinear and marginal notes studied below.[25]

A little over two centuries after it was owned by Master Alfred, AS82 came into the hands of a third recorded owner, Henry Penwortham, who spent the last twenty years of his life as registrar and treasurer of Archbishop Chichele, the founder of All Souls College.[26] In Penwortham's hands, the manuscript formed part of a collection slightly more historical and belletristic in character than that of "Magister Aluredus." Along with a manuscript of homilies and sermon material by various authors (All Souls 19), Penwortham also owned a manuscript (All Souls 37) containing historical and antiquarian works such as the *Flores historiarum* of Matthew of Westminster, and Nigel Whiteacre's *Brunellus*. The text of Virgil has moved here into the more public and secular world of high church power, and an owner whose use for the manuscript would appear to have been more readerly and historical than teacherly, grammatical, or rhetorical. Certainly the fourteenth century witnessed an increased respect for the therapeutic and recreational value of literary pleasure, for clerics as well as princes.[27] While the manuscript's last layer of notes was (to judge from the handwriting) probably entered in the generation or so before Penwortham, these notes nonetheless reflect a setting and set of interests consonant with the later owner, as we will see below (pp. 68–80).

Penwortham left his Virgil and a number of other manuscripts to All Souls College.[28] With this bequest of 1438, he moved the manuscript on to the next stage in the typical history of high medieval Virgils, which by the end of the Middle Ages often find their way into the universities. There they share with imported Italian manuscripts the attention of the English humanists. Compare, for example, the intriguing history of Cambridge, Jesus College 33 (Appendix I, no. 12), written in England in the twelfth century. Lost leaves were replaced in the fifteenth century, and by mid-century it was privately owned by the early English humanist John Free. Free took it with him to Italy, where he learned humanist minuscule; in this hand he added extensive notes from his studies with Guarino da Verona. Free willed the manuscript to John Gunthorpe, who in turn left his books to Jesus College.[29]

The most significant aspect of the history of AS82 – and here again it is typical of English Virgils – is the very duration of its use and the variety of contexts, institutional and intellectual, to which it was relevant. From this point of view, the English manuscripts of Virgil which we know today represent a far greater impact on the intellectual life of the nation than is suggested by their simple numbers. The duration and variety of use met by a manuscript like AS82, however, is best seen not in the bare facts of history and ownership, but in the nature of the commentaries by which the text is surrounded. Before investigating the layers of annotation in AS82, though, we need to turn briefly to that monumental pedagogical introduction to Virgil, universally used throughout the Middle Ages and Renaissance, the commentary of the late-antique grammarian Servius.

SERVIUS AND THE CONTINUITY OF PEDAGOGICAL EXEGESIS

Scholarship on the interpretation of Virgil in the Middle Ages has tended to concentrate on allegoresis, and this focus has led to a limited sense of Latin Virgilianism in the period.[30] As is inevitable where the terrain is so incompletely mapped, scholars have sought out those data which reinforce their presuppositions, and the two medieval *Aeneid* commentaries that have appeared in modern editions are both purely allegorizing.[31] Thus the very decision to print the Fulgentius and Bernard Silvestris commentaries (first modern editions 1898 and 1924, respectively) may represent more their affiliation with contemporary notions of medieval readership than it does their actual manuscript diffusion in the period.[32] It is of course true that allegorical approaches – themselves quite varied – played an important role in the medieval reception of the *Aeneid*, and they will receive detailed attention in chapters 3 and 4. But these two published commentaries represent at most only one approach to the classics, among others which medievalists are now exploring more fully. In sheer numbers, the allegorizers do not even begin to approach the influence of those commentaries I am calling, in a fairly narrow sense, "pedagogical" – the Virgilianism of the lower schools.[33] AS82 is merely one example among many; the pedagogical tradition represents the single most important channel of medieval Virgilian commentary.[34]

At the same time that its dominant method has been taken to be allegorical, classical readership in the Middle Ages has been considered unable or unwilling to understand ancient texts as set in a past which must be imaginatively recaptured. In fact, though, as I will show in this and the following sections, the central tradition of medieval Virgilian commentary consistently aims to regain some sense of the original setting of the *Aeneid* (or at least of Virgil's Rome), perceived as different in language, religion, social order, and geography.

This preponderant interest in the letter of the text, as it is reflected in the twelfth-century annotation of AS82 and similar Virgil manuscripts, is fully coherent with contemporary developments in biblical exegesis. The middle quarters of the twelfth century saw a concern for the literal exegesis of the Bible returning to prominence along with the established traditions of Gregorian allegoresis. Beryl Smalley locates the initial resurgence of such study in the *Notulae* of Hugh of St. Victor, in which "the importance of the letter is constantly stressed" as a crucial preparatory to spiritual interpretation.[35] But it was Andrew of St. Victor who, for Smalley, best carried out Hugh's exegetical principles in the following generation, whence they influenced the great commentators of the later twelfth century, like Peter Comestor and Peter the Chanter.[36] Andrew was a persistent literalist, with widespread "interest in the chronology and geography of the Old Testament."[37] Where (as we will see) the twelfth-century annotators of

AS82 turned to Macrobius and Roman historians to help with literal understanding, Hugh and Andrew turned to Jewish scholars and sources.[38]

The dominant Virgilian exegesis of the high and later Middle Ages, however, also has far earlier roots, and can in fact be summarized in one word: Servius.[39] In clearing the ground for the Harvard Edition of this late classical commentator, Charles Murgia has revealed for medievalists the extraordinary diffusion, throughout the period, of Servius or Servian-based commentaries, with their emphasis on literal explanation and pedagogical exposition of grammatical, historical, and geographical detail.[40] Murgia's *Index Codicum Siglorumque* lists over three-hundred twenty manuscripts containing some Servian commentary.[41] A similar, indeed closely derivative, Virgil commentary associated with Anselm of Laon confirms the dominance of this pedagogical approach to the letter of the *Aeneid*, as I will show below (pp. 63–68). The manuscript tradition of the allegorical Bernard Silvestris commentary is much smaller, and by comparison to Servius it is tiny.[42]

If medieval Virgilianism is centrally Servian, it is also centrally pedagogical. However varied the success of this pedagogical approach during the Middle Ages, these school commentaries display a continuous impulse to grasp or reconstruct the difference of the Virgilian world, an impulse which unites late-classical Virgil exegesis with that of the Middle Ages and of the Renaissance.[43] Narrowly defined, the Virgilian exegesis offered by the lower schools – late classical, medieval, and renaissance – aimed to provide readers with sufficient information such as history, mythology, geography, and grammar, to understand Virgil's works in something like the historical and social context of antiquity. So narrow a definition, of course, sets aside the problem of the shifting purposes of exegesis: whether a work should ultimately serve the ends of grammatical imitation, rhetorical analysis and the empowerment of Christian eloquence, aesthetic pleasure, historical information, or political or ethical guidance and imitation. But the kind of fundamental material provided by Servius or (in more fragmentary fashion) the margins of AS82 can move in any of these directions.

Servius provided a wide range of the kind of information I associate with pedagogical exegesis. He wrote at a crucial moment at the end of the fourth century: the imperial system was under stress, and there was considerable need for a magisterial and point-by-point description of a fading Virgilian language and world. Servius constructs a summary commentary for an educational system that can no longer be counted on to absorb the great variorum reading partly preserved in *Servius auctus*, nor the specialized treatises on particular aspects of Virgilian wisdom which he mentions in relation to Book Six, much less the Greek and early Latin works from which he constructs his intertextual apparatus. At the same time, Servius still had available to him the earliest Virgilian commentators, most of the ancient Latin writers, and at least some command of Greek history and literature.[44] It is almost exclusively through his work that the Virgilian knowledge of late antiquity reached the high Middle Ages.

Servius simplifies a great deal from his sources, silently making choices among various possible interpretations or references in different passages. We will see this process of selection and simplification progress further in the earlier annotations to AS82. Nevertheless, Servius "distinguishes himself by the clear simplicity which characterizes the great and successful teacher."[45] His clarity and decisiveness combined with his pedagogical technique to produce a commentary magnificent in its command and presentation of local detail in the *Aeneid* and the other works of Virgil. Servius provided for the medieval reader of Virgil that dense and nuanced sense of the Virgilian imaginative landscape which later exegetes struggled so hard to recover for other authors, very often with the aid of Servius himself. Even in the great modern works of Virgilian scholarship, like R. G. Austin's editions, it is the rare page of notes which does not still depend at some point on Servius's knowledge of Virgil's world.

Although his broader intentions tend to disappear under the minuteness of his notes and the need for local pedagogical explanation, Servius nonetheless provides a wide range of the kind of information and interpretation that makes possible an imaginative reconstruction of the Virgilian world.[46] He gives a sense of place, both geographical and historical, explaining place-names and races, describing legal and military antiquities. He explains mythological background, religious belief, and religious ritual. He covers the whole range of language, from basic points of grammar and syntactic order, to praise for the *peritia* (skill, cleverness) of Virgil's choice of the etymologically correct word. He explains Virgil's rhetoric on many levels, identifying simple tropes or analyzing whole speeches. He is also, of course, sensitive to allegorical suggestions, both political and (especially in Book Six) spiritual.[47] But such notes are rare in comparison to the informative and linguistic topics I mention above, though as I will show in chapter

3 they can be selected and expanded to generate a more primarily allegorical set of marginalia.

Like the humanists later on, Servius sees literature also as a model for ethical imitation; he praises Aeneas's *pietas*, Anchises's fatherhood, Ascanius's virtues as a son; he criticizes Dido (despite his fascination with her) for her fall from queenly dignity. More than the virtues of character, though, Servius sees the well made, courtly speech as the important object of imitation.[48] This emphasis on verbal skill too will find echoes in the rhetorical preoccupations of the medieval trivium and the Renaissance. Finally, Servius makes an attempt, if rather a feeble one, to place the *Aeneid* in the context of its literary background of Greek literature and earlier Roman epic.[49]

Let us consider from this point of view Servius's comments on the opening of the *Aeneid*. He explains "Arms" in the first line as a metonymy for war, comparing it to the toga as a metonymy for peace and citing a similar example in Cicero. He points out the three possible meanings of "cano" (to praise, prophesy, or recite), explaining that the last sense is used here. He says that Troy is a region of Asia, but that in this case the name of the region is used to indicate its capital city, which is correctly called Ilium. He explains how Aeneas can be said to have come "first" to Italy, though we later learn that Antenor was in fact there before him: at that time, "Italy" referred only to the land as far as the Rubicon, so that Antenor had really come to Cisalpine Gaul.[50] In the first line alone, then, rhetoric, lexicography, geography, and the history of place names are all used in an attempt to give a historical sense of Virgil's meaning, distinguishing semantic nuance, and resolving confusions that have arisen from changes in words. All these notes have as their basic impulse the pedagogical ends of giving a clear sense of time and place, of linguistic and historical difference, and of stylistic and rhetorical refinement.

In a superb new study, Robert Kaster has shown the extent to which these notes, especially those dealing with verbal usage, operate within a complex framework of social power.[51] Servius's pedagogy, like that of other late-classical grammarians, was an indispensable pathway to social prestige and the linguistic elegance by which the social elite was defined and its power exercised; but at the same time the grammarian's power was effective only and exactly in so far as it was left behind by the student who moved on to rhetoric and thence to active authority. The grammarian himself tended to be socially marginal and static, and his guardianship of his learning was thus all the more jealous. The grammarian's power over language was threatened on the one hand by the vagaries of common usage, and on the other by the idiosyncracies in authoritative texts such as Virgil; between these he set up his own dominant rules and defined the true nature of proper language.[52]

This latter aspect of the commentary is what tends most to drop out of Servius as he is used in the Middle Ages. Servius's vast and essentially pedagogical commentary was wholly available to the high and later Middle Ages, but after the Carolingian period occasions when it was used in its entirety are increasingly rare. The big, stately, squarish manuscripts in which we typically find Carolingian copies of the Latin classics leave a great deal of marginal space for commentary, and often such Virgils include full texts of Servius.[53] The major codicological change in school manuscripts between late Carolingian times and the Renaissance of the twelfth century was the narrowing of the codex, as Virgil became less the author of imperial pretension and royal monasteries, and more the daily bread of the young clerk working his way through *grammatica*. This left less and less marginal space around the text; and as a result it was no longer possible, or it was increasingly difficult, to include the very full kind of commentaries found in the Carolingian codices. Some compression had to take place, and this most often occurred through selection or simplification of Servian entries. Sometimes this is just a series of apparently random selections or abbreviations, particularly in sparsely annotated manuscripts. But often there is some sense of more specific aims being pursued. These aims produce somewhat more limited readings of the *Aeneid* and, as we will see in chapter 3, ultimately point the text in new directions.

Moreover, verbal elegance of the sort so painfully mastered by Servius's students was now far less relevant to pedagogy. It had been challenged by patristic debate over classical *versus* biblical eloquence,[54] and even where verbal elegance was openly sought, the Latin language and literary context in which Servius had operated were so changed as to make much of his advice scarcely recognizable. What remained, and what we will see the annotators of AS82 exploiting, was (first) Servius's more basic grammatical and lexical material, (second) his rhetorical analysis, often expanded, and (third) his substantive information on history, geography, and myth. This narrowing of attention responds intriguingly to the two main roles of the *grammaticus* as summarized by Quintilian: *recte loquendi scientia* on the one hand, and *poetarum enarratio* on the other.[55] Both the nature and centrality of *recte loquendi* had radically changed by the high Middle Ages, while *poetarum enarratio* and its attendant apparatus of historical learning remained crucial to education. Indeed, to the extent that it went beyond basic grammar and syntax, elegant usage had moved away from any contemporary teacher and back to the *auctores* in distinction to whom (as Kaster has shown) the late classical *grammaticus* staked out his position and power.[56]

Different kinds of selection and reduction from Servius produced rather different kinds of sub-commentaries. In the following sections on AS82, we will see two different uses of Servius at work. In the earlier of the two major sets of marginalia, dating from the mid-twelfth century, Servius is compressed and often severely reduced, producing, I will argue, a "flattened" and vague, though still literalist, sense of the Virgilian landscape. But a later fourteenth-century annotator will be seen to revive the more fully detailed exegesis of the original Servian notes, particularly in reference to history and rhetoric, adding more from Servius and composing fresh marginalia which address those pedagogical interests discussed above. Thus we will find an English reader of Virgil in the age of Chaucer already re-emphasizing aspects of pedagogical exegesis which have generally been associated, for England, only with the middle or end of the following century.

THE TWELFTH-CENTURY ANNOTATIONS: DIFFERENCE ERODED

Commentary I

The two earliest layers of annotation in All Souls 82 are probably contemporary with the manuscript and possibly by the scribe of the main text. Two scripts are involved which, however, may be by the same hand. The simpler script provides interlinear glosses, rare variants, and brief marginal notes in the very small bookhand used for such purposes in the first half of the twelfth century. The simple graphs required by the small size of the script make the question of scribal origin difficult. The second early script in the manuscript is used for longer marginal notes and has qualities of the *notularis* that became widespread later in the century: tall proportions and slightly curved descenders, especially to the tall *s*. The two kinds of script do overlap at mid-century, and the differences here could be ascribed to a single hand moving from the discipline of interlinear space to the relatively greater spaces of the margins.[57] These differences in the script might even mirror differences in the content, brief glosses *vs.* more extended marginal notes. In any case, the content of the two scripts is different enough to justify considering them separately as Commentary I and IA.

Commentary I is, essentially, a typical and literal gloss of the text. Most of its entries are of one or two words, and by far the greatest proportion of them are interlinear. These entries are frequent in the first three books of the *Aeneid*, but increasingly sparse in later books, also a typical pattern. Books Nine through Twelve have only very sporadic glosses. It is worthwhile to examine this material in some detail, though, because it *is* so basic and representative. It displays the variety possible in such notes and the errors to which they are sometimes prey, and it shows some of the ways in which even such brief glossing can alter, if only slightly, the impact of the text.

Most of the interlinear glosses are quite straightforward.[58] Lexical glosses usually stay between the lines. Occasionally, grammatical and syntactic glosses of slightly greater length move into the margins. Sometimes these merely rearrange word order to make the syntactic relationships clearer.[59] Or the hand will sometimes offer a looser paraphrase of the passage it is treating.[60] But the notes headed *ordo* are more typical than paraphrases, and in this they are of a piece with most school-commentaries in the period.

Glosses such as these simply help the reader with obvious lexical or syntactic difficulties. But there are other glosses, again usually of a single word, which may be said to color the reader's reception of the text. Most of these would doubtless have been perceived as straightforward lexical aids, but they do alter the text in one of two subtle ways. First, they may silently choose between possible alternate interpretations, or make precise a word intended to be ambiguous; uncertainty is replaced by precision. Second (and far more frequent), the gloss may reduce a reference – historical, geographical, or mythological – with a swift general explanation which obviates any longer note; thus the precise but obscure is replaced by the general and the accessible.

Let us consider the first case. At 1.107, in the midst of the tempest scene, Virgil writes "furit aestus harenis" ("surge that seethes with sand"). Now the gloss of "aestus" ("fever, seething, tide, anxiety") is "periculum" ("danger"), which fixes the word in a metaphorical rather than a literal sense. Again, at 2.310–11 ("The spacious palace of Deiphobus / has fallen, victim of the towering Vulcan"), "Volcano" is glossed not in the mythological but in the metonymic sense, with "igne" ("fire"). A double reference is avoided or, at the least, its impact is reduced.[61] At 4.31, "luce" (Anna's "Sister, you more dear / to me than light") is glossed metaphorically with "uita" ("more dear than life"). Examples could be multiplied. Such glosses never twist the sense of the text, but they do make choices for the reader, providing a single sense where a double reference is possible.

The second case, that of glosses which generalize a specific reference, is far more widespread and has more effect on the flavor of the text. Consider a few examples from Book One. "Samos" (16) is glossed "an island"; "Symois" (100), "a river"; "Lycians" (113), "a name"; "Capys" (183), "a name"; "Vesta" (292), "a goddess"; "Eurotus" (498), "a river"; "Oreads" (500), "nymphs"; "Atlas" (741), "a jester, a joker."[62] Such notes can be found throughout the *Aeneid*.[63] Often a name is simply glossed "p.n." – probably "proprium nomen."[64] On rare occasions, glosses like these introduce actual errors, as at 1.535 where the constellation "Orion" is glossed "uentus" ("a wind"), and at 1.403 where "ambrosiae" (Venus's "ambrosial" hair) is glossed "genus herbe" ("a kind of plant").

It is, of course, in the nature of an interlinear gloss to be succinct, and detailed explanations of obscure words are beyond its range. So I do not suggest that the effect of such glosses is deliberate, but they have an effect nonetheless. By reducing geographical, historical, and mythological terms to generalities, these glosses "flatten" the text. They abrade the particularity of its referential landscape even while aiming to minimize its obscurity, and help to soften or efface those elements which distance the text from its medieval readers.[65] They thereby make it slightly easier for the reader to place the text in his own imaginative landscape. From this point of view the generalizing glosses can be seen as potentially aiding the tendency of some medieval readers to domesticate the *Aeneid*, to see it in terms of their own time and place, as we will see when we turn to vernacular retellings in chapters 5 and 6. Alternatively, once the text is somewhat detached from its geographical and historical framework, a more exclusively symbolic, even allegorical, understanding becomes possible. In chapter 3, we will examine fragments of two allegorical commentaries which have been added at the beginning and end of an *Aeneid* manuscript whose original marginal annotation is fundamentally similar to that in AS82.

Again, this effect does not seem to be conscious, nor in any way systematic, although it is widespread. For there are also rare notes in Commentary I which explain precise details of history, geography, and mythology, and the glossator does occasionally try to supply a historical note. For example, at 1.292–93, "And aged Faith and Vesta, / together with the brothers, Romulus / and Remus" ("Remo cum fratre Quirinus"), the glossator provides two notes. First, Quirinus is glossed "the one who married the sister of Augustus"; then in the margin next to 1.292 is a vaguer note, "Caesar Augustus, as if a brother."[66] Servius associated Augustus Caesar with Quirinus, a traditional cognomen for the emperor, and Remus with Agrippa, who was however Augustus's son-in-law, not his brother. Some manuscripts of Servius, possibly influenced by the mythological brothers, have Agrippa marrying Augustus's sister. Despite its uncertainties about imperial marriage, the note displays a rare attempt to elucidate a historical detail.

Geography also receives an occasional longer note, as at 7.302: "The Syrtes are shallow places in the sea where ships sometimes get stuck."[67] Mythological references, which are those most flattened by the generalizing glosses, nevertheless receive some fuller explanations. Latona (1.502) is correctly described as "the mother of Diana."[68] The mother of the Nereids (3.74) is specified as Tethys, an identification which could stem from Servius at *Georgics* 1.31: "Tethys is the wife of Oceanus, and mother of the nymphs."[69]

Most of the material from Commentary I discussed so far falls into the class of explanatory glosses – brief elucidations of difficult words or phrases. But we encounter rather a different kind of analysis when this hand enters an occasional rhetorical note.[70] Of such notes, and there are not very many, only a few are to be found in Servius. This suggests a certain amount of original analysis in the glossator or his source, and points once again to the study of the trivium in the kind of school we know this manuscript served, at or soon after the time of these glosses. The rhetorical notes also remind us of the mingling of *grammatica* and *rhetorica* in the twelfth-century schools, not surprising given the textual (rather than oratorical) focus of medieval rhetoric.[71]

This group of rhetorical notes leads us to the difficult question of the source of the glosses. As we have seen, many are traceable to Servius. But many others provide correct and incorrect information from independent sources. And moreover, though a majority of the longer entries derive their information from Servius, we cannot infer from this any direct contact with a full Servian text, for the phrasing is almost always independent. The commonest of such notes radically simplify Servius, often silently choosing only one of several proposed explanations; this extends the process which Servius had begun with his own sources.[72] Longer notes are less frequent but are nonetheless important because they display indubitable Servian derivation.[73] On at least one occasion, access to Servius is demonstrated by a near-quotation; this case also betrays contact with Servian format in that it provides a *lemma*, uniquely in Commentary I.[74]

This first layer of annotation is by no means exclusively Servian, though. Most of the brief, simple glosses could come from any decently educated master of the time. But there are also a number of more recondite marginal notes which are clearly independent of Servius, even if specific alternate sources cannot be identified.[75] Some of these independent notes need have no specific source, but could derive, like the glosses, from context and general knowledge.[76] But Commentator I seems to have consulted Isidore or some glossary dependent on him for notes like the learned etymology of "Oenotri" at 1.532: "They are called Oenotri from the cultivation of the vine, which used to abound there. 'Enos' in Greek is 'wine' in Latin. Thus 'enophorium': a wine vessel."[77] A source ought also to be sought for the mistaken explanation at 6.803 of "Lernam," here certainly intended as a poetic name for the Hydra. Our commentator notes, "Lerna is a mountain in Arcadia where there are very swift wild boars."[78] But the commentator is both correct and well informed in his note at 6.844: "Serranus was a poor farmer whom the Romans elected consul. And he came into the theater with his cart. And on account of this the Romans held the cart sacred."[79] A note like this suggests a respectable knowledge of Roman history (not at all surprising in the time that was producing some of the great Anglo-Norman historians), although like the other notes just discussed it may well come from secondary sources or scholia to other classical texts.

Altogether, then, the glosses and brief marginalia of Commentary I show a desire to make the language and substance of the text accessible to a new and different age. This attempt generates obvious glosses, but also certain simplifications which tend to move the *Aeneid* away from its complex framework of local reference and mythological imagery. This may have opened the text to interpretations not limited by the specific imaginative geography and historical assumptions of its author and first readers. The commentator depends on Servius, on the grammatical and lexical knowledge of the schoolroom, and on certain independent sources which suggest that his learning was perhaps not merely typical. Indeed, our commentator's learning was quite good if he was responsible for the *notularis* script of Commentary IA.

Commentary IA

Theoretical statements about the proper order of explaining texts, such as that in Hugh of St. Victor's *Didascalion*, distinguish between the strictly grammatical exposition of *littera*, the more substantive matter of *sensus*, and the doctrinal *profundior intelligentia* of the text's *sententia*.[80] We have already seen that the first two functions tend to mix in the notes of Commentary I. The group of annotations discussed here as Commentary IA corresponds more closely to Hugh's notion of *sensus*, the clear meaning of the literal level (though details of that literal level can raise challenging problems for the exegete), and at one point at least commentary IA can be said to move into the highest and last of Hugh's levels, *sententia*, the spiritual or philosophical implications of the text. This general (but by no means systematic) division of emphasis between brief, literal interlinear notes and longer, more ambitious marginal notes also corresponds to medieval distinctions, themselves inconsistent, between *glosa* (even when grouped together away from the margin of the *auctor* and called *glosule*) and *commentum*.[81]

The generally longer notes of Commentary IA also include many of Servian derivation; these often provide accurate explanations of obscure references.[82] But these notes treat their Servian source with considerable liberty, not just by paraphrasing and summarizing, but also by adding material and wholly recasting its presentation. Most of the notes in Commentary IA, however, are completely independent of Servius and display a most interesting variety of sources. Straightforward syntactic and lexical glosses like those of Commentary I are found here in longer form. These may further serve to connect the two sets of notes, and like the earlier notes probably come from no single source. Also like Commentary I, these independent notes are not altogether accurate, as at 3.211, the beginning of the Harpy passage: "Phineus is the father of these Furies" – an error possibly derived from context.[83] In such notes it is useful to distinguish between errors deriving from incorrect or misapplied sources, and errors stemming from attempts to make sense of the text in the *absence* of sources. The distinction can be crucial.[84] Consider for instance one interesting mythological note. The commentator describes Minos (6.432): "Minos was a most just king; therefore he was made the inquisitor of sins."[85] Now Minos was a widely known figure and appears in several Servian notes, but his role is nowhere so neatly stated in Servius. Is the commentator dipping into his memory and producing this succinct note *ad hoc*?

Other notes, by contrast, provide a nicely specific sense of the unusually sophisticated framework of learning brought to bear upon Virgil by Commentary IA. Commentary IA names its source on three occasions, twice citing Macrobius's *Saturnalia* and once Boethius's *Consolation of Philosophy*. In a long note, the commentary directly quotes selections from Macrobius's discussion of *Aeneid* 2.352 ("the gods on whom this kingdom stood").[86] The commentator had access, it is clear, to a good text of the *Saturnalia*. Macrobius is again quoted at length in explanation of *Aeneid* 2.632 ("guided by a god"), and Virgil's reference there to Venus as grammatically masculine.[87] It is interesting enough to know that this annotator was consulting a late-classical discussion to help explain his Virgil. I know of no other English Virgil commentary that cites the *Saturnalia*.[88] But we must also inquire why these particular passages were chosen for quotation. Both have reference to elements of pagan belief and the role of the gods in human fate, which might well have roused the special interest of a medieval reader. The passages give specific, detailed information that helps reconstruct the religious beliefs and practices of the ancient past.

Even more interesting is a long note at 3.21, where Aeneas is "slaughtering along that beach a gleaming / white bull to the high king of the heaven-dwellers." The note here uses, without citation, still another passage from the *Saturnalia* dealing with the pagan gods and ritual practice. Commentator IA lifts whole phrases from Macrobius, but he adapts them for the schoolroom as a *quaestio*, a form that was gaining ground in biblical exegesis at the same period:[89]

HEAVEN-DWELLERS: It is asked why Virgil, as though he did not know what should be slaughtered on which altars, had a bull sacrificed to Jupiter. That is not permitted, except to Apollo, Neptune, and Mars. Solution: Virgil was not ignorant of the fact that a bull ought to be sacrificed to Neptune and Apollo; he said "a bull to Neptune; one to you, Apollo" (*Aen.* 3.119). But in this passage he said that a bull was sacrificed to a god to whom it was not permitted, so that he could create a passage with a portent to follow. Thus he adds below, "I ... see an awful omen, terrible / to tell" (*Aen.* 3.26)[90]

This gives us a glimpse of the teaching of the *Aeneid* in a twelfth-century classroom. It has none of the technical elaboration of the later scholastic *quaestiones*, but it does suggest a more sophisticated level of address than in the notes of Commentary I. A master writing or using these notes has students well in command of the basic text, and capable of appreciating detailed questions about pagan ritual practice. Far from judging or avoiding realities of pagan belief in Virgil's time, far from suppressing the difference and pagan quality of the epic, the master in this setting wants to get the story straight in terms of ancient belief and ritual.

The commentator's adaptation of Macrobius's dramatic setting is equally suggestive. In the *Saturnalia*, it is the obnoxious Evangelus who challenges Virgil's religious expertise, and the dignified Praetextatus who defends it. In the *quaestio*, then, the commentator takes to himself the dignity and authority of Praetextatus. This may reflect the exegete's sense of his own position in regard to this text and his students.

But probably the most significant, and surely the longest, entry in Commentary IA is at 6.724 ff., the great cosmological passage spoken to Aeneas by Anchises. Commentary IA, fascinatingly, explains this section by reference to Boethius's famous cosmological verses in the *Consolation of Philosophy* III, metrum 9, "O qui perpetua mundi ... ," an extremely popular passage in the Middle Ages. The commentary quotes III, metrum 9.13, and appends a long note lifted directly from a commentary on the *Consolation*: this particular Boethius commentary is otherwise unknown, although its closest textual affinities are to a commentary in another twelfth-century insular manuscript: Glasgow, Hunterian Library, U.5.19.[91] (I include a transcription of the entire entry from Commentary IA, as Appendix III.)

The use of Boethius to explicate a passage of *Aeneid*, Book Six is of considerable significance. It participates in a widespread association throughout the Middle Ages between the cosmologies of Boethius and *Aeneid* 6. This association can move in the reverse direction as well: in the ninth century Bovo of Corvey cites Virgil in his commentary on *Consolation of Philosophy* III, metrum 9, as does William of Conches in the twelfth century, and the two passages are linked in a number of other twelfth-century contexts.[92] The parallels between these two specific passages are close; both grew out of the same platonic tradition, and Boethius would have had Virgil's lines well in mind. But this citation is simply part of a broader tendency to compare the two entire works, explaining one through the other. Such a habit points to the understanding of the *Aeneid*, and *Aeneid* 6 especially, as a record of spiritual education rather than a simply historical epic; here the commentator arguably moves to Hugh of St. Victor's final level of reading, the *sententia*, though in a text where Hugh himself might not approve of such reading.[93] To this extent, the citation of Boethius by Commentary IA shares in the same impulse which takes its exaggerated form in an allegorical treatment like that attributed to Bernard Silvestris. But the attraction of the *Aeneid* 6 passage into memories of Boethian platonism is perhaps the more striking in AS82, which is otherwise so much interested in a very different, historical reading of the epic. In chapter 3, I consider in detail the associations between Virgil and Boethius in the interpretive tradition.

Commentaries I and IA, then, whether or not they are from the same hand, move in divergent but not contradictory directions, and would appear to address two levels of student, or students moving on from simple grammatical reading to more sophisticated questions. Commentary I shows only sporadic dependence on learned sources. Rather, as we have seen, it offers a wide range of brief entries, the bulk of which tend to simplify or "flatten" the text. The *Aeneid* is thus left without its framework of local reference: it is somewhat denatured. To a small extent, the flattening of the text by Commentary I is counteracted by the much more sporadic entries of Commentary IA, which shows real learning and even active research. Macrobius is rifled to help explain pagan ceremony, and a fragment of Boethian commentary is applied to Virgilian cosmology.

The flattening of the text by its twelfth-century apparatus, then, is not conscious or systematic. On the contrary, some of the impulses defined above as typical of pedagogical Virgilianism are operating here, but ignorance or haste leaves those impulses for the most part unfulfilled. It could be claimed, and rightly, that these notes do not constitute a failure to read or contextualize the *Aeneid*; rather, they fulfill the very different intentions of the twelfth-century schoolroom in opening the *Aeneid*, intentions which focus on basic instruction in grammar and rhetoric and on some limited knowledge of classical lore. In this system, it could be argued, the real work of the manuscript occurs in the annotations, not in the text they divide and surround. This was, after all, a manuscript owned during its early history by Master Alfred and by a house of learned canons.

Insofar as the manuscript functioned only in the context of fairly basic education, this reply would be true. In the medieval schoolroom, as long before in the school of Servius, reading the epic was more a means for teaching language than *vice versa*. The *Aeneid* circulated in other contexts, however, both simultaneously and diachronically, in manuscripts of which AS82 is fairly typical. In the twelfth century, there were ambitious readers like Walter of Châtillon and (in England) Joseph of Exeter, who were to produce Latin poems that imitated not just the style of the *Aeneid*, but also its antique setting.[94] There were also readers like those in the orbit of the Angevin court, whose interest was so much in the epic as model of imperial foundation rather than container of grammar and lore, that they moved it altogether out of Latin and into the vernacular. (And this context is particularly of interest if the Alfred who owned AS82 was indeed the man who tutored Henry II.) As we will see in chapter 5, the redactor of the *Eneas* made use of annotations just such as I have examined here.

In contexts like these, the kind of reading generated in the early notes of AS82 does indeed leave the epic incompletely contextualized, with parts of its originally imagined world lost. We need not see this effect in only a negative sense, though. Rather, the sort of non-specific, "flattening" glosses examined above could be said to open up new and alternate spaces for the epic's reception, expanding the systems of "blanks" (as Iser calls them) in which the reader can operate.[95] Such a situation arguably helps give rise to the kind of anachronistic domestication found in the *Eneas*, or the sort of spiritual allegoresis we will see in the following chapter.

This particular manuscript, moreover, also moved into new settings diachronically. And as I will show next, its later users also changed the emphasis and the extent of contextualizing detail in its margins. In Commentary III, a fourteenth century annotator, responding to those aims in the original commentary, proceeded to provide fresh material to carry them out.

Commentary II

Commentary II can be summarized very briefly. It is almost exclusively a series of brief lexical and grammatical glosses, the great majority of them interlinear. These appear only in Book One, and become rarer even as this book progresses; they scarcely merit being called a commentary. Their interest for us lies only in the proof they provide that the text was being read systematically, though not perseveringly, in the second half of the thirteenth century, to which time the hand of the glosses can be dated.

As we will see again in Commentary III, this series of glosses makes use of the previous layer of commentary, expanding rather than ignoring the earlier work. At 1.77, for example, Commentary I glosses

Virgil's "capessere" with "frequenter facere." Commentary II adds, "id est perficere." There are several other similar instances. The brief entries could have come from almost any decently educated reader, while the rare longer notes derive entirely from Servius, though none of them are textually identical to any passage in Servius. Thus the commentary repeats the pattern of selection and redaction pointed out in the briefer notes in Commentary I. Finally, a single vernacular gloss should be mentioned. At 1.213, "aena" ("bronze vessels") is glossed as "les caudrans." As might be expected, the literary vernacular of a reader of Virgil at this time is French.[96] It is not until well into the fourteenth century that I find Virgil manuscripts with vernacular glosses in English.

"ANSELM OF LAON" AND SERVIAN TRADITION IN THE HIGH MIDDLE AGES

Not long before the early layers of annotation were being entered in AS82, a much fuller continuous commentary with similar aims and sources was produced on the Continent. It soon arrived in England and was, as we will see, an important source for the last and most extensive layer of annotation in AS82. It is to this commentary, written in the late eleventh or early twelfth century and attributed to Anselm of Laon, that we now briefly turn our attention.

Despite the dominance of the Servian commentary and selections from it in the Carolingian and later periods, new commentaries did develop in response to changing levels of education and more specialized interests. As of now, no full Virgil commentaries by the great masters of the ninth or tenth century have been uncovered, although there are marginalia that seem to show the influence of Remigius of Auxerre and Gerbert of Reims.[97] Even these marginalia, however, appear as insertions into fairly full marginal texts of Servius.

A dependence on Servius comparable to that we have seen in AS82, with occasional independent additions, is evident in the extensive but little-studied commentaries on all three of Virgil's works tentatively attributed to Anselm of Laon.[98] By their considerable twelfth-century manuscript attestation, these commentaries would appear to date from the later eleventh or earlier twelfth century. Although still unedited, they are now emerging as, after Servius, the most widespread and influential Virgil commentaries of the Middle Ages.[99] I have identified seventeen manuscripts, and in a recent article Virginia Brown names five more; other copies, from the twelfth through the fifteenth centuries, continue to appear.[100] Moreover, occasional borrowings from "Anselm" are to be found in the margins of many Virgil manuscripts.

The *Aeneid* commentary, on which I focus here, exists in the highly fluid state typical of eleventh- and twelfth-century commentaries. Redactors and copyists felt free to introduce minor textual adaptations as they wished, and as a result each manuscript represents at least a slightly independent version. Beyond these individual distinctions, the manuscripts appear to divide into two major redactions, a longer and a shorter.[101] The predominant pedagogical impulses I wish to point out are common to both.

"Anselm's" *accessus* is much briefer than that of Servius, but covers exactly the same traditional topics – "poetae uita, titulus operis, qualitas carminis, scribentis intentio, numerus librorum, ordo librorum, explanatio" – though "Anselm" follows a different order and does not name each topic.[102] The commentary begins with the *intentio*.

For he intended to praise Augustus through his forebears. And he does this by describing the deeds of Aeneas, namely how, after the fall of Troy, he came sailing to Italy after much wandering, and how he made war there against the opposing Rutilians and Latins. Indeed, since he wrote in praise of Augustus, therefore suppressing much historical truth he quite becomingly added certain poetic fictions ... And truly, if he had only followed the truth of history, he would not certainly have seemed a poet, but an historiographer.[103]

Like Servius, then, "Anselm" begins with a political, even an imperial reading of the *Aeneid*. Dido disappears into the "multos errores" which here cover wanderings both geographical and erotic. "Anselm" is brief on Virgil's life, probably because the topic is covered in greater detail in his *Eclogues* commentary. He says nothing of the three styles – "humile, medium, grandiloquum" – over which Servius pauses, and instead of the Servian *ordo librorum*, he outlines the opening order of Book One: "Proponit. Inuocat. Narrat."[104]

"Anselm's" commentary on the *Aeneid* clearly shares many of the pedagogical preoccupations described in the discussion of Servius above; indeed, wide stretches of the commentary on the *Aeneid* merely paraphrase or quote Servius, with or more often without attribution.[105] Let us consider these pedagogical emphases in terms of the opening lines of the *Aeneid*. "Anselm's" very first note on the text of the *Aeneid* is typical. He takes the substance from his source, deletes Servius's specific parallel examples (from Cicero), and adds new rhetorical details, naming one figure which Servius only describes (hysteron proteron), and analyzing another not in Servius (hendiadys).[106] Such use of Virgil's text as a medium for expanded rhetorical instruction continues throughout the commentary, again reflecting the interests of the schools as did the rhetorical notes in Commentary I above. And Virgil's literary preeminence makes him a source of grammatical example as well, as in Priscian whom "Anselm" often cites.[107] In these notes, where Virgil (rather than the grammarian himself) becomes the dominant master of usage, we again see the slippage of authority from the master (so jealously guarded by Servius) to the ancient text.

"Anselm" shortens the Servian note on the polysemous quality of *cano*, and goes on, like his source, to explain the geographical and poetic sense of *Troiae* (cited above, note 105). When Virgil says that Aeneas "came first" to the Lavinian shores, "Anselm" follows Servius very closely in explaining that the region above the Rubicon already occupied by Antenor was not yet called Italy. This interest in the changes of geographical terminology across time is perhaps surprising in a medieval commentator, but we will see repeated interest in chronological change in this commentary, as when it explains that a verb used actively in Virgil's time had become deponent in usage by his own.[108] "Anselm" also summarizes Servius's comments on the founder of Italy (Italus), on the use of prepositions in reference to provinces and cities, and on the several names of the city Lavinum. He further notes, with Servius, Virgil's care in emphasizing that Aeneas came to Italy "driven by fate" (*fato profugus*), not through any criminal intent or desire for empire.

While these early notes largely paraphrase Servius and continue to add some rhetorical and metrical detail,[109] they also respond to places where Servius may not have been clear to late eleventh- or twelfth-century students. Thus "Anselm" converts Servius's reference to *miliaria* into leagues, thereby retaining a useful geographical detail.[110] At the same time, he usually (but not universally) suppresses Servius's frequent long citations of parallel effects in other classical authors. Elsewhere, he often simplifies Servian mythography to provide briefer, clearer explanations.

Imperial destiny, geographical detail, authorial command of rhetoric and poetic effect, the historical change in word meanings – all these are recognizable as aspects of that "pedagogical" impulse which attempts to restore to the commentator's audience as full a sense as is manageable of the difference of the Virgilian world. This commentator is in great part dependent on Servius for his information, although we have already seen his skills in adding new rhetorical analysis. But this only points up the continuity of pedagogic intention between the two. There are, though, occasional moments where "Anselm" explores the relevance of the *Aeneid* to his own spiritual and literary world and where new exegetical priorities begin to emerge.

Such moments occur most often when "Anselm" compares narrative details in the *Aeneid* to scriptural events. When Jupiter is prophesying the future of the Trojans (1.265–71), for instance, and says that Ascanius will succeed his father, "Anselm" notes, "For the blessed Augustine relates that the fall of Troy was in that time when Moses led the Israelites across the Red Sea."[111] This implies a developed, even Eusebian, sense of parallel histories, for it is predicted here that Aeneas, like Moses, will lead his people to their promised land, but not live long enough to see them in their imperial city. But it is precisely the historical aspect of links between pagan and Christian worlds that rouses the commentator's interest here, not the sort of parallel spiritual histories that are explored by the allegorizers. Far from "Christianizing" the *Aeneid*, then, such a note provides it with a historical context of biblical history more easily accessible to "Anselm's" students than a purely classical chronology.[112] At the same time, this kind of historical alignment is suggestive of the new and lower status of classical reading compared to the late antique world. Here the *Aeneid* narrates events which are part of an array surrounding the more central history of the Bible, and study of the *Aeneid* is only part of an intellectual ascent to the central text of *sacra pagina*.

But something much closer to Christian allegorization occurs at 1.291 ff., where Jupiter predicts that peace will come under Augustus, and that "cana Fides et Vesta" will set the laws:

While Augustus lived there was peace through the whole world, which Virgil fictively attributed to Augustus. But it was because of the peacemaker which was born through Jesus Christ, namely "venerable Faith." Faith is called venerable (*cana*) either because it is found in dogs (*canibus*), or because one sacrifices to her with the hand wrapped in a white cloth, through which he shows that one must be secret in faith. Vesta is the goddess of religion; this is the fire of the holy spirit.[113]

Even this note, though, is not inconsistent with the commentary's constant interest in Virgil's intent to praise Augustus through fictions.

Indeed, the commentary adds independent details relating to Augustus and his achievements; we will return to some examples later in the chapter.

A similar concern with ideas more immediately relevant to his audience is evinced by "Anselm's" long note at 1.32, "driven by fate," which makes careful distinctions between fate, free will, and divine will. "Anselm" cites Servius's note here at some length, but then goes on to propose an alternate sense, introducing it as do most commentators with *uel*:

Or FATE. Some things happen from the free will of men; some from the necessity of fate, such as a man being born and dying; some from the will of divine powers, such as attaining honors, [or] gaining office. That Aeneas came to Italy was in the will of the divine powers.[114]

There are also in this commentary occasional brief hints of the kind of numerological exegesis that is found, in more fully developed form, in the commentary attributed to Bernard Silvestris. When Aeneas speaks for the first time, calling them "three and four times blessed" who died at Troy (1.94), "Anselm" explains the outburst in terms of standard numerological associations. As usual, he offers Servius's explanation before his own: "He has put a finite number for the infinite, that is, 'many times.' Or, some relate it to the body and the soul. Four in respect to the body, because it is made of four elements. Three to the soul, because it is irascible, concupiscible, rational."[115]

The most extensive notes suggestive of incipient spiritualizing allegory are found, not surprisingly, in Aeneas's descent to the Underworld in Book 6. The proximity of the shrine of Apollo and temple of Diana is because they are brother and sister, "Anselm" explains, but also

because Apollo is the god of wisdom, Diana of eloquence, and the one is scarcely effective without the other. Whence it is necessary that we first be instructed in grammar, which teaches us to speak, then in dialectic which teaches us how to prove something, then in rhetoric which teaches right living.[116]

This note places Aeneas's movements, though only implicitly, in the context of that educational process which in "Bernard Silvestris" is explicitly a preliminary to spiritual development.

The golden bough (6.136–37) is also the subject of long notes that vary considerably both in detail and substance among the various manuscripts of the commentary; it is therefore difficult to say what parts of its allegorization derive originally from "Anselm" and which were added by later redactors whose interest was raised by the passage. What most versions have in common is the Servian material on the branch as an image of the Pythagorean "Y" and symbol for moral decisions in the course of adolescence.[117] Other notes describe previous descents to hell, such as those of Orpheus, Theseus, Hercules, Euridice, and Ulysses; these are identified with the descents of virtue, vice, and artifice in more fully allegorical commentaries.[118]

These sporadic and relatively isolated moments of spiritual and ethical application, hinting at later allegorical developments, should not lead us to ignore this influential commentary's predominant place in the pedagogical, historicist tradition deriving from Servius. The great bulk of the notes come directly from Servius, and most of those that are not from Servius merely extend certain of his emphases, especially on the history of Augustus and, even more, on the figures of rhetoric. Whatever its occasional glances toward other, more domesticating methods of exegesis, the "Anselm" commentary centers on the Servian, "pedagogical" intent to establish the difference of the Virgilian world and the stylistic effects through which Virgil created that world. And, as we will now see, it is with the aid of "Anselm" that the last commentator in AS82 attempts to reconstruct the particularity of the Virgilian past which had been abraded to some extent in the glosses of Commentary I.

RECONSTRUCTING DIFFERENCE IN THE LATER ANNOTATIONS

Commentary III

By the later twelfth century, as we have seen, All Souls 82 was provided with an extensive set of brief interlinear glosses and related marginal notes (Commentaries I and IA) largely Servian in content although independent in phrasing. The major impulses behind these notes were lexical and syntactic: they aimed to make the text linguistically comprehensible to readers of unsophisticated Latinity. As a further part of this program of basic pedagogy, the annotations also provided occasional details of history, geography, and mythology. But such specific, informative notes are neither extensive nor numerous. On the contrary, as I have argued above, the earliest layer of annotation tended to generalize the imaginative landscape of the epic. This produced a book at once more accessible to readers ignorant of the historical and religious details of Virgil's world, and potentially more assimilable to spiritual and moralizing interpretations. The early annotator's longest single note, the reference to the Boethian cosmic vision, might itself seem to hint at such preoccupations.

In a sense, then, this codex – text and early commentary taken together – shows us the *Aeneid* at a delicate and crucial moment in the history of its reception in medieval England. Still supplied with some localizing detail, the epic is nonetheless partly shorn of its foreignness, its imaginative difference. From here interpretation can proceed, on the one hand, in the direction of such thoroughgoing spiritual allegory as that present in England in Cambridge, Peterhouse College 158 (see chapter 3), or such moralizing, explicitly Christian interpretation as we will see in London, BL Additional 27304 (see chapter 4). On the other hand, a reader with more historical interests can still make use of such a codex, expanding on the material already present and adding further information of a sort to revalidate the historicity, the difference, of the text.

It is this latter alternative that is followed in the third and last layer of notes in All Souls 82, Commentary III. Here a well-trained medieval mind with access to an apparently decent library makes selective use of earlier commentaries such as Servius and "Anselm" to reinstitute, indeed to emphasize, those differentiating details of the Virgilian imaginative landscape which we saw beginning to melt away in Commentaries I and II. Commentary III is particularly important because, while it offers no evidence as to its place of origin, it can nevertheless be dated paleographically to the second half of the fourteenth century, roughly the period that produced the moralizing and allegorical commentary we will examine in BL Add. 27304. These separate commentaries suggest the diversity and richness of thought being applied to the *Aeneid* in the England of Chaucer's time; the intense contrast of their interpretive approaches is the more striking in light of their numerous parallels of structure and method.

Before considering in detail the content of Commentary III, it is well to pause over the many difficulties facing the student of marginal notes, difficulties especially acute in fourteenth-century marginalia. The neat and tiny *notularis* hand of the twelfth- and early thirteenth-century notes, written in fine dark ink, is often perfectly legible today. But much-read manuscripts, which are exactly those of interest to the student of interpretation, suffer most of all in their margins, where centuries of dirty thumbs have often rubbed away crucial bits of tantalizing entries. Damage done by binders, too, is particularly destructive of the later layers of commentary in a manuscript, which of course had to be squeezed into the outermost spaces of already crowded margins. Finally, the inks used in the fourteenth century were often much paler, and are now more faded, than those of earlier centuries. Even with the benefit of infra-red and ultra-violet light these notes – truncated, faded, and worn – often resist decipherment. Commentary III of All Souls 82, unfortunately, suffers from all these problems, and yet one more: tightly sewn into a historically important and now fragile binding in the mid-fifteenth century, the commentary's inner margins are today rendered virtually inaccessible by the spine's refusal to open flat. What follows, then, as often in later chapters, is an analysis of remnants.

This commentary, like the late fourteenth-century commentary we will study in BL Add. 27304, appears to have been original to this manuscript and not a copy of a previously extant series of notes. Rather, the commentator seems to have had before him a fairly full and accurate copy of Servius and "Anselm of Laon," possibly in the margins of another Virgil manuscript from whose text he occasionally corrected or supplemented the text in All Souls 82. Along with these, he had access to other source books whose specific identity is not yet clear, all of which he exploited to create his own series of notes. Sometimes copying directly from his sources, he more often para-phrased or expanded them, or combined material from two sources in a single note. The impression of a commentary composed as the reader progressed through the book is reinforced by certain visual details of the notes. At several points in the manuscript the hand appears to have gone through the text a second time, adding new notes or expanding old. These double sets of notes can be distinguished by differences in the shade of ink, size of graphs, or thickness of duct, yet they are indubitably by the same hand.

The writer of Commentary III appears nowhere to reject the information or methods of the earlier notes; rather he seems to see himself as making more complete and specific the material already present. This is again graphically evident at several places where Commentary III adds directly to a note entered by Commentary I or II.[119] The commentary also continues the work of Commentaries I and II by providing additional literal glosses and marginal paraphrases of difficult syntax, particularly the latter. These are sometimes (as in Commentary I) based on the Servian entry, but just as often they are original and display the commentator's own knowledge and ingenuity.

Many other general explanatory notes which extend the techniques of Commentary I most probably derived not from specific commentaries or written sources but from general knowledge and an appreciation of the context. So Commentator III enters a sensitive explanation of 3.302, "false Simois": "A certain stream which they called Simois, so they might have some memory of the Simois that was at Troy."[120] The note also shows a nice sense of the Trojans' desire to re-establish some vestigial symbols of their past, to remake Troy not through empire building but by "false" naming. Such explanatory notes are very frequent.

Another aspect which appears to be the work of the commentator himself, but quite unlike the preoccupations of Commentaries I and II, is the habit of providing plot summaries and topic headings. These helped the reader through the text, and probably aided in locating specific passages. This development is especially noteworthy because it is paralleled, though with greater frequency, by the contemporary commentary in BL Add. 27304. Such similarities of preliminary method are significant in commentaries with interpretive preoccupations which are otherwise, as we shall see, so very different. These summaries and headings occur throughout the commentary. So at 1.12 ("There was an ancient city"), the commentator mentions that Virgil here "explains the cause of Juno's enmity."[121] A lengthier summary appears at 1.180: "After Aeneas's companions roasted food thus at the fire, Aeneas went out from his ship to the cliff mentioned above, to see if he could see his lost companions anywhere."[122] Entries of this sort can be much briefer: "a portent" (at 7.59).[123] Or they can remind the reader of the plot immediately preceding a new section or book, as at 9.1: "Thus Venus had brought to her son the arms and shield."[124]

This provision of topic-headings, pointing out major new sections of the text, suggests a reader accustomed to return to well-known or well-liked parts of the epic, and an attention to the text that goes beyond its passing use as a tool in the teaching of grammar and rhetoric. We have already seen that this particular commentator went over some episodes more than once, and we will see that the fourteenth-century commentator of BL Add. 27304 did the same.

These hints at rereading make it possible to conjecture a reader sensitive to the repeatable pleasures of the text, a reader of the *Aeneid* not just as a schoolbook and guide to grammar or rhetoric, but as enjoyable history or ethical guide, or even to some extent *belles-lettres*. It is well to remember that by the beginning of the fifteenth century this copy of the *Aeneid* was part of a collection, Henry Penwortham's, that included historical texts and Whiteacre's *Brunellus*. This response to the epic of course remains conjecture, but it is a conjecture reinforced by other though sporadic details of the commentary. There are a few notes which show the commentator's efforts to supply imaginatively the dramatic details of certain passages. In Book Two, for example, Aeneas disguises himself and his comrades in the armor of murdered Greeks and strongly defends the subterfuge: "If that be guile or valor – who would ask / in war?" (2.390). Our commentator at this line seems to imagine the dramatic situation, and posits an interlocutor: "In response to what someone could have said, that it wasn't good to gain victory through craft."[125] In Book Three, Aeneas describes his terrifying encounter with the ghost of the murdered Polydorus. He goes on to tell briefly the story of Polydorus's death. Our commentator seems to wonder what prompted the explanation, and supplies an answer which again shows a lively imaginative grasp of the dramatic situation surrounding Aeneas's book-long speech: "Because Dido could have asked about this Polydorus, therefore, since he had made some mention of him, he went on about him."[126]

Such notes, rare as they are, hint at an active imaginative engagement with the letter of the text and its implied dramatic setting. And it is just such a commitment to the letter, to apprehending a series of historically independent though artistically conditioned moments, that is confirmed in the more transparently "pedagogical" nature of the bulk of the notes in Commentary III. Drawing on Servius, "Anselm," and other sources, the notes both emphasize and explicate those specific details of the text which lend complexity and weight to the reader's experience of the difference of the epic.

Many of these substantive notes derive very closely from Servius; a few indeed are almost textually identical, though they nearly always show some activity of selection. It is likely, then, that a good text of Servius was available to our commentator, though just how full a text is uncertain.[127] However compressed a text of Servius Commentator III used, portions at least were quite free of intermediate alteration. Sometimes the entries from Servius amount virtually to quotation.[128] More often, though, Commentator III (or the tradition on which he draws) takes a far more active attitude toward the Servian material. He energetically rephrases Servius, summarizes him, often simplifies entries by selecting among alternate interpretations or expands them by offering new ones. In all these activities he is comparable to "Anselm."

In a situation where quotation, compression, redaction, and suppression are all taking place, some principle of selection, however apparently random, must be involved. Our commentator's pattern of selection and suppression, especially in the case of those longer notes which are textually close to Servius – the Servian entries he apparently most valued – is consistent and significantly reinforces those notions of imaginative readership perceptible in other aspects of his commentary. The notes so selected show the commentator's consistent impulse to explore the verbal nuance of artistic realization and the social and factual nuance of past time and foreign place. The commentator largely ignores Servius's own notions of Virgilian political allegory and his exploration of philology and grammar. Instead he draws most extensively from the notes on rhetoric, mythology and religion, history, and especially geography. The following paragraphs review these four areas of interest in Commentary III. I show how the annotator regularly draws on Servian material, but also uses "Anselm" and other sources to explore each topic yet further.

Commentator III shows a consistent interest in rhetorical aspects of the *Aeneid*, often identifying individual instances of figurative language, but also pointing out broader aspects of the structure of the epic. He uses Servius, but contributes much analysis that appears to be his own. Commentator III uses the Servian entry at 1.77, for example, to explain the reference to *litotes* in Commentary II (see note 119). This is typical of the commentator's expansion of earlier notes. He again quotes a relatively long rhetorical note at 1.159 (the description of the Libyan bay), distinguishing between descriptions of fictive and actual places – "topotesia" and "topografia."[129] On the other hand, Servius's long and learned note on grammatical usage relating to names, in the same entry, is completely ignored.[130] Such close adherence to Servius's rhetorical notes continues throughout the commentary.

Most non-Servian notes on rhetoric in Commentary III are so brief and general as to make the identification of an immediate source difficult.[131] Like many of the glosses and syntactic paraphrases discussed earlier, most of the independent rhetorical notes could have come from any reader with a solid command of the *trivium*. Nevertheless, they are very interesting for the way in which they extend an aspect of Servius already much explored by "Anselm." And they demonstrate the commentator's interest, similar to "Anselm," in the details of Virgil's verbal artistry. Indeed Commentator III appears to derive from "Anselm" an isolated note displaying appreciation of semantic detail. When Achaemenides describes his wretched existence among the Cyclopes, he uses the phrase "uitam traho," "I drag out my life" (3.646–47); the commentator delicately notes, "it is for the noble and fortunate to lead a life, but it is for the wretched to drag it out."[132]

From the start, Commentator III also displays an awareness of larger structural strategies, especially in the conflicts between the details and sequence of Trojan history and Virgil's presentation of those events. The distinction between *ordo naturalis* (the narration of events in chronological order) and *ordo artificialis* (narration through flashback and indirect report) is fundamental to all rhetorical analysis of the *Aeneid's* structure, as appears to be recognized here in a long note (at 1.34) which is unfortunately so faded and trimmed as to be practically indecipherable.[133] The crucial first words, though, are legible: "He proceeds according to the artificial order."[134] There follows a summary of the *Aeneid* in *ordo naturalis*: "First Ilium fell, then he built the fleet ..."[135] These legible passages, and a few other fragments, show remarkable similarity to "Anselm's" note on the same passage.[136]

The distinction between history and fiction is also carefully noted, but at a peculiar moment. The conversation between Juno and Aeolus is passed over; only when Neptune rises to calm the winds (1.124) does Commentator III feel the need to distinguish fact from fancy: "the author passes from history to fiction."[137] This kind of rhetorical and factual distinction provides the pagan gods with an implicit metaphorical quality; they are mere fictions, artistic effects. Such an attitude may help to explain the commentator's apparent acceptance of the pagan gods, combined though with a hesitation to credit them with a major role in history.

This leads us to the exploration of mythology and pagan religion in Commentary III. The commentator appears eager to take from Servius information about religious beliefs and practices and the history of the pagan gods, which he almost always records without demur or judgment. Thus, when Neptune reproves the winds (1.132), the commentator borrows from Servius to explain the meaning of "generis uestri" ("your race"): "The winds were born of Astraeus, who fought along with the Titans, and of Aurora."[138] Religious practices also engage the commentator's attention: he repeatedly takes pains to provide background information which would differentiate the religion of the epic moment from his own. He quotes Servius at 3.24, explaining the appropriateness of myrtle to the worship of Venus, and he paraphrases Servius at 3.111, giving background on the Corybantes. Again, when Helenus prophesies Aeneas's meeting with the Sibyl (3.444), the commentator quotes Servius on the three modes of prophecy. This learned interest in the details of pagan belief shows important continuity with the earlier annotator's citations of the *Saturnalia*, discussed above.

At the same time, nonetheless, Commentator III seems to resist open acknowledgment of any direct role of the pagan gods in history. He completely ignores Servius's long note (at 2.166) on the theft of the Palladium, the anger of Athena, and the ultimate fall of Troy entailed by the loss of the divine image. On the other hand, he quotes at length Servius's euhemerist rationalization of Aeolus (at 1.52) and Servius's remark that, while the gods can delay events, they cannot prevent them (at 7.315). To an extent, then, this commentator "re-historicizes" the epic, emphasizing human agency where Virgil and Servius both affirm divine mystery.

Equally interesting are the uses Commentator III makes of medieval mythography. Clearly his interest in the details of classical lore is not limited to classical sources, and odd figures pop up unexpectedly in the general flow of Servian information. The commentator seems to be subscribing to the typically hostile medieval view of Venus when he explains her attribute "alma" ("gentle, bountiful") at 1.618 : "Venus is called 'alma' because she nourishes ("alit") the lecherous in her lust."[139] Again, when Juno bribes Aeolus with the offer of a lovely nymph as a wife (1.72), our commentator explains "Deiopea": "the nymph's name, which is interpreted as serenity."[140] This suggests a connection, though probably distant, with the allegorical *Aeneid* commentary attributed to Bernard Silvestris. At the same line Bernard allegorizes the fourteen nymphs of Juno as seven airs and seven tempests, all her servants. Of the airs, "the loveliest is serenity, that is the splendor of air, whom we understand to be Deiopea."[141] A number of other notes show an accurate knowledge of classical mythology which appears not to derive from Servius.

In his notes on history and geography, we see most clearly the commentator's impulse to give a specific and nuanced picture of the time and place of the *Aeneid*, its legendary background and physical setting. Here he makes wide use of Servius, and is especially active in seeking notes often far from the passage being annotated. When Aeneas first sees Dido's temple to Juno (1.441 ff.), our commentator rearranges and slightly expands Servius's long note on the history of Dido's flight and the foundation of Carthage (Servius, at 1.443; the note in "Anselm" is quite different). He again quotes Servius at length to explain the history of Polyxena. Instances of this sort abound, showing a distinct pattern of selection.[142] Some of the same notes, though, also show the commentator's pattern of suppression. Thus in the note concerning Priam and Hector, Servius's preliminary note on the archaism of "in hoste" is omitted. At such a point, history is more important than verbal detail.

Our commentator's use of independent sources to flesh out specific areas of interest is most apparent in his notes on history and geography, and it is in these notes too that his use of "Anselm" is most sustained. The commentator's typical pattern in these historical notes, like "Anselm's," is to begin with the Servian entry at the relevant line, then to expand it with information either from elsewhere in Servius or from clearly independent knowledge. For instance, Commentary III discusses at some length the history of Troilus, whose death Aeneas sees depicted on the temple wall (1.474). Commentator III expands the details of the Servian note, detailing the drama of the scene from an independent source or, just as likely, from his own imagination.[143] Yet elsewhere, Commentator III will ransack Servius to provide a general background note where Servius does not, as at 1.619 where Dido mentions her early knowledge of the Trojan Teucer: "Indeed, I still remember banished Teucer." The opening lines of this long note are particularly important because they connect the commentator's historical preoccupations with his interest, mentioned earlier, in establishing the precise dramatic context of speeches: "Someone could have said, 'How do you know Aeneas so well?' To this she would answer, 'Indeed I well recollect . . .' "[144]

While these expansions of Servian materials do form the bulk of the historical notes in Commentary III, there are also additions which clearly show use of other sources, especially "Anselm." These most often link Servian notes with individuals in Roman history, and most particularly with the Caesars. The generations of the Trojans noted at 1.285 (which follow most closely the list in the First Vatican Mythographer)[145] have the name of Caesar added as an end point (". . . Anchises fathered Aeneas; and Aeneas, Julius Caesar"[146]), an addition not found in any of the sources.[147] The suggestion would of course be in front of our commentator's eyes, in the "Trojan Caesar" of 1.286. But the commentator's special interest in and independent knowledge of Caesar is clearer in the following note, to 1.289, "weighted down with Oriental booty." Servius takes this to refer to

Julius Caesar's victories over Pharnaces and at Alexandria, and mentions these in his note. Commentator III mentions only the victory over Pharnaces and then adds a detail, wholly lacking in Servius, about Caesar's victory after Pompey's failure to conquer Pharnaces.[148] This he takes from "Anselm."[149]

Soon after, Commentator III makes another historical addition to Servius, at 1.294, "the gates of war." Here he closely follows the Servian note which explains the gates in the temple of Janus, their first closing by Numa Pompilius, and their opening during the Civil Wars. Our commentator, however, interpolates a section on the two other closings of the gates, concluding with Augustus Caesar.[150] Yet another historical detail regarding the Caesars is taken from "Anselm" to buttress a Servian note at *Aeneid* 3.80 ("King Anius, both king of men and priest / of Phoebus"). Servius explains the ancient custom of the king being also *pontifex*, but our commentator adds to this a specific example: "In antiquity it was the custom that the king should be both king and supreme pontiff; thus it is read regarding Julius Caesar that he was supreme pontiff, which was the greatest honor."[151] This is not just antiquarian lore stuck in the margin. Rather, Commentator III is carefully elucidating the very relevance of Trojan history to Augustan Rome, the Rome of the Caesars that Virgil had so elaborately woven into the *Aeneid*. This is historically oriented reading of a high order.

Equally sophisticated is the commentator's constant interest in questions of geography and nationality, place-names and race-names. Here Servius provides him with abundant material which he quotes and paraphrases copiously. Again and again he uses Servius's helpful identifications of races and locales with varying names, as at 1.22, "Libya": "LIBYA, that is Carthage; the province instead of the city;"[152] or at 1.416, "Sabaean": "Arab. Sabaea is a region in the east where incense is abundant."[153] Servius also provides the commentator with more general descriptions, as for Megaros and Thapsus (3.689); it is significant, though, that in this note Commentator III deletes Servius's information on the physical position of these places in relation to Syracuse. Our commentator is indeed providing geographical descriptions, but his interest and information do not extend to any sense of cartographical relationships. These cities, rivers, mountains, and islands are radically elsewhere, but do not appear to exist for our commentator in the ordered spaces they must have occupied in the better-informed mind of Servius.

Indeed, our commentator's geographical interest is most aroused by

Servius's explanations of the derivation and meaning of names, what R. G. Austin nicely calls "the romance of geographical history."[154] He closely paraphrases Servius's note on "Oenotrian men" (3.165) – their name comes either from a king or from the vines they grow – and Servius's longer note on the tale behind "the Lydian Tiber" (at 2.781-82). Perhaps our commentator's longest sustained Servian quotation comes at 1.468, "Phrygians," where Servius discusses the different names given to the Trojans in different situations. When cowardly, as here, they are called *Phryges*; when treacherous, *Laomedontiadas*; when brave, *Troas* or *Hectoreos*. It is not surprising that this entry should gain the attention of Commentator III, as it addresses at once his interest in the relation of names to geography and history, and his previously mentioned concern with verbal precision.

As in his historical notes, moreover, Commentator III expands upon and adds to Servius in order to provide further details about the geographical and racial references of the *Aeneid*. The pattern of additions is like that of the historical notes. Most often Servius is expanded in the interest of specificity; at other points Commentator III quotes the Servian note to a different part of the *Aeneid*; and in some cases independent material is introduced, often from "Anselm."[155] Commentator III is especially interested in racial names and characteristics. When Sinon is said to be instructed "in Pelasgan trickery" (2.152), our commentator explains Pelasgan: "that is, deceitful, because Greeks are deceitful by nature."[156] There is no such note in Servius. Again, at the end of Sinon's speech, Virgil's "Asia" (2.193) is explained by Servius with "Asians." But Commentator III adds detail on locations and national characteristics: "ASIA, that is Asians. Sinon says this fawningly, because Asia is the third part of the world. Troy is a region of Asia. 'Asia' is used here for Troy, which is in Asia."[157] Again the source here is "Anselm," whose note is very similar.[158]

The additions to Servius made by Commentator III are not, of course, strictly limited to the sort of factual notes examined in detail in the paragraphs above. In occasional notes justifying the actions of Aeneas, our commentator also shows himself to operate within ethical aspects of the pedagogical tradition, in which Aeneas is depicted as an ideal prince and object for worldly imitation. A medieval reader of the *Aeneid*, as we have seen in chapter 1, had to contend with widely known rival versions of the Troy story, many of which saw Aeneas as a traitor for fleeing Troy, and a cad for abandoning Dido. Commentator III is at pains to refute both accusations. At 2.298, when Aeneas first awakens during the sack of Troy, our commentator reproduces "Anselm's" close paraphrases of Servius's justification of the hero.[159] Again, when Helenus is prevented from knowing or speaking all the events in Aeneas's future (c. 3.379), Commentator III paraphrases Servius's strong note of justification: "The prophet knew everything, but Juno did not allow him to tell everything, namely the death of his father and the storm sent by Aeolus and the love of Dido. For if Aeneas had known he was going to leave Africa, he would not easily have consented to the love of Dido."[160] Such a note rests on the assumption of Aeneas's unwaveringly virtuous intentions and implicitly rejects the rival tradition.

Altogether, then, Commentator III shows a systematic and intelligent effort to fulfill those exegetical aims described in the beginning of this chapter as "pedagogical." He begins with the inadequate but generally correct notes of the two (or three) earlier annotators already present in All Souls 82. To these he adds a mass of new marginalia which consistently attempt to restore for the reader a detailed sense of the historical, geographical, religious, and mythological difference of the world of the *Aeneid*. He has an active and energetic grasp of the dramatic reality of certain scenes. He shows considerable interest in rhetorical technique; on rare occasions he notes details of stylistic and semantic elegance. At a few, but significant, points he defends Aeneas against the hostile views of the counter-tradition.

Most of this could have been accomplished by a careful use of Servius. Commentator III, however, goes further. He does indeed use Servius, but not merely as a continuous commentary. Rather he treats Servius as a reference tool, moving backward and forward through the commentaries on all of Virgil's works and gathering disparate details into new notes. He regularly consults a second influential commentary, that of "Anselm of Laon." Even more important, Commentator III does a certain amount of fresh research, probably in geographical and historical texts, to improve the notes in those areas of particular interest to him. Most striking, perhaps, are those aspects of the available exegetical tradition that he studiously ignores. Aside from one very brief note, there is no material here from the allegorization attributed to Bernard Silvestris. Commentator III, despite his extensive borrowing from "Anselm," makes no use of the occasional allegorizing or Christianizing notes mentioned in the discussion of "Anselm" above. Indeed, he adds no notes at all to that most allegorizable of books,

Aeneid 6. Instead, he carefully exploits "Anselm" for those notes that can be used to establish details of rhetorical style and a sense of historical difference. In particular, he shares with "Anselm" a continuing interest in Virgil's *intentio* to praise Caesar through the epic. This political emphasis in his reading connects Commentator III with social and ethical aspects of the pedagogical tradition that extend from Servius to the Renaissance, and it is to continuities between this tradition and the Virgilian exegesis of the Renaissance that we now turn.

PEDAGOGICAL EXEGESIS, MEDIEVAL AND RENAISSANCE

To close this chapter, let us consider briefly the extensive continuities that link much of the pedagogical tradition discussed above with the teaching of Virgil, at least at the basic levels, among the Italian humanists. Since this chapter has proceeded by close study of a manuscript whose history can be traced through particular owners and institutional settings, we may best continue with another such specific case, Basel, Öffentliche Bibliothek der Universität F II 23 (hereafter "B").[161] This copy of Virgil's works is roughly a century older than AS82, but like AS82, it received successive layers of annotation across the centuries. The most interesting notes here are those entered by Coluccio Salutati (1331–1406). Craig Kallendorf has argued convincingly that Salutati purchased the manuscript in 1355 and annotated it between then and 1375; the notes by this leading Italian humanist would thus be roughly contemporary with those of the English Commentator III in AS82.[162]

There are important correspondences between the notes added to the manuscript by Salutati, and those examined in the section above. In part, these similarities result from the frequent use of Servius by both annotators.[163] But even the broad influence of Servius marks their participation in a common tradition; the next annotator of B, Giovanni Tortelli (1400–1466), would by contrast make very little use of Servius. Further, the very entries which Salutati selected from Servius parallel the interests we saw in Commentator III of AS82. The "vast majority" of Salutati's annotations, as Kallendorf notes, are literal and procedural, explaining difficult vocabulary or providing paraphrases; "all function to clarify the literal meaning of the text."[164] This sort of assistance was already partly in place when Commentator III came to

AS82, and he extended it with his constant provision of plot summary and topic headings.[165]

A smaller number of notes by Salutati, moreover, show specific topical interests similar to those in Commentator III. Like Commentator III, Salutati occasionally pointed out rhetorical figures, going beyond Servius at some points.[166] And in four distinguishable areas Salutati set out, as did Commentator III, to provide information on details and mores of the ancient world: myth, geography, ancient history, and "ancient religious rites and festivals."[167] In all these, Salutati shows his participation in a literal and pedagogical tradition strikingly similar to Commentator III who, as I have shown above, draws most extensively from Servius's notes on rhetoric, mythology and religion, history, and especially geography.

In all these regards, both Commentator III of AS82 and Salutati are pursuing the common aim of literal exegesis and of providing some sense of the differences between their own and Virgil's world. But they are doing so, for the most part, by exploiting little ancient material beyond the text of the poet himself and his most ancient accessible commentator. That is, they are both trying to construct something of a "free-standing" manuscript of Virgil, one whose own margins contain the basic elements of its comprehension. Tortelli, as we will see, changes this orientation.

But Salutati was typical of the earlier humanists, both in his interests and in his dependence on Servius as a source of information. As Anthony Grafton and Lisa Jardine have recently shown, the educational manuals and commentaries of Guarino da Verona (1374–1460) and his school followed medieval precedents, and drew much of their erudition from Servius.[168] Their general aim "was not a deep knowledge of any one subject or subjects, but as comprehensive a catalogue as possible of disconnected 'facts' necessary for informed reading and writing in the classical tradition: etymological, geographical and mythological points have equal value for this purpose, and demand equal attention."[169] Except for the aspect of "writing in the classical tradition," all the elements of this pedagogy can be recognized in the medieval English commentator we have examined above.

This was not to remain the central emphasis of classical reading during the fifteenth century. Grafton and Jardine, among others, have noted the increasing specialization of the humanists as they became more numerous and institutionalized, and as the range of texts they studied increased. The broad education practiced by Guarino and later Landino came to be challenged by proponents of narrower and more rigorous study.[170] Grafton sees this change reflected in part in the move from commentary to "the late fifteenth-century monograph, with its tightly-organized series of quotations marshalled to solve a single difficulty."[171] To return to the Basel manuscript of Virgil, this signal turn is apparent in its last layer of marginalia, entered by Giovanni Tortelli, whose "annotations differ radically" from Salutati's in being "relentlessly philological."[172] Tortelli is concerned to establish specific and nuanced word meanings through a system of marginal references to other uses of problematic words, both in Virgil and in eighteen other ancient writers.[173]

The far narrower focus of Tortelli's commentary has two general implications, both of which suggest a turn in the study of Virgil away from the pedagogical tradition we have seen in fourteenth-century England and Italy. First, Tortelli's exclusive attention to vocabulary itself corresponds to the kind of new specialization discussed by Grafton and Jardine; he was also author, we may note, of a specialized monograph, the *De orthographia*.[174] Second, and perhaps more significant, Tortelli exploits parallels in ancient usage, rather than authoritative commentary, to explain and contextualize difficult vocabulary. In Tortelli's approach, the largely self-supporting structure of interpretation written into AS82 or B by the late fourteenth century begins to be replaced by a Virgil text that functions only within a much broader network of other ancient texts. This presupposes a genuinely new and different range of accessible texts, and an altered interpretive emphasis.

Yet, let us note in closing, Tortelli's is not necessarily a *different* emphasis but rather an *added* emphasis in the context of the Basel manuscript. Like readers of B for four hundred years, and like the readers of AS82 for three hundred years, Tortelli did not efface the earlier marginalia in B, but rather read them and added to them.[175] One good reason that he could pursue his particular bent is the presence of an adequate traditional annotation by Salutati and others before him. The traditions of literal and pedagogical exegesis were not so much abandoned in this case, as they were used as a basis for new advanced applications. As we will see in the following chapter, other advanced kinds of interpretation, though of a very different sort, already existed during the Middle Ages along with the kinds of literal exegesis studied here.

In All Souls 82, then, we have examined a manuscript which continuously displays a literal and pedagogical approach to Virgil. Its earliest notes show only a very indifferent attitude toward achieving those goals, sporadically supplying useful and detailed notes, but far more often simplifying to a point where much of the difference – the historical, cultural, and verbal setting – of the *Aeneid* may be lost to the reader wholly dependent on the learned support of the annotation. The late-fourteenth-century Commentator III, however, had real success in carrying out his interests, and he leaves later medieval England a copy of the *Aeneid* to which much of the sense of difference has been restored. While this manuscript illustrates the major tradition of Virgilian reading in medieval England and Europe, it was by no means the only path a manuscript of the *Aeneid* might take. In the following chapter we will examine a manuscript which, in the late twelfth century, was supplied with fragments of spiritualizing allegory. By at least the beginning of the fifteenth century, like All Souls 82, it too had moved into the universities. And in chapter 4 we will study a commentary contemporary with Commentary III above, but far more interested in using the *Aeneid* for examples of imitable Christian morality and Christian allegory.

Spiritual allegory, platonizing cosmology, and the Boethian Aeneid in medieval England: Cambridge, Peterhouse College 158

The incremental layers of pedagogical exegesis in All Souls 82 show only one path of Virgilianism in medieval England, although it is a far more important path than has been recognized heretofore. In the case of All Souls 82, a text of the works of Virgil was produced as a conscious unit, and initially surrounded by a predominantly Servian apparatus, with brief but significant additions from the *Saturnalia* of Macrobius. Later notes reinforced and elaborated the literal and "pedagogic" emphasis of the Servian entries, providing yet more details of grammatical and lexical exegesis, and especially, more historical and geographical information.

This was not, however, the only exegetical path a manuscript could take as it gathered to itself layers of marginal notes, additional leaves of commentary material, and whole new texts. Cambridge, Peterhouse College 158 offers an important example of a manuscript annotated and adapted to suit a different level and focus of readership, interested in a very different kind of Virgilianism – the Virgilianism of spiritual pilgrimage, arcane science, and Platonizing cosmology. Indeed, even in All Souls 82 we witnessed a moment that briefly moves in the direction of such concerns, when the earliest annotator cites a *Consolation* commentary to explain Anchises's speech on the World Soul. That note evinces, though only in passing, an interest in cosmology and its links to similar themes in Boethius. Such annotation, which is only a minor note in AS82, becomes the major interpretive preoccupation in exegetical materials bracketing the beginning and end of the *Aeneid* in Peterhouse 158 (hereafter P158).

The allegorization of Virgil's *Aeneid* was extremely important for the reception of the epic in the high and later Middle Ages and on into the Renaissance; central texts like Dante's *Divine Comedy* and (as I will show in chapter 6) Chaucer's *House of Fame* attest to that. Yet we possess, in fact, rather few actual witnesses to the process, particularly the early stages, of that allegorization. Fulgentius's late-antique *Continentia Virgiliana* was widely known, and there was also the far more subtle and extensive twelfth-century commentary of "Bernard Silvestris"; we will turn to both of these below.[1] But besides these, we have rather little to go on, before the early Italian humanists began reading and adapting "Bernard."[2] John of Salisbury briefly mentions the allegorization of the *Aeneid* as the ages of man, in a passage that appears to be related to "Bernard."[3] The Third Vatican Mythographer includes a considerable amount of Virgilian exegesis dependent on Fulgentius and the more allegorizing moments in Servius, perhaps also on the commentary of "Bernard," discussed below. And the widely influential William of Conches is reported to have written a *Philosophia … super libris Eneidos Virgilii*.[4] "Bernard's" commentary itself was in wider circulation than is realized by his recent editors, but we nonetheless lack a sense of the wider variety of approaches to the text of Virgil that must have been available in the twelfth century.

In this chapter I will discuss a manuscript in whose annotation such cosmological, and more explicitly allegorical content in the *Aeneid* becomes a major though not exclusive focus, as the manuscript is progressively supplied with its own layers of exegesis. The *Aeneid* in P158 is bracketed at beginning and end with two allegorizing commentaries, the second much more persistent and systematic than the first. The first of these (hereafter "Peterhouse I"), squeezed in between two very traditional introductory *accessus* and appearing sporadically in the marginal notes as well, was until recently unknown. The second commentary (hereafter "Peterhouse II"), on three leaves added at the end of the *Aeneid*, is a fragment centering on Book Six, and is either an early version of the longer commentary attributed to Bernard Silvestris, or possibly that commentary's immediate (and, if so, deeply influential) source.[5] Between them, these two fragments show us two important moments in the progress of Virgilian allegory in the high Middle Ages, and witness the presence of such allegorical exegesis for readers of the *Aeneid* in high and later medieval England.[6]

Using this manuscript and its elaborate exegetical apparatus as my central example, I will also introduce some of the late antique discussions of Virgil, and more general developments in the allegorical reading of ancient fable, which stand behind these high medieval allegorical approaches to the epic. I will examine the uses of Virgil in Peterhouse I and II, and the latter commentary's problematic relationship to the allegorical commentary attributed to Bernard Silvestris. I will try to establish (see pp. 120–30) the specifically Boethian optic which I believe provides the controlling perspective for the exploration of spiritual pilgrimage in Peterhouse II and "Bernard Silvestris." And finally, I explore the broader climate of classicism in twelfth-century England which provides the setting and audience for the kind of sophisticated and creative approaches to Virgil that we find in P158.

EXEGESIS AND ITS FORMATS: FROM *GLOSAE* TO *COMMENTUM*

Quite probably as a part of its original production, the manuscript of the *Aeneid* in P158 was provided with the single leaf, containing a group of introductory texts, which is now folio 42.[7] This leaf comprises two *accessus*, both quite traditional in content but differing in their organization and, sandwiched disconnectedly between them, the beginning of the partly allegorical commentary "Peterhouse I"; see plate 3a.[8] None of these texts has any heading, which is typical, and they are distinguished from one other only by beginning at the top of a new column, and by the presence of a simple paragraph mark. Then, after the close of the *Aeneid*, are three further leaves (fols. 169–71, the modern foliation is inaccurate), copied in the late twelfth century but bound in with this manuscript at an uncertain date; see plate 4. These contain a systematic allegorical commentary ("Peterhouse II") interpreting the *Aeneid* in terms of the ages of man and spiritual progress through study of the *artes*.

The very presentation of this exegetical material in the codex, bracketing the *Aeneid* but separate from it – and thus to an extent independent of any immediate, local reading of the text itself – serves as an index of the quite different approach to the epic we encounter in P158. The systematic introduction provided by the two *accessus* was wholly absent in AS82, as was any hint of allegorical interpretation and the fairly elaborate theoretical justification thereof, which we will encounter in "Bernard" and Peterhouse II. Instead, in AS82, the *auctor*'s text itself consistently dominated (despite occasional marginal hints of the voice of a *magister* or his students), and the order of the marginal notes was dictated strictly by the primary text and closely linked to it, creating a sequence of disconnected entries organized and justified only by reference to the middle of the page.

The codicological organization of P158, on the other hand, asserts the presence of the *magister* or reader as an agent far more independent of the *auctor*, and, both before and after a reader turns to the central poem, this manuscript offers on separate leaves an active, even creative mediating consciousness engaged with, yet distinct from, that *auctor*. Both of the initial *accessus* have a connected story to tell (if an ancient and traditional one) about Virgil's life and the historical and political causes that brought about the writing of the *Aeneid*. And Peterhouse II, at the end, while it follows the order of the books in the epic, nonetheless also constructs from them, as we will see, its own independent narrative of human life on earth and the course of its spiritual development. This para-narrative could not be further from the disconnected sequence of annotations dotting the margins of AS82. Even the much less persistent, less systematic allegorization of Peterhouse I operates through careful selection and artful emphasis within the master text. Such physical organization of the material, then, suggests at once a greater distance, a more aggressive willingness to assert the reader's presence in regard to the text, and an urge to domesticate, even control the *auctor*, in effect to generate a second book by reading *mistice*.

This increased independence from the local lexical and grammatical demands of the authorial text as we shift our attention from AS82 to P158 corresponds rather neatly to broad distinctions between "gloss" and "commentary" current in the twelfth century. As noted in chapter 2, Hugh of St. Victor distinguished three aspects of a text that can receive the attention of its expositor: *littera*, *sensus*, and the *sentencia* that involves a *profundior intelligentia*.[9] The notes on AS82, I suggested, address the first two of these levels, but at points like the Boethius citation, they reach briefly toward *sentencia*. This increasing distance from the local letter of the text is reflected in contemporary distinctions between *glosa* (or *glosule*) and *commentum*, though these are only two among a wide and inconsistent array of terms for exegetical activity and its resultant texts.[10]

There is little indication that most exegetes worried themselves about the terminology of their activities, and what titles exist are more likely to be scribal than authorial.[11] William of Conches, however, who is very influential for the exegesis studied in this chapter, offers the following distinctions:

Nowadays we call *commentum* only an explanatory text. Hence it is different from the *glosa*, for a *commentum* deals only with the *sentencia*. It says nothing about the *continuatio* or the *expositio* of the *littera*. But a *glosa* takes care of all these factors. That is why it is called *glosa*.[12]

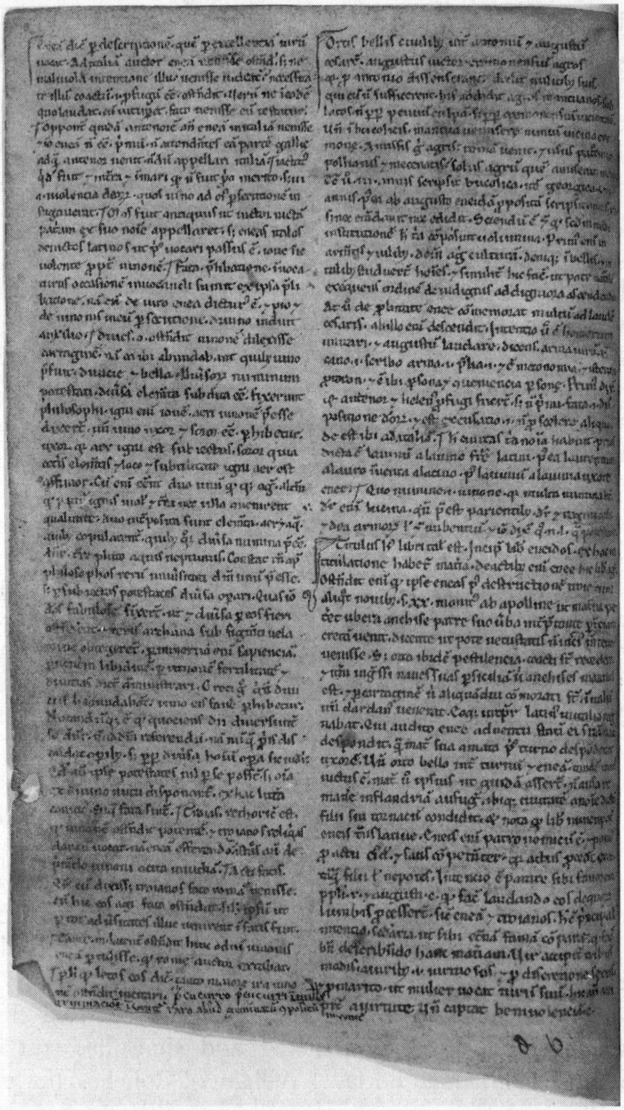

Plate 3a Cambridge, Peterhouse College 158, fo. 42 *verso*.
At right (3b), the opening of the *Aeneid*, with the earliest layer of marginal commentary, and some added notes in a later hand. The left-hand page of the same opening (3a) contains introductory material, including a quite traditional life and *accessus* (in column B), and the beginning of an allegorical commentary (in column A, "Peterhouse I"). The latter is connected to the notes in the margins of the text. Published with permission.

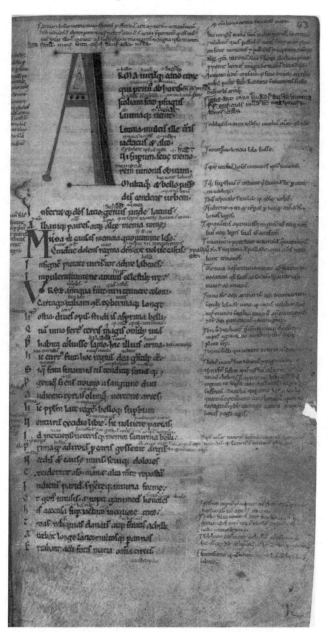

Plate 3b Cambridge, Peterhouse College 158, fo. 43 *recto*.

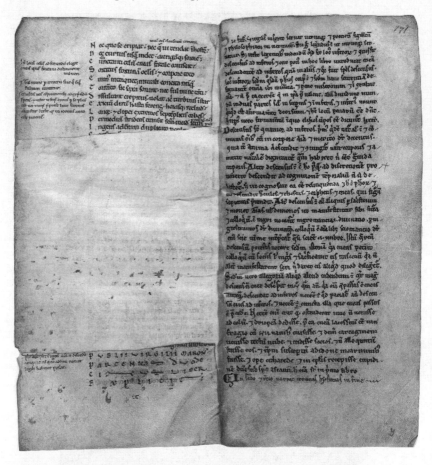

Plate 4 Cambridge, Peterhouse College 158, fo. 167 *verso*–169 *recto* (the modern foliation is inaccurate). At left, the end of *Aeneid* 12, with the early marginal annotation. The blank section at left is the *verso* of an interleaved scrap (fo. 168) containing, on its hidden side, the one-line summaries of all twelve books of the *Aeneid* and the one- and ten-line summaries to Book One. At the right, the opening of an allegorical commentary on *Aeneid* 6 ("Peterhouse II"), closely related to the commentary attributed to Bernard Silvestris. Published with permission.

William's *glosa*, then, addresses the basic level of the text that Hugh also calls *littera*, while William gives the name *commentum* to more advanced kinds of exegesis that leave the letter aside and concentrate only on what, like Hugh, he calls *sententia*. *Glosa* is generally associated with briefer interlinear and marginal notes, such as we witnessed in AS82.

Separate collections of such notes, sometimes little adapted toward consistency, are often called *glosule*.[13] Häring records an interesting notice by Robert of Auxerre of this shift from notes in the margins, to a separate collection of more or less disconnected notes, to a separate exegetical text. "Peter Lombard, [Robert] related, 'has given a clearer and more detailed exposition of the *glosatura* on the Psalms which Anselm had divided into short interlinear and marginal glosses and which Gilbert then transformed into a coherent text.' "[14]

The commentaries in P158 offer us an unusually clear instance of two different moments in the process described by Robert. For, as I will show in greater detail below (pp. 101–07), Peterhouse I proves to be a fairly advanced set of notes at a liminal moment in the move from the margins to an independent text. It begins separate from the Virgilian text, on fol. 42vb, but then continues in the margins themselves; in another manuscript, however, these notes are presented only in the margins. So in Peterhouse I, loosely connected marginal notes are beginning to emerge into the form of a separate set of *glosule*. And as we will see, the occasional but unsystematic allegorical content in these notes corresponds to Hugh's notion of *sententia* and approaches William of Conches's idea of a *commentum*.

Peterhouse II, on the other hand, is wholly separate from the text of the *Aeneid*, and as I will argue it can really only function as a separate *commentum*; it is too selective in its focus, and for the most part too far divorced from the details of the primary text, to work effectively as marginal notes.[15] P158, then, offers us not only two related stages in the development of Virgilian allegoresis, but also a fascinating moment in their emerging codicological presentation. In this codicological move from marginal notes closely tied to the authorial text, to a separate *commentum* more loosely inspired by that text, I will try to show the simultaneous emergence (or splitting off) of a new Virgilian myth. A new *fabula* is written in these separate commentaries, deriving as much from Boethius and late antique Platonism as from the letter of the *Aeneid*; and this new *fabula* visually brackets the *auctor* from which it derives.

LATE ANTIQUE VIRGILIANISM AND MEDIEVAL MODES OF ALLEGORICAL INTERPRETATION

Behind the emerging codicological independence of Peterhouse I and Peterhouse II, and their implicit assertion of the exegete as an intervening textual presence, there lies, paradoxically, a near-religious reverence for Virgil's text as the repository of profound learning and philosophical wisdom. Inherited from late antiquity and widely available throughout the Middle Ages, this approach claimed, at least in theory, to discover in the *Aeneid* all the *scientia* – especially the arcane wisdom – of Virgil's, but more particularly the exegete's own, ambient culture. This gave rise, from an early point, to the articulation of Stoic, Pythagorean, and more importantly of Neoplatonic themes in the epic, most densely in commentary on Aeneas's descent to the Underworld.

Servius expresses such reverence in his much-quoted opening lines on Book Six:

Truly, all of Virgil is filled with learning, in which this book holds preeminence ... And some things in it are put straightforwardly, many are from history, and many concern the profound learning of the Egyptian philosophers and theologians, so much so that a great many [commentators] have written separate treatises on each of the book's topics.[16]

Writing about a generation after Servius (and making Servius a character in his *Saturnalia*) Macrobius displays, much more persistently, a similar sense that Virgil's knowledge is virtually limitless. Virgil is considered "an authority in every branch of learning,"[17] and whole books of the *Saturnalia* are devoted to demonstrating Virgil's command of philosophy, astronomy, religious law, sacrificial practices, and augury.[18]

This assertion of Virgil's universal learning combines in Macrobius with an almost slavish regard for his stylistic perfection. At certain high points in the discussion, the poet's art is explicitly said to imitate the harmony of nature itself and to approach the skill of a world-creating divinity. The character Eusebius, depicted as a Greek rhetorician, demonstrates Virgil's command of all oratorical styles, then adds:

And thus it was that with the universal mother, Nature, for his only guide he wove the pattern of his work – just as in music different sounds are combined to form a single harmony. For in fact, if you look closely into the nature of the universe, you will find a striking resemblance between the handiwork of the divine craftsman and that of our poet.[19]

From a book so woven (*praetexuit*) like the world itself, it is not a long step to the twelfth-century commonplace of the world as something to be read as a book, and the epic hero as a character undergoing an education in the *artes* that will allow him to read his fallen world wisely and find in it the work of his Creator.[20]

But such a text, both stylistically and philosophically universal, demands a readership itself learned and skilled enough to articulate the text's profundities. It is exactly in the gap thus opened by their reverence for Virgil that exegetes like Servius and Macrobius position themselves and insert their models of culture and social order.[21] Servius's sense of his special place is most apparent in his local pronouncements on proper usage,[22] but Macrobius is often more explicit about the social power standing behind the ability rightly to explicate Virgil. After Praetextatus – who embodies the traditional patrician virtues – has demonstrated Virgil's "knowledge of both the divine and civil law," the company makes him almost a modern Virgil: "Hereupon all the others were unanimous in asserting that Vergil and his interpreter, as men of learning, were equally matched."[23]

Virgil's more obscure passages, "dug out from the hidden recesses of Greek literature," require an equally sensitive and learned reader ("drunk deep of the learning of Greece"), better than "the rank and file of schoolmasters."[24] But if Virgil's Greek learning often comes from hidden recesses (*de ... penetralibus*), his own poetry too is figured by Macrobius as a holy place, like a temple, with hidden inward spaces (*reclusa penetralia*) and secret chambers (*abstrusa ... adyta*) which can be opened only by elect readers – virtually as elect, in fact, as Virgil himself – such as the company of the *Saturnalia*.[25] Symmachus, the most distinguished among them, asserts the near-divinity of the poem, the unique access of his class to its mysteries, and their condescending generosity in sharing such wisdom with others:

> But we, who claim to have a finer taste, shall not suffer the secret places of this sacred poem to remain concealed, but we shall examine the approaches to its hidden meanings and throw open its inmost shrine for the worship of the learned.[26]

As Kaster has put it, "The text readily becomes a pool of Narcissus: in admiring the poet's *occultissima diligentia* one is admiring one's own."[27] Symmachus thus makes his kind of elite readers almost an initiatory priesthood, providing entrée to the hidden, quasi-religious mysteries of Virgil, but also positioned between those mysteries and any vulgar readership. A similar sense of simultaneous access and distance, of the exegete's presence between the reader and the cryptic text, and his resulting power, is implicit in the codicological presentation and, as we will see, textual tone of Peterhouse I and II and "Bernard Silvestris."

As suggested above, however, a paradox inheres in such reverential assumptions of Virgil's inexhaustible but largely hidden wisdom; for while it renders hostile criticism of the poetry scarcely imaginable, it also lays open broad fields for the play of the exegete's own ingenuity, and for the insertion of his own cultural values.[28] Despite this theoretical space for explication of hidden mystery by an exegetical elect, though, neither Servius in his commentary nor Macrobius in the *Saturnalia* give much sustained attention to hidden or allegorical content. Instead, their explication of Virgilian obscurity is largely directed toward questions answerable by means of an enormous but largely literal body of linguistic, literary, historical, and religious knowledge.[29] It is from this body of learning, Servian and Macrobian, that the "pedagogical" notes studied in AS82 derive.

There is, nonetheless, both in Servius and in Macrobius's *Commentary on the Dream of Scipio*, passing reference to specific allegorical ideas and to Platonic notions of human life and the cosmos, sufficient to lay the groundwork for the more systematic commentaries of Fulgentius and "Bernard Silvestris." Servius introduces allegorical interpretations, particularly in Book Six but elsewhere as well, from which two great strands of later systematic allegoresis derive: first, the interpretation of moments in Aeneas's journey in terms of moral or spiritual progress; and second, the interpretation of the gods as forces of the physical universe.[30]

The second of these is fairly straightforward, with the gods resolved into the elements or their effects. So Jupiter is aether (1.47); Juno is air, whose movement creates wind and the storm that shipwrecks Aeneas (1.78), and her attendant nymphs are seen as the water that derives from clouds in the air (1.71). In a closely related move, the gods can be interpreted astrologically (*secundum mathesin*), so that when Jupiter and Venus cross, Aeneas is certain to have good luck through the agency of a woman (Dido, 1.223).[31]

Notes interpreting characters or events as stages in Aeneas's moral status are rather more numerous. As early as the first book, Aeneas's constant companion Achates is interpreted as the anxiety (*sollicitudo*) that is the constant companion of kings (1.312); this interpretation is arrived at through Greek etymology, which will provide an enormously rich medium of exegesis for later commentators. Such notes become quite dense in Book Six, where the entire underworld is seen as an image of our life on earth, virtue mixed with vice (6.477).[32] This points toward "Bernard's" systematic approach to Book Six as Aeneas seeing life on earth in a second way, but now equipped with philosophical maturity. The nine circles of the river Styx, for Servius, represent the nine planetary and stellar spheres (6.439).

Within this symbolic world, Aeneas, and implicitly any moral agent, is presented with a sequence of challenging choices. They begin, symbolically, with the golden bough, interpreted by Servius as the Pythagorean *bivium*, where man makes his first moral choice in life as a youth:

> We know that Pythagoras of Samos divided human life like the letter Y, namely because the first age of life is undecided, since it has not yet given itself over to vices or virtues; however, the dividing point of the Y begins at youth, at which time men follow either the vices (that is, the left side) or the virtues (that is, the right side).[33]

The image of the *bivium*, with reference to Virgil's golden bough, also arouses discussion in Lactantius Placidus and other Christian writers after him. Lactantius introduces the idea – itself Pythagorean and Neoplatonic – that the youth will begin on the way of virtue by study of the liberal arts. This notion will be crucial both to Fulgentius and, after widespread development among high medieval Christianizing Platonists of several stamps, to "Bernard." The golden bough, then, provides one of several pregnant images by which the late-antique Platonism associated with Virgil in Servius and Macrobius takes on Christian overtones that will be exploited by later allegorists.[34]

The challenges of the underworld/world are the greater in this system of interpretation, because Servius introduces as well the Platonic notion that the soul, in descending through the planetary spheres, forgets its former virtues and takes on weaknesses: torpor from Saturn, wrath from Mars, lust from Venus, longing for profit from Mercury, desire for power from Jove (6.714).[35] A few notes (at 6.426 and 6.705) suggest that the nine circles of hell represent the progress from infancy to old age, beginning with birth in the approaches to the underworld (6.286), another idea that will have great consequence for later allegorists.

It is important to recall, nonetheless, that these allegorizing notes by Servius are sporadic even in Book Six, and quite rare elsewhere. Indeed, Jones counts only one hundred eighty-two such notes, including the euhemerist and historical allegories, among the tens of thousands of entries in Servius.[36] But their suggestive yet transient nature leaves the field open for very creative responses among later interpreters for whom the *Aeneid* was far less a public epic than the record of private development. Like the awed respect for Virgil's poem registered by Macrobius and Servius, these notes had the paradoxical effect of opening the text to the imagination of this new kind of reader.

The first of these was Fulgentius. This earliest surviving systematic allegorization of the *Aeneid* makes explicit if clumsy use of the idea of human life as a journey through nature to knowledge, and finally to happiness. Fulgentius's *Expositio Virgilianae Continentiae*, probably written in the late fifth or earlier sixth century, is fundamental to all later Virgilian allegory.[37] Unlike the self-approving, grand commentators of the late fourth and early fifth century, Fulgentius depicts himself in a minor role; by dramatizing his interpretation as a vision, he can cast Virgil himself – depicted as a stern *magister* – as the interpreter of his own text.

After a very brief overview of the allegorical content (*misticae* ... *rationes*[38]) of the *Eclogues* and *Georgics* in Fulgentius's own voice, Fulgentius's Virgil claims that "in the twelve books of the *Aeneid* I have shown the full range of human life." Fulgentius begins the habit, followed later, of allegorizing the *Aeneid* in the order of its telling, not in the chronological order of its events. His broad structure relates the individual books to the ages of man. Thus Fulgentius's Virgil "introduced the shipwreck as an allegory of the dangers of birth."[39] Book One is infancy, Books Two and Three allegorize youth. The Cyclops shows youth's pride, and the death of Anchises its rejection of parental discipline. Book Four is adolescence, and there Aeneas appropriately discovers lust. Mercury, or intellect, causes him to leave this, and passion (Dido) then burns to ashes. Book Five marks Aeneas's return to the values of his father.

In his allegorization of Book Six, Fulgentius begins to address far more closely the issues of worldliness, learning, and transcendence. Here Aeneas "reaches the temple of Apollo, that is, studious learning." But before he can "penetrate obscure and secret mysteries," he must bury Misenus, "the illusion of vain praise," and take up the golden bough, "the study of philosophy and letters."[40] Thus Fulgentius sees true maturity as a weaning away from love of worldly praise, and an eagerness for study of traditional learning. We have seen, above, that this idea had already been appropriated to Christian ideas of spiritual development by some of the fathers. Fulgentius is hesitant, however, to attribute to Virgil himself any conscious Christian intent; when he suggests that the initial depiction of Aeneas, combining virtue and wisdom, somehow predicts Christ, "Virgil" insists that this is the work of Fulgentius's insight, not his own.[41] We will see a similar hesitancy in "Bernard Silvestris."

Fulgentius's notions of release, however, have little of the exalted tone found in later allegories. His Virgil is more a harsh pedagogue than a spiritual guide, and his Elysium is merely the freedom from a student's fear of his teachers: school days are past.[42] The summary treatment of the later books shows that Fulgentius's idea of Aeneas's reward is thoroughly worldly, if quite virtuous. Lavinia, whom he marries, symbolizes "the road of toil, for at this stage of life, Everyman learns the value of toil in furthering his worldly possessions."[43] As Whitbread points out in his introduction, Fulgentius's "emphasis is on material prosperity, on making good, not on reaching a wise old age or a final sanctity."[44] For all its barrenness of detail and limited vision, however, Fulgentius's commentary lays the essential structure for the much richer, later allegorizations of the *Aeneid* in terms of the ages of man.

The *Expositio* survives in many manuscripts; they are particularly numerous from the tenth to the earlier twelfth centuries.[45] It is perfectly clear that Fulgentius's work provided the general model for the major statement of twelfth-century Virgilian allegoresis, the commentary of "Bernard Silvestris." "Bernard" follows the broad outlines of the earlier allegory, but as we will see his own commentary is far more energetic, imaginative, graceful, and nuanced than that of Fulgentius. A major reason for the greater elaboration and sophistication of "Bernard's" and related high medieval commentaries is their extensive use of interpretive ideas inherited predominantly from Macrobius in the *Commentary on the Dream of Scipio*, and elaborated by commentators like William of Conches and "Bernard" himself.

Toward the beginning of his enormously influential *Commentary*, Macrobius pauses to articulate the subdivisions of fable (*fabula*), and judge which are appropriate to philosophical interpretation, and just what – rather strictly limited – philosophical topics such interpretable fable (*narratio fabulosa*) hides under its pious veil (*sub pio figmentorum velamine*).[46] Having made these rather elaborate distinctions, Macrobius goes on to justify the purposes of fable, in language that recalls several passages from the *Saturnalia* quoted above:

But in treating of the other gods and the Soul, as I have said, philosophers make use of fabulous narrative; not without a purpose, however, nor merely to entertain, but because they realize that a frank, open exposition of herself is distasteful to Nature, who, just as she has witheld an understanding of herself from the uncouth senses of men by enveloping herself in variegated garments (*vario rerum tegmine operimentoque*), has also desired to have her secrets (*arcana*) handled by more prudent individuals through fabulous narratives. Accordingly, her sacred rites are veiled in mysterious representations (*figurarum cuniculis*) so that she may not have to show herself even to initiates. Only eminent men (*summatibus viris*) of superior intelligence gain a revelation of her truths.[47]

This passage presses even further the *Saturnalia*'s tone of a small, elect readership empowered both to reveal and to protect textual secrets. Whereas in the refined company of Praetextatus and his guests all Virgil's mysteries could be spoken, here Macrobius suggests another audience (*vulgaribus hominum sensibus*) to whom the deeper secrets are denied, forever hidden under their covering. The implied architecture of the text, with its inner rooms requiring an initiated guide, explicit in the *Saturnalia*, is again suggested here in the figural use of *cuniculis* – literally, underground passages. Most important, perhaps, is Macrobius's intricate comparison of natural and textual secrets, elaborating the idea introduced by Eusebius in the *Saturnalia*. But while Eusebius was instituting a neatly controlled comparison, Macrobius here never fully distinguishes – nor, I think, does he mean to – between the mysteries of the fabulous text and the covered body of nature. The two elements remain densely interplicated, a near-unification of world and text that will have important implications for "Bernard's" later exploration of scientific truths found almost anywhere in the hidden sense of the *Aeneid*.

Later discussions of hidden senses and the multiple modes of their interpretation, derived largely from commentaries and reflections on this chapter in Macrobius's *Commentary*, are equally important for the allegorical approach to the *Aeneid* in "Bernard" and other twelfth-century interpreters.[48] The most influential development of Macrobius is found in passages from William of Conches's commentary on Macrobius, edited and brilliantly analyzed by Peter Dronke.[49] As he shows, William takes pains in his discussion to expand the definition of fable, and to reopen the range of fables susceptible of philosophical interpretation, which had been narrowly restricted by Macrobius.[50] Whereas Macrobius limits interpretation to fables that report seemly acts by the gods, William sees the greater need to interpret unseemly fables, and thereby to uncover the quite proper truth they hide: "for [William] the seemliness of the *significatio* genuinely eclipses and renders unimportant the unseemliness of the words."[51] To describe the technique of interpreting such fable, and often as a word for the fable itself, William invokes the term *integumentum* – a covering.[52] Unseemliness in fables is irrelevant for William (or demands interpretation all the more) exactly because fables are but a covering for philosophical truth.

Yet in his most elaborate discussion of the term among the notes published by Dronke, William hesitates intriguingly, and ultimately leaves in place some of Macrobius's sense of a nudity that resists uncovering, a mystery that reveals even as it remains mysterious. Discussing the passage from Macrobius I quote above (pp. 97–98), William equates Nature's nudity with being *sine integumento* – at once a body without clothing and textual truth without fabulous covering.[53] William then goes on to interpret Macrobius's "mysterious representations" (*figurarum cuniculis*, for which Dronke's translation "labyrinths of imagery" is more effective) as the *integumentum* itself:

A *cuniculus* is a subterranean passage by which a man walks under cover from one place to another; so too an animal, a rabbit, is called *cuniculus*, because it dwells in the burrows underground. But here it is *integumenta* that are called "labyrinths of imagery" – for as rabbits take cover in such labyrinths, so truth is enclosed, in darkness as it were, in *integumenta*.[54]

William thus emphasizes the literal, architectural sense of *cuniculus* that links it, I have suggested, with other textual hidden spaces adumbrated in the *Saturnalia*. But the implications of his comparison go further; for if an integumental narrative is indeed a *cuniculus*, then like Nature's body it cannot be definitively uncovered. Uncovered, a *cuniculus* ceases to exist; and an *integument* so figured, and so treated, consumes itself. In regard to moments like this, Dronke seems quite right to claim that for William "there are certain vital aspects of metaphysics where we can proceed only by images – where *imago* is our only hope for knowledge."[55]

Another aspect of William's argument here is exemplary of the procedures both he and "Bernard" bring to their analyses of fabulous texts. Within Macrobius's discussion of fables and their secrets, William takes a single term (*cuniculis*) on which briefly to focus his argument. Drawing on a literal meaning somewhat distant from the metaphorical sense primarily intended by his *auctor*, William then creates, as it were, his own secondary *narratio fabulosa* within the master text: a little story of men moving from place to place by the hidden route of underground passages, or rabbits in their warrens. It is this interior story – itself almost a *cuniculus*, something hidden under the ground of the text –

that provides the integument to justify his argument about *integumenta*. There is a sense almost of creating the very secret spaces (or *adyta*, to use Macrobius's term) that the exegete then opens to the reader. This mode of reading, by generating a fable for interpretation, allows for a vast amount of learning to be discovered within the text, but it also provides tremendous creative opportunities for the exegete qualified by education and position to undertake such reading.[56] While "Bernard's" theoretical explication of *integumentum* suggests rather a less mysterious notion of reading, I will suggest that his approach to the *Aeneid* works through self-generated fables and – either by intention or hesitation – leaves certain mysteries untapped, in ways that reflect his profound debt to William of Conches.

"Bernard's" own statement on textual mysteries and their modes of revelation, in his commentary on Martianus Capella, has been the single most cited passage in recent discussions of twelfth-century secular exegesis.[57] It demands little further comment, except to note its simultaneous urges to tidy up and systematize a range of current technical terms, and to reinforce – even extend – the power of the exegete who uses such techniques. "Bernard" begins:

The form of instruction [of *De nuptiis*] is figurative (*Genus doctrine figura est.*) Figurative discourse (*Figura*) is a mode of discourse which is called "a veil" (*involucrum*). Figurative discourse is twofold, for we divide it into allegory and *integumentum*. Allegory is a mode of discourse which covers under an historical narrative a true meaning which is different from its surface meaning, as in the case of Jacob wrestling with the angel. An *integumentum*, however, is a mode of discourse which covers a true meaning under a fictitious narrative, as in the case of Orpheus. For in the case of the former history, and in the latter fiction, contains a profound hidden truth, which will be explained elsewhere. Allegory pertains to Holy Scripture, but *integumentum* to philosophical scripture.[58]

"Bernard" here seems to see the fabulous covering of *integumentum* as more fully and neatly uncoverable than did William of Conches in the passage discussed just above. The two discourses are quite separate, and lack the interdependent quality that is implicit both in Macrobius and William. At the same time, whereas William was eagerly reopening the ranges of interpretable fable and the topics they could cover, "Bernard" here again introduces distinctions and limits. The narrative mode of integument is carefully separated from that of biblical allegory.

Moreover, recalling Macrobius once again, "Bernard" restricts the topics that integument can cover:

However, a philosophical treatise does not allow use of a "veil" everywhere, as Macrobius bears witness. For he states that, when the pen dares to approach the highest divinity, it is wrong to admit even the permissible kind of fiction. But when the soul or the powers of the upper or lower air are discussed, *integumenta* have their place. Hence Vergil, when describing the temporal life of the human spirit within the body, used *integumenta* . . .[59]

But these restrictions also generate mysteries even in those antique fables which "Bernard" seems to consider so fully uncoverable. Using a perspective very different from William's, then, this statement nonetheless, like William, leaves certain matters ultimately uncovered in (uncovered *by*) the text of the antique *auctor*. Following a distinction of biblical and philosophical scripture, as this paragraph does, it seems particularly to delimit theological truth from the purview of the reader of secular fable.[60]

But even if these hierarchical distinctions limit (at least in theory) the hidden subjects of *integumenta*, the modes in which *integumenta* operate leave great responsibility and great power in the hands of their exegete:

It should be noted that *integumenta* have double and even multiple meanings (*equivocationes et multivocationes*). For example: in Vergil the name Juno is an equivocation for the lower air and the practical life . . . In Vergil there are multivocations as well, because Jupiter and Anchises are names for one and the same [i.e. God] . . . And therefore the reader must take great care in making these distinctions.[61]

Equivocation expands a single integumental figure into a whole range of potential senses (though these do tend to be largely traditional). And multivocation, by which any number of figures can cover a single concept, allows many moments in the text to converge on one dominant idea. While this imposes care on the exegete, though, like other ideas discussed above it also generates tremendous potential for the exegete to thematize the text toward his own ends. It is this room (again to use Macrobius's metaphor) for the exegetes' own skill in fable-making that we will see progressively exploited in the group of allegorizing commentaries I explore in the following two sections.

PETERHOUSE I: THE EMERGENCE OF ALLEGORY

On the leaf that precedes the text of the *Aeneid* in P158 (at some point the beginning of a manuscript containing only the epic, and now fol. 42), a single column contains the beginning of a commentary that then continues in the margins of the text itself. This commentary contains much that recalls the early layer of annotation in AS82, both in style and content; but it also features a series of allegorizing notes. These notes make "Peterhouse I" an important example of a kind of unsystematic integumental reading of parts of the *Aeneid* that would appear to develop before or along with the more systematic allegoresis we will see in "Peterhouse II" and the commentary of "Bernard."

When I first described the materials that I now call Peterhouse I, I took the single column containing the beginning of that commentary to be independent of the occasional allegorical notes in the margins themselves.[62] Since that time, however, I have discovered another witness to this commentary (Biblioteca Apostolica Vaticana, Vat. lat. 1574) in which all these notes appear, but exclusively in the margins of the text.[63] What we seem to be witnessing in P158, then, is a moment when a kind of commentary, whose interest is shifting from *littera* to *sententia*, is also beginning to move codicologically, from the margins to the separate space of an independent commentary.

Since the allegorizing notes in Peterhouse I mix in with a predominant group of notes that reflect the "pedagogical" tradition explored in AS82, we should pause first to consider how literal exegesis operates in Peterhouse I. The initial series of marginal notes around the *Aeneid* in P158 are largely (and, as the commentary proceeds into later books, increasingly) pedagogical. These notes, however, are not so often from Servius as those in the All Souls manuscript.[64]

Most of the non-Servian material deals with rhetorical analysis of the text. The commentary introduces a number of technical terms not found in Servius at the same points in his commentary. So at 1.1, "Arms," the notes include the Servian description of metonymy, but the opening phrase is also described as hendiadys and hysteron proteron.[65] Similar rhetorical analysis of the first few lines can be found in other twelfth-century manuscripts, but it is not usually as persistent as in P158. The notes go on to say that Virgil divides his material in two parts, the wanderings and the hardships which Aeneas suffered on land and sea.[66] Other early entries include alternate meanings of words not provided in Servius,[67] and notes on the kinds of language to be used in various social situations.[68] The notes also give mythographical information not found at the same points in Servius.[69] For example, when Neptune calms the seas (1.138), his trident is explained: "The trident is assigned to Neptune, because the sea is said by some to be the third part of the world, or because there are three kinds of water – the sea, the streams, the rivers – over which Neptune presides."[70] The non-Servian material becomes less frequent in the later books, but some independent rhetorical and mythographical material continues to appear.[71]

The allegorizing material in Peterhouse I is concentrated in the notes on the beginning of the *Aeneid*; the commentary then returns to its dominant pedagogical mode except for one moment in Book Six. And its discussion of the methods of allegorical exegesis, not surprisingly, occurs close to the start, in the notes on folio 42vb. Although this discussion is quite brief, careful examination can localize it in the traditions of scientific and spiritual integumental reading that were discussed above. If we can draw conclusions from so brief a passage, though, certain details of language will suggest that the commentator was not working in the specific milieu of "Bernard" or William of Conches, and instead derives his technical language from rather earlier sources.[72]

Insofar as we can judge from Peterhouse I and related notes preserved in Vat. lat. 1574, this commentary did not have the kind of sophisticated overall allegorical structure found in "Bernard." Rather the entries at each lemma move back and forth between the pedagogical topics described above, general ethical comments – praising the virtues of Aeneas, for instance – and scientific allegory of the gods. This commentary, then, may give us another precious glimpse of the kinds of sporadic allegorizing materials that stand behind the commentary of "Bernard," and that he then systematized around the structure provided by Fulgentius.[73]

Peterhouse I's comments on the opening lines of Book One concentrate on showing Virgil's intention of praising Aeneas as an unblemished model of ethical action:

Through a description he speaks of Aeneas, whom he calls MAN on account of his excellence. The author shows that Aeneas came to ITALY. But lest he should seem to have come there with some evil intention, Virgil shows him to have been forced by necessity, that is, BANISHED. Indeed, lest he should censure Aeneas in that very thing for which he praises him, the author shows him to have come THROUGH FATE ... In fact, he was CAST ABOUT both on land and at sea, which was not of his own deserving, but BY THE POWER that is the violence of the gods, whom Juno had incited to persecute him. (1–6.)

The commentator is at particular pains to justify Aeneas's invasion of Italy. Behind this careful demonstration of his virtue lies the historical tradition of Aeneas the traitor and profiteer, a tradition which

"Bernard" will accept as historical, reserving the truth of the text for his allegorical exegesis. Clearly this commentator is not willing to discard even the literal level.

Peterhouse I becomes far more interesting, however, when it turns to the passage on Juno's affection for the Carthaginians. Here the commentator includes a methodological digression on the allegorical significance of the pagan gods:

(11) RICH IN MEANS: He shows that Juno loved Carthage, for there was an abundance there of those things over which Juno presided: riches and wars. (12) Philosophers used to think that the various elements are set under the power of different divine authorities. (13) They said that Jove presided over fire, Juno over air, and thus Juno is said to be his wife and sister: his wife because air is subordinate to fire, and his sister because air is closer to fire, in position and fineness, than are the other elements. (14) For whenever there are two things, there is one which acts, and the other which suffers. (15) And the mass of fire and earth do not meet in any property. (16) Two elements are placed between, air and water, by which they [i.e. fire and earth] are bound together, and over which different divine authorities are said to preside: Pluto over the earth, Neptune over the waters. (17) It is agreed, however, among the philosophers that one god presides over the universe of things, but that he carries out various things through subordinate powers, which they represented fictively as gods, so that they might show various things to come to pass through them, and so they might hide the secrets of things under the veil of fiction. (18) For they say that wisdom is administered through Minerva, lust through Venus, fertility and riches through Juno. (19) Thus when the Greeks are abounding in riches, Juno is said to favor them. (20) And it should be noted that, whenever the gods are said to differ among themselves, this should not be referred to God. (21) For He is never discordant in his own works, but he seems so on account of the diverse works of men. (22) Because, moreover, these powers can do nothing by themselves, but all things are disposed through the divine will. (23) This is inferred from this phrase: IF THE FATES ALLOW.

Even this brief explanation provides enough detail to allow a fairly precise identification of the intellectual milieu from which the commentary drew. In its broad outlines, the passage is traditional enough: an allegorization of the gods as physical elements or human desires, and a brief explanation of the habit of ancient "philosophers" (including Virgil) of veiling secret learning under fictive stories. But comparison with contemporary and earlier statements of the same range of ideas shows three details in which the Peterhouse commentator is unusual. First, he is more specific than are other mythological allegorists about certain details of element theory. His argument for the necessity of intervening elements between fire and earth shows a command of element theory based on six properties and deriving from Plato's *Timaeus* – an approach gaining renewed currency in the twelfth century – rather than the analysis based on four properties popularized through Macrobius's *Commentary* and more generally used by literary commentators like "Bernard."[74] Second, and perhaps pointing toward an earlier intellectual setting, he uses literary terminology which was beginning to be old-fashioned by the time commentaries like those of "Bernard" and William of Conches began circulating. Specifically, he speaks of philosophical truth as covered by fiction's "veil" (*velamine*); he thus uses the term favored by Macrobius, while as we have seen commentators like William and "Bernard" were predominantly employing *integumentum* and *involucrum*.[75] And Peterhouse I's general idea of hidden truth also derives closely from Macrobius. Third, he is uncommonly explicit about the relationship of his allegorical gods to the Christian God.[76]

Given a text like this, dateable only on paleographical grounds, it is imprudent to talk of sources and influences when comparing it to other twelfth-century allegories. In his general allegory of the gods and in his relation of them to the Christian God, Peterhouse I is in line with an ancient and continuing tradition of allegoresis. The commentator seems to be most closely influenced, however, not by writers contemporary with the manuscript like "Bernard" and William of Conches, but rather by much earlier mythographers like Servius and Macrobius. Yet both these writers were actively used in the first half of the twelfth century. Peterhouse I, then, fits well with general trends of twelfth-century mythographical allegory, although it appears also to reach back to far earlier sources for the details of its work. His references to element theory are considerably more sophisticated than those to be found in the other allegorizers, and some details of his language may justify us in associating him with new trends in natural philosophy just before mid-century.

We cannot be sure where this text was copied; many simple mid-century text hands are virtually indistinguishable between England and northern France. Moreover, as noted above, a somewhat fuller version of Peterhouse I circulated on the Continent at about the same time. Nonetheless, the *Aeneid* in P158 was being annotated by a distinctively English hand by the middle of the thirteenth century, and some of these notes occur in two other English manuscripts, so we can be comfortably certain that these ideas were circulating in England in the twelfth century and after. In fact, the "Third Vatican Mythographer," Albericus of London, who flourished around 1160, shows a number of very similar ideas, and some parallel terminology. Their mutual knowledge of element theory is particularly striking.[77] Here again the vagueness of dating makes questions of source unanswerable; the two texts must simply be treated as arresting analogues, both demonstrating the presence of closely related ideas in England around and soon after mid-century. As we will see, Albericus is related in turn to "Bernard's" commentary on the *Aeneid*, which also proves to have intriguing English connections.

The allegorizing material in Peterhouse I does not end with the opening fragment on fol. 42va. Rather, a group of marginal notes shows continuing interest in allegorical approaches to certain moments in the epic, though no such systematic reading as we have seen in Fulgentius and will see again in "Bernard." These are infrequent, and they do not alter the essentially "pedagogical" emphasis of the other marginalia, but they deserve to be noted in detail. In the margin at 1.81, where Aeolus is creating the storm that will shipwreck Aeneas, there is a long note not found in Servius:

This poet carefully observes the particular qualities of things. For first he represents Aeneas as a youth, and timid, not yet troubled by adversities, and as if oppressed by an ecstasy, but nevertheless contemplating virtue in some way. He thereafter displays such perfection of soul that Virgil shows him having descended to hell. For he says Aeneas was at first timid, then somewhat comforted. This is natural for the virtuous man, for at first he is terrified of unexpected adversities, then strengthened by virtue he withstands them.[78]

This somewhat confused note clearly reflects the allegorization of the *Aeneid* as the ages of man and stages of virtue. It is not precisely parallel to "Bernard," however, who interprets the storm as shipwreck and birth, not (as apparently here) as boyhood or youth. The allegory is very insightful, nevertheless. Aeneas's chill and weakness, and his inactivity in the face of the storm, are most interestingly allegorized as a youthful spirit "oppressed by an ecstasy." This is only a very brief glimpse, however, and is not pursued elsewhere in the notes.

The notes also introduce occasional scientific allegorizations of the gods, similar to if simpler than those we saw above. Some of these are very ancient, and only made unusually explicit here. At 1.15 (where Juno is mentioned in association with Carthage) the gods are allegorized as the elements: "The gods were said to preside over each of the elements: Jupiter over fire, Juno over air, Neptune over water, Pluto over earth."[79] This material is indeed available in Servius, but it is never stated so synoptically there. Again at 1.6, where it is said that Aeneas "carried the gods into Latium," the gods are allegorized as "the good laws."[80]

Two other non-Servian allegorical entries seem to be independent both of Servius and of the allegories of Fulgentius and "Bernard." When Aeneas emerges from his surrounding cloud in Carthage, an independent explanation is offered:

Because the author, writing poetically, says that Aeneas was encompassed by a cloud. This signifies the cares which he had in his soul, which cares vanished when his companions were received and Dido's friendship was obtained.[81]

Much later, the golden bough is allegorized.

This bough signifies the virtues by which men are liberated from the hell of this life, and are borne to heaven. Or, by the bough are understood the riches which cast many men down to hell. It is said to lie hidden in forests, because truly in the confusion of this life and the very great extent of sin, virtue and integrity lie hidden.[82]

It seems probable that marginal commentaries like this one, grounded in the school tradition but hesitantly exploring allegorical possibilities, lie behind the fuller allegories of the twelfth century. Indeed, nothing in Peterhouse I departs from allegorical possibilities implicit in Servius himself, as we saw, although Peterhouse I greatly extends some of these implications. He is closest to Servius in choosing not to press these scattered allegorizations toward a systematic integumental reading of the epic. It is always possible, of course, that the few notes cited above merely reflect established traditions, which intrude here only in passing. Indeed, there is more allegorizing and scientific material in Vat. lat. 1574 and BL Add. 32319A, often mentioned in the notes above, than is to be found here. Peterhouse I seems to be using some of this material but still preserving the fundamentally Servian, pedagogical emphasis which makes up the bulk of his notes. As we will see now, the *Aeneid* is bracketed at the other end of P158 by a far more systematic allegorical fragment, based on a reading of the *Aeneid* in terms of the ages of man and spiritual development.

FABULIZING VIRGIL: INTEGUMENTAL READING AND THE POWER OF
THE EXEGETE

At the end of the *Aeneid* in P158, the epic is again bracketed by three
more leaves of interpretive material, which proves to be a systematic
(though, in this copy, fragmentary) allegorical interpretation of Book
Six. The commentary includes a brief summary and allegorization of
earlier books, but concentrates on Aeneas's descent to the Underworld
as the culmination in a fable of spiritual development through study of
the *artes* and rediscovery of virtues initially lost and forgotten in the
fallen world. This reading of the *Aeneid* privileges its allegorical subtext,
and approaches the poem through a profoundly Boethian optic, one
which already had been progressively associated with the *Aeneid* in a
sequence of influential *Consolation* commentaries of the twelfth century
and earlier.

This second commentary at the close of P158 ("Peterhouse II") has
dense and extensive connections, both procedural and verbal, with the
much longer commentary attributed to "Bernard Silvestris."[83] In my
earlier discussion of Peterhouse II, I proposed that it preserved an early
version of the commentary of "Bernard Silvestris," transmitted
through the doubly confusing filters of aural reception (presumably
swift and highly abbreviated notes taken from a classroom lecture) and
poor copyists.[84] Based on this identification of Peterhouse II as a
redaction of "Bernard" copied in England about a generation earlier
than any manuscript then known, I went on to suggest the possibility
that the commentary – whose association with Bernard Silvestris rests
on a single, much later manuscript – might have been written in
England. Such a possibility is further supported by a complex network
of parallels between the texts and diagrams in the two "Bernard"
commentaries (on Virgil and Martianus Capella), and those in two
other works known to have an exclusively English manuscript tradition.

Recently, however, Julian W. Jones has reviewed the evidence and
argued that Peterhouse II does not represent an early redaction of
"Bernard's" Virgil commentary, but rather – and more excitingly –
that it may be an indirect witness of the lost Virgil commentary by
"Bernard's" single most influential source, William of Conches.[85] Jones
identifies a series of details in Peterhouse II which suggest to him
"significant differences" with "Bernard," and others which seem
"exotic or eccentric" compared to "Bernard's" usual religious and
exegetic conservatism.[86] He also finds the organization of Peterhouse II

sufficiently unusual to distinguish it from "Bernard."[87] Jones proposes William as an author whose strong philosophical bent could account for some of the anomalies he finds; further, if William is the "author" (a problematic term in commentaries like these, where virtually each manuscript can represent a separate version), this would account for a group of notes in Peterhouse II that are much closer to notes in William's *Timaeus* commentary than to anything in the later redactions of "Bernard."[88]

Jones's argument does indeed press further several points of distinction between Peterhouse II and "Bernard" which I had insufficiently articulated in my earlier article.[89] But his work convinces me, above all, that we can neither quite make our claims, given the transmission and textual state of Peterhouse II. If Peterhouse II was, as I argue, subjected to the double opportunities for alteration and corruption inherent in (1) rapidly written class notes, followed by (2) flawed scribal transcription, then it becomes rather difficult for either Jones or myself to nail down our identifications definitively.[90] There have been too many occasions for omission and for the introduction of odd terms.[91] Both Jones and I find ourselves making special pleas based on the complex transmission of Peterhouse II: I to explain the often imprecise parallels, and certain real divergences, between Peterhouse II and "Bernard"; and Jones to explain "added comments from other sources" which would not sit well with authorship by William.[92]

Jones sees what survives this ordeal of ear and pen as an indirect version of William, reported with occasional inept additions by "some anonymous figure,"[93] and a text that later had enormous impact on "Bernard"; I continue to see it as a rough early redaction by "Bernard," with its sources – William chief among them – still cobbled together in a very exposed fashion, and a number of alternate interpretations not yet resolved or discarded. Indeed, were it not that William of Conches is so towering a figure in the intellectual life and heritage of the twelfth century, the distinction between these two theories might be seen as not greatly consequential; but a new commentary by William – if Peterhouse II finally proves to be that – does matter. Until and unless new witnesses emerge, though, I fear we must both resign ourselves to Peterhouse II being an intriguing *tertium quid*, though we can disagree as to whether it is the work of a *tertius quis*.

For the purposes of this study, with its focus on the presence and influence of competing traditions of Virgilian commentary in medieval

England, however, it is the circulation of this kind of allegorical approach in Britain, and not its origin there, that most matters. In fact, at the beginning of his article, Jones shows that the allegory of the *Aeneid* summarized in John of Salisbury's *Policraticus* represents yet another permutation of the allegorical approach based on the ages of man – still another version of Virgilian allegoresis circulating in England.[94] In what follows, then, I will not restate my arguments for possible English origin, but rather explore the exegetical implications of the kind of approach that fundamentally characterizes both "Bernard" and Peterhouse II.[95] Since "Bernard" survives in much fuller form, I will focus on his commentary, but I will discuss parallels and independent material from Peterhouse II.[96]

As his last challenge before the descent to the Underworld and its accompanying visions of history and cosmos, Aeneas is sent by the Sibyl to find a bough, golden in its leaves and slender stalk, that lies hidden in a shady tree: "latet arbore opaca / aureus et foliis et lento uimine ramus ... " (6.136–37). The extraordinary image of the golden bough, as we have already seen, held the attention of Servius, who associated it with the Pythagorean *bivium* and interpreted it as a figure of choices between virtue and vice that begin to be made at youth. I will argue that this bough, encountered at the moment where the epic itself divides from Aeneas's wanderings to his conquest of Latium, is the fundamental image around which a more systematic fable of private spiritual development and moral choice began to be inserted into allegorical readings of the *Aeneid*.[97]

Patristic writers like Lactantius Placidus recalled Virgil and the golden bough in their own thinking about the *bivium*, as we have also seen; and they further associated study of the *artes* with the progress of the soul toward virtue. This double association – of events in Aeneas's career with steps in private moral evolution, and the aid of the *artes* in that evolution – virtually encapsulates the exegetical program, however enormously elaborated, that we have already reviewed in the commentary of Fulgentius, and that we will now see in "Bernard" and Peterhouse II.[98] I will suggest in what follows, moreover, that the golden bough is not merely an early focus from which much of the substance in these two commentaries derives, but that its form (once the letter Y of the Pythagorean *bivium* is imposed on it) is virtually an emblem of their structure and exegetical methodology.

Interpretation of the golden bough undergoes considerable development between the patristic period and the twelfth century; it is worthwhile to pause over some of these interpretations, since they help establish other aspects of the exegetical milieu from which "Bernard" draws. Fulgentius, for instance, already explicitly interprets the bough as "the study of philosophy and letters."[99] It is only with this tool that Aeneas can proceed to study the *secreta scientiae*.[100]

The increased interest this image was raising, as we approach the time of Peterhouse II and "Bernard," can be seen in the very long and surprisingly varied entries it received in various manuscripts of "Anselm of Laon."[101] "Anselm" begins with a close paraphrase of the material in Servius, including its connection with the flight of Orestes to the temple of Proserpine; and a second, allegorical interpretation (also from Servius) of the gold in the bough as the wealth that easily kills mortals. "Anselm" then goes on to the Pythagorean interpretation of the bough as the letter Y, and the beginning of moral choices at youth. But his language here approaches the *bivium* more directly as an allegorical image than does Servius; while Servius explains the connection as a comparison, "Anselm" uses terms implying a more direct symbolic equation, like *designatur* or *intelligitur*.[102] Further, "Anselm" extends Servius's comparison by allegorizing particular parts of the branch. The lower part of the branch, before it divides, thus "designates" boyhood. And the two paths – of sin and virtue – are initially wide then narrow and painful, or *vice versa*.[103] Notes in other manuscripts of "Anselm" articulate the implications of following the right branch for the soul's return from the lower realms.[104] Finally, "Anselm" introduces yet a fourth interpretation, saying that the bough has many leaves signifying the many branches of lust.

Peterhouse I, as seen above, also elaborates on Servius's allegorization, calling the bough the "virtues by which men are liberated from the hell of this life, and are borne to heaven."[105] Between them, then, these interpretations include the ideas of progressive ages and the achievement of moral choice, but further graft that idea of appropriate moral choice with a Neoplatonic notion of the soul's return to heaven from a fallen temporal life, as in Peterhouse I. The explicit association of the golden bough and the progress of the soul with study (seen in Fulgentius and patristic authors) is again implicit in the interpretation offered by Peterhouse II:

He finds that golden bough which is dissimilar to the tree on which it grows and which it illuminates. Through the tree, man is understood, because man, as Pythagoras says, is a tree turned upside down (*arbor inuersa*), whom wisdom, unlike himself, illuminates. That branch he received from a tree, that is, from another man, his teacher.[106]

This interpretation, whose innovation is well discussed by Jones, makes explicit the role not just of study, but of the teaching master, in the correct development of the soul. Whether the formulation is "Bernard's" own or that of William of Conches, we will see that this emphasis is certainly influential for the general approach of "Bernard's" fuller commentary.

"Bernard's" own comment on this passage is nearly as long as those in "Anselm." But he begins here, intriguingly, with an explanation of the bough so generalized as to make it almost infinitely applicable: "Allegorically, anything which is composed of diverse parts (*quodlibet quod in diuersa scinditur*) (such as the virtues, the vices, and knowledge) is called a branch."[107] He then proposes just such a division of the parts of philosophy, and appends one of the diagrams in which he delights, adding "It is golden because we interpret gold to be wisdom ... ."[108] There follows a comparison of mankind and the tree which would seem to combine the notion of choice between virtue and vice, with a hint of Peterhouse II's comparison of the tree and man's body: "Pythagoras called humanity a tree which is divided into two branches, that is, into virtue and into vice. For although they are joined together in the beginning, some people divide themselves to the left and some to the right, some in vice and some in virtue."[109]

By the twelfth century, thus, the golden bough as *bivium* had attracted to itself a range of interpretations linking it to ages in human life, stages of spiritual growth, right (or wrong) moral choices, and the soul's escape from the fallen world with the aid of learning, particularly through the aid of a master. Together, this range of interpretations virtually summarizes "Bernard's" integumental reading of the *Aeneid*. I suggest that the figure of the *bivium* is a model for the way "Bernard" structures his commentary. By constructing a sequence of *bivia*, "Bernard" at once acknowledges but turns from other paths of interpretation and implicitly, I think, asserts his superiority over them. One might go so far as to suggest, even, that the commentary is structured so as to imitate the series of choices and divided paths which "Bernard" sees as the fundamental integumental story of the *Aeneid*. Certainly, I will argue, he wishes for his readers to perceive themselves after the model of the allegorized Aeneas.

"Bernard" prepares his students for this system of divides in the *accessus*, which is itself a carefully presented double argument for Virgil's intentions and *modus agendi*. The very first words of the commentary introduce doubling and division: "Gemine doctrine observantiam perpendimus in sua Eneide Maronem habuisse" ("We hold that in the *Aeneid* Virgil has 'the observance of twofold teaching,'" quoting Macrobius), including both philosophical truth and poetic fiction.[110] He then proposes, in effect, a double introduction, covering three standard topics of the "modern *accessus*" from these two perspectives:

Si quis ergo Eneida legere studeat, ita ut eius voluminis lex deposcit, hec in primis oportet demonstrare, unde agat et qualiter et cur, et geminam observationem in his demonstrandis non relinquere. [Therefore, anyone who wishes to read the *Aeneid* as the nature of this work demands must first of all indicate the intention, the mode, and the objective of the work and then not fail to observe the double point of view of philosophy and poetic fiction in discussing these matters.][111]

This is to observe the "law" of the book (*voluminis lex*). The term suggests an inner working in the poem, a doubleness inherent and inborn, more the quality of the text's own logic than that of an intentional author; while Virgil's "intention" is mentioned (once) in the *accessus*, it drops out in the real work of the commentary. Even here, the term does not generate any particular focus on Virgil, but is rather part of "Bernard's" list of standard topics.

"Bernard" begins by going through these topics from the perspective of Virgil as poet and fiction maker. Virgil's intention (*intentio*, corresponding to *unde*) is to tell the story of Aeneas and the Trojans, by which means he may obtain the favor of Augustus. His mode of procedure (*modus agendi*, corresponding to *qualiter*) is to imitate Homer, but also to introduce pleasing fictions about Aeneas. The third topic, why Virgil writes (*cur agat*, or *causa*) is itself subdivided into pleasure (*delectatio*) which the reader derives from his style, and usefulness (*utilitas*). This in turn proves to be twofold: approached as a fictive poet, Virgil teaches the reader both skill in writing (an *utilitas* implicit everywhere in the pedagogical tradition), and examples of correct behavior (*recte agendi prudentia*) such as Aeneas's patience or piety.[112] In Chapter Four, we will see the idea of proper behavior and moral example, treated here very much in passing, raised to a central concern by a late fourteenth-century commentator. In covering the *Aeneid* as

poetic fiction in this first part of his *accessus*, then, "Bernard" acknowledges alternate approaches to the poem; but he then puts them aside,
and pursues what he sees as the higher path – as it were, the right
turn in the *bivium* – of philosophical truth.

Between the second and the third topic I have just mentioned,
"Bernard" pauses over another standard topic of the "modern"
accessus, the *ordo libri*, which he says is also double in the *Aeneid*. One is
historical, and is told out of order, starting first with the Trojans and
Dido, and then circling back to the fall of Troy; this is called *ordo
artificialis*. But stories can also be told in *ordo naturalis*, following the
actual sequence of time and events. Bernard will return to this
distinction when he proposes a second approach to Virgil in terms of
philosophical truth, through what is in effect a second *accessus*:

> Nunc vero hec eadem circa philosophicam veritatem videamus. Scribit ergo
> in quantum est philosophus humane vite naturam. Modus agendi talis est: in
> integumento describit quid agat vel quid paciatur humanus spiritus in
> humano corpore temporaliter positus. Atque in hoc describendo naturali
> utitur ordine ... [Let us now consider these same topics with regard to
> philosophical truth. Insofar as he is a philosopher, Virgil writes about the
> nature of human life (*intentio*). His procedure (*modus agendi*) is this: he describes
> in an integument what the human spirit does and endures placed temporally
> in the human body. Virgil uses natural order when writing about this ...][113]

The *utilitas* gained from reading Virgil as a philosopher is self-
knowledge. Such an approach recasts the *Aeneid* as a journey of self-
discovery, told in natural order. But it must be interpreted as an
integument, a covering fable to be decoded by the *magister*.

This fable "Bernard" now proceeds to construct (or repeat from a
source very like Peterhouse II) out of the master text, by offering a
summary made up from selected details in the *Aeneid*, presented in the
order they occupy in the text. In effect "Bernard" takes a narrative that
could have happened (and in part, he believes, shorn of its flattering
fictions, did happen); he then reinscribes it in a way that could not have
happened. So "Bernard" creates an anti-historical fable from the
quasi-historical stuff of the *Aeneid*; thus it is not just the myths of the
gods that demand integumental exegesis (as, for instance, in Peterhouse
I), but the entire reordered narrative.[114] Such a summary generates, in
effect, a doubled narrative branching away from the poeticized history
of the literal level: a fabulous narrative that can only make sense with
the help of integumental exegesis, and thus absolutely requires the aid

of the *magister*, who becomes as powerful and necessary as the prior *auctor*; such a text must be bracketed by commentary, as it is in P158.

In Peterhouse II most of this Virgilian fable is covered at once (notes 17–27), followed by summary interpretation; while in "Bernard" the summaries (textually quite close to Peterhouse II) are distributed at the beginning of the commentary on Books Two through Five. Indeed, most of the time in these first five books, rather than quoting the text of Virgil for integumental interpretation, "Bernard" quotes bits of his own summary fable as lemmata.[115] The Virgilian fable produced by "Bernard," moreover, includes a certain amount of minor alteration to suit Virgil to the purposes of the integumental narrative. For instance, in order to interpret Aeneas as wandering between his corporeal and divine nature, "Bernard" must report that Aeneas (and not, as in Virgil, Anchises) misinterprets the oracular command to "seek your ancient mother."[116] Later, to interpret the funeral games in Sicily as the four virtues, "Bernard" has to reduce the number of contests from Virgil's five, lumping together the foot race and horse race.[117]

At the same time, the *Aeneid* is in itself already dense with episodes and imagery that invite integumental reading: exile, journey, homes lost and regained, deprivation and reward, opaque prophecies and obscure symbols such as the golden bough. By allegorizing these features of the *Aeneid* as reordered in his fabulous narrative, "Bernard" inserts the epic into the tradition that Winthrop Wetherbee elegantly calls "intellectual pilgrimage, the experience of the spirit in its attempts to rise above its earthly situation through an understanding of *naturalia* and attain a vision of truth."[118] It is within this fundamental model of pilgrimage that we should understand "Bernard's" frequent and often lengthy digressions on scientific aspects of the cosmos.

What emerges as "Bernard" progressively articulates and uncovers his Virgilian fable, however, is yet another sequence of ramifications, an attention divided between the microcosmic progress of the individual soul through the ages of man, and an explication of the scientific macrocosm through which that symbolic everyman moves.[119] The two are of course connected: the hero's spiritual progress is achieved through study of the *artes*, and "Bernard's" frequent learned and scientific digressions transmit some of that very learning to the reader. He pursues this dual focus by interpreting his reformed narrative in terms of the ages, and by inserting creative and sometimes fanciful exploitations of more local etymology. And the two trains of attention join together again in the person of the very reader who would be absorbing the commentary: the twelfth-century student trying to progress in imitation of the allegorized Aeneas, and approaching the crucial precondition of such progress, the *artes*, through studying one of the central *auctores* with the help of his master.

The integumental narrative of the ages does not depart radically from Fulgentius. So the shipwreck of Book One is birth; the tale of the fall of Troy in Book Two, historically earlier, is the age of boyhood when speech is gained. Book Three describes the nature of adolescence. Troy is the human body; its burning (actually from Book Two) symbolizes the natural fervor of the first age. Aeneas wanders, but is finally advised by Apollo to "seek his ancient mother." There are two ancient mothers, though, which are the two constituent parts of Aeneas himself. One is Crete, his corporeal nature, and the other Italy, his divine nature. Aeneas errs (in a non-Virgilian detail, as we saw above) by seeking his wrong, worldly self; there he cannot rule. But the family gods he carries with him (wisdom and virtue) advise him to seek his better self: Italy.[120] Aeneas is prevented from doing so in Book Four, "the nature of youth." Having arrived at adolescence, Aeneas resides in Carthage, the city of this world (*civitas mundi*), where Dido (*libido*) reigns. Here he feeds on the goods of the world. For "Bernard," then, the implicit story of the *Aeneid* is not just that of the ages of man. Far more, it is the soul's journey through the city of this world to the city, never quite explicitly stated, of God. Finally Mercury (eloquence) orders him to leave Carthage. Dido then, like spent passion, turns to ash.[121]

The funeral games of Book Five ("the nature of manhood") symbolize the cardinal virtues, again by means of an adaptation practiced in the fable. In a vision at the end of the book, Aeneas is told by his dead father to seek him in the underworld. Virgil's underworld is interpreted as the human body and the world it enters at birth. Although the creator (Anchises, the father) lies above and cannot be known through mere thought, he can be known by properly comparing the creation below to things above. "For although he is not in his creatures, the father (that is the Creator) is nonetheless known by knowing his creatures."[122]

But the fabulous tale, the "natural" narrative of fallen birth and the acquisition of philosophical maturity, itself divides into a double plot soon after the incidence of the central image of the *bivium*, the golden bough. For, as Schreiber and Maresca point out in the fine introduction to their translation, there is a double spiritual biography here.[123] The first five books are allegorized as early life and its vicissitudes, by which the soul achieves a willingness to undertake serious study and approach the world once again from a philosophical perspective – to see the creator in the creation. But this is then followed, in the descent to the underworld of Book 6, by a second birth and upward progression undertaken in the age of maturity, this time aided by philosophical perspective and the spiritual guidance of the Sibyl. Thus at the entryway to the underworld, the jaws of Orcus are interpreted simply as "birth."[124]

The allegory of Book Six is very detailed indeed, interpreting many words and incidents as parts of the necessary education of a rational spirit, the study of *trivium* and *quadrivium*. The golden bough is philosophy, the wood it inhabits is sin, the two doves guiding Aeneas to it are reason and virtue.[125] Beyond the rivers of hell, Aeneas reaches the contemplative life (*vitam quietam*), cleansed of grief and sadness. There the spirit, now free, can review in contemplation the images of its past life, and acknowledge its calamities.[126] Thus the descent to hell is virtually a second birth, but a birth by a soul now resistant to worldly temptation, and able instead to use worldly phenomena as a *via ad patrem*.[127] The commentary, however, breaks off soon after this, before Aeneas's meeting with the father, Anchises, and his prophecy of the future in the third city, Rome.

Yet even this much-divided procedure, into two modes of writing (poetic and philosophical), two plots (historical and integumental), and the fabulous plot divided into a double biography, finds itself further and multiply divided. Indeed, as the commentary proceeds into Book Six it becomes so ramified, repeating itself around so many points, that it virtually comes to a standstill. I want to suggest that this is not merely the result of a commentator moving from narrative summary to a reading *ad litteram*, but also a slowing – and finally a halt – in the face of "Bernard's" own sense of the limits of spiritual progress possible through the *artes*.[128]

Some of the commentary's tendency to ramification is expressed in its many scientific and learned digressions by which the very substance of the *artes* is inserted into the journey through the Underworld.[129] More frequent in Book Six is a tendency to replicate large parts of the entire allegorical ur-plot in briefer integuments so that, implicitly, the same plot of spiritual education is proceeding at several stages simultaneously. To take a prominent instance, *studium* – the eagerness to learn that is the precondition for Aeneas's spiritual advancement in the book – is figured at various points by Achates, the frenzy (*rabie*) which overcomes the Sibyl, Aglaia, Aeneas's footsteps toward the golden bough, one of Aeneas's eyes following the doves (the other eye is wit), Hercules burning the Hydra, and Tityus whose rape of Latona represents the eagerness of study.[130] This is an extreme instance of that *multivocatio* which "Bernard" carefully pauses to explain in both his commentaries.[131] But it is also symptomatic of the problem "Bernard" has moving past the stuff of the *artes* and into the higher wisdom for which Aeneas is ever more ready. Even if it were theoretically possible to extract that higher theological or philosophical wisdom from secular *auctores* (and surely a follower of William of Conches might think it possible), this teacher also faces the problem of his own audience – students still of the *trivium*, though clearly at a higher level of sophistication than those addressed in a "pedagogical" commentary like that in AS82.

In this protracted liminal moment, with Aeneas and figures around him repeatedly at the threshold of true wisdom, yet another implicit plot, or setting, begins to emerge: the narrative of the very schoolroom in which the reading took place. We will recall the unusual note in Peterhouse II where the golden bough was interpreted as the wisdom a student takes from his teacher; this is particularly fascinating, since it not only casts the teacher as a figure of great power, but seems specifically to cast the student – who receives the bough – as an integumental Aeneas. The same idea is operative, though never so explicit, when "Bernard" begins to allegorize the golden bough in its tree and Virgil's comparison of the bough to mistletoe in winter (6.204–11):

Viscum: as if Virgil had said "*gummi*," "gum," for just as that liquid gum goes from the interior to the exterior of the tree, so wisdom, flashing from the mind of man, also comes to the exterior either through instruction or action ... For just as the exterior moisture moves from the earth by means of roots and the innermost pith, so too wisdom from a teacher flashes through the mind or speech or deed of a pupil.[132]

Later, Aeneas's first entrance into the Underworld is elaborately compared to the combination of wisdom and eloquence that is a necessary preparation for teaching.[133] This extends the figuring of Aeneas as student, to Aeneas as potential *magister*.

But this insertion of the educational process into the integumental narrative is not just a pedagogue's myopia. Far more important, it also structures into these particular readers a sense of emulation; if Aeneas is like a schoolboy, they too read like Aeneas, they strive toward his wisdom, and their project takes on heroic implications. If Aeneas is inserted into the twelfth century in such a reading, just as surely his readers are inserted into his allegorized trials. The idea of reader as a spiritual pilgrim guided by elements of the authoritative text, of course, is basic to the roles of Dante and Virgil in the *Divina Commedia*. And we will see the closely related idea of the reader as an Aeneas used, not without parody, by Chaucer in the *House of Fame*.

If the commentary of "Bernard" does take Aeneas as far as the contemplative life and the incipient capacity for true wisdom, it nonetheless breaks off, in every one of the growing number of its manuscript witnesses, well short of the visionary and cosmological core of the *Aeneid* – the speeches of Anchises on the rebirth of souls and the inward spirit (*spiritus intus*) of the world (6.703–51). The commentary on Martianus similarly stops short of the most challenging passages in the *Marriage of Philology and Mercury*: the robing of Jupiter and Juno and the council of the gods.[134] Both commentaries thus fall silent just where they might be called upon to articulate that spiritual wisdom toward which they have, ever more slowly, been moving. The *artes* offer a road to spiritual wisdom, but leave Aeneas (and the exegete/reader who emulates him) always and repeatedly at the doorstep to such wisdom.

It is of course perfectly possible that the fragmentary state of both commentaries is purely an accident of transmission. But is it not also possible that it is no accident, that "Bernard" (whose intellectual conservatism has been noted) quailed in the face of his texts' highest and potentially heterodox challenges? Or, I would further suggest, did "Bernard" desist because his integumental narrative (having taken a path splitting ever further from the literal narrative whence it first branched) had reached its logical conclusion before – to pursue the simile – the other, literal path ended? "Bernard" felt that while the arts of the schoolroom might bring a student to readiness for higher spiritual education, they could not perform that education itself. That project is left to the yet higher study of theology.

So having repeatedly asserted and demonstrated the glories of the *artes*, I suggest, the commentary also progressively adapts itself to their limitations. It most radically rewrites the *Aeneid* by stopping its Virgilian fable at just that point where the integumental plot could proceed no further, but only (as we have seen) repeat itself in ever subtler variations. This sense of the limits of the *artes* and their *auctores* is already adumbrated early in Book Six when Aeneas approaches the grove of Trivia and the temple of Apollo, decorated by Daedalus:

Dedalus: Virgil says that Aeneas approaches the grove of Trivia (*Trivie*), that is, the study of eloquence, and he shows the nature of it. This is done by instruction in the authors. Indeed, the poets introduce one to philosophy ... Those who enter Apollo's temple see the pictures of history and fable on the outside. The temple of Apollo is the philosophic arts ...[135]

But it is exactly from his involvement with these poetic illustrations, significantly outside the temple, that Aeneas is called peremptorily by the Sibyl, the priestess who "reveals the principles of both philosophy and eloquence."[136]

Aeneas, and the reader whose study of the *artes* emulates him, is left perpetually and repeatedly on a threshold of higher wisdom, always approaching but never finally encountering Anchises, "the father of all who presides over all."[137] As the sight of Anchises approaches (6.679), the commentary reaches the logical close of its progression and its own internal fable (6.636). From this perspective, the commentary is logically complete but functions as a self-limiting artifact that brings its student along to the point where the very stuff he is studying needs (like the decorations of Daedalus's temple) to be abandoned. In chapter 6, I will argue that this same integumental logic helps explain much of the Virgilian echoes in the *House of Fame*, and perhaps even its own tantalizingly fragmentary state.

"BERNARD" AND BOETHIAN READING OF THE *AENEID*

Let us return once again to Aeneas's search for the golden bough and its allegorization by "Bernard." Before the twin doves arrive to lead him toward the hidden tree near the mouth of Avernus, Aeneas wanders in the ancient forest, uncertain how to proceed. The wood in which he finds himself is twice explained by "Bernard" as the goods of the world:

Itur in silvam (6.179): Aeneas "enters the woods" – he advances with the steps of contemplation (namely by wit and study) in the multitude of temporal goods (*temporalium bonorum*), which are shady and trackless.[138]

This echoes an earlier interpretation of the same groves in Aeneas's prayer to the Sibyl:

Virgil calls temporal goods groves (*lucos*) since they have three qualities similar to those of a grove. Just as groves are dark because of the lack of sun, so too temporal goods are dark because of the lack of reason. And just as woods are impassable places because of the multitude and variety of paths, so too are temporal goods impassable because of the various paths which seem to lead to the highest good (*summum bonum*) but which do not. And *Avernus* means "woods without spring" (*nemus sine vere*), as if without delight; and thus the groves lack true delight.[139]

This exegesis in terms of the *bona temporalia*, and their capacity to make the wanderer confuse them with the true, highest good (the *summum bonum*), inserts this moment in Aeneas's journey into yet another implicit narrative, the particular kind of symbolic pilgrimage explored by Boethius in the *Consolation of Philosophy*. In this pilgrimage, the wanderer has forgotten his true home and the real good that resides there; it is Lady Philosophy who begins to guide him back. I left this aspect of the pilgrimage largely aside in my discussion above, but I now want to argue for its centrality to the allegorization of the *Aeneid* offered by "Bernard" and Peterhouse II. First, however, I want to recall the use of Boethius which we also witnessed in AS82, and the intermingling of *Aeneid* and *Consolation* as early as the latter text's very composition, and certainly in the commentary tradition which came to surround them both.

For an early layer of marginalia in All Souls 82, we will remember, also includes an intriguing note at *Aeneid* 6, lines 724 and following, the great cosmological passage spoken to Aeneas by Anchises, which the two commentaries discussed above do not cover. The long marginal note at that point in AS82 is not from any commentary on the *Aeneid*. Rather, we saw, the annotator explains this moment in Virgil's epic by reference to Boethius's equally famous cosmological verses in the *Consolation of Philosophy*, Book Three, metrum 9, "O qui perpetua mundi …" After quoting Boethius's opening lines, the annotator simply inserts in the margin a section from a twelfth-century *Consolation*-commentary.

The full significance of this use of Boethius to explicate a passage of the *Aeneid*, and especially of Book Six with its themes of Platonic spiritual education and Pythagorean cosmology, begins to emerge in the context of the allegorical tradition that has just been discussed. All Souls 82 offers only one passing instance of a widespread association throughout the Middle Ages between the cosmologies and ethics of Boethius and *Aeneid* Six. Through the nexus of commentaries the two texts virtually interpenetrate. In certain commentaries, especially those we associate loosely with the school of Chartres, there arises an allegorical monomyth, a single structure of explication deemed adequate to both texts; basic approaches, and indeed whole passages, from this allegorical monomyth can be lifted from commentary on one text and inserted, in the case above *verbatim*, into commentary on another.

In this exegetical project, Boethius's *Consolation* appears to be the dominant text. This association can move in the reverse direction as well, though: as early as the ninth century, Bovo of Corvey cites Virgil in his commentary on *Consolation* III, metrum 9, as does William of Conches in the twelfth century. But these instances are merely part of that broader tendency to compare the two entire works, explaining one through the other. The two primary texts thus become intertextually linked through the agency of commentary. It is arguable, moreover, that this tradition responds to echoes and parallels already present in Boethius's own text.

It has long been recognized that, as we might expect, Boethius was steeped in the language of Virgil.[140] Extensive quotations and echoes of Virgil have been identified in the *Consolation of Philosophy* by Courcelle, Bieler, Gruber, and others.[141] Such references to the great Latin epic seem to have been perceived by these scholars, however, merely as rhetorical or illustrative – fine phrases used in a new context, and appropriately sententious quotations. To a considerable extent, this is a true perception of Boethius's Virgilian echoes. To a man like Boethius, possessed of a superb knowledge of classical Latin literature, useful tags and images from Virgil would be automatically at hand; no special significance need be attributed to their use.

To my knowledge, however, it has not been suggested that Boethius's use of Virgilian echoes and parallels follows any consistent or significant pattern.[142] Yet I think just such a pattern can be shown to exist – a loose but persistent series of linkages and echoes, particularly in the early books of the *Consolation*, between Boethius's progress and that of Virgil's hero Aeneas. A thorough study of this relationship would have to take into account the literary mediation of Augustine's *Confessions*, whose geographical structure carefully follows that of the *Aeneid*.[143] But my concern here is to establish the intertextual connection between Boethius and Virgil around which later commentary will form.

This use of the *Aeneid* by Boethius suggests not just a grammarian's knowledge, but an interpretive grasp of the text comparable to, though far subtler than, that of Fulgentius. Indeed, knowledge of the *Expositio Virgilianae Continentiae* would not have been impossible for Boethius, though it is unlikely: Boethius was writing the *Consolation* in AD 523–24, and we know of "Fulgentius" (whoever he was) only that he wrote the *Expositio* sometime in the late fourth or early fifth century. But Fulgentius merely, and somewhat crudely, systematizes ideas about Virgil's hidden wisdom that, as we have seen, were already widespread in more voluminous, less focussed commentaries like that of Servius and Macrobius's *Saturnalia*. A learned reader like Boethius (himself a writer of allegorical and cosmological verse) could have arrived at an allegorical interpretation of the *Aeneid* quite on his own. He was more than capable of making imaginative associations between Virgil's troubled hero, striving for stability among forces far beyond his control, and Philosophy's student, desperately seeking sanity in the wreckage of his past and striving to reach that new, true home which is soon promised him.

The *Consolation* begins, then, with a clear echo of the "spurious" opening lines of the *Aeneid*. Boethius starts:

> Carmina qui quondam studio florente peregi
> Flebilis heu maestos cogor inire modos.
>
> (I, met. 1.1–2)
>
> [Verses I once made glowing with content;
> Tearful, alas, sad songs I must begin.]

This invokes Virgil's autobiographical lines, now discredited but available to early readers in the *Vita Donatiana* and in Servius:

> Ille ego, qui quondam gracili modulatus auena
> carmen, et egressus siluis uicina coegi
> ut quamuis auido parerent arua colono,
> gratum opus agricolis, at nunc horrentia Martis.[144]
>
> [I am that poet who in times past made the light melody of pastoral poetry. In my next poem I left the woods for the adjacent farmlands, teaching them to obey even the most exacting tillers of the soil; and the farmers liked my work. But now I turn to the terrible strife of Mars.][145]

The reader is alerted thereby not only to possible later echoes of the *Aeneid*, but is further reminded of parallels between the disenfranchised Boethius and the exiled poet-pastor of the *Eclogues*.

Our attention shifts quickly, however, from parallels between Boethius and Virgil to parallels with Virgil's hero Aeneas: "Et veris elegi fletibus ora rigant" ("And with unfeigned tears these elegies drench my face," I, met. 1.4). This echoes Aeneas, as he tried in the

Underworld to embrace his father's shade: "sic memorans largo fletu simul ora rigabat" ("His face / was wet with weeping as he spoke," *Aen.* 6.699). In each case the protagonist is attempting tearfully to cling to a lost past, either by sentimental mourning or by physical embrace.[146] This should not imply, though, a straightforward parallel with the *Aeneid*. For it must be remembered that Lady Philosophy is soon to cast out as "theatrical tarts" those poetic Muses through whose agency Boethius is indulging in his grief.

But poetry can also express higher truths, and Lady Philosophy so uses poetry (and Virgilian echoes) elsewhere in the *Consolation*. The parallels with the *Aeneid* are reinforced in metrum 2, where Philosophy uses the first of her two major metaphors for Boethius's unenlightened lethargy: danger at sea, and enchainment.

> Ah! How steep the seas that drown him!
> His mind, all dulled, its own light fled,
> Moves into outer dark, while noxious care
> Swollen by earthbound winds
> Grows beyond measure.
>
> (I, met. 2.1–5)

The ship endangered by storm and its search for safe haven is of course a very widespread trope. But given the context established in metrum 1, the memory of Aeneas's disasters in *Aeneid* I and III seems clearly to be invoked here. The image of the wise man or hero caught in an uncontrollable storm at sea is invoked again and again, each time reminding us, I think, of the essential similarities between Aeneas and Boethius.[147]

Specific narrative parallels, however, also continue to appear. Tied to worldly goods and concerns, Boethius has strayed, says Philosophy, far from his original homeland, and must seek it again: "cuius oriundus sis patriae reminiscare" ("You must remember what your native country is," I, pr. 5.9–10). This vague and oracular statement reminds us of the Delphic command to Aeneas to seek out the lost motherland: "antiquam exquirite matrem" (3.96). The parallel is perhaps extended in prose 6, where Philosophy speaks further of Boethius's self-ignorance in terms of exile, wandering, despoliation, and purposelessness. These parallel the spiritual and physical miseries that plague the wandering hero in *Aeneid* 3 and 5. At the end of *Consolation* I, though, as at the end of *Aeneid* 5, a promise is made of ultimate fulfillment, of return to the lost and original homeland.[148]

Once past the initial dangers, and aware of Philosophy's promise, Boethius is led through ascending levels of vision and independence from worldliness in *Consolation* II through V. This parallels the process which early allegorizers like Fulgentius saw Aeneas undergo in *Aeneid* Six:

As I said before, having obtained the golden bough – that is, learning – he enters the lower world and investigates the secrets of knowledge. But on the threshold of the lower world he sees "grief, diseases, wars, strife, old age, and want." For only when all things are considered in the heart and mind of man, when the study of learning is carried through and the darkness penetrated by higher knowledge, only then can the close kinship of old age to death be recognized as the inflated and illusory deception of a dream ... So Aeneas goes down to the lower world and there, looking on as an eyewitness, he sees both the punishments for the evil, the rewards for the good, and the sad wanderings of those given over to passion.[149]

In *Consolation* II and III there are again prominent though less frequent reminiscences of the *Aeneid* and its hero, as Boethius is led to reject the goods of Fortune and Fame and to seek the true good. Philosophy reminds Boethius that Fortune has not quite turned against him, echoing Aeneas's prayer to Jupiter not to turn against the Trojans altogether.[150] Here, I think, Boethius is consciously portraying himself as a type of Aeneas.

Just as he is made to turn away from the gifts of fortune, Boethius is also instructed to relinquish the attractions of glory, or Fame. In Book Two, metrum 2, Philosophy describes the figure of Fame in language that again brings to mind the *Aeneid* and its description of Fama.[151] Having passed beyond worldly goods, Boethius must still rediscover his lost, true self and his lost, true homeland: the true good, "the appearance of true blessedness" (III, pr. 1.25–26). Fulgentius, as I have noted, sees Aeneas's descent to the underworld as a process of philosophic education. The arrival at Elysium is thus interpreted as the life of peace ("feriatam vitam"), and Anchises there symbolizes, etymologically, "living in one's own land. There is one God, the Father, King of all, dwelling alone on high, who yet is revealed whenever the gift of knowledge points the way."[152] This is exactly the truth Boethius is shown by Philosophy, that the lost home is God himself: "therefore true happiness must reside in the most high God" (III, pr. 10.38–39). At the allegorical level at least, then, Boethius seems to be extending here the linkages between Philosophy's student and Virgil's hero.

Books Four and Five of the *Consolation* contain no such overt evocations of the *Aeneid* and its hero. But the implicit relationship between the two texts does not therefore completely lapse. For *Consolation* IV and V do not themselves possess the sort of narrative characteristics or exposition of personality found in the earlier three books. Instead, Lady Philosophy enters into extended and abstract discussions, attempting to explain the apparent evil and confusion of the world from which Boethius has now begun to disentangle himself. I think the parallel here is to the "secreta scientiae" which Fulgentius sees,[153] or the "lofty knowledge of the philosophers, theologians, Egyptians," which Servius finds, in the whole of *Aeneid* 6.[154] Boethius is literally led to kinds of wisdom which these early readers saw Aeneas achieve only allegorically.

This elaborate linkage between the *Consolation* and the *Aeneid*, carried out in verbal echoes, parallel imagery, prophecies, and aspects of character, lends an epic character to the intellectual journey of the *Consolation*. It specifically enhances our sense of Boethius's pathos and the tragic losses he has endured. In turn, the parallels suggest an understanding of the *Aeneid* which, if it is not systematically allegorical, is at least symbolic and spiritualizing. The *Aeneid* as echoed in the *Consolation* is personal rather than political, spiritual rather than historical. As we have seen, "Bernard" also constructs his commentary in such a way as to make another company of spiritual itinerants – the readers themselves – figures from the epic. It is a lesson he could have learned from his dense command of the *Consolation*.

The intertextual relationship described above is, however, admittedly fleeting and allusive rather than explicit. But as we will now see, the relationship was perceived and expressed, with increasing sureness and elaboration, in the commentary tradition which came to surround the two texts in the ninth through twelfth centuries. In these commentaries we can see the one text repeatedly invoked to explain the other, though the *Consolation* seems to dominate.

The earliest manuscripts of the *Consolation of Philosophy* date from the ninth century, and from the beginning the text is encased in a rich and shifting nimbus of commentaries.[155] The most widely influential early commentary is that of Remigius of Auxerre, written in the earliest years of the tenth century.[156] Remigius's commentary is still unedited but another commentary, edited by E. T. Silk,[157] is apparently a compilation based largely on Remigius.[158] Remigius, insofar as he is represented in the Silk text, cites the *Aeneid* only occasionally and then only as an illustration.[159] He indicates no sense that the *Consolation* has any special affinity to the *Aeneid*.

Remigius's assumption that Boethius's content was entirely Christian raised considerable controversy. In a reply attacking Remigius's Christianization of the Boethian world soul (III, met. 9), Bovo of Corvey cites extensive parallels between Boethius and the *Aeneid*.[160] Bovo argues that Boethius conceals philosophical truths – that is to say pagan truths – in his verses, just as Virgil did in his. Bovo specifically cites passages from Anchises's visionary description of the world soul in *Aeneid* 6.[161] Much of the explicit comparison between Virgil and Boethius would continue to center around these two passages and, although the Christianizing view of Remigius prevailed (his commentary alone was copied in the eleventh century[162]) commentators went on citing and expanding thematic and textual parallels with the *Aeneid*.

The twelfth century, deeply imbued with Christianizing platonism, was very open to the ideas of the *Consolation*, particularly as domesticated by Remigius. New commentaries appeared, extending the Christian–platonic themes already present in the tradition. Most important among these was the commentary of William of Conches.[163] William's commentary, too, used the Virgilian world soul to explain the Boethian.[164] At least one other twelfth-century commentator also does this, and at one point Abelard makes the comparison as well.[165] William also apparently used Fulgentius's commentary on the *Aeneid* to allegorize certain mythological figures mentioned in the *Consolation*.[166]

From the fragments available in print, it does not appear that any of the above commentators recognized the explicit Virgilian echoes by Boethius that I have discussed, though as I have suggested, "Bernard" seems to have responded to connections between the two. Rather, they discovered new linkages between the *Aeneid* and the *Consolation*. Moreover, the intertextuality moved in both directions, and the *Consolation* was often cited in commentaries on the *Aeneid*. I have already shown that one Virgil commentator in twelfth-century England, in his marginalia to *Aeneid* 6.719 ff., quotes *Consolation* III, metrum 9 and appends a long note from an otherwise unknown Boethius commentary.[167] Boethius, and his commentary tradition, begin to be used to gloss Virgil: the texts interpenetrate within the learned tradition.

There is at least one commentator of the twelfth century, however, who explicitly recognizes an imitative relationship, though an indirect one, between the *Aeneid* and the *Consolation*: "Bernard Silvestris." In his Martianus commentary, he discusses the polyvalent symbolism of the classical gods with frequent reference to their role in the *Aeneid*. He goes on:

In fact, this is imitation of an authority, because Martianus is emulating Virgil. For in Virgil, Aeneas is led through the underworld by his teacher the Sibyl, and finally to Anchises; similarly, here Mercury is led through the world's regions by his teacher Virtue, and to Jupiter. Similarly also, in the *Consolation*, Boethius ascends through the false goods to the highest good, led by Philosophy. And these three figures express almost the same thing. So Martianus imitates Virgil, and Boethius imitates Martianus.[168]

This overt connection of Virgilian descent and Boethian ascent provides a central nexus of meaning in the *House of Fame*, as we will see.

In "Bernard's" *Aeneid* commentary, indeed, the *Consolation* provides a dominant and explicit pattern of interpretation. Boethius is by far the most frequently quoted author in the commentary. When Aeneas gazes in fascination at the pictures on Juno's temple at Carthage (*Aen.* 1.464 ff.), for example, "Bernard" interprets the moment by reference to Boethius's enchainment to the goods of the world. The *Consolation* thus glosses the *Aeneid*. Again, when Aeneas is ordered to seek his ancient mother (*Aen.* 3.96 ff.), his erring quest is allegorized in Boethian terms:

But Aeneas misunderstands the oracle, and when he is commanded to go to Italy, he seeks Crete. He errs in Apollo's oracle thus: wisdom asks man, as one can read in Boethius (*Consolation*, bk. 2, prose 4, l. 23), whether anything is valuable in itself. When he responds "very little," he is commanded to seek beatitude in himself. He interprets "in himself" to mean "in the nature of the body," not "in himself" to mean "in the nature of the spirit," and he descends completely into pleasures of the flesh. And thus Aeneas comes to Crete when he is ordered to go to Italy.[169]

Many other passages of this sort could be quoted,[170] but perhaps the most fascinating example comes at *Aeneid* 6.3–4, where Aeneas's ship finally anchors on the shore of Italy: "tum dente tenaci / ancora fundabat navis," "then the anchors began to secure the ships with their sharp teeth." As we saw above, this passage is already echoed in the *Consolation*. Within "Bernard's" allegorical scheme, this is the moment when Aeneas leaves behind carnal and worldly desires and undertakes the pursuit of true wisdom. He explains the situation, again, by appeal to Boethius:

Tum dente tenaci: since Virgil said that Aeneas and his companions, that is, the spirit and the spiritual desires, are opposed to the passion of the flesh and excitement of temporal things. And it is most difficult to show how they are able to do this with their ships, but Virgil narrates thus: they are able to turn the prows to the beach since "the anchor (*anchora*) holds the ship fast." We interpret the anchor here to be the same thing as in Boethius: "The anchors hold fast" (*Consolation*, bk. 2, prose 4.9). Indeed, in both works we interpret the anchor as hope. Hope is the expectation of future good and is properly designated by the anchor, because, just as that instrument does not allow the ship to drift, so hope does not permit desire to vacillate.[171]

Here once again the two texts interpenetrate through the learned tradition. For the passage quoted from Boethius (II, prose 4) immediately follows a sentence in which, as discussed above, Boethius has quoted Virgil. At such a moment the heroes are virtually an interchangeable type.

But there is a subtler, and perhaps a more significant way in which this commentary manifests the intertextuality of the *Consolation* and the *Aeneid*. We see this at the many points where "Bernard" silently transcribes whole passages from William of Conches's *Consolation* commentary, applying them instead to the *Aeneid*. Anchises's description of the world soul is glossed by a passage borrowed without acknowledgement from William's explanation of *Consolation* III, metrum 9.[172] It is in this that the *Consolation* can be seen most clearly to impose a dominating pattern on spiritual allegoresis of Virgil. A text drawing its meanings in part from the *Aeneid*, is in turn imposed upon the *Aeneid* by the commentary tradition of the Middle Ages.

In the commentary of "Bernard," then, we find perhaps the fullest expression of a profound intertextuality: a complex and ramified bonding between the *Aeneid* and the *Consolation*, a relationship entrenched in the texts themselves and in centuries of commentary surrounding them – so entrenched, in fact, that the one is almost automatically read in terms of the other. A single set of moral and allegorical responses becomes adequate to both; the reading of one text inextricably involves the other.

Later commentaries on both the *Consolation* and the *Aeneid* have a more moral and ethical, less spiritual and allegorical, emphasis.[173] We will see analogous developments in the late fourteenth-century *Aeneid* commentary in BL Add. 27304. The important *Consolation* commentary from fourteenth century England by Nicholas Trevet concentrates on encyclopedic and ethical aspects of the text, although Trevet does offer occasional interpretations that could be called integumental.[174] This change in emphasis does not mean, though, that the intertextual linkages between the *Aeneid* and the *Consolation* ceased to be recognized and important, or that they failed to be influential in England, where our immediate interest lies. Quite the contrary. "Bernard's" commentary (or a version that was overwhelmingly influential on it) was available in England, at least in summary, and some of the basic thrust of his approach to the text could also be found in Albericus of London, the Third Vatican Mythographer, as well as in other English writers whose works were copied and read throughout the Middle Ages.

A widely studied English author like John of Salisbury, for instance, also provides a summary allegory of the ages of man in the *Aeneid*.[175] But John's own use of the intertextuality between Boethius and Virgil has not been recognized. John introduces his Virgilian allegoresis as part of an argument against "Epicureans" and in favor of indifference to fleshly desires and the goods of the world. John defines the Epicureans very broadly, as any men "who desire to fulfill their own will in all things ... So the world is full of Epicureans."[176] John then attacks the Epicureans with arguments and imagery highly reminiscent of Boethius: the poverty of the rich, the weakness of the powerful. John says that any man who cannot understand his argument "is indeed blind,"[177] precisely the metaphor Lady Philosophy used for Boethius in *Consolation* I. John finishes, like Philosophy, by saying that men tied to worldly sins are mere animals; he assigns various sins to particular beasts. While the lists differ in detail, this is the argument found in *Consolation* IV, prose 3. In this Boethian context, John introduces the example of Aeneas and his growth by stages to true wisdom. He takes up his Boethian arguments again in the chapter immediately following.[178] In such a way, awareness of the linkages between Boethius and Aeneas is again manifested and extended into Chaucer's period in the works of a widely read author.[179] As we have seen, however, the platonizing approach to Virgil, and the Boethian optic through which it largely operated, were also available in medieval England in the more immediate context of manuscript commentaries such as Peterhouse II.

PETERHOUSE 158 AND CLASSICISM IN HIGH MEDIEVAL ENGLAND

The presence of allegorizing commentaries bracketing the *Aeneid* in P158 raises questions not just about the possible English origins of the "Bernard Silvestris" commentary, but also more generally about audiences for such sophisticated readings of the epic in twelfth-century England. In fact, from the point of view of the general intellectual history of northwestern Europe in the twelfth century, the question of

English or French composition is not centrally important. In most fields, the French were the intellectual leaders of the period.[180] The English were only eager consumers of French education and texts.

> Culturally the most obvious thing about England in the twelfth century is its dependence on France. It was a colony of the French intellectual empire, important in its way and quite productive, but still subordinate.[181]

Richard Southern's argument may be overstated, but its broad implications cannot be denied. The English studied in France, and they imported both teachers and texts from France; the textual history of many major works of twelfth-century French humanism proves this.[182]

Both the Martianus commentary and the Virgil commentary constantly show the marks of French learning; only the Third Vatican mythographer provides a major source of apparently English genesis, and even that has recently been cast in doubt (see below). Not only French teachers, but also French monks, abbots, and ecclesiastical and secular administrators – often very learned men – were brought into England beginning even before the Conquest. Lanfranc and Anselm were French, as were many members of their entourages, and Thomas Becket's famous *eruditi* included a number of Frenchmen.[183]

But Southern also points out that the English did indeed have their own contributions to make to the intellectual life of the twelfth century, particularly in the fields of science and history.[184] The early and continuing role of Englishmen in the transmission of Arabic learning has been studied by Dorothée Metlitzki,[185] and the quality of twelfth-century English historiography has long been recognized. The education of the future king, Henry II, may not have been atypical; he received his early education in France, continued it in Bristol where he had some kind of contact with the astronomer and Arabist Adelard of Bath and completed his studies back in France once again under the great master William of Conches.[186]

In an important article responding to and expanding on Southern's arguments, Rodney M. Thomson points to two other major developments in English intellectual activity of the twelfth century, the production of high-quality books and "the renewed study of the literature of pagan Rome."[187] Thomson cites the activity, especially in south-west England, of a group of classicizing poets, glossators, anthologizers, and particularly the renowned historian William of Malmesbury.[188] Should we expand this area of English expertise to include some fairly widespread interest, even something approaching a

school, in the allegorical exegesis of classical texts? Certainly, even if
my arguments regarding the origins of the *Aeneid* and Martianus
commentaries are accepted, their contribution cannot be seen as in any
way uniquely English. The apparatus of sources in Jones and Jones
shows us the extent to which French materials influenced the
commentary.[189] But a further review of English interest in the Latin
classics, even excluding the two commentaries now under consideration, shows a broad and, more important, continuing study of the texts
of the classics.

English acquaintance with the *Aeneid* can be found in almost any
learned text of the twelfth century, and the accessibility of the *Aeneid* is
demonstrated by the existence of the manuscripts under study in these
chapters and in Appendix I. John of Salisbury's interest in the Latin
classics is very widely known, and his student Peter of Blois – a
Frenchman living in England – thought enough of the classics to
plagiarize John's proposed list of classical readings.[190] John of
Salisbury, however, lived in a period when the humanist interests of
Chartres and Paris were beginning to enter their decline. As early as
1159, in the *Metalogicon*, John attacked the "Cornificians" who
advocated a far briefer and more professionally orientated study of the
artes; and his was only one in a chorus of voices protesting the
narrowing of studies and cold professionalism of the new scholasti-
cism.[191] Yet John's work was very successful in England; and a number
of his compatriots continued to produce works in the "Chartrian"
tradition throughout the twelfth and well into the thirteenth century.

This continuing interest in the classics and in platonizing humanism
need not be seen as a sign merely of English backwardness. For it is
strongly associated with at least one school which made major
contributions to the most advanced kinds of learning throughout the
century: Hereford. Hereford's early and continuing role in the
transmission and dissemination of Arabic astronomy and Aristote-
lianism has been well studied. But its associations with classical studies
and more traditional Chartrian learning have not been fully explored.
Yet this is an important strand in the learning of Hereford and the area
of western England known as the West Country.

Important classical manuscripts are loosely associated with this area,
going back at least as early as the collection of classical and school texts
known as the Dunstan Classbook,[192] and the *Aeneid* manuscript in
English Caroline minuscule from Worcester.[193] The mid-twelfth-
century Virgil manuscript AS82, as we saw in chapter 2, was owned by

a Master Alfred who was perhaps the tutor of Henry, and it has early associations with the learned West Country Abbey of Cirencester.[194] Two of Hereford's bishops in the decades after mid-twelfth-century were school masters who had spent time studying and teaching in France: Gilbert Foliot and Robert of Melun.[195] Cirencester's early thirteenth-century abbot, the humanist Alexander Neckam, links together Hereford and Cirencester through a network of dedications.[196] While the content of Alexander's *De naturis rerum* draws from Arabic learning, its fourfold organization based on the elements harkens back to the encyclopedic traditions of France in the first half of the century.[197] Alexander also wrote a very old-fashioned commentary on Martianus Capella.[198]

Simund de Freine, who wrote poetry in French and Latin, was a canon at Hereford around the turn of the thirteenth century.[199] Among his two preserved French poems is a free version of Boethius's *Consolation of Philosophy*. Simund's work also draws into the milieu of Hereford another continuator of humanist ideals, Gerald of Wales. Gerald, twice disappointed in bids for the bishopric of St. David's Asaph, was seeking in 1203 some place of refuge and retirement. Simund wrote him a letter in Latin elegiacs inviting him to come to Hereford. Gerald, the glory of the arts, would be warmly welcome in the city of the arts, "in which is the true house of the trivium and quadrivium."[200] It is significant that at this date Simund praises Hereford not only for its excellence in scientific and astronomical learning, and its reading of the old and new law, but also for its emphasis on the old-fashioned study of the trivium.

In his younger days, Gerald had written a brief cosmological Latin poem, strongly reminiscent of the Platonic cosmologies of the French around mid-century.[201] This poem, incidentally, provides another index of Virgilian influence among such English writers; its opening couplet contains a clear verbal and metrical echo of the beginning of Aeneas's speech describing the fall of Troy.[202] Yet further humanizing interest in the classical past, in the general milieu of the West Country, is to be found in Latin poems like Joseph of Exeter's *De Bello Troiano*.

Chartrian Platonism and humanist interest in the classics, then, was a major strand in the milieu of English culture, and moreover a strand whose importance continued well after similar interests had begun to die down on the Continent. It is interesting to speculate whether this combination of classicism and scientific expertise might be the cause of the particular scorn which "Bernard's" Martianus commentary seems to hold toward the ignorant and superstitious French.[203] Scorn for the obsolete French teaching of sciences is a tradition particularly among English Arabists stretching back through Daniel of Morley to Adelard of Bath in the early years of the twelfth century.

Hereford, however, provides us with only one well-documented example of an English center of learning combining a tradition of scientific scholarship and associations with a range of classical and humanist interests. In fact, the Martianus and *Aeneid* commentaries are far more intimately connected with a text from the other end of the country, the *Allegoriae Poeticae* of Albericus of London, also known as the Third Vatican Mythographer. This text, while it contains indubitable parallels with the *Aeneid* and Martianus commentaries, provides only equivocal evidence for their English origin.

Of the forty-three manuscripts listed by Elliott and Elder, ten attribute the text to an Albericus; four call him Albericus of London; none of these manuscripts are earlier than the end of the thirteenth century, and none are identified as being of English origin.[204] The earliest manuscript listed, from the late twelfth century, is at least now in France. Ten attributions, however, are fairly convincing evidence, and in 1941 Albericus was identified as a canon of St. Paul's Cathedral around 1160.[205] The *Allegoriae Poeticae*, then, may be late enough that it should not be cited as a "source" of the "Bernard" *Aeneid* commentary. But no matter which text was influencing which, the parallels between the two are very striking. Most of them are cited in the apparatus to Jones and Jones.

The numerous references to Virgil in Albericus make it practically a commentary on the *Aeneid* in itself. At seven points Albericus enters into fairly extensive allegorization of episodes in the *Aeneid*.[206] Three of these come very close indeed to "Bernard," and at each of these three points Albericus uses and explicitly cites Fulgentius. These are the allegorization of Juno and Aeolus as forces of air and wind; the explanation of the nine circles of hell as the sins of the world; and an astrological allegory of Venus's role in the events following Aeneas's shipwreck in Libya. Since Albericus is fairly open about citing his sources, and since he mentions no other source for his *Aeneid* allegoresis, his may well be the earlier text. If this is so, it may help to explain other points where "Bernard" appears to be borrowing from Albericus in allegorizations of the classical gods.[207]

Together, these materials provide eloquent witness to the presence and, just as important, the continuity of classical reading and, more important for our concerns in this chapter, classical allegoresis in medieval England. Whether these texts represent a "school" of English classicists, based on and continuing the traditions of Paris, Chartres, and Orléans, must await further research and publication. Whatever the final verdict, study of the Peterhouse commentaries raises interesting and important questions about the contribution of England to the renaissance of the twelfth century.

Virgilian allegory, then, was widely accessible in high and later medieval England, in a number of forms. It could be found, in marginalia, in manuscripts like P158, BL Add. 32319A, and Pembroke 260. The tendency of such marginal notes is strongly reinforced, in this case, by the added frame of opening and closing texts containing explicit allegorical commentary. Further, as we have seen in these final pages, a manuscript like P158 came out of a milieu where there was considerable interest in the *Aeneid*, and considerable exegetical activity.

This allegorizing text, moreover, continued to be used and came into university circles no later than 1418. Medieval English readers of the *Aeneid* thus had multiple means of access to that tradition of interpretation which responded to deeply felt needs for transcendence and vision. If the "pedagogical" tradition studied in chapter 2 is one great stream of medieval Virgilianism, the vision of Virgil in Peterhouse 158 surely represents the other.

CHAPTER FOUR

Moral allegory and the Aeneid in the time of Chaucer: London, BL Additional 27304

"PLATONIZING" VERSUS "MORALIZING" EXEGETICS

Previous chapters have addressed two traditions of Virgilian interpretation and annotation deriving from largely independent, though overlapping, milieux. Using the example of Oxford, All Souls 82, I have tried to demonstrate in chapter 2 the continuity of a literalist and pedagogical vision of the *Aeneid* witnessed by layers of commentary stretching across three hundred years of the high and later Middle Ages. The glosses and notes of All Souls 82, grounded in the commentary of Servius and his medieval followers such as "Anselm of Laon," and nourished by independent learning, show a desire to make the text accessible on its own historical terms. This was especially clear in the early commentator's use of an unusual source for information on ritual practice, Macrobius's *Saturnalia*. If the scholarship is sometimes inadequate and the leap of historical imagination (as we know from other kinds of evidence) unsuccessful, the persistent impulse toward historically informed reading, must nonetheless be acknowledged.

Another vision of Virgil, through allegoresis of spiritual ascent, natural science, and platonizing cosmology, appears predominantly in independent tracts rather than in the margins of manuscripts. The commentary attributed to Bernard Silvestris is the most famous of these. Chapter 3 explored the presence in England of this and closely related commentaries. I also showed there how a limited number of marginalia surrounding the *Aeneid* in Peterhouse 158 and a few other English and continental manuscripts may have paved the way for such systematic allegoresis.

In chapters 5 and 6 we will examine a third and better known approach to the *Aeneid*, the "romance" vision of Virgil, especially as it is exemplified by some Latin versions of the story, by the *Roman d'Eneas* and by Chaucer's retelling in the *House of Fame* and the *Legend of Good*

Women. This vision of Virgil is witnessed most often in the vernacular. It participates, as do the other approaches, in the ambivalence toward Aeneas, created by that hostile counter-tradition described in chapter 1, and complicated by the paganism of Virgil's epic. The Aeneas of the romance vision is often a cad who flees Troy and abandons Dido. But at the same time he is a founder of empire and a splendid martial hero, possessed of ideal courtly manners: a model prince for an imperial culture. This divided narrative and exegetical tradition will be richly exploited by Chaucer.

These three visions of Virgil have their origins in different historical and educational circumstances. The early pedagogical response is the product of the monastic scriptorium and schoolroom and the cathedral schools, later readapted for higher studies as some manuscripts migrated to the universities. The allegorical tradition stretches from Fulgentius to renaissance commentators like Cristoforo Landino, but it is consistently associated with a sophisticated and speculative level of intellectual activity: the late classicism of north Africa, twelfth-century platonism, and later Italian humanism. The romance Virgil has more popular roots, and only here can we feel certain of a widespread secular audience for Virgilian story in the high Middle Ages.

By the fourteenth century, however, many of the institutions that gave rise to these traditions were in decline or vigorously changing. The basic education earlier provided only by the monasteries and cathedral schools was available from other sources such as friars, university masters, and emerging civic grammar schools. The growth of the universities created a larger educated elite, as did other centers of learning like the Inns of Court.[1] The audience of the vernacular romance tradition grew in size as moneyed bourgeois gained an interest in history and literature, and it grew in scope as secular education improved and expanded.[2] At the same time, in response to increased lay and university interest in the ancient stories – not necessarily classical Latin literature – a series of adventurous friars in the first half of the century began introducing extensive classical *exempla*, suitably moralized, into their sermons and the biblical commentaries which stood behind those sermons.[3] The traditions began to mix. An audience was coming into existence with an interest in, and access to, all these visions of Virgil as well as many other versions of the Troy story. One specific manifestation (and in turn source) of such complex access will be the subject of this chapter.

Before analyzing the layers of commentary in BL Add. 27304,

though, we should consider briefly a broader development in the exegesis of classical myth that affected the particular role of allegory in that manuscript. The later thirteenth and fourteenth centuries saw a turn away from the kind of exclusively spiritual allegory, deeply influenced by medieval natural science and platonism, that we have studied in Peterhouse I and II and in "Bernard." In some ways, allegorical exegesis became more daring, overtly comparing classical heroes and gods to Christ, Mary, and God the Father. But interest in classical texts as extended allegorizations of Everyman's spiritual life or platonic cosmology seems to have waned. Instead, texts from Latin antiquity were increasingly approached as models for life in this world, rather than as means of transcendence and contempt of the world. The exegesis, literal and allegorical, took on a more strongly moral tone, and explication of the literal level shifted much of its attention from historical difference to contemporary analogy, that is, to classical characters as exemplary or cautionary figures.

In England, this approach to classical texts as sources of exemplary models is especially associated with the activities of the "classicizing friars" mentioned above. They rifled classical literature for brief moral *exempla* to be inserted into their scriptural commentaries and sermons; they wrote commentaries on ancient Latin historians, and on some other ancient texts. (Nicholas Trevet, an influential forerunner of their work, wrote a commentary on Virgil's *Eclogues*, though it circulated only in Italy.[4]) But the same general approach is also applied to whole works of classical literature. The most widespread and widely studied instance of this is the allegorization of Ovid's *Metamorphoses*.[5] Two enormously influential works apply moral allegory to Ovid: the *Ovide Moralisé* and Pierre Bersuire's *Ovidius Moralizatus*.[6] The same kind of interpretation, however, was to be found in the Latin marginalia in manuscripts of the *Metamorphoses*.[7] The tradition was extremely widespread, and we will see its influence in the third layer of marginal commentary in BL Add. 27304 (hereafter Add27304). It is particularly conspicuous in that commentator's apparent attempt to divide the *Aeneid* into smaller units of plot, more readily reducible to the style of contemporary Ovidian allegory. Indeed this commentator provided his most coherent and energetic allegories for a few self-contained episodes in the *Aeneid*, like the Hercules and Cacus story in Book Eight, or the epyllion of Nisus and Euryalus in Book Nine.

This fragmentation of the text by the fourteenth-century commentator in Add27304 is part of a significant paradox in the development of later medieval Virgilianism. For this most flexible and complex of readers is also annotating the epic in such a way as to break it up. He identifies episodes that can be treated as limited *fabulae* more easily susceptible of explicitly Christian allegorization; but he creates other subdivisions as well that could then be distributed into other texts, or could render the *Aeneid* merely a study resource for the reading or creation of other texts. We will recur to this paradox below.

We have already seen an example of juxtaposed interpretations in Peterhouse 158, where a text surrounded by largely pedagogical marginalia is bracketed at beginning and end by two slightly later commentaries in the tradition of spiritual, platonizing allegoresis. Add27304 offers another fascinating case of new traditions accreting around the text as each century adds its layer of commentary. More important, it shows us in its last and longest series of notes an individual reader who registers some contact with all three approaches to Virgil. This last commentator seems able to absorb all three visions of Virgil, moving among them with no apparent sense of contradiction or incoherence. As we will see in later chapters, this commentator's contemporary, Chaucer, recognized just such contradictions and consciously exploited them. Finally, this commentary suggests one major pathway through which sophisticated literary reading of the *Aeneid* could have reached an audience much wider than that of the particular manuscript. But we must first give brief attention to the original state of the manuscript and its earlier layers of notes.

THE EARLY MARGINALIA

In the method and quality of its original production, Add27304 contrasts strikingly with the consistent format and single disciplined hand of All Souls 82; see plate 5. Quite aside from the changes in handwriting wrought by roughly a half century separating the two manuscripts, the hands of Add27304 nowhere display the high level of skill seen in All Souls 82. Furthermore, there are perhaps a dozen different hands involved in the production of the later manuscript, alternating without apparent system. As noted in the technical description (Appendix I, no. 18) the ruled format makes a sudden change at the beginning of the eleventh quire. The greater number of lines in the new format may simply reflect a desire to economize on membrane; it is not an isolated instance. (See App. I, no. 21, where a number of hands also appear.)

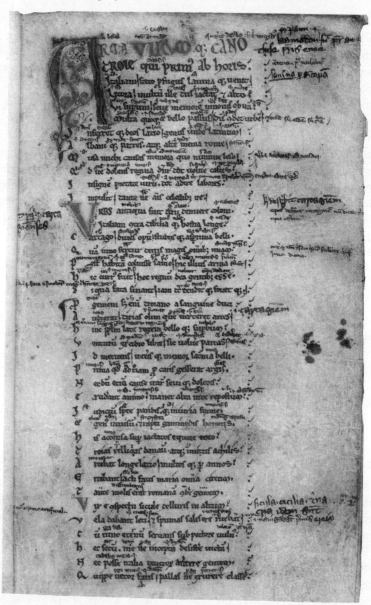

Plate 5 London, British Library, Additional 27304, fo. 5 *recto*. The opening of the *Aeneid* lacks the typical introductory summary lines; they are present (though usually incomplete) in later books. The three layers of marginal annotation, including the late-fourteenth-century "Norwich commentator" are all visible here. Pulished with permission.

Nonetheless, this casual approach to the production and physical appearance of the text suggests two things. First, Virgil manuscripts of the late twelfth and early thirteenth centuries were produced in a variety of scriptoria, sometimes with very low standards, and not just in limited centers of great intellectual activity and high-quality book production. Interest and demand appear to have been widespread, and exemplars were widely distributed. Second, however, the production of these manuscripts was perhaps not the primary or most careful activity of a scriptorium. There appears to have been no need to copy a scarce exemplar swiftly; rather, a number of hands work on the manuscript, apparently quite casually. Sometimes a hand will contribute as few as half a dozen lines. In some cases, where occasional hands appear to be quite uncontrolled, we may be witnessing the work of a master and pupils.[8] An exaggerated instance of this is London, BL Burney 269 (App. I, no. 20), which appears to come from a center quite unaccustomed to disciplined writing and book production.

The earliest layer of glosses and marginalia in Add27304 is approximately contemporary with the text. These are written in a tiny, neat *notularis* hand typical of the late twelfth and earlier thirteenth centuries. They appear not to be the work of the scribes of the text, since the hand of the notes bridges changes in the hands of the text. It also bridges, though barely, the change in format, the final entries falling on the *verso* of the new format. Like so many school commentaries, these notes are most abundant in the early books; they cease altogether after Book Eight. They are also like other sets of notes in the great difficulties they pose the modern transcriber: generations of greasy hands and the trimming of at least one binder have made many entries practically illegible.

In content, Commentary I of Add27304 displays the general pedagogical impulse studied in detail in Commentary I and IA of All Souls 82. These early notes provide brief lexical glosses, simple grammar and syntax, and some rather longer notes with historical, mythological, and geographical information. There is more emphasis on history here, though, and less on grammar and syntax, than in All Souls 82.

Commentary I of Add27304 offers only a few rhetorical or metrical notes, but where these do occur they appear to be the result of independent analysis, and not dependent on a Servian source. At *Aeneid* 1.34, where the narration turns to Carthage, the commentator follows traditional lines in noting that Virgil "uses the artificial order."[9] Again, at 5.33 "fertur cita gurgite classis," "the fleet runs swift across the surge," the commentator identifies the figure tapinosis ("by which one demeans the solemnity of his theme by the crudeness of his language").[10] Presumably he is objecting to *gurgite*. Hypermetric lines are noticed on three occasions. The first reference (1.332) is drawn from Servius. The second two (5.422 and 432) are independent, but both betray ignorance of technical aspects of classical metrics.[11]

This commentary makes things even easier for the reader than did Commentary I and IA of All Souls 82, by regularly supplying summaries and plot background. When Venus appears to Aeneas as a huntress, the commentator explains: "He shows how Venus, concealing herself, came to Aeneas."[12] There follows, as the notes point out, the "questioning of Venus."[13] This running list of contents is continued casually in the following books. Book Two is headed: "In this book is contained the Trojan War."[14] There are also longer summaries, as at 2.57: "He shows how the shepherds found and treated Sinon, who later betrayed them."[15] This is followed by a long prose summary of Sinon's speech, filling in the background of his story.

Information on history, mythology, and geography is presented in a manner similar to that detailed in the analysis of Commentary I and IA of All Souls 82, although the notes in Add27304 betray more clearly their Servian sources. As in All Souls 82, there are few direct textual parallels to Servius, but Add27304 orders its information more closely along Servian lines and has less independent material. Like All Souls 82, it typically simplifies the Servian notes, relates them closely to the plot, and often repeats only one of several interpretations offered by Servius. The commentary is unusual in one respect, in that it apparently had some access to the notes of Servius *auctus*, though possibly through a third source. Its note about Polydorus at *Aeneid* 3.13 is clearly drawn from Servius *auctus*.[16] Occasionally the Servian explanation is thoroughly garbled, as when the commentator gives background on the golden bough at 6.136.

In the latter half of the thirteenth century a second layer of glosses and very brief notes was added to Book One. It appears nowhere else in the manuscript.[17] This set of notes consists almost exclusively of one-word grammatical and lexical glosses, most of them interlinear. Occasional marginal notes add to the summaries of Commentary I. At *Aeneid* 1.8, Commentary II provides the heading "The words of the author to the Muses";[18] at 1.46 it notes, "These are Juno's words to herself."[19]

By the beginning of the fourteenth century, then, Add27304 was provided with a learned apparatus much like that of All Souls 82: it was a well notated school book, pedagogical in impulse and largely Servian in background. Both manuscripts seem to have rested during the first half of the fourteenth century. If read, they were not much annotated. Add27304 has a few hands making single entries, always too brief to date with certainty, which may nonetheless show that it was being read during the first half of the century.

In the later decades of the century, however, both manuscripts were in active use again, though their paths diverged radically. All Souls 82, as we have seen, came into the hands of Archbishop Chichele's registrar Henry Penwortham, acquired yet another layer of pedagogical commentary, and moved to Oxford when it was willed to All Souls in 1438: all this not necessarily in the order of my list. Add27304 had quite a different fate, and gained a last layer of commentary reflecting altogether different preoccupations and a very different intellectual milieu.

COMMENTARY III, NORWICH, AND THE PEASANTS' REVOLT

The last set of notes in Add27304, its Commentary III, is by far the most copious of the three. It is written in a fully developed *cursiva Anglicana*, showing no sign of the French graphs which began to infiltrate English cursive in the later part of the fourteenth century.[20] Indeed, on paleographical grounds alone the commentary might be dated about mid-century, or even as early as its second quarter.[21] We must now turn to internal evidence, however, which allows us to locate the origin of the commentary and date it with some certainty in the last two decades of the century. A brief journey into local history at this point will lead to clues for the only closely dateable Virgil commentary from medieval England.

The annotator makes a local reference in the notes to *Aeneid* 8.95, where Virgil describes the twisting course of the Tiber. Our commentator adds, "This was a twisting river just like that between Norwich and Yarmouth."[22] There are many twisting rivers in England other than the Yare; this choice for comparison suggests a commentator in or very interested in the area around Norwich and Yarmouth. This is supported by another geographical comparison at 2.21 ("Before their eyes lies famous Tenedos"): "In relation to Troy just as Flanders is now in relation to England."[23] Of course, much of the east coast of

Britain is almost in sight of Flanders, but the reference again appears to situate the commentator in the east. Another series of references, moreover, buttresses the association with Norwich and makes possible a fairly certain dating.

In *Aeneid* 1, at lines 123 and following, Neptune calms the tempestuous winds by the power of his words and authority. There follows the famous simile about a seditious crowd calmed by some grave and *pius* man:

> And just as, often, when a crowd of people
> is rocked by a rebellion, and the rabble
> rage in their minds, and firebrands and stones
> fly fast – for fury finds its weapons – if,
> by chance, they see a man remarkable
> for righteousness and service, they are silent
> and stand attentively; and he controls
> their passion by his words and cools their spirits:
> so all the clamor of the sea subsided
> after the Father, gazing on the waters
> and riding under cloudless skies, had guided
> his horses, let his willing chariot run.
>
> (1.148–56)

The first three lines of this simile seem to have struck a responsive chord in our commentator, and brought to mind some event in his own memory. He writes two notes to line 148: "Because where it is crowded with people there is often insurrection,"[24] and "Note how the peasants and the low-born and the townspeople rise up against their betters."[25] And there is a longer note at line 150: "Here he shows what such a throng does when it rises up. John Latimer in Norwich, and Horyn in London."[26] This is excruciatingly ambiguous. Are Latimer and Horyn the rabble-rousers or the peace-makers? Fortunately, in this case, documents offer some answers.

John Latimer was a wealthy but not a noble citizen of Norwich in the second half of the fourteenth century. A considerable landowner, he was freeman in 1349, bailiff of Norwich on five occasions between 1364 and 1388, Member of Parliament for Norwich in 1371 and 1380. He bore arms for the Leet of Conisford in 1355. In 1378-79 he paid the highest taxes in Mancroft Ward and the third highest in all of Norwich; in 1390-91 he contributed the second greatest sum toward bringing the coveted wool staple to Norwich; sometime before 1368 he made generous gifts to the important church of St. Peter Mancroft. His will was proved in 1392. None of the records, however, associate him with seditious activities in any role.[27]

The single name "Horyn," on the other hand, is a small needle, and London a large haystack. There was, however, a London alderman named John Horn whose life parallels Latimer's so closely, and whose activities suit the note so precisely, that it seems fairly certain he is the man intended by the commentator. John Horn enters the records the same year as does Latimer. In 1349, as a fishmonger, he was part of a suit against other fishmongers for using "false nets." He was the king's inspector for the building of a barge to defend London in 1372, and gave surety for another fishmonger in 1373.[28] Horn was a London Alderman in 1379, and Alderman again when he was involved in the disturbances accompanying the Peasants' Revolt of 1381. He was indicted in 1382, accused of having betrayed his trust as a messenger to the rebels outside London. Witnesses claimed that rather than trying to persuade Tyler's men to disperse, Horn incited the rebels to assault the city, and even arranged a meeting in his own home between the Kentish leaders and discontented men of London. He was accused also of leading a rebel mob through the streets of the city the next day.[29]

Recent historians have cast doubt on Horn's actual treachery in the Peasants' Revolt,[30] but what matters for our purposes is that he was popularly rumored to have encouraged the rebels. He was in fact acquitted of the charges, but disappears completely from the records after this time.

Could John Latimer have played a similar role in Norwich? To my knowledge all the records are silent on this point. But Latimer certainly had a political and social position like that of Horn in London. Latimer did hold office after the Peasants' Revolt, but then so did several London men indicted and acquitted along with Horn.[31] And a Norwich commentator might well have known local rumors which never led to indictment and the kind of permanent legal record it supplied for Horn. Or alternately, did both men possibly have reputations as peace-makers? Horn, as we have seen, was an ambassador to the rebels, and it remains uncertain whether he deserved his indictment.

Taken together, though, these two biographies and the commentator's strong response to Virgil's image of *seditio* make it seem clear that he was thinking of the events of the Peasants' Revolt. The settlement of the uprising also parallels part of Virgil's simile. The rebellion in Norfolk was dispersed largely through the actions of one man of great

authority and some *pietas*, Bishop Despenser.[32] Although he spoke
through blood rather than words, the sudden calming effect of
Despenser's actions suits Virgil's language rather closely.

Our commentator's references, then, confirm the likelihood that he
wrote in Norwich or its environs, and provide a *terminus a quo* for the
date of the commentary. Of course, the memory of such a major
uprising can last a long time. But I have already pointed out that the
hand of the commentary is more typical of the middle of the century,
and, while an older man may well continue to write the hand he
learned as a boy, an archaic hand is not likely to survive longer than a
generation in a major urban center like Norwich. Further, it is
probable that the details of the seditious activity of secondary figures
like Horn and Latimer would not stay in mind as long as the memory
of men such as Tyler and Litester. It seems fairly safe, then, to date
Commentary III in the decade or so following the Peasants' Revolt of
1381.

PEDAGOGICAL ANNOTATION IN THE NORWICH COMMENTARY

This Norwich commentary of the late fourteenth century is important
not only for the light it casts on the development of established
interpretive traditions, but also for the insight it provides regarding the
mind of a sensitive and independent reader. Past tendencies and
current exegetical fashions are reflected in these notes on the *Aeneid*, but
an individual personality and interpretation emerge as well. The
commentary does not offer a consistent and formal analysis. Rather,
we can follow the commentator's vagaries as he reads. His emphasis
and enthusiasm shift as different aspects of the text gain his attention.
Sometimes differences in the shade of ink and the size of his script
suggest that the commentator has returned to a passage to add a few
more notes. We have already found similar signs of rereading in the
contemporary Commentary III of All Souls 82.

The Norwich commentator, however, is not writing his notes as if on
blank margins. On the contrary: the fourteenth-century history of
Add27304 offers another excellent example of a later layer of notes
responding to and complementing an earlier layer. Text and apparatus
shift almost organically, receiving new contexts without rejecting old
ones. The early thirteenth century, as we have seen, had provided the
Norwich commentator with a very useful pedagogical apparatus:
glosses, a few summaries, historical, geographical, and mythological

notes. Several details prove that the later commentator made serious use of the earlier material. Frequent use of the manuscript may already by his time have rendered some of the early entries barely legible, and the Norwich commentator several times retraces an earlier note in his own ink to make it clearer for himself or later readers.[33] On at least two occasions he adds directly to a thirteenth-century note. At Book One, line 321, for example, where the disguised Venus first approaches Aeneas, the early commentary gives a topic heading: "The questioning of Venus."[34] To this the Norwich commentator adds directly: "to teach men how to speak with others on certain occasions."[35]

As I suggested earlier, the Norwich commentator not only alters the manuscript by adding a wholly new kind of interpretation, but he also combines within his own notes aspects of all three visions. To begin with, he greatly extends the qualities of the manuscript as a school book by expanding on the work of the thirteenth-century notes. An examination of only the first 150 lines of *Aeneid* 1 will make this process quite clear.

The first few books are extensively glossed by the earliest commentator, and only a few simple glosses are added by Commentator III. Some national names are glossed, as at line 12, "Tyrians." In the margin the Norwich commentator writes, "TYRIANS, that is Carthaginians."[36] This is only the first instance of a consistent pattern by which the commentator simplifies national and place names (1.196, "CICILIA, TRINACRIA, and SICULA are the same thing"; 1.235, "Teucrians, Dardanians, and Trojans are the same thing, also Phrygians"; 1.366, "Carthaginians, Tyrians, Punics, Libyans are the same thing, also Pelasgians").[37] So whereas Commentator III in All Souls 82 reverses the effacement of nuance he inherited in earlier notes, the Norwich commentator in Add27304 to some extent continues it. There are also rare English glosses in the Norwich commentary; I count only eight.

Like the thirteenth-century commentator, the Norwich commentator often paraphrases the text directly, simplifying the syntax and clarifying the sense. At 1.77 ("explorare labor," Aeolus's "O queen, your task / is to discover what you wish"), the commentator writes, "YOUR TASK TO DISCOVER, as if he should say, you think about what you desire and I will give it to you."[38] Again, at 1.93 when Aeneas stretches his two hands to the stars he writes, "He was entreating the gods with both hands."[39] And at 1.104–05 he cuts through the difficult syntax, "That is, the flank of the ship was turned to the waves";[40] while at 1.123 ("the ships accept the enemy waves") he disposes of a metaphor: "That is, the sea water entered."[41]

The Norwich commentator greatly expands the earlier commentator's habit of providing topic headings and narrative summaries. When Juno approaches Aeolus at 1.65, we read in the margin, "Here Juno speaks to the god of the winds, saying as follows."[42] Two lines later he adds, "She complains about Aeneas and his people,"[43] then at 1.71, "She praises the reward which she promises to the god of the winds,"[44] and the scene concludes at 1.76 with the note, "Here the god of the winds responds to Juno, 'I grant your request,' giving his reasons."[45] This is an exaggerated instance, but parallels could be cited. We have already witnessed a similar provision of summaries in the roughly contemporary All Souls 82, Commentary III. The Norwich commentator, however, is rather less systematic about it; he seems to busy himself most with summaries and topic headings when no other matters engage his attention. He appears determined to be copious, and when he has no fresh information to add he fills in the margins with plot outlines. In a later book he even starts making a list of verbs in the text, but soon abandons the project.[46] The very persistence of these headings and summaries, though, is another sign of the paradoxical potential for a break-up of the epic at the hands of this commentator. Despite the energy of his own reading, he is making it possible for later users of the manuscript to locate and contextualize episodes without reading the work as a whole.

Under the hand of the Norwich commentator, then, the manuscript is improved as a glossed school book, if only in a wayward fashion. But this commentator also continues the fuller pedagogical, informative impulse of the earlier notes; he provides new information, and notes on some technical points of grammar and rhetoric. At *Aeneid* 1.2 his manuscript has the spelling *lavina*; he knows the alternate (and today the accepted) spelling *lavinia* and explains the manuscript spelling "through syncope."[47] At 1.99, he explains (incorrectly) the reference of "savage," "SAVAGE, that is savage lord Achilles,"[48] and at 109 he describes the *Aras*, "Altars," "The altars were rocks in the middle of the sea between the two countries."[49] These concerns with details of grammar and geography are comparable to those we witnessed in "Anselm of Laon" and Commentator III of AS82, though none of the notes here appear to derive from "Anselm."

The pedagogical notes just cited appear to reflect independent and usually accurate learning, but other notes both reveal the commenta-

tor's major source and, occasionally, betray his ignorance. He
sometimes gets his gods wrong. Vesta, for example, is described (at
1.297) as the goddess of love. Classical genealogy is not consistently
accurate, either: "Atridas" (at 1.458) is called the *mother* of Menelaus
and Agamemnon.[50] More often, though, his pedagogical notes are
accurate and predictably Servian in origin. The port of Carthage is
described at 1.159, and the commentator adds a longish note:
"Topothesia, that is the fictional description of a place. Topographia is
the true description of a place. Here he uses topothesia."[51] This is
clearly a paraphrase from Servius and could be found in many places;
in fact it is quite close to the formulation found in "Anselm of Laon,"
but the absence of other close parallels to his commentary suggests
some alternate source. But our commentator does seem to have had at
hand at least parts of a fairly good text of Servius, as can be seen at
1.171, ("magno telluris amore," "with great desire for land"). Here the
Norwich commentator tells us that Virgil is using Tellus, the goddess,
for the element earth, just as elsewhere Vulcan is used for fire and
Ceres for grain.[52] This is merely copying part of Servius's entry.[53] But
while the text may be directly Servian, the choice of entry, as we will
see, is significant – a physical allegory of classical gods.

It seems likely, then, that the Norwich commentator was working
with a manuscript containing incomplete but accurate Servian notes.
Such a source manuscript would help to explain the commentator's
combination of accurate Servian entries and occasional errors where a
complete text of Servius would have given correct explanations. An
alternate manuscript would also explain the commentator's acquaintance with the spelling *lavinia*, mentioned above, and his single textual
emendation. The original text has an incorrect reading at 4.471: "aut
Agamenonius furiis agitatus Orestes." (The standard text reads
"scaenis agitatus.") The error, possibly the conscious alteration of a
confused scribe, is understandable given an audience that may have
known the story of Orestes but did not understand the reference to
stage production. Our commentator, working with a more correct text,
alters the reading to *scenis agitatus*, "harrassed on the stage," and adds a
marginal note – not Servian – that suggests some information on a
point that vexed many a medieval reader: "HARRASSED ON THE
STAGE, that is recited on theater platforms, in the manner of the
ancients who used to recite there various deeds, while others close by
mimed in accordance with the songs."[54] He seems to have a notion of
combined declamation and mime, shared by others in the Middle

Ages, but he does successfully explain the gist of the metaphor. There are other manifestations of a pedagogical interest in the historical details of classical life, as at the Sibyl's instructions for Misenus's burial (6.154): "She teaches the ancient way of burials."[55]

The Servian sources of much of the pedagogical commentary are clear. But our commentator did not make a regular habit of citing his authorities, and indeed most of his non-Servian information goes no further than the learned apparatus of a decently educated man of the time.[56] When Virgil mentions the story of Hippolytus and his son Virbius (7.761 ff.), however, the commentator gives an indication of other parts of his reading: "Note, this story is in Theodulus and in Bernard Sil," surely meaning Silvestris.[57] The story of Hippolytus is found in Theodulus's tenth-century *Ecloga*, popular throughout the Middle Ages, but not in any work of Bernard Silvestris.[58] Probably the commentator is thinking of the commentary on the *Ecloga* by another Bernard, of Utrecht.[59] The error is intriguing, given my sugggestion in the last chapter that the allegorical commentary discussed there might also have been by a different Bernard, then similarly attached to a more famous writer of the same forename.[60]

Despite his general dependence on Servius and Servian-derived commentary, then, the Norwich commentator is also ready on occasion to use other, independent sources. It is significant, though, that at least in this instance he does not seek out a learned commentator like Anselm, or an ancient informant as a genuine "humanist" later might. Rather, he cites two medieval poets and, as we will see now, a patristic authority. His interest in establishing the genuine nuance and difference of Virgilian references has quite narrow limits.

At one of the moments of rereading mentioned earlier, the Norwich commentator was also going through three chapters in Augustine's *De civitate Dei*.[61] He reviews some seven hundred lines of the *Aeneid* at the end of Book Six and through much of Book Seven, noting six occasions where Augustine refers to Virgilian passages or characters.[62] The first cluster of references comes in Anchises's long prophetic passage about the future kings and leaders of Rome.[63] When Juno sends Allecto to rouse Amata's fury (7.341 ff.), the commentator again cites a brief reference in Augustine.[64] This is little more than note-taking, though, not a critical or interpretive use of Augustine.[65] The Norwich commentator registers the parallels, but takes no notice of the fact that Augustine's message in these chapters is hostile to the ancient Romans.

Indeed, these references point once again away from annotation as an explanation of the epic, and toward annotation as a preparation of the manuscript for use in other settings. Augustine is not being introduced to explain Virgil here; rather, the *Aeneid* is marked in such a way as to aid the reader of the *City of God*. Along with the commentator's genuinely engaged reading, this nonetheless hints once again at the commentary's potential for decomposing the book of Virgil, and redistributing its parts across a series of alternate texts.

ETHICAL EXAMPLE AND CHRISTIAN ALLEGORY IN THE NORWICH COMMENTARY

There is another exegetical mode which our commentator pursues with much more consistency and enthusiasm. This is his habit of moralizing on proper and improper behavior: individual, social, and religious. I have already quoted the commentator's earliest manifestation of this interest, in the section on dating and location. The events of the Peasants' Revolt are cited as examples of the crowd's improper behavior and the calming impact of an august aristocrat. This already suggests the commentator's very conservative social ethos, and his reading of the *Aeneid* as a prescriptive model of ordered political behavior, a model he will equally reinscribe in the zones of social and religious action. After this point, most such comments are positive and generalized. They are innumerable, and while they point out proper behavior in any form, they naturally concentrate on the hero. When, after the tempest, Aeneas gives his great speech of comfort to the surviving Trojans (1.208), the commentator notes that Virgil "describes the way a consoler acts."[66] Venus, speaking of Dido, says that she was given "intact" to Sychaeus, and the note adds, "He shows how a woman should be given to her husband" (1.345).[67] Aeneas answers Venus's questions politely, even reverently, and the commentator tells us: "Behold how suitably he answers, and men should answer questions to the point."[68]

Such generalizations regarding proper manners continue throughout the commentary. The reader is told to notice how to come to the table (1.697), that one should say prayers before drinking (1.736), that prayers should be offered for peace (3.261), the proper address on leaving a place (3.492), the proper speech to the fatherland when returning from afar (3.522), how to approach an enemy (3.598), and how to approach a friend (8.143).[69] The reader is reminded, too, that one does not have to speak against oneself unless it is unavoidable (3.609), that it is good to encourage men with prayers (5.291), that a man must think how to help himself and avoid danger (8.21), that one good man can stop many evils (in regard to Hercules, 8.570), and that we should celebrate the feasts of saints (responding to Evander's ceremonies, 8.281).[70]

We have already seen the Norwich commentator at work on a project of geographical domestication when he explains Virgilian geography in terms of the river Yare or the coastlines of England and Flanders. Elsewhere he compares Evander's primitive dress to that of Welshmen.[71] But the examples in the paragraph above suggest an equally important gesture of domestication. That is the appropriation of the *Aeneid* as a normative text sustaining a dominant social and ethical order. Again and again, as in the instances above, the Norwich commentator makes Virgil's heroes models for proper contemporary action. But this is not just a reading of the *Aeneid* as a kind of courtesy book. Such explicit use of an authoritative text to support an established but threatened ideology is particularly telling after the disruptions of the Peasants' Revolt.[72]

The comment on Evander's religious ceremonies, cited above, gives a clue to the more particular impulse behind these apparently tepid generalities. The commentator is making a marginal list of social, but also specifically Christian, virtues. The precise language of these notes makes his intent even more clear. One of the entries is called an *exemplum* (1.242, about Antenor), as is another at 2.355 (on Aeneas), and at 2.379 (on Androgeus). A more frequent opening is *nota modum*, "note the way," usually indicating the proper way of behavior. Even more often we see *debent* and *debemus*, "they ought" and "we ought." In these frequently iterated phrases, the *Aeneid* is rendered a hortatory text, constantly urging the reader to participate in the social and religious structures which the marginalia are progressively deriving from the authoritative work.

This is not simply a list of virtues, then, but a list of *exempla*. In the Norwich commentary we are witnessing a rare instance of a classical text on its way to becoming an entry in a medieval *exemplum* book or a lively anecdote in a sermon. We have endless examples of the final products, both *exemplum* books and sermons, and we know of many encyclopedic works and florilegia from which classical material was selected.[73] But excepting Ovid, whose works were themselves regarded as encyclopedias, I know of no other classical manuscript, certainly no other English Virgil, where we see a reader (almost certainly clerical) moving in this fashion between literary analysis and external applications. With these notes, even more emphatically than in the citations of Augustine mentioned above, we witness the manuscript being marginally unpacked, its content parceled out for use in new contexts, and made accessible without an extended reading of the poem.

This particular approach to *exemplum*, however, also associates our commentator with another interpretive tradition, the romance Virgil. It shares with the romance vision a preponderant emphasis on the virtues of the hero, his outstanding qualities as a model of social manners and political leadership. Like the romance vision, too, this aspect of the commentary concentrates on Aeneas's imitable rather than his historical character. In this desire to see Aeneas as a wholly admirable hero, the chivalric tradition joins with the pedagogical, which has its own prejudices in seeing Aeneas as an unblemished political figure and ideal prince. This leads both traditions, and the Norwich commentary, to defend elaborately Aeneas's most dubious action, the abandonment of Dido. The defense is particularly necessary in view of the widespread interest in the counter-tradition of Aeneas the cad and traitor, discussed in chapter 1. This interest was accompanied, even in the pedagogical Virgil, by great sympathy for and fascination with Dido.

Consider the defense. Mercury has given his warning, and Aeneas realizes he must leave Carthage. The Norwich commentator contrasts this noble resolve with common men who do not obey preachers: "Note, Aeneas flees Dido at the order of Mercury and Jupiter. And mankind does not flee sin at the order of God and the preacher."[74] This not only glorifies Aeneas but casts Dido as a source of sin, an identification quite possibly deriving from earlier allegories like that of "Bernard" and the Peterhouse fragment. This implicit allegorization of Aeneas and Mercury, moreover, is another hint of the Norwich commentator's preoccupation with preaching. (Mercury is, after all, a god noted for eloquence.) The commentator attributes Aeneas's decision exclusively to the prompting of the gods: "Note what Aeneas did, and that he fulfilled the commands of the gods."[75] And he is at pains to explain Aeneas's speech of self-justification, at 4.347: "Aeneas answers Dido, offering herself as an example – how through the will of the gods she fled from Phoenicia to Carthage, which she loved, and that similarly he had to go to Italy, and he adduced many reasons."[76] The object of so many *exempla* must be unspottedly virtuous.

Hortatory examples are also drawn from aspects of the text other than simple social propriety. Later in the section examined above, Virgil compares Aeneas to an oak tree in a storm (4.441–49). The commentator spies this out immediately: "A good example for the steadfastness a man should maintain, also for humility, etc. 'He humbled himself,' etc."[77] The biblical citation with which the note closes (Philippians 2:8) is part of a habit we will see elsewhere, of comparing specific moments in the *Aeneid* to the life of Christ. Other notes are more general, linking images and episodes to virtues and vices. Earlier, when Polydorus speaks from the bleeding myrtle, the commentator sees another good *exemplum* and writes, "Note, on avarice" (at 3.44).[78] And when the Virgilian narrator breaks in to apostrophize ("To what, accursed lust for gold, do you / not drive the hearts of men?"), the commentator notes, "a good passage on Avarice."[79] Under the power of love, Dido neglects to pursue the building of Carthage, and the commentator finds another *exemplum*: "Note that lechery hinders many good things."[80] Even Dido's powerful and frightening curses have a possible application: "by so much more strongly is excommunication to be feared."[81]

The Norwich commentator, then, draws upon and expands the school and pedagogical traditions of the early thirteenth-century commentary he found already in the margins of Add27304. His social and heroic *exempla* associate him, though only distantly and partially, with the romance vision of the *Aeneid*, while at many other points he seeks out *exempla* of more specifically Christian virtues and vices. But this moralizing, hortatory impulse in the commentary, for all its domestication of the epic to Christian virtues and contemporary social propriety, is far indeed from the allegorical mode we witnessed in the "Bernard" and Peterhouse commentaries. Here there is no extraction of platonic cosmology or natural science, no overarching allegorical program of education in the liberal arts as a pathway to *contemptus mundi*.[82] Rather, in his array of *exempla* the Norwich commentator shows a dogged attention to applications of the literal level, even if that is a literal level often temporarily denuded of its historical specificity.

We now turn, though, to another aspect of his interpretation of the *Aeneid*, which shows an acquaintance with and an enthusiasm for another major tradition of later medieval classicism, the tradition of Christianizing allegoresis. The specific manifestation of this tradition in the Norwich commentary, further, allows us with some certainty to identify the intellectual milieu from which it grew.

I have already suggested that there is a significance to the commentator's choice of the Servian entry which he transcribes with such accuracy at 1.171, explaining "Tellus" as a metaphor for earth. This is only one example of the way that Servius's vast but basically pedagogical commentary can be used selectively to inform interpretations of a far different color. The commentator begins with this physical allegory from Servius, but he goes on to use the same idea in places where Servius makes no such suggestions, although the commentator makes only traditional associations.[83] So for example, using the technique of physical allegory, Nereus, god of the sea, "is interpreted as the sea."[84]

More often the allegories and moralizing parallels are overtly Christian. Juno, nursing her own wounds, mentions Athena's vengeance on the entire Greek fleet for Ajax's rape of Cassandra (1.41). The commentator explains: "Note that many died on account of one. Note, this is about our first parent and the originators of evil."[85] Ajax will be used for an *exemplum* describing Adam. More interesting is the allegorization of Jupiter's great prophecy of the Augustan peace and the binding of Furor: "on the binding of Satan."[86] Jupiter himself is Christianized as God the Father and Augustus cast as a Christ figure, bringer of the new dispensation. When Dido prays to Jupiter at her banquet to make this a "joyful day" (1.732), the note adds: "In our own language, 'may God make us joyful,' because all joy is from him."[87]

As might be expected, the secular hero of the moralizing *exempla* examined above is allegorized as well. The process is occasional and inconsistent, mixing allegory with simpler literal moralization. It begins with Aeneas's speech of comfort after the tempest in *Aeneid* 1 which, as mentioned above, is cited as an *exemplum* of the good *consolator*. But lines 204-06 ("Through / so many crises and calamities / we make for Latium ... ") are explained with clear Christian meaning: "Harsh is the way to heaven."[88] Here again, the implicit framework of allegoresis is most provocative. The Norwich commentator seems to assume, if only in passing, the traditional interpretation of the quest for Italy as a soul's pilgrimage to heaven, as we have already seen in "Bernard." This silent assumption is yet another proof of how widespread was such an allegorizing approach to the *Aeneid* in later medieval England. If Aeneas is the leader of those seeking such an end, his Christological role also becomes clear.

The ramifications of this approach to Aeneas are not however articulated in the commentary until Aeneas descends into hell, where he speaks with Deiphobus: "Here Deiphobus asks Aeneas how he came to hell, and this can be applied to Christ."[89] The *Ovide Moralisé* also tells the story of Aeneas's descent to the Underworld, in a version based on Ovid but expanded to include some Virgilian details such as Anchises's prophecy of the Trojan lineage and foundation of Rome.[90] Later the descent is allegorized in a manner similar to that of the Norwich commentator:

> Par Eneas puis droitement
> Noter le piteuz Rambeour,
> Le debonaire Sauveour,
> Le fil Dieu, qui deigna venir
> Des cieulz en terre, et devenir
> Vrais homs, et enfer visiter,
> Pour ses amis d'enfer giter.
>
> (xiv.978–84)

The Ovidian moralizer then pursues the allegory further than does the Norwich commentator, to include the tree as the Virgin Mary (sprung from the root of Jesse), and the golden bough as the fleshly form Christ takes from her (xiv.998–1007).[91] It is important to note that at this point the Norwich commentator not only abstains from so extended a treatment, but also stops short of thoroughgoing allegory, offering instead a likeness or comparison: "potest applicari ad cristum." This is simile, not metaphor, *exemplum* rather than identity.

In fact, the whole Virgilian Underworld undergoes a domesticating transformation in the Norwich commentary, being seen in light of a Christian purgatory and hell. When he begs Aeneas to give him burial, Palinurus is said to be *in purgatorio* (at 6.364). Anchises's description of the universe and its souls is domesticated with a similar Christian parallel: "In the beginning God made heaven and earth, etc. Note the concord. The spirit of the Lord was born upon the waters."[92] Anchises's prophecy of Caesar is twice said to be *de Christo* (at 6.781 and 793). This goes very much further than did "Bernard," offering explicit parallels where the previous allegorizer made only the most hesitating and vague analogies. Here, too, the allegorizing of Aeneas has moved from Everyman to his Savior. Where the twelfth-century commentators drew comparisons and commentary from Boethius's prisoner (see chapter 3, pp. 120–30), the Norwich commentator goes straight to Christ himself and the Bible. Aeneas's likeness to Christ is again mentioned in Book Eight when Evander sends him off to battle ("But you, whose years and blood are blessed by fate, / whom gods have called, take up your way ... " 8.511–12). Here as before the commentator limits himself to citing the parallel as an *exemplum*: "Apply the story of Aeneas to Christ."[93]

The implications of this are carried even further. Aeneas's mother Venus is naturally compared to the mother of Christ: "Apply to Mary all good things about Venus" (at 2.632).[94] And again: "Apply the story of Venus to the blessed virgin Mary" (at 8.532).[95] But the commentator is definitely not engaged in sustained and programmatic allegoresis at this point, and alternate *exempla* for Christ and Mary are offered elsewhere. Galaesus, for example, is to be applied to Christ (at 7.535), and Camilla "ad beatam uirginem" (at 7.803). We will return to this reduction of allegoresis to brief divisions of text.

Something much closer to programmatic allegory, treating an entire narrative, occurs in the notes to the Hercules and Cacus episode in Book Eight, although it is still limited to the function of *exemplum*. The allegory is outlined as the episode opens: "Note the place of Cacus and apply it to hell, Christ to Hercules, the cattle to those held in Limbo."[96] Another suggestive parallel is noted soon after: "Note here how Hercules was a shepherd" (at 8.203).[97] And finally: " 'to leap,' and note, regarding Christ, how he killed the devil. Nearby ... 'o death I will be your death.' "[98] This allegorization of Hercules is well established and could have come from many sources, but I know of it in no other commentary on the *Aeneid*. It was made very famous in the earlier fourteenth century by inclusion in the *Ovide Moralisé*.[99]

This treatment of Hercules and Cacus, along with the reading of Aeneas's descent to the Underworld in terms of Christ's harrowing of hell, and the parallels to both in the *Ovide Moralisé*, all point to a reader influenced by contemporary traditions of Ovidian exegesis. In its willingness to identify Aeneas overtly with Christ, and other epic players with characters in the drama of salvation, such Ovidian allegory is much more daring in its anachronism than the exegesis practiced by "Bernard" and his contemporaries. But at the same time, in limiting itself to brief episodes rather than whole narratives, fourteenth-century Ovidianism is less ambitious than the programmatic allegorizers of the twelfth century. The Norwich commentator, too, like his Ovidian models, moves toward allegory in those episodes that can be treated as brief, self-contained units. The story of Hercules and Cacus is just such an episode, as is the epyllion of Nisus and Euryalus to which we will turn toward the end of this chapter. Indeed, even at moments which do not lend themselves to narrative dissection, the Norwich commentator will tend to make his allegorizing points in isolation, and without regard to context.[100]

The casting of Christian allegory largely in the form of explicit *exempla*, moreover, further allows us to identify the precise intellectual milieu in which the commentary as a whole developed. It seems almost certain that the commentary's interpretive models, its impetus to moralizing applications, and its general hortatory tone were inspired by the group of classicizing friars I mentioned early in this chapter, whose activities have been the object of Beryl Smalley's pioneering study and the later, more literary investigations of Judson B. Allen.[101] These friars, a small group centered in Oxford and Cambridge but also working in some of the provincial *studia*, made extensive use of classical history and literature in their Bible commentaries. The commentaries in turn were meant for use by practicing preachers, who would be able to draw from them classical *exempla* for their sermons.[102] Manifestly, it is just such a service that the Norwich commentator is trying to provide with his moralized and allegorized *exempla*. The language of the allegorical notes particularly seems to speak, almost in the form of instructions, to sermon-writers: *applica, applica, applica.*

A number of other details suggest that the manuscript was being prepared, however haphazardly, for easy access in annotating scripture or enlivening sermons. We have noted the commentator's great extension of topic headings already present in the earlier notes; usually underlined or circled, these would help a user avoid extended reading in pursuit of a specific point. The occasional word lists, arranged vertically at the extreme edges of the margins, may also be entered for later use in a glossary. At other points, the Norwich commentator will number a sequence of events, places, or characters, presumably for ease of reference.[103] And this commentary also includes the earliest instance I know of numbered *capitula* in an English Virgil manuscript.[104]

At the time of Smalley's work on the classicizing friars, it appeared that they drew their quotations of classical verse largely from secondary sources.[105] The Norwich commentary of Add27304 provides proof that in one case at least a reader in exactly this milieu used a complete manuscript of classical verse, and as a part (though only a part) of his commentary arranged it for use as a source of *exempla* in preaching. Perhaps more important, if my dating is correct, the commentary extends the activity of the classicizing friars by at least three decades. Smalley argues that the classicizing activity had only a brief florescence, roughly from 1320 to 1350.[106] The Norwich commentary may of course be only a secondary manifestation of the classicizing friars, its ideas deriving from some of the widely distributed manuscripts of their work. It nonetheless demonstrates a continuity of interest in the classics, and a fascination with their potential Christian content, maintained right into the last decades of the century, and therefore into the most active period of the great vernacular poets whose classicism is the ultimate object of this study.

Aside from manuscript circulation of their commentaries, which was considerable and continued well after the period of their florescence, it is not clear how the direct influence of known classicizing friars would have been felt in Norwich; only one of them, Thomas Ringstead, has any Norfolk connections, and there is no evidence that he returned there in his productive years.[107] But, as William Courtenay has pointed out, Norwich was a flourishing center of education beyond the universities, it possessed "a vigorous and famous grammar school," and all "four major mendicant orders had convents in the city that were *studia particularia* both for philosophy and theology."[108] This reputation lasted well into the second half of the century.[109]All of them sent students on to Oxford and Cambridge. Thus both the Franciscans and the Dominicans, the orders of the classicizing friars, had flourishing houses and important schools in Norwich, so direct influence remains possible.[110] In any case the thirty years which elapsed between the classicizing Bible commentaries and the Norwich Virgil commentary provide more than enough time for their ideas and methods to have spread in manuscript.

THE NORWICH COMMENTATOR AS READER

The analysis above violates to some extent the flexibility and integrity of the Norwich commentary by dividing its activities into three separate areas, of pedagogical interests, moral applications, and Christian allegory. But probably the most exciting aspect of the commentary is the way it allows us to watch an individual of the fourteenth century work at reading his Virgil. He is certainly a wayward reader and unsystematic commentator, his attention shifting from one topic and approach to another, making much of an occasional obscure point, ignoring another which seemed important to other medieval readers, and switching from one emphasis and format to another. And he is not altogether persistent, his notes breaking off suddenly at 9.504. But above all his very waywardness provides the traces of an enthusiastic reader and re-reader of Virgil.[111]

The vexed question of what could be called "literary" reading, in its modern senses, hangs over any study of medieval classicism. It is simple to prove that manuscripts of the classics were available in the Middle Ages, and just as easy to prove that they were used: mere signs of wear show that. But were they ever read as people might have read, say, Chaucer?[112] The Latin classics were certainly read as encyclopedias of lore; Ovid in particular provided the period with a vast amount of information about classical deities and myths. And they were used constantly as rhetorical models, Virgil especially. Sometimes they were read as history. But none of these activities alone combines emotional involvement, stylistic sensitivity, historical imagination, and interpretive response – the pleasures of the text. The allegorizers, "Bernard" in particular, seem to be reading in a way we can easily recognize as symbolic (probably more easily than we could have done twenty years ago). But here too the response seems limited, reducing the text to a new paraphrasable fable and then applying a systematic interpretation; thoroughgoing allegory of this sort effaces, or at least puts aside, the emotional and stylistic appeal of the literal level.

In its very complexity, however, in its waywardness and odd combination of approaches, even in its incompleteness, the Norwich commentary strikes me as transmitting a readerly experience we can recognize as interestingly parallel to our own. The commentary does have external ends, of course, but they are only a part of the reader's activity. Beyond the search for *exempla*, the commentator seems intensely involved with his reading and reaction. The only nuance that lacks, as in most marginalia then and today, is the record of emotional response. (There are occasional hints of real enthusiasm, as when Bitias drinks deeply from the cup proffered by Dido, and the commentator notes in large, underlined letters, "A sign of good wine!"[113]) But the above analysis, dividing the commentator's work into three sections for the purpose of comparison and historical argument, does an injustice to his variety and inventiveness. This section will close, therefore, by examining in detail and in its original order one of the Norwich commentator's most sensitive passages of readership, his notes on Nisus and Euryalus.

The epyllion of Nisus and Euryalus is among the most moving and disturbing sections of the *Aeneid*, combining as it does martial bravery and selfless friendship with avarice and bestial slaughter.[114] The patriotic resolve of Nisus and Euryalus, to find a way through the Latin siege and carry a message of the Trojans' extremity to Aeneas is soon sullied by their lust for blood and booty. The response of this fourteenth-century reader, while different from ours and not altogether consistent, is nevertheless insightful and brilliant in its audacity.

The Norwich commentator opens the episode, as is his habit, with a topic heading, "de Niso et euriolo" (at 9.176), then notes his main theme at 9.182: "amor." "Fierce avarice" ("dira cupido," 9.185) will soon prove the heroes' downfall, and the commentator is very perceptive when he notes in the margin that this is "a sign of things to come."[115] Euryalus refuses to let Nisus go into danger without him, and the commentator draws a moral: "One companion should not send his fellow into danger alone."[116] Another habit mentioned earlier, the listing of verbs, surfaces briefly in the margin at 9.203: "erudire." Nisus replies that Euryalus, who is young and has his life ahead of him, should not expose himself to such danger; the commentator approves, "because one companion does not always accept his fellow in danger, but sometimes sends him away."[117] In a further entry the commentator seems to be suggesting that Nisus is undertaking his mission only on behalf of Euryalus: "A friend should put himself in danger for his friend."[118] Besides, Nisus argues, he wants his friend to outlive him, "because men wish ... also that their friends live after their own deaths,"[119] and if necessary bury him: "let him celebrate the burial rites."[120] Nisus also hesitates to take Euryalus away from his mother, who bravely journeyed on with him rather than stay behind with the other old women in Sicily: "what a man's mother does for him."[121] But Euryalus, firm in his loving friendship, will not be persuaded to let Nisus go alone.

They seek out the prince, Ascanius, to offer him their services as messengers to Aeneas. All the other Trojans are asleep: "the rest after labor."[122] The Trojan elders, however, are holding, as the commentator notes, a *consilium*, deciding who will act as messenger to Aeneas. Nisus and Euryalus make their brave offer: "Note, about Nisus and Euryalus."[123] They have discovered a safe place to sneak out of the encampment and past the Latins: "A man should first seek out the right place for artifices. Thus the devil acts."[124] The aged Aletes thanks the gods for such young men, then embraces them, weeping: "Signs of love. Thus we should remember the passion of Christ, hold out our arms and weep."[125] This begins to hint at the overt Christological

allegory that is to follow. Ascanius then swears to reward them richly if
they bring back Aeneas. This, the commentator notes, is "a son's love
toward his parent."[126]

Euryalus cannot face the parting with his aged mother; her
tears would weaken his resolve. But he asks Ascanius to give her
the protection and comfort she deserves. The commentator
compares her to the Virgin: "That is, great thanks are owed her
on account of such an offspring. By so much the more is it owed
to Mary on account of Christ her son."[127] The two friends go
out into the Latin camp and, rather than pursuing their mission,
they engage in an orgy of murder and spoils-taking. The
commentator falls rather silent here, offering only a few subject
headings; he seems as uncomfortable as is many a modern reader
with this side of the brave men. It certainly assorts oddly with the
allegorizing to follow. He does acknowledge sensitively, however,
that an ugly kind of pride has overtaken the heroes. When the
Latin forces see Euryalus's captured helmet gleaming in the
moonlight, he adds the comment, "against Pride."[128]

They flee the Latins, but Euryalus is slowed by the weight of his
booty and, without intending to, Nisus gets far ahead of him: "A man
should not wander from his friend and leave him in danger. Nor
should he be separated from him, because this will separate us from
the charity of Christ."[129] At once Nisus turns back: "Note what a
friend should do for his friend when he is in danger, and what Nisus
did for Euryalus."[130] Before hurling his spear at the Latins, Nisus
utters a prayer to Diana: "A man in danger should pray to the saints
for aid, and especially in time of war."[131] The Latins cannot see who
is throwing the deadly spears, but prepare to take vengeance on
Euryalus instead. Trying to divert attention, Nisus shouts out where
he is: "Note what a friend did for his friend."[132] But it is too late.
Volscens has already thrust his sword through Euryalus. Nisus rushes
in wildly, determined at whatever cost to kill Volscens in return. Here
the commentator rises to perhaps his most audacious allegory, seeing
the avenging Nisus as a type of Christ: "Note that Nisus killed
Volscens. Thus Christ killed the devil on account of a man who was
killed."[133]

This episode shows us the Norwich commentator at his most subtle
and flexible as a reader. He provides school notes, topic headings,
moralizations, and bold but suggestive allegorical readings. It is also his
most creative passage of commentary. All the previous comparisons

have precedents in allegorizing we have already studied. But to my knowledge, the Norwich commentator's interpretation of Nisus and Euryalus is altogether new. It is a pity, then, that his commentary breaks off just as it arrives at its most startling inventiveness.

Add27304 shows us the text of Virgil being adapted to new interests in the moralizing and allegorical applications of classical story. It shows a complex reader moving with ease though not perhaps with a sense of critical consistency among the three major traditions of Virgilian interpretation, and shaping them to his own professional ends. Further, in the applications suggested by the moralizing and allegorical notes, the manuscript points out one way in which Virgilianism reached a wide audience, through the preaching activities of the friars. Although in original production a less distinguished manuscript than All Souls 82, Add27304 shared with it a nearly parallel history through the end of the thirteenth century. After that point they veered sharply. All Souls 82 gained a last layer of medieval pedagogical commentary and then moved into the university. Add27304 moved into (or stayed in) the hands of the friars, and entered the more popular tradition of sententious moralizing.

The fourteenth-century annotations and ownership of these two manuscripts typify two major strands in late medieval reading of the Latin Virgil. On the one hand, there is the controlled, learned, pedagogical approach, born in the monastic schoolroom and destined for the university. This is a distanced and distancing reading of the epic, which achieves its ends only insofar as it meticulously (and always incompletely) reconstructs in its own margins the world from which the text arose. On the other hand, and growing out of a very similar set of high medieval glosses, is the Norwich reading of the *Aeneid*, aimed largely at persuasion and the hortatory application of the letter to local place and contemporary time. Even the setting of the epic, in this reading, is partly reimagined in terms of insular geography. We are at an opposite pole from the readings of Commentator III in AS82, with his studied efforts to reconstruct the historical, geographical, and religious difference of the Virgilian *Aeneid*. Here instead, as Judson Allen put it, "All exemplary existences inhabit, ultimately, the same world."[134] The Norwich commentator acknowledges Virgilian difference in his pedagogical notes, but he also overcomes (or suppresses) it in the interest of using Virgilian *auctoritas* to describe and advance a contemporary social, ethical, and religious order.

These three chapters have tried to show, by specific examples, something of the variety of approaches to the *Aeneid* accessible to later medieval England through the immediate matrix of the manuscripts. In these examples, we have seen two major visions of Virgil in action, one pedagogical and the other allegorical. This fastidious bipartite division, though, should not be allowed to obscure the considerable variety and even inherent contradiction within each of these two central interpretations of the epic.

We have seen in All Souls 82 how an early layer of notes, pedagogical in impulse and very largely Servian in background, can by its brevity and simplicity act to "flatten" the text, effacing (even if by necessity) a detailed sense of Virgilian time and place. This flattened text, I have argued, can open a way for the kind of abstract spiritual allegorizing seen in "Bernard." The early marginalia of Peterhouse 158, also largely Servian, show again how essentially pedagogical notes can provide a background for spiritual allegoresis through a certain pattern of selection from Servius and occasional extension or emphasis of Servian allegory.

At the same time, the bulk of commentaries within the pedagogical tradition are more directed toward providing the reader with a rich sense of the "difference" of the Virgilian world. Many do so simply by offering a wide variety of accurately preserved Servian entries. (See for example Appendix I, nos. 7, 10, 12 [layer I], and 15.) Others, most notably the notes in All Souls 82, establish or re-establish a pedagogical vision through independent research, recourse to independent medieval commentaries, and fresh notes.

There is variety, too, within the allegorical vision of the *Aeneid*. In chapters 3 and 4, we have studied two very different kinds of Virgilian allegoresis present in medieval England. The "Bernard" and Peterhouse commentaries approach Aeneas as a figure of Everyman, enacting the pilgrimage of the human soul through the fallen world toward a state of transcendent vision and renewed grace, all within a framework of Platonic cosmology. The Norwich commentator of Add27304 is far less systematic, and at the same time more extreme. His allegories address only brief sections of text and tend to interpret Aeneas (as well as other characters) as a figure of Christ, rather than as the questing human soul. Aeneas figures the virtuous Everyman only insofar as he is a literal model of worldly manners and morality. He is a hero in uncomplicated service to the Norwich commentator's contemporary religious and political ideology.

Major studies by Judson Allen and Alastair Minnis have delineated simultaneous but contrary developments in later medieval habits of interpretation which bear interestingly on these two major strands of fourteenth-century Latin Virgilianism. On the one hand, Minnis, working largely from biblical commentary, has shown a growing interest in the human authors of Scripture, and in their individual historical situations and intentions. The human mediator of divine inspiration becomes increasingly important in such exegesis, and with this new importance there comes as well fresh attention to the author's historical circumstance, rhetorical technique, and aims of literary unity.[135] On the other hand, Allen (and before him, Paule Demats) has looked at later medieval classical study and discovered there a growing exegetical independence from the historical situation of the author, a tendency to register but then ignore authorial intention.[136] The interpretation of Ovid, in particular, so subdivides his stories as to efface their unities, and focusses instead on the Christian and moral implications of each individual fable.[137] *Divisio*, itself a universal habit of scriptural exegesis, becomes the most crucial moment in such classical *lectio*. And through *divisio* and its suppression of context a radical domestication of the text becomes possible, whereas attention to unity, historical situatedness, and authorial intention might resist such reading.

But while real differences lie between these two approaches to late medieval readership, the two strands of exegesis we have seen linked in Add27304 suggest that Allen and Minnis are not necessarily at odds. Rather, the contrasting emphases they each document respond to two of the major and simultaneous traditions of Virgil study which have been examined here. The "pedagogical" tradition, with its careful attention to the historical reference of the text, and its focus on the rhetorical and grammatical methods of the poet, helps produce that very historicizing *lectio divina* which Minnis studies. And the later allegorical tradition, with its diminishing attention to literary cohesion and authorial intent, further documents the emphasis followed by Allen. Both, as we have seen, operate in the activities of the Norwich commentator. We are not witnessing a scholarly argument about the one late medieval way of approaching texts; rather, it seems to me, Allen and Minnis document two parallel but interestingly contrary developments in readership.

It is not surprising that both Demats and Allen find much to support their positions in late medieval commentaries on Ovid. From an early date, the *Metamorphoses* in particular were seen as an encyclopedic collection of fables, an attitude which encouraged readers to focus on the individual unit rather than aspects of broader structural coherence. The *Aeneid*, on the other hand, for all its mythological content, has the inherent unity of a single narrative, and could be said to resist Ovidian treatment. Where such local allegorization does occur, as at certain points in the Norwich commentary, it is at the cost of subverting narrative coherence. From this perspective, the tendency of the Norwich commentary to take the epic to pieces, both by the provision of topic headings and in local allegorizations – the preparation of the manuscript thereby for piecemeal external application – can be seen as a kind of breakdown of Virgilian reading, in which the search for ethical relevance and contemporary application finally and radically subverts narrative coherence. The commentator's sporadic struggle to impose an ultimately incompatible mode of exegesis on his text may be reflected in the incompleteness and tentativeness of his annotation. The impulse to application sometimes even ends by silencing him, as in a note he just leaves incomplete. At 2.390 ("If that be guile or valor – who would ask in war?"), he comments "a good phrase for ...," but cannot think for what, and so leaves the note unfinished.[138]

As we have seen in the past three chapters, the marginal notes and systematic commentaries bearing these approaches to the epic can be found in separate manuscripts or, as in Peterhouse 158, they can compete for a reader's attention within a single manuscript. In the latter case the text's progressive encrustation by different visions creates an exegetical framework of great depth and complexity, but equally of great potential conflict. The visions approach a single authoritative text through multiple and inconsistent exegetical postures, thus jeopardizing to an extent the very authority of that text.

The Norwich commentary in Add27304 is significant as a witness of a reader aware of these multiple visions and moving among them. We have already seen how the Norwich commentary introduces a new aspect of allegoresis, and how that allegoresis nonetheless seems to presuppose a knowledge of the kind of spiritualizing approach made by "Bernard." We have also seen how the commentary seeks out exemplary moments and characters and suggests moral applications strongly reminiscent of the classicizing friars. This in turn suggests another means of access to the *Aeneid* for a large and less well-educated audience.

For the purposes of this study, however, the greatest importance of the Norwich commentator is the complexity of his readership and the ease and unconcern with which he moves among the visions of Virgil. He is a reader, as we have seen, of considerable insight and even greater ingenuity. He moves back and forth, with no apparent sense of discomfort, among the pedagogical and allegorizing approaches to the *Aeneid*, adding new Servian notes and creating a moral commentary and Christian allegory very much his own. In his use of Aeneas as a model for contemporary manners and everyday morality, moreover, he participates to an extent in the third vision, the romance Virgil, which we shall consider in chapter 5.

This uncritical embrace of the three visions of Virgil is not the only possible response to the presence of multiple interpretations. The Norwich commentator's contemporary, Geoffrey Chaucer, is similarly aware of these approaches to the *Aeneid*, but he is vastly more conscious of their potential for conflict and the extent to which they may impair the authority of Virgil's text. In the following chapter we will turn to the romance vision of Virgil in the *Roman d'Eneas*. In chapter 6, we see how Chaucer used this as a source of simultaneous sentiment and irony in *The House of Fame* and "The Legend of Dido." Finally, in a brief conclusion we see two late medieval Virgil redactors, William Caxton and Gavin Douglas, one of whom draws wholly on the romance tradition, while the other attempts to create codicological space for a genuine Virgilian *translatio*.

CHAPTER FIVE

The Romance Aeneid

In or about the mid-twelfth century, the Virgil manuscript All Souls 82 was receiving its early apparatus of pedagogical annotation, and allegorical commentaries like Peterhouse II and "Bernard Silvestris" were appearing in England and France. Around the same time, still another audience and another claim on the authority of Virgil and the example of the *Aeneid* story began to emerge. This was an audience of male and female aristocratic readers (or listeners) of the Norman vernacular, a company that in those years spanned England and northwest France. In those years, too, the young King Henry II was heir at once to a British and continental empire still in some need of historical self-justification, and to an intellectual milieu steeped in texts of the Troy tradition. All these forces – the Latin book, a growing audience for the vernacular, the Angevin appetite for genealogical prehistory and models of empire – converge in the writing of the *Roman d'Eneas*. The shifting of Virgil's story from Latin to romance, and from a Europe-wide to a French and Anglo-Norman readership, creates a flashpoint. In the resulting poem a literary and political community registers both its sense of its power and ancient antecedents, and its nervousness over competing emergent powers, in particular the powers of women and of mercantilism. For all its subtle dialogue with its Latin source, the *Eneas* makes place for new explorations of feminine will and of trade, both signal challenges to the ancient social model of a militant aristocracy. More intriguingly still, as we will now see, the poem tends persistently to figure the one emergent power in terms of the other.

LAVINE AT HER BOOK

Lavinia, who will be Aeneas's second wife and his race's link to native Latin lineage, exists only as a name in Virgil's *Aeneid*. But in its most noted and audacious innovation, the *Roman d'Eneas* invented a character

for Lavine and an elaborate romantic involvement between her and
Eneas.[1] As she meditates on her sudden love for the Trojan invader
Eneas, the Latin princess begins the first of several long and intellectually
sophisticated internal dialogues. Partway through, she shifts from self-
address and begins speaking to a personified figure of Amors:

> Amors a escole m'a mise,
> an po d'ore m'a molt aprise.
> Amors, molt sai bien ma leçon;
> or ne m'as leü se mal non,
> del bien me redevroies lire . . .
> Ge sui une meschine fole,
> novelement m'as a t'escole,
> tot ai apris an moins d'un jor,
> les maus, la poine, la dolor;
> forment me plain, griément me dueil.
> Amors, car retorne ton foil,
> de l'autre part me fai garder!
>   (8183–87, 8211–17)

[Love has sent me to school, and in a little while has taught me much.
Master Love, I know my lesson very well: until now you have read me
nothing but the bad; you should in turn read me the good . . .
I am only a foolish maiden, and you have me newly in your school, but
I have learned in less than a day all the ills, the pain, and the sorrow.
Bitterly I complain, grievously I lament. Love, turn over your page,
make me look in another place!][2]

I begin this chapter with Lavinia, and will end with her, not just for
the daring of the passage, but also because it incorporates a whole
series of themes and gestures – particularly in regard to women, their
power, and its containment – typical of the *Roman d'Eneas* and more
generally of the "romance" approach to the *Aeneid*. Most overtly, the
redactor suggests here the specifically learned and pedagogical context
of his vernacular project. At the very moment when he begins to
intertwine his own non-Virgilian erotic episode into the directly
Virgilian military narrative surrounding it, the poet brings back to his
vernacular audience's attention the situation of the schoolroom and its
study of Latin books, which is his poem's immediate background. Thus
he calls in the figures of the master, the student, the book, and the
technical language of reading just when he most signally expands his
primary curricular text, the *Aeneid*.[3]

The poem's additions to Virgil have been the objects of long and
fruitful study: they include whole narratives like the affair of Lavine

and Eneas, scientific comment, and exotic descriptions to which I will return below. But we are only beginning to appreciate the extent to which the *Eneas* self-consciously incorporates the full inherited Virgil of the classroom and its Latin manuscripts, both in the narrow sense of minor explicatory detail and in the broader influence of existing interpretive traditions. There is much to be said about these influences of the Latin book on the vernacular poem, but the pointed manner in which the poet here alerts us to his departure from the *Aeneid* of the schoolroom has its own thematic impact. This gesture, however local and playful, typifies the poem's pattern of articulating traditional modes of power and its transmission (here educational, elsewhere imperial and genealogical) even as it displays its capacity temporarily to subvert or challenge them.

Indeed, the figure of Amors as teacher, which reminds us at once of Latin sources and the poet's independence from them, is itself a nod to the Latin poet Ovid, from whom much detail in the Lavine episodes is borrowed.[4] The whole setting of the internal dialogue and its love casuistry derive from Ovid and other elegiac poets.[5] Ovid styled himself the *praeceptor Amoris* in the *Ars amatoria* (1.17), and the *Eneas* goes further here by assigning the role of love-pedagogue to Amors himself, a step apparently parallelled in Latin poems of the *Carmina Burana*.[6] As he moves into Ovidian themes and conventions, the redactor acknowledges this other and, as I will argue, competing master of the Latin book. In doing so, he extends and emphasizes a pattern of alternation between Virgilian and Ovidian, and masculine and feminine perspectives in his version of the fate of Eneas. Ovid himself had a well-articulated sense of responding to Virgil, particularly by giving voice to female desire, and the competing traditions represented by Virgil and Ovid clash or interpenetrate in a number of medieval Latin Troy poems that circulated in England.

This competition between Ovid and Virgil in the *Eneas*, however, is not simply between poetic voices. Rather, it is part of a broader and more complex thematic negotiation in the poem between, on the one hand, feminine desire and feminine efforts to claim voice and power and, on the other hand, the genealogical and territorial demands of patriarchy as represented by Eneas's divinely fated empire and the war through which he will claim it. Below, I will focus on this tension and its ultimate reconciliation. It is enough here to recall that the passage quoted above occurs during an eight-day truce between the decision to settle Lavine's fate by single combat and the (ultimately delayed) combat that Eneas wins. Her interior discovery of Amors is bracketed, textually contained at beginning and end, by the military and judicial discussions among men that will actually decide her future; and her "independent" desire for Eneas only aligns her, however fortuitously, with a preference that her father, guided by the pantheon, has already expressed. This narrative containment of Lavine climaxes a whole series of strategies by which the poem contains feminine challenges to the order of patriarchal will or divine power.[7] The first instance of this procedure is of course Dido, who poses a many-sided danger to Trojan destiny.

Lavine's address to Amors also, however, situates her more locally within this exploration and ultimate containment of feminine voice and power. For Lavine figures herself as a grammar student in the schoolroom, reading a hard passage and begging the teacher to turn the page, and thus places herself where a Norman princess was unlikely to be.[8] She thus usurps, but only figuratively and only temporarily, the reader's place that in fact has been occupied by the clerk who now controls the redaction. (This metaphoric usurpation is extended soon after, but then literally, when Lavine writes Eneas a letter explicitly said to be in Latin, lines 8776–77.)[9] Finally, of course, this playful and paradoxical moment dissolves itself because it is wholly metonymic – a mode of articulating internal psychology. As we will see, much of the accommodation between feminine and masculine power and discourse in the *Eneas*, and much of the final containment of the feminine, is accomplished in a similar sequence of linked moves between the literal and the metonymic.[10]

What little we know about patronage of vernacular writing in the twelfth century suggests that it was in good part the result of wealthy women without Latin, seeking access to texts that were central to the self-conception of male power.[11] It is perhaps not surprising then that we witness the redactor inventing a role for Lavine neatly converse to the role of such books. That is, Lavine becomes the key to lineage and empire in the *Eneas*, and her extended role exists only in the vernacular version, yet makes playful if temporary reference to schoolroom learning and the Latin language. The erotic will of the vernacular female character is, as we saw above, figured in terms of the Latin book which her Norman counterparts are unlikely to have known.[12] But insofar as the *Eneas* is a doorway to ancient *auctoritas* for readers of limited or no Latinity, it is a doorway opened only through the Latin-reading clerk and only to the extent he chooses; and analogously, insofar as Lavine in this episode discovers her own will within her crucial imperial role, it is a moment of power bracketed by male decisions already taken – thus only a suspension of the imperial narrative – and equally bracketed by a narrative from the Latin source of which she is an excrescence, an interruption.

There are two broad implications of this situation, which together comprise the center of what I call the "romance *Aeneid*" in the Middle Ages. First, the two-sidedness of the *Eneas* as an access to normative Latin epic allows it both to set forth openly the culture it would seek to have its readers imitate, and to record covertly its fears about outsiders, particularly women, gaining access to the power described and transmitted in that text. The poem achieves the prior end by narrating the triumph of Eneas in terms reminiscent of Norman social order, especially its growing organization through genealogy and law. Yet the *Eneas* simultaneously carries out the latter project through bookish echoes or allusions that would have been accessible only to the most learned and Latin-educated portions of its audience; I explore a prominent instance in the divine arming of Eneas below (pp. 180–84).

Second, the presence of Lavine and the passage discussed above constitute fundamentally a delay in the imperial narrative that precedes and follows it. Yet Lavine, because of her genealogical role, is the one female character whose will, once acknowledged, must finally be integrated by the epic. All other feminine and erotic resistance to the progress of empire is indeed expressed but then contained, ever more firmly if always incompletely, in various structures of suspension, delay, and postponement. In her study *Inescapable Romance*, Patricia Parker aptly characterizes romance "primarily as a form which simultaneously quests for and postpones a particular end, objective, or object ..."[13] It does so, she argues, by strategies of extended liminality, "the dilation of a threshold rendered now both more precarious and more essential."[14] In the *Eneas* and, as we will see, in some of its medieval Latin analogues, eroticism and feminine power are almost always engaged and contained in evasions of their own end, strikingly similar to the generic motives articulated by Parker. They undertake such evasion through evolving strategies of dilation, both temporal and narrative. These can be as straightforward as Dido's efforts to delay the Trojans in Carthage, or scientific efforts to resist time, as in the tombs studied below (pp. 203–06). More often, romance dilation is practiced by narrative techniques of suspension, as in the episode already discussed. Yet other strategies involve narrative anomalies such as anachronism that create double moments in which chronology itself dilates; we will see this first in a Latin plaint of Dido and then in her epitaph in the *Eneas*.[15]

In what follows, then, while I pursue some of the themes of love psychology and courtly manners that have preoccupied much of the commentary on the *Eneas*, I am more concerned with the political and narrative context of these erotic episodes.[16] As I will try to show, romance dilation does not merely empower eroticism, giving it a new and expanded place in the vernacular Virgil. It also uses temporal anomaly to move endangered and endangering figures beyond the reach of time; and it thereby defuses their historical impact, even while it fixes them indelibly in written and even architectural space. It is this double power of dilation – both to make space for the feminine and erotic, and to contain their effects by making them into artifacts – that most deeply characterizes the "romance *Aeneid*."[17]

THE CLERK AT HIS BOOK

Whatever the broader thematic burden of Lavine's internal address to Amors as a schoolmaster, the trope also draws, as I have suggested, more immediate attention to the kind of classroom setting in which the clerkly redactor himself would have gained his command of Virgil. The three previous chapters, and their detailed examination of manuscript commentaries, provide the context in which I will begin a more detailed examination of the competing thematics of the *Eneas*. I do not undertake here a systematic analysis of specific links between Virgil manuscripts of English or Norman provenance and the *Eneas*.[18] Rather, in this section I want to sketch, first, a few instances where fairly minor textual details in the French poem demonstrate the redactor's dependence on glossed manuscripts and fuller commentaries, particularly such manuscripts of the basic pedagogical tradition as are exemplified by All Souls 82 in chapter 2. The absorption of marginal comment and even, as we will see, of marginal episode into the vernacular narrative is itself a part of the poem's romance dilation, by which it looks backward to the mythic roots of its history, and forward to the imperial genealogy its hero will engender.[19]

The reading of the *Aeneid* reflected in the pedagogical annotations and their surrounding apparatus of *accessus*, whatever its overt and primary attention to simple grammar and historical information, is of course not an unselective or uncolored approach to the epic. As we have seen, the central interest of the "pedagogical" tradition was language, but even by itself this study helped prepare for the exercise of a language, Latin, whose empowering command was largely limited to men. In fact, however, scattered details in the school apparatus of twelfth-century Virgil manuscripts – to which I turn later in this section – more openly suggest preoccupations extending well beyond clerical interest in language and learning, preoccupations that we will see to be central to the imperial discourse of the *Eneas*, as opposed to the erotic discourse that threatens to subvert it. In turn, I consider a contemporary Latin Troy poem, itself connected with the Anglo-Norman court, which displays these themes in concentrated, even exaggerated form.

Finally, this section closes with a specific instance – the arms of Eneas – in which the redactor plays with learned Latin reference in a way that acknowledges the dangers of feminine power even while it describes the divinely wrought implements of militant conquest. But at the same time, the episode's recondite references hide that acknow-ledgement from the less Latin-reading members of the audience, including of course most of its women. In later sections of this chapter, I will show that these themes of patriarchy and empire in the learned Troy tradition are at the center of the *Eneas*, although they co-exist and ultimately negotiate with a nervous acknowledgement of the power of women, in figures like Dido, Camille, and Lavine. These themes of women's power and the disruptive potential of feminine erotics can also be identified in aspects of the Latin Troy tradition.

A number of details in the French poem suggest the redactor's close dependence on an annotated manuscript of Virgil. The redactor's procedure is dense with brief instructive asides reminiscent of the sort studied in Commentary I of All Souls 82 and identified in the earlier annotations of Peterhouse 158 and Additional 27304; these might be called "glossing lines." Most obvious are the redactor's passing identifications of the roles of the classical gods.[20] While it has been widely noted that the *Eneas* tends to downplay the direct intervention of the Pantheon in human events, nonetheless the poem does not suppress them entirely.[21] On the contrary, the redactor makes regular efforts to inform or remind his audience of mythological detail, if usually in the brief and general fashion characteristic of Commentary I in All Souls 82. For instance, the appearance of Venus is repeatedly "glossed" with the information that she is "la deesse d'amor" (lines 32, 102, 769, etc.); Juno is identified as "del ciel deesse" (line 93), Pallas as "deesse de bataille" (line 147), Aeolus ("Oleüs") as "li deus des vanz" (line 1016).[22] This kind of elementary mythography was widely available in sources like Servius and the Vatican Mythographers, but in this setting it reflects most closely the schoolroom study of Virgil.[23] The redactor is responding not just to an isolated text of the *Aeneid*, but also to the sort of information with which we have seen it surrounded in twelfth-century manuscripts. He is working with the entire codex.

Other sorts of glossing information enter into the more general flow of the story. When Eneas visits the Elysian Fields (in a passage much shorter than in the *Aeneid*), we are twice reminded that only virtuous souls, "li buen home," reside there (lines 2793, 2809). This reflects a detail twice provided by Servius and expanded yet further in the commentary of "Anselm."[24] Mythological background also enters the poem more overtly in such digressions as the Judgment of Paris and the adultery of Venus and Mars.[25] I will turn to the latter story below, when I discuss the arms of Eneas; the Judgment of Paris in the *Eneas*, as Barbara Nolan has proven, corresponds more closely to marginalia in Virgil manuscripts (one of them definitely English) than to other known versions in the Latin mythographical tradition.[26]

Exegetical emphasis on rhetoric in the Latin Virgil tradition has an even greater impact on the redactor's art. The frequent expansion of major speeches as they move from the *Aeneid* to the *Eneas* no doubt derives in good part from the more general schoolroom study of rhetorical *artes* popular in the period. But that interest is equally reflected in the study of Virgil and its record in the rhetorical marginalia of many of the more sophisticated twelfth-century (and earlier) Virgil annotators. For instance, as we have seen, rhetorical notes appear regularly in the commentary of "Anselm" and in the early marginalia of Peterhouse 158.[27] The pattern of rhetorical expansion in the *Eneas* occurs as early as the redactor's version of Aeneas's monologue during the storm in *Aeneid* 1 (lines 94–101). Aeneas's seven lines turn into Eneas's twenty (lines 211–30), a far longer speech even given the shorter French octosyllabic line. In general, the speeches are most highly crafted and elaborate when they occur in more judicial contexts, as in the exchanges between Turnus and various opponents at the court of Latinus. This suggests a link between such "pedagogical" attention to rhetoric (both in Latin manuscripts and the vernacular poem) and the *Eneas*'s wider interest in law and the administration of empire.

Religious ritual and other practices of ancient society provide still another area in which substantive preoccupations of the twelfth-century Latin marginalia appear to have influenced the redactor of the *Eneas*.[28] We saw in chapter 2 (pp. 59–60) that the mid-twelfth-century Commentary IA of All Souls 82 displayed sophisticated interest in details of pagan religious ritual. Such attention to ancient practice seems to be reflected in moments like Sinon's description in the *Eneas* of preparations for his sacrifice. Virgil's passing reference to salted meal ("salsae fruges," 2.133) is expanded here to include its being sprinkled on the victim (information available in Servius) along with wine, oil, and ashes (possibly a pseudo-learned expansion).[29] Along with his invention of new episodes and other gestures of domestication, then, the redactor also repeatedly reminds his audience of differences in time, place, and society. This is especially the case in his frequent and specific accounts of cremation and burial practice, where he regularly refers to the difference of "lor loi" and "la costume de lor loi."[30]

The interest in the ancient "law" of burial seems to extend in occasional marginalia to a more general attention to the law and running of society. As we saw in chapter 3, when Virgil says that Aeneas brings his "gods" into Latium (1.6), the early annotator of Peterhouse 158 notes, "gods, that is good laws."[31] An early thirteenth-century *accessus* copied in England makes the skillful waging or entire avoidance of warfare, not (as is usually found) ethical character formation, the central *utilitas* of the epic.[32] Even the *Eneas*'s use of *ordo naturalis* rather than Virgil's *ordo artificialis* has a background in marginal explanations, and implications beyond just the arrangement of events.[33] For when certain notes and *accessus* undertake to summarize the epic in *ordo naturalis*, they betray centers of attention symptomatic of the legal, military, and imperial preoccupations mentioned above.

An *accessus* at the end of BL Add. 32319A gives a particularly telling summary of Virgil's *materia*:

For he shows that Aeneas, after the destruction of Troy, was counselled by Apollo that he should seek his mother's breast – words interpreted by Aeneas's father Anchises – and came with a number of ships (namely twenty) via Thrace to Crete, whence Anchises, since he was not ignorant of antiquity, said Teucer had come. But when a great pestilence arose there they were forced to depart. They entered their ships a third time and, passing through Sicily where Anchises died, and Carthage where they finally lingered a long while, they came to Italy, whence Dardanus had come. At the time when Aeneas came to Italy, Latinus reigned there. Hearing of Aeneas's arrival, Latinus immediately promised him the hand of his daughter, whom her mother had earlier promised to Turnus. For this reason a war arose between Turnus and Aeneas; finally Turnus was defeated. But his mother, not daring to remain, fled to Flanders and founded there a city called Tournai from the name of her son. These brief points are made about the book's content.[34]

Several points emerge from this passage. First, the *accessus* lays primary emphasis on lineage and social foundation, both of Rome and Tournai. The prominent details about Teucer and Dardanus derive more from preoccupations in the commentary tradition than from Virgil. Second, and linked to the issue of lineage, is an interest in the naming of places. Significantly, the *Eneas* too closes with a reference to Romulus's foundation and naming of Rome. Third, this is a summary about knowledge and empire passing from father to son, rather than about historical or erotic loss. Troy is quickly dismissed; Lavinia does not possess a name here and no reference whatsoever is made to Dido.[35] (We will see the same narrative silence about Dido in a Latin poem examined below.) Finally, the passage shows a fascination with the continuing westward movement of those touched by the Trojan war. This of course is exactly the context in which the *Eneas* was produced – an audience of Angevins for whom imperial expansion into England was neither old nor uncontested history. Such a context is further marked by the manuscript association of the *Eneas* with the *Brut* (see chapter 1, p. 20).

Interest in lineage, and the particular attention to a theme of lineal return through Teucer and Dardanus, is very widespread indeed in the commentaries and recurs regularly in the *Eneas*.[36] (Such lineal return of course corresponds nicely to the Normans' original claims to English kingship.) Servius outlines the ancestry of the Trojans in several places, and simplified versions occur in many manuscripts.[37] An entry in Additional 27304 is especially intriguing: "Teucer and Dardanus were Aeneas's original fathers, and thus Aeneas heard in the oracles 'Seek your first father.'"[38] The oracle "quoted" in the final words is not Virgilian and seems to usurp Virgil's oracular counsel to seek the *antiquam . . . matrem* (*Aen.* 3.96).

If these themes of empire, westward-moving power, genealogy, and social order emerge only glancingly in the learned annotation of the *Aeneid*, they appear far more coherently in some Latin poems of the twelfth century. Shorter Latin poems retelling the matter of Troy and its victims are very widespread in the high Middle Ages, especially during the twelfth century, and circulate widely thereafter.[39] By their very brevity, these poems offer particularly concentrated developments of the thematics examined above, and provide yet a further context for the imperial theme in the *Eneas*. I would like to consider just one such poem here, frequently copied both in France and England and closely connected to the intellectual milieu of the *Eneas*. In this poem, as in the Latin summary quoted above, we see the threat of feminine eroticism displaced, and emphasis placed instead on the direct line of narrated history, figured particularly by the genealogical line.

The 124-line "Viribus, arte, minis" ("Through the power, fraud, threats of the Greeks, Troy is delivered to destruction ... ") was written by an early tutor of Henry II, Pierre de Saintes.[40] According to the *Chronicle* of Richard of Poitiers, because Pierre was learned in poetry beyond all those of his age as far as the Pyrenees, he was chosen to teach the young Henry.[41] His poem is in fact a somewhat stilted affair, an overtly, even pretentiously learned work, full of indirect allusion to ancient names ("Pelides," not Achilles; "Sponsus Penelopes," not Ulysses) and Trojan episodes. It is not a redaction that would open the story to a wider audience, but rather a poem for the *illuminati*, as might be expected from a royal tutor. Whatever its virtues as a poem, though, its widespread and enduring manuscript tradition suggests real impact, and it provides a significant context for the far more ambitious *Roman d'Eneas* which was to be produced in the milieu of Henry's court.[42] It will be remembered that All Souls 82 may well have belonged to another of Henry's tutors (see chapter 2, pp. 44–46); between them, then, these two artifacts provide a good sense of the vision of Troy and Rome to which the future king was educated.

Pierre's poem narrates the fall of Troy and the foundation of Rome, but simply omits any reference to Aeneas's delay in Carthage. (This is comparable to the strategy in the *accessus* quoted above.) Instead, it casts the subversive danger of woman onto the earlier figure of Helen, thus producing an Aeneas of uninterrupted imperial intention and marital purity. The ambivalence of eros is suppressed here, to be replaced with repeated diatribes against Helen for the grief she caused Troy and the Trojans ("Such a woman, alas! the cause of such evils!"[43]), and overt warnings against illicit sexuality: "Lest anyone love rashly, let overthrown Troy teach him to beware, / Which by Paris's crime is made nothing ... "[44] Pierre organizes his narrative around an uncomplicated symmetry between imperial fall resulting from adulterous sin, and imperial refoundation through Aeneas's battles and marriage: "Thus Romulus's race rises up from Hector's" provides a neat closing line.[45]

Pierre makes his poem an imperial genealogy starring, toward its end, a normative Prince Aeneas thoroughly inscribed with the virtues to be imitated by a young Duke Henry. The adulterous Paris (whose sin is doubled by having insulted Juno) is balanced by the reverent and militant Aeneas: "Your piety keeps you safe, that you may seek new realms."[46] The poem thus extends Virgilian narrative into a wider pattern of prior sin, redemption through virtue and conquest, and later political resolution through imperial marriage:

> Ergo damnatae spe firmus, fidus Achate,
>   Hesperiae latae tendis in arva rate.
> Plurima bella geris, tibi dum loca debita quaeris;
>   sed fretus superis obvia quaeque teris,
> Turnus ut elatus tibi fata tuisque minatus
>   occubuit stratus, dum fodis ense latus.
> Pro qua certatur tibi regia virgo dicatur,
>   paxque reformatur, dum tibi nupta datur.
> Hinc processerunt qui Romam constituerunt,
>   qui, dum bella gerunt, fortia quaeque terunt
> Et sibi fecerunt nomen, quod in astra tulerunt,
>   ut, qui scripserunt pristina gesta, ferunt.
> [Therefore, sure of your hope in what is promised, trusting in Achates,
>   You strive by ship toward the plains of wide Hesperia.
> You wage many wars, while you seek the places owed to you,
>   But relying on the gods you crush what lies in your way.
> Haughty Turnus who threatened your fates and your people's
>   Has fallen slain, when you mutilate[d] his side with the sword.
> The royal virgin for whom you fought is declared yours,
>   And peace restored, once she is given you as bride.
> From her proceeded those who built Rome,
>   Who waging war crushed all fierce foes,
> And made for themselves a name, which they bore to the stars,
>   As they who have written of ancient deeds maintain.][47]

Thus Pierre narrates a simplified version of Aeneas's adventures, a version that privileges imperial and genealogical concerns and silences erotic and private dilations both Ovidian and Virgilian. This echoes those interests in genealogy, historical cause and imperial refoundation identified in the pedagogical marginalia. And it corresponds closely to the *Eneas*, with its expanded narration of the Judgment of Paris and the pacification of Latium by Eneas and his offspring.

Both in the inheritance of the pedagogical annotations surrounding the *Aeneid*, then, and in learned poems like Pierre's, the redactor of the *Roman d'Eneas* would have encountered a vision of Virgil and the Troy story in which the values of militant male conquest and empire building dominate. Below, I will be concerned to demonstrate the centrality of just such preoccupations in the long middle section of the *Eneas* (see pp. 200–10). There, the narrative of battle, truce, and ultimate settlement in Latium not only centers on empire, but inscribes through its Virgilian tale a legitimating prehistory for a whole gamut of political and legal values being pursued in Henry II's Anglo-Angevin empire.

This, however, is only part of the story of the "romance *Aeneid*" we encounter in the French poem. For balancing this middle section of the poem are long narratives of erotic delay, greatly expanded from Virgil, which explore the subtleties of feminine desire and its potential to subvert patriarchal history. But at his subtlest – and most playful – moments, the *Eneas* redactor can enfold both thematics simultaneously. At such moments, the redactor at once overtly narrates the work of male militancy and, by rather obscure references likely to have been fully understadable only to his learned and male readers, covertly acknowledges its endangerment by feminine desire and quest for power. I close this section on the links between learned Latinity and the vernacular poem by examining one such instance, the arming of Eneas.

In *Aeneid* 8, Virgil constructs a sequence of geographical and historical links between his own place and time and that of Aeneas. Virgil's Aeneas, seeking military alliance with Evander against Turnus, unwittingly visits the future site of Rome (8.97–101, 337–61); on his return toward Latium he finds the arms prepared for him by Vulcan at Venus's intercession, among them a shield that elaborately depicts his race's own future glory as late as Augustus Caesar in Virgil's own day (8.626–731).

At this point in the narrative, the redactor of the *Eneas* abandons Virgilian history for Ovidian erotics in the form of two excursus by which he fills in some mythological background to which Virgil alludes only briefly if at all: the adultery of Venus and Mars, and the story of Arachne's weaving contest with Athena.[48] He tells the story of Venus's adulterous affair with Mars, and Vulcan's vengeance by capturing and exposing the lovers in a fine net of his own making (lines 4353–93). It is for this reason, the redactor explains, that an angry Venus has avoided her marriage bed. The effect of the mythological excursus is not merely informative, though; this expansion gives fuller space to an instance of the power of feminine erotics to stir enmity between males, human or divine.[49] This kind of explicit attention to such stories, at which Virgil glances only in passing, had already ballooned into the margins of the Latin manuscripts, and here makes space for a brief Ovidian episode.[50]

But Venus, as narrated both in Virgil and in the *Eneas*, ultimately schools her own desires to serve the needs of her son and the threatened Trojan nation, returning to her spurned marital bed in the interests of military protection and the Latin line that will spring from military triumph. In both versions, the goddess of desire comes at this moment to serve history and imperial genealogy. The hero's arms, in the *Eneas* as in the *Aeneid*, are the product of a negotiation among gods regarding the possession of one female between two males. This is perhaps more pointed in the *Eneas* than in the *Aeneid*. For in Virgil, Aeneas receives arms that are wholly the product of Vulcan's work; but in the *Eneas*, while the arms themselves are Vulcan's, Venus adds to them a pennon which originally belonged to Mars. The ensemble thus more fully incorporates the Olympian competition over Venus, and in turn more neatly echoes the very battle over Lavine on which Eneas is engaged.

Where Virgil's shield is inscribed with the martial triumphs and imperial line guaranteed by Venus's return to her marriage bed, however, the arms in the *Eneas* are startlingly different, marvelous rather than historical and, as we will see, simultaneously referring to erotic conflict rather than patriarchal genealogy. Here (lines 4411–529) there is no ecphrasis of imperial danger and triumph: Eneas's arms are lovingly described wonders of natural power (marvelous stones and impenetrable fish skins) and divine technology (inlay, enamel, unbreakable steel).

Whatever their miraculous attributes, the arms of the *Eneas* are a fully recognizable set of twelfth-century aristocratic military regalia: hauberk, helmet, shield, sword, and lance. Suspended from the lance, however, and thereby incorporated into the equipment of military conquest, is the pennon added by Venus, which leads to a second Ovidian excursus and another containment of subversive feminine power:

> bien fu tissue et bien ovree
> et par listes fu d'or broudee;
> cent torsels valut d'altres dras.
> Par anvie l'ot fet Pallas:
> ele l'ovra par grant mestrie,

quant Arannes l'ot aatie;
els ovrerent a entençon,
dont fist Pallas cest confanon.
Por ce qu'el fist meillor ovraigne,
Aranne mua an iraigne,
qui contre li s'ert aatie;
s'entente ot mis tote sa vie
en tailes faire et an filer,
por ce ne puet ancor finer:
toz tens file iraigne et tist,
sa filace de son vantre ist.

(4527–42)

[It was well woven and finely worked, embroidered with gold in bands, and worth a hundred pieces of other cloth. Pallas had made it out of envy. She had worked it with great skill when Arachne had provoked her to a contest. They vied with each other in weaving, whence Pallas made this pennon. Since she made the better work, Pallas changed Arachne, who had challenged her, into a spider. She had devoted herself all her life to making cloth and spinning; therefore, she cannot stop yet: always the spider spins and weaves, with thread which issues from her belly.]

This apparently odd insertion of the pennon, and the bit of Ovidian mythology (*Metamorphoses* 6.5–145) hanging from it in the poem, bring to our attention two famous pieces of weaving, created in the competition between Athena and the human maiden Arachne.

The two tapestries which Ovid describes raise conflicting models of patriarchal justice and sexual violence, but only for those readers whose learning would have let them pursue their implications. In the surviving textile now adorning Eneas's lance, Athena records a quarrel between gods – herself and Neptune – over the allegiance of Attica and the very name of Athens, and depicts the judicial council of twelve gods settling the dispute (*Met.* 6.70–102). Only in its corners does Athena display human revolt and its swift suppression (*Met.* 6.85–102). The disagreement was decided in favor of Athena, the most patriarchal of the goddesses, the goddess of battle and reason; Athena of course is male-born, sprung from the head of Zeus split by an axe blow from Vulcan, whose arms her weaving now decorates.[51] Even the triumph of the goddess is thus encircled by a sequence of patriarchal powers, and even the woven scene of her triumph here becomes a merely decorative embellishment hanging from the arms of Vulcan. This scene of calm judgment is the ensign, provided by Venus but woven by

Athena and earlier owned by Mars, under which Eneas will conquer Turnus and Latium.

But, significantly, the *Eneas* does not describe or dwell upon the pennon itself. Rather, the redactor narrates at some length the conflict which led to its production and the fate of Athena's challenger, Arachne, a figure of willful feminine revolt against the gods, whose own tapestry tauntingly reminds them of their own habits of sexual deception and violence, with scenes of Europa, Leda, Danae, Proserpine, and others (*Met.* 6.103–28). This narrative attention, moreover, ironically privileges Arachne's weaving over Athena's.

Arachne perfectly embodies the female challenge to patriarchal order and values which always ends in the *Eneas* by being suppressed, bracketed, or suspended. Indeed the story itself delays the description of Eneas's martial gear, and thus its record of erotics and feminine power also performs the romance structure of narrative dilation. If Arachne's subversive potential is technical rather than erotic, that of a weaver rather than a lover, she nonetheless weaves the story of the pantheon's sexual violence against mortal women. We will see a related theme of *un*weaving and spatial dilation in the narrative of Dido in the following section. Arachne's punishment is not just her transformation, we are reminded, but a permanent if asexual dilation, endlessly carrying out that most centrally female task of spinning and weaving. Athena's weaving, on the contrary, affirms the order of the pantheon, including herself, and banishes to the corners, the margins, her four scenes of futile human striving with the gods.

This last detail – the pennon on the arms of Eneas and its mythological background – thus inscribes not just the dominance of a patriarchal pantheon over the threatening ambition of a mortal woman, but also the suppression of her woven reminder of the violence characteristic of that pantheon. At a climax of Enean triumph and access to imperial power, the pennon nonetheless provides a brief moment of ironic Ovidian viewpoint on that triumph. The arms of Eneas move from the historical and prophetic thematics of Virgil to negotiations over control of the feminine – both in the divine order of the sexual enjoyment of Venus, and in the human order of sexual violence visualized, then suppressed. The reminder of a contest between women is rendered a part of the tools of aristocratic battle over land. The narration, too, perfectly enacts the suppression that cannot resist telling what it suppresses. While it is Athena's pennon that Eneas carries, and not that of the defeated Arachne, it is nonetheless

Arachne's challenge and defeat, not the pennon of the patriarchal goddess, that is fully narrated. Yet even the full tale of that subversion would be partly hidden from all but the text's more classically educated readers.[52]

Between these two mythological excursus on Venus and Arachne lies the elaborate description of Eneas's wondrous arms (lines 4411–522). But these arms themselves also practice a simultaneous recapitulation and cooptation of a prior and subversive female presence in the narrative – that of Dido and Carthage, her city of marvels – to the ends of militant male aristocracy. For Eneas's arms revive a dense and distinct pattern of images and themes earlier encountered in more overwhelming form during Eneas's own erotic dilation in Libya, and later to be associated with the equally unsettling figure of Camille. The arms are wonders of technical skill, though divine here rather than human; they have extraordinary strength and resistance and are decorated with such luxuries as inlay, gold, and enamel plates. But they also benefit from natural marvels: the helmet and shield made from skins of fish, the helmet decorated with precious gems and its nose plate protected by an unbreakable stone, and the shield also decorated with gems and lit by a carbuncle set in the boss. The sword's pommel is of emerald, its scabbard made from the tooth of a fish. Much emphasis is placed on the mercantile value of the arms, the helmet worth one hundred forty besants (4430), Venus's pennon worth one hundred pieces of any other cloth (4529). Finally, writing comes into play with Vulcan's inscription of his mark and his name in letters of gold on the blade of the sword (4481). As we shall now see, these images of technology, natural marvel, and mercantile exchange are all linked to the central erotic danger posed by the story's most challenging woman, Dido.

CONTAINING DIDO

As we see in the allusive structure of the arming of Eneas, the French poem's redactor was not writing just a straightforward hymn to imperial conquest and patriarchal lineage in the mode of Pierre de Saintes's Latin poem. Rather, the *Eneas* redactor incorporates, if nervously and covertly, competing subversive powers of feminine eroticism (Venus) and quest for power (Arachne). Other moments in the poem, to which we now turn, explore more openly a tension between, on the one hand, the preoccupations of empire and male lineage, and on the other, the potentially subversive, dilatory voice of female will, both erotic and political. Such a tension between eros and history lies at the center of what I am calling the "romance *Aeneid*," particularly as it enters the vernacular literatures of the high and later Middle Ages. These potential dangers to imperial history are registered especially in the figure of Dido. But the themes that cluster around Dido and her city themselves have roots in aspects of the Latin Troy tradition.

Dido has long been a center of critical attention in scholarship on the *Roman d'Eneas*, especially because her romance with Eneas, accompanied by extended dialogues and plaints, marks a significant entry of Ovidian erotic psychology into early French vernacular literature.[53] This is indeed a centrally important element in the *Eneas*, balanced toward the end of the poem by the even more original love affair between Eneas and Lavine. Both these expansions by the *Eneas* redactor are major incidents of erotic dilation typical of the "romance *Aeneid*," delaying imperial fate through the pressure of an inserted Ovidian casuistry. Their resistance to historical development (a resistance finally controlled in the case of Lavine, as we will see) pursues thematics of longing and erotic death-wish.[54]

The *Eneas* redactor would have found an authoritative model for his exploration of women in the Troy story in that other great Latin school author of the high Middle Ages, Ovid. Ovid gave voice to a whole range of women connected directly or indirectly to Troy and its aftermath. The fall of Troy in *Metamorphoses* 13 is dense with women's splendor and anguish: the sufferings and transformation of Hecuba, Polyxena's courageous speech before being sacrificed to the spirit of Achilles, the mourning and fury of the Trojan women. Ovid makes space here for women who are left silent or near-silent in Virgil's narrative of the fall of Troy, and these female voices emerge with their own power and potential violence from the military battles surrounding them. The letters of the *Heroides* give almost exclusive attention to the desires and laments of women, many of them connected to Troy.[55] And Ovid's Dido in the *Heroides* provides a particularly telling counterbalance to Virgil, for she reformulates the grandeur and tragic historical destiny of the Virgilian Dido in a character at once more intimate, more sentimental, and perhaps more accessibly human.

Virgil's Carthage and Virgil's Dido are elaborately interplicated in the historical fall of Troy, and prophesy, for Virgil's readers,

Carthage's future destruction by Rome. In the epic's most famous use of *ordo artificialis*, the very events of Troy's fall are narrated by Aeneas at Carthage, at the banquet during which Dido falls in love with her guest. The broken walls by which the Trojans admitted the horse (2.234) are later echoed by Carthage's half-built walls (4.86–89), left unfinished by the love-sick queen. Dido's deepening and uncontrollable love is figured by flood and fire, both of which revive patterns of imagery from *Aeneid* 2. And the literal flames and toppling towers of Ilium recur in Dido's flaming pyre, on which she kills herself with the arms Aeneas had once used at Troy. Her final speeches, notoriously, call her people to perpetual enmity with the Romans. Particularly in these speeches, love and rancor link together erotic humiliation with pride in the city she has founded:

> I have built a handsome city,
> have seen my walls rise up, avenged a husband,
> won satisfaction from a hostile brother...
> I shall die unavenged, but I shall die.
>
> (4.655–60)

By contrast, the Ovidian Dido positions herself domestically rather than historically, between wives and husbands rather than cities; hers is "a softer emotional world" than in Virgil.[56] Whereas the declining nightmares of Virgilian Dido are indeed populated both by the voice of Sychaeus and the pursuit of "ferus Aeneas," they always close with Dido as leader of a nation, however maddened and solitary, burdened with the work of empire and the fate of her people in a strange land (e.g. *Aen.* 4.460–68). Ovidian Dido, on the other hand, weaves herself into a sequence of marital partners and domestic groups, in which women appear as helpmeets (however betrayed) and mothers, rather than destroyers or founders of empire. Even when Ovidian Dido calls upon Venus and Amor, she does so in terms of family relation ("nurus" and "frater," *Her.* 7.31–32). And in Ovid's most striking innovation, his Dido claims to be pregnant with Aeneas's child (133–34). Ovid's Dido does cast herself both forward and back in Aeneas's history, but in terms of wives, not cities, predicting an *altera Dido* to come in Rome (*Her.* 7.17), and promising to appear to Aeneas as a shade just as Creusa (and the betrayed, bloody Hector) did while Troy burned (69–70). I will argue that much of Lavine's role in the *Eneas* is to function exactly as an *altera Dido*, but in a version rendered safe and containable.[57]

Removed from the context of history, her voice is preserved in the moment of the letter whereas the Virgilian Dido is ultimately silenced in ashes. Forever fixed in contemplation of her death, centered on her private loss, the Ovidian Dido is at once more pathetic, more persistent, and less dangerous than the Virgilian. These two Didonic voices, Virgilian and Ovidian, predominantly historical and predominantly erotic, exercise continuing and competing influences in the Troy story as it descends to the Latin and vernacular traditions of the high Middle Ages. Dido, and the feminine sentiment and power she carries, is alternately privileged and silenced in these versions. We have already seen her left aside in a twelfth-century summary of the *Aeneid* and in the Troy poem of Pierre de Saintes. I turn now to another high medieval Latin poem in the Troy tradition which provides an intensive instance of the Ovidian Dido in the imagination of the Middle Ages, and provides in turn an analogue in the Latin tradition for the thematics we will find associated with Dido in the *Eneas*.

The lovely brief sequence "Anna soror, ut quid mori / tandem moror?" ("Sister Anna, why do I so long delay my death?"), survives in an early thirteenth-century anthology produced in England, although it has extensive textual connections to a more widely attested Dido lament, Carmina Burana no. 100.[58] Written entirely in the voice of the abandoned Dido contemplating (and thus postponing) her death, it also explores the emotional and political disasters which have lead to her moment of final collapse. The poem opens and closes in direct address to Anna (1a "Anna soror ...," to 5b "O luce clarior, / Anna ..."), but moves into an internal monologue (2b, 3b–5a) which in turn is interrupted by an imagined speech of dismissal to the now-absent Aeneas (2b–3a, "Hospes, abi!" "Off with you, sojourner!"). Anna's role here is quite innovative. She is dramatically present throughout, listening to Dido's obsessive wish for death ("Mors michi uiuere," "It is death for me to live," 3b, 8).

The sequence exploits with extraordinary dexterity verbal and tonal echoes of both *Aeneid* 4 and *Heroides* 7. If it begins and ends with a domestic setting and private pathos reminiscent of the *Heroides*, it also rises to an angry if brief dismissal of Aeneas that better recalls the Virgilian Dido:

> Off with you, sojourner!
> Why exert yourself
> to slip away and secretly
> take flight?

> Dido isn't hurrying
> to weave any delays;
> although under a wintry sky
> she'd spare you
> and your tender son,
> not surrender you
> to torments of the sea.[59]

Dido's passing effort at anger here is close to, though less violent than, Dido at *Aeneid* 4.380–81: "I do not refute your words. I do not keep you back. / Go then, before the winds, to Italy."[60] The following two strophes in the sequence further call to mind preceding passages in the *Aeneid* (4.365–70), where Dido accuses Aeneas of having tigresses, not Venus, as a mother, and of being unmoved by her plaints. The sequence then goes on to lament the political consequences of the affair, both to Dido's city and to her personal power, surrounded as she now is by hostile Libyans, her brother, and her disenchanted Tyrians: "Should I await the destruction / of what I built up, / the walls of my new city?"[61]

Of course this latter topic, as well as Dido's reference to the dangers of the wintry sea and the life of Iulus, equally echo topics in *Heroides* 7, as Dido attempts to delay Aeneas's departure.[62] But the double echo is crucial to the sequence's skilled balance. For the poet also, even more cleverly, uses Ovid's own signal quotation of Virgil – "Anna soror" (*Aen.* 4.9, *Her.* 7.191) – to establish his very complex temporal setting of confession and delay. The sequence, in effect, sets itself simultaneously at the Ovidian moment preceding death – the close of the letter – and at the Virgilian moment of late-night erotic confession – the opening of *Aeneid* 4. Thus, while it inscribes a Virgilian Dido fixed in her fullest initial servitude to desire, that desire, in this version, has from the start already led to the death-wish. And if the poem gives ear to Virgilian political crisis and anger, that is nonetheless both surrounded and eclipsed by Ovidian pathos.

Moreover, the Dido of this sequence speaks in an abnegation even deeper than either Ovid's or Virgil's. She knows what she has lost, both romantically and politically; but she exploits neither the resources of full Virgilian fury nor of Ovidian delay. Except for the very brief reference to the wintry sea, this Dido uses none of the Ovidian Dido's ploys to slow Aeneas's departure, omitting particularly Ovid's invention of a pregnancy by Aeneas. At the same time, she shows none of the Virgilian Dido's passing hopes of military or divine vengeance.

Indeed, at the crucial moment she lacks even the will for suicidal self-vindication, turning instead to her sister for release. As Dronke puts it, "through that unheroic weakening this Dido is revealed in her most lovable aspect."[63]

The sequence's pathetic intensity derives, I believe, from this double echo and double time-scheme, producing a Dido whose loss is fully Virgilian (both civic *and* erotic) and whose delay is largely self-directed, even sadder and more powerless than the Ovidian. Her almost erotic servitude to fire and sword ("gladii ... obsequio," 5a, 11–12), as the sequence nears its close, is so complete that she cannot even use the sword against herself. Instead, both Dido and the poem remain trapped in that same moment of delay at which they began, which she explicitly calls a "mortis dilatio":

> Oh! too bitter
> this manner of life!
> This delay of death
> is another death to me!
> (1a, 6–9)

Whatever the abasement of Dido's voice in the sequence, however, it is that voice alone that speaks here; the Aenean, the divine, the imperial are surrounded, usurped by the dominant female voice and the cause of erotic desire and mortal *dilatio*. The thematics of imperial foundation and loss are bracketed by those of love and death which are, as we will further see, the central urges of the romance *Aeneid*.[64]

The sequence "Anna soror," then, acknowledges the Virgilian Dido and the political context of her plight in a series of verbal and topical reminiscences of the *Aeneid*, but simultaneously folds her in a double moment of private erotic and mortal longing which literally brackets the Virgilian: a female voice, however weak and pathos-ridden, controls the entire poem. The voice remains moving and insistent, but loses its imperial aspect. This Dido no longer threatens to suspend Aeneas's fate either by tempting him into her own *dilatio* (as the Ovidian Dido still tries to do), or by her aetiological call for perpetual enmity between Carthage and Rome. We will witness a closely similar structure of bracketing off Dido in the *Eneas*, though in the French poem she is enclosed in space – the little urn that holds her ashes and its enclosing tomb – rather than suspended in time.

In what follows, however, I primarily want to pursue several related aspects of the queen and her city which I think pose threats as consequential to Eneas and the imperial aristocracy he represents as does her strictly erotic danger. I am especially interested in the depiction of Carthage as a focus of moveable wealth, technology, and trade – sources of power that implicitly challenge the military ethos of the Trojans and their destiny of empire through conquest. Dido's seductive dilation, moreover, is figured in the *Eneas* exactly in terms of those dangerous civic qualities. Finally, I will suggest that the containment of those combined threats is as much imagistically enacted by the arms we have just studied as it is literally enacted by Dido's political fall and death.

The *Eneas* redactor begins his story of Dido like Virgil's, with the murder of her husband Sicheüs by her brother, but with a significantly altered motivation: Virgil's Pygmalion kills through blind love of gold ("auri caecus amore," 1.349), whereas in the *Eneas*, Dido's unnamed brother wants political power ("por ce qu'il volt avoir l'enor," 386). This leaves Dido, who flees Tyre with "great treasures of silks and cloth, silver and gold,"[65] more the exclusive figure of moveable wealth, while her men fight to control land. Almost as important to the redactor as her initial wealth, though, is Dido's great skill ("grant angin," 393) in the arts of profitable trade. Her first and fundamental gesture in the *Eneas* is one of expansion and financial multiplication – another form of dilation – told in yet another excursus making space for a story to which Virgil (*Aen.* 1.367–68) only glancingly, even nervously, refers:

> An cel païs est arivee;
> au prince vint de la contree,
> par grant angin li ala querre
> qu'il li vandist tant de sa terre
> com porprendroit un cuir de tor,
> doné l'an a argent et or;
> et li princes li otroia,
> qui de l'engin ne se garda.
> Dido trancha par correetes
> lo cuir, qui molt furent grelletes;
> de celes a tant terre prise
> c'une cité i a asise;
> puis conquist tant par sa richece,
> par son angin, par sa proëce,
> que ele avoit tot le païs
> et les barons a soi sozmis.
>
> (391–406)

[She arrived in this land and went to the prince of the country. With great cleverness she went to ask him if he would sell her as much of his land as the hide of a bull would enclose, and she gave him gold and silver for it. The prince, not suspecting a trick, granted it to her. Dido cut the hide into very thin thongs; with these she took so much land that she founded there a city. Then she conquered so much by her wealth, by her cleverness, and by her prowess, that she possessed the whole country, and the barons submitted to her.]

The redactor thus opens space in the Virgilian narrative for the story of Dido opening space for herself in the prince's domain.[66] If Arachne challenged the pantheon by her weaving, Dido's *angin* succeeds through a kind of unraveling that puts her in the company of Penelope, who unwove to create time as Dido undoes the hide to create space. Dido's subterfuge links in one direction to her gender by its power of multiplication through the establishment of an empty zone,[67] and in the other direction it links to her compatriots' skills in technical production, particularly of fabric, and the multiplication that comes from trade.[68]

Dido's *angin*, a capacity thrice noted in this brief passage and made part of her triad of powers (*richece*, *angin*, and only lastly *proëce*), also harkens back to an earlier trade similarly though less directly connected to an erotic heroine and the downfall of a city: the Judgment of Paris (99–182), the very first of the redactor's mythological excursus. For Paris too considered "par grant angin" (131) how he might best profit from his choice among wealth, courage in battle, and the world's most beautiful woman.[69] But both subversive traders, and the feminine eroticism that fuels their danger, are to be echoed and contained in the arms of Eneas, themselves laden with gold and silver, produced by Vulcan's "workmen (*jingnor*) who were beating the gold and silver."[70]

The civic space opened by Dido's *angin* is itself a marvel of production and multiplication, both economic and literal. Virgil describes Carthage as "extremely rich / and, when it came to war, most fierce."[71] But the depiction of Carthage in the *Eneas* cuts this emphasis in half, for while the later Carthage is *dives opum*, there is little recognition given there to Virgil's *studiisque asperrima belli*. Carthage is indeed depicted as a wondrously devised military structure, but that structure and its wonders are entirely defensive. Situated behind elaborate outworks, this Carthage has impenetrable walls of marble and adamant, themselves made "par grant anging" (424), and supplied with magnets that hold fast any armored aggressor (433–40).[72]

On the inside of these same protective walls is an arcade housing Carthage's central activity – not war, but trade:

> grant marchié i avoit toz dis;
> la vendoit an lo vair, lo gris,
> coltes de paile, covertors,
> porpres, pailles, dras de color,
> pierres, espices et vaiselle;
> marcheandie riche et bele
> i pooit l'an toz tenz trover;
> ne se poüst hom porpenser
> de richece que el mont fust,
> dont en cel leu planté n'eüst.
>
> (449–58)

[There was always a large market there, where men sold silk, furs, quilts of satin, coverlets, purple cloth, gowns, colored clothes, precious stones, spices, and plate. Rich and beautiful merchandise could always be found there. One could imagine no luxury in the world which was not there in plenty.]

The city's elaborate architecture and gorgeous decoration reflect both the technical abilities on which this trade is based (enamel, metal, and marble work), and the multiplication of value to which it gives rise. Even the much-discussed natural marvels of Carthage explicitly serve its technology and wealth. The little fish found near their shore are used to produce "la porpre chiere" (477) already mentioned as a feature of the market, and the *cocadrille* whose digestion is performed by birds is similarly used for a black dye (483–96).

The description of the city is almost obsessively numerate – one hundred colors of marble on the decorated walls, two hundred arches in the capitol, five hundred towers – and features a sequence of multiplication by tens that ends up surrounding Dido: seven principle gates, each of whose counts owes seven hundred knights to their ruler, whose fortress wall has seven thousand enamel plaques.[73] Such numbers further figure the unnerving power of expansion by which Dido tricked the obliging local prince, and which links her city's mercantile *angin* and her gender. The nearby temple to Juno, goddess of both wealth and childbirth according to the Second Vatican Mythographer,[74] is "riche a desmesure" (517), "rich beyond measure" as Yunck translates, but also rich excessively, beyond normal limits.[75] This tone of possible excess is part of a broader pattern in which, as we will see, imperial rule is associated with measure, and threats to it (particularly erotic threats) are described in terms of excess or "desmesure."

The expansion of wealth through the mere manipulation of capital, either in usury or trade, was of course deeply suspect in the Middle Ages, and especially so when trade began to exert new pressures on society in the eleventh and twelfth centuries. Neither merchants (whose practice was called *ignobilis mercatura* in the eleventh century) nor moneylenders could follow their trade without sin, according to theologians like Peter Damian, Peter Lombard, and Honorius of Autun.[76] But even money itself, as Lester Little writes, "was seen as an instrument of exchange that had devil-like, magical powers of luring people and then of corrupting them."[77]

It is just the lure of this dangerous *desmesure*, commercial and erotic – figured in the city, its queen, and its goddess – that threatens both the imperial military ethos of the aristocratic Trojans, and the marital fate of their leader.[78] The narrative itself will contain the erotic threat, but it is the arms of Eneas (and later the tombs of the dead around him) that at once revive and cooptate to imperial ends the riches of Carthage. The arms are also feats of technology, marvels (4417, 4449) now made to serve military conquest. Their extraordinary strength and resistance translate Carthage's impenetrable defensive walls to purposes of imperial aggression. They are made largely of silver and gold, the source of Dido's initial power, and almost each piece has enamel-work decoration, like Dido's own palace. The helmet and shield are fashioned from wondrously strong skins of fish (4428, 4445– 47), recalling and transforming the sea creatures that served Carthaginian trade. The helmet, further, is decorated with precious gems ("pierres naturaus," 4438) which at once duplicate the rich gems sold in the Carthage market (453–4) and the hogshead of precious stones ("chieres pieres naturalz," 508) set in the walls of Dido's palace. And, as noted earlier, the great exchange value of the arms is twice repeated, the helmet worth one hundred forty besants (4430), Venus's pennon worth one hundred pieces of any other cloth (4529).

Dido's political power, as we have seen, is presented in terms of her skillful purchase and her city's trade; but so, equally, is her eroticism, to the extent that her sexuality is ultimately encoded through the commodities of her city's mercantile splendor. Dido is easily convinced by Anna that she can abandon her oath to remain faithful to Sicheüs, but she remains uncertain of Eneas's love. Following this conversation, her first effort at seduction is by the display of the city itself:

Lo Troïen prent par la main,
de s'amor n'ert ancor certain;
demeine lo par la cité,
se li mostre sa richeté
et son chastel et son palés.
(1393–97)

[She takes the Trojan, of whose love she is not yet certain, by the hand,
leads him through the city, and shows him its wealth and her castle and
her palace.][79]

But this simultaneously endangers Dido's own power. In recentering
public wealth around her body, exchanging *onor* for *amor* (1431–32),
Dido abandons the building and protection of Carthage, cooling
toward her public role ("A nonchaloir a mis lo regne," 1427, see also
1411, 1417) as the erotic flame (776, 809, 814, 1385) grows hot within
her. Her men begin to murmur against her, and the redactor here
begins to join with their voice, as he will do more explicitly later on.

Dido's mercantile eroticism intensifies on the hunt as the affair
approaches consummation. In a passage close to Virgil, but with the
extra impact of echoing a dominant theme of wealth and trade, Dido is
enrobed in the symbols of her city's wealth:

La raïne se fu vestue
d'une chiere porpre vermoille,
bandee d'or a grant mervoille
trestot lo cors desi as hanches
et ansemant totes les manches.
Un chier mantel ot afublé,
menüemant ert d'or goté;
a un fil d'or ert galonee,
et sa teste ot d'orfrois bandee.
Aporter fist un coivre d'or,
qu'el fist traire de son tresor;
cent saietes i ot d'or mier,
les fleches erent de cormier.
(1466–78)

[The queen had dressed herself in an expensive purple material banded
very beautifully with gold all over the body as far as the hips, and
likewise all over the sleeves. She wore an expensive cloak, finely
decorated with gold in drops, trimmed with a golden thread, and on her
head she had a band embroidered with gold. She had brought with her
a golden quiver which was taken from her treasure. There were a
hundred arrows of pure gold, and the arrows were of fruitwood.]

The poetry echoes *or* even more densely and repetitively than Virgil's does *aurum*, in a virtual incantation of gold.[80] Dido's dress of *chiere porpre* clothes her in the stuff of Carthage's production and trade; even her horse is "all covered with gold and precious stones."[81]

If, as we have seen, the goods and architecture of Carthage are repeated, cooptated and thus contained by the arms of Eneas, this Dido and her gold-decorated purple are recapitulated in Eneas's first pennon, the one he abandons for the pennon of Athena and its thematics of patriarchy:

> Cent ansoignes mist el donjon
> et en mileu son confanon,
> qui fu de porpre o listes d'or ...
> (4267–69)

[He placed a hundred ensigns on the fortress, and in the center his own pennant, of purple silk with bands of gold.]

This recapitulation of Dido's erotic value in the pennon, which disappears in favor of Athena's, further reinforces the thematics of a suppressed feminine challenge to male will and control.

Dido might appear to be exercising choice in her decision to turn from mourning Sicheüs to her desire for Eneas, and in her shift of civic wealth to erotic value. But we have already noted the complaints of her male retainers at such a choice, and the language of the sexual encounter in the cave further serves to undermine this apparent exercise of female desire:

> Estes les vos andos ansanble,
> il fait de li ce que lui sanble,
> ne li fait mie trop grant force,
> ne la raïne ne s'estorce,
> tot li consent sa volenté;
> pieça qu'el l'avoit desirré.
> (1521–26)

[Here are the two of them together. He does with her what he wishes, nor does he use very much force at all, nor does the queen resist: she consents to him with all her will, for she has long desired him.]

Significantly here, male *force* – however restrained – precedes and obviates feminine *volenté*. He does not use too much force, but he does use force, and the implication is that Eneas takes a sexual decision, by which Dido's willing desire is rendered almost superfluous. Like Lavine later, such a Dido does have desire, even a kind of choice, but a choice pre-empted and effectively obviated by prior male decision.

Indeed, as David Shirt has pointed out in a study of the language of death in the Dido episode, the very "choice" offered by Anna, between Sicheüs and Eneas, is no choice at all. "Of course, Dido has no such choice: in giving way to her feelings for Eneas, and ostensibly opting for life, Dido takes her own life. Anna's life/death argument is fabricated merely to persuade Dido that she is free to act of her own accord ... "[82] Because of her prior oath to remain faithful to Sicheüs, any act of sexual choice by Dido must be a choice of death. We have seen Dido similarly boxed within mortal alternatives in the sequence "Anna Soror." Dido is fixed, despite her apparent agency, in a closed system of patriarchal power. She must remain faithful to the dead Sicheüs or die in her exercise of choice and desire for Eneas.[83]

But Dido does *appear* to be choosing, and this raises the wrath of all the surrounding barons whom she had earlier rejected. In the *Aeneid*, it will be remembered, the local prince Iarbas alone complained to Jupiter, who in turn sent Mercury to press Aeneas back upon his way. Here, male hostility is broader, more corporate; even the divine messenger, in a much abbreviated appearance, will be sent not by Jupiter but by "les deus" (1616).[84] To this company of male protest, the redactor emphatically adds his own voice:

> Antr'els dïent, et si ont droit,
> molt par est fous qui feme croit ...
> (1589–90)

[They say among themselves, and they are right, that he who believes a woman is very foolish ...]

Moreover, the very language of their anger again links Dido's sexual crime with a perceived misuse of her wealth, expressed both explicitly and by etymological association.[85] Fame spreads word that Dido holds Eneas "an putage" (1572), literally buying his sexual services; and that the two live "An luxure" (1573), which primarily suggests debauchery in Old French, but whose immediate source in Virgil ("luxu," 4.193) perhaps attracts it more closely to the Latin sense of extravagant wealth. Particularly interesting in this context is the repeated term *talant* (1596, 1607). Yunck is right to translate this by "will" and "desire," but the term's Latin origin (*talentum*, a weight of precious matter, usually gold) gives it suggestive economic resonance, verbally combining Dido's wealth and her desire.[86]

But the barons' most explicit concern is that Dido has broken her word to another man, her dead husband, undermining thereby a kind of feudal pledge:

or est mantie la fience,
trespassee est la covenance
qu'a son seignor avoit plevie.
(1597–99)
[now she has belied her promise and broken the agreement she had
pledged with her lord.]

This is her central challenge to their notion of order. It is the danger
Dido poses to possession and fidelity, and her replacement of feudal
relation with a private and movable *talant*, that troubles the noblemen,
not sexual morality. And it is only when Dido's ability to change is
definitively controlled in the suicide which is, ironically, her final
expression of *angin*, that a communal male voice once again can
approve of her.[87]

The affair between Dido and Eneas continues to be figured in the
language of money and feudal service as it moves to its conclusion.
After receiving his message from the gods, Eneas decides to leave
Carthage in secret: "en larrecin" (1646) and "a larron" (1694). But
again the word choices seem to bear echoes of their Latin sources, *latro*
and *latrocinium*; Eneas would leave Dido like a robber, as if her wealth
had been absorbed into his act of sexual possession. When Dido
challenges him, Eneas acknowledges that he has had her kindness
"molt richemant" (1778), and that he cannot now repay her
("gueredoner," 1781). In response Dido displays "mautalant" (1792),
"anger" as Yunck translates it, but also a loss or reversal of her earlier
talant. Her power of erotic delay, like her control of her rich city, is now
leaving her.

While the surrounding barons complain of Dido's broken *convenance*
with Sicheüs, Dido now comes to complain that love itself has broken
faith with her: "amors n'est pas vers moi loials," "Love is not loyal to
me" (1826). Here, a personified Ovidian figure of *Amor* is cast as the
disloyal feudal servant.[88] Dido's explanation of love's disloyalty in the
following line – "quant ne senton comunalement," "since we do not
feel alike" – extends the context of public, social relation. Dido's
feelings have indeed failed to work in a way acceptable to her *commun*,
leaving her increasingly isolated from the male voices rising around
her.[89] In a final plaint before her suicide, Dido returns to her broken
faith and makes Love virtually a military enemy:

por coi trespassai ge la foi
que ge plevi a mon seignor?
Ja me venqui ansi amor.

> Or est la fiance mantie ...
> (1988–91)
> [Why did I break the vow which I pledged to my lord? Thus Love has
> destroyed me indeed. Now the promise is belied ...][90]

The plaint ends with Dido's thoughts returning to those very rejected
barons whose protests against her lack of faith we have already seen.

Already dying from her self-inflicted sword wound, Dido delivers her
final speech (2039–67). This, it has often been noted, is utterly unlike
the Virgilian Dido.[91] Far from the queenly glory and furied prediction
of perpetual enmity found in the *Aeneid*, this Dido's speech is one of
final forgiveness and private, enfeebled pathos, very like the tone we
witnessed in the sequence "Anna soror." Here she admits that she has
cast away her public power and has at the same time failed to
guarantee the continuity of her rule by producing an heir:

> ci lais m'enor et mon barnage,
> et deguerpis sanz oir Cartage,
> ci perc mon nom, tote ma glore,
> mais ne morrai si sanz memore
> qu'en ne parolt de moi toz tens ...
> (2051–55)
> [Here I have thrown aside my honor and my power, and left Carthage
> without an heir; here I have lost my name and all my glory. But I will
> not die so utterly without remembrance that men will not forever speak
> of me ...]

Dido's assurance that she will remain indelibly in male *memore*,
especially that of the Trojans, replicates the situation of other
subversive women such as Arachne and, later, Camille: disempowered,
finally marginalized, she is nonetheless a persistent memory. If she is
denied the erotic dilation and public impact of restraining Trojan fate,
she feels assured of the temporal dilation of permanent presence in the
private Trojan imagination.

The mourning and burial of Dido perfectly enact this simultaneous
containment and temporal dilation of her threat. Once she is dead,
and her capacity for shifting and transforming value is thus
permanently controlled, she regains the praise of her people, who
"formant regretent sa proëce / et son savoir et sa richece" (2127–28,
"lamented deeply her courage and her wisdom and her wealth"). But
here Dido's dangerous *angin* is suppressed; she is dead now and can be
praised while disregarding her most subversive quality. This containment of Dido's *angin* and its capacity for dilation is literally practiced

with the immuring of her ashes in "une asez petite chane" (2131, "a very small urn").[92]

The urn then is placed in a tomb which repeats in miniature the wealth and artisanal skill of her city:

> puis i firent molt gent tombel,
> fait a esmals et a neel;
> un plus riche nus hom ne vit.
> Un epitaife i ont escrit;
> la letre dit que: "Iluec gist
> Dido qui por amor s'ocist;
> onques ne fu meillor paiene,
> s'ele n'eüst amor soltaine,
> mais ele ama trop folemant,
> savoir ne li valut noiant."
>
> (2135–44)

[Then they built a very noble tomb, made of enamel and inlay: no man has ever seen one more rich. On it they inscribed an epitaph, whose letters say: "Here lies Dido, who killed herself for love. There would have been no better pagan if solitary love had not seized her: but she loved too madly, and her wisdom availed her nothing."]

Dido is allowed her excessive value ("un plus riche nus hom ne vit," 2137) in the one situation she is certain not to transform.[93] And once again, she is placed in workmanship that is to be echoed in the arms of her abandoner, Eneas. The ashes of her body, dead from his sword in an act that clearly repeats his earlier phallic penetration, are placed in a tomb whose enamel and inlay ("a esmals et a neel") will in turn occur on the scabbard of Eneas's new imperial sword ("antaillié et neelé," 4510).[94]

Whatever the containment of her subversive eroticism and value by death and the little urn, Dido predicts for herself, as we have seen, a temporal and memorial dilation that will challenge all efforts finally to banish her danger from the text or its narrative. And this prediction is guaranteed not only by the tomb itself – the first of three that echo one another and mark turning points in the narrative – but even more by its epitaph, Dido's first moment of inscription, to be followed by a whole sequence of memorial texts emphasizing the temporal dilation that writing itself produces, including the *Eneas* itself. But if the epitaph serves to immortalize Dido, it also sets her floating in a temporal double bind as peculiar as that in the sequence "Anna soror," though broader in scale. For the most extraordinary element of Dido's epitaph is its egregious and surely self-conscious anachronism, describing the dead queen as one who could have been the best of pagans ("onques ne fu meillor paiene," 2141) but for her excessive love. The effect here, I think, is analogous with the double time-scheme of "Anna soror," placing the heroine in a perpetual dilation. For the epitaph, which itself intends to give Dido a tragic immortality, also vibrates tensely between its ancient "historical" moment and that of the Christian redactor and reader. It inscribes the reader in the past, or the ancient inscribers in the present, and Dido virtually out of time, literally monumental but historically ineffectual. Virgil's Dido, we remember, ended her life cursing Aeneas's people to perpetual enmity with her own race (4.621–29). It is in the context of the epitaph, and its denial of specific historical moment to Dido, that the redactor's suppression of this historical impact is most significant.

HISTORY AT THE CENTER: EMPIRE IN THE ENEAS

The final containment of Dido in her little urn, and her further suspension from linear history by the playful anachronism of her epitaph, produce one of the high moments in the *Eneas*'s repeated efforts to negotiate with feminine power and eroticism through strategies of containment, bracketing or marginalization. Indeed, the episodes of Dido and Lavine are themselves placed at the margins, the outer edges of the poem, in roughly its first and last two thousand lines. But Dido and Lavine, because they provide much of the overtly original material in the poem, have so interested critics that their centrality has been exaggerated; critics have tended to ignore the narrative's competing and finally greater attention to themes of patriarchy: militant aristocracy, the foundation of empire, and the establishment of royal power through battle, public argument, law, and lineage.[95]

The central bulk of the poem, roughly six thousand lines intervening between the two great erotic episodes, is occupied by the doings of a war of imperial conquest between the Trojans and the Latins. This alone shifts thematic weight from the *Aeneid*. Virgil's twelve books hinge on Aeneas's descent to hell and arrival in Latium (*Aeneid* 6–7), while the *Roman d'Eneas* centers around feudal war and disagreement over legal possession of land and woman, the matter only of Virgil's later books. In fact, the numerical center of the French poem, the exact middle ground between Dido and Lavine, is held by the heroic sacrifice of

Nisus and Eurialus (4906–5278), a decentered and less positive though equally pathetic episode in Virgil (9.176–502).[96] Where Virgil's *Aeneid* thus centers on the transformation of the hero and his historical and Pythagorean education in the underworld, the center of the *Eneas* is the entirely male, military, and amatory though not explicitly erotic union of Nisus and Eurialus.[97]

This latter episode is among the most extended close redactions of Virgil's text, although the *Eneas* shares none of Virgil's moral ambivalence about Euryalus's eagerness over booty. The only considerable narrative element that is left out by the French redactor, significantly, is any of the Virgilian reference to Euryalus's mother, the heroes' fears for her, or her mourning (*Aen.* 9.216–18, 283–302, 473–502). The female, even the maternal, is wholly suppressed at the poem's center, leaving all the more prominent its focus on male militarism and fidelity. There is in this pair no particular suggestion of homosexuality (as there will be later in Amata's accusations against Eneas), but what could reasonably be called a homosocial bond, based on established sentimental attachment, the link of youth and age, and militant virtues, and issuing in a glorious and sacrifical death in arms.[98]

Such elision of the feminine at the French poem's central point, and its broader emphasis on imperial conquest, recall the preoccupations of the Latin poem "Viribus, arte, minis . . . ," written by a tutor of Henry II, whose court later provided the audience for the *Eneas*. For "Viribus," we remember, dealt similarly with the story's most dangerous woman, Dido, by leaving her out altogether, to concentrate instead on the story's historical setting, on male militarism, and on the establishment of genealogy.[99] These, and related themes of imperial power such as law and rhetoric, occupy the center and the real bulk of the *Eneas*. Through these topics, the *Eneas* redactor is able to inscribe and thereby validate the modes of his own imperial society in the authoritative ancient tale he recounts.

We have already noted the *Eneas* redactor's insertion of his narrative into earlier history, when he recounts the Paris episode which resulted in the Trojan war. And equally like "Viribus," the *Eneas* closes by extending the Virgilian narrative into later history, looking forward to the nation and imperial lineage which will arise from the marriage of Eneas and Lavine (10131–56).[100] The extended sources and results of imperial war thus occupy brief parts of the poem's opening and close, while it centers on the mechanics of military conquest, the specific rhythms of siege, battle, truce, and council.[101]

The *Eneas* mirrors contemporary values, for example, in its frequent recursion to lineage and the establishment of genealogy, discussed above, in relation to the commentary tradition. R. Howard Bloch has pointed to the increasing transmission of land through blood kin, ever more narrowly conceived in terms of patrilineal descent, during the twelfth century.[102] And the *Eneas* makes the attachment of land to a new race a central theme, carefully looking forward (as we have seen) to its extension and link to Trojan blood through Eneas's offspring. Indeed, in the much reduced underworld episode in the *Eneas*, the redactor does nonetheless retain most of the information about Eneas's line, although trimmed of much of Virgil's historical and mythological elaboration.[103]

Even more interesting is the role of law and debate in the *Eneas*.[104] The poem gives repeated emphasis to baronial councils in which leaders take the advice of their nobles. Between them there is a shared thread of judicial rhetoric which has much in common with the rhetorical emphasis observed in the pedagogical tradition of *Aeneid* commentary. These councils gain prominence as Eneas approaches Latium (with, for example, the council in Sicily, 2228–41), and thereafter become part of the narrative rhythm of battle and truce. Legal terminology also strongly colors Eneas's later encounters with Dido in Carthage and the underworld, as he separates himself from her in preparation for his genealogical destiny. Whereas Virgil's Aeneas merely weeps and blames the gods for his unwilling departure from Carthage (6.455–66), the French Eneas engages in legalistic self-defense. He insists that while he may have been the immediate occasion ("acheison") for her death, he is legally blameless: "ge n'i oi colpes ne tort" (2634, "I have no guilt or wrong in it"). This final dismissal places Dido in the context of Eneas's move to a quite new intellectual system, one that demands legal responsibility over erotic fidelity.

These social processes emerge far more clearly in the challenge posed to them by Turnus, to whom I turn at the close of this section. Along with Turnus's genuinely historical danger, however, the central section of the *Eneas* also sees potential danger to its aristocratic order and historical destiny from two other fronts, erotic and feminine, though now in separate persons: Pallas and Camille.[105] And it responds to these dangers as it did to Dido, by enclosing and inscribing them in increasingly elaborate tombs which stand almost (but, crucially, not quite) outside of time.[106] Versions of dilation thus continue to haunt even the poem's historical middle as Eneas moves toward his imperial triumph over Turnus. The latter (Camille) links back to Dido through her appropriation of a traditionally male role and thus her threat to imperial patriarchy, and through the tomb where her remains are interred. The former (Pallas) links both to Dido and Camille through death and the tomb, and forward to Lavine by the love of Eneas; but Pallas also raises the spectre of a homosexual desire that could block Trojan lineage as surely as an erotic triumph by Dido or a military triumph by Camille would have done.[107]

The entire procedure of marking Pallas's death recapitulates, intensely if briefly, the tone and imagery of Dido's power and end. His elaborate bier is of silk, ivory, and gold, the stuff of Carthaginian wealth, topped with a feather bed or quilt ("colte de paille," 6117). This quilt has enamel plaques in its four corners, an echo at once of the enamels decorating Dido's palace and their recuperation in the pommel of Eneas's helmet.[108] Pallas's corpse is then dressed in a robe that was the gift of Dido to Eneas "quant elle l'anama" ("when she loved him," 6124). This garment answers the gift of clothing from Eneas to Dido, which she embraced as she approached suicide. Pallas's final covering literally implicates him – folds him – in the erotic danger earlier posed by Dido.

The lament of Pallas's father Evander in Pallantee (6301–14) echoes none of the Virgilian reference to *sors* or *fortuna* (*Aen.* 11.165, 180), nor the comfort the Virgilian Evander takes in the broader historical glory of dying in the service of Aeneas and Trojan destiny. Rather, he voices the more practical concern of how to retain baronial fidelity when there is no heir or *linnage* (6311), a fear which recalls Dido's sense of political isolation, herself without heir, as Eneas prepared to leave her.[109] In addition, the *Eneas* includes a long, entirely invented lament by Pallas's mother (6317–70), providing yet another voice of female hostility to Trojan conquest: "maudite soit lor sorvenue, / tote ma vie an ai perdue" ("Cursed be their coming, for I have lost all my life from it!" 6323–24). Pallas's mother not only revives Dido's language of a life lost to the Trojans, but twice echoes Dido's accusation of Trojan bad faith.[110]

With Pallas's splendid tomb, the language of *desmesure* again enters the poem, for the first time since Dido's Carthage, and the glory of artisanal ingenuity again blossoms forth around death.[111] The tomb's walls have stones of one hundred colors, decorated with animals and flowers, like those of Carthage; and like Carthage it is decorated with

gold, enamels and precious stones.[112] Yet this workmanship, meant for
Eneas's political ally Evander, but now serving his military companion
Pallas, again equally evokes the magnificence of Eneas's arms. Pallas's
entombment suspends him between eroticism and militarism.[113]

Fascinated attention is paid here to the medical preservation of
Pallas's body through a sort of closed recirculating system of balm and
turpentine (6468–84), which will keep the corpse from putrefaction
"toz tens," unless water should touch it. Whereas the striking
anachronism of Dido's epitaph strove to move her outside of time
altogether, the effort here is to create an endless suspension within
time, but one which, because physiological, is therefore inevitably
under some threat. This mood of physical preservation forever
endangered is reinforced by the vault's seal of bitumen. For the
redactor makes an almost coyly mysterious remark that only a thing –
"une rien" (6501) – which should not be named openly can penetrate
bitumen. John Yunck has suggested convincingly that the redactor
draws here from a passage in Isidore of Seville, where it is said that
bitumen can be broken only by "muliebribus inquinamentis" –
presumably menstrual blood.[114] The very learned obscurity of this
reference, characteristically, hides from the unlearned the female
power that it reveals, even while it acknowledges their politely
unspeakable danger. The site of perfect militant male eroticism, the
preserved body of the untouched prince loved by Eneas, is thus left in a
setting that can be subverted, returned to time, by feminine pollution.
The female remains, however playfully unnameable, at the center of
masculine loss, the suppressed, unspeakable voice of change at the door
of an artificial permanence.

The entombment of Camille takes this tone of threatened containment to a yet more elaborate stage. Camille's challenge to lineage and
male militancy clearly fascinated the redactor and his later readership.
The *Eneas* not only expands her role greatly from Virgil, but some of its
manuscripts illustrate her and her warrior maidens in battle.[115]
Camille's challenge is militant, not sexual, and she gains the
admiration, however uncomfortable, of the redactor. It is important
that the incongruity of her role, fighting on the battlefield rather than
in bed, is articulated by the thoroughly unpleasant Tarcon (7073–106),
in a speech that nonetheless voices the male fear of her feminine
desmesure.[116] For even if he can get Camille off the battlefield by paying
her gold, Tarcon taunts, her sexual voracity will take on a hundred of
his men without satisfaction. He thus again links female sexual power,

trade, and *desmesure* in a fashion that recalls Dido and Carthage, though in a different combination.

If anything, Camille is more dangerous to the renascent Trojan empire than was Dido, because she is touched by none of the erotic weakness that led to Dido's downfall. She combines queenship and kingship in a whole that is the more threatening because it appears to be self-sufficient. Camille opens herself to armed male penetration (and that in an ambush) not through eros, but only in her desire for the helmet of Cloreus.[117] But Cloreus's helmet is not just the golden one of Virgil (*Aen.* 11.774–75). Rather, in the *Eneas* it is further decorated with a seven-colored stone, other precious stones, and enamels (7169–76), all of which, especially the number, serve to recall qualities of Carthage and its queen.[118] And in a detail exactly like Virgil, Arranz's spear enters Camille just below the breast ("soz la memelle," 7202, cf. *Aen.* 11.803); but this in turn recalls the suicide of Dido, who also struck herself "soz la memelle" (2032).

These echoes of Dido are reinforced by the splendor of Camille's bier, and by the brief reappearance of natural wonder in the pillow stuffed with the feathers of the miraculous *calade* (7464–78). This linkage continues in Camille's tomb, whose pillar is decorated with flowers, beasts, and birds ("a flors, o bisches et oisiaus," 7553), at once recalling the tomb of Pallas and the walls of Carthage.[119] The tomb, with its series of concentric circles expanding at each level above the pillar, and topped with a miraculous mirror that shows all enemies as they approach, is the poem's crowning instance of human technology striving for an ever more unlikely dilation in the face of mortality, even as it encloses yet another threat to patriarchy and the Trojan empire.[120] Indeed, Camille's epitaph encodes the perfect values of militant male aristocracy:

> En porter armes mist s'entente,
> ocise an fu desoz Laurente.
>   (7667–68)
> [She gave herself to the bearing of arms and by arms was killed beneath Laurente.]

But this praise can finally be accorded to Camille, with whatever regret, only once she is dead and her real threat to Trojan empire is over.

The permanence of Camille's tomb and its inscribed praise of a virtue now rendered ineffectual, however, are the most endangered of them all. Not only is its architecture precariously balanced on a single pillar, but over the tomb, suspended from a chain "par grant mestrie" (7672), is a lamp that will burn forever ("toz jors," 7680, just like the preservation of Pallas's corpse), "se l'an ne la brise ou abat" ("if it is not broken or struck," 7681). Here, the slightest touch can undo the brightly burning suspension (perhaps a final echo of Dido's fire), and send it crashing back into time.[121]

Pallas and Camille – these twin threats to the work of history through genealogy and warfare, swiftly if precariously placed beyond the touch of time – are only punctuations, turning points within far more persistent rhythms of military conquest and the genuinely historical danger posed to Eneas by Turnus.[122] It is through Turnus, and by contrast to him, that the social model of the newly translated empire is articulated; and while Turnus's threat is indeed historical, it is the threat of archaism, of a history that could easily run backwards. If Dido's Carthaginian mercantilism posed a new danger to the kind of militarist, aristocratic ethos Eneas represents, then Turnus poses an old danger, the danger of decentralized, early feudal rule and the chaos of private war.[123]

Beginning with the Trojans' arrival in Latium, the *Eneas* employs, with increasing prominence, Virgilian themes of paternal genealogy and divine destiny to justify their imperial claims.[124] Even much earlier in the narrative (1186–89), Venus ordered Eneas to go to the land whence came his ancestor Dardanus, thus clearly establishing his twin genealogical and divine claim to the country. In Virgil, by contrast, it is only after much confusion and wandering that a definite geographical paternity succeeds (3.167–68) the initial ambiguity of the oracular instruction to seek an *antiquam ... matrem* (3.96).[125] Virgil's Trojans arrive already announced to Latinus in two prophecies as the fated rulers of Latium but, it is equally emphasized, as strangers.[126] In the *Eneas*, on the other hand, only their genealogical link and divine destiny are emphasized.[127]

These themes of course would ring loud in the ears of an audience accustomed to Norman propaganda justifying its own recent conquests in England. Moreover, as Bloch has reminded us, the twelfth century generally, and particularly the Anglo-Norman world, saw the older control of land through feudal relation being replaced by control through the relation of blood:

The transformation of fiefs into heritable *patrimoines* was accompanied by a growing consciousness of blood relations in distinction to those by marriage. The kin group as a spatial extension was displaced from within by the notion of the blood group as a diachronic progression ... Nobility became, in the period under consideration, synonymous with race (*sanguine nobilitatis*), as the undifferentiated bilateral mixture of agnatic and cognatic kin ceded to the enhanced prestige of a unilateral descent group.[128]

An audience sensitive to such a change (and even to the tenuousness of their ruler's claims thereby), would see Turnus arguing from the declining system of personal oath and expandable family, and Eneas buttressed by paternal genealogy and narrowing notions of family relation. Eneas's claim to Latium thus is simultaneously modern and, in its appeal to divinity, beyond historical challenge.[129]

If the argument of blood will leave Turnus with the declining claims of feudal oath, the argument of the gods will leave him in the company of dangerous women. Once past the very beginning of the poem and the story of Juno's hostility issuing from the Judgment of Paris, conflict among the gods disappears in the *Eneas*, and increasingly their intentions are spoken only through the genealogical heirs of Latium, the two kings Latinus and Eneas.[130] Instead, the opposition which in Virgil resides in the female divine (Juno, Allecto, Iris) is transferred to women (Pallas's mother, and an Amata whose role is much expanded even if her name is suppressed) whose very humanity diminishes their threat.

It is thus a messenger from Amata, not the Virgilian Allecto, who first brings word to Turnus that his engagement with Lavine, and indeed all of Latinus's prior "covenance" (3424), have been abrogated.[131] In the face of these broken oaths, the messenger further urges Turnus to undertake what emerges more and more clearly as a private war against Eneas:

> Prent soldoiers, asanble gent,
> ne te tarder mes de noiant,
> lo Troïen coite de guerre,
> tant qu'il te guerpisse la terre,
> ou que l'aies vencu ou pris
> ou qu'il s'an alt par mer fuitis.
>   (3431–36)

[Take soldiers, gather an army without delay, and press the Trojan with war, until he abandons the land to you, or you have conquered or captured him, or he departs a fugitive by sea.]

Private war, skipping over any legal recourse that might be available (however weak), was the aristocratic course to justice in the earlier feudal period, and of course remained a temptation for any sufficiently powerful baron. "A persistent fact of life in the Middle Ages, vengeance carried out independently by private individuals did not necessarily involve either public or semipublic legal process."[132]

Turnus's response here and after hinges on the power of prior oath and the rights thereby guaranteed him, to Lavine and to her lands:

> Li mes s'en vet, Turnus remaint,
> a ses amis privez se plaint
> del roi, qui ne li tient convent
> ne fiance ne seremant.
>
>   (3491–94)

[The messenger departs and Turnus remains, complaining to his close friends about the king, who has not kept covenant with him, or faith, or oath.][133]

Turnus's objection thus is to the breaking of specific feudal covenants; Latinus and Eneas will respond with the superior (and, in the twelfth century, contested) claim of lineage, and the desires of a pantheon to which they have exclusive access.[134]

Ascanius's slaughter of Silvia's stag, in a scene far uglier and bloodier than Virgil's, gives Turnus the "occasion" ("acheison," 3497, 3507) he has been seeking to initiate his war; he calls together his barons to hear his complaint and render counsel. From this point on, however, simultaneous with the armed struggle on all sides, efforts are made in council to move Turnus's war into a legal setting, or at least to limit it to a judicial duel between himself and Eneas. Along with the rise of patrilinear inheritance, the period of Anglo-Norman consolidation was also an era of judicial duel (*judicium Dei*) and early efforts to suppress even that mode of justice in favor of legal procedure.[135] When Turnus first appeals to Latinus, already figured as a traditional weak feudal king, Latinus initially refuses to involve himself, leaving it to these two barons to settle the matter in battle. But even in Turnus's initial meeting with his barons, one of them, Mesencius, counsels "measure" and an appeal to steps of legal procedure:

> mes nos devons faire mesure,
> ce m'est avis que est droiture:
> faire les doiz araisoner
> et de tort fait lo fai reter,
> que droit t'an face an ta cort,

> ainçois que a noalz li tort;
> se il de droit faire s'estorce,
> ainz que sor lui ailles a force,
> anprés lo fai donc desfier
> et de ta terre congeer.
> (4201–10)

[But we should act with moderation. It seems to me that the just way is this: you should have him approached and accused of wrongdoing, and then informed that he should make due amends for it in your court, before affairs become worse for him. If he evades doing you justice, before you go against him by force, you should first have him challenged and dismissed from your land.][136]

This is rejected by the violent Mesapus, who prefers the swifter and old-fashioned recourse to vendetta (4211–36). His advice prevails, but it is significant that the good counsellor, Mesencius, goes on to an explicitly noble death in battle on Turnus's behalf.

Once the war between Latins and Trojans is under way, its sure movement, however often delayed and frustrated, is from the earlier feudal model of private war to the high medieval model of judicial duel, with Turnus or his allies repeatedly dragging it back toward the more archaic form. It is Drances, as unattractive in the *Eneas* as in Virgil, who again proposes a *judicium Dei* in Latinus's council (6699–706). But Drances has been preceded by the admirable Mesencius in calling for the control of law. And this time the call for judicial duel succeeds:

> se cors a cors la puet conquerre,
> si ait la feme o tot la terre.
> (6801–02)

[If he can win her, man against man, then let him have the girl and all the land.]

The judicial duel is interrupted as in Virgil, but not through another intervention by Juno. Rather, one of Turnus's own knights articulates for a final time the old aristocratic resistance to individual *judicium Dei*, and then reignites general battle:

> Franc chevalier, nel dretés ja,
> combatons nos o çals dela,
> ne nos metons an tel mesure
> sor un sol home an aventure.
> (9421–24)

[Noble lords, do not allow it; let us do battle against our enemies, and not place our fortunes to such an extent on the action of a lone man.]

Finally, again as in the *Aeneid*, Turnus sees his fortune in decline and calls for a renewal of the single combat. At this point, as in Virgil, his historical fate crosses with the suspended memory of Pallas through the relic Turnus reserved to himself, in this case a ring. Pallas, so elaborately preserved from time in the *Eneas*, becomes the central agent in Turnus's death and thereby guarantees Eneas's historical success. Eneas even speaks of Pallas as the literal killer (9809–10).

It is not surprising that these moves from private warrior to peacemaker, from fighter to talker, from open and group battle to something very like judicial duel, and from weak king to the promise of a strong king, should all come in a text of Norman or Anglo-Norman origin. For as Bloch and others before him point out, the Normans were among the first to codify the legal processes that slowly replaced private war with judicial combat, and ultimately judicial combat with legal inquest.[137] It was William the Conqueror who first tried to restrict private campaigns, and Henry II who was most effective in his time working against judicial duel and toward legal procedure.[138] If the Anglo-Angevin empire was at a delicate point of transition from feudal assignment to patrilinear inheritance, from open warfare to *judicium Dei*, then Eneas's language of lineage, law and divine right looks forward, while Turnus's and his cohort's preference for swift and wholesale war looks back.

At the same time, the French poem's insertion of feudal obligation and law into an ancient epic context, far from being a naive "modernization" by a redactor unable to understand his source, is a canny legitimation of his culture's feudal war over imperial inheritance in England. His thematics and his narrative converge with Virgil's as he moves into the imperial half of the Latin source, at the same time altering Virgil's focus by rendering that imperial half his own center. And his use of Turnus shows a brilliant sensitivity to the Homeric fury and archaism of Virgil's Latin prince, genuinely translating him into the embattled protector of values newly archaic in the twelfth century. The *Eneas* centers around ancient imperial history, but a history that simultaneously validates the political changes occuring in the redaction's own time.

LAVINE AND CONTAINMENT THROUGH METONYMY

This chapter closes where it began, at the period of narrative suspension during which Lavine debates Amor, internally articulating the complex effects of her sudden desire for Eneas, whom she has just sighted from a tower.[139] This psychological version of dilation, we can now see, is signally different from Dido's wish to delay her lover, or from her lover's later wish to suspend Pallas from the corruption of time, or from the even more threatened suspension of Camille's tomb and the woman warrior it contains. Instead, the internalized and lyrical mode of erotic delay here moves Lavine toward her imperial destiny. It initiates Lavine's turn from the influence of her mother to the wishes of her father and the gods whose intentions he and Eneas alone can voice.[140] Dilation in this instance thus does not resist history but rather helps to accommodate feminine desire to history's work; romance comes to serve the ends of epic. The vernacular romance, having made a space (however marginal) for a woman ignored in its Virgilian source, simultaneously begins to reabsorb her into Virgil's imperial program.[141]

While the two great erotic episodes of Dido and Lavine may bracket the poem's central action of military combat and conquest, the latter of these two is itself folded into the final battle of the romance. Lavine's and Eneas's desire for one another emerges from (almost literally, as we will see) and returns to the work of men on the battlefield and the issue of kingship. As the poem approaches the climax of its military conflict in Eneas's judicial duel with Turnus, then, it simultaneously re-engages its negotiation with the power of women and the force of heterosexual eroticism. And it does so, appropriately, during a suspension of hostilities, the truce between the burial of Camille and the duel itself. Moreover, whatever its cautious limitation of Lavine's power, this last erotic episode also shows the male hero in a genuine dialogue with the feminine. Eneas suffers from erotic woes hitherto limited to women, and himself engages in an internal debate that acknowledges his own capacity for desire and *desmesure*, qualities that until now have been seen only in women.

As she discovers her love for Eneas and then informs him of it, Lavine revives a dense pattern of diction and gesture already repeatedly associated with the feminine usurpation of or challenge to male power. But whereas such threats were previously contained by the literal action of the narrative, in the case of Lavine their containment is subtler, even wittier. Lavine's exercise of potentially subversive feminine power and her assumption of traditionally male power, is in almost every case suppressed through a reduction toward metonymy. If Dido is stabilized in her urn and Camille in her tomb,

Lavine is stabilized in the book itself, by tropes. The earlier epitaphs, acknowledging the power of those now dead, are answered by the book's inscription of a Lavine whose threatening echoes are almost purely verbal and thus, like the tombs, beyond history.

The *Eneas* begins its creation of a non-Virgilian Lavine in a scene with her mother, whose own role is greatly expanded from Virgil though her Virgilian name, Amata, is ignored.[142] As in Virgil, Amata here wants to secure Lavine for Turnus, and pursues that aim by inquiring of her daughter whether she has yet learned about love and its tricks (*angins*, 7881), using the term that figured so largely in the episode of Dido. Amata goes on to describe the god Amors, his twin arrows tipped with gold and lead, and his medicine box. But, she adds, this description is figurative, "tot par figure" (7983); the force of Amors is wholly psychological. Amors again echoes Dido through the golden arrows she carried on the hunt with Eneas, but also renders them figurative, no longer physically effectual.[143] The golden arrows of Dido's burgeoning love, and her death by the sword "soz la memelle" (2032), are soon linked when Lavine is hit figuratively by Cupid's dart "desi qu'el cuer soz la memelle" (8067, "as deep as the heart beneath her breast"). And this simultaneously recalls and metaphorizes Camille's death, also, we recall, by "un dart" (7198) which "struck her in the heart ... below the breast" ("la fiert el cuer soz la memelle," 7202). The double echo is finally less about love, I think, than about the recuperation by figurative language of earlier literal feminine threats to Trojan destiny.

It is not such metonymic language alone, however, that enacts a limitation to feminine challenge. Lavine's wakening desire and her growing sense of self both serve to align her with her father and against her mother.[144] As if to establish this point all the more strongly, the *Eneas* includes a long, learned debate between Lavine and Amata, in which Lavine first denies any love at all, then denies love for Turnus. She finally acknowledges her love for Eneas in a quasi-grammatical division of his name into syllables, which are only "read" as the full name by an astonished Amata (8553–60). Thus Eneas's erotic triumph, and Lavine's rejection of maternal domination, are announced in a moment of specifically verbal, even pedagogical play, recalling once again the implicit setting of the traditionally male schoolroom in which Lavine first debated Amor.[145]

The theme of writing and its dangers in the midst of Lavine's accomodation to Trojan destiny continues, as she decides to announce her love to Eneas. After further internal debate, Lavine resolves to write him a letter, explicitly said to be "an latin" (8778). This not only extends the topos of learned activity with which the whole episode is replete, but equally recalls that best-known sequence of women's Latin letters, the *Heroides*, and the record many of them carry of disruptive feminine agency in desire.

Lavine sends her letter to Eneas by a means that more than any other embodies this episode's play between the literal and figural. Seeing Eneas within bowshot of the city, Lavine ties her letter tightly around an arrow, and instructs an archer to shoot it at him; she justifies this in terms of military defense, calling the Trojans spies (8817). The archer refuses her demand, fearing that his shot may endanger the truce; Lavine then convinces him to shoot so that the arrow will fall as a warning, just short of the enemy. Eneas does initially take this as a breaking of the truce by the Latins, though as before he plans to respond through legal protest rather than immediate violence (8841–60). But as soon as he reads the letter, Eneas recognizes that the gesture has only erotic significance: it is figural, not an act of military defiance. Lavine's brief control of the arrow is thus immediately emptied of political significance, and the actual arrow is implicitly transformed into Amor's dart as Eneas finds himself in his brother's power, touched to the heart by pain: "al cuer li toche la dolor" (8921).[146] The arrow is soon further reduced toward metaphor when Eneas links the letter with Amor's dart:

> Tu m'as de ton dart d'or navré,
> mal m'a li briés anpoisoné
> qu'entor la saiete trovai.
> (8953–55)

[You have wounded me with your golden dart. The letter which I found around the arrow has poisoned me badly.]

At the same time, however, Lavine's brief usurpation of the arrow and her use of Latin have also initiated Eneas's experience of erotic suffering, its first appearance in a male character.

When Eneas's men later recognize his condition, they explicitly invoke the metaphor of Amor's dart by speaking of Lavine as an archer in the tower:

> mais il c'i esta uns archiers
> qui molt trairoit ça volantiers.
> (9249–50)

[... but there is an archer standing there who would be very happy to shoot here.]

But this is merely the close of a joking exchange in which the Trojans metonymize Lavine herself as the tower, pillar, and window. That is, Lavine is figured as the architecture Eneas will possess, aided by Lavine's desire, upon their marriage (9241–52). Thus, once again, the literal elements by which female challenge has earlier been articulated and contained – the architecture of castle, tower, tomb – are echoed in figural and even better-controlled language, and the metonymized figure is now aligned with the interests of imperial destiny. The sort-crossing of this densely metaphorized argument of love works to inscribe in Lavine the whole social system which will emerge from Eneas marrying her: she herself is figured by the castle she will deliver, her relation to Amors by scholarly study and pliant feudal servitude.[147]

Thus Lavine's potentially dangerous intervention in signs of male warfare – the arrow, and its brief threat to the truce – is finally only a mild usurpation, a complicating not a causal factor, easily enclosed by Eneas's measured response and his followers' practice of metonymy. The letter it carries rouses the spectre of Ovid's letter-writing women (especially Helen and the Dido whose letter predicted Lavine as *altera Dido*), only to allay that spectre. The earlier violence of feminine eros is again brought to our attention only to be swiftly reintegrated into the structure of male power and its finally ordered lineal transfer.

The interpenetration of military and erotic experience, and of the literal and metonymic, is yet further extended in the melee that interrupts the first effort at single combat between Eneas and Turnus. There, Eneas is hit accidentally by an arrow (9468–74), and cured with medications from a box (9560), that neatly literalize the arrow and box of Amors, which, we will recall, exist for Amata "toz par figure." Such an invasion of the male arena by elements now dense with erotic and feminine associations has however been predicted by Eneas's experience of the pains of love, and by his internal debate (8940–9099). Versions of psychological debate have already been explored in female characters, in Dido's conversations with Anna, and in Lavine's earlier inner dialogues. But Eneas is the first male character to undergo such conflict and the narrative dilation it entails, and the voices of his debate display within this single character (as they have already done in Lavine) simultaneous capacities for practical reason and emotional *desmesure,* capacities which up until this point have been distinguished as masculine and feminine, and placed in opposition.

Lavine engages in a whole sequence of internal debates, culminating (8676–774) with her decision to write to Eneas. This final debate, before her brief usurpation of Latin and the truce-threatening arrow, articulates within Lavine opposing voices of logic and emotion, *mesure* and impetuosity; but rather than leaving them in final opposition, it begins a rapprochement between the two qualities that is extended in Eneas and then in the marriage of the two characters. A first voice in this debate tells Lavine to show *mesure* (8679; it later counsels *sens,* 8736), and to send no message to Eneas. Any direct advance is a *vilenie* unworthy of her rank (8720–21), and will lower her value in the eyes of her lover. Instead, Lavine should hide her feelings, leave open the possibility of either champion winning, and let the battle itself decide her preference (8729–42). This voice thus counsels Lavine at once to practice a rational discretion, to preserve her value in the market of lineage – her *parage,* and to let herself be the prize of male debate, to hide if not deny her *volente.*

But an answering and finally dominant voice speaks for the claims of Amors and feminine agency in desire. Amors, this voice says, holds her in his *baillie* (8686), and can do as he wishes with her (8693). In this voice, Lavine claims she doesn't care about harm to her public reputation so long as she has her *volente* (8718–19). But, in a crucial move, the debate ends with Lavine's insistence that her *volente* in communicating her love will make Eneas stronger for his upcoming combat (8759–62). So the voice of desire shifts its focus by claiming to aid the ends of military conquest. Female *volente* makes its final argument in the context of the male arena; it insists on action but claims that action will aid Trojan destiny.

This negotiation moves in two directions, however, just as we saw it do in the imagery of Cupid's arrows and box. For Eneas too has an internal debate, between strikingly similar voices, that sees feminine transgression as finally helping his cause.[148] The voice of practical militancy in Eneas reads Lavine's arrow and letter in the simplest literal sense, as objects that failed to have military impact, and suggests he ignore them. He will get no justice over an arrow that fell short of him, or over a piece of parchment; instead he should concentrate on his upcoming duel (8961–83). Love, this voice reminds him, is irrelevant to Lavine's fate; it is the winner of the duel who will get her, not the lover. This articulates overtly the primacy of the military procedures of *judicio Dei* over any action of desire or any preference held by Lavine. Besides, the voice points out, women are skilled at *enginier mal* (8998), and Lavine may be showing equal favor to Turnus (a ruse indeed suggested to Lavine by the more practical voice in her earlier debate, but rejected). Her letter may be false, this voice adds, and if he answered it Eneas would be mad (*fous*, 9073, just as the related voice earlier called Lavine *fole*, 8679).

The second voice of Eneas's debate, much closer to the voice of Lavine's erotic *volenté*, understands the full metonymic potency of the arrow and letter; both have wounded him (8962–73). This voice approves of Lavine's *angin* (9020) in sending him the letter since (as the related voice in Lavine had predicted) it makes him stronger for battle (9051–56); thus here again feminine *angin* is approved when it serves the ends of men in battle. The first voice of military practicality and diplomatic hesitation is not finally quashed here, however. The voice of desire argues that Eneas should answer Lavine's letter (9070–99), but he does not do so, in part because he is too much overcome by his emotion.

In these arguments between practicality and erotic desire, between *mesure* and *volenté*, then, previously conflicting patterns of masculine and feminine behavior begin to accommodate one another and even to coalesce in single characters, though still within a hierarchy clearly headed by the historical demands of empire. Unlike the love of Dido, whose quest for private power ended in metaphors of poison and destruction, and in literal death, the love of Lavine – her *angin* and *volenté* – is figured under, and subtends, an ordered hierarchy of male power.

Once Turnus is dead, the narrative further explores Eneas's and Lavine's acceptance and experience, each of the other's powers. In yet a final narrative suspension between the duel and the marriage which is its legal reward, the poem engages in a sort of lyrical delay through more internal discourses by Lavine and Eneas. In Lavine's final debate, the terms have significantly altered, from the earlier simple exchange between manipulative reason and impulsive eros, to a debate in which both elements are present in each voice. Now the debate is more between, on the one hand, a fearful assumption that male and female experience, empire and eros, are wholly divided, and on the other hand a stronger voice (using the vocabulary earlier reserved for reason) that sees the two elements in a comfortable if still distinctly hierarchical relationship.

The voice of eros is now fearful, and assumes that Eneas's world is limited exclusively to his interest in empire; once he has Lavine's castles, he will despise her because she was impulsive (*prinsaltiere*, 9863) earlier; he will triumph over her, and will want to have the empire without her (9895–96). But the second voice sees the two forces in balance, not battle:

> Fole Lavine, ne t'enuit,
> s'il vaint lo jor et tu la nuit.
> (9867–68)
> [Foolish Lavine, do not be angry if he wins in the day and you at night.]

In calling her *fole* and later saying she lacks *mesure* (9873) this voice echoes the earlier voice that counselled dissembling; now the voice acknowledges woman's need to speak her love, but sees it nonetheless as part of a necessary social arrangement, since Lavine's barons would hardly accept Eneas unless he married her (9902–05).

The conquering Trojan responds exactly to Lavine's voice of *mesure* and its accomodation of empire and eros. Eneas has no time in the day for love (9922), but at night he regrets his delay of the marriage, in a scene that recalls both Dido's and particularly Lavine's erotic turmoil.[149] Lying in bed, Eneas replicates Lavine's earlier suffering, even speaking quietly ("soëf," 9928) as she had done ("tot soavet," 8424). But the bulk of his long monologue is less about love itself than about the effect love has on his perception of time. His own discovery of desire thrusts Eneas into a world where normal time itself is dilated, an experience he explores through rhetorical amplification, as when he contemplates the apparent slowing of the firmament (10027–47). At this point, however, such romance delay is no longer the fault of women who would hold him back from the work of history; rather Eneas repeatedly blames himself for naming so long a period betwen battle and marriage. Even the dangers of such delay are now his fault; he would not blame Lavine for losing her love since he failed to give sufficient sign of his own love. This failure he significantly calls "grant desmesurance" (10001), imputing to his own nature the quality earlier reserved to Dido and Lavine.

Finally, of course, Eneas's rhetorical dilation gives way again to epic time and the celebration of his marriage with Lavine. This moment literalizes the text's earlier moves toward treating Lavine as herself a metonym for the empire to be transmitted through her and her offspring:

tot li a otroié lo jor
que il sa fille a esposee.
(10100–01)
[He [Latinus] granted everything to Eneas on the day when he married
his daughter.]

Thus, even while the preceding passage shows Eneas in the throes of
erotic experience and romance time, his incorporation of such
previously feminine experience comes just at the moment when his
military might most fully makes Lavine part of his imperial destiny.

Eneas's approach to empire, then, moves from Dido, to battle, to
Lavine. He passes out of the realm of a threatening feminine *angin* and
dominance, and a form of dilation which proves to be solitary, mad,
and suicidal. He moves thence through the exclusively male preserve of
the poem's military center, particularly as exemplified by Nisus and
Eurialus. And he returns finally to a link to woman, *angin* and dilation,
but now hierarchically inscribed within the processes of patriarchal
dominion, lineage, and logic. At the same time, and in a move by now
predictable, the poem records Eneas's final joy in a comparison that
calls back to mind the original figure of moveable feminine desire that
led to the Trojan war:

Unques Paris n'ot graignor joie,
quant Eloine tint dedanz Troie,
qu'Eneas ot, quant tint s'amie
en Laurente ...
(10109–12)
[Never did Paris have greater joy when he had Helen in Troy than
Eneas had when he had his love in Laurente.]

But if the poem does circle back nervously to the dangers of desire, the
differences too are telling. Helen, who set off the first war when a
Trojan stranger took her from her husband, is balanced by Lavine,
who set off the second war when a Trojan stranger took her from her
fiancé. Helen, though, was taken from a husband, at the behest and
with the support of a goddess. Lavine is taken from Turnus with the
support of a man, her father, and at the behest of his male gods, in
defiance of a powerful woman's vain wishes. And whereas it is at least
partly Helen's desire that helps set off the Trojan War (especially as
Helen is presented by Ovid), Lavine's love is only and explicitly
secondary, starting as the war is grinding down to its end, distinctly an
epiphenomenon, not an agent in events. And the poem finally closes, as
I noted earlier, far from the question of eros in something close to a

genealogical table of Eneas's male line. The *Roman d'Eneas*, for all its exploration of desire and romance delay, ends reminiscently of Anchises in *Aeneid* 6, and the genealogical marginalia of the pedagogical tradition, listing the transmission of empire from fathers to sons.

CHAPTER SIX

Writing the reading of Virgil: Chaucerian authorities in the House of Fame and The Legend of Good Women

The second half of the fourteenth century witnessed a revival of interest in classical story and particularly in the *Aeneid*. Chapters 2 and 4 analyzed the layers of commentary which were written in the margins of All Souls 82 and Additional 27304 at that time. Other manuscripts were re-annotated in the same decades, and a number of new copies were made in England, the first significant group of Virgil manuscripts produced there since the end of the twelfth century.[1] Simultaneously, a manuscript of the *Roman d'Eneas* was copied in an English hand for Henry Despenser, bishop of Norwich 1370–1406, and a major supporter of Richard II.[2] So, roughly, while the Norwich commentator was writing his allegoresis and its comments on political power, an aristocrat known as a fighting bishop owned the *Eneas*, with its own much more elaborate focus on imperial and military power. And in the same generation, Geoffrey Chaucer began to write his own Troy poems, including two works that specifically claimed to represent the Virgilian story of Aeneas and Dido.

The classical tradition, and especially the Virgilian tradition as received by a late-medieval reader like Chaucer, was in a very complex state, as the previous five chapters have shown. The medieval vision of antiquity and of antiquity's central Trojan narrative involved, among yet other things, ever more heavily annotated older Latin manuscripts; newer Latin manuscripts, some of them largely free of extra-textual apparatus – "naked texts"; a relatively fresh tradition of illustration; a growing corpus of encyclopedic mythography, often daringly allegorized; and a burgeoning library of classical story in the vernacular, from important reformulations like the *Roman d'Eneas* to an infinite regress of translations of redactions in the various Troy-books. These many media of access produced a floating body of "classical story," capable of being viewed and told from multiple perspectives.[3] Moreover, these varied media and the many audiences they addressed (monastic, university, courtly, mercantile) generated shifting centers of focus in which Latin text, platonizing allegory, ethical exegesis, vernacular version, even illustration, or some combination of these, could variously function as the primary carrier of the tale.

In this welter of conflictingly pre-read Latin texts, vernacular versions, and free-standing mythography, where might a medieval reader locate an authentic voice of the classical Latin poets, a transparent source of their revered *auctoritas*? Further, was such an "authentic," originating voice even available or desirable?[4] Or had the gesture of cultural appropriation become more important, more reassuring, than its ever more distant source? These questions are at the center of Chaucer's ruminations on Virgil and the Troy story in the *House of Fame* and the "Legend of Dido" in the *Legend of Good Women*.

Twice in his career – at the end of the 1370's and again in the second half of the 1380's – Geoffrey Chaucer explicitly summarized the events of the *Aeneid*, particularly the affair of Dido and Aeneas, with subtly modulated fidelity and infidelity to Virgil's text.[5] These two poems were by no means the beginning or end, though, of Chaucer's life-long redeployment of the Matter of Troy. Troy literally illuminates the dreamer's room as early as the *Book of the Duchess*, and helps provide mock epic tone as late as the Nun's Priest's Tale, written well into the period of the *Canterbury Tales*.[6] In the broader context of his meditation on Troy, Chaucer's two quite different redactions of Virgil show us one writer, increasingly aware of his own cultural authority, in the process of receiving and recreating an earlier great writer, and taking his measure by his predecessor, even challenging that predecessor. Chaucer overtly manipulates and refashions Virgilian themes of passion, pathos, and power. In both poems, at the same time, he wrestles with the great problem of Virgilian authority in the face of competing versions and conflicting interpretations, and with his own ambitions toward authority.

Along with the *Book of the Duchess* and the *Parliament of Fowls*, the *House of Fame* has generally been classed as an "early poem," part of Chaucer's extraordinary absorption and readaptation of ancient Latin literature, the exegetic developments of late antiquity, and the forms of medieval French and Italian vernacular culture. The Virgilianism of the *House of Fame* centers around the private crisis of the reader/narrator and his negotiation with tradition, especially concurrent versions of the *Aeneid* itself, and with conflicting versions of Aeneas's heroism. In the *House of Fame*, I will show, Chaucer stages a visionary journey through the reception of Virgil's Trojan narrative, and a quest for a mode of heroism upon which he can model his own readerly experience and his growing authorial ambition. In this early work, though, he casts himself less as an independent writer than as a confused, passive, and almost a defeated reader. Chaucer's narrator in the *House of Fame* records the experience of working through an ancient and prestigious text overloaded with almost irreconcilable meanings and challenged by a growing body of alternate versions. The question becomes whether a just interpretation of Virgil's text, and a just knowledge of the past, are possible at all.

Certainly Chaucer's greatest encounter with the Matter of Troy, though only tangentially with its Virgilian version, is his *Troilus and Criseyde*, from the middle years of the 1380's.[7] This poem, Chaucer's longest sustained narrative and arguably his own best claim to epic, restricts its story to the prehistory of the *Aeneid*, though at crucial moments Troilus can be seen as a figure of Dido, and Criseyde as a figure of Aeneas. It is only in the aftermath of the *Troilus*, and with an invigorated capacity for historical and political imagination gained in writing that poem, that Chaucer returns explicitly to Virgil's narrative – however multiply challenged – of Dido and Aeneas, in the *Legend of Good Women*. This return, moreover, is fictively sited within readerly responses to *Troilus and Criseyde*, especially its depiction of women.

Chaucer's sense of his own readerly and poetic position in regard to his epic predecessor alters enormously in the years between the *House of Fame* and the "Legend of Dido."[8] In the *Legend of Good Women*, Chaucer begins to insert himself, modestly but firmly, in the company of the great *auctores*. Historical truth may be evasive and poetic truth multiple, but both these problems open up the possibility for Chaucer to articulate his own versions of antique narrative, and especially of its heroines. Moreover, the multiplicity of authority and interpretation in the *Legend of Good Women* lets Chaucer claim for his own voice a valid place in that irreducible complexity. The later version of the story of Dido and Aeneas, whose text is often much more verbally faithful to Virgil than is the *House of Fame*, nonetheless presents itself as a worthy revoicing and revision of its antique sources "In thyn Eneyde and Naso."[9] This chapter will trace Chaucer's movement, then, from a poetry of bewildered readership to a self-authenticating and self-canonizing authority even through the very words of Virgil, in these two redactions of the *Aeneid*.

AENEAS AND GEFFREY AS HERMENEUTIC HEROES

Chaucer's use of Virgil in the *House of Fame* goes far past the poem's famous summary of the Troy story in Book One, with its notoriously wavering allegiances to the versions and sympathies of Virgil and Ovid. Rather, Chaucer's narrator Geffrey enacts profoundly if also parodically, three interlocking aspects of Virgil's hero.[10] First, Geffrey is a witness of narratives recorded through human artifice, specifically visual art, and through this he recalls two crucial episodes in Aeneas's history. Second, by extension, Aeneas and Geffrey both become conspicuously hermeneutic figures, heroically or comically trying to negotiate these and many other kinds of (often visionary) sign. Third, Geffrey undergoes other more overt parallels of Aeneas's narrative situation, though often as rendered through the optic of Boethian allegoresis.[11] Geffrey's inadequacy to the prototype who is proposed by these similarities is sometimes comic, but the reader's laughter at a character who is himself so readerly is at best uncomfortable. Geffrey's hesitations and inadequacies may also be the reader's own, faced with the multiplication of inherited *Aeneids*. I will suggest that the entire poem reviews the *Aeneid* at least twice, from the conflicting perspectives of the three dominant visions of Virgil which have been the subject of earlier chapters.[12]

There is a useful distinction to be drawn, when we think about a poem and its past, between those myriad influences that may touch the poet in his process of *inventio*, and the referential landscape the poet may more or less overtly propose to his readers in the poem itself. Neither by "influences" nor by "referential landscape" do I mean only objects of close imitation; rather I want to suggest the whole range of associations, contrasts, and optics by which both poet and reader can use earlier works of art to approach a later one. Of course the cultural forebears that automatically influence a poet, and the models consciously offered to readers in the text, often do overlap. Dante not only steeped himself in the *Aeneid* but made its author a central character in his narrative. Poetic influence and readerly model need not cross, however, and Chaucer's career often exemplifies an anxious separation of the two. Chaucer did not just suppress Boccaccio as the source of his *Troilus*, he went to the length of inventing (or conscripting) Lollius as a stand-in. He thus proposes to his readers a referential landscape of ancient authority and Latin literature, however spurious, in which to approach his vernacular poem.

This distinction invites a simple observation: that Chaucer proposes Virgil's *Aeneid* to his readers as the dominant though by no means exclusive referential landscape of the *House of Fame*. Of course this is Chaucer's most obviously bookish book, and a small army of other writers is mentioned in its course: Ovid, Dante, Claudian, Boethius, Alan of Lille, and Martianus Capella, not to mention all the pillar dwellers Geffrey encounters in the Palace of Fame.[13] The ground-breaking work of Sheila Delany set out a broader intellectual backdrop: the contemporary philosophical problem of knowing the ineffable – what she and others call "skeptical fideism" – and the late medieval "awareness of the coexistence of contradictory truths" on which so much of the poem plays.[14] Others have also explored the critique of textual authority and exegesis in the poem.[15] The approach pursued below could make little sense without the contexts this kind of work has provided.

It is Virgil, however, whose story Chaucer openly recounts in the *House of Fame*, though in a version where Ovid competes for our attention – a point to which I will return later. Beyond Virgil and Ovid, only Boethius is openly named and then quoted in the poem. Equally important "influences" have far less place in this explicit referential landscape, if any at all: Dante is named only once, as an authority on hell along with Claudian, and the name of Boccaccio appears nowhere. And it is the *Aeneid* to which our minds return at later moments like the description of Fame and the reference to Domus Dedaly, where once again single images also call to mind Ovid and Boethius. The *Aeneid*, then, is a more immediate and overt context in which Chaucer explores themes also present in his covert sources: the broad problem of knowledge posed by skeptical fideism, the question of secular texts and sacred wisdom posed by Dante's reading of Virgil, the question of dream posed by Boccaccio.

I will approach Chaucer's use of the *Aeneid*, further, in terms of those other two major players in the referential landscape already mentioned above. For if the Virgil of Chaucer's cultural world carried a dense context of multiple and often conflicting redaction and interpretation, two of its major streams – the romance and allegorical – may be characterized as "Ovidian" and "Boethian." I am interested, then, in Chaucer's *book* of Virgil, both in the general sense of an auctor's cultural reception, and in the narrow sense of the codex.[16]

This approach to the *House of Fame* begins as Virgil begins his *Aeneid*, out of order and in the middle of things, by drawing attention to two places where Chaucer's narrator witnesses stories. After complaining of how hard it is to interpret dreams correctly, the narrator curses anyone who interprets *his* dream wrong, and then tells how he fell asleep one day "wonder sone" (114), as no aspiring lover should. As his dream begins, though, Geffrey finds himself in Venus's temple:

> But as I slepte, me mette I was
> Withyn a temple ymad of glas,
> In which ther were moo ymages
> Of gold, stondynge in sondry stages,
> And moo ryche tabernacles,
> And with perre moo pynacles,
> And moo curiouse portreytures,
> And queynte maner of figures
> Of olde werk, then I saugh ever.
>
> (119–27)

These "queynte maner of figures" tell the story of the *Aeneid*, which begins "writen on a table of bras" then seems to continue in "ymages" or "portreytures." The setting of this pictorial narrative reminds us powerfully of its hero Aeneas when he first arrives in Libya. Like Aeneas at the opening of the *Aeneid*, Book One, Geffrey is disoriented, uncertain of his whereabouts ("I nyste never / Wher that I was," 128–29) and, like Aeneas, he wanders around trying to find out. In the *Aeneid*, the interview with Venus follows (Geffrey of course has already seen Venus in her temple), and then Aeneas's approach to the city of Carthage and Dido's temple to Juno, where he tearfully regards, in "the handiwork / of rival artists," the depiction of his own past on the walls of Juno's temple: "With many tears and sighs he feeds / his soul on what is nothing but a picture" (*Aen.* 1.455–64). At the analogous point in the story of his dream, Geffrey, already in a temple, wanders up to the tables of brass and sees the story of Aeneas himself:

> I fond that on a wall ther was
> Thus writen on a table of bras:
> "I wol now synge, yif I kan,
> The armes, and also the man
> That first cam, thurgh his destinee,
> Fugityf of Troy contree,
> In Itayle, with ful moche pyne
> Unto the strondes of Lavyne."[17]
>
> (141–48)

Geffrey witnesses the Trojan past in a setting reminiscent of Aeneas's when he too witnessed that past.[18]

The links between the two scenes are even denser, though, and more synthetic than just narrative. The friendly reception promised by Dido's sympathy for Troy introduces the theme of Fame as a positive force: "this fame will bring you some deliverance" (*Aen.* 1.463). The table of brass echoes the very metal used in Juno's temple: ".... flights of steps led up to brazen thresholds; / the architraves were set on posts of brass; / the grating hinges of the doors were brass" (1.448–9).[19]

The glittering richness of Venus's temple, its jewels and gold, also gather to this single structure a second Virgilian space where Aeneas himself will soon become a narrator and where Venus's influence is so powerful: Dido's luxurious palace, where there are "engraved in gold, / the sturdy deeds of Dido's ancestors," and "ceilings rich with golden panels" (*Aen.* 1.637–42 and 726–27). This impaction of two structures from *Aeneid* 1, with their twin heroic picture cycles, may prepare us for Geffrey's divided attention and sympathies, alternately Trojan and Sidonian, in his redaction of the story. At a moment like this, Aeneas with his own divided loyalties does indeed become a "queynte maner of figure" for Geffrey, as both witness and teller of the Trojan saga. The new Aeneas, suitably dwarfed and comic for his own age, re-enacts a crucial moment in the history of his prototype. As Aeneas gazed at his own past, Geffrey gazes at the past of his double.

But the effect of the "empty picture" on Aeneas is not necessarily positive. It delays him, makes him stop and sigh, and it will do so again. As he moves toward the second great episode in the epic, the descent to the Underworld in Book Six, Aeneas comes to another temple, Apollo's, and again loses himself in Daedalus's engravings on its doors instead of praying for the god's assistance. Here he is explicitly rebuked by the Sibyl: "This is no time to gape at spectacles" (*Aen.* 6.37). Art here is truly seen as an ambiguous medium, moving, but also dangerously tempting.

The episode of Aeneas gazing at Daedalus's engraved doors is recalled by a second moment in the *House of Fame* to which I would draw attention. Geffrey has now left the temple of Venus, only more confused than before; an eagle has carried him, initially terrified, through the heavens to the House of Fame, where he witnesses further confused testimony to the vagaries of history and reputation; and he finally leaves Fame's palace, still seeking the true "tydynges / Of Loves folk" (644–45) the eagle had promised him.

Tho saugh y stonde in a valeye,
Under the castel, faste by,
An hous, that Domus Dedaly,
That Laboryntus cleped ys,
Nas mad so wonderlych, ywis,
Ne half so queyntelych ywrought.
(1918–23)

It is after descending to this house that Geffrey hopes finally to receive the tidings he has so long been promised. The House of Twigs, like the Temple of Venus, actually conflates several Virgilian (as well as Ovidian and Boethian) moments, to which we will return. For the moment I simply want to show Geffrey once again re-enacting the situation of his "figure" Aeneas at a house of Daedalus toward the close of the *House of Fame*, and as he is about to witness stories.

Both these episodes link Geffrey to Aeneas not as a martial or erotic conqueror, but rather as a gazer in moments of narrative suspension. At both points, Aeneas is a reader of events (almost literally – the Trojans at Apollo's temple "perlegerent oculis," *Aen.* 6.34), and at the latter he is reproached by the Sibyl for allowing himself to be trapped by his sentimental response. So Geffrey is – at these moments anyway – linked to Aeneas as a "reader," someone responding to the problematic power of human artifice to draw him away from his role as an actor.

Geffrey's specifically readerly role goes even further here. Venus's temple itself, like the Palace of Fame later on, has strong overtones of the architectural spaces of the arts of memory.[20] Moreover, pagan temples in the French "romances of antiquity" are sometimes figured almost as books.[21] So if Geffrey is linked on the one hand to Aeneas as reader, he is also on the other hand enacting the difficulties faced by Chaucer's or Virgil's own readers in the fourteenth century. This crossing of epic hero and mundane reader in the figure of Geffrey is not surprising when we recall that the whole program of "Bernard's" allegory was to refigure Aeneas as a spiritual Everyman; the insertion of the contemporary reader's experience into the epic has ancient roots by the time Chaucer invokes it here.

These two moments of viewing visual narratives in the context of sacred architecture, though, are only the most explicit enactments of much broader and subtler thematic parallels between the *Aeneid* and the *House of Fame*, related to signs and their problematic exegesis. For if human signs briefly tempt Aeneas out of the epic's action, if indeed his own human sign-making as narrator of the Troy story helps seduce Dido and extend that delay, then divine signs repeatedly though confusingly thrust him back into his heroic destiny. Especially in the first six books, Aeneas is a hermeneutic hero, constantly faced with dreams, omens, and prophecies, often ambiguous or incomplete. His own and his people's survival depend upon the proper interpretation and execution of these supernatural counsels. Yet, particularly in Books Two through Four, we see Aeneas (as well as Anchises) misinterpreting or even resisting these signs.[22]

The beginning of Aeneas's story in Book Two describes a whole nation wilfully refusing the warnings of Laocoön, Cassandra, and the very clash of arms in the belly of the horse. Aeneas then ignores the dream-counsel of Hector to flee Troy and save its "holy things and household gods" (2.293), and instead rushes into battle. What finally sends Aeneas back to his family and the escape for which he is intended is not the worldly event of Troy's actual fall, but rather the visionary perception, unclouded by mortal sight, of the gods tearing the city apart (2.604-06). Aeneas would again rush to his death in battle were it not for the yet stronger omens of Iulus's tongue of flame and the shooting star. These, and the words of Creusa's shade, finally propel him from Troy. Book Three is a literal map of misreadings, as the Trojans wander through a series of false foundations, misnamings, and misinterpretations, most notoriously Anchises's wrong reading of the Delphic instruction to seek out his "ancient mother" (3.96). Only when, in yet another dream, Aeneas's family gods interpret Apollo for him (3.147–71) – a vision reading a vision – does he finally understand his destination. Even then he will approach Italy only after more wanderings, the evil portents of the Harpies, and the incomplete prophecy of Helenus (3.374–462). And Helenus only promises still more signs and sends Aeneas on to another potentially confused prophecy, that of the Sibyl of Cumae. It then takes the vision of Mercury, the appearance of Anchises in his dreams, and finally the stern warning by Mercury in yet another dream to push Aeneas away from Dido. Anchises again comes to the hero in Book Five, instructing Aeneas to find him in the Underworld; and the central episode of the entire work, the descent to Anchises, closes on a note that suggests it too may be a dream. *Aeneid* 6, quite apart from its atmospherics (monsters, allegorical figures, swords that do not cut, embraces that do not clasp), shows us the hero in his most exaggerated, dream-like state of powerlessness and passivity. His journey completed, Aeneas returns to the upper world, notoriously, through the ivory gate of false dreams (6.893–99).[23]

In the epic he summarizes, then, Geffrey has a heroic precedent in undertaking a bizarre journey intertwined with confusing signs and the experience of dream. As interpreters more than anywhere else, though, Geffrey and Aeneas are at once compared and sharply contrasted. Aeneas as a viewer delayed – even tempted – by the persuasions of human artifice is closely doubled by Geffrey. But Geffrey's confusions are puny and comic next to Aeneas's heroic exegesis of supernatural signs. Aeneas quite literally shoulders interpretation when he carries his father and *penates* from the flames of Troy, whereas Geffrey can refuse to interpret (as in the extended *dubitatio* on dreams with which the poem begins, 1–58), shrug his shoulders and let the reader deal with the problem. To this extent, Geffrey pushes the heroic role onto the reader: "Devyne he" (14). Further, whatever Aeneas's difficulties with interpreting other forms of visionary experience, the messages conveyed to him by dream are clear and unambiguous, even if usually fearful and not always obeyed.

Because Aeneas is himself such a double and conflicted reader of signs – willingly seduced from his path by human artifice and simultaneously pressed (however resistantly) toward his destiny by divine omen – Chaucer can construct in Geffrey an avatar at once serious and comic, straightforward and parodic. Geffrey as reader of *auctoritee* is best understood as a character already enacting, refiguring the hero he will read, and who will enact that hero again at the close of the poem. For the *Aeneid* as inherited by Chaucer's culture and experienced by Geffrey had become so densely figured, so multiply interpreted and redacted, as to elicit either a frustrated refusal to understand it coherently, or a readership almost heroic in its complexity. Not only was the *Aeneid* replete with the thematics of Fame, positive and negative, but its own burden of conflicting cultural reception made Virgil's book itself a perfect emblem of Fame.

The "queynte maner of figures" in Venus's temple take on their full significance when considered in terms of this culturally weighty text they report. A story like the *Aeneid*, surrounded as it is by ancient and multiple traditions of exegesis, is figural in the most complex and difficult sense. It is as superabundant, figurally, as the details of Venus's temple. And as we will see, Geffrey will wander among the *Aeneid*'s meanings as uncertainly as he "romed up and down" among the temple's "queynte maner of figures."[24]

Such a codicological situation, with inherited alternate meanings at once authoritative and conflicting, and a hero considered at once admirable and villainous, places great strain on a text and on its reader. The reader too is thus put in a situation analogous to that of Aeneas himself in the face of visions and prophecy. Multiple interpretations are posited, and the reader must make the right choice, if a right choice is even possible.[25] Chaucer, I would argue, exploited the aesthetic possibilities of this exegetical overload in the *House of Fame*. For Geffrey's redaction of the *Aeneid* lies at the center of complex layers of dramatic and aesthetic distance – dream, ecphrasis, text, memory – which qualify, both by limitation and suggestive extension, the possibilities of significance in the narrative. It is also surrounded, at the outermost level, by a viewing narrator who himself is in a situation similar, if only parodically, to that of Aeneas. So the aesthetic structure of Book One of the *House of Fame* mimics the codicological complexities – even the shape – of Virgilian narrative, encrusted with conflicting potential meanings. The various buildings of the *House of Fame* can be seen, from this perspective, as the Virgilian book architecturalized, pushed into a third dimension. The parallels between Geffrey and Aeneas, and the dubious mediation of the *Aeneid* itself, both relate complexly to the theme of Fame which Chaucer will develop explicitly in Book Three.

I would propose, further, that Geffrey not only occupies a double role, linking himself parodically to Aeneas in his quest and wanderings (on the one hand), and to the arguably heroic reader of the received *Aeneid* (on the other), but that in his own wanderings Geffrey moves among the three major and conflicting approaches that were taken to the *Aeneid* in its medieval reception. I will try to show that Chaucer is, in a sense, splitting up the complex received tradition into its separate and now competing strands, and exploring the exegetical crisis this creates. While I do not suggest that he programmatically sets out these different interpretive possibilities in the progress of the *House of Fame*, I do think he was aware of their multiplicity and inherent incompatibility, and that they played through his mind as he summoned up various aspects of the *Aeneid* in his poem.

DECENTERING AUTHORITY IN *HOUSE OF FAME* I

As many critics have noted, Geffrey's narrative in the *House of Fame* Book One tells the story of Aeneas mostly at its popular, literal, and sentimental level; it clings largely (but, we will see, not exclusively) to the "romance" vision of Virgil, and takes crucial passages from Ovid.[26] And the visual presentation of the story in books of the romance tradition may influence the architectural setting of Geffrey's dream. At least one splendid *Eneas* manuscript (see plate 1, and discussion pp. 26–27) illustrates the opening episodes as a series of vignettes on a diapered gold ground, separated by pillars and Gothic arches; the similarity to Venus's temple is striking.

But Geffrey's narration also participates in other approaches to the *Aeneid*. Geffrey's summary begins, as quoted above, by combining ecphrasis and textuality, with a close translation of the opening of the Virgilian *Aeneid*. Translation, with its close grammatical attention to the letter of the text, parallels the pedagogical vision of Virgil. It offers an accessible but relatively unmediated book (although the modesty of "yif I kan" speaks more from Geffrey's mouth than Virgil's).[27] It is distanced and authoritative, presented without apparent interference by the viewing narrator or the artist of the brass tables. Much of Book One's history of the Trojan fall and the foundation of Rome is also consistent with the generally factual emphasis of the pedagogical tradition, including its frequent provision of abbreviated historical summaries in the *accessus*.[28]

Further, a certain amount of the narrator's awkwardness in the *House of Fame* – his summary deflation of epic tone, his sometimes comically simple-minded didacticism – can be traced, I think, to the reductionist impact of some pedagogical glossating.[29] As I showed in chapter 2, there are aspects of annotation in the pedagogical manuscripts that tend to simplify the text even while explaining it. Such notes reduce geographical, mythic, or historical specifics to their most general terms.[30] I also suggested that this kind of textual flattening is almost inevitable in any elementary parsing of a foreign text and culture; and it was probably the more necessary in earlier medieval scholastic settings that lacked the range of secondary and parallel sources available later. Nonetheless, the elementary kinds of explanation noted in many of these manuscripts could seem over-simplified when the same manuscripts were reread in the later fourteenth century. By that time, there was in circulation a varied body of systematic source materials, such as the ever more wide-ranging mythographical surveys of the period or the encyclopedic exegeses of Ovid's *Metamorphoses*. The period also saw a revived use of quite detailed ancient history and learning, displayed for instance by the classicizing friars and by annotators like Commentator III of All Souls 82.[31] To a reader commanding some of this kind of information, yet re-using a much earlier manuscript (as each of the three manuscripts studied in chapters 2, 3, and 4 were in fact re-used), the early brief glosses could have appeared almost comically insufficient.

Geffrey will occasionally fill out a line of his Troy narrative in Book One with what is in effect a gloss. At such points the impact is very like the simpler pedagogical Latin glosses. So he comments on "Lete, / That is a flood of helle unswete... " (71–72), and explains that Creusa is "daun Eneas wif" (175); he refers to "cruel Juno, / That art daun Jupiteres wif" (198–99), or to "Eolus, the god of wyndes" (203).[32] Most of these explanations have no exact counterparts in *Aeneid* glosses, but they correspond neatly to the methods and tone of the elementary notes in pedagogical manuscripts.[33]

This arguably intentional, and mildly amusing, narratorial pedantry does not account for several fairly minor errors of scholarship in the poem, which have gained a modest notoriety among Chaucer critics.[34] In the Troy summary of Book One, Geffrey says that Creusa fled the burning city with "hir yonge sone Iulo, / And eke Askanius also" (177–78), thus burdening her with an extra son.[35] Approaching the actual palace of Fame, Chaucer has his narrator see "Marcia that lost her skin" (1229), mistaking the gender of the musician Marsyas.[36] And Chaucer describes Fame herself as having not the swift wings she is given by Virgil, but rather "Partriches wynges" (1392).[37] Scholars have made special pleas for each mistake, and each plea has some weight.[38] But Chaucer need not have an impeccable philological command of the *Aeneid*, nor infallible mythological scholarship, in order to have achieved a substantial and complex reaction to the epic, and to have sensed the inadequacy of literal-minded pedagogical glossing. Indeed, we have encountered just such a reader, who makes an analogous mistake about the gender of a mythological figure, in the "Norwich" commentator of Add27304.[39] Like many readers today, with limited Latin but good guidance in the form of translations and commentaries, Chaucer could gain a subtle sense of the poem that was also nonetheless idiosyncratic and occasionally inaccurate.[40] As earlier chapters have demonstrated, just such an artillery of redaction (if not translation) and intriguing interpretation was circulating in England by Chaucer's time. Indeed, the very emphasis on multiple visions of the *Aeneid* across the *House of Fame*'s three books suggests a reader still as much engaged with the materials of reception and interpretation as with the original text. And in the actual Troy narrative to which we now turn, Geffrey moves among versions of the story that many readers would have recognized as stemming at once from Virgil, from Ovid, and from their medieval redactors and commentators.

The story of Aeneas and Dido in the *House of Fame*, Book One follows the pattern of "romance" redactions in using *ordo naturalis*, presenting events in their chronological not their Virgilian sequence.[41] This is the mnemonic *Aeneid*, the *Aeneid* of Venus's temple and of her worldly servants. Not only the order, but also the relative emphasis of the popular redactions is followed – the tradition of Aeneas's splendor and misconduct, of Dido's voluntary generosity and erotic tragedy. Geffrey reacts most sympathetically to this aspect of the Virgilian narrative, and the intensity of his response is reflected in the temporary, but almost surreal, breakdown of aesthetic conventions in these passages.

Chaucer's mode of presenting the *Aeneid* entails a complex series of narrative strategies. Put briefly, Geffrey's report of the story in the temple combines ecphrasis and textuality in a whole that could be experienced only in memory or dream.[42] Once past the initial lines, it becomes emphatically clear that what he is summarizing is visual, not textual: "First sawgh I ... And aftir this was grave,... And next that sawgh I ... And I saugh next..." (151–74). Then, in a surprising piece of sympathetic perception, Geffrey begins briefly to *hear* the story (though he uses only indirect discourse) when Creusa's ghost appears to Aeneas (187–92). It is symptomatic that this penetration of aesthetic levels and conventions occurs at a moment of heightened sympathy for a feminine character.[43]

After this point, both the sources and the narrative mode change. We have reached, for Geffrey and the romance tradition, the crisis of the narrative: the seduction and abandonment of Dido. As Geffrey's sentimental pity is aroused and his emotional involvement increases, the artifice of dependence on some ancient source completely crumbles, and Geffrey's narrative again moves from ecphrasis to the report of a speech directly overheard:

> In suche wordes gan to pleyne
> Dydo of hir grete peyne,
> As me mette redely –
> Non other auctour alegge I.
> (311–14)

At what is for Geffrey the heart of the story, he finds not his *auctor* or his epic hero, but rather himself – "non other auctour alegge I" – and the reshaping power of his response to the text.[44]

Another peculiar break characterizes Geffrey's narrative. While the emotional core, for Geffrey, is clearly Dido's passion and abandonment, this episode is, in fact, almost not narrated at all. By contrast, the imperial history of Virgil's Aeneas, before and after Carthage, is told, although swiftly, nonetheless in some detail. We learn about the fall of Troy, about the intervention of Venus in Eneas's survival and his escape with Anchises and the household gods, about Creusa's death and ghostly prophecy. We learn about the quest for Italy, about Juno's storm, and its abatement through divine intervention. After the affair, we hear about the death of Palinurus, Eneas's descent to the Underworld, his arrival in Italy, marriage to "Lavina," war with Turnus and final triumph.[45]

Compared to this, the seduction and betrayal of Dido in the *House of Fame* remain almost a narrative blank.[46] Ascanius disappears along with Virgil's story of his replacement by Cupid; there is no report of Dido's erotic intoxication, her confession to Anna, or the hunt and storm during which she and Eneas consummate their passion; and we are ultimately told only that "he betrayed hir" (294), without elaboration.[47] Only the suicide is actually narrated, and even that is shorn of much detail.[48] Instead, the actual events of the affair disappear into various ellipses: "shortly for to tellen" (242), "Hyt were a long proces to telle" (251), "shortly at oo word" (257). What remains, floating almost outside of narrative time, are the twin arias of Dido's and the narrator's laments, both of them in effect acting as readers of what has already taken place.[49] Both voices gloss what has been practiced on them by the text or the seducer, though Geffrey's gloss is far more moralizing (if no less emotional) than Dido's. "The narrator interjects himself as a commentator," as Fyler puts it,[50] and the act of reading itself (Dido's or Geffrey's) occupies the emotional high point of the first book of the *House of Fame*.

And, not surprisingly, at this point Geffrey also shifts fully into the Ovidian rhetoric and sentimentality which characterize the whole Dido episode:

> And after grave was how shee
> Made of hym shortly at oo word
> Hyr lyf, hir love, hir lust, hir lord.
> (256–58)

This is the Ovidian *Aeneid*, taken without irony.[51] Geffrey identifies with the distraught Dido, and constantly adds his own rather superfluous interjections. Geffrey and Dido, indeed, vie for the most frequent use of "allas!" Both fall into elaborate repetitions and overstatement. They share identical preoccupations about appearance and truth, and the loss of Fame in the sense of good repute.

> Allas! what harm doth apparence,
> Whan hit is fals in existence!
> For he to hir a traytour was;
> Wherfore she slow hirself, allas!
> (265–68)

Drawing from the Epistle of Dido in Ovid's *Heroides*, Geffrey's imaginative re-enactment puts into Dido's mouth speeches of inflated rhetoric that quickly pass into bathos ("O Eneas!... O wikke Fame!").

> "Allas!" quod she, "what me ys woo!
> Allas, is every man thus trewe,
> That every yer wolde have a newe,
> Yf hit so longe tyme dure,
> Or elles three, peraventure?
> (300–04)

This Dido is quite without her Virgilian magnificence. Rather she is plaintive, almost mawkish, a fit subject for Geffrey's reductive moralizing.

Like that hero in the scenes explored above, then, Geffrey is rather more a reader here than a narrator. His interjections, his constant recursion to his own emotional response, get him lost in glossating rather than moving along with his story. The themes of fame and authority, too, suffer a peculiar diminution as Geffrey and Dido lament over them in this episode. The difficulty of finding authority, of establishing the truth of vision, has been raised in the initial passage on dreams. The grandeur and potential of visionary experience increase as potential similarities develop between Geffrey and Virgil's hero. The first section of ecphrastic narrative in the temple shows the prototype as divine imperatives affect his world. From these elevated echoes, though, we see Geffrey turn to reflections on fame not as heroic renown, but as worldly Rumor. From the questioning of divine authority, we see him turn to sentimental reflections on the worldly lies of man. This is not so much a false reading as it is a deflated "romance" reading, a worldly reading that pulls the poem from grand problems into almost tawdry sentiment.

Geffrey is no more eager to abandon this emotional ensnarement than is Aeneas. No divine authority calls him away from his love-affair, but the authority of the Virgilian text does. After the death of Dido and a series of moralizing exempla about as well-organized as his tract on dreams, Geffrey finally returns to the plot he is summarizing.[52] He also makes a spectacular return to ecphrasis and the distanced, pedagogical attention to the detail of the text with which he began.

> But to excusen Eneas
> Fullyche of al his grete trespas,
> The book seyth Mercurie, sauns fayle,
> Bad hym goo into Itayle,
> And leve Auffrikes regioun,
> And Dido and hir faire toun.
>
> (427–32)

"The book" – the authoritative Latin *Aeneid* – justifies Aeneas, as neither Geffrey nor the romance tradition does. With Dido gone, Geffrey is less involved and acknowledges the authority of the Virgilian text. Interpretive traditions clash again.[53] This renewed emotional distance also allows resumption of the original narrative mode: "Thoo sawgh I grave..." (433). Aeneas is heroic again; the epic apparatus of gods returns to the tale. But the emotional center of the poem is past for Geffrey, and he races through the last eight books of the *Aeneid* in thirty-five lines.

ALLEGORICAL VIRGILIANISM IN *HOUSE OF FAME* II AND III

Although torn away from his sentimental involvement, Geffrey leaves Venus's temple no more enlightened than when his dream began, and his search – for simple information if not for wisdom – must start over. In particular, as at the start (128–29), he simply does not know where he is.

> But not wot I whoo did hem wirche,
> Ne where I am, ne in what contree.
> But now wol I goo out and see,
> Ryght at the wiket, yf y kan
> See owhere any stiryng man,
> That may me telle where I am.
>
> (474–79)

Outside the temple, he finds himself in a wasteland, as sandy and barren as the desert of Libya. Looking up, he is terrified to see a gigantic eagle swooping down toward him. As Steadman long ago noted, this scene recalls Aeneas just after his shipwreck in *Aeneid* 1.[54] Indeed, the lines just quoted consciously echo the grammar, rhyme, and some of the phrasing of the beginning of Geffrey's translation:

> "I wol now synge, yif I kan,
> The armes and also the man
> That first cam, thurgh his destinee. . ."
>   (143–45)

Chaucer's meditation on the epic, and Geffrey's enactment of its hero, thus circle back to a point even slightly earlier in the epic than that of Juno's temple, as if to close but also close off the Dido episode. (It should be remembered that Aeneas too comes back to the Libyan coast after leaving Dido at the close of Book Four, sleeps there, and is warned to depart by the winged god Mercury.)[55] Geffrey and the reader embark instead, I think, on other ways of seeing epic, other visions of the *Aeneid*, in which Dido has little more role than that of delay. I will suggest that Geffrey moves through themes raised by the pedagogical and allegorical visions of Virgil, but moves through them in a fashion ever more comic and surreal. He is literally carried through questions of imperial and racial history, and through the Boethian epic of vision and spiritual education. Rather than the Aeneas of moral weakness, lost in fruitless contemplation of empty images of the past, we now see Geffrey re-enacting the more taxed but promising Aeneas of the original search, the Aeneas of shipwreck and the Libyan shore.

It is a highly exaggerated version of that most traditional of inherited forms, personification allegory, that provides Chaucer the space (literally) in which he can assume a comic posture toward the very serious themes of historical authority, vision, and spiritual ascent he evokes in Books Two and Three. The pattern he employs here may be better called systematic reification than just allegory. There are, of course, personified figures like Fame and allegorically laden gods like Venus in the poem. But more peculiar and effective (and comic) are the moments where not just ideas but metaphors and other verbal constructs – even literal graphs – become things, possessing agency and acting in the narrative. When the eagle carries him off (541–48), Boethius's feathers of philosophy – the metaphoric medium of ascent –

literally swoop down and lift Geffrey up (see below), and that idea
made flesh in turn articulates the principles of sound being made flesh
which allow Geffrey to see the equally reified figures of rumor in the
House of Fame. But this making of images and ideas into objects and
characters extends to the codex itself. Stories have become spaces in
which the narrator can roam, and figures clad in red or black – letters
come to life – will later run around the House of Fame.

The scheme of reification has of course already had its place in Book
One, with its book turned into a temple of Venus by way of the
traditional arts of memory. But it is far more overt in Books Two and
Three, and exploits especially a series of images made prominent in the
allegorical vision of the *Aeneid*, particularly the spiritual allegory
inspired by Boethius. We have seen in chapter 3 that throughout the
Middle Ages there is a widespread association between the cosmologies
and ethics of the *Consolation of Philosophy* and *Aeneid* 6. Boethius, and his
commentary tradition, are used to gloss Virgil: the texts interpenetrate
within the learned tradition. The connection thus generated between
Virgilian descent and Boethian ascent as parallel exercises in spiritual
re-education provides a central nexus of meaning in the *House of Fame*.

Especially in the commentary of "Bernard," we find a complex and
ramified bonding between the *Aeneid* and the *Consolation*. And as we
have seen, such a commentary was available in England, at least in
summary in Peterhouse 158, and the basic thrust of his approach to the
text could also be found in Albericus of London, the Third Vatican
Mythographer, as well as in other English writers like John of
Salisbury. Readers and writers of the later Middle Ages, then, inherited
a pair of texts linked by nearly a thousand years of echoes and mutually
referential interpretations. The commentary tradition, in particular,
established such parallels that on at least one level of interpretation the
texts virtually coalesced. It is this aspect of Chaucer's referential
landscape – its solidity and tradition, its very obviousness – that
allowed Chaucer to use it at once seriously and parodically.[56]

The eagle and Geffrey's flight gather together and reify a series of
thematically loaded images that explore these Virgilian/Boethian
associations. Geffrey's ignorance of his true whereabouts already re-
enacts Aeneas. But being lost is also among Lady Philosophy's central
metaphors for Boethius's spiritual plight, so Geffrey's literal situation
also links him to Boethius through the strategy of reification. The eagle
(*ales Iovis*) allows Geffrey to re-enact Aeneas's sighting of the eagle and
swans (*Aen.* 1.393–400). And as the winged messenger of Jupiter, the

eagle replicates the role of Mercury come to awaken the sleeping Aeneas at the end of *Aeneid* 4. The eagle also reifies a Boethian metaphor that is particularly appropriate to this stage in the *House of Fame*: the feathers of philosophy.

Geffrey and his model, Aeneas, have both at this point just broken away from a worldly enchainment, however attractive; both are now ready to approach the real end of their tasks, literal and spiritual. The analogous moment in the *Consolation* falls at the beginning of Book Four. Lady Philosophy has persuaded "Boethius" away from his own enslavement to worldly goods; she now promises, metaphorically, to show him the way to "verray blisfulnesse" and his true home:

> I schal shewe the the weye that schal bryngen the ayen unto thyn hous; and I schal fycchen fetheris in thi thought, by whiche it mai arisen in heighte; so that, alle tribulacioun idon awey, thow, by my gyding and by my path and by my sledys, shalt mowen retourne hool and sownd into thi contree.
>
> I have, forthi, swifte fetheris that surmounten the heighte of the hevene. Whanne the swifte thoght hath clothid itself in tho fetheris, it despiseth the hateful erthes, and surmounteth the rowndenesse of the gret ayr; and it seth the clowdes byhynde his bak, and passeth the heighte of the regioun of the fir... (*Boece* IV, prose 1.64–metrum 1.7)

The parallel careers of Aeneas, Boethius, and Geffrey are thus brought together in the single figure of the eagle.

The rest of Book Two parodies its prototypes more overtly than did *House of Fame* 1. Rather than seeking the love which moves the world, Boethius's cosmic love, Geffrey serves and seeks only the worldly love of man and woman. Even in this, as the eagle says, Geffrey is almost hermetically sealed from reality, only writing and reading about love, never experiencing the thing itself. Geffrey's world is the world of books, of mediated and predigested experience. And his promised reward is not "verray blisfulnesse" nor the true "hous" and "contre" promised by Lady Philosophy. Rather, the eagle offers Geffrey "tydynges" of his worldly neighbors and a trip to the House of Fame "To do the som disport and game" (664). This is an awful parody of the true home and country promised to Aeneas and his avatar Boethius in the allegorical vision of the *Aeneid*, but in a deeper sense it is appropriate. The House of Fame is the proper home and country of this modern Boethius whose only interest in love is in the sense of "affairs."

The eagle is a perfect guide for this parodic ascent.[57] Garrulous and self-satisfied, he has a talent amounting almost to genius for misusing Boethian arguments. At every possible point, the eagle makes mechanical and mundane those explanations which Lady Philosophy presented as metaphoric and spiritual. In a funny way, then, the eagle reifies concepts just as does Chaucer. The eagle presents as a mechanical proof, for instance (730 ff.), the descriptions of proper place in the cosmic order found in the *Consolation* (III, metrum 2 and prose 11, and IV, metrum 6).

The obfuscating role of false interpretation enters the structure of *House of Fame* 2 just as it did in Book One. Here the false interpreter is the guide himself. Even when dull Geffrey slowly realizes the Boethian parallel to his journey ("thoo thoughte y upon Boece," 972) and quotes from *Consolation* IV, metrum 1, the eagle quashes any spiritual meaning. He offers instead to expound the physical properties of the universe:

> With that this egle gan to crye,
> "Lat be," quod he, "thy fantasye!
> Wilt thou lere of sterres aught?"
> (991–93)

This perverse misinterpretation characterizes the eagle's entire, seemingly endless speech. Rather than leading Geffrey to Boethian truth, the eagle clouds it.[58]

After his reified and parodic Boethian ascent, Geffrey is indeed deposited at a house that again echoes Lady Philosophy's metaphors of the lost home, but hardly of the sort she meant. Instead, Geffrey finds himself in the House of Fame, where the previous doubts about untrustworthy visions, the dubious authority of human language, conflicting interpretations, and the gap between appearance and truth, are all embodied – reified – and acted out in yet more exaggerated form. Where Venus's temple in Book One was decorated with scenes from one poem, here the structure is decorated with figures of the word-mongers themselves. This broader perspective, nonetheless, does not depart entirely or finally from the sequence of imagery, grounded in the *Aeneid*, that we have already explored.

The figure of Fame gathers details from the *Aeneid* (4. 173–90); from Ovid, whose authority has already contested Virgil's in Book One; and from the *Consolation*, from which she adopts qualities of Fortune (I, prosa 5 and II, prosa 2) and the physical aspect – cruel parody – of Lady Philosophy herself (I, prosa 1).[59] The texts intersect again. But this is not "Fame" in the positive sense of virtuous repute or heavenly glory. Rather it is Fame in the sense of unpredictable rumor and worldly approbation.

Her house is the house of authority, the house of words. It is held up by pillars occupied by the creators of Fame, the great writers (1419–25). These are writers, however, whose reliability has been cast into doubt by the previous books and whose authority is now further deflated. Among them, these writers present the whole of ancient Mediterranean history – Jews, Thebans, Greeks, and Romans – and encompass both the world and the underworld. Yet even they can offer no consistent record. Particularly in the matter that has troubled Geffrey most, the history of Troy and Aeneas, there is disagreement.

> But yet I gan ful wel espie,
> Betwex hem was a litil envye.
> Oon seyde that Omer made lyes,
> Feynynge in hys poetries,
> And was to Grekes favorable;
> Therfor held he hyt but fable.
> (1475–80)

It is indeed, as Geffrey remarks, "a ful confus matere" (1517).[60]

Rather than being raised to an apprehension of some supreme truth in Fame's palace, then, Geffrey seems (though unwittingly) to parody the elevated aims of the Boethian, allegorized *Aeneid*. He arrives in a place which only confirms our prior fears about the unreliability of authority, the impossibility of true interpretation, the emptiness of vision. Geffrey himself is relatively unmoved; he has only wanted the tidings promised him by the eagle. But the aim of the visionary ascent has failed.

At this point in the *House of Fame*, however, Geffrey begins once again to re-enact rather closely the experiences of Aeneas. For not all possibilities of vision, of some more authentic and profitable experience of the postlapsarian world, have been exhausted. There remains, within the allegorized Boethian vision of Virgil, the alternative offered to Aeneas. This is the way to vision and truth not through abandoning the world, but by re-entering it – the descent to vision that we see in *Aeneid* 6. Through his creatures, as explained by "Bernard," the Creator reveals himself; and through contemplation of his own life and world, Aeneas may grasp cosmic truths. But the successful descent to vision entails some true interpretive ability and a capacity for mature contemplation. Once past the engraved doors of Daedalus in Book Six, Aeneas abandons that tearful and sentimental contemplation of the past seen also at Juno's temple in Book One. He has reached the point where he may undertake what "Bernard" calls "the virtuous descent."

In this, a wise man descends to worldly things, not placing his attention in them but seeing through their fragility to invisible truths.[61] We may well wonder whether Geffrey, like his model Aeneas, will be receptive to this new vision of worldly reality.

With an anonymous guide who mysteriously turns up, Geffrey leaves the House of Fame, and literally descends to the House of Twigs, which stands "in a valeye" (1918).[62] In this, too, he enacts the role of Aeneas, who is repeatedly forced to leave splendid but sterile enclosures, places of civilization (the city of Helenus and Andromache, Carthage, Sicily) in favor of the unmediated, ferocious realities of desert, sea, and battle. In order to found an authentic civilization or create an authentic artifact, the hero/poet must achieve the kind of controlled, authoritative contact with unmediated reality toward which, at several levels, Aeneas and Boethius both strive. Geffrey thus once again embodies Aeneas's pilgrimage in his descent to the Babel of the House of Twigs: the unmediated world of man, the radical source of unreliable words.

The structure Geffrey now approaches again yokes together two closely related Virgilian moments, as well as echoes of another text, the *Consolation*.[63] Geffrey begins by comparing the building to "Domus Dedaly, / That Laboryntus cleped ys" (1920–21), and this, as we have already seen, calls to mind Aeneas's delay before the artwork of Daedalus in *Aeneid* 6.[64] But the house itself closely replicates imagery of that Underworld to which Aeneas then descends.

> And eke this hous hath of entrees
> As fele as of leves ben in trees
> In somer, whan they grene been;
> And on the roof men may yet seen
> A thousand holes, and wel moo,
> To leten wel the soun out goo.
> And be day, in every tyde,
> Been al the dores opened wide,
> And be nyght echon unshette;
> Ne porter ther is noon to lette
> No maner tydynges in to pace.
>   (1945–55)

The house has a thousand holes in its roof to let the sound out, and doors with no porters that open during the day and are unlocked at night. In addition to Ovid (*Metamorphoses* 12.39–63), this surely recalls Virgil's Euboean cave with its hundred doors and the voices of the

Sibyl issuing from each, its doors suddenly flung open (*Aen.* 6.42–81). Even the leaf simile may recall Helenus's prophecy of the Sibyl, and the chaos of her omens when the wind blows the leaves upon which they are written (3.444–47). Both structures provided entryways to true experience and exits for chaotic language. The comparison to Domus Dedaly, and the description of the House as at once the House of Twigs and the cave of Avernus, all link together to create an image of wandering and uncertainty – a place that at once reminds us, as in the allegorized Virgil, of the Underworld as the world itself, and of that world as an entangling labyrinth in which we are caught first by our limited experience and second by our circle of words.[65] At the same time, the house's very shape ("hyt was shapen lyk a cage," 1985) recalls the Boethian image of the earth as a prison house where our vision is inevitably obscured.

Rejoined by his dubious guide, the eagle, Geffrey prepares to enter the House,

> For yit, paraunter, y may lere
> Som good theron, or sumwhat here
> That leef me were, or that y wente.
>   (1997–99)

As when he left the temple of Venus at the close of Book One, here again Geffrey seems to be circling back to a starting point. The eagle had promised "here I wol abyden the" (1086) when he dropped Geffrey near the House of Fame, and it is to "here," apparently, that Geffrey now returns. If the parodic Boethian ascent has failed him, "paraunter" the Virgilian descent – another way to vision – may now offer some help. The eagle now takes on yet another role as guide, that of the Sibyl: he is the companion both of Geffrey's Boethian ascent and of his Virgilian descent. The whispers of events that fill the house suggestively overlap the allegorical figures occupying the vestibule of Virgil's hell.[66] Within the house, Geffrey sees a vast crowd, similar to that Aeneas sees in the Underworld (*Aen.* 6.305 ff.):

> But which a congregacioun
> Of folk, as I saugh rome aboute,
> Some wythin and some wythoute,
> Nas never seen, ne shal ben eft;
> That, certys, in the world nys left
> So many formed be Nature...
>   (2034–39)

In this labyrinthine Underworld to which he has circled back, then, Geffrey finds the "man of gret auctorite" (2158) who remains forever silent, because here the poem itself falls silent.

By the end of the *House of Fame*, Geffrey – whether we take him as poet or as clownish would-be lover – finds himself virtually where he began. He has sought vision and truth, though usually of the wrong kinds. He has seen the story of, and even identified himself with, the heroes in two texts of great cultural authority, the *Aeneid* and the *Consolation*. The usefulness of authority has been cast into doubt, however, by Geffrey's own inadequacy as an avatar and reader of those two intimidating figures, Aeneas and Boethius. But in the end, Geffrey only finds himself where most of humankind does in a fallen world. Like his model Aeneas, Geffrey must make a descent before he can hope for any true visionary flight. If we leave him waiting attentively before an Authority who never speaks, the resolution is no more ambiguous than that of Aeneas who learned the truths of cosmogony and history, then left the Underworld through the gate of false dreams.[67]

GEFFREY IN THE CIRCLES OF NARRATIVE, COSMOS,
AND HERMENEUTICS

A central pattern of imagery in Boethius, as often noted above, is the wanderer in search of his lost homeland; and it is in terms of return there that Philosophy marks the major steps of her instruction. *Consolation* III draws to a close with a sequence of reminders about the ultimately circular path of this return. In metrum 11 Lady Philosophy reminds Boethius that he must bend the long motions (*Longos ... motus*) of his thought back in a circle (*orbem*) in his soul in order to escape the darkness of the body and regain the light of wisdom. But this instance of an enlightening circularity is followed by two cautionary examples. In prose 12, Boethius protests briefly against Philosophy's subtle arguments, wondering whether their circularity mimics the perfect form of the cosmos, or whether instead they are an inextricable "hous of Didalus," an argument whose circularity can lead nowhere. The book then closes with the fable of Orpheus, whose ascent to the light of wisdom is arrested (specifically because of human love, like Geffrey and Dido) "whanne he looketh the helles, that is to seyn, into lowe thinges of the erthe" (*Boece* III, metrum 12.68–69). This sequence of references to circularity not only reminds us of the topos of hell as the "lowe thinges of the erthe," but also establishes the simultaneous need and danger of turning back upon the self and the world. The cosmic circle can recall to the blinded soul the perfection of its creator, but the glance back to earthly things, as earthly things, will only restore the fall. The world is at once cosmic circle and the "hous of Didalus," image of liberty and bondage. It is this context which "Bernard" brings to his interpretation of the descent in *Aeneid* 6 (as discussed in chapter 3), and the context I think we are invited to call to mind when Geffrey undertakes his own approach to the House of Twigs, which is also a descent and, as I have suggested, possibly a circle.

The comparison of the House of Twigs to Domus Dedaly thus creates a multiple linkage – to Boethius and the problem of language as circular and entrapping, to Aeneas and his descent to hell, and to the imagery of the world itself as a prison and labyrinth, an idea embodied by this last house of fame. Indeed, the three buildings of the *House of Fame* follow a sequence of ever more general, less reliable and simultaneously less mediated report.[68] The unreliability of Geffrey's redaction of the *Aeneid* in Book One was clear to the reader but not apparently to Geffrey himself. In the House of Fame he witnessed the uncertainty of textual tradition, in the shoving that goes on among the *auctores* in the pillars. He now witnesses the production of conflicting report in the House of Twigs. In a sense, then, he circles through the same house and the same epic three times. In this too he may re-enact and exceed the double birth of the allegorized Aeneas, who must twice descend to the world, first in his physical birth, and then again in his philosophical descent to the Underworld which symbolizes the world.

Even these structures in which the truth value of verbal authority is set increasingly in doubt, however, are at the same time monuments to the dazzling power of artifice, the shining and fascinating power of human craft to involve us in report – and comfort us by report – even if that report is false or incomplete or subverted by its audience. This is exactly the tempting comfort and fascination Aeneas found in the two temples, and from which he had to be practically torn away. Both these episodes on which Geffrey's initial re-enactment of Aeneas is based, moreover, address incomplete projects. The temple of Juno is still being built (*condebat*, *Aen.* 1.447) when Aeneas sees it. And Daedalus's engravings on the gates of Apollo's temple are also incomplete work, in which the artificer's own emotions overcome him and prevent his finishing (*Aen.* 6.32–33).[69] These two fundamental moments of

Virgilian prefiguration thus also prepare us for the incompleteness of the *House of Fame*.

What is more, these two moments themselves enact the failure of intention in the life of the artifact, and the power of its audience to wrest it away from the artificer. The pathos of the engraved doors to the temple of Apollo in *Aeneid* 6 lies largely in what Daedalus could *not* bring himself to depict – the fall and death of Icarus. The Trojans' gaze and attention, just as the scene is interrupted by the Sibyl's arrival, seem to rest on the blank where "twice a father's hand had failed" (6.33). And the hero's tears in *Aeneid* 1 respond to images that intend to depict a triumph of Juno over her enemy, Troy; he subverts that intention and makes the pictures into a tragic revery on his lost past.[70] So while I agree with Piero Boitani that in the temple of Venus "Chaucer contemplates the *Aeneid* as a supreme model of art" and there "re-enacts the *Ur*-poem," I think Chaucer consciously does so precisely by re-enacting the moment where the "supreme model" marks out its own and all art's limitations, its inevitable embedding in and unbinding by time and the audience.[71]

The very incompleteness of the text, the power of the audience explicit both in Aeneas as gazer and Geffrey as redactor, the ever less mediated forms of report and the ultimate silence of authority, all imply a realization that exactly by emulating Aeneas Geffrey can abandon him.[72] Geffrey can move past a tradition that has become binding, even enslaving – and not only because of the easy and dangerous sentimentality into which we saw him (like his model Aeneas) briefly slip in Book One, but also because it has become so profoundly encumbered by conflicting exegesis that it carries confusion more than meaning for him. Yet like Aeneas descending to "Bernard"'s underworld/world, or like Boethius, Geffrey may finally be learning to *use* the originally enslaving literary "world" to move past its enslavement. In the House of Twigs he witnesses the radical origins of a world no less verbal than that of the House of Fame, but nonetheless closer to its source in the silva of originary whispers. Here the link between receiving and transmitting verbal "reality" is far closer than it was in the House of Fame where the mediating auctors, however dubious and contradictory, held up the roof and restricted at least a little the range of possible versions. Rather than authoritative and finished works, the House of Twigs shows us verbal generation, and the role of hearer as transmitter becomes central. This is of course the central gesture of the Virgilian redaction with which the poem began, at whose center Geffrey has claimed "non other auctour alegge I."

I turn now to the fifteenth-century objects to which Chaucer's text gave rise: the manuscripts of the *House of Fame*, in the context of the House of Twigs, and its hearer/retellers reconstituting the reader/redactor of Book One, and diverting central attention from authority to transmission. In the closely related Bodley and Fairfax manuscripts, the *House of Fame* is by far the most heavily annotated Chaucerian poem, and indeed it is among the most annotated of any work by Chaucer, with fifteen Latin citations in its margins.[73] So the poem is distinguished by its scribal transmission as the most classically Latinate and bookish in these collections.

Indeed the poem's format and brief notes in these two manuscripts are strikingly like a number of less heavily annotated Virgil manuscripts that were being produced in later fourteenth- and fifteenth-century England.[74] This phenomenon is not unique. Nigel Palmer has pointed out the extent to which deluxe manuscripts of vernacular *Consolation* translations seem to imitate the format of Latin manuscripts, especially by including Latin commentaries and Latin lemmata in the margins.[75] In these cases, the manuscripts seem to mediate between an only slightly Latin-reading audience and the fully learned tradition to which it aspires. The *House of Fame's* mediation is far more complex, with several authors competing in the marginal "lemmata" (as they might be considered) and unresolved in the vernacular text they surround. But the learned, Latin books which the poem is made visually to echo are significant nonetheless of the authorities it at once emulates and subverts.

This is not merely a learned poem codicologically imitating its authorizing sources, though. For we encounter here a radical codicological subversion, in which the "authorities" are mixed up as in the poem itself, Virgil alternating with Ovid and others. Moreover, this text about reading – that activity of the codicological margins – usurps the center space which is the usual place of the auctor, and pushes the Latin sources to the margins. In the two best manuscripts of this poem, then, as in its text, Virgil is at once central but decentered, honored but ignored, cited but marginalized. Instead, it is that figure of the margins, that negotiator squeezed in the disappearing space between marginalia and text, Geffrey the reader, who usurps the page, thrusting a confused sequence of *auctoritates* into the margins. It is not the "man of gret auctorite" but his readings and reader who occupy the center of the page and poem. In this context, it is no longer surprising that the Aeneas Geffrey most intensely enacts is the marginalized and liminal hero – the invisible Aeneas not yet quite in Carthage and not yet descending to the Underworld.

Let us return to a poet I dismissed at the beginning of this chapter. Dante turns to the close of his own, partly Virgilian epic with the poignant image of a book's scattered leaves being bound into a single volume, and the implication of a world known before only in parts but now as a whole.[76] In an opposite move that still takes on its richest implications only in the context of Dante, Chaucer ends the *House of Fame* with an *un*binding, an unfinished sentence that defies all the parsing and skills of *grammatica* to which we are alerted in Books One and Two. And that unreadable fragment occurs inside a labyrinthine space that images our restricted vision of the world and recalls the Sibyl's scattered and therefore incomprehensible, unbindable leaves. If at the close of the *House of Fame* we are left with authority unbound, reduced to its most primitive, unmediated, and disorganized elements, this is nonetheless not a moment of despair. On the contrary, Geffrey is suddenly buoyant, and energy has returned to the poem after the rather sagging sequence of petitioners in the House of Fame. We are back to the world of tidings, from which new art may be made; and we are brought back in a circle – as has been Geffrey himself – to a new authority.

Despite his humor, or better yet through his humor, Chaucer responds in the *House of Fame* to the same yearnings for truth and transcendence addressed by the allegorical vision of the *Aeneid*. This is a parodic poem, but a parody whose point is directed against Geffrey, not against the Virgilian and Boethian quests he re-enacts. Chaucer makes fun of this particular incarnation of Aeneas, but not of the model. Serious archetypes always hover behind their momentary and comic manifestation. As Doob puts it, "However deft its touch, ... *The House of Fame* means business."[77] The transcendent pilgrimage and the enchained pilgrim – Aeneas, Boethius – remain intact, mysterious, and poignant. No matter how lightly we choose to take it, the *House of Fame* begins with "God" and ends with "auctorite"; and it is in the troubled relationship between the latter and the former that the poem's thematic weight ultimately lies. Just what that relationship may be is left up to the reader, as it is in any hermeneutic situation, to ... figure.

AUTHORITY: TYRANNY VERSUS DIALOGUE IN THE PROLOGUE TO *THE LEGEND OF GOOD WOMEN*

After writing *Troilus and Criseyde*, one of the great Troy poems in our language, and approaching the years of the *Canterbury Tales*, Chaucer returned once again to the story of Dido and Aeneas, and to the divisive authorities of Virgil and Ovid therein. To this pair of authorities in the "Legend of Dido," however, Chaucer decisively adds a third: himself. In the final two sections of this chapter, I approach the "Legend of Dido" not as a free-standing redaction of Virgil's and other versions of her story,[78] but rather through the hermeneutic, erotic, and political framework provided by the *Legend*'s Prologue.[79] The Prologue, especially in its probably later "G" text, explores versions of readership as wide-ranging and problematic as any in the *House of Fame*, but with two signal developments. First, the authorial epicenter for conflicting readership has undergone a profound shift, from Virgil in the *House of Fame* to Chaucer himself in the *Legend*; Chaucer inserts his own earlier poems as books approaching canonical status, worthy to be scrutinized as closely as the Ovidian and Virgilian tales that follow. Second, the readers in this Prologue are powerful and quasi-royal deities, Cupid and Alceste, the latter of whom is clearly linked to Queen Anne in the "F" Prologue; they articulate their contrasting expositions of readership, intriguingly, in the language of good and bad governance; and since they present themselves as a romantic couple, their versions of readership and governance are distinguished by gender as well as by method. Both these moves reflect a dramatic shift away from the largely private, passive readerly themes of the *House of Fame*, and toward an aggressive approach to the poet's own work and to his narrative, sited within a more public and politicized sphere. The goodness of the women in the legends themselves, and especially of Queen Dido, calls for a readerly response as politicized yet flexible as that demanded by their figure in the Prologue, Alceste.

For his Prologue to the *Legend of Good Women*, Chaucer returns to the structure of the dream vision. After a May day of self-consciously literary devotion to the daisy, his favorite flower, the narrator returns home to sleep, and finds himself dreaming in a scene that mirrors his waking love-service. Within the dream, the daisy is doubled by Alceste, who arrives with the "myghty god of Love" (G 158), and followed by "ladyes nyntene / In real habyt" (G 186–87) who will prove to be the intended subjects of the legends that follow. As he had done in the *Book of the Duchess*, the *House of Fame*, and the *Parliament of Fowls*, Chaucer casts his dreaming narrator as a marginal figure, polite and hesitant in the presence of a courtly superior: "And I answerde / Unto his axynge ... / And seyde, 'Sire, it am I,' and cam hym ner, / And salewede hym" (G 238–41). But those courtly superiors in this poem are readers of Geoffrey Chaucer's own work, especially the *Troilus*. This distinction of the narrator and his work within the dream vision aids Chaucer's procedures of autocanonization in the Prologue. Chaucer elevates the prestige of his earlier texts without needing to abandon his traditional narratorial stance of slightly befuddled modesty.

Cupid, enraged, accuses the dreamer of having defamed the followers of love in *Troilus and Criseyde*: "Thow art my mortal fo and me werreyest, / And of myne olde servauntes thow mysseyest" (G 248-49). Cupid's notion both of his own followers ("alle wyse and honourable," G 247) and of romantic narrative is splendidly egomaniacal and monolithic. All the servants of love are good in his view, and "al the world of autours" (G 308) supports his position, depicting lovers "evere an hundred goode ageyn oon badde" (G 277). Cupid is angry about the potential of Chaucer's work to make "wise folk fro me withdrawe" (G 257). Still, Cupid sees the dreamer not as a significant poet but rather as a wilfully perverse redactor. The narrator has real *auctores* in the "sixty bokes olde and newe" (G 273) he owns, but he fails to read them Cupid's way. Cupid's is an amusingly but also tyranically self-centered form of readership: all books are about him, he assumes, and all are positive, even works like "Jerome agayns Jovynyan" (G 281), a notorious source of anti-feminist examples. Cupid's readership thus lays claim to virtually any text, from a literally Erotic perspective.[80]

Alceste then speaks. She intercedes for the dreamer, and proposes to read his texts with a very different approach, in which multiple explanations are discoverable, and the text operates in dialogue with its reader.[81] Alceste insists that the text, or its representative within the dream, should be allowed to speak back: "Ye moten herkenen if he can replye" (G 319). More importantly, Alceste couches her promotion of responsive voices within the text in terms of proper governance and judicial procedure. She suggests a number of possible rereadings of the dreamer's anti-Erotic texts: perhaps he is falsely accused, or wrote out of habit and without malice, or was ordered to write, or now regrets having done so (F 350–68, G 328–52). Cupid, she says, ought not to respond to the dreamer's poems "lyk tyraunts of Lumbardye, / That usen wilfulhed and tyrannye" (G 354–55). Her discussion of right royalty that then follows is largely about the king hearing his people's responses and behaving with justice and moderation. Alceste thus demands that Cupid encounter the threatening work through a model of quasi-judicial dialogue between text and reader, a model explicitly based on notions of clement kingship, as opposed to Lombardic or Erotic tyranny. She returns, however, to the dreamer's poetry, and offers a list of his own works "in preysynge of youre name" (G 404). This balances Cupid's list of the authoritative works in the dreamer's book chest, and provides another of the Prologue's gestures of autocanonization. Cupid finally places the dreamer's fate in the judgment of Alceste, and she orders him to devote his time to "makynge of a gloryous legende / Of goode women" (G 473–74).

Cupid is not quite done, however. He turns back to the kneeling dreamer, and identifies the lady who has rescued him as Alceste:

> Hast thow nat in a bok, lyth in thy cheste,
> The grete goodnesse of the queene Alceste,
> That turned was into a dayesye ...?
> (G 498–500)

Cupid's "learned" reference provides the Prologue's most cunning moment of inserting Chaucer into the canon of *auctores*. For this bit of pseudo-Ovidian metamorphosis in fact appears to be Chaucer's own invention; it has no antique source, no place (yet) among the authoritative tomes in the dreamer's chest. If the story *is* among those books at all, it is there only once the Prologue itself rests among them, adding Chaucer's version to the received myth of Alceste.[82] Through Cupid's own voice, then, Chaucer writes himself into the "sixty bokes olde and newe" that Cupid had accused him of perverting.

Chaucer thereby inserts his own book among the *auctores*, and his Prologue explores readerships modeled on tyranny or judicial dialogue, respectively proposed by a male and a female speaker. These initial themes of literary recreation, just kingship, and flexible reading are complicated and problematized throughout the Prologue, however, by two interconnected clusters of imagery: first, imagery of gleaning and seasonal cycle, and second, imagery of nakedness and veiling. The two image clusters imply another gendered argument about reading, literary recreation, and male power; this more shadowy argument adumbrates (even while it leaves incompletely articulated, veiled) a connection between literary renewal and fertility, yet a renewal always equally and uncomfortably threatened by versions of masculine, tyrannical violence.

At the Prologue's opening, the narrator bemoans his inability adequately to praise the daisy, the object of his adoration and gaze. The best of poetry is already written, and he remains like a gleaner, picking up what may be left behind:

> For wel I wot that folk han here-beforn
> Of makyng ropen, and lad awey the corn;
> [And] I come after, glenynge here and there,
> And am ful glad if I may fynde an ere
> Of any goodly word that they han left.
>
> (G 61–65)

The image of the poet as autumnal gleaner, picking up after his greater predecessors, creates an initial tone of modesty. Cupid later adapts this harvest image to serve his own notions of the monolithic tradition of Erotic literature, and similarly dismisses the modern writer, when he ends his accusations against the dreamer: "But yit, I seye, what eyleth the to wryte / The draf of storyes, and forgete the corn?" (G 311–12). But gleaning can also be an assertion of equality; the modern gleaner discovers and exploits what the *auctores* failed to notice or left behind. Gleaning, after all, finds corn – the lost ears, and by analogy the suppressed but valuable versions of literary tradition, not just Cupid's "draf." Poetic equality between ancients and moderns, of course, is precisely what the narrator slyly achieves with his version of Alceste and its self-inserted place among the *auctores* in his chest of books.[83]

Such local references to harvest and gleaning participate in the Prologue's broader evocation of seasonal cycle and renewal, inevitable in a poem about the courtly rites of May. Winter here is a time of violence, defeat, and sterility, and the emergence of spring calls the birds forth to mock the fowler whose craft would have killed them – another, darker and violent version of harvest. These uncomfortably connected ideas, suggesting the poet himself as a crafty fowler in the sterile nakedness of winter, converge in a textual image that lies between them in the Prologue:

> For myn entent is, or I fro yow fare,
> The naked text in English to declare
> Of many a story, or elles of many a geste,
> As autours seyn; leveth hem if yow leste.
>
> (G 85–88)

These famous lines possess an irresolvably multiple valence beyond even the monolithicizing capacities of Chaucer's Cupid. They propose a version of authoritative story liberated from authority, and particularly from Latinity and the marginal impositions of the Latin page.[84] Yet they make this claim in terms of a nakedness at odds with the linguistic revestiture inherent in the translation or redaction. Moreover, these "naked texts" of famous women's lives suggest an unwilling exposure to the narrator's or reader's gaze, a nudity that will often recur literally in the stories to follow.[85] Finally, as in the narratives, this nakedness has as much to do with fantasies of male dominance (the narrator's or a sexual aggressor's) as with the subjects of the legends.

By contrast with this vexed imagery of literary renewal through divestiture, the Prologue explores vernal renewal emphatically in terms of desirable *re*vestiture and a retreat from violence:

> Forgeten hadde the erthe his pore estat
> Of wynter, that hym naked made and mat,
> And with his swerd of cold so sore hadde greved.
> Now hadde th'atempre sonne al that releved,
> And clothed hym in grene al newe ageyn.
> (G 113–17)

The sword of winter and its violence against the nudity of a helpless (but male) earth will reappear in the legends, especially those of Dido and Lucrece, in the guise of sexualized swords and suicidal, not quite veiled female bodies. If, as we have seen, modes of readership are figured in terms of tyranny and justice, and of gendered and sexualized relations, so (though far less explicitly) the modes of translation and literary renewal are contradictorily linked to nakedness and reclothing, to violence and its departure, both sets of images also irreconcilably pulled between seasonal cycle and sexuality.

Spring's peaceable revestiture of the earth and the occasion it provides for song and poetic creation, then, seem to pull against the narrator's pursuit of a denuded authoritative text, the fowler's ploys, and the violence of winter's sword. Further, in a Prologue so much devoted to exploring eroticized versions of writing and reading, all this language of veiling and unveiling, covering and uncovering recalls ancient tropes for writing and hermeneutics, tropes that themselves imply the text as a body susceptible of undress and sexual investigation, even violation. In an ancient and dominant metaphor, the text is seen as a veil covering truth, and calling out for exegetical undress in a traditionally male scholastic setting. Yet the uncovering of an implicitly (or explicitly) feminine core also suggests violence and transgressive exposure, the laying bare to vulgar eyes of truths that Nature wishes reserved for a company of initiates.[86]

Just like the narrator's very gaze and the dance of her lady attendants, so all these topics and images in the Prologue converge on the person and story of Alceste, the dream's fulfillment of womanly goodness. Alceste of course is the proponent of a responsive and variable reading of texts, and it is she who introduces the model of tyranny and justice for these conflicting hermeneutics. But if she articulates a way of reading, and a reading that is responsive, engaged, flexible, non-tyrannical, she is also something to be read, investigated by the narrator and explicated by Cupid. Alceste is thereby susceptible of the very tyrannical readings, the violation and readerly undress which her logic resists. She is after all the dream-double for the daisy which is the day-long and immobile object of the narrator's erotic gaze, and she is the God of Love's beloved, thus the literal object of Erotic gaze and desire. Further, the myth of Alceste's return from the Underworld is analogous with the Prologue's themes of cultural and seasonal renewal.[87]

Alceste is, I would propose, the achieved version of an enhanced, but still limited and always endangered feminine power; she enacts a queenly power necessarily in erotic, political, and hermeneutic dialogue with manhood – qualities toward some of which each of the Good Women in the legends will strive. Yet Alceste is no solitary queen like Cleopatra or Dido, no unprotected woman like Lucrece or Tisbe, no usurper of male order like Medea. Alceste's power, however openly articulated, exists only in so far as she is in dialogue with, and is the erotically desired consort of, the God of Love. Her double situation as reader and as what is read – at once a carrier of themes and proposer of responsive readership, and (as the daisy) the static object of admiring or eroticizing gazes – thus also foreshadows the double reactions, sympathetic yet often leering, that the narrator will carry into the legends.[88] Both her power and its limits set up Alceste as an almost typological fulfillment of the powers and threatening transgressions enacted by the individual heroines of the legends that follow. She bears, as the ladies of the F Prologue put it, "our alder pris in figurynge" (F 298), but price, like so much else in the Prologue, has a troublingly double valence, suggesting both the rewards and the mortal costs of womanly goodness.[89]

The G Prologue to the *Legend of Good Women* thus proposes both a range of themes, and a double, unresolved hermeneutics by which those themes may be approached in the legends to follow. All these elements center on contested literary and political authority, couched in terms of gender and sexuality. Thematically, the Prologue juxtaposes tyranny with balanced and responsive kingship, and displays Alceste – a regal, feminine figure – both encouraging and playing a part in judicial dialogue. It proposes modes of cultural renewal both by acknowledging ancient authority and by seeking out what that authority has left aside: another form of dialogue juxtaposed with the potential tyranny of textual authority. But the Prologue creates a narrator whose own dream preparation for writing the lives of ancient women floats uncertainly between imagery of tyranny and dialogue, nakedness and revestiture, sexualized wintry violence and gentle vernal renewal. All of this presses us, as readers, to be prepared for tales whose very narration may be uncertain, unresolved in its judgments and attitudes toward the good women depicted therein, and their versions of selfhood and power. It also presses us to read the tales as themselves responsory, speaking back at once to the authorities that are often so explicitly their sources, and to the notions of womanhood and goodness proposed by Cupid, Alceste, or their narrator. It is in terms of these themes and this double hermeneutics that we now turn to Chaucer's last telling of the story of Dido and Aeneas.

THE TEMPTATION OF AUTHORITY IN THE "LEGEND OF DIDO"

The emotional passivity – the victimization, even – of the *House of Fame*'s Dido, and the hermeneutic passivity of her narrator there, have largely disappeared when her story re-emerges in the "Legend of Dido." Instead, in Chaucer's return to this story, both the heroine and her narrator display forms of will and choice that respond suggestively to the themes of political power, hermeneutic dialogue, and readerly flexibility just investigated in the G Prologue. If the *House of Fame*'s narrator modeled himself primarily on aspects of Aeneas as a passive sufferer and troubled intrepreter, the narrator of the "Legend of Dido" by contrast imitates active aspects of Dido as a seeker of power in her world. Both this Dido and this narrator are willing even to commit certain kinds of misreading and transgression of authority in their pursuits. The "Legend"'s narrator does not finally create a Dido at once queenly and abandoned, but he nonetheless does assert temporarily both her glory and his own honor, and they both provide models, we may even say types, for the more accomplished assertions of Alceste's influence and Chaucer's canonicity in the G Prologue.[90]

The "Legend"'s agonistic treatment, both of Virgil and of Ovid, is intriguing in this context. It reveals the narrator's sense of his own power to reshape his inherited sources, and thus to remake ancient authority as his own.[91] "Throughout the poem," Götz Schmitz writes, "he has a voice of his own and interferes more and more freely as he progresses with his tale."[92] This new sense of freedom operates within a double irony, however, for the "Legend of Dido" is at once closer to Virgil in text, and to Ovid in plot and focus, than the comparable episode in the *House of Fame*. Moreover, while the "Legend of Dido" does reflect some elements of the late-antique or medieval Troy tradition, it remains in general closer – and explicitly closer – to the classical Latin poems than does the *House of Fame*, whose narrator's wanderings among centuries of reception were studied above. In the "Legend of Dido," instead, the struggle by which the narrator asserts his own viewpoint is far more directly with what he had called "naked text" in his Prologue. Yet the very exposed fashion with which he uses Virgilian (and some Ovidian) text only serves to remind his readers of what a new work he patches together, the new veil he weaves from those masters. Famous passages from either *auctor* repeatedly lead to some signal moment of Chaucerian disagreement or refusal to continue redacting his source.

This narrator begins his bold project of syncretizing and superseding Virgil and Ovid with the very opening of his legend:

> Glorye and honour, Virgil Mantoan,
> Be to thy name! and I shal, as I can,
> Folwe thy lanterne, as thow gost byforn,
> How Eneas to Dido was forsworn.
> In thyn Eneyde and Naso wol I take
> The tenor, and the grete effectes make.
>
> (924–29)

His sweeping compliment to the status of Virgil as the story's dominant poet is immediately qualified by the inclusion of Ovid as an equal source, and the bland claim that a single "tenor" can be drawn from them.[93] The narrator's mode of addressing Virgil here may imply virtual equality with his predecessor: he will tell about Dido "as I can."

There may reside some question of skill here, but no doubt of the project's possibility; indeed the phrase may mean "in my manner." This speaker "wol... the grete effectes make," with that verb's full implication of original poetic creation, even while following the lantern of Virgil. If the Aenean narrative of the *House of Fame* wrenched itself painfully from Virgilian tone to Ovidian and back again, this version of the Dido and Aeneas story abuts these conflicting authorities from the very start. Yet the narrator does so, here, with no display of interpretive anxiety. Instead, he adopts for himself a calm, almost magisterial position of reconciler.[94]

His effort at syncretism has its most daring expression in the tensions between a text that is openly, even provocatively Virgilian (drawn from *Aeneid* 2 and 4), and a plot that is largely Ovidian.[95] The "Legend"'s focus, appropriately, is primarily restricted to plot elements that appear in the *Heroides*, whose heroines populate the dream scene in the Prologue. It begins with a fairly brief summary of the fall of Troy, Aeneas's escape therefrom with Anchises and Ascanius, the loss of Creusa, and the Trojans' arrival at Carthage (930–1001); *Heroides* 7 never narrates this material in so linear a fashion but makes reference to most of it.[96] The "Legend" then goes on to tell "How Eneas to Dido was forsworn" (927) – the seduction, abandonment, grief, and death of Dido – a narrative all found quite openly in *Heroides* 7.[97]

Within these Ovidian narrative constraints and the Ovidian focus on Dido, however, important passages of the text itself, some of its local ordering, and elements of its tone follow Virgil in an almost obtrusive fashion. The earlier parts of the narrative use the order and some notable details from *Aeneid* 1 and 2. So we are reminded that Eneas is shipwrecked in Libya with only "shipes sevene and with no more navye" (960, cf. *Aen.* 1.170), and that he goes to scout the countryside taking only Achates (964–66, cf. *Aen.* 1.312). When these two encounter Venus in the guise of a local huntress, the "Legend" almost translates their famous encounter from the *Aeneid* (970–93; cf. *Aen.* 1.314–41).[98] Again, when Dido and Eneas first meet, Chaucer carefully echoes another famous speech; Virgil's "tune ille Aeneas quem Dardanio Anchisae / alma Venus Phrygii genuit Simoentis ad undam?" (*Aen.* 1.617–18) becomes Chaucer's slightly more terse "Be ye nat Venus sone and Anchises?" (1086). Such echoes persist throughout the "Legend," though they slowly taper off, for reasons discussed below.

Two elements pull against the textual Virgilianism of the "Legend," however. First, as already noted, the Ovidian narrative focus on Dido and her fate minimizes Virgilian elements external to that topic. The fall of Troy is reduced to a list; the death and ghostly reappearance of Creusa (which receive a fair bit of attention in the *House of Fame*, 181–92) get a single line here (945); Eneas's departure for Italy and harrassment by Juno are given only four lines (949–52). Indeed all of Eneas's imperial destiny is virtually suppressed; instead he tends to be a creature of quick and high emotion comparable, if anything, to the Dido of the *House of Fame* and many women of the *Heroides*.[99] When he sees the destruction of Troy depicted on Dido's temple wall, Virgil's Aeneas weeps, but does so while delivering a grave and measured speech to Achates: "quis iam locus, / ... quae regio in terris nostri non plena laboris?" (*Aen.* 1.459–60). Chaucer's Eneas sees this as a matter for shame, "And with that word he brast out for to wepe / So tenderly that routhe it was to sene" ("Legend of Dido," 1033–34); the second line cleverly undoes the hero's Virgilian dignity, along with most of his Virgilian story.[100]

A second force in the "Legend," though, equally and more explicitly contests the *Aeneid*: the narrator himself, who repeatedly brings Virgilian detail or text to the reader's attention, then refuses to continue redacting that text, or openly disagrees with it.[101] Most often, this is a way of closing off the prospect of Virgilian narrative, and restricting it to the Ovidian plot of the "Legend." The assertiveness with which this is done, however, also begins to insert the Chaucerian narrator as an equal player in the Troy canon. After his Virgilian summary of Eneas's escape from Troy, for instance, just when the reader might expect some reference to his imperial destiny, the narrator closes off that path. Eneas, he says,

> sayleth forth with al his companye
> Toward Ytayle, as wolde his destinee.
> But of his aventures in the se
> Nis nat to purpos for to speke of here,
> For it acordeth nat to my matere.
> But, as I seyde, of hym and of Dido
> Shal be my tale, til that I have do.
>
> (951–57)

Again, when Eneas meets Venus in the nearly translated passage mentioned above, a reader of Virgil would expect her famous summary of Dido's history, which follows in the *Aeneid*; instead, the narrator again asserts the force of his own focus, and abandons a Virgilian moment "Of which as now me lesteth nat to ryme" (996). He goes on to reveal Venus's identity, as in Virgil, but then dismisses his source yet again: "I coude folwe, word for word, Virgile, / But it wolde lasten al to longe while" (1002–03). This in turn is followed by the narrator's own recital of Dido's life (1004–14), with an emphasis and voice quite distinct from Virgil.

The narrator shifts at other points from such not-quite-respectful refusal, to open doubt of the "autour" or his "bok." When Eneas enters the temple where Dido is at worship,

> I can nat seyn if that it be possible,
> But Venus hadde hym maked invysible –
> Thus seyth the bok, withouten any les.
>
> (1020–22)

The narrator's refusal to verify this detail provides a further stage in the reduction of Eneas, pulling him away from the dictates of historical destiny and the miraculous aid of the gods. In general, the "Legend" does not suppress pagan divinity itself; rather, it resists gods in the direct service of Eneas. (Instead, as we will see, it briefly elevates Dido herself to a status near divinity.) At the same time, though, this very rewriting of the Virgilian Aeneas calmly presumes the Chaucerian narrator's right to create his own version of Troy and alter the links between Trojan fate and Aenean eroticism. A similar refusal to accede to Virgil arises when the narrator reports the incident of Ascanius's replacement by Cupid (*Aen.* 1.657–94). He records the story as "oure autour telleth us" (1139), but then dismisses it: "Be as be may, I take of it no cure" (1145). The impact of the Virgilian Venus and Cupid will be replaced, in this version, by an elaborate psychologizing of Dido's reaction to her first sight of Eneas (1061–81).[102]

If the narrator thus tells the bulk of his tale by at once echoing and contesting Virgil, he also evokes then refuses to report Ovid's *Heroides* 7 at the close of the narrative, where Dido's erotic tragedy can no longer be evaded. Dido approaches her suicide with a complaint to Anna, which may remind medieval readers of lyric plaints (examined in chapter 5) rather more than it recalls Ovid.[103] But Dido's final words are as close to a translation of the opening of *Heroides* 7 as anything above was to the *Aeneid*:

> But, as myn auctour seith, yit thus she seyde;
> Or she was hurt, byforen or she deyde,
> She wrot a lettre anon that thus began:
> "Ryght so," quod she, "as that the white swan

Ayens his deth begynnyth for to synge,
Right so to yow make I my compleynynge.
Not that I trowe to geten yow ageyn,
For wel I wot that it is al in veyn,
Syn that the goddes been contraire to me.
But syn my name is lost thourgh yow," quod she,
"I may wel lese on yow a word or letter,
Al be it that I shal ben nevere the better;
For thilke wynd that blew youre ship awey,
The same wynd hath blowe awey youre fey."
But who wol al this letter have in mynde,
Rede Ovyde, and in hym he shal it fynde.

                                                    (1352–67)

Here again, we see the narrator assert his own authority by closing off the very *auctor* he has just introduced and briefly translated. Even more intriguing, though, is the apparent ease with which the narrator has dropped his earlier primary "auctour," Virgil, and replaced him with Ovid.

Against the background of these challenged "auctours" and the unlikely assertion of a single tenor between them, a narrative voice and a Dido that are very much Chaucer's own emerge during the "Legend"'s climax of seduction and betrayal. Simply put, the narrator at this point moves into a world that is ever closer to the erotic modes of his own time, and populates that world with a Dido who manages briefly to be at once Virgilian and Ovidian, at once queenly and erotic, and thus a type for the Prologue's Alceste, who is at once beloved and powerful. At the same time, though, the intensifying eroticism of the narrative, and its ever sharper focus on the physical attraction of Dido and Eneas in these passages, lead the narrator into the same troubling imagery, the same themes of masculine sexual transgression, and the same temptation to his own erotic voyeurism that subtly darkened the argument of the G Prologue.

The persistence in the "Legend" of a regal and powerful Virgilian Dido, even as her destiny moves toward tragedy and suicide, is clearest perhaps in the narrator's constant attribution to her of the epithet "queen." From her entrance into the narrative, Dido is most often shown doing the work of her people's queen. That is how Venus first identifies her – "This is the reyne of Libie there ye ben, / Of which that Dido lady is and queen" (992–93) – and how she is named another twenty times, almost until the end of the "Legend."[104] Such a title connects Chaucer's Dido to her initial role of leader, city-builder, and lawgiver in the *Aeneid*: "dux femina facti," as Venus says there (1.364). Virgil only once explicitly calls Dido a queen ("regina," 1.496), but elsewhere calls her "regalis" (1.686), and often names her in terms of her nation and the people she leads: Phoenissa, Sidonia, Tyria.[105] By contrast, in *Heroides* 7 Dido identifies herself mostly in terms of domestic roles: wife (22, 69), daughter-in-law to Venus and sister to Amor (31-32), and finally, pregnant ("grauidam," 133).[106] In the *House of Fame*, similarly, Dido is only once called "quene" (241), and is otherwise "woful" (318, cf. *Her.* 7.7) and "wrechched" (335). In the "Legend," Dido remains "queen" even as her story moves ever more pathetically toward its Ovidian close, as she protests Eneas's departure and indulges in sacrifices to keep him with her. This Dido retains an almost hyper-Virgilian queenliness, that is, until near the very end, in no way diminished by her passion and its pursuit.

Indeed, Dido's erotic attractiveness and her regal practices are interwoven and interdependent in the central passages of the "Legend," where the narrator does synthesize Virgilian and Ovidian themes, and relates them in a voice that is his own, and is increasingly medieval and courtly. This begins when the narrator, having refused to redact Venus's (and thus Virgil's) version of Dido's history, launches instead into his own:

> This noble queen that cleped was Dido,
> That whilom was the wif of Sytheo,
> That fayrer was than is the bryghte sonne,
> This noble toun of Cartage hath bigonne,
> In which she regneth in so gret honour
> That she was holden of alle queenes flour
> Of gentillesse, of fredom, of beaute,
> That wel was hym that myghte hire ones se;
> Of kynges and of lordes so desyred
> That al the world hire beaute hadde yfyred,
> She stod so wel in every wightes grace.
> (1004–14)

This Dido is drawn from her Virgilian story, but is described in a tone and vocabulary closer to the eroticism and courtly modes of the Prologue and Alceste. Dido here is still a "queen," and the founder of a city; but she is also fairer than the sun and "flour" of queens "Of gentillesse, of fredom, of beaute" – an almost formulaic triplet of attributes for a courtly heroine.[107] In an image that fuses her eroticism and queenliness, Dido's beauty is said to attract so many kings and lords that it fires the world.[108]

Such description of Dido as at once erotic and powerful reaches its high point when the narrator suggests she might make a consort for a god whose status as pagan or Christian is left nicely ambiguous:

> This fresshe lady, of the cite queene,
> Stod in the temple in hire estat real,
> So rychely and ek so fayr withal,
> So yong, so lusty, with hire eyen glade,
> That, if that God, that hevene and erthe made,
> Wolde han a love, for beaute and goodnesse,
> And womanhod, and trouthe, and semelynesse,
> Whom shulde he loven but this lady swete?
> Ther nys no woman to hym half so mete.
>
> (1035–43)

Moreover, this Dido, with her "estat real" and her "eyen glade," at once "yong" and "lusty," draws from a romance vocabulary that suggests male heroism as much as feminine beauty.[109] By this point, Dido is crossing many lines at once: from her earlier antique textual derivation to a narrative tone and locus far more of Chaucer's time, from pagan eminence to an almost Marianic status as potential wife of God.[110] All this draws Dido still further into the imaginative conventions of the narrator's own time, and thus closer to the courtly setting, the power, and the Christian overtones of Alceste.[111] Even while the narrator uses elements from the romance tradition to achieve these effects, further, they work to expand his voice and confirm a perspective and authority independent either of Virgil or Ovid.

If, however, this melting of gender and the melding of Dido with Christian imagery do generate a high point, the tone of the passage also tends to overextend itself, even a bit comically, and thus perhaps leads toward its own undoing. When Dido begins to feel an attraction for Eneas soon after, she is inevitably pressed back toward her gender and an increasingly private aspect of desire that, in both the Virgilian and the Ovidian versions of her tale, will finally undermine her political standing and take her life. At the same time, the narrator here makes his tale and his Dido most his own, in an omniscient report of her interior feelings and thoughts.

> The queen saugh that they dide hym swych honour,
> And hadde herd ofte of Eneas er tho,
> And in hire herte she hadde routhe and wo

That evere swich a noble man as he
Shal ben disherited in swich degre;
And saw the man, that he was lyk a knyght,
And suffisaunt of persone and of myght,
And lyk to been a verray gentil man;
And wel his wordes he besette can,
And hadde a noble visage for the nones,
And formed wel of braunes and of bones.
For after Venus hadde he swich fayrnesse
That no man myghte be half so fayr, I gesse;
And wel a lorde he semede for to be.
And, for he was a straunger, somwhat she
Likede hym the bet, as, God do bote,
To som folk ofte newe thyng is sote.
Anon hire herte hath pite of his wo,
And with that pite love com in also;
And thus, for pite and for gentillesse,
Refreshed moste he been of his distresse.

(1061–81)

This passage, with its elaborate psychologizing, its measured analysis and subtle movement from physical impact to emotional response, marks the apex of the narrator's implicit assertion of his own creative authority; the canons of medieval courtly eroticism move to the center of the reader's attention, and the echoes of antique sources are left behind.[112]

At the same moment that the Chaucerian narrator most clearly and calmly takes over the tone of the "Legend," though, he also begins moving toward some of the imagery and attitudes that formed such an uncomfortable subtext in the Prologue. The passage quoted above emphasizes pure physicality – a body anatomized – and initiates an increasingly voyeuristic exploration of Dido's carnal reaction to Eneas. Dido and the narrator thus shift simultaneously into habits of "amorous lokyng and devys" (1102), and the narrator uses Dido's own gaze, ironically, to penetrate her psyche. He begins turning Queen Dido into a victim not of her political plight, but of her sight and of Eneas's body. And that victimization will soon lead Dido to die by the agency of cloth and sword, the very images through which sexual violence and penetration pulled against the Prologue's (and specifically Alceste's) logic of justice, dialogue, and readerly balance.[113]

The banquet Dido gives Eneas (1098–105), another famous Virgilian moment now almost obtrusively medievalized by the narrator, is followed by a careful list of Dido's gifts:

> There nas courser wel ybrydeled non,
> Ne stede, for the justing wel to gon,
> Ne large palfrey, esy for the nones,
> Ne jewel, fretted ful of ryche stones,
> Ne sakkes ful of gold, of large wyghte,
> Ne ruby non, that shynede by nyghte,
> Ne gentil hawtein faucoun heroner,
> Ne hound for hert or wilde bor or der,
> Ne coupe of gold, with floreyns newe ybete,
> That in the land of Libie may be gete,
> That Dido ne hath it Eneas ysent;
> And al is payed, what that he hath spent.[114]
>
> (1114–25)

This munificence, and especially the closing detail that Dido paid all Eneas's bills, extend the emphasis on her wealth and power, and his reduction toward a weepy kept man. This implication takes on a nasty edge when Eneas too sends off for "riche thynges," but not all to be used as gifts: "Some for to were, and some for to presente / To hire that alle thise noble thynges hym sente" (1132–33). At the same time, though, the eroticizing of their relationship reduces Dido's power, as the imagery of fire re-enters the "Legend." The fire that had expressed the global impact of Dido's beauty and queenship now becomes the physical passion for Eneas that penetrates her body:

> Of which ther gan to breden swich a fyr
> That sely Dido hath now swich desyr
> With Eneas, hire newe gest, to dele,
> That she hath lost hire hewe and ek hire hele.
>
> (1156–59)

This is the first time, too, that Dido's habitual epithet, "queen," is replaced by the pathetic "sely."[115]

In the later scenes of the "Legend" – Dido's plaint to Anna, the hunt in which Dido and Eneas consummate their passion, and Eneas's departure – Virgilian and Ovidian incidents and echoes again begin to intrude upon the narrator's and reader's attention, though they remain in contest with the narrator's perspective. Dido is further reduced toward her status in *Heroides* 7: a passive, private body, the object of entrapment, possession, transgression, and, finally, abandonment. And the narrator moves further into imagery and attitudes reminiscent of the dark side of the Prologue. Dido's conversation with Anna initiates this final section of the "Legend"; it is, the narrator says, "th'effect,"

the "fruyt of al, / Whi I have told this story, and telle shal" (1160-61).
The narrator not only emphasizes his presence (using "I" at 1161,
1162, and 1167), he also invokes imagery of fruition that recalls the
Prologue's exploration of harvest. In the Prologue, too, such imagery
was linked both to seasonal fertility and to a naked wintry violence.
Winter had a sword, and the fowler gathered birds through the
"sophistrye" of his "net" (G 125, 119). The moment of Eneas's sexual
conquest, too, will be part of a hunt, with its own habits of entrapment
("nettes") and violence ("speres brode and kene," 1190).

In the "Legend"'s version of the hunt scene, Dido is implicitly seen
as herself a horse ("so priketh hire this newe joly wo," 1192) and,
increasingly, a possessible object, "the last and richest gift of all she has
to give."[116] Her entrance before the hunt again makes her the object of
the narrator's gaze, and she arrives like an offering, encased by many
of the precious goods that had been catalogued among her gifts to
Eneas:

> Upon a thikke palfrey, paper-whit,
> With sadel red, enbrouded with delyt,
> Of gold the barres up enbosede hye,
> Sit Dido, al in gold and perre wrye...[117]
> (1198-201)

Eneas in turn rides "Upon a courser stertlynge as the fyr − / Men
myghte turne hym with a litel wyr" (1204-05). This horse's aptitude
for control, its "bit of gold" (1208), and its association with fire, all
serve to connect it too with the "amorous queene" (1189) who is both
riding on and figured as a horse.[118] Dido is thus placed at another and
critical crossing point here, from ruler to ruled, from agent to object,
even perhaps from queen to beast. And though she is still called a
"noble queen" (1210), it is Eneas now who enacts the vocabulary of
rule, over the horse whose bit "Governeth he ryght as hymself hath
wold" (1209).

The cave to which Dido and Eneas retreat from the storm has divine
occupants in Virgil's version. In the "Legend," the narrator hedges this
detail ("The autour maketh of it no mencioun," 1228), but implicates
his own voyeuristic presence at the scene by the detail and
medievalizing courtliness of his description:

> For there hath Eneas ykneled so,
> And told hire al his herte and al his wo,
> And swore so depe to hire to be trewe

> For wel or wo and chaunge hire for no newe;
> And as a fals lovere so wel can pleyne,
> That sely Dido rewede on his peyne,
> And tok hym for husbonde and becom his wyf
> For everemo, whil that hem laste lyf.
>
> (1232–39)

Chaucer's narrator not only invents a scene of kneeling and avowal of love, but also explicitly domesticates the relationship thereby initiated, at least from Dido's point of view: the "Legend"'s Dido takes Eneas as her husband, whereas in the *House of Fame* he became her lord. This again implies the narrator's own authority within the tradition, yet also presses Dido still further into the domestic role she adopts in *Heroides* 7.

When king Yarbas, who "hadde hir loved evere his lyf" (1246), hears of the affair through the agency of "wikke fame" (1242), he mourns like a spurned lover. The narrator thus again treats the affair in terms of private, courtly love-play; he drains Dido of the regal role she had earlier played, and ignores (for the moment) the territorial threat offered by Iarbas in Virgil's and other versions of her tale. Indeed, the mention of Yarbas is followed immediately by the narrator's own moralizing gloss on the events soon to ensue (1254–76), a gloss in which he reduces all "sely wemen" (1254) into powerless innocents and pure victims. To do so, the narrator must quite leave behind the Virgilian Dido of the earlier part of the "Legend," and equally suppress the power of his fictive patroness, Alceste. He must also mentally reinvent Eneas wholly in the guise of a wooing medieval courtier, who "feyneth hym so trewe and obeysynge" (1266, see 1263–76), and who acts outside the claims of history that even *Heroides* 7 acknowledges. This Eneas has received both Dido's body and her "reame" (1281), but abandons her, as the narrator sees it, only because he is "wery of his craft" (1286). The role of Anchises and the visit by Mercury in prompting the departure become the untrustworthy material of Eneas's excuses. The narrator thus presses Eneas too into the mode of entrapment and transgressive danger ("craft") that was one posture of manhood in the Prologue, especially figured by the wintry violence of the fowler "And al his craft" (127).[119] Yet, with such a monolithic reinterpretation of male sexuality and passive woman-hood in his "gloss," the narrator also places himself in the camp of the fowler and his "sophistrye." He adopts just such a monolithic, narrow, even tyrannical reading as Cupid proposed and Alceste resisted in the Prologue.

The final two scenes, in which Dido begs Eneas to remain with her and then carries out her own suicide, draw quite openly upon Virgil and Ovid once again. But the narrator also adapts those sources toward his own ends, and quietly adds new details. Dido's position as a Virgilian queen is again prominent (1306, 1309) and for the first time she articulates the territorial danger under which she rules: "These lordes, which that wonen me besyde, / Wole me distroyen only for youre sake" (1317–18). Even this renewed political aspect, though, renders Dido's fate the result of a contest among men; and the revival of Dido's regal station occurs only as she is about to lose both her queenship and her life. This is followed by Dido's claim, deriving from *Heroides* 7.133, that she is pregnant (1323). The pathos of this claim is extended by other details of Chaucer's invention or selected from post-classical versions: Eneas cynically pretends to weep when first confronted by Dido (1301), she offers to be his thrall or servant (1313), and he abandons Dido in her sleep "And as a traytour forth he gan to sayle" (1328).[120]

The dominant objects in the "Legend"'s final passages, though, are Eneas's "cloth" (1332, 1336, 1338) and "swerd" (1321, 1332, 1351), and these again return us to the troubling imagery of the Prologue. The first of these is a Virgilian detail ("Iliacas uestis," *Aen.* 4.648), its source emphasized by another moment of near translation as Dido addresses it:

> "O swete cloth, whil Juppiter it leste,
> Tak now my soule, unbynd me of this unreste!
> I have fulfild of fortune al the cours."[121]
>
> (1338–40)

The sword is Dido's way of suicide both in Virgil and Ovid, but Ovid stresses the presence of the sword in Dido's lap even as she writes her final letter (*Her.* 7.184: "scribimus, et gremio Troicus ensis est"). With the imagery of cloth and sword, and with the comparison of Dido and a swan – "'Ryght so,' quod she, 'as that the white swan / Ayens his deth begynnyth for to synge'" (1355–56) – the close of the "Legend" re-echoes suggestively the darker imagery of the Prologue. This is a Dido who combines Virgilian power and Ovidian eroticism only briefly. As her narrator asserts his own growing cultural power and independence from antique authority, he is also attracted into the Prologue's subtle and unresolved attitudes of violence and dominance: entrapment, the voyeuristic gaze, and the sterile transgression of the wintry sword.[122] In the Prologue, Alceste and her explicit arguments for judicial dialogue and readerly flexibility are a bulwark against the impact of this imagery. But in the individual legends, like that of Dido, the narrator's own self-assertion, his efforts to enact Chaucerian canonicity, connect him – quietly but inextricably – to violence and dominance. Dido explicitly wishes to be freed of the cloth in which she has been netted, possessed by Eneas, reread and progressively divested of queenliness by the narrator: "unbynd me." But her queenliness, and even her claim to fertility, are both finally blasted, transfixed by the sword of Eneas. She does not survive the sophistry and craft of fowler, narrator, or lover. She remains only a temporary and incomplete type for the kind of feminine power (and even that is limited) achieved by Alceste.

The Dido of most of the "Legend," then, is not the Dido Cupid might have expected in a paeon to courtly eroticism: she is not the besotted, hand-wringing Dido of the *House of Fame*, wholly shorn of public role and title. Instead, she is (as is almost endlessly restated) a queen, even if her queenliness leaves her in the central episodes of her legend. Whatever her final fate, she begins as a Dido more for Alceste than for Cupid, and her reader must at various points contest her narrator as much as Alceste contests Cupid. It is only the final Dido, erotically as well as politically dependent, but now abandoned by Eneas and exposed to the dangers of attack, who satisfies the God of Love's narrow definitions of eroticism and feminine power. For Cupid, she can be acceptably regal only when she is the queen of a king, and she can be that queen only within canons of profound dependence.

The very mode of Dido's textual veiling – Virgilian text limited within Ovidian narrative constraints and persistently re-read by the redacting narrator – makes her the center of an unresolved hermeneutic dialogue between literary traditions, and between political and erotic versions of womanhood: the dialogue of the good woman. Thus, despite (or, finally, through) the narrator's initial claim to reconcile his *auctores*, the Aeneas and especially the Dido of Virgil and Ovid are ultimately left in unresolved dialogue in the "Legend": she hovers between erotic servitude and queenly power, between private and public life, between the narrator's admiring language of queenship and his almost leering tale of passion and death. This dialogue, of course, is just the sort of readerly response that Alceste herself proposed. Like any naked text, Dido is reveiled, but also transfixed by the sword, and left victim of both the narrator and Eneas, tricked out of her regality and power by their fowler's craft. The "Legend of Dido," more than any other of the *Legends of Good Women*, faces up to the uncomfortable and ultimately political implications of any author's claim to canonicity and to a cultural status equal to the great antique authorities. Still, in the poem as a whole, Chaucer makes just such a claim, forever aware of the violence he may do to the characters he thereby controls.

Envoi, to the Renaissance: books of Aeneas and of Dido

The end of a book carries temptations of false closure or specious order, and aiding those temptations come the siren calls of organic form or rigid literary periodization. These closing pages will try to evade such models, and yet point toward some genuine changes that take place as the *Aeneid* and related narratives of Troy move from the later Middle Ages into the English Renaissance. In a tradition that becomes ever more ramified (another organic metaphor, granted) as redactions multiply across languages and across time, a few themes do gain notable new importance in the later fifteenth and the sixteenth centuries: the place of women in the story of Troy and Rome, and their challenge to what had been primarily a narrative of male empire; an awareness of increasingly divided audiences for such narratives – men, women, knights, clerks, and burghers; and with such divided audiences, an enlarged attention to agents other than armed male aristocrats in the movement of empire – agents such as trade, wealth itself, and (as we will see in Spenser) the woman warrior. These emergent players, I will suggest, operate most vigorously around the Dido episode, and contribute to the growing centrality of her story in an important group of Troy texts.

This is a shifting, but clearly not a wholly new dynamic. Earlier chapters have noted the increased (but contained) place of women, themes of mercantile power, and textual nods toward more than one audience, particularly in the *Roman d'Eneas*. Also constant, though inexplicit, is the ambition to mastery, we may even say to authority, among certain retellers of the Virgilian story as they struggle with the competing exegetical, narrative, and social claims laid upon that Ur-*auctor*.

The career of Geoffrey Chaucer, we have seen, traces these twin shifts as he twice retells the story of Dido and Aeneas. Chaucer begins, in the *House of Fame*, with an expanded Dido episode that is nonetheless

270

still contained within a Virgilian narrative of Aeneas's Trojan and Roman fate; and he speaks there through a fairly passive narrative voice that, even thereby, mirrors some aspects of Aeneas's experience. In his *Legend of Good Women*, on the other hand, Chaucer's Dido stands alone, not bracketed by any story of imperial militancy. The Prologue to the *Legend* is both a site of divided readership (the militant God of Love *versus* Alceste), and a bookish drama in which Chaucer lays decisive claim to his own canonicity, his book's right to accompany if not to supersede the source books of Latin legend and myth; and thereby Chaucer also lays claim to the authority of English.

These developments, however, as well as resistance to them, become much more pronounced in the period at which I now glance. Unsurprisingly, such trends toward new players and ambitions for poetic mastery within the Virgilian tradition accelerate in a period when the hermeneutic fields around the text of Virgil, indeed the very question of what comprised the "text" of Virgil, have become exceptionally divided, open, and fluid. The early chapters of this book display the burgeoning of hermeneutic approaches to the Latin *Aeneid* during the high and later Middle Ages. The number and accessibility of such competing approaches only increase in the fifteenth century, and still further with the advent of print. At the same time, the number and forms of Troy narrative expand and alter as vernacular versions, such as the *Roman de Troie*, move into the more authoritative Latin of an influential redaction like Guido delle Colonne's *Historia Destructionis Troiae*, and then back again into a number of European vernaculars in the later Middle Ages.[1] Other redactions begin to collapse such hierarchies of linguistic authority, and choose at will between ancient Latin and medieval vernacular texts; the *Histoire Ancienne jusqu'à César*, for instance, refers back and forth, explicitly, to Virgil and the *Roman d'Eneas*.[2] Still other versions, we will see, insist they possess an exclusively Virgilian authority despite their heteroglot sources. And at the same time, as noted in a number of contexts, the codicological hierarchy distinguishing the Latin primary text from its marginal commentary starts to blur when the Latin book is vernacularized. In the face of such dizzying multiplicity, finally, the task and situation of the redactor can take on nearly heroic, and in this tradition therefore Aenean, proportions.

In the century after Chaucer, a vast redistribution and hybridization of classical story began again in France among translators and redactors like Octavien de St. Gellais, Raoul Lefevre, and Christine de

Pizan.[3] From this fecund but tumultuous recombination and re-redaction of polyphonic sources – classical Latin, medieval Latin, Italian, and French – newly configured chunks of classical tale emerged. They generate a floating and sometimes chaotic pool of classical story for readers of the fifteenth century. This setting of vastly multiplied, variant and repetitive sources presents a fascinatingly levelled field of narrative play.

The English vernacular too witnessed an explosion of classical story during the transition of later manuscript and incipient print culture. When the French and other classicizing material comes into English circulation, we witness what I would call a tertiary hermeneutic negotiation with classicism. The traditional hierarchy of textual authority is annulled. Commentary infiltrates primary text, especially when that text undergoes translation. Redactors and translators are not judging conflicts among dominant ancient authorities or versions of Latin exegesis. Rather, they are playing among long-established floating stories, balancing, challenging, sometimes refusing to choose within the multiplying variance of late medieval textuality. From this fecund combination, new preoccupations and new viewpoints can take hold of classical Troy narrative and recast it, often radically.

William Caxton's 1490 *Eneydos* offers a sort of limit case for the indiscriminate hermeneutic levelling and appropriation of multiple traditions outlined above.[4] The *Eneydos* is almost a transliteration of a 1483 French *Livre des Eneydes*.[5] It reduces all information from its sources, narrative or explanatory, to a virtually unexamined level of even, scarcely characterized voice.[6] Literal story, major speeches, learned exegesis, and narratorial comment all occupy a single and minimally varied thread of discourse.

In the book's broad structure, this flattening of distinctions displays itself notably in an even-handed report of *both* the dominant versions of Dido's life: the chaste widow, in the version by Boccaccio, and then the suicidal lover, probably drawn indirectly from the *Histoire Ancienne jusqu'à César*.

Soo thenne we shall leve to speke of Eneas, And shalle retorne to speke of dydo. And firste to shewe the dyfference of Iohn bochace and of vyrgyle, to putte in bryef the falle of the sayd dydo recounted by bochace, and after by the sayd virgyle.[7]

The tale offers no preference between the two stories, and scarcely registers any tension between them. More important, perhaps, is the way that a fascination with Dido, in whatever version, takes over Caxton's text, filling more than half his book and threatening to eclipse the hastier story of Eneas that functions as little more than a pendant before and after the double tragedy of Dido. This is Didonic expansionism with a vengeance, but only extends patterns by now centuries old.

The effect of this blending of sources can be equally bizarre on the local scale. The narrative absorbs a tremendous amount of largely traditional commentary information, and inserts it with no shift of register, wherever it becomes relevant. So we witness the near-mad Dido pause in her diatribe against Eneas, to launch into an explication of Trojan genealogy and then the geography of the Caucasus:

o man right false and untrue, that, what somever men sayen, was never borne of no goddesse, nor procreated of Royalle lynee comyng of the puissant dardanus, fyrst founder of the grete cyte of troye, but arte engendred of Caucasus whiche is a mountayne terryble in ynde, all full of harde stones of dyverse fygures, of merveyllous height that recheth almost unto the hevyns ... (p. 71)

Dido's auto-glossation continues for most of a page before she returns her attention to Eneas. Such digressions occur regularly throughout the work, often (as here) inserted into the mouth of whomever may be speaking when the topic arises. Moments like these – and they produce the dominant tenor of the *Eneydos* – erase traditional distinctions of primary narrative and secondary comment, of codicological center and margin. Instead, the text embraces a kind of universal but homo-genized encyclopedism, in which all information, plot and cultural background, is presented without distinction to the audience's attention.[8]

Caxton's *Eneydos* simultaneously subverts and pays homage to Virgil, though; it at once tells an ever less Virgilian story and yet claims Virgilian authority. Caxton says of his source, the "lytyl booke in frenshe," that it was "translated oute of latyn by some noble clerke of fraunce, whiche booke is named Eneydos made in latyn by that noble poete & grete clerke vyrgyle" (p. 1). In this, Caxton trusts his French book, which also asserts that "this present booke, compyled by virgyle, ryght subtyl and Ingenyous oratour & poete, Intytuled Eneydos, hath be translated oute of latyn in-to comyn langage" (p. 10). Yet this claim is soon followed by the calm move, quoted above, to Boccaccio's version of Dido's fate; and even the Virgilian portions of the story derive from a vernacular intermediary.

Caxton and his French book are similarly multiple and unresolved in the audiences they propose to address. The French Prologue presents the book as an account

In whiche may alle valyaunt prynces and other nobles see many valorous fayttes of armes. And also this present boke is necessarye to alle cytezens & habytaunts in townes and castellis, for they shal see, How somtyme troye the graunte and many other places stronge and inexpugnable, have ben be-sieged sharpely & assayled, And also coragyously and valyauntly defended. (p. 10)

This suggests, again without registering any sense of conflict, another sort of divide in the narrative, between a story of traditional aristocratic battle, and a lesson for burghers in protecting their towns (against, among other foes, those very aristocrats who are also invited to read the book). In his own prologue, Caxton further elaborates the mix when he considers what level of diction he should use, "playn" for the gentlemen or "curyous" for clerks:

And for as moche as this present booke is not for a rude uplondyssh man to laboure therein ne rede it, but onely for a clerke & a noble gentylman that feleth and understondeth in faytes of armes, in love, & in noble chyvalrye, Therfor in a meane bytwene bothe, I have reduced & translated this sayd booke in to our englysshe, not over rude ne curyous ... (p. 3)

Together, then, the prologues address a triple audience, excluding only the "rude uplondyssh man," and placidly ignoring the divided, even conflicting, interests of so socially varied a readership.

Irreconcilable stories, collapsed codicological layers issuing in a near-monophone, denial and assertion of Virgilian authority, and multiple audiences: all these help create a disconcertingly slippery, yet remarkably open and absorptive text. And the disruptive potential of a text like the *Eneydos* within the Virgil tradition may be all the greater exactly because of its uncritical, even-toned narrative voice. The text is open, it seems, to whatever elements, however irreconcilable, may rise to the redactor's attention from the vast pool of Troy narrative and surrounding commentary. It is precisely this permeability in the *Eneydos*, I think, that allows it to register, inconsistently but often quite clearly, a number of the cultural pressures and fixations of its several audiences.

Even as the text centers its attention on the nobility and erotic tragedy of Dido, for instance, it also enfolds a sense of Dido's disruptive and transgressive properties. The explanatory material links her to classical Bacchic and matricide figures.[9] The sense of Dido's inextinguishable presence in the later history of Rome is similarly exaggerated here by a great expansion of her Ovidian threat to pursue Eneas as a spirit.[10] An urban audience, too, might be unnerved by the suspension of building activities at Carthage that results from Dido's infatuation with Eneas; this is described in anxious and technical detail, with only a brief nod to the simultaneous lapse of chivalric exercises:

The werkes of the grete yates, toures, and othre edyfyces that were begonne for the perfectyon of Cartage, be lefte wythout eny more werkyng, alle Imperfyt: the exercyse of armes is dyscontynued; the noble men were robuste and rude, wythout exersice of fayttes of werre; The brydges, poortes and passages ben lefte wythoute warde, And the deffences ben voyde and emptye wythoute entreteynynge, redy to receyve the enmyes wythoute ony contra-dyctyon: Alle werkes ceassen and appyeren interrupte for defaulte of conductours. The stones of the walles that are bygonne, whiche appyeren alle awry sette, croked, bowed, and counterfette, by cause thei be not fully made and polisshed ... The grete edyfyces are lefte uncovered in dyverse places. And shortely, alle falleth in-to ruyne, by cause of her grete furoure. (p. 49)

Such nervous attention to urban technology and its lapses is common throughout the book.

The most telling of the *Eneydos*'s anxieties, probably, is its sense of manhood endangered, and gender distinctions undone, by Dido's command of Carthage and her temporary influence over Eneas. It tells both stories of Dido's famous tricks – to escape Tyre with her husband's wealth and to purchase all Carthage by requesting only the space of a bull's hide – in an almost collapsed version.[11] In the narrative borrowed from Boccaccio, Dido is a lawgiver, comes to be called "moder of theyr countrey," and is "honowred as a goddesse" (p. 36). More important, the effeminization of Eneas at Carthage is carefully documented. Yarbas complains that Eneas

kepeth himself in maner as a woman, in their companye, wyth his longe heres that he maketh to be enoynted & kemed for to be yelow as golde, makyng theym to be bounden in a coyffe rounde a-boute his hed, without to thynke upon none other thynges, but only the delites of wymenly love, wherein he is contynuelli ocupyed wyth her ...[12] (pp. 60–61)

Mercury is even more direct when he orders Eneas to leave Carthage, calling him a "Man effemynate, wythout honour, ravysshed in to dilectacion femynyne" (pp. 63–64). It is only once past the nearly-divine mother of her country that Eneas once again begins to act like a founder of empire. These and other preoccupations enter the narrative through the redactor's willingness to dilate his narrative and to fold commentary material within it.

A number of the points sketched above, and especially Caxton's ballooning and doubling of Dido's story, arouse the wrath of Gavin Douglas in the Prologues to his 1513 *Eneados*.[13] Working from a renewed, direct contact with the Latin Virgil and the textual canons of resurgent humanism, Douglas's translation lays claim to a purer, originary Virgilianism, and an original imperial theme, which his work will make available to his aristocratic patron and relative Henry Sinclair.[14] Douglas's restricted notion of the Virgilian text and theme also entails a notion of audience much narrower than the multiple readerships embraced by Caxton. Douglas speaks emphatically to his own aristocratic class – his highborn patron and the other nobles whom he invites to cast aside Caxton's book:

> Ʒhe worthy noblys, redis my wark for thy
> And cast this other buke on syde far by,
> Quhilk vndir cullour of sum strange Franch wycht
> So Franchly leys, oneith twa wordis gais rycht.[15]

As a translator, Douglas joins this select class of aristocratic readers, and strives to write for them in a "ryall style" and "knychtlyke stile": "Thar suld na knycht reid bot a knychtly taill."[16] Again at the end of the translation, Douglas pictures himself reading his Virgil in the company of Sinclair "And other gentill companʒeonys."[17]

Douglas angrily articulates and rejects much of what goes on in the syncretistic Virgilianism of Caxton and of Chaucer before him:

> Thocht Wilʒame Caxtoun, of Inglis natioun,
> In proyss hes prent ane buke of Inglys gross,
> Clepand it Virgill in Eneadoss,
> Quhilk that he says of Franch he dyd translait,
> It hass na thing ado tharwith, God wait,
> Ne na mair lyke than the devill and Sanct Austyne.
> Haue he na thank tharfor, bot loyss hys pyne,
> So schamefully that story dyd pervert.[18]

Paradoxically, though, Douglas's very anger suggests how personal a project this is for him, and how much he has emotionally (and even politically) invested in it. Such emotional involvement by a redactor/ translator harkens back to the narrators of Chaucer's Virgilian tales, and those narrators' ambition to emulate, in the poetic sphere, a kind of Aenean or even Virgilian heroism.

Despite his claim to an austere textual purity, further, Douglas makes elaborate and canny use of the late-medieval book of Virgil, with its hierarchical system of *accessus, vitae,* verse summaries, and commentaries.[19] Upon that system Douglas models his own apparatus of vernacular Scots summaries, prologues, afterwords, and prose marginalia.[20] This codicological superstructure, neatly separate from the central Virgilian text, becomes the arena for Douglas's own voice, his readerly preoccupations, and his poetic ambitions. Indeed, the justly famed Prologues are a virtual conspectus of late-medieval vernacular forms, and make up an almost competitive dialogue with the varieties of Virgilian style that Douglas registers, often dazzlingly well, in the translation itself. At the same time, the codicological framing provided by these extra-Virgilian materials creates a place for Douglas to engage in a sequence of textual conflicts with other redactors (like Caxton, as we have already seen) and with varied opponents and non-Virgilian sources he feels unable to ignore.[21] Douglas thus uses the inherited framework of the Virgilian book at once to acknowledge, contest, and yet (quite literally) marginalize contending traditions.

The codicological frame also provides a place where Douglas, like Chaucer before him, explores his own quasi-heroic similarities with Aeneas and with Virgil, and thereby asserts the claim to mastery, to authority, earned by his poetic skill and effort.[22] Douglas's sense of himself as an avatar of Aeneas emerges, predictably, when the two are called upon to recount the same tale of the fall of Troy. Douglas includes Aeneas's opening of the tale of Troy at the close of Book One, and then echoes Aeneas's words in his own voice in the Prologue to the second book.[23] Then in the Prologue to Book Three, when he prepares to relate Aeneas's wanderings in the Mediterranean, Douglas invokes the trope of his own work as a ship, navigating the same geography as does Aeneas: "By strange channellis, fronteris and forlandis, / . . . Now goith our barge."[24] Again, in the Prologue to Book Six, Douglas calls upon the same guide who will lead Aeneas through the Underworld: "To follow Virgil in this dyrk poyse / Convoy me, Sibil, that I ga nocht wrang."[25] And Book Eight, that opens with Aeneas's dream of Tiber and Tiber's counsel, is prefaced with a Prologue that places Douglas as well in a dream vision.

Douglas develops more fully the interweaving of his own poetic

ambition (and hope for aristocratic favor) with that of Virgil. Addresses
to his patron Sinclair, as a sort of combined Maecenas and Augustus,
provide much of the setting for these comparisons. In the first
Prologue, Douglas explains at length that he undertook his translation

> At the request of a lord of renown
> Of ancistry nobill and illustir baroun,
> Fader of bukis, protectour to sciens and lair,
> My speciall gud Lord Henry, Lord Sanct Clair.[26]

But Douglas is more direct and explicit in his claim to Virgilian
accomplishment in the "Conclusio," one of several poems that close
the whole translation:

> Throw owt the ile yclepit Albyon
> Red sall I be, and sung with mony one.
> Thus vp my pen and instrumentis full 3or
> On Virgillis post I fix for evirmor,
> Nevir, from thens, syk materis to discryve.[27]

Douglas hangs up his pen, like a triumphant warrior's lance, on Virgil's
post, and thereby lays claim to Virgil's glory. This explicitly chivalric
metaphor, further, links Douglas's heroic Virgilianism with his
repeated assertion of himself and his readers as knightly aristocrats; and
it helps to close the translation on a combined note of literary and
social mastery.

Given these poetic and personal commitments to Aeneas and Virgil,
and to an imperial and aristocratic notion of the epic, Douglas strives
to project a wholly virtuous picture of the epic hero. He does much of
his battling with medieval ambivalence toward Aeneas in the Prologues
and marginal notes; but at times he also subtly cants his translation in
Eneas's favor. Douglas presents an idealized, princely Eneas, a model
for the Christian knight, who possesses "euery vertu belangand a nobill
man,"[28] and who is (in explicit opposition to Chaucer's report) neither
a traitor nor forsworn to Dido.[29] Not surprisingly, Douglas underplays
hints of the hero's effeminacy in Book Four, particularly when
compared with the exaggeration of this theme in Caxton and other
medieval redactions.[30] At the same time, the translation persistently
adds public and honorific titles to Eneas's name: "manfull," "gret
prynce," and "kyng."[31] Douglas closes his work with a boast to Eneas
that the translation has restored his repute and undone medieval
tradition of him as a traitor:

> Be glaid, Ene, thy bell is hiely rong,
> Thy faym is blaw, thy prowes and renown
> Dywlgat ar, and sung fra town to town,
> So hardy from thens, that other man or boy
> The ony mair reput traytour of Troy,
> Bot as a worthy conquerour and kyng
> The honour and extoll, as thou art dyng.[32]

This cleansing of Eneas's image, plus the aristocratic and political values of the translation's framework, place Gavin Douglas's *Eneados* squarely in the camp of Aeneas in the growing rift of attention and narrative that has been developing even as early as the time of the *Roman d'Eneas*.

Of course, the contesting focus of this rift in the Virgilian tradition, and the greatest threat to Aeneas's reputation, is Dido. If Douglas's prologues and notes are concerned to reject alternate forms of Aeneas, they are equally eager to dismiss alternate and expanded versions of Dido. He is especially outraged that Caxton has allowed a single book of the Virgilian epic to expand into half the *Eneydos*.[33] Indeed, Douglas's Prologue to Book Four seems intent on extracting the Dido episode from the general tenor of the epic, to render it instead a rather disconnected *exemplum* about lust and unregulated love, a brief but separate "tragedy."[34]

> Zour ioly wo neidlyngis most I endyte,
> Begynnyng with a fenzeit faynt plesance,
> Continewit in lust, and endyt with pennance.[35]

Despite the tears he admits (like Augustine) to shedding for Dido, he still closes his address to her on a strong moralistic note: "Throw fulych lust wrocht thine awyn ondoyng."[36] The Prologue pulls Book Four away from any question of the ongoing Trojan destiny, and instead presents it as almost a self-contained story of erotic fall, in which the real agents are Dido's excessive passion and Venerian desire.

On either side of this developing gap in late-medieval Virgilianism – the political book of Aenean empire *vs.* the erotic book of Didonic tragedy – the Queen of Carthage is consistently a figure of pathos (when she is not, in some "Aenean" narratives, ignored entirely), though this pathos may result from widowed fidelity or erotic excess. In an inspired departure, however, Christine de Pizan's *City of Ladies* situates Dido in such a way that she is (if only temporarily) a figure of a woman's civic triumph, and an agent in Christine's re-education in the native virtue of women.[37] Christine wrote at the turn of the fourteenth and fifteenth centuries; she had a considerable vogue in England, from her own lifetime right through the sixteenth century. Much of her work was translated, including the *City of Ladies* in the translation of Bryan Anslay, published in London in 1521.[38]

In this book, Christine presents herself as an almost autobiographical narrator, beaten down by the apparent universality of male misogyny, almost to the extent of accepting it as fact, and regretting her own gender. But in a quasi-dream state, Christine is approached by three allegorical ladies who promise to re-educate her in what she already naturally knows, that women are virtuous. Through this reversal in Christine's estimate of her own sex, her visionary advisers will build for her a new city, a kind of architecturalized universal feminine history in which those virtuous women will reside, ruled ultimately by the Virgin Mary. Within this project of revising and reinscribing women's history, Dido plays a fascinating role. She takes a central place in two of the work's three books, all of course in the context of building a women's city for which Dido, as founder of Carthage, is a natural exemplar.

Christine tells the story of Dido, though in an intriguingly divided version. Toward the end of Book One, she uses Dido as an example of women's prudence and civic foundation. One of her allegorical teachers, Reason, tells Christine the story of Dido's escape with her husband's treasure and her purchase of Carthage with the unravelled bull's hide.

Prudence so as thyselfe hast sayd before is to have advyse and a beholdynge upon thynges that one wyll take on hande howe that they sholde be determyned; and that women sholde be in suche respecte advysed in grete matters. I shall gyve the yet ensample of some puyssaunt ladyes, and fyrst of Dydo. This Dydo was fyrst named Elyxa. the connynge of her prudence shewed well by her werkes as I shall tell the. She founded and edyfyed a cyte in the lande of Auffryke named Cartage of the whiche she was lady and quene.[39]

Dido goes on to govern well, and the chapter ends on a high note that nonetheless returns to the convergence of gender around her achievement:

But as moche for hardynesse of the fayre entrepryse that she had made and for the grete prudent governaunce they chaunged her name and called her Dydo whiche is as moche to say in latyne as Virago, that is to saye she that hath vertue and strengthe of man. and thus she lyved gloryously a grete whyle and longer had done if fortune had ben favourable to her, but as she often tymes envyous (*sic*) to them that ben in prosperyte dystempered to her an harde draught of drynke at the last so as here after in tyme and place I shall tell the.[40]

This detail of "Dido" as a Punic word for "virago" goes back to late-antique commentary, but it is telling that Christine chooses to so feature it in her story.

By breaking off her narrative of Dido at this point in the first book of the City, Christine uses her in the positive light of a foundress of a nation, a role parallelled soon after by Christine's story of Lavinia as foundress of the imperial Roman line. Christine thus structurally bifurcates her Dido – she is queen and only later martyr, in widely separate episodes. And, by emphasizing Lavinia as the foundress of imperial Roman genealogy, Christine nearly erases Aeneas as a player in the history of either city.

Christine returns to Dido, then, only in Book Two, as an example of women's fidelity, even to death. Another teacher, Rectitude, speaks:

It shall suffyse to prove it by the ensample of them that have perceyvered unto the dethe. And fyrst I shal tell the of the noble Dydo quene of Cartage of whome it is spoken here above of her grete valoure as thyselfe hathe touched other tymes.[41]

Christine inserts her own history as a writer at the moment she again approaches the story of Dido. If redactors like Chaucer or Gavin Douglas played on parallels between themselves and Aeneas, the widow Christine seems to suggest an emulation of the virtues of Dido.

Probably the best measure of how widely known were these fractured, contested, but simultaneous versions of Virgil can be seen in the confident way that a poet like Edmund Spenser can enfold them all, and play one tradition against another, even within quite brief episodes, in his epic of English faith and empire, the *Faerie Queene*.[42] Spenser engages virtually all the themes raised by Caxton, Douglas, and Christine, but perhaps chiefly enacts the tradition of the redactor's mastery by proposing a reconciliation of roles that have become divided along the antinomies of gender, as well as a narrative reconnection of the divided themes of eroticism and militarism in the Troy tradition. I close this glance toward English Renaissance Virgilianism with a single episode in Spenser's narrative of Britomart, the woman warrior in his *Faerie Queene*, first published in 1590.

In the third book of the *Faerie Queene* where we first encounter her, Britomart pursues a quest for her destined husband, Artegall, in response to a vision presented in explicitly genealogical and imperial terms: their marriage will renew the Trojan line, restore the fortunes of the Britons, and descend ultimately to Elizabeth I.[43] Much of the book's narrative, though, comprises a sequence of episodes in which various forces try to entice Britomart herself, or the reader's attention, from her historically oriented quest and into scenes of erotic repetition and delay. The entire book thus contains telling analogies with Aeneas's imperial and genealogical quest, and with the challenges to that quest posed by characters like Dido. But in Britomart – perhaps responding to interrogations of gender assumptions like Christine's in the *City of Ladies* – Spenser inverts the gender orientation of erotic delay in the *Aeneid* and most medieval Troy tradition: a woman, Britomart, is the heroic but tempted quester here.

The echoes of Troy and the *Aeneid* become much denser, though, and their challenge to received stereotypes more complex, in Cantos nine and ten. There, along with two other knights (Satyrane and Paridell), Britomart takes refuge from bad weather in the castle of an unwilling host, Malbecco, who fears for his wealth and the fidelity of his wife Hellenore. After a graceless dinner that recalls and parodies Dido's banquet at Carthage and her passion for Aeneas, the enraptured Hellenore asks Paridell – now the object of *her* passion – to recount his "deeds of armes" and his kindred. In terms that clearly echo the opening of Aeneas's account of the fall of Troy in *Aeneid* 2, Paridell mourns the "direfull destinie" of Troy and recounts his descent from the Trojan prince Paris.[44]

Immediately thereafter, though, Britomart (until now linked to an Aenean quest for lineage and empire) briefly takes up the Didonic role. She asks, however, not for a further tale of passion and vengeance but rather for a historical narrative of "countries cause" and particularly the fate of Aeneas.[45] Paridell responds as asked, with an account of patriarchal refoundation in Latium, entirely omitting reference to Aeneas's affair with Dido. Paridell's two stories thus split and distribute across two sets of characters the ambivalence present in Virgil and ever more strained in later tradition. In the narrative to follow in Books Three and Four, it is Paridell who will disappear into an endless if unreported repetition of seduction and abandonment. And it is the female knight, Britomart, who will continue her Aenean quest for a predestined consort and empire.

Britomart's story thus registers Spenser's own mastery, his assertion of his own powers in the face of the daunting authority and hermeneutic polyphony of the inherited Virgilianisms of his literary culture. Britomart plays both Dido and Aeneas, both curious audience to Paridell and fated founder of empire. But even more, Britomart's political destiny is predicated on her erotic quest, and it is she (her gender significant in the England of Elizabeth) whose search for a completed chastity links back together the largely divided romance and historical, female and male Virgilianisms of Spenser's medieval and Renaissance heritage.

Britomart, then, combines the visionary, imperial quest of Aeneas, with that part of the Dido tradition that casts her as a chaste civic leader. But Britomart also reconciles visionary eroticism with imperial quest. The empire of the *Faerie Queene* will arise only in the achieved desire of her marriage to Artegall. Cantos nine and ten, however, also imprint upon other characters, and then leave aside, dangerous figures and counter-versions from the Troy tradition: Helen, Paris, Aeneas as treacherous abandoner, Dido as a figure of excess wealth and erotic entrapment. Spenser thereby profits, quite brilliantly, from the rifts and divisions that had grown up around the ever multiplied forms of medieval Virgilianism. He re-uses and reconciles these very gaps, and enfolds them within his own evolving imperial myth, a myth that can encompass and indeed require feminine militancy and feminine eroticism.

This book about the medieval artifacts of ancient texts ends with a final, exemplary artifact of the movement from medieval to Renaissance Virgilianism. The printed book Wood 106 in the Bodleian Library at Oxford is a copy of Richard Stanyhurst's 1583 translation of the first four books of the *Aeneid* (Appendix I, no. 6; see plate 6). This particular copy is, in effect, a sixteenth century paperback. The gatherings are loosely sewn together but were never put between boards. Instead, the book is protected by a "wrapper," in this case a stout piece of vellum. The wrapper covering Stanyhurst's Virgil in Wood 106 is not blank, though. It is recycled from a medieval manuscript, and happens to be a leaf from a fine English twelfth-century copy of the *Aeneid*. The single leaf is written in a stately mid-century hand, in large double-column format, the only surviving example of this format in England before the fourteenth century. It must once have been part of a splendid volume. Another hand, from the first half of the thirteenth century, supplies occasional interlinear glosses: still another instance of the ongoing study of Virgil in England after the twelfth century. Whether this combination – the English

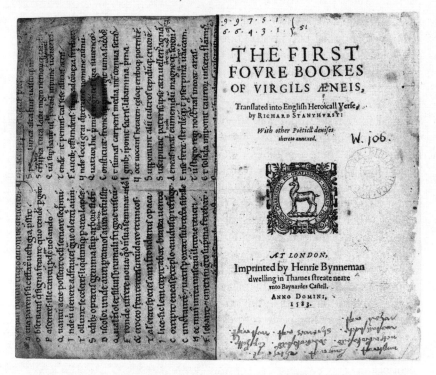

Plate 6 Oxford, Bodleian Library, printed book Wood 106, *verso* of wrapper and frontispiece. At right is the title page of the 1583 translation by Richard Stanyhurst. At left is the inner side of the book's wrapper, made from a recycled piece of stout parchment, which (by chance or choice) is a leaf from a twelfth-century manuscript of the *Aeneid*.

translated book and the wrapper in its original Latin – occurred through an elegant accident of history or the inspired agency of a Renaissance wit, we will never know. But it provides a closing icon of the continuities in English Virgilianism which are a central argument of this book: Stanyhurst's translation is literally wrapped in that very medieval past which the Renaissance thought to put behind but which nonetheless inextricably embraced it. The visual conceit seen in plate 6 expresses, I think, as well as any words can, the figure of the *Aeneid* of the English Middle Ages in its Renaissance heritage.

Manuscripts of Virgil written or owned in England during the Middle Ages

This Appendix lists manuscripts of the *Eclogues*, *Georgics*, and *Aeneid* copied in England during the Middle Ages, or produced elsewhere but owned in England, up to the dissolution of the monasteries in 1542. Manuscripts containing only works from the *Appendix Virgiliana* or spurious attributions are not included, nor are manuscripts with Virgil represented only as selections within a *florilegium*. Surviving fragments which appear to have been part of full texts are, however, listed. Poems from the *Anthologia Latina* I.1 and I.2 ("*AL*"; see Abbreviations) are cited by the continuous numbering in the two parts of that volume.

The main intention here is to present information on contents of the manuscripts, including commentary and other texts present with Virgil. All descriptions are based on direct observation, except for the following, where I have used microfilms and the catalog entries noted in the bibliography: 2, 3, 4a, 4d, 7, 19, 27, 35, 37. No attempt is made to offer complete codicological descriptions. Information on each manuscript appears in the following order:

1 Contents, with folio references:
  (a) *Eclogues*, *Georgics*, and *Aeneid* (hereafter *E*, *G*, *A*)
  (b) Works from the *Appendix Virgiliana*
  (c) Spurious works attributed to Virgil in the manuscript
  (d) Verse arguments prefixed to the *E* (hereafter "*AE*," see *AL*, no. 2, lines 5-8), *G* (hereafter "*AG*," see *AL*, no. 2.I-IV), and *A* (hereafter "*AA*"). The *AA* are of ten lines for each book, though they are often prefixed with a monostich summary of the book (*AL*, no. 1.I–XII, indicated here by Munk Olsen's convention of book number and superscript 10 or 11, e.g. "I^{10}" or "IV^{11}." In instances where lines are missing from the 10-line summary, this is indicated with superscript 1+ the number of lines present; in the single instance (no. 25) where two monostich summaries are prefixed to books, superscript 2+10.) A separate 12-line summary to the entire *A* (*AL*, no. 634) is frequently present elsewhere in the manuscript, most often with the materials before *A*.
  (e) *Vitae* and *accessus* separate from the Virgil text.

(f) Annotation (interlinear and marginal glosses, marginal notes and fuller commentary) accompanying the Virgil text.

(g) Other texts present in the manuscript.

2 Brief description of manuscript:

(a) Period and place of original production.

Discussion of the manuscript's association with England (hand-writing, ownership, etc.; with s. XII text hands, often difficult to distinguish as French or English, I frequently rely on the more idiomatic hands of later marginal annotators).

(b) Material (all manuscripts are membrane unless noted); number of folios (I do not include flyleaves unless stated); gatherings and signatures.

(c) Dimensions of folio; dimensions of written space, in square brackets. Width of written space refers to average width of the written column of verse, not the ruled column, unless noted.

(d) Number of columns; lines per column.

(e) Hand or hands of the text, if notable.

3 History of the manuscript: private and institutional owners, indication of donors, etc.

4 Bibliography, including references to Munk Olsen and Allessio. I indicate catalog descriptions only where they contain information not provided in this Appendix.

Elements of the above are reduced or absent where other catalog descriptions are available and accurate.

(1) OXFORD, ALL SOULS COLLEGE 330, nos. 60 and 61 (formerly ee.4.6), binding fragments

Aeneid 12.1–12.69. Brief glosses, some variants.

s. ix, probably France.

Two narrow binding fragments, cut from the same folio. The binding from which these fragments were recovered is English, *c.* 1523–57 (Oldham roll HM.a.7); the manuscript was therefore presumably in England by the end of the Middle Ages.

The text is written in a fine Carolingian minuscule; the glosses and variants are in two roughly contemporary hands.

Richard W. Hunt, "Pastedowns from All Souls College Books," in Sir Edmund Craster, *The History of All Souls College Library*, ed. E. F. Jacob (London: Faber and Faber, 1971), no. 21, p. 105. J. Basil Oldham, *English Blind-Stamped Bindings* (Cambridge University Press, 1952), p. 51, and plate XLVII, no. 776. Not listed by Munk Olsen or Allessio.

(2) LONDON, COLLEGE OF ARMS, ARUNDEL 30, fols. 5–10, 208

Aeneid 5.708 (fol. 9r); at inner margin in a gathering of six heavy leaves, otherwise palimpsest. A related singlet at fol. 208. One gloss, in the hand of the text.

s. x, England.

The text is written in Anglo-Saxon minuscule.

The rescript portion (and the rest of the manuscript) was written at Bury St. Edmunds, s. xiv.

W. H. Black, *Catalogue of Arundel Manuscripts in the Library of the College of Arms* (London, 1829), pp. 44–57. Helmut Gneuss, "A Preliminary List of Mss Written or Owned in England up to 1100," *Anglo-Saxon England* 9 (1981), no. 503, p. 33. *T&T*, xxxii, note 128. Munk Olsen, B.106. Allessio, no. 423.

(3) VATICAN, BIBLIOTECA APOSTOLICA VATICANA, REG. LAT. 1671
Eclogues (fols. 1r–15r), *Georgics* (fols. 15r–52r), *Aeneid* (fols. 52v–218v).
Fragment of *Culex* (fol. 218v). "Ille ego…" (fol. 52v, hand of s. xi). *AG* I–IV; *AA* I^{11}, II^{10}–IV^{10}, VI^{11}–IX^{11}, XII^{10}. *AL*, no. 634 (fol. 52r).
Interlinear glosses and marginal notes in several hands. Frequent notes from Servius in *E* 1–6, rare after. Occasional brief glosses in *G*. Two groups of annotation in *A*. (1) In the outermost margins, words from the text, with vowel quantities marked; frequent in 1, 4–6; rare in 7 and after. (2) Glosses and longer notes, frequent in 1, 6, 10–12, only occasional glosses in 4-5, 7–9, none in 3. Some notes derive closely from Servius, others provide independent information, especially about mythology. These notes merit further study.
Other texts: *AL*, nos. 256–57, 392–93 (fol. 218v, in a different but contemporary hand).
s. x second half, England, probably Worcester.

For full description, see *MCLBV* II, 1, pp. 352–54. Hands and probable origin are discussed by T. A. M. Bishop, *English Caroline Minuscule* (Oxford: Clarendon, 1971), no. 19, p. 17. Gneuss, "Preliminary List," no. 919, p. 58. *T&T*, xxxii, note 128. Munk Olsen, B.248. Allessio, no. 886.

(4a,b,c,d) Fragments probably from one manuscript in English Carolingian Minuscule
(4a) DEENE PARK LIBRARY, KETTERING, NORTHAMPTONSHIRE, binding fragment
Georgics 2.503–19 and 2.535–3.7.
One squarish fragment, recovered from a London binding *c.* 1535–49 (Oldham roll FP.a.6).
(4b) LONDON, BL SLOANE 1044, fol. 60, binding fragment
Aeneid 4.88–119 and 120–51.
From a collection of binding fragments made by John Bagford, mostly of English provenance.
(4c) OXFORD, BODLEIAN LIBRARY, LAT. CLASS. C.2, fol. 18, binding fragment

Aeneid 4.222–55 and 256–290.

(4d) CAMBRIDGE, CORPUS CHRISTI COLLEGE, binding fragment from
printed book EP–O–6

Aeneid 5.469–525. I am grateful to Dr. David Ganz for notice of this
fragment.

Interlinear glosses in two roughly contemporary hands. Rare glosses in
later hands.

s. x/xi, probably England.

The text hand is a stately English Carolingian minuscule, which Dr.
Bruce Barker-Benfield identifies with the style of St. Augustine's
Canterbury, noting though that it could be a very stately French
hand, s. ix.

I am grateful to Dr. Barker-Benfield for bringing fragment 3a to my
attention and providing description. For the binding of 4a, see
Oldham, *English Blind-Stamped Bindings.* Gneuss, "Preliminary List,"
no. 648, p. 41. *T&T,* xxxii, note 128. Munk Olsen, B.162. Allessio,
nos. 130a, 421a, 612 (Oldham roll number of the Deene Park
binding fragment there mistaken for a manuscript number), 615.

(5) LONDON, BL ROYAL 8.F.XIV, fols. 3–4

Aeneid 8.302–425.

Many interlinear and marginal glosses, in a roughly contemporary hand:
Servius and paraphrases closely based on Servius.

s. xi in., France?

This bifolium is now at the center of a six-leaf gathering of fly-leaves,
originally paste-downs. On fol. 6v is a Bury St. Edmund's shelf mark,
G.15, and a contents-list by Henry de Kirkstede. Thus the s. xiii
philosophical text making up fols. 1, 2, 5, and 6 in the gathering was
bound into the manuscript at least by the end of s. xiv when
Kirkstede was active. The *A* fragment was therefore probably also in
Bury St. Edmund's by that time.

25-

0 x 190 [217 x 105]. 1 column, 31 lines.

Munk Olsen suggests the hand of the text may be English, but Prof. T.
Julian Brown, who kindly examined the hand for me in 1979,
believed it to be French. Prof. Brown also felt that the marginalia,
though in a better hand, were comparable in date and origin with
the text.

For full contents of the manuscript, George F. Warner and Julius P.
Gilson, *Catalog of Western Mss in the Old Royal and King's Collections,* I
(London: British Museum, 1921) pp. 270–72. On Henry de
Kirkstede, see Richard H. Rouse, "Bostonus Buriensis and the
Author of the Catalogus Scriptorum Ecclesiae," *Speculum* 41 (1966):
471–99. Gneuss, "Preliminary List," no. 477, p. 31. *T&T,* xxiv note

159. Pattie, no. 80, pp. 137–38. Munk Olsen, C.104. Allessio, no. 419.

(6) OXFORD, BODLEIAN LIBRARY, PRINTED BOOK WOOD 106, wrapper
Aeneid 6.116–274.
Occasional interlinear glosses, s. xiii.
s. xii first half, England.
This single leaf is found as the wrapper to Richard Stanyhurst, *The First Foure Bookes of Virgils Aeneis Translated into English Heroicall Verse* (London, 1583).
Original dimensions over 214 x 159 [206 x 145]; 2 cols., 39 lines per col.; one line per column now trimmed off. (The only English Virgil in two-column format, to my knowledge, before s. xiv.)
The text is written in a fine, unusually careful bookhand.

Not listed by Munk Olsen or Allessio. I am grateful to Dr. Bruce Barker-Benfield for bringing this fragment to my attention.

(7) VATICAN, BIBLIOTECA APOSTOLICA VATICANA, OTTOB. LAT. 1410
Eclogues (fols. 1v–13v), *Georgics* (fols. 14r–46r), *Aeneid* (fols. 49r–196r).
AL, nos. 256, 257, 674a, 1 *Praefatio* (fol. 196v). Verse argument to *E* (*AL*, no. 2, lines 5–8, fol. 1r and again 197v); *AL*, no. 634 (fol. 48v); *AL*, no. 1 *Praefatio* (fols. 196v–197r); *AG* I–IV; *AA* I^{11}–II^{11}, III^{10}, IV^{11}–XII^{11}. *Vita Bernensis* (*Vitae*, pp. 66–67), damaged at beginning (fol. 1v).
Numerous interlinear and marginal notes in one contemporary hand, less frequent after *A* 7. These derive mostly from Servius, frequently verbatim. But they show particular interest in mythographical information found in Servius, sometimes embroidering on such entries.
Distich and tetrastich epitaphs on Virgil (*AL*, nos. 507–18, fols. 46v–47r; *AL*, nos. 555–66; fol. 47r–v); Martial, Epigram I.19 (fol. 196v); *AL*, no. 160 (fol. 196v, the four-line version); *AL*, no. 672 (fol. 197r–v).
s. xii, England.
One of a group of English manuscripts, many once belonging to the Cambridge friars, sent to Rome during the dissolution of the monasteries; they entered the collection of Cardinal Cervini and passed into the Vatican Library. There are several s. xv English glosses. Dr. Ker, who brought the manuscript's English connections to my attention, thought the hand to be s. xii first half, perhaps second quarter.
The *E* and *G* are in a separate booklet from the *A*; cf. no. 9 below.
The text is in a fine bookhand, probably English.

For full description, see *MCLBV* I.1, pp. 550–52. On the Cervini manuscripts, Neil R. Ker, "Cardinal Cervini's Manuscripts from the

Cambridge Friars," in *Books, Collectors, and Libraries*, ed. Andrew G. Watson (London and Ronceverte: Hambledon Press, 1985), pp. 437–58. Fraŋois Fossier, "Premières récherches sur les manuscrits du Cardinal Marcello Cervini (1501–1555)," *Mélanges de l'école franqise de Rome* 91 (1979): 418. Murgia, p. 62. Munk Olsen, C.234. Allessio, no. 846.

(8) EDINBURGH, NATIONAL LIBRARY OF SCOTLAND, ADV. 18.4.13
Aeneid
$AA\ II^{11}$, III^{10}, IV^{11}-VI^{11}, IX^{11}-XII^{11}.

Fragmentary opening of a commentary, badly rubbed, s. xiii, fol. 1r, right margin. Inc., "materia uirgilii eneidos est fortia gesta enee uiri troihani transeuntis a troiha combusta in italiam." Exp., "quod elie filia iunonis prius habebat et hoc fuit alia causa."

Interlinear glosses and brief marginal notes in a number of hands, s. xii to s. xiv, largely lexical and grammatical. The s. xii marginalia, largely in one hand, show considerable independence from Servius; they are typical pedagogical notes, comparable to the early layers in All Souls 82 (see pp. 53–62).

s. xii, England?

Cunningham identifies the present binding as French, s. xvi. The boards and sewing, however, are earlier, later recovered in velvet. Dr. Neil Ker kindly examined the manuscript and suggested that boards and sewing are both English. The rather narrow hand of the text could be northern French or English, however, and there is a suggestion of French ownership, s. xviii. But there are extensive marginalia, s. xiii second half, which are undoubtedly English.

114 fols., 225–30 x 143 [180–85 x *c*. 60], one col., 36 lines.

On first membrane flyleaf at back of manuscript: "Robertus filius Roberti ffolwode," s. xiv? On paper flyleaf, fo. ii *verso*: "ex libris D D Robert de Saint Victor," s. xviii? Could the latter be an antiquarian's reference to the former?

For further description, see I. C. Cunningham, "Latin Classical Manuscripts in the National Library of Scotland," *Scriptorium* 27 (1973): 77–78. Munk Olsen, C.42 (which lists *AA* differently). Allessio, no. 140.

(9) OXFORD, ALL SOULS COLLEGE 82
Eclogues (fols. 1r–10r); *Georgics* (fols. 10v–35r); *Aeneid* (fols. 36r–150v).
"Ille ego qui quondam..." (fol. 36r, upper right corner); *AL*, nos. 256, 257 in the four-line version, 674a (fol. 151r); *AG* I–IV; $AA\ I^{11}$, II^{10}, III^{11}-XII^{11} (the summary at Book Three comes from a different series, Baehrens, p. 151); verse summary to *A* (*AL*, no. 1 *praefatio*, fol. 151r); *AL*, no. 634 (fol. 151v).

Three major layers of glosses and commentary are distinguishable, s. xii, xiii, xiv. For discussion see ch. 2.

Other texts: *AL*, no. 672 (fols. 148v–149r); "Exprobacio in uetulam" (inc. "Quattuor ut memini...," Walther, no. 15333, cf. Martial I.xix, fol. 151r); Proverbs (fol. 151v); *AL*, no. 160 with explanatory verses (fol. 149v, left margin).

The content of this manuscript is strikingly similar to that of no. 7 above; it is notable that both manuscripts similarly place the *A* in a booklet separate from the *E* and *G*.

s. xii med., England

s. xiv + 151 + iv (iv is a stub) fols. (pencil foliation inconsistent and incorrect); 257 x 130 [195 x *c.* 67]; one col., 44 lines.

The *E* and *G* are in a separate booklet from the *A*, and have an independent sequence of signatures.

Despite the presence of two booklets, the entire text is written by a single, well-disciplined bookhand.

On flyleaf ii there is an incompletely erased inscription (s. xiii), "liber ecclesie Sancte Marie de (Cyrence)st(r)'," common also in other Cirencester books. On flyleaf iii *verso*, "Liber magistri Aluredi." Aluredus also owned Oxford, Jesus Coll. 26 (Ivo of Chartres, *Panormia*, s. xii) and Hereford Cathedral O.2.iv (Gilbert de la Porrée on the Pauline Epistles, s. xii). For discussion of his identity, see pp. 44–46. By the early fifteenth century, the manuscript was owned by Archbishop Chichele's registrar, Henry Penwortham, who left it to All Souls in 1438. He also owned All Souls 19 and 37.

For further discussion, see ch. 2. R. W. Hunt and others, *The Survival of Ancient Literature* (Oxford: Bodleian Library, 1975), no. 25. Neil R. Ker, *Medieval Libraries of Great Britain: A List of Surviving Books* (London: Royal Historical Society, 1964), pp. 51–52. Neil R. Ker, "Sir John Prise," *The Library*, 5th ser., 10 (1955): 1–24. Munk Olsen, C.163. Allessio, no. 616. I am deeply grateful to Professor A. G. Watson, who reviewed and corrected this description; Prof. Watson's forthcoming catalog of the All Souls manuscripts will provide a much fuller description.

(10) CAMBRIDGE, PEMBROKE COLLEGE 260 (C.M.A. 2048)

Aeneid (fols. 1r–122r); *Eclogues* (fols. 123r–133r); *Georgics* (fols. 133r–159r). (The manuscript was originally ordered *E, G, A*, as indicated by the original quire numbering.)

"Ille ego qui quondam..." (fol. 1r, added by hand of commentary layer III, see below); Virgilian epitaph "Mantua me genuit..." (*AL* I.2, p. 62, fol. 123r); *AL*, no. 222 (fol. 123r); *AG* I-IV.

Three major layers of annotation. (I) The earliest was part of the original production of the manuscript. Several different hands are involved in this set of notes, but one hand follows another without overlap, presumably working from an exemplar. There are few of these notes in *E*. They are frequent in *G* 1 and 2 and throughout *A*. Interlinear glosses and longer marginal notes, mostly from Servius, range from loose summaries to near-quotation. In the *G*, they show particular interest in astronomical information from Servius; a few lexical and astronomical notes appear to be independent. Most notes in *A* are quite close to Servius and provide information similar to that in layers I and IA in All Souls 82 (no. 9 above, and see pp. 53–62). A few non-Servian notes are very close to notes in London, BL Add. 32319A (no. 14). (II) A less frequent group in an English cursive hand, s. xiv. They do not appear in *E*, and make only sporadic glosses in *G*. They reappear in *A* 6–8, mostly brief lexical glosses, and a few longer notes on mythology. This hand also provides occasional glosses in English. (III) A large cursive hand, perhaps later than group II, written in pale grey ink, now very faded. While there are brief marginalia and frequent glosses in this hand, it is mostly characterized by topic headings in the margins, written very large and usually enclosed by a line: names of characters and places, and summaries of major events. This group of notes is particularly notable for its lack of interest in *A* 4 and 6; it has far more entries in the battle books of the second half of the epic.

Other texts: *AL*, nos. 256–257 (fol. 123r).

s. xii med. or xii², England.

159 fols.; 253 x 150 [written space varies considerably, 180–95 x *c*. 65]; one col., 40–42 lines.

Three rather undistinguished hands are involved in the text, changing at the end of quires: i-xv, xvi-xvii, xviii-xix. Several other hands make brief appearances in the last four quires.

The manuscript was given to Pembroke by Thomas Westhaugh; flyleaf ii^r, "liber aule ualencie marie de cantabr. de dono m(agist)ri Thome Westhaghe quonda(m) perpetui socii eiusd(em)"; see the entry in Emden, *BRUC*. Flyleaf ii^v, s. xv: "M. Edwardus G., ex mutuo habens librum a Ma(gist)ro thoma"; in a different hand, "Precium istius libri [erasure]."

M. R. James, *A Descriptive Catalogue of the Manuscripts in the Library of Pembroke College, Cambridge* (Cambridge University Press, 1905), pp. 237–38. Emden *BRUC*, pp. 630–31. Munk Olsen, C.32. Allessio, no. 100.

(11) CAMBRIDGE, PETERHOUSE COLLEGE 158 (I.6.3)
Eclogues (fols. 1v–12r); *Georgics* (fols. 13r–39r); *Aeneid* (fols. 43r–167v). (Modern foliation inaccurate.)
AG II-IV; *AA* V^11–VIII^11; *AL*, no. 634, *AA* I^11 (fol. 168r).

The *E* contain rare contemporary glosses, and marginal notes in an English cursive hand, s. xiv. The same, or a very similar hand provides brief marginal notes to *G* 1, citing new topics and difficult words; and one long note explaining proper names at the beginning of 3.

The *A* is surrounded at beginning and end by several *accessus* and commentaries, all s. xii. (1) An *accessus* (fol. 42r a–b), unpublished but closely related to the *vita Noricensis* and *Periochae Bernensis* II (Bayer, pp. 282–90), with some details from Servius and the *vita Donatiana*, inc. "Quattuor a doctissimis solent percunctari doctoribus: locus, tempus, persona, scribendique occasio. Siquidem hec quattuor in carmina uirgilii reperiuntur..." Exp. "ac per hoc omnes suos libros uiginti et uno anno composuit. uixit autem quinquaginta duo annis." (2) Another *accessus* and fragmentary opening of a commentary (fol. 42v b), beginning with Servius, then mixing details from the *vita Donatiana* and fresh material, including a prose narrative of the *A*, breaking off with an entry on "uir" (1.1). Inc. "Ortis bellis ciuilibus..." Exp. "Vir accipitur tribus modis. a uiribus, id est uirtuosus, et pro discretione sexus, et pro marito, ut mulier uocat uirum suum. hic autem accipitur a uirtute. Unde captat beneuolenciam c(esaris)." (3) Fragmentary opening of an allegorical commentary (fol. 42v a), discussed pp. 101–07 and printed in "Allegorization," Appendix I. Inc. "Eneam dicit per descriptionem, quem per excellentiam uirum uocat." Exp. "per hoc quod letos eos dicit, tanto maiore ira iunonem ostendit incitari." This item is connected to marginal notes in the text (see pp. 106–07); this leaf was thus probably added when *A* was first annotated, quite likely as part of its original production. (4) An allegorical commentary on *A* 6 (fols. 169r–171r [incorrectly foliated 174]), closely related to the commentary of "Bernard Silvestris." Discussed pp. 108–20, and printed in "Allegorization," Appendix II. Inc. "Sic fatur. Virgilius in sexto seruat utrimque et poeticum figmentum et philosophiam rei ueritatem." Exp. "et pallada id est sapientia, et probitate attulit ENEAS."

s. xii (*A*), s. xiii in. (*E*, *G*), England.

The two booklets were apparently bound together by 1418, when this manuscript appears as no. 228 ("opera") in the Peterhouse catalog, printed by James (see below), p. 17. But they may have still been independent s. xiv, since the hand that makes many marginal entries in *E* and *G* at that time appears nowhere in *A*.

173 fols., 222 x 115 [167–72 x *c*. 65 (*E*, *G*), 176–80 x *c*. 60 (*A*)], one col., 40 lines (*E*, *G*), 39–40 lines (*A*).

A single hand, recognizably English, writes *E* and *G*; another single hand writes *A*. The commentary fols. 169r–171r is distinctively English, s. xii last quarter.

M. R. James, *A Descriptive Catalogue of the Manuscripts in the Library of Peterhouse* (Cambridge University Press, 1899), pp. 186–87. Christopher Baswell, "The Medieval Allegorization of the *Aeneid*: MS Cambridge, Peterhouse 158," *Traditio* 41 (1985): 181–237. Julian W. Jones, "The So-Called Silvestris Commentary on the *Aeneid* and Two Other Interpretations" *Speculum* 64 (1989): 835–48. Not listed by Munk Olsen. Allessio, no. 101 (listed as "Peter's College 163").

(12) CAMBRIDGE, JESUS COLLEGE 33 (Q.B.16)
Aeneid, lines 1.1–229 now missing (fols. 2v–103r).
"Epitaphium uirgilii": "Pastor oues, arator agros, et prelia / miles instruxi. Eterno clarus honore maro" (Walther, no. 13785, fol. 103r); *AA* VII[11]–XII[11].

Five layers of annotation can be distinguished, of which (I) and (III) should perhaps be further divided into independent but contemporary hands. (I) A contemporary layer of mostly interlinear glosses; a few longer marginal notes, especially in the later books, deriving closely from Servius. (II) A fully formed English cursive hand, s. xiii-xiv; this hand appears to write in two colors of ink, going through the text more than once. (III) An English cursive hand, s. xv, various gray inks; James associates these notes with the hand that supplied missing leaves. (IV) Humanist minuscule, s. xv, second half. This is the hand of the early English humanist John Free; English symptoms include the use of the 2-chambered *Anglicana a*. Free sometimes writes the lemmata in a larger, more clearly English hand. (V) A stiffer, more stately humanist minuscule hand, s. xv/xvi? It appears mostly in the earlier books, often seriously faded.

s. xii[2], England; erased and missing portions rewritten s. xv (fols. 2r, 93v), and missing leaves inserted s. xiv? (fol. 86) and s. xv (fols. 3–4, 94–103).

103 fols. (modern pencil foliation begins with fly-leaf ii, two leaves mistakenly numbered 83). 237 x 112 [192 x *c*. 60, some variation], one col., 47 lines (not 49 as in Munk Olsen), later additions 42–46 lines.

The original production was by three hands: (1) fols. 2, 5–39; (2) fols. 40–50r line 6; (3) fols. 50r line 7–85, 87–93r. (1) and (2) are typical mid-century bookhands, (3) is more old-fashioned.

The manuscript must have travelled with Free to Italy, where he studied with Guarino da Verona and learned humanist minuscule. He never returned to England, but left his manuscripts to another early English humanist, John Gunthorpe, who in turn left many of his books to Jesus College; this manuscript is not recorded among them. The manuscript is recorded as "E dono Thomae Wood." Three such names are linked to Jesus, 1575–93 (*Alumni Cantabrigiensis*, pt. 1, IV, pp. 454–55).

M. R. James, *A Descriptive Catalogue of the Manuscripts in the Library of Jesus College Cambridge* (London and Cambridge: Clay and Sons, 1895), pp. 42–43. On John Free, see Emden, *BRUO*, pp. 724–25 and references there. I am grateful to Prof. Albinia de la Mare for confirming that the hand of annotation layer (IV) is by Free. Munk Olsen, C.30. Allessio, no. 99.

(13) CAMBRIDGE, TRINITY COLLEGE 623 (R.3.50)
Aeneid (fols. 1r–140r).
Annotation falls into two groups. (I) Sporadic literal glosses in a hand s. xii/xiii, which occasionally also inserts a missing word or line. At Book Eleven, these become more frequent and a little longer. They show contact with Servius but are often independent and sometimes inaccurate. Two or three hands may be involved; the notes in Book Eleven (and the few in Twelve) are in a single, distinctive, rather crude hand. (II) Marginalia in an English cursive hand, s. xiii/xiv, frequent in Book One, rare after. Aside from literal glosses, it gives plot summary, and grammatical and rhetorical notes.
s. xii ex., England?
The manuscript was given to Bury St. Edmunds by Willelmus Curteys, abbot 1429–45. There are s. xiii annotations in distinctively English hands.
140 fols., 172 x 98 [145-51 x *c.* 50], one col., 34–36 lines.

M. R. James, *The Western Manuscripts in the Library of Trinity College Cambridge* (Cambridge University Press, 1901), II, p. 119, with owner and donor information, and accurate collation. Ker, *Medieval Libraries*, pp. 19, 233. Munk Olsen, C.34. Allessio, no. 106.

(14) LONDON, BL ADDITIONAL 32319A
Eclogues (fols. 4r–13r), *Georgics* (fols. 13v–37v), *Aeneid* (fols. 38r–148v).
AL, no. 257 (fol. 37v); "Ille ego. . ." (fol. 37v); *AL*, no. 256 (fol. 150va); *AG* I, III–IV; *AA* I^{11}, II^{10}–III^{10}, V^{11}–VIII^{11}, X^{11} (*AA* IX^{11} is prefixed to Book Four, correct *AA* supplied s. xv in lower margin); *AL*, no. 634 (fol. 38r). A group of *accessus*, *vitae*, and verses, accurately described by Munk Olsen (fols. 149r–150v); several link this manuscript with the apparatus in Brussels, Bibl. royale 10014–10017 and Leiden, Bibliotheek der Rijksuniversiteit, B. P. L. 92A.
A densely annotated manuscript, with marginalia falling into three major groups. (I) *E* and *G* have numerous interlinear and marginal notes in a hand contemporary with the text, probably part of the original production; largely Servian, but providing more narrative summary than Servius; they emphasize the political allegory of *E*. Two other hands, roughly contemporary with the text, also add occasional notes. (II) *A* has extensive interlinear and marginal notes, part of

original production, but in a different hand. They derive closely from Servius, but show particular interest in rhetoric and mythology, especially physical allegory of the gods; in this area they have entries independent of Servius, some of which overlap with entries in the early annotation in Peterhouse 158 (no. 11). Two other roughly contemporary hands make brief entries in A. (III) Three different English cursive hands, as. xv, make brief notes including a few English glosses.

Other texts: *AL*, no. 664, lines 3–11 (fol. 148v).

s. xii ex., England?

The hand of the text could suggest, I think, either France or England; there are brief marginal glosses in distinctly English hands of s. xv (a few in English); but neither the ruled format nor the quiring (gatherings of 12, final gathering of 15) are typical of English Virgils of the period.

148 fols.; 245 x 145 [195 x *c.* 65]; one col., 45 lines.

Catalogue of Additions to the Manuscripts in the British Museum 1882-1887 (London, 1889), p. 101, which believes the text and marginalia are Italian; neither suggestion seems convincing on close examination of the manuscript, and particularly its marginalia. Valerie Edden also suggests Italian provenance; see "Early Manuscripts of Virgiliana," *The Library*, 5th ser., 28 (1973): 24. Pattie, no. 26, p. 129. Brummer, *Vitae*, pp. viii–ix. Munk Olsen, C.93 (who also proposes "Angleterre?" as place of origin). Allessio, no. 367.

(15) LONDON, LAMBETH PALACE 471

Eclogues (fols. 1r–9v), *Georgics*, now lacking 2.453–3.93 (fols. 10r–32v), *Aeneid* (fols. 33r-135v).

AG I–II, IV; *AA* I^{11}–II^{11}, III^{10}–IV^{10}, V^{11}–XII^{11}; *AL*, no. 634 (fol. 32v).

Annotation is in three groups. (I) Probably by the hand of the text. Interlinear and marginal notes, frequent in *E* and *G* Book One, *A* Books One–Three and the first page of Four. These derive almost completely from Servius; the selection concentrates on lexical and grammatical information, with some notes also on history and geography; there is no special interest in mythology or rhetoric. A few lexical glosses are independent of Servius. (II) An English hand, s. xiv (ex.?), enters a few lexical and grammatical notes. (III) A cursive Secretary hand with some English forms, s. xv, more frequent than group II, also makes lexical and grammatical notes. (A few other English hands, s. xiii–xv, make rare entries.)

Other texts: *AL*, no. 392 (fol. 9v); Walter of Châtillon, *Alexandreis* (originally a separate manuscript, now fols. 136v–203r).

s. xii ex., England.

The hand of the Virgil portion of the manuscript could be northern French or English. There are marginalia in distinctively English hands as early as s. xiii, though; there seems little reason to doubt its English origin.

The two portions of the manuscript were originally separate but bound together by s. xiv when a continuous sequence of signatures was entered. The following information refers only to the Virgil sections.

133 fols. (now 203 fols.); 237 x 125 [178 x *c*. 50]; one col., 49–50 lines. *E* and *G* have original signatures separate from *A*, though apparently part of a single production; cf. no. 7 and no. 9 above.

The entire Virgil text is in a single, typical small bookhand.

The most elaborately decorated English s. xii Virgil, including a unique historiated initial at *E* 1.1. See description in James and Jenkins (see below).

The gift of Archbishop Abbot (d. 1633).

M. R. James and Clive Jenkins, *A Descriptive Catalogue of the Manuscripts in the Library of Lambeth Palace* (Cambridge University Press, 1930–32), pp. 646–48. Neil R. Ker, "Archbishop Sancroft's Rearrangement of the Manuscripts of Lambeth Palace," in E. G. W. Bill, *A Catalogue of Manuscripts in Lambeth Palace Library: MSS 1222-1860* (Oxford: Clarendon Press, 1972), pp. 6–7. Munk Olsen, C.107. Allessio, no. 425.

(16) PARMA, BIBLIOTECA PALATINA 2662
Aeneid (fols. 8r–125v).
AA III^{10}–IV^{10}.

Infrequent interlinear and marginal glosses in several hands, mostly s. xiii, using distinctively English forms. Most entries are lexical and syntactic; a few rhetorical glosses. Very rare after Book Four.

Fols. 1–7, 126–31 are flyleaves, apparently from one manuscript, a theological text.

s. xii ex., England?

The text hand could be northern French or English. Marginalia are indisputably English.

131 fols. Following information pertains only to part 2, *A*: 118 fols. Early quire signatures, in Roman numerals, on final *verso* of each quire. 240 x 140 [193 x *c*. 65], one col., 40–44 lines.

Fol. 7v, s. xvii: note of gift from Thomas Barlow (1607–91) to "D. Sam. Tennulio," dated 1650.

Munk Olsen, C.206. Allessio, no. 699.

(17) EDINBURGH, NATIONAL LIBRARY, ADV. 18.5.12
Aeneid (fols. 100r–210r)
AA III^{10}–IV^{10}, V^{11}–VI^{11}, VIII^{11} (on inserted slip), IX^{11}, XI^{11}.

At least three hands, roughly contemporary with the text, enter glosses and brief notes, mostly derived from Servius. The rare longer notes are usually quite close to Servius. There are, in addition, many one-word rhetorical marginalia (and a few metrical), many of them independent of Servius. This group of notes thins out after Book Two, though it occurs throughout, and with some frequency again in Six. There are a few brief notes in a humanist minuscule, s. xv.

Other texts: Statius, *Thebaid* (fols. 1r–99v).

s. xii/xiii, England or France

The single hand of the *A* could be English or northern French. The manuscript was in England at least by s. xiv ex., already combined with the originally separate manuscript of Statius, when the Dover Priory librarian's note on fol. V^v lists both texts.

Virgil and Statius portions originally separate, in different though roughly contemporary hands.

210 fols., (following information applies only to *A*) 215 x 104–10 (*pace* Cunningham) [180–95 x 60–70, much variation], one col., 46–49 lines.

For further description, see I. C. Cunningham, "Latin Classical Manuscripts in the National Library of Scotland," *Scriptorium* 27 (1973), pp. 80–81. Ker, *Medieval Libraries*, p. 59. Munk Olsen, C.43. Allessio, no. 142.

(18) LONDON, BL ADDITIONAL 27304

Aeneid, now lacks 10.275–379, 10.486–890, 11.75–178, 12.950–52 (fols. 5r–112v).

AA II^{10}, III^{10}, IV^{11}–V^{11}, VI^{1+9}, VII^{1+9}, VIII^{1+9}, IX^{11}, X^{1+9}, XI^{11}, XII^{11}.

Three major layers of annotation. (I) Near-contemporary with the text, largely literal and heavily dependent on Servius; (II) occasional glosses and a few brief notes, s. xiii^2; (III) an extended marginal commentary s. xiv, with much narrative summary and Christian allegorizing. These are discussed on pp. 143–63.

s. xii/xiii, England.

108 folios (4 membrane flyleaves foliated); 236 x 130. Two different formats: (a) fols. 5–84 [181–84 x *c.* 55, except for fols. 77–84, 190 x *c.* 55], one col., 40 lines (fols. 77–84, 41 lines); (b) fols. 85–112 [196–204 x *c.* 50], one col. 48–52 lines.

As many as ten hands are involved in the text, though they divide into two major groups with the change in format at fol. 85.

Fol. 2v, s. xvii: "Richard Shuttleworth / Joh(n) Rudd / William Shuttleworth." Fol. 4v, s. xix?: "Luke Yarker."

Not listed in Munk Olsen. Allessio, no. 365.

(19) VATICAN, BIBLIOTECA APOSTOLICA VATICANA, OTTOB. LAT. 1373

Eclogues (fols. 1r–11v), *Georgics* (fols. 11v–39r), *Aeneid* (fols. 39v–162v; fols. 73–74 should follow 162).

AG I–II; *AA* I^{10}–IV^{10}, V^{11}–XII^{11}; *AL*, nos. 256–57 (fol. 11v); *AL*, no. 634 (fol. 39r).

Infrequent contemporary glosses in *E*. No glosses in *G*. *A* has extensive marginalia, Books One–Six, in a distinctively English hand, s. xiii/ xiv, including English glosses. This hand has two distinguishable activities: (a) lists of words from the text, entered vertically in the outer margin, only some glossed; (b) regular interlinear and marginal notes, showing some influence of the "Anselm" commentary (see ch. 2, pp. 63–68). Brief entries in a variety of later hands.

s. xii/xiii, England? Fols. 1 and 73–74 (should appear after 162) supplied later.

The first layer of annotation in *A* is in a distinctively English hand and includes English-language glosses. The supplied folio i shows English characteristics and appears to be earlier than s. xiv (as indicated in *MCLBV*). This would seem to be another of the Cervini manuscripts that came from the Cambridge Friars and ended among the Ottoboni, studied by Ker and Fossier (see no. 7 above); neither scholar, however, lists this manuscript.

162 fols.; 222 x 118 [187 x *c*. 63]; one col., 40 lines.

Although most of the text is written in hands that could be English or northern French, fol. 1 is written in a distinctive hand with several English characteristics such as trailing-headed *a*, *x* with its lower left stroke curling around the preceding letter, and characteristic treatment of the headstroke of final *t*. (See Neil R. Ker, *English Manuscripts in the Century after the Norman Conquest* [Oxford: Clarendon Press, 1960], p. 35.)

MCLBV I, pp. 540–41. Munk Olsen, C.233 (where it is said to be French). Allessio, no. 843.

(20) LONDON, BL BURNEY 269
Aeneid, now lacks 1.1–81, 1.576–656, 12.896–952 (fols. 1r–120v).
AA II^{10}–IV^{10}, V^{11}–XII^{11}.

Three hands, roughly contemporary with the text, enter interlinear and marginal glosses, and occasional longer notes. These are frequent in the early books, rarer thereafter. They are largely informational, grammatical, and lexical, generally dependent on Servius. Occasional rhetorical and lexical glosses are independent. In general level and emphasis, these are comparable to group I in no. 9. There is a very sporadic group of notes and glosses, in pale gray ink, s. xiii–xiv, with English cursive forms.

s. xiii^{1}, England?

120 fols. 228 x 130 (frequent variation) [173 (varies, 160–75) x *c*. 60], one column, 41 lines (quire ii, 35–39 lines; quire xi, 42 lines).

As many as nine hands contribute to the text, none especially disciplined or consistent; some enter only very briefly. Punctuation is inconsistent and idiosyncratic. Both in writing and format, the manuscript has the aspect of an amateur production.

Pattie, p. 130, no. 32. Allessio, no. 371.

(21) LONDON, BL ROYAL 15.B.VI
Aeneid (fols. 4r–121r).
AA I^{11}, III^{10}–IV^{10}, V^{11}–XI^{11}, XII^{10}.
Rather few glosses, in many hands from contemporary with the text to s. xv English cursive. Mostly lexical and grammatical. A number of indications of "C(omparati)o" in hands of text. Two brief *accessus* to *A*, badly rubbed (fol. 121v). (1) Inc. "Virgilius utebatur triplici stilo scilicet grandiloco, et mediocri, et umili stilo...," exp. illegible. (2) Almost wholly illegible; enough words can be read to make it clear that this conformed to the "modern" *accessus* (Hunt, type "C").
s. xiii^1, England.
121 fols.; quiring i–xiv^8, xv^6; 240–45 (quire ii, 235) x 123. Three formats: (1) quires i, iii–viii [192–95 x *c.* 48], one col., 40 lines; (2) quire ii [186 x *c.* 45], one col., 36–40 lines; (3) quires ix–xv [192–202 x *c.* 50], one col., 43–47 lines.
A number of hands contribute to the text, usually changing at the beginning of quires.
Belonged to St. Augustine's Canterbury: fol. 4r, "De librario sancti Augustini Cantuariensis." Fol. 2r: "Laurens Goldstoy."

Sir George F. Warner and Julius P. Gilson, *Catalogue of Western Manuscripts in the Old Royal and King's Collections* (London: Trustees of the British Museum, 1921), II, p. 155. M. R. James, *The Ancient Libraries of Canterbury and Dover* (Cambridge University Press, 1903), p. 368, no. 1476. Ker, *Medieval Libraries*, p. 45. Pattie, p. 138, no. 81 (there identified as 15.B.iv). Allessio, no. 420. On the model for *accessus* (2), see A. J. Minnis, *Medieval Theory of Authorship*, 2nd ed. (Philadelphia: University of Pennsylvania Press, 1988), pp. 18–28.

(22) LONDON, BL HARLEY 4967
Eclogues (fols. 126v–138v).
Extensive notes in the hand of the text, concentrating on grammar and rhetoric, but ranging widely, and including much traditional political and biographical allegory. They draw on Servius, sometimes quite closely, but also make considerable independent analysis. These notes merit much further study, in the context of the rest of the s. xiii portion of the manuscript.
Other texts: The manuscript was originally in three parts (I) Fols. 1–76 are s. xii^2, and contain mostly legal texts including the *Liber Prometheus* and *Institutes* of Justinian. (II) Fols. 77–185, mostly s. xiii, are largely

by one hand but include six booklets, often with their final leaf originally blank and filled by several later hands. Works copied by the original hand make up an intriguing collection of ancient and medieval Latin poetry, and liberal arts texts, particularly on grammar, rhetoric, and metrics. They include: a collection of hymns with an *accessus* (fols. 78r–91v), inc. "lux beata trinitas et principalis unitas...," exp. "Gloria eterno patri et cristo uero regi paraclito que sancto in sempiterna secula. amen."; Avianus, *Fables* (fols. 92r–102v); Persius, *Satires* (fols. 139r–149r); Alan of Lille, the *Liber parabolarum* (fols. 151r–160v); the *cento* of Proba (fols. 169r–174v). (III) Fols. 186-93. A single hand, s. xiv/xv? A metrical Latin text on synonyms.

s. xiii^2, England.

189 fols. Following applies to part II only: 241 x 188 [167 x 105 (prose), x *c.* 65 (verse)], one col. (two cols. fols. 161–68; marginal cols. ruled for notes throughout), average 33–35 lines with great variation.

Part I was probably at Worcester.

A Catalogue of the Harleian Manuscripts in the British Museum (London, 1808), III, pp. 233–34. Ker, *Medieval Libraries*, p. 207. Not listed by Pattie. Allessio, no. 414.

(23) OXFORD, BODLEIAN LIBRARY, AUCT. F.1.17 (S.C. 2506)

Eclogues (fols. 19rb–24rb), *Georgics* (fols. 24va–38rb), *Aeneid* 1–12.431 (fols. 46va–108vb).

Culex (fols. 39rb–41vb), *Dirae* (fols. 41vb–43ra), *Copa* (fols. 43ra–b), *De est et non* (fol. 43rb), *Vir bonus* (fol. 43rb–43va), *De rosis nascentibus* ("Rosetum," fol. 43va–b), *Moretum* (fols. 43vb–44va); "Mantua me genuit..." (fol. 44va, 45rb); *AL,* nos. 256, 257 (fol. 44vb); "Ille ego..." (fol. 46va, upper margin, not in hand of text); *AL,* no. 634 (fol. 46rb–va); *AG* I–IV; *AA* II^{11}, III^{10}–IV^{10}, V^{11}–XII^{11}.

Interlinear and marginal glosses to works of Virgil in two s. xiv hands, frequent only in *E*, first eighty lines of *G*, and beginning of *A* 1 and 6, mostly lexical and grammatical. The second hand provides occasional glosses in English, and sometimes numbered divisions within books of A (e.g. 1.67 "2^a pars"). A third hand enters a few glosses at the beginning of *A* 6.

Other works: *AL,* no. 160 (four-line version, fol. 44vb); distich and tetrastich epitaphs on Virgil (*AL,* nos. 507–518, 555–566, fols. 44vb–45rb); *AL,* no. 264 (fol. 45rb); *AL,* no. 727 (= Walther, no. 14964, fol. 45rb–vb); *AL,* no. 672 (fol. 46ra–b); *AL,* no. 392 (fol. 46rb); Alan of Lille, *Liber parabolarum* (fols. 1ra–4vb); Matthew of Vendôme, *Tobias* (fols. 5ra–18vb); Marbod, epigrams (fols. 38rb–39rb); Geoffrey of Vinsauf, *Poetria Nova* (fols. 109ra–121va); Ovid, Works, see *Summary Catalogue* (below) for full list (fols. 121va–283rb); Sedulius, *Carmen*

Paschale (fols. 283rb–294va) and *Elegia* (fols. 294va–295rb); Prudentius, *Psychomachia* (fols. 295rb–301va).

s. xiv[1], England

301 fols. 348 x 250 [ruled frame 263 x 200], 2 cols., 40 lines.

Two good gothic bookhands write the entire manuscript, changing at fol.
283rb.

Falconer Madan and H. H. E. Craster, *A Summary Catalogue of Western
Manuscripts in the Bodleian Library at Oxford* (Oxford: Clarendon,
1922), II, pt. 1, no. 2506, pp. 401–02. M. D. Reeve, "The
Textual Tradition of the *Appendix Vergiliana*," *Maia*, n.s. 3 (1976):
242. Otto Pächt and J.J.G. Alexander, *Illuminated Manuscripts in the
Bodleian Library*, III: *British, Irish, and Icelandic Schools* (Oxford
University Press 1973), p. 615. Eva M. Sanford, "The Use of
Classical Latin Authors in the Libri Manuales," *Transactions and
Proceedings of the American Philological Association* 55 (1924): 238–39,
no. 395. Susan Gallick, "Medieval Rhetorical Arts in England and
the Manuscript Traditions," *Manuscripta* 18 (1974): 78, 82. Allessio,
no. 575.

(24) LONDON, BL ADDITIONAL 16166

Eclogues (fols. 10r–20v), *Georgics* (fols. 20v–48r), *Aeneid* (fols. 54r–184r),
with later erasures.

AG II–III; *AA* I[11]–XII[11] (fols. 48v–50r, now largely erased); the
"flyleaves," apparently original, may have been intended to hold
commentary matter and related Virgiliana.

Interlinear glosses and brief marginal notes in the hand of the text.
Sparse in *E*, more frequent in *G* 1, absent *G* 2–4; dense again *A* 1 and
6, sparse or absent in other books. Largely informational, only partly
drawn from Servius. The marginalia also include many independent
plot summaries and paraphrases, comparable to the roughly
contemporary activity in no. 18, annotation layer III.

Other texts: the early or original flyleaves (fols. 1–9, 186–91) now have a
variety of unrelated texts, mostly recipes, s. xv and xvi, in Latin and
English, many in the hands that also fill erased portions of the
original text.

s. xiv, England.

193 fols. (including original flyleaves; 2 folios skipped in the modern
pencil foliation); 9 membrane flyleaves at beginning, 6 membrane
flyleaves at end; 203 x 102 [151 x *c.* 67], one col., 36–42 lines.

Text and annotation in a single, rather undisciplined English cursive
hand, except for a second text hand fols. 151r line 20–161v.

Fol. 1v: "cum Wyl(elm)o Walde(n) monacho de bery" (s. xv). Fol. 2r:
"Thomas Warner" (s. xvi?). Fol. 188v, at the end of one of the s. xvi
recipes: "William Rabon."

Catalogue of Additions to the Manuscripts in the British Museum (London: 1846–47), pp. 156–57. Pattie, no. 17, pp. 127–28. Allessio, no. 359.

(25) OXFORD, NEW COLLEGE 271

Aeneid (fols. 1r–155v).

"Ille ego…" (fol. 1r, hand of annotator), AA I^{10}–IV^{10}, V^{2+10}, VI^{11}–IX^{11}, X^{2+10}, XI^{11}–XII^{11} (books Five and Ten have both the standard monostich and the appropriate line from *AL*, no. 634).

Extensive marginalia are provided as part of the original production of the manuscript, on the first page of Book One, and resuming again in Book Six. Other hands make brief notes and glosses.

The "thirteeth book" of the *Aeneid*, by Mapheus Vegius (fols. 157r–167r), and his *De morte Astyanactis* (fols. 167r–172).

Italy (Florence), *c.* 1400.

The manuscript was owned in England in the second half of s. xv, and given to New College by John Russell in 1482.

170 fols. 290 x 210 [193 x *c.* 90], one col., 32 lines.

The first booklet (*Aeneid*) is by one Italian hand; the second by two English humanist scribes (see Hunt and de la Mare), the first of which (copying the "thirteenth book") is Thomas Candor, an Englishman who had learned humanistic script in Italy.

Owned by William Brygon and John Russell, s. xv second half. Russell left the manuscript to New College.

For discussion of the manuscript, its English scribes and ownership, see R. W. Hunt and Albinia de la Mare, *Duke Humfrey and English Humanism in the Fifteenth Century* (Oxford: Bodleian Library, 1969), no. 59, pp. 34–35, and p. 32. For Russell's gifts and the scribe Thomas Candor, see R. W. Hunt, "The Medieval Library," in *New College Oxford 1379–1979*, ed. John Buxton and Penry Williams (Oxford: Warden and Fellows of New College, Oxford, 1979), pp. 327–29. Not listed by Allessio.

(26) OXFORD, BODLEIAN LIBRARY, ASHMOLE 54

Eclogues (fols. 1r–13v), *Georgics* (fols. 14v–46v), *Aeneid* (fols. 56r–199v, now lacks 12.905–52; 2.567–88 supplied fol. 53v, with prose explanation, drawn from Servius, of their deletion by Varrius and Tucca.)

"Ille ego…" (fol. 50r). *AL*, nos. 256, 257 (fol. 54r). A genealogy of the Trojans, closely related to the text printed by W. Speyer (*RM* 107 [1964], p. 91) and to the "First Vatican Mythographer" (see below), no. 135; followed by a summary of Aeneas's wanderings, related to the "First Vatican Mythographer," no. 202; inc. "Dardanus ex Ioue et Electra filia…," exp. "Ubi ab incolis deus ingens nominatus est" (fol. 48r–v). A genealogical chart of the Trojans (fol 48r) and a further chart of Aeneas's wanderings (fol. 48v). *AL*, no. 634 (fol. 50v); *AA* I^{11}, II^{10}–V^{10}, VI^{11}–X^{11}, XI^{10}, XII^{11} (fols. 50v–52v).

There are two groups of annotation. The first is by the scribe of the text; it gives rhetorical and topic headings, as well as more substantial informative notes, often drawn loosely from Servius, but also showing research in other texts; it mentions Guido delle Colonne's *Historia destructionis Troie* ("in guidone de bello troiano"), Ovid (on several occasions), and "Ebrardus" (probably Eberhard of Bethune's *Graecismus*). The second group, s. xv, provides only glosses, many in English. Both groups tend to cluster around the beginning of each work.

"Iusserat hec rapidis..." (*AL*, no. 653 note), *AL*, no. 1 *Praefatio*, *AL*, no. 2 lines 1–4, *AL*, no. 257 (fol. 48r); *AL*, no. 740 (fol. 48v); epitaphs on Virgil (*AL*, nos. 507–18 555–66, fols. 48v–49v); *AL*, no. 672 (fols. 49v–50r); "Ouidius dicit," inc. "Hoc omne uirgilius felix eneidos autor...," exp. "...clarius exta opus" (fol. 50r, Walther, no. 13785).
s. xv, England.
199 fols. (one remains unnumbered between 98 and 99); 255 x 140 [186 x 75], one col., 34 lines.
The entire manuscript is written in a good text hand.
Fol. 1r: "Parcyuall Martyn / precium ii s uiii d"

W. H. Black, *A Catalogue of the Manuscripts Bequeathed unto the University of Oxford by Elias Ashmole* (Oxford, 1845), cols. 92–93. For the "First Vatican Mythographer," see Bode, ed., *Scriptores rerum mythicarum*. Not listed by Allessio.

(27) CAMBRIDGE, QUEENS' COLLEGE K.17.5, three pastedown fragments
Eclogues, fragments.
Interlinear glosses, some English.
s. xv, England.
Neil R. Ker, *Fragments of Medieval Manuscripts used as Pastedowns in Oxford Bindings, c. 1515–1620* (Oxford University Press, 1954), p. 228. Not listed by Allessio.

(28) CAMBRIDGE, ST. JOHN'S COLLEGE 54 (C.4)
Eclogues (fols. 1r–14v), *Georgics* (fols. 15r–54r), *Aeneid* (fols. 54r–228v).
12 monostichs, "Ille ego..." (fol 54v); *AG* II–IV; *AA* II[11], III[10]–IV[10], V[11]–XII[11].
Copious marginalia in a humanist minuscule hand, *A* 1, 2, and first half of 3. Sporadic interlinear and rare marginal glosses, in Latin and English, in the hand of the early English humanist Robert Flemmyng.
s. xv, Italy. Copied by Johannes Hornsen of Münster (fol. 228v: "Ioan. de Monasterio scripsit.").
In England by 1474; the manuscript is identifiable as no. 73 in the Lincoln College inventory of that date.

228 fols., 300 x 190 [196 x *c.* 100], one col., 29 lines.
Owned by Robert Flemmyng.

M. R. James, *A Descriptive Catalogue of the Manuscripts of St. John's College Cambridge* (Cambridge University Press, 1913), p. 72. On Flemmyng, see Roberto Weiss, *Humanism in England during the Fifteenth Century* (Oxford: Blackwell, 1957), pp. 101–05; and Emden, *BRUO*, II, pp. 699–700. The Lincoln College inventory is edited by Roberto Weiss, "The earliest catalogues of the Library of Lincoln College," *Bodleian Quarterly Record* 8 (1937): 343–59. I am grateful to Prof. Albinia de la Mare for identifying the English marginalia as in the hand of Flemmyng. Allessio, no. 102.

(29) CAMBRIDGE, TRINITY COLLEGE 457 (R.I.40)
Aeneid (fols. 2r–203v).
AL, no. 634 (fol. 1v); *AA* I^{11}, II^{10}, III^{11}–XII^{11}.
Numerous interlinear glosses and sporadic marginal notes throughout, showing little direct dependence on Servius. Some interlinear glosses are English, most provide literal synonyms, though there are consistent rhetorical glosses. Marginal notes are also largely informational and rhetorical; many help with syntactic order ("ordo"); they are rare in the later books.
s. xv, England.
203 fols., paper; 210 x 143 [140–50 x *c.* 65], one col., 20–26 lines.
Fol. ir: "Ioh(ann)es Walsyngh(a)mes huius libri est uere possessor," "John Raynoldes," s. xvi. The latter may be the John Raynolds described by Emden (*BRUO*) as a Dominican Friar who became a reformed preacher, references from 1513-49.

M. R. James, *The Western Manuscripts* (1901), II, p. 10. Allessio, no. 105.

(30) LONDON, BL ADDITIONAL 11959
Eclogues (fols. 1r–24v), *Georgics* 1.1–2.13 (fols. 25r–36v).
A brief *vita* (fol. 1r), inc. "Virgilius mantue natus a patre figulo, matre uero maya. Studuit athenis. Plures libros composuit, sed tres principales...," exp. "Unde illum librum incendi precepit. Sed augustus ne tantum opus periret tuscam et uarrum duos peritissimos poetas ad corrigendam adhibuit, tali lege, ut suo operi nichil adderent, sed quecumque superflua abraderent."
Extensive commentary in the hand of the text, crossing the whole column every few lines of verse, with briefer notes also in the ruled outer margin. The commentary provides simple explanations of plot and content, with some political allegory in *E*, but its greatest emphasis is on grammatical construction.
s. xv med., England.

36 fols. 287 x 205 [entire frame 200 x 145], elaborate frame with ruling for text and commentary, one col., lines per col. vary.

A single, fine English cursive bookhand writes text and commentary. Some French Secretary forms in text, fewer in commentary.

Pattie, no. 13, p. 127. Allessio, no. 355.

(31) LONDON, SOCIETY OF ANTIQUARIES 44
Eclogues (fols. 64r–80v), *Georgics* (fols. 80v–123v).
AL, no. 2 lines 1–4 (fol. 64r); *AL*, no. 634 (fol. 123v); "Origo troianorum," followed by a summary of Aeneas's wanderings–the same text as in no. 26 above, fols. 48r–v (fols. 123v–124v); Servius's *accessus* to the *A* (fols. 124v–127r).
Interlinear glosses and marginal notes to *E* and *G* in the hand of the text. Those on *E* derive closely from Servius, except for the introductory note at 1.1, inc. "Hic loquuntur duo pastores inter se, melibeus qui et cornelius gallus uel unus ex mantuanis a quo agri adempti sunt, tytirus qui et uirgilius, cui sunt agri redditi...," exp. "Scopon id est intencio Telos prima finis. Que sunt in hoc libro semper ad laudem et amorem cesaris pertinent." Those on *G* are verbatim selections from Servius.
Prudentius, *Hamartigenia* (fols. 1r–42v), *Psychomachia* (fols. 42v–63v).
s. xv, England.
127 fols. 217 x 150 [135 x *c.* 70], one col., 26 lines.
Text and annotation in a single cursive bookhand.
Given to the Society by a member, George Allan, 1798.

Neil R. Ker, *Medieval Manuscripts in British Libraries*, I: *London* (Oxford University Press, 1969), pp. 300–01. Allessio, no. 426 (there listed as *sine numero*).

(32) OXFORD, BODLEIAN LIBRARY, AUCT. F.2.7 (S.C. 4030)
Aeneid 5.183–7.195.
AA VI[11].
Frequent interlinear and marginal glosses, mostly one-word lexical information.
s. xv^2, England.
Mixed membrane and paper, 21 fols. 295 x 208 [208 x *c.* 85], one col., 40–50 lines.

Allessio, no. 578.

(33) CAMBRIDGE, ST. JOHN'S 205 (H.2)
Eclogues (fols. 1r–18r); *Georgics* (fols. 18v–63r); *Aeneid* (fols. 65v–270v); "Thirteenth Book" by Mapheus Vegius (fols. 271r–283v).
"Ille ego qui quondam..." (fol. 63v); "Epigramma P. V. M." ("Mantua me genuit...," Walther, no. 13785 [inc. "Pastor boues et arator

agros et prelia miles. . ."], *AL*, no. 800) (fol. 284r); *AL*, no. 634 (fol. 64v); *AG* I–IV; AA I–XII[10] (occasional rearrangement of line order) and a decastich summary of the "Thirteenth Book" (in a hand different from the rest of the text but part of original decoration), inc. "Victori enee subdit se rutula manus. . .," exp. "Diua parens Iouis imperio astra ad summa beatum."

"Origo troianorum et totius Enee uite decursus totiusque libri eneidos pulcherrima prefatio" (a genealogy of Aeneas and prose summary of the *Aeneid* including the "thirteenth book" of Mapheus Vegius, inc. "Dardanus ex Ioue et electra filia athlantis. . .," exp. "In celo ubi esse creditur deus ingens nominatus est"; fol. 64r).

Very little annotation. *A* Books Three–Five have some interlinear glosses and and a few marginalia in a sprawling cursive hand, providing lexical material and occasional plot summary, identifying some rhetorical tropes, and occasionally scanning lines. A brief, second set of notes occurs in Book Eight, in a good small humanist minuscule; it largely enters topic headings.

Nine-line acrostic on Natalis (inc. "Nunc canit enean. . .," exp. "Brixia quem genuit tellus saturnia pinguis," fol. 284r); *AL*, no. 672 (fols. 284v–285r).

s. xv[2], Flanders? The manuscript was in England at least as early as its ownership by Richard Nykke (fl. 1473–1536); he is called bishop of Norwich in the manuscript ("Liber Ric. Nykke episcopi Norwicensis"), a post to which he was named in 1501.

286 fols. One col., 24 lines.

The manuscript was a gift to St. John's of "domini Shelletoe," 17 December 1624.

James, *Manuscripts of St. John's College Cambridge*. On Richard Nykke, see Emden, *BRUC*. Allessio, no. 103.

(34) EDINBURGH, UNIVERSITY LIBRARY 195
Eclogues, Georgics, and *Aeneid,* with the "thirteenth book" of Mapheus Vegius
No annotation.
Paris, *c.* 1460.
The royal arms of Scotland appear in the decorated borders to the four full-page miniatures.
For full description, see Borland.
Given to the University Library by John Colville, 1654.

Catherine R. Borland, *A Descriptive Catalogue of the Western Medieval Manuscripts in Edinburgh University Library* (University of Edinburgh, 1916), pp. 281–83. Allessio, no. 143.

(35) LONDON, B. L. Burney 277, fol. 73
Aeneid 1.61–120.

s. xv^2, England.

I have not examined this folio. I am grateful to Prof. Albinia de la Mare for bringing it to my attention.

(36) CAMBRIDGE, PETERHOUSE COLLEGE 159 (I.6.3*)

[Folio numbers below correspond to the early pen foliation, not James's (or a predecessor's) pencil foliation, which becomes confused early in the manuscript, in an effort to account for cancelled and lost leaves.]

Eclogues (fols. 1–15r), *Georgics* (fols. 15v–57v), *Aeneid* (fols. 62–234v).

Copa and several other works from *AV* (fols. 57v–59v); *Moretum* fols. 59v–61v; *AG* I–IV; *AA* I^{11}, II^{11}, III^{10}, IV^{11}, V–IX^{11}, X^9, XI–XII^{11}; *AL*, no. 634 (fol. 62r).

Extensive marginal and interlinear annotation appears to be in the hand of the text.

Bound with the manuscript is an incunabulum of the *Satires* of Juvenal and Persius (printer, John of Westphalia, Louvain, 1475).

s. xv, last quarter; possibly s. xvi in. The manuscript's watermarks can mostly be identified with Briquet marks of the last quarter of the century. The blind-stamped binding is by the Cambridge binder W.G. or G.W., active 1478–1533 (Oldham, pp. 14, 16–17).

Paper. 234 fols. 281 x 210 [*c.* 210 x *c.* 90]; one column, 20–32 lines with great variation.

The entire text and annotation is written by one rapid, cursive hand.

This binding is noted by G. D. Hobson, *Bindings in Cambridge Libraries* (Cambridge University Press, 1929), p. 46, no. II; its two stamps are illustrated plate XV, nos. 34 and 35. For the work of the binder G.W. or W.G., see Oldham, *English Blind-Stamped Bindings*, pp. 14–17. Not listed by Allessio.

(37) SHREWSBURY SCHOOL IV (Mus. III.40)

Eclogues 1.1–26, 3.110–6.26, 6.41–42, 6.45–60 (fols. 53v–57v); leaves are missing after fol. 53; blank spaces for missing lines in *E* 6.

A very few glosses.

Other texts: fragments of Aesopic fables and metrical texts on grammar.

s. xv ex., England

Paper, 78 fols., 214 x 145 [*c.* 150 x *c.* 85, varies], one col., lines vary.

The manuscript is probably in the hand of Thomas Fane, who writes, fol. 18v: "si tho scribatur et mas simul accipiatur / Et fane addatur qui scripsit sic nominatur."

Not listed by Allessio.

Doubtful, rejected, and ghost manuscripts

(1) "CAMBRIDGE, CLARE COLLEGE 205" (Allessio, no. 97)
   Clare College possesses only thirty-one manuscripts. This citation
   presumably derives from confusion with St. John's 205 (no. 33
   above), which Allessio identifies correctly at his no. 103.

(2) "CAMBRIDGE, PETER'S [PETERHOUSE] COLLEGE 163" (Allessio, no. 101)
   Manuscript 163 in M. R. James's catalog of the Peterhouse collection is
   a copy of the *Manipulus florum*. Peterhouse 158 (no. 11 in Appendix I)
   carries the old shelf mark I.6.3.

(3) "CAMBRIDGE, ST. JOHN'S 226" (Allessio, no. 104)
   This manuscript does not contain the works of Virgil, as recorded in
   Allessio; it does include (fols. 151–73) a *vita* and *accessus* of Virgil.
   Allessio correctly notes that the manuscript was once owned by the
   early English humanist John Tiptoft (Emden, *BRUO*, p. 1879).

(4) LENINGRAD, ACADEMY OF SCIENCES Q.443 (once Phillips
   16366)
   Eclogues (fols. 17–21) and *Georgics* (fols. 22–51).
   AG II–IV.
   A brief *accessus* ("clausula") to *E* and *G*, fol. 52r–v, very close to the
   Servian introductions.
   Marginal and interlinear notes in a contemporary hand, deriving very
   closely from Servius.
   The manuscript also contains the *Cento* of Proba (fols. 1–8), Cicero's
   Paradoxa Stoicorum (fols. 53–63), pseudo-Ovid, *De pulice* (ed. Friedrich
   W. Lenz, "De pulice libellus," *Maia* 14 (1962): 299–333) (fol. 64r–
   v), Geoffrey of Vinsauf's *Poetria Nova* (fols. 65–96), rhetorical text,
   inc. "Artis rethorice doctrinam duppliciter..." (fols. 97–98).
   1345 (fol. 96v: "Expletum hoc opus fuit anno domini m°III^c XLV die
   XXVIII mensis decembris tempore pape Clementis VI").
   Written probably in Italy. Kiseleva identifies the manuscript's origin as
   "Anglia," perhaps influenced by the Phillips provenance and

possibly by the presence of "Gualfredus Anglicus" (though the *Poetria nova* had very wide Continental distribution). Neither the text nor the marginal hands strike me as English; Dr. Adelaide Bennett has kindly examined some samples of the pen-drawn decorated initials and suggests northern Italy as the likely place of origin.

L. I. Kiseleva, *Latinskie rukopisi Biblioteki AN SSR. Opisanie rukopisei latinskogo alfavita X–XV vv.* ("Latin Manuscripts of the Library of the Academy of Sciences: A Catalog of 10th-15th-Century Latin-Alphabet Manuscripts"), ed. A. D. Lyublinskaya (Leningrad: 'Nauka,' 1978), pp. 123–25. L. I. Kiseleva, "Medieval Western Manuscripts in the Academy of Sciences Library, Leningrad," *The Book Collector* 28 (1979): 393, 396.

(5) LONDON, BL BURNEY 273
Aeneid (fols. 1–115r).
Fragment of the *Culex* (fol. 115v).
Interlinear and occasional marginal glosses.
s. xii ex., France?
Munk Olsen suggests France or England as the origin of this manuscript. The text hand could indeed be either; but the later marginal hands, which tend to betray local idiosyncracies, show no distinctive signs of English origins.

Munk Olsen, C.94. Pattie, no. 36. Allessio, no. 375.

Glosses to Boethius at Aeneid 6.719 in Oxford, All Souls 82[1]

Celum accipit hic pro igne quia (.../
ior uis est ibi ignis quam aliorum elemen<to/
rum. Constet ibi quattuor esse elementa. Hic ing<re/
ditur loqui de spiritu id est de anima mun<di./
De qua Boetius: tu triplicis media<m/
nature cuncta moventem. et c. Ist<e/
spiritus triplicis nature perhibetur esse id est <rationis/
concupiscentie, ire. Ratio qualis est dat<a/
ne bono irascatur. Concupiscentia <ut/
cupiamus bonum. Ira ut irasc<amur/
malo. uel triplicis id est uegibilitatis, sen<si/
bilitatis, sensibilitatis (*sic*), rationabilitati<s./
uel triplicis id est idemtitatis (*sic*), diuersita<tis,/
mixti id est de eo quod est. Ecce idem de <eo/
quod non est. ecce diuersum de eo quod est et (..../
ecce mixtum. In firmamento quod (..../
in idem uoluitur. identitatem seru<it/
anima. diuersitatem, qui currunt co<ntra/
firmamentum, quod est irracionabilis (..../
et appositus racionabili. Mixtum uero in <ipsis/
planetis, potest intelligi. nam finito curs<u/
redeunt ad idem.[2] et quamuis contra fir<ma/
mentum nittantur, tamen trahuntur a fir<ma/
mento, et sic est in eis mixtum. Etiam eod<em/
tempore. Eodem modo est in hominibus idem spiritus. nam/
idem consideratur, in animabus sanctorum que semper <ten/
dunt ad idem id est ad deum.[3] Diuersitas/
animabus malorum. Mixtum uero in animab<us/
illorum qui modo hoc modo illud uolunt id est \modo/ bonum/
modo malum.[4] uel triplicis nature, quia talis est/
facta a deo, quia potest cognoscere illud quod <idem/
id est deum, et illud quod est diuersum id est malum. et/
illud quandoque bonum est quandoque in quo notatur mixtum.

Ostenditur etiam cuncta mo(.../
sua ui. quia quicquid mouetur, per animam mouetur. Agitari
proprie dominus, ut arbores per uentos.

The Aeneid-*accessus of "Anselm of Laon"*[1]

Auctor iste sicut bucolica scripsit rogatu pollionis, georgica uero rogatu mecenatis, ita et eneidem ad laudem scripsit augusti cesaris. Intendit enim augustum[2] a parentibus[3] laudare et hoc[4] describendo[5] facta enee. Qualiter scilicet post excidium troianum in italiam post multos errores deuenerit nauigio.[6] Et qualiter rutilis et latinis resistentibus ibidem bella composuerit.[7] Verum quia ad laudem augusti scripsit, idcirco de ueritate historie multa reticendo poetice quedam figmenta[8] satis competenter apponit.[9] Neque enim ut ipse refert eneas in nece turni bella terminauit, sed longe ante in numicium[10] fluuium submersus periit.[11] Vnde iuuenalis cum de hercule et enea[12] loqueretur ait, "alter aquis alter flammis ad sidera missus."[13] Si tantummodo uero ueritatem[14] historie sequeretur[15] non utique poeta sed historiographus uideretur.[16] Et hoc est[17] primum capitulum.

Est autem carmen hoc heroicum constans ex diuinis humanisque personis, continens uera cum fictis. Nam eneam at italiam uenisse manifestum est. Venerem uero cum[18] ioue loquutam, missumue[19] ad didonem mercurium[20] hoc totum constat esse compositum et ficticium.[21] Et ecce secundum capitulum.

Scripsit autem eneidem undecim annis, sed morte preuentus nec correxit nec edidit. Vnde moriens eam incendi precepit. Augustus uero ne tantum opus deperiret uel deperderetur[22] thuccam et uarum duos peritissimos poetas hac lege ad emendandum adhibuit, ut de suo nichil adderent,[23] sed queque superflua[24] demerent.[25] Vnde et[26] quosdam uersus inuenimus[27] semiplenos,[28] ut ibi, "hic cursus fuit,"[29] quosdam omnino[30] demptos, ut in principio. Non enim ab armis incepit, sed ita,

> Ille ego qui quondam gracili modulatus auena
> Carmen, et egressus siluis uicina coegi
> Vt quamuis auido parerent arua colono,
> Gratum opus agricolis, at nunc horrentia martis
> Arma uirumque cano.

Illi autem dignitatem et altitudunem carminis considerantes[31] humilitatem detraxerunt principii.[32] In secundo autem libro uiginti et duo insimul subtracti sunt.[33] Et ecce tercium capitulum.

Sicut autem theocritum in bucolicis, et sicut esiodum in georgicis, ita in

313

eneide imitatur homerum. Hec autem de uita poete sufficiant. Et ecce quartum capitulum.

Titulus talis est, Publii uirgilii[34] primus liber eneidos incipit. Bene dicit primus nam sequitur et secundus.[35] Sunt et enim duodecim. Publius est cognomen a cognacione. Publia enim fuit[36] quedam familia mantue, unde uirgilius dictus fuit publius. Virgilius uero agnomen fuit ab euentu. Maia autem mater sua dum pregnans esset sompniauit quod uirgam pareret, que usque ad celum attingeret, quod nichil aliud fuit quam[37] quod uirgilium pareret, qui sapientia sua loquendo de astris[38] tangeret. A uirga ista dictus est uirgilius.[39] Maro uero proprium nomen est.[40] Eneis est femininum patronomicum ab enea, uel[41] historia est de enea facta, sicut theseis de theseo, thebais de thebis. Ecce quintum capitulum.

Opus suum in tria distinguit: proponit, inuocat, narrat.[42] Proponit, ubi ait, "arma uirumque cano" et cet.[43] Inuocat, ubi difficultati operis subcumbens ait, "Musa mihi causas memora" et cet.[44] Narrat ibi[45] "Vix e conspectu siculis telluris in altum," et cet.[46] Hiis finitis et prelibatis literam exponamus.

Notes

INTRODUCTION MANUSCRIPTS AND THEIR CONTENTS

1 Dom Jean Leclercq, "Virgile en enfer d'après un manuscrit d'Aulne," *Latomus* 17 (1958): 731–36.

2 Ibid., p. 733.

3 Ibid., p. 734. Virgil's own harsh and impatient tone derives from his ancient association with the classroom, and has models as early as his representation by Fulgentius; see J. W. Jones, "Vergil as Magister in Fulgentius," in *Classical, Mediaeval, and Renaissance Studies in Honor of B. L. Ullman*, ed. C. Henderson, Jr. (Rome: Edizioni di Storia e Letteratura, 1964), I, pp. 273–75.

4 Comparetti's survey of clerical ambivalence toward Virgil and other pagan classics, ch. 6, pp. 75–95, is dated but very useful for its breadth of references.

5 Ed. Hans–Jürgen Gräbener (Münster, Westfallen: Achendorffsche Verlagsbuchhandlung, 1965).

6 "Hec positio semper quandam prerogativam notare debet. Ut hic: Apostolus dicit, id est Paulus. Poeta, id est Virgilius" (*Ars Poetica*, ed. Gräbener, p. 68). Hugh of St. Victor, in a homily on Ecclesiastes, similarly cites Virgil with the simple term "poeta": see Patrologia Latina 175, 136.

7 *English Friars*, pp. 13–14.

8 The only commentator I know to have treated all three works was "Anselm of Laon" (see ch. 2, pp. 63–68), whose three commentaries did travel together widely. It was certainly perfectly possible, then, to study all the works of Virgil with a good school commentary for help.

9 See for instance the densely annotated copy of the *Eclogues*, separate from the other works of Virgil, Appendix I, no. 22; see also no. 37. The *Eclogues* and *Georgics* appear together, without the *Aeneid*, in no. 31; no. 30 is a fragment that could once have contained the *Aeneid*. By contrast, the *Aeneid* appears alone in nos. 8, 12, 13, 16, 17, 18, 20, 21, 25, 29.

10 This is not to say that the work was unread. Individual passages were widely known, and circulated separately from the rest of the work. For instance, the description of the five zones of the earth (*Georg.* 1.233 ff., "Quinque tenent caelum zonae...") was excerpted and anthologized,

315

and so heavily annotated that charts and even extra pages were sometimes inserted at this point in manuscripts.

11 The study of medieval texts in terms of, and as conditioned by, their presentation in manuscripts is a central focus of "New Philology." Stephen Nichols, introducing a special issue of *Speculum* on this topic ("Introduction: Philology in a Manuscript Culture," *Speculum* 65 [1990]: 1–10), issues a call "that the language of [medieval] texts be studied not simply as discursive phenomena, but in the interaction of text language with the manuscript matrix and of both language and manuscript with the social context and networks they inscribe" (p. 9). This kind of attention to the book is not, by itself, strikingly "new." Minus the label, it has been exploited to strikingly effective critical ends in recent publications such as Sylvia Huot's *From Song to Book* (Ithaca, N.Y. and London: Cornell University Press, 1987).

12 See Barbara Nolan, "The Judgment of Paris in the *Roman d'Eneas*: A New Look At Sources and Significance," *The Classical Bulletin* 56 (1980): 52–53. This absorption of the margins has been shown also to be the case among numerous late-medieval translators of the classics by Jacques Monfrin, "Humanisme et traductions au moyen âge," *Journal des savants* 148 (1963): 161–90, and "Les traducteurs et leur public en France au moyen âge," *Journal des savants* 149 (1964): 5–20.

13 A fine recent study of this is by Tim William Machan, *Techniques of Translation: Chaucer's "Boece"* (Norman, Okla.: Pilgrim Books, 1985), especially chs. 4 and 5.

14 For a fuller discussion, see Christopher Baswell, "Talking Back to the Text: Marginal Voices in Medieval Secular Literature," in *The Uses of Manuscripts in Literary Studies: Essays in Memory of Judson Boyce Allen*, eds. Charlotte Morse, Penelope Reed Doob, and Marjorie Curry Woods (Kalamazoo, Mich.: Medieval Institute, 1992), pp. 121–60.

15 *Sir Gawain and the Green Knight*, ed. J. R. R. Tolkien and E. V. Gordon, 2nd ed. rev. Norman Davis (Oxford: Clarendon Press, 1967), p. 20, line 690.

16 "... sed ubique ut Augusti Cesaris gratiam lucraretur, Enee facta fugamque ficmentis extollit," Jones and Jones, p. 1. This commentary is translated, with a perceptive introduction, by Earl Schreiber and Thomas E. Maresca (Lincoln: University of Nebraska Press, 1979); I use their translation with occasional minor changes. The translation is not always reliable, however, especially in technical passages; see the review by Charles Burnett, *Notes and Queries*, n.s. 28 (1981): 329–31.

17 "veritatem philosophie docuit," Jones and Jones, p. 1.

18 A similar tendency to acknowledge categories of intention in the *accessus*, then leave them behind in the actual discussion of the text, has been noted in non-allegorical school commentaries on Ovid. See Hexter, pp. 163, 173–74, 203, 212.

19 See for instance Cambridge, Jesus College 33 (Appendix I, no. 12),

where two hands in humanist minuscule (one that of the early English humanist John Free) sometimes erase sections of earlier marginalia in order to make space for their own notes. In Free's case, these notes derive from his study with Guarino da Verona – an interesting example in England of humanist reading suppressing an earlier style of interpretation.

20 These two poles of approach – through indirect access and through reconstructing immediate study of the ancient text – are typified by two recent books specifically devoted to Chaucer and the ancients. In *Chaucer and Pagan Antiquity* (Cambridge: D. S. Brewer, and Totowa, N.J.: Rowman and Littlefield, 1982), A. J. Minnis investigates the medieval transmission of classical story and belief, and especially vernacular tradition – that is, those works demonstrably connected to Chaucer himself or his intellectual world – as the functioning context of his classicism. Minnis describes moralized mythography on the one hand, and the insertion of classical story into romance and history on the other, arguing that Chaucer's real interest lay with the latter (p. 21). Winthrop Wetherbee, in *Chaucer and the Poets: An Essay on "Troilus and Criseyde"* (Ithaca, N.Y.: Cornell University Press, 1984), interests himself in Chaucer's ability, as a great reader, to make direct contact with the authoritative vision of the classical Latin poets, without the mediation of (even in conscious contradistinction to) later commentary or redaction. But while he posits a less mediated readership, Wetherbee's arguments are at their strongest and subtlest when he uses Dante as a mediating reader, through and in response to whom Chaucer approaches the Latin *poetae*. At his best, then, Wetherbee has used Dante as I will try to use manuscript study, to establish the classical reading through which Chaucer would have approached his Statius or Ovid or Virgil.

21 Sir Roger Mynors's edition of Virgil (Oxford: Clarendon Press, 1969), for example, cites no manuscripts later than the ninth century. Murgia, however, in preparing his text for the Harvard edition of Servius, has surveyed many high medieval manuscripts, thereby fortuitously producing one of the very few detailed discussions of some medieval Virgil commentaries.

22 See, however, the important early work of Vladimiro Zabughin, *Virgilio nel rinascimento italiano*, 2 vols. (Bologna: Zanichelli, 1921–23).

23 See Suerbaum, pp. 346–48.

24 Several more recent catalogs, such as the excellent survey of Latin classical manuscripts in the Vatican now being produced by the CNRS (see *MCLBV*), give much improved descriptions of marginalia.

25 This is the approach taken in Courcelle I.

26 *L'Etude des auteurs classiques latins aux XIe et XIIe siècles*, 3 vols. (Paris: Editions du CNRS, 1983–87). Despite the title, the catalog includes earlier material as well.

27 The systematic survey that will appear with the Virgil volume of the

Catalogus translationum et commentariorum (*CTC*), general editor Professor Virginia Brown, will do much to clarify the patterns and geographical detail of Virgilian reading across the period.

28 The massiveness of available material has led to a split between ambitious but imprecise work, and a narrow focus that can preclude useful synthesis. So for example Comparetti tried to cover the whole field in *Virgilio nel Medio Evo*; the expanded edition of this work by Giorgio Pasquali, 2 vols. (Florence: La Nuova Italia, 1937–41), provides far better documentation. Elizabeth Nitchie attempted the same sort of global survey in *Virgil and the English Poets* (New York: Columbia University Press, 1919). Vastly more detail but far less effort at synthesis is found in the very focussed studies of Pierre Courcelle (gathered in Courcelle I). While Courcelle provides a magisterial and extraordinarily wide–ranging survey of echoes or citations of the *Aeneid*, the volume does little more than compile details. For a bibliography on Virgil in the Middle Ages, by far the most complete yet assembled, see Suerbaum.

29 These older assumptions of an almost monolithic, allegorizing approach, extending to all the classics in the Middle Ages, have been challenged on many fronts, but they remain current nevertheless. They were reflected and reinforced by influential books like Jean Seznec's *La Survivance des dieux antiques* (1940, English trans. by Barbara F. Sessions, *The Survival of the Pagan Gods* [New York: Harper, 1953]), which works, however, almost entirely from iconographic and mythographic materials, rather than from actual commentaries on classical texts. Similarly, Judson Allen's *The Friar as Critic* (Nashville, Tenn.: Vanderbilt University Press, 1971), while it makes use of little known works of the "classicizing friars" uncovered by Beryl Smalley, and acquaints us with an important new range of medieval classicism, restricts its focus to a narrow, allegorizing aspect of their writings. To cite just one alternate witness, Nicholas Trevet's *Consolation* commentary is almost entirely literal; see Minnis, *Chaucer and Pagan Antiquity*, pp. 17, 145–50. Even scholars widely read in medieval Virgilianism continue to assume universal habits of Christianizing mythology in the Middle Ages. For instance, Eberhard Leube writes, "In dem lateinischen Epos Petrarcas wird danach zum ersten Mal die heidnische Götterwelt frei vom mittelalterlich-christlicher Denaturierung und Interpretation in formaler Schönheit im Bilde dargestellt bzw. beschrieben": *Fortuna in Karthago: Die Aeneas-Dido-Mythe Vergils in den romanischen Literaturen vom 14. bis zum 16. Jahrhundert* (Heidelberg: Carl Winter, 1969), p. 22.

30 In two closely related articles, Lewis Brewer Hall offers an extensive comparative study among medieval, largely vernacular redactions of the Dido-and-Aeneas story. See "Caxton's 'Eneydos' and the Redactions of Virgil," *Mediaeval Studies* 22 (1960): 136–47; and "Chaucer and the Dido-and-Aeneas Story," *Mediaeval Studies* 25 (1963): 148–59. Hall finds five "primary techniques of medievalizing the *Aeneid*" ("Chaucer," p. 149): a

tendency to reduce or ignore Books Two and Six, the use of *ordo naturalis* (relating the narrative in chronological order), an extension of Virgil's story forward and backward in time, exaggeration and idealization of character and setting, and exploration of the motivations behind the characters' actions.

31 For a superb overview of this material, see Jacques Monfrin, "Les *translations* vernaculaires de Virgile au Moyen Age," *Lectures*, pp. 189–249.

32 Daniel Porion, "De l'*Énéide* à l'*Eneas*: mythologie et moralisation," *Cahiers de Civilisation Médiévale* 19 (1976), 213–29.

33 The most penetrating recent challenges to this assumption have been made by Bernard Guenée and his students. See for instance *Histoire et culture dans l'occident médiévale* (Paris: Aubier Montaigne, 1980).

1 AUCTOR TO AUCTORITAS

1 Similarly, though with perhaps more limited intentions, the compiler of the early thirteenth-century *Li Fet des Romains* (1213), who was thoroughly versed in a wide range of classical historians, consciously adopted anachronism to make his histories more clearly relevant to the nationalism and imperial preoccupations of his noble readers. See Jeanette M. Beer, *A Medieval Caesar* (Geneva: Droz, 1976), esp. pp. 74–91.

2 The finest work on Virgil's early literary and social power is by Robert Kaster, *Guardians of Language: The Grammarian in Antiquity* (Berkeley: University of California Press, 1987), especially chs. 5 and 6. For further bibliography, see Suerbaum, pp. 319–27.

3 Servius's introduction to *Aeneid* 6 is perhaps the most important and seminal statement of this attitude toward Virgil; see below, ch. 3, pp. 91–93.

4 See ch. 1 of his *Exposition of the Content of Virgil*, trans. Leslie G. Whitbread, *Fulgentius the Mythographer* (Columbus, Ohio: University of Ohio Press, 1971), pp. 119–20.

5 The best survey is Pierre Courcelle, "Les exégèses chrétiennes de la quatrième Eclogue," *Revue des études anciennes* 59 (1957): 294–319. See also Comparetti, ch. 7.

6 John Wells Spargo, *Virgil the Necromancer: Studies in Virgilian Legends*, Harvard Studies in Comparative Literature X (Cambridge, Mass.: Harvard University Press, 1934), especially pp. 60–68. Comparetti is still the most wide–ranging study of Virgil as a figure of learned authority and popular legend.

7 The *cento* of Proba accompanies the *Eclogues* in one English manuscript of the earlier fourteenth century (App. I, no. 22). For bibliography on the *sortes* and *centones*, see Suerbaum, p. 318. See also Rosa Lamacchia, "Centoni," *Enciclopedia* I, pp. 733–37, and Mario Spinelli, "Proba Petronia," IV, pp. 283–84.

8 For a series of entries on the legends and iconography of Aeneas, pre- and

post-Virgilian, see *Enciclopedia* II, pp. 221–36. See also J. P. Callu, "'Impius Aeneas'? Échos virgiliens du Bas-Empire," *Présence*, pp. 161–74.

9 On the early Aeneas tradition, see G. Karl Galinsky, *Aeneas, Sicily, and Rome* (Princeton University Press, 1969). For a survey of medieval developments hostile to Aeneas, see Meyer Reinhold, "The Unhero Aeneas," *Classica et Mediaevalia* 27 (1966), 195–207; and Vicenzo Ussani, "Enea traditore," *Studi italiani di filologia classica*, n. s. 22 (1947): 109–23. The best general narrative survey of the Trojan story is Margaret R. Scherer, *The Legends of Troy in Art and Literature* (New York and London: Phaidon Press for the Metropolitan Museum of Art, 1963). See also Werner Eisenhut, "Spätanike Troja-Erzählungen – mit einem Ausblick auf die mittelalterliche Troja–Literatur," *Mittellateinisches Jahrbuch* 18 (1983), 1–28. For the text of Dares, see Ferdinand Meister, ed., *De Excidio Troiae Historia* (Leipzig: Teubner, 1873). For Dictys Cretensis, see *Ephemeridos Belli Troiani Libri*, ed. W. Eisenhut (Leipzig: Teubner, 1973). See also the relevant articles in *Enciclopedia* I, pp. 1000–02, and II, pp. 109–10. Translations of Dares and Dictys, with basic bibliography, are in R. M. Frazer, *The Trojan War: The Chronicles of Dictys of Crete and Dares the Phrygian* (Bloomington and London: Indiana University Press, 1966). Other early Latin versions include the *Excidium Troiae* (far closer to classical Latin sources than are Dictys and Dares), ed. E. Bagby Atwood and Virgil K. Whitaker (Cambridge, Mass.: Medieval Academy of America, 1944); a fuller edition has now appeared by Alan Keith Bate (Frankfurt and Bern: Peter Lang, 1986). Vernacular expansions began in the twelfth century with Benoît de Ste. Maure's *Roman de Troie*, whose great influence was exercised through the Latin redaction by Guido de Columnis (Guido delle Colonne), *Historia Destructionis Troiae*, ed. Nathaniel E. Griffin (Cambridge, Mass.: Medieval Academy of America, 1936). Guido's redaction had great influence in the widespread vernacular Troy books; it came into the Middle English vernacular tradition at an early point, and most fully in Lydgate's *Troy Book*. The multiplicity of French versions is suggested by the entries under "Troie" in Brian Woledge, *Bibliographie des romans et nouvelles en prose française antérieurs à 1500* (Geneva: Droz, 1954), pp. 125–31. Guido in Middle English has been studied by C. David Benson, *The History of Troy in Middle English Literature* (Cambridge: D. S. Brewer; Totawa, N.J.: Rowman and Littlefield, 1980). See also Suerbaum, pp. 343–46.

10 Birger Munk Olsen, "Virgile et la renaissance du XIIe siècle," *Lectures*, p. 39, note 28: "c'est cet ouvrage qui accompagne le plus souvent l'*Énéide* au Moyen Age."

11 For a recent discussion of both works, see James G. Farrow, "Aeneas and Rome: Pseudepigrapha and Politics," *The Classical Journal* 87 (1992): 339–59. On Dares, see also *Enciclopedia* I, pp. 1000–02; and on Dictys, II, pp. 108–10.

12 Frazer, *The Trojan War*, p. 97.

13 Ibid., p. 143.

14 "Intendit itaque casus Enee aliorumque Troianorum errantium labores evolvere atque hoc non usque secundum historie veritatem, quod Frigius describit; sed ubique ut Augusti Cesaris gratiam lucraretur, Enee facta fugamque ficmentis extollit." Jones and Jones, p. 1.

15 "Tantum ualuit pulchritudo narrandi, ut omnes Phoenissae castitatis conscii, ... coniueant tamen fabulae, et intra conscientiam ueri fidem prementes malint pro uero celebrari quod pectoribus humanis dulcedo fingentis infudit." See Courcelle I, p. 376, note 714 for citations from Servius, Macrobius, and John of Salisbury.

16 "... defectum magnorum auctorum, Virgilii, Ouidii, et Homeri, qui in exprimenda ueritate Troyani casus nimium defecerunt, quamuis eorum opera contexuerint siue tractauerint secundum fabulas antiquorum siue secundum apologos in stilo nimium glorioso, et specialiter ille summus poetarum Virgilius, quem nichil latuit": *Historia destructionis Troiae*, ed. N. E. Griffin (Cambridge, Mass.: Mediaeval Academy of America, 1936), p. 276; trans. Mary E. Meek (Bloomington: Indiana University Press, 1974), p. 265. For the negative portrait of Aeneas in Benoît's *Roman de Troie*, see Jerome E. Singerman, *Under Clouds of Poesy: Poetry and Truth in French and English Reworkings of the "Aeneid," 1160–1513* (New York: Garland, 1986), pp. 138–47.

17 Ed. Atwood and Whitaker, p. xiv (see note 9 above).

18 For a full description of the manuscripts, see the Introduction to J.-J. Salverda de Grave's first edition, *Eneas: texte critique* (Halle, 1891). Jacques Monfrin has made the suggestion in a recent article that these manuscripts may represent part of a broad effort at constructing a British (or at least, one might add, Anglo-Norman) imperial history, "une sorte d'histoire ancienne qui établit les origines troyennes des habitants de la Grande-Bretagne, qui relie le monde arthurien aux héros antiques": "Les *translations* vernaculaires de Virgile au Moyen Age," in *Lectures*, pp. 197–98.

19 Monfrin, "Les translations," *Lectures*, pp. 200–11. Over seventy manuscripts survive, of which about forty are fourteenth century (including those dated to the very turn of the century) or earlier; see Woledge, *Bibliographie* (note 9 above), pp. 56–58, and *Supplément 1954–1973* (Geneva: Droz, 1975), pp. 42–44. The role of the *Aeneid* as a principal source was established by Paul Meyer, "Les Premières compilations françaises d'histoire ancienne," *Romania* 14 (1885): 43–46, and confirmed by Guy Raynaud de Lage, "Les 'romans antiques' dans l'Histoire ancienne jusqu'à César," *Le Moyen Age* 63 (1957): 297–305. By contrast, Raynaud de Lage notes, the other sections of the *Histoire* depend heavily on vernacular redactions; the author did know the *Roman d'Eneas*, but made only occasional and secondary use of it. The Dido episode in the *Histoire* (in the second redaction) is discussed by Eberhard Leube, *Fortuna in Karthago*, pp. 30–36; Leube concentrates on the role and rationaliza-

tion of the gods in the *Histoire*. For a very good discussion of the Aeneas story in the *Histoire*, and its dependence on the Latin *Aeneid*, see Singerman, *Under Clouds*, pp. 152–79.

20 Don Cameron Allen, "Marlowe's *Dido* and the Tradition," in *Essays on Shakespeare and Elizabethan Drama in honour of Hardin Craig*, ed. Richard Hosley (London: Routledge and Kegan Paul, 1963), pp. 55–68. The historical tradition of Dido has been admirably studied by Mary Louise Lord, "Dido as an Example of Chastity: The Influence of Example Literature," *Harvard Library Bulletin* 17 (1969): 22–44, and 216–32.

21 Monfrin, "Les translations," *Lectures*, p. 207.

22 Courcelle II; Hugo Buchthal, *Historia Troiana: Studies in the History of Medieval Secular Illustration*, Studies of the Warburg Institute, 32 (London: The Warburg Institute and Leiden: E. J. Brill, 1971). See also Fritz Saxl, "The Troy Romance in French and Italian Art," in *Lectures* (London: Warburg Institute, 1957), I, pp. 125–38 and plates 72–81; and *Enciclopedia* III, pp. 428–32, 443–50.

23 Terence is an important exception. Illustrations of his plays are fairly frequent, and their iconography descends directly from late-classical exemplars. See L. W. Jones and C. R. Morey, *The Miniatures of the Manuscripts of Terence* (Princeton University Press, 1931).

24 Among medieval manuscripts of Virgil, Courcelle detects contact with antique models only in the tenth-century Beneventan manuscript, Naples, BN lat. 6. See Courcelle II, pp. 9–33 and figs. 1–8.

25 Buchthal, *Historia Troiana*, p. 9. There is in fact one earlier illustration in a Benoît manuscript, a single illuminated initial in Paris, Arsenal 3340, fol. 1, written in 1237. I am grateful to Prof. M. Alison Stones for this information.

26 Courcelle II, pp. 35–66 and figs. 22–156. There is a facsimile edition: *Heinrich von Veldecke: Eneit. Die Bilder der Berliner Handschrift*, ed. Albert Boekler (Leipzig: Harrassowitz, 1939).

27 Courcelle II, p. 37.

28 When Aeneas is shown sending out a search party, for instance, he says, "Go scout the country and come back quickly" ("Ritet schowen daz lant und chomt her wider zehant"), Courcelle II, p. 40, note 27.

29 Heidelberg, Universitätsbibl., palat. germ. 403; see Courcelle II, pp. 67–75 and figs. 157–95.

30 Paris, Arsenal 5077. Only six miniatures illustrate the portion of the history pertaining to Aeneas. See Courcelle II, pp. 104–07.

31 Courcelle II, pp. 28–29 and figs. 10 and 11. For a color reproduction of the initial at *Aen.* 1.1, see *Enciclopedia* III, plate XXXIII.

32 François Avril, "Un manuscrit d'auteurs classiques et ses illustrations," in *The Year 1200: A Symposium* (New York: Metropolitan Museum of Art, 1975), pp. 261–82.

33 Ibid., p. 265. Avril adds, "Tous ces exemples suggèrent fortement que les enlumineurs ont travaillés d'après un receuil de modèles d'illustration

bibliques." A closely similar model is used to depict Mercury's descent from the heavens in Book Four. The miniatures are so similar, in fact, that they are reversed in Courcelle II (figs. 16 and 19).

34 Courcelle II, p. 33 and fig. 20.

35 Courcelle II, p. 111 and fig. 253.

36 Courcelle II, pp. 95–96, 98, and fig. 223. Professor M. Alison Stones informs me that some of the *Bibles historiales* are from the same workshop as BN fr. 60.

37 See for instance The Hague, Rijksmuseum 76 E 21, *c.* 1470, probably from Bruges (Courcelle II, pp. 141–49); Ghent, Cathedral library 9, late fifteenth century, Ghent or Bruges (Courcelle II, pp. 151–62); Harvard University, Richardson 38, late fifteenth century, France (Courcelle II, pp. 191–202); Dijon, Bibl. mun. 493, late fifteenth century, central France (Courcelle II, pp. 203–12). The first illustrated printed edition of Virgil (Strasbourg, 1502), produced under the direction of the humanist Sebastian Brant, still places its classical events in a contemporary and northern European world.

38 Courcelle II, fig. 224a.

39 Courcelle II, p. 31 and fig. 14 (the caption has been mistakenly placed under the image at fig. 15).

40 Courcelle II, pp. 44 and 52, and figs. 41 and 78. Courcelle suggests an oriental image as the source of the tree.

41 *Aeneid* 4.68–73 and 7.483–510; *Eneit*, trans. J. W. Thomas (New York: Garland, 1985), pp. 22–23 and 53. The deer imagery in von Veldeke makes the linkage even clearer than in the *Aeneid*, for von Veldeke's metaphor overtly casts Aeneas as the huntsman: "The game had been hunted down. The man who shoots to his advantage has a pleasant hunt" (p. 23).

42 The Klosterneuburg manuscript has only three miniatures. Two show Aeneas (at Book One alone, and at Book Five with Palinurus); a third (at Book Seven) is hard to interpret, but shows a man gripping the trunk of a tree. Courcelle argues that it may illustrate a reference to Circe at lines 10–25 (Courcelle II, p. 28). In any case it is a manuscript visually conceived to emphasize the experience of men in the epic.

43 Courcelle II, figs. 249, 251, 252, 253, and 258.

44 See *Eneas*, lines 2125–44, and Monfrin, "Les *translations*," p. 226.

45 Courcelle II, figs. 218–23.

46 Courcelle II, figs. 224a and 224b.

47 Courcelle II, fig. 224a.

48 Courcelle II, p. 90 and fig. 197.

49 Courcelle II, p. 89.

50 Paris, BN fr. 9682 and fr. 20125. Courcelle II, p. 91 and figs. 198–201.

51 Paris, BN fr. 9685. Courcelle II, pp. 94–95 and figs. 214–17.

52 Courcelle II, pp. 101–04, and figs. 231–42.

53 Courcelle II, 104–07, and figs, 243–48. This MS contains a different universal history, the *Trésor des hystoires.*

54 Courcelle II, p. 48.

55 Courcelle II, p. 41 and fig. 29.

56 Courcelle II, p. 47.

57 "Hie macht man dem tugentrichen degen. aine bar als wir noch hiute pflegen": Courcelle II, p. 60, note 95, and fig. 118.

58 Buchthal, *Historia Troiana,* p. 34.

59 There are of course yet other extra-textual materials which, at different times and places in the Middle Ages, would have affected the understandings of Virgil. There exists, for example, a small group of late-Carolingian *Aeneid* manuscripts in which a few major passages are superscribed with musical notation, suggesting some habits of chanted performance. See Suerbaum, p. 338; Munk Olsen, p. 686, nos. 130–49. I have encountered musical notation in England only in App. I, no. 3, which has neumes at 2.274–86, the passage most frequently accompanied by neumes. But I find no evidence that this extended to later periods.

60 Munk Olsen, pp. 673–826.

61 "Tradizione manoscritta," *Enciclopedia* III, pp. 432–43.

62 See also Valerie Edden, "Early Manuscripts of Virgiliana," *The Library,* ser. 5, 28 (1973): 14 and notes.

63 For editions and excellent discussion of these lists, see Michael Lapidge, "Surviving Booklists from Anglo-Saxon England," in *Learning and Literature in Anglo–Saxon England: Studies Presented to Peter Clemoes,* ed. Lapidge and Helmut Gneuss (Cambridge University Press, 1985), pp. 33–89. Lapidge's useful bibliographical notes go well past the Anglo–Saxon period.

64 Ibid., pp. 46, 70.

65 James Stuart Beddie, "The Ancient Classics in Medieval Libraries," *Speculum* 5 (1930): 10. More can be found in M. D. Knowles, "The Preservation of the Classics," in *The English Library before 1700,* ed. Francis Wormald and C. E. Wright (London: Athlone 1958), pp. 136–47. For more recent discussion and bibliography, see Helmut Gneuss, "Englands Bibliotheken im Mittelalter unt ihr Untergang," in *Festschrift für Walter Hübner,* ed. D. Riesner and H. Gneuss (Berlin: Schmidt, 1964), pp. 91–121. The greater incidence of Virgil manuscripts on the Continent, as reported by J. de Ghellinck in *L'Essor de la littérature latine au douzième siècle,* 2nd ed. (Brussells and Bruges: Desclée de Brouwer, 1955), p. 296, probably reflects the more complete study and editing of continental book lists by Max Manitius (for example his indispensable *Handschriften antiker Autoren in mittelalterlichen Bibliothekskatalogen* [Leipzig: Harrassowitz, 1935]), Lehmann, and others by that time. As Michael Lapidge points out ("Booklists," pp. 37–38), the editing of continental booklists continues to outpace that of British lists. Much attention is paid

to the reading of ancient Latin poets, and especially Virgil, by Günter Glauche, *Schullektüre im Mittelalter: Entstehung und Wandlungen des Lektüre-kanons bis 1200 nach den Quellen dargestellt*, Münchener Beiträge zur Mediävistik und Renaissance–Forschung 5 (Munich: Arbeo-Gesellschaft, 1970). Glauche works both from booklists such as those mentioned above, and from surviving descriptions of education (sometimes used rather uncritically); he is especially good on the reintroduction of classical reading into the canon in the late tenth and eleventh centuries; see pp. 62–100.

66 Suerbaum, pp. 308–48.

67 For a brief survey of Virgil in early Christian writers, see also Aldo Ceresa-Gastaldo, "Cristianesimo," *Enciclopedia* I, pp. 934–37.

68 Any list of instances is inevitably anecdotal. Jerome cites the "imago mortis" in falling Troy (2.369) to describe the effects of the Germanic invasions (Courcelle I, p. 177). A poem about Charlemagne borrows widely from *Aeneid* 1, especially comparing Charlemagne's sight of the rising Aix-la-Chappelle to Aeneas viewing the walls of Carthage from a hill (pp. 99–100). William of Poitiers, in the *Gesta Guillelmi*, compares William the Conqueror crossing the Channel and arriving in England to Aeneas in the tempest and his arrival at Carthage (pp. 46–47). And Henry of Huntingdon again evokes the fall of Troy to describe an army ravaging Winchester (p. 178, note 207).

69 Courcelle I regularly cites Virgilian echoes in Christian epitaphs; see also p. 139.

70 Prudentius and Sedulius, writing on Christ calming the waters, use reminiscences of Neptune calming the storm caused by Aeolus (Courcelle I, pp. 38–39, 55). In Juvencus, Virgil's Jupiter looking down from the heavens to Libya and predicting Aeneas's future is used to describe Christ (p. 70). The star which Aeneas and his family see fall into the forests of Ida, is seen by several early medieval writers as the star which leads the Magi to Christ (pp. 208–09).

71 Ambrose compares the refuge which the Trojan ships seek at Carthage to the refuge faith offers to believers (Courcelle I, p. 113). Adso of Montier-en-Der uses Aeneas's speech on striving always toward Latium (*Aen.* 1.204–06) with an implicit allegorical sense of man's pilgrimage on earth, always straining toward the divine fatherland (p. 66, note 296). The flight of Daedalus is made to parallel the upward flight of the Christian soul (p. 425–26). And Lactantius makes a long comment on the *bivium* in the inferno (6.540) as a moment of moral choice (442–43).

72 See H. Hagendahl, *Latin Fathers and the Classics* (Göteborg: Göteborgs Universitets Årsskrift, 1958), and his *Augustine and the Latin Classics*, 2 vols. (Göteborg: Göteborgs Universitets Årsskrift, 1967).

73 See Hagendahl, *Augustine and the Latin Classics*, and John J. O'Meara, "Augustine, the Artist, and the *Aeneid*," in *Mélanges offerts à Christine Mohrmann*, ed. L. J. Engels *et al.* (Utrecht: Spectrum, 1963), pp. 252–61.

74 Hexter, pp. 3–4, note 4. Hexter's note must represent untold hours of counting.

75 See James F. Mountford, *Quotations from Classical Authors in Medieval Latin Glossaries*, Cornell Studies in Classical Philology, 21 (New York and London: Longmans, Green, and Co., 1925). Studying only two important but rather brief glossaries, Mountford lists sixty-four Virgil quotations, twenty-four of them from the *Aeneid*. See also Cataldo Roccaro, "Glossari medievali," *Enciclopedia* II, pp. 773–74. The marginal word-lists in Vatican, BAV Ottob. lat. 1373 (App. I, no. 19) may reflect the link between Virgil's text and the glossaries.

76 Consider the provision of vowel quantities over words listed in the margins of Vatican, BAV Reg. lat. 1671 (App. I, no. 3).

77 *Institutionum Grammaticarum Libri XVIII*, ed. Martin Hertz, in *Grammatici Latini*, gen. ed. Heinrich Keil, II and III (Leipzig: Teubner, 1855–1859; repr. Hildesheim: Georg Olms, 1961). Priscian also wrote a less widely studied *Partitiones duodecim versuum Aeneidos principium*, in *Grammatici Latini*, III, pp. 457–515. The first line of each book is studied in great detail for meter, grammar, and vocabulary.

78 *Donati de partibus orationis ars minor*, ed. Heinrich Keil, *Grammatici Latini*, IV, pp. 353–402.

79 G. Paré, A. Brunet, and P. Tremblay, *La Renaissance du XIIe siècle: les écoles et l'enseignement* (Paris: Vrin; and Ottawa: Institut d'études médiévales, 1933), chs. 1–3, especially pp. 116–17.

80 Louis John Paetow, *The Arts Course at Mediaeval Universities with Special Reference to Grammar and Rhetoric* (Urbana-Champaign, Ill.: University of Illinois Press, 1910). Paetow's analysis is not essentially changed in this respect by the more up-to-date work of Gordon Leff, *Paris and Oxford Universities in the Thirteenth and Fourteenth Centuries* (New York: John Wiley and Sons, 1968), ch. 3, "The Curriculum at Paris and Oxford."

81 Paetow, *The Arts Course*, pp. 33–66.

82 "The Classics in the Thirteenth Century," *Speculum* 4 (1929): 249–69. Also "A Friend of the Classics in the Times of St. Thomas Aquinas," in *Mélanges Mandonnet*, II (= *Bibliothèque Thomiste* 14) (Paris: Vrin, 1930), pp. 261–74. Indeed, in the fifteenth century, Eberhard is used to gloss Virgil; see App. I, no. 26.

83 Ed. Dietrich Riechling, in *Monumenta Germaniae Paedagogica*, XII, gen. ed. Karl Kehrbach (Berlin: Hofmann, 1893). It should be noted, however, that most of Alexander's classicism consists of unacknowledged echoes; see Riechling's secondary apparatus, "Testimonia et explanationes." Thus, while he is a witness to classical reading, he cannot be seen as a major means of access to those materials.

84 A useful if unselective gathering of material was made by Eva M. Sanford, "The Use of Classical Latin Authors in the Libri Manuales," *Transactions and Proceedings of the American Philological Association* 55 (1924):

190–248. The most important recent investigators are Richard and Mary Rouse, and Birger Munk Olsen: see Richard Rouse, "Florilegia and Latin Classical Authors in Twelfth- and Thirteenth-Century Orléans," *Viator* 10 (1979): 131–60, with references to his earlier publications; and B. Munk Olsen, "Les Classiques latins dans les florilèges médiévaux antérieurs au XIIIe siècle," *Revue d'histoire des textes* (part 1) 9 (1979): 47–121, and (part 2) 10 (1980): 115–64.

85 Olsen, "Les Classiques latins," pp. 49–55.

86 Rouse, "Florilegia."

87 For popular Virgilian passages, see B. L. Ullmann, "Virgil in certain medieval florilegia," *Studi Medievali*, n. s. 5 (1932): 59–66. Ullmann does not cover many *florilegia*; a wider range is accounted for by B. Munk Olsen, "Vergil i middelalderen," *Museum Tusculanum* 32–33 (1978): 96–107.

88 Olsen, "Les Classiques latins," section AI, no. 4, pp. 60–61.

89 Oxford, Bodleian Library, Add. A. 208 (England, s. xiii) has over one hundred eighty lines from the *Aeneid*. Oxford, Bodleian Library, Digby 65 (England, s. xiii) gives the entire *Fama* passage from Book Four, all of *Eclogue* Four (here called "prophetia de Christo" and in a very bad text), and other selections from the two works. Oxford, Merton College 248 (England, s. xiii) has one page (fo. 40v) devoted to Virgil. Virgil provides much of the material for a very casual and sloppily organized classical *florilegium* in the first three leaves of the Oxford, Lincoln College 58 (s. xv). This shows only what is to be found in Oxford manuscripts; further searching would certainly provide many more examples. Olsen, "Les Classiques latins," mentions two other English *florilegia* with brief Virgil quotations: his numbers 83 and 86.

90 For instance, the brief Virgil extracts in Oxford, Merton College 248 have several intriguing glosses which impose a moralizing allegory on the quotations. In a quotation from *Eclogue* 5.36–37, the sowing of seed in furrows is glossed as "opera carnalia"; it gives rise only to unlucky darnel ("id est peccatum") and sterile wild oats ("id est desperatio").

91 J. M. C. Toynbee, *Art in Roman Britain* (London: Phaidon, 1963), plate 235; and her *Art in Britain Under the Romans* (Oxford: Oxford University Press, 1964), plate 58.

92 A. A. Barrett, "Knowledge of the Literary Classics in Roman Britain," *Britannia* 9 (1978): 307–13.

93 See Michael Lapidge's excellent article, "Gildas' Education and the Latin Culture of Sub-Roman Britain," in *Gildas: New Approaches*, ed. Lapidge and David Dumville (Woodbridge, Suffolk and Dover, N.H.: Boydell, 1985), pp. 27–50.

94 Lapidge, "Gildas' Education," esp. pp. 38–47. See also F. J. E. Raby, "Some Notes on Virgil, mainly in English authors, in the Middle Ages," *Studi Medievali*, n. s. 5 (1932): 359.

95 L. D. Reynolds, "Introduction," in *Texts and Transmission: A Survey of the Latin Classics*, ed. Reynolds (Oxford University Press, 1983), p. xvii.

96 Vivian Law, in *The Insular Latin Grammarians* (Woodbridge, Suffolk: Boydell, 1982), provides a useful account of the earliest grammatical texts, discriminating nicely between the Irish and English contributions to the tradition.

97 A superbly lucid exposition of the vexed and complicated Servian tradition is found in George P. Goold, "Servius and the Helen Episode," *Harvard Studies in Classical Philology* 74 (1970): 101–68. The manuscript evidence is summarized by Charles H. Beeson, "Insular Symptoms in the Commentaries on Virgil," *Studi Medievali*, n. s. 5 (1932): 81–100. Early medieval classicism in the British Isles is magisterially surveyed by T. Julian Brown, "An Historical Introduction to the Use of Classical Latin Authors in the British Isles from the Fifth to the Eleventh Century," *La cultura antica nell'occidente latino dal VII all'XI secolo*, Settimane di studio del centro italiano di studi sull'alto medioevo 22 (Spoleto: Presso la sede del Centro, 1975), pp. 237–93, with discussion by Ludwig Bieler, Diaz y Diaz, and Bernhard Bischoff, pp. 295–99. See also W. Berschin, "Glossierte Virgil-Handschriften dreier *aetates Virgilianae*," in *The Role of the Book in Medieval Culture*, ed. Peter Ganz (Turnhout: Brepols, 1986), II, pp. 121–25.

98 The use of such evidence is discussed by Brown, "An Historical Introduction," pp. 283–85.

99 J. D. A. Ogilvy, *Books Known to the English, 597–1066* (Cambridge, Mass.: Harvard University Press, 1967), pp. 241–42; Lapidge, "Surviving Booklists," pp. 46, 49.

100 Goold, "Servius," p. 116; see also p. 104.

101 E. A. Lowe, *Codices Latini Antiquiores* (Oxford: Clarendon Press, 1934–66), supplement, no. 1806. The fragment is now in Spangenberg. See also Murgia, p. 71. Murgia points out that this earliest witness to Servius Auctus may point to England, not Ireland, as its place of compilation.

102 Beeson, "Insular Symptoms," pp. 94–100. See also Goold, "Servius," pp. 119–20; and Brown, "An Historical Introduction," p. 287 and p. 293, note 1. For a recent survey of positions, with bibliography, see David Daintree, "Glosse Irlandesi," *Enciclopedia* II, pp. 774–76.

103 See Brown, "An Historical Introduction," pp. 248–49, and 272–73. Also Louis Holtz, "La redécouverte de Virgile aux VIIIe et IXe siècles d'après les manuscrits conservés," *Lectures*, pp. 9–30; "La Survie de Virgile dans le haut Moyen Age," *Présence*, pp. 219–21; and Law, *Insular Latin Grammarians*, p. 9.

104 Raby, "Some Notes on Virgil" (see note 94 above), p. 362. For brief comment and recent bibliography see Neil Wright, "Aldelmo," *Enciclopedia* I, pp. 89–90.

105 Brown, "An Historical Introduction," p. 260. See also Jacques Boussard, "Les influences Anglaises sur l'école Carolingienne des VIIIe et IXe siècles," *La Scuola nell'occidente latino dell'alto medioevo*, Settimane di studio

del Centro italiano di studi sull'alto medioevo 19 (Spoleto: Presso la sede del Centro, 1977), pp. 417–52.

106 Brown, "An Historical Introduction," p. 262. See also M. L. W. Laistner, "Bede as a Classical and Patristic Scholar," in *The Intellectual Heritage of the Early Middle Ages*, ed. Chester G. Starr (Ithaca, N.Y.: Cornell University Press, 1957), pp. 93–116. Laistner's conclusions, however, have been convincingly challenged by Neil Wright, "Bede and Vergil," *Romanobarbarica* 6 (1981–82): 361–79; Bede himself certainly knew and made use of Virgil, especially in his metrical *Vita Cuthberti*. For a recent survey see Mariangela Scarsi, "Beda," *Enciclopedia* I, pp. 473–74.

107 Brown, "An Historical Introduction," pp. 290–91.

108 D. A. Bullough, "The Educational Tradition in England from Alfred to Aelfric: Teaching *Utriusque linguae*," *La Scuola*, Settimane 19, pp. 473–75; J. Armitage Robinson, *The Times of St. Dunstan* (Oxford: Clarendon Press, 1923), pp. 82–87. See also T. A. M. Bishop, *English Caroline Minuscule* (Oxford: Clarendon Press, 1971), p. xviii.

109 F. A. Rella, "Continental Manuscripts Acquired for English Centers in the Tenth and Early Eleventh Centuries," *Anglia* 98 (1980): 107–16. Appendix I, nos. 1, 4, and 5 date from this period, but they all survive in much later flyleaves and binding fragments; their arrival in England cannot be exactly dated.

110 See Ludwig Traube's famous lecture, reprinted in *Vorlesungen und Abhandlungen 2, Einleitung in die lateinische Philologie des Mittelalters* (Munich: C. H. Beck'sche, 1911), p. 113.

111 "Virgile et la renaissance du XIIe siècle," in *Lectures*, pp. 37–38.

112 *Imtheachta Æniasa*, ed. and trans. Rev. George Calder, Irish Texts Society 6 (London: Irish Texts Society, 1907). Gerard Murphy, "Vergilian Influence upon the Vernacular Literature of Medieval Ireland," *Studi Medievali*, n. s. 5 (1932): pp. 379–81. Robert T. Meyer, "The Middle-Irish Version of the *Aeneid*," *Tennessee Studies in Literature* 11 (1966): 97–108. Robert J. Rowland, Jr., "Aeneas as a Hero in Twelfth-Century Ireland," *Vergilius* 16 (1970): 29–32.

113 James A. Weisheipl, "The Place of the Liberal Arts in the University Curriculum during the XIVth and XVth Centuries," in *Arts libéraux et philosophie au moyen âge*, Actes du quatrième congrès international de philosophie médiévale (Montréal: Institut d'études médiévales; and Paris: Vrin, 1969), p. 209.

114 These men were the object of Beryl Smalley's superb study, *English Friars*.

115 *English Friars*, pp. 147–48. Judson B. Allen, *The Friar as Critic* (Nashville, Tenn.: Vanderbilt University Press, 1971), pp. 91–92.

116 The central agent in this genealogical program was Geoffrey of Monmouth's *Historia regum Brittanniae*; for his enormous influence on English historical imagination, see Hugh A. MacDougall, *Racial Myth in*

330   Notes to pages 40–45

English History: Trojans, Teutons, and Anglo–Saxons (Montreal: Harvest House and Hanover, N.H.: University Press of New England, 1982), ch. 1; and J. S. P. Tatlock, *The Legendary History of Britain* (Berkeley, Calif.: University of California Press, 1950; repr. New York: Gordian Press, 1974).

117 Mary Giffin, "Cadwallader, Arthur, and Brutus in the Wigmore Manuscript," *Speculum* 16 (1941): 109–20.

118 *The Complete Peerage*, ed. H. A. Doubleday, Duncan Warrand, and Lord Howard de Walden (London: St. Catherine Press, 1926), VI, p. 469.

2 PEDAGOGICAL EXEGESIS OF VIRGIL IN MEDIEVAL ENGLAND

1 For a fuller description of the manuscript, see App. I, no. 9.

2 App. I, no. 7 is also very well produced, and shares a number of features with AS82. Another such well disciplined manuscript is App. I, no. 15.

3 See London, BL Add. 27304, discussed in chapter 3, App. I, no. 18; also nos. 20, 21.

4 For complete contents, see the technical description in App. I, no. 9.

5 For the text of these lines, with discussion, see R. G. Austin, ed., *P. Vergili Maronis Aeneidos liber primus* (Oxford: Clarendon, 1971), pp. 25–27.

6 The earliest notating hand does enter a considerable number of textual variants, but no explanatory glosses, in the first few *Eclogues*.

7 The inscription appears on the third flyleaf, *verso*. In the twelfth century, "magister" almost always denoted a teacher, or someone with sufficient educational advancement to be a teacher, although a man might continue to use the title after having passed on to other duties. For a review of the considerable and unsettled scholarship around the term, see Julia Barrow, "Education and the Recruitment of Cathedral Canons in England and Germany 1100–1125," *Viator* 20 (1989): 118–19.

8 The Hereford manuscript dates roughly from the middle or third quarter of the twelfth century. In the discussion that follows, I have benefited from suggestions communicated by Dr. Christopher de Hamel and Dr. Michael Gullick. They are not of course responsible for any conclusions I draw.

9 AS82 was at Cirencester, the Gilbert manuscript is now at Hereford, and many Jesus College manuscripts are of west country provenance. Moreover, the Hereford and Jesus College manuscripts were owned by Sir John Prise, most of whose collection came from the west. See Neil Ker, "Sir John Prise," *The Library*, 5th ser., 10 (1955): 1–24; repr. Ker, *Books, Collectors, and Libraries: Studies in the Medieval Heritage* (London and Ronceverte: Hambledon, 1985), pp. 471–96.

10 "Sir John Prise," p. 17; A. T. Bannister, *A Descriptive Catalogue of the Manuscripts of the Hereford Cathedral Library* (Hereford: Wilson and Phillips, 1927), p. 19.

11 Christopher F. R. de Hamel, *Glossed Books of the Bible and the Origins of the*

Paris Book Trade (Woodbridge, Suffolk: D. S. Brewer, 1984), pp. 4–9. De Hamel's observations are based on a massive command of the manuscript evidence.

12 R. Hunt *et al.*, *The Survival of Ancient Literature* (Oxford: Bodleian Library Exhibition Catalogue, 1975), p. 11. See *The Cartulary of Cirencester Abbey*, ed. C. D. Ross (London: Oxford University Press, 1964), p. 54. "Magister Alveredus" also witnesses three charters for Henry II between 1155–58, see Léopold Delisle and Elie Berger, *Receuil des Actes de Henri II* (Paris: Imprimerie Nationale, 1916), I, nos. xliii, lxx, lxxxiii, and p. 354.

13 W. St. Clair Baddeley, "Early Deeds Relating to St. Peter's Abbey, Gloucester," *Transactions of the Bristol and Gloucestershire Archaeological Society* 37 (1914): 225. The deeds are undated, but are grouped with material of the 1130's and 1140's. This grant corresponds to a series in the cartulary of St. Peter's (clii–clvi); the closest wording occurs in clii, which lists no witnesses. *Historia et cartularium monasterii Sancti Petri Gloucestriae*, ed. William Henry Hart (London: Rolls Series, 1863), I, pp. 239–40.

14 See Dom David Knowles *et al.*, *The Heads of Religious Houses, England and Wales, 940–1216* (Cambridge University Press, 1972), p. 165. A tutor of Henry would presumably be titled *magister*. Aluredus felt close enough to his former student to ask him a favor in granting custody of his abbey to the FitzAlan family; this is done, the charter states, "Ad preces Aluredi Abbatis de Haghmon, nutricii mei"; see *The Cartulary of Haughmond Abbey*, ed. Una Rees (Cardiff: Shropshire Archaeological Society and University of Wales Press, 1985), no. 411, p. 93. Abbot Aluredus is named in Pope Alexander III's letter of 1172 confirming the Abbey's possessions and privileges (*Cartulary*, p. 248).

15 See Richard W. Hunt, "English Learning in the Late Twelfth Century," *Transactions of the Royal Historical Society*, 4th ser., 19 (1936): 19–42; repr. in *Essays in Medieval History*, ed. R. W. Southern (London: Macmillan and New York: St. Martin's, 1968), pp. 106–28, esp. 114–21. David Postles, "The Learning of the Austin Canons: the Case of Oseney Abbey," *Nottingham Medieval Studies* 29 (1985): 32–43. Postles points out the order's interest in law (pp. 34, 36), an intriguing detail in view of Magister Aluredus's copy of Ivo's *Panormia*.

16 For the early and sustained prosperity of Haughmond and its Angevin patronage, see Marjorie Chibnall, "The Abbey of Haughmond," in *VCH Shropshire*, (1973), II, pp. 62–64.

17 Cirencester had a large and varied collection. Haughmond had a respectable collection of books, but mostly on religious topics; see Chibnall, "Abbey of Haughmond," p. 67.

18 In the 1130's and 1140's, Prince Henry of France – the son of Louis VI, who ended his life as archbishop of Rheims – also owned Gilbert on the Pauline Epistles and the letters (though not the *Panormia*) of Ivo of

Chartres, as well as other, mostly glossed biblical manuscripts. See de Hamel, *Glossed Books*, pp. 5–7.

19 Winthrop Wetherbee, *The "Cosmographia" of Bernardus Silvestris* (New York: Columbia University Press, 1973), p. 58 and references; Austin Lane Poole, *From Domesday Book to Magna Carta*, The Oxford History of England 3 (Oxford: Clarendon, 1955), p. 161.

20 In 1153, when Henry was still prince, Osbert of Clare could address to him a begging poem couched in terms of Maecenas's and Augustus's patronage of Horace and Virgil. See F. J. E. Raby, *A History of Secular Latin Poetry in the Middle Ages* (Oxford: Clarendon Press, 1957), II, pp. 139–40.

21 André Boutemy, "Le poème *Pergama flere uolo* . . . et ses imitateurs du XIIe siècle," *Latomus* 5 (1946): 233–44, esp. 237–39. I will examine this poem as part of chapter 5.

22 The inscription is on the *recto* of the same leaf as Aluredus's. The last word is mostly illegible, but the manuscript is further linked to Cirencester through Sir John Prise, most of whose manuscripts came from Cirencester (see note 9 above). See also N. R. Ker, *Medieval Libraries of Great Britain* (London: Royal Historical Society, 1964), pp. 51–52.

23 Dom David Knowles and R. Neville Hadcock, *Medieval Religious Houses: England and Wales* (London: Longman, 1971), p. 154. See also Knowles, *The Monastic Order in England* (Cambridge University Press, 1966), pp. 175 and 359.

24 On the considerable role of canons' schools in the absence of or in addition to cathedral schools, see Emile Lesne, *Les Ecoles de la fin du VIIIe siècle à la fin du XIIe*, Histoire de la propriété ecclésiastique en France 5 (Lille: Facultés Catholiques, 1940), pp. 416–17, 449–50; Philippe Delhaye, "L'Organisation scolaire au XIIe siècle," *Traditio* 5 (1947): 241–46.

25 Still another possible identification for "Magister Aluredus" should be mentioned in connection with Cirencester. This is the English Arabist Alfred of Sareschal, who appears in documents as "Magister" and dedicated his best known work (the *De motu cordis*) to Alexander Neckham, who was abbot of Cirencester 1213–17. However, the books owned by "Magister Aluredus" would be even more old-fashioned in the time Alfred of Sareschal flourished, around the turn of the thirteenth century; and their content is foreign to his interest in Aristotelian science. See Dorothée Metlitzki, *The Matter of Araby in Medieval England* (New Haven, Conn.: Yale University Press, 1977), pp. 38–41; James K. Otte, "The Life and Writings of Alfredus Anglicus," *Viator* 3 (1972): 275–91.

26 Emden, *BRUO*, pp. 1459–60. See also E. F. Jacob, *Henry Chichele* (London: Nelson, 1967), pp. 26, 62, 80, 83.

27 See Glending Olson, *Literature as Recreation in the Later Middle Ages* (Ithaca, N.Y.: Cornell University Press, 1982), esp. pp. 107–19.

28 This gift is recorded in the manuscript's last ownership inscription, on the

second *verso* of the first gathering, "Liber collegii omnium fidelium defunctorum Oxonii datus per Henricum Penwortham." For the relevant extract from Penwortham's will, see Neil R. Ker, *Records of All Souls College Library 1437–1600* (Oxford Bibliographical Society, 1971), p. 122.

29 Roberto Weiss, *Humanism in England during the Fifteenth Century* (Oxford: Blackwell, 1957), ch. 7, esp. pp. 111–12, 125–27; and entries in Emden, *BRUC*. Neither scholar appears to have known Jesus 33. It is not clear that this manuscript came to Jesus College among Gunthorpe's gifts; for donor information, see the Appendix entry.

30 See Introduction, pp. 9–10.

31 Fabius Planciades Fulgentius (Fulgentius Mythographus), *Expositio Vergilianae continentiae*, ed. and trans. T. Agozzino and F. Zanlucchi (Padua: Istituto di Filologia latina, 1972); the first edition appeared in 1898, in *Fabii Planciadi Fulgentii V. C. Opera*, ed. Rudolph Helm, rev. ed. Jean Préaux (Stuttgart: Teubner, 1970). *The Commentary on the First Six Books of the "Aeneid" Commonly Attributed to Bernardus Silvestris*, Jones and Jones (first edition 1924, *Commentum Bernardi Silvestris super Sex Libros Eneidos Virgilii*, ed. William Riedel [Griefswald: Julius Abel]).

32 A much more widely distributed medieval commentary is discussed below, pp. 63–68.

33 This is not to suggest that allegorizers like Fulgentius and Bernard Silvestris were not, in their own eyes, pedagogical. But the learning they wanted to transmit in their commentaries – scientific or spiritual – was not immediately about Virgil and his time, nor was it aimed (especially by Bernard) at the student of the lower schools.

34 For manuscripts with broadly similar marginalia, see App. I, nos. 7, 8, 10, 12, 15, 18, 20, 24, and 26.

35 *The Study of the Bible in the Middle Ages* (Oxford: Blackwell, 1952; repr. University of Notre Dame Press, 1978), p. 89; see also pp. 85–106.

36 Ibid., pp. 178–80.

37 Ibid., p. 140.

38 Ibid., pp. 102–05, 149–72.

39 For a survey of issues and recent scholarship, see *Enciclopedia* IV, pp. 805–13.

40 Murgia in turn is much indebted to the groundbreaking work of John J. Savage, for which see Murgia's bibliography.

41 Murgia, pp. 199–207.

42 Jones and Jones identify four manuscripts, and four more have emerged since; see chapter 3, note 83. By comparison, the witnesses to the "Anselm" commentary number over twenty; see note 100 below.

43 A similar predominant emphasis in the medieval reading of Ovid also begins to emerge. Hexter shows the rarity of any allegoresis or Christianizing reference in the wide range of commentaries he studies, and also notes the present-day orthodoxy based on a limited number of edited commentaries. "The earlier, mostly neglected texts are surprising

in the relative scarcity ... of allegorizing and Christianizing comment"
(Hexter, p. 11). Rather, Hexter finds the kind of broadly literal,
pedagogic emphasis in the teachers of Ovid that I find in the Servian
and related commentaries on Virgil. Despite a general interest in those
aspects of rhetorical strategy that were receiving emphasis in the
developing medieval *artes dictaminis*, the most important aim of these
commentators was "to explicate Ovid, that is, to explain him to their
students as best they could on his own terms" (p. 212).

44 See Henry Nettleship, "The Ancient Commentators on Virgil," in *Works
of Virgil*, ed. John Conington (5th ed., London: Bell, 1898; repr.
Hildesheim: Georg Olms, 1963), p. xcvii.

45 Goold, "Servius," p. 115.

46 R. R. Bolgar seems unduly harsh in his dismissal: "Servius does not
make the slightest attempt to reconstruct the personal or cultural
background of his poet or of the period in which the action of the poem
is ostensibly set. His explanations deal exclusively with matters of detail
which he discusses in a spirit of antiquarian curiosity" (*The Classical
Heritage and its Beneficiaries* [Cambridge University Press, 1958], p. 42).
Indeed, Servius provides one of the fullest of the early *vitae*, and cites
literary parallels (especially with Homer, Appollonius of Rhodes, and
Ennius) which survive throughout the Middle Ages. While he has no
archeological command of the Trojan world, neither did Virgil himself.
A detailed and convincing argument for Servius's commentary as an
agent (or at least a reflection) of imperial Roman ideology is offered by
Martin Irvine in the chapter "Commentary on Vergil: Donatus to
Fulgentius" of his forthcoming book *The Making of Textual Culture:
Grammatica and Literary Theory, 350–1100* (Cambridge University Press,
1994).

47 This aspect of Servius is surveyed in the very useful doctoral dissertation
by Julian W. Jones, "An Analysis of the Allegorical Interpretations in the
Servian Commentary on the *Aeneid*" (diss. Ph.D., Univ. of North
Carolina, 1959); summarized in "Allegorical Interpretation in Servius,"
Classical Journal 56 (1960–61): 217–26.

48 Philip N. Lockhart, "The Literary Criticism of Servius" (diss. Ph.D.,
Yale University, 1959), pp. 95–102.

49 Ibid., pp. 208–210.

50 This last note is among the most consistently copied in the margins of
medieval Virgil manuscripts. It may reflect interest in establishing the
historical accuracy of Virgil's version of events. But it also suggests an
awareness of historical shifts in word-use, an interest which we will see
again in "Anselm of Laon."

51 *Guardians of Language: The Grammarian and Society in Late Antiquity* (Berkeley,
Calif.: University of California Press, 1988), esp. pp. ix–xii, 12–14.

52 Ibid., pp. 17–19, 175–79. See also Kaster's "The Grammarian's
Authority," *Classical Philology* 75 (1980): 216–41.

53 For one example, see John J. Contreni, "A propos de quelques manuscrits de l'école de Laon au IXe siècle: découvertes et problèmes," *Le Moyen Age*, 4th series, 27 (1972): 5–39. Louis Holtz discusses the medieval origin of such "editions commentées," probably in pre-Carolingian Ireland, and specifically connected with the study of Virgil; see "Les Manuscrits Latins à gloses et à commentaires," *Atti del convegno internazionale "Il Libro e il testo,"* ed. Cesare Questa and Renato Raffaelli (Urbino: Università degli studi di Urbino, 1984), pp. 141–67.

54 See Kaster, *Guardians of Language*, pp. 70–95.

55 Quoted and discussed by Robert Kaster, "Macrobius and Servius: Verecundia and the Grammarian's Function," *Harvard Studies in Classical Philology* 84 (1980), 220–21.

56 These altered priorities, and a new sense of history as a record of events now distant and needing explanation, may be reflected by the different order in which Rabanus Maurus, for instance, lists the elements of grammar: "Grammatica est scientia interpretandi poetas atque historicos et recte scribendi loquendique ratio" (*De institutione clericorum*, Patrologia Latina 107, 395).

57 For discussion of an analogous hierarchy of text hands, see T. Julian Brown, "The Palaeography," in *The Hortus Deliciarum of Herrad of Hohenburg*, ed. Rosalie Green *et al.* (London: Warburg Institute, and Leiden: Brill, 1979), I, pp. 81–85.

58 For example, "dum" (1.5) is glossed "donec," and "tantaene animis" (1.11) has the grammatical explanation "an sunt"; "olim" (1.20) has "id est in futuro"; "dicabo" (1.73) has "consecrabo."

59 Such is the case at 1.736 ff.: "Ordo. libauit inmensum id est magnum honorem. propter magnum ciphum." What appears to be a slightly later hand then adds: "uel aliter. libauit honorem id est uinum in mensâm id est super mensam. primaque libato id est fusa super." This gloss also shows access to variant readings; All Souls 82 and its initial gloss read "inmensum," but the slightly later glossator clearly knows the better reading "in mensam" as well. The note is not Servian; so this is not an instance of a correct text descending from an ancient commentary, rather than from a good manuscript. Other such elaborate examples can be found, as at 3.484, 5.751, and elsewhere.

60 As at 8.12: "Et qui edoceat illum eneam dicere se posci a fatis regem id est ut sit rex." Again, at 11.227: "Hec responsa nil actum esse omnibus impensis."

61 The same approach is used in glossing "Martem" (6.165) with "bellum" ("war"), and "Cerealia" (1.177) with "pistoris" ("the baker's"). Thus the elevated "arms of Ceres" are reduced to "the baker's tools."

62 "Samo" (1.16), "insula"; "Symois" (100), "fluuius"; "Litios" (113), "proprium nomen"; "Capin" (183), "proprium nomen"; "Vesta" (292), "dea"; "Eurote" (498), "fluuius"; "Oreades" (500), "nimphe"; "Athlas" (741), "ioculator."

63 As at 4.52 where "orion" is glossed "signum," and 6.576 where "hydra" is glossed "serpens."

64 See Hexter, pp. 37–38, 48.

65 Let me not exaggerate the effect of such glosses, nor suggest that the effects I propose are necessary or universal. The glosses' establishment of accurate general categories for obscure words could help point some readers toward the particular. Readers with sufficient energy or learning to make such use of these glosses might have been rare, but the record of one survives in the marginalia that make up Commentary III.

66 "qui sororem augusti duxerat," and "cesar augustus quasi frater"; the second note appears to be in a slightly later hand.

67 "Sirtes sunt loca uadosa in mare ubi aliquando herent naues"; this may derive from Servius at *Aeneid* 1.111.

68 "mater diane."

69 "Tethys est uxor Oceani, nympharum mater."

70 At 3.423, "uerberat" is glossed "tangit. hiperbole dictura est." The entire line at 4.412 is described as "exclamatio poete." Again at 6.62, "hac troiana tenus" is glossed "temesis." This last may be a slightly later hand.

71 See for instance Lesne, *Les Ecoles*, pp. 597–99, 625.

72 At 3.402, for example, Philoctetes is explained as "the shield–bearer of Hercules" ("armiger herculis"); this takes the essential information from a long Servian note which tells a great deal else about the adventures of Hercules and Philoctetes. Again, 5.24 "eryx" is glossed "the king of Sicily" ("regis sicilie"), which ignores Servian doubts about his parentage.

73 Servius's well-known rationalizing explanation of "lupae nutricis" (1.275: Romulus is "joyful in the tawny skin of his nurse the she–wolf") is briefly summarized by our commentator: "That is, of (his nurse) Acce, the wife of a certain shepherd named Faustulus. She nursed Remus and Romulus. She is said to be a she-wolf because she was a prostitute" ("Id est Acce uxoris faustuli pastoris cuiusdam. qui nutriuit remum et romulum. que fingitur lupa esse quia fuit meretrix"). A rare metrical note to 2.16 "abiete costas" also derives from Servius: "proceleumaticum pro dactilo."

74 At 2.1: "INTENTIQUE ORA T. Aut intue<b>bantur ora loquentis. aut <t>enebant uultus suos immo<b>iles."

75 In these notes we again encounter the problem of scripts discussed earlier. They are mostly in the small bookhand of the interlinear glosses, but show occasional aspects rather like the *notularis* script which is more consistently present in Commentary IA. They also parallel Commentary IA in their use of non-Servian sources. It is these notes, intermediate in length and script, which suggest the likelihood that I and IA may indeed represent two scripts and two commentating impulses from a single writer.

76 Context could have suggested the explanation of "tanto cardine"

(1.672): "Vel iuno haut cessabit tanto cardine id est tanto introitu. quam (*sic*) habet aditum nocendi. cardo est per quod intratur in domum." Popular attitudes toward pagan religion might have given rise to notes like those at 6.565, "Dii non habent penam, sed pene tamen sunt deorum," and at 6.743 "manes," "infernales penas." And widespread notions of physiology and psychology could have provided background for the rather sophisticated note to *irrigat* (3.511): "Bene dicit irrigat. notans phisicam. dum autem aliquis dormit, humores melius per corpus diffun\dun/tur. quia natura non diffusa per sensus corporis, tamen interiora curat."

77 "Oenotri dicuntur a cultu uini quod ibi habundabat. enos. grece. uinum. latine. unde enophorum uas uinarium." Cf. Isidore, *Etymologiarum* lib. XX.vi.1. While the bare suggestion for this might have come from Servius (*ad loc* or at 3.165), he supplies neither the Greek nor the parallel example. The gloss could, however, derive from "Anselm" (see below, pp. 63–68), who writes: "OENOTRI. Oenotria dicta est. uel a uino bono. quod ibi nascitur. Nam oenos uinum est. inde oenoforum uas uinarium. uel ab oenotro rege sabinorum."

78 "Le\r/na mons est archadie ubi apri sunt uelocissimi."

79 "<S>eranus erat pauper agricola quem <el>egerunt romani consulem. et ip<se> uenit cum carruca in theatrum. et <Ro>mani carrucam ex hinc habu<er>unt in sacrosanctum." A number of sources for this note are possible, including Cicero (*Rosc. Am.* 50, *Sest.* 72), Pliny (*NH* 18.20), and Valerius Maximus (4.4.5).

80 Quoted and discussed in Paré, Brunet, and Tremblay, *La Renaissance du XIIe siècle*, p. 116. See also Pierre Riché, *Ecoles et enseignement dans le Haut Moyen Age* (Paris: Aubier, 1979), pp. 247–48.

81 Paré *et al.*, *La Renaissance du XIIe siècle*, p. 118.

82 As at "conum" (3.468), "septemque" (6.783), "mephitim" (7.84), and "Arruncos" (7.206).

83 "Fines pater est harum Furiarum."

84 One such note (to 2.316, "animi"), by its length and subtlety, surely invites further source-hunting: "Animus. aliquando singularis ponitur, pro plurali. aliquando pluralis pro singulari. ut hic. quando autem singularis pro plurali ponitur, causa curialitatis est. Quando pluralis pro singulari, significantie causa est. sicnificat enim quod animus unius ualet animos multorum et sapientia unius sapientiam multorum." This is completely independent of Servius.

85 "Minos fuit rex rectissimus. ideo quesitor peccaminum factus est."

86 "Macrobius saturnalium. De uetustis<si>mo romanorum more. et de occultissimis <s>acris prolata est uox. constat enim omnis urbes in alicuius dei tutela esse. morem\que/ romanorum archanum. et multis ignotum fuisse. ut cum obsiderent urbem hostium eamque iam capi confiderent. certo nomen carmine euocarent tutelares deos..." (*Saturnalia* 3.9.1–3 and 14).

87 *Saturnalia* 3.7.8–3.8.2, and 3.8.4.

88 The *Saturnalia* was a fairly uncommon text in the high Middle Ages; only twenty-five manuscripts survive from the twelfth century and before. But copies did exist in England (e.g. Cambridge, Corpus Christi College 71, s. xii, from St. Albans; and Cambridge, University Library Ff.3.5, s. xii, from Bury St. Edmunds). And the work was known to John of Salisbury and Gerald of Wales; see *T&T*, pp. 222, 224, 234–35.

89 Beryl Smalley, *The Study of the Bible*, pp. 72–73. On the *quaestio* in the twelfth-century schools and earlier, see also Lesne, pp. 630–33; Paré *et al.*, pp. 124–28.

90 "CELICOLUM. Queritur cur uirgilius, quasi quid, apud quas aras mactetur ignorans, taurum ioui fecerit immolari. quem nisi apollini neptuno et marti non licebat. Solucio. Non ignorabat uirgilius taurum neptuno et appoloni esse immolandum, qui ait, TAURUM NEPTUNO, TIBI TAURUM PULCHER APOLLO [*Aen.* 3.119]. Sed in hoc loco taurum immolari dixit deo cui non licebat ut locum faceret monstro secuturo unde subdit HORRENDUM, ET DICTU VIDEO MONSTRUM [*Aen.* 3.26]." Cf. *Sat.* 3.10.2–7. The commentator uses whole phrases from Macrobius, but deletes reference to obscure sources like Labeus and Ateius Capito.

91 I am grateful to Diane K. Bolton, of the Institute for Historical Research, London University, who examined this fragment and suggested its connection with the Glasgow manuscript. Ms. Bolton also kindly supplied me with transcriptions of the unpublished Glasgow commentary and other unpublished commentaries on III, met. 9. For brief discussion of the Hunterian commentary, see Jacqueline Beaumont, "The Latin Tradition of the *De Consolatione Philosophiae*," in *Boethius: His Life, Thought and Influence*, ed. Margaret Gibson (Oxford: Blackwell, 1981), pp. 296–97.

92 For citations and further discussion, see the treatment of Virgil and Boethius in chapter 3.

93 Winthrop Wetherbee discusses Hugh's criticism of the allegorical reading of secular classics in "Philosophy, Cosmology, and the Twelfth-Century Renaissance," in *A History of Twelfth–Century Philosophy*, ed. Peter Dronke (Cambridge University Press, 1988), p. 39.

94 *Alexandreis*, ed. M. Colker, Bibliotheca scriptorum latinorum mediae et recentioris aetatis 17 (Padua: In aedibus Antenoreis, 1978); *Daretis Yliados libri sex*, ed. Ludwig Gompf, in *Josephus Iscanus Werke und Briefe*, Mittellateinische Studien und Texte 4 (Leiden: Brill, 1970). For the modes and limitations of Virgilian imitation in these and three other twelfth-century Latin poems, see the excellent article of Jean-Yves Tilliette, "*Insula me genuit*: L'Influence de l'*Enéide* sur l'épopée latine du XIIe siècle," *Lectures*, pp. 121–42.

95 Wolfgang Iser, *The Act of Reading: A Theory of Aesthetic Response* (Baltimore, Md.: Johns Hopkins University Press, 1978), esp. pp. 194–213.

96 For a magisterial survey of French and Middle English glossing, see now Tony Hunt, *Teaching and Learning Latin in 13th-Century England*, 3 vols. (Cambridge: D. S. Brewer, 1991), esp. I, pp. 3–55.

97 John J. Savage, "Notes on Some Unpublished Scholia in a Paris Manuscript of Virgil," *Transactions and Proceedings of the American Philological Association* 56 (1925): 229–41, and "Mediaeval Notes on the Sixth *Aeneid* in *Parisinus* 7930," *Speculum* 9 (1934): 204–12.

98 At the beginning of the commentary to *Aeneid* 2, most manuscripts refer to "magister ansellus uel anselmus." London, BL Add. 33220, for instance, reads: "<C>ONTICUERE OMNES ET C. Hic respirat auctor. Hoc dicebat magister anxellus. duobus de causis fiunt distinctiones in libris, propter fastidium uitandum, et ut preterita ad memoriam reducantur." That the commentator knew of a Master Anselm, though, does not seem clear evidence for Anselm's authorship of the Virgil commentary; indeed, I should think that the commentator here borrows a generalization about the division of books from another source, Magister Ansellus, whom he names just as he elsewhere often names sources like Servius or Priscian. However, Max Manitius mentions the commentary under Anselm's name (*Geschichte der lateinischen Literatur des Mittelalters* [Munich: C. H. Beck, 1931], III, p. 238), and the association has stuck. I will refer to the author as "Anselm" to underscore the uncertainty of the attribution.

99 Dr. Robert Babcock, of the Beinecke Library, Yale University, has worked on the *Aeneid* commentary; and Catherine Emerson, a student of Virginia Brown at the Pontifical Institute of Mediaeval Studies, is working on an edition of the *Eclogues* commentary.

100 Baswell, "A High Medieval Commentary on the *Aeneid*," in David Anderson, ed., *Sixty Bokes Olde and Newe* (Knoxville, Tenn.: New Chaucer Society, 1985), pp. 60–63. Brown, "A Twelfth-Century Virgilian Miscellany–Commentary of German Origin (Vatican MS. Pal. Lat. 1695)," in *Scire litteras: Forschungen zum mittelalterlichen Geistesleben*, ed. Sigrid Krämer and Michael Bernhard (Munich: Bayerischen Akademie, 1988), p. 82, note 25. Among these, London, BL Add. 16380 was copied in England and circulated in the environs of Canterbury and Rochester by about 1200. Citations below are taken from BL Add. 33220, unless otherwise noted. As we will see, the last annotator of All Souls 82 also had access to a manuscript of the commentary. For help in locating these manuscripts of an unedited and usually uncatalogued commentary, I am grateful to my colleagues in the Virgil project of the CTC, Professor Brown and Professor Mary Louise Lord.

101 My suggestions here are quite preliminary, and must await fuller investigations for confirmation; there is not yet even a full handlist of extant manuscripts. These differences do not appear to derive from long-term developments in the transmission of the text; they are quite clear in the twelfth-century manuscripts, and may reflect multiple versions by the

original master. The *accessus* are fairly consistent; the two versions are most distinguished in those longer notes, particularly in Book Six, where "Anselm" shows non-Servian interests. Typical of the "shorter" version are Berlin, Staatsbibl. lat. fol. 34 (fols. 43–85, s. xii), and London, BL Add. 16380 (fols. 2–72, *c.* 1200); while the "longer" version is found in Bern, Bürgerbibl. 474 (fols. 1–40, s. xii), and London, BL Add. 33220 (fols. 30v–84, s. xiii med.). The two traditions do not descend independently, though; a manuscript of the "short" redaction will sometimes carry the "long" version of a note, and *vice versa*.

102 A. J. Minnis provides a full discussion of the organization and topics of medieval *accessus* in *Medieval Theory of Authorship*, 2nd ed. (Philadelphia: University of Pennsylvania Press, 1988), pp. 15–28. "Anselm's" *accessus* is closest to Minnis's "first type," which was associated with Servius; see pp. 15–16.

103 For the Latin text of "Anselm's" *accessus* to the *Aeneid*, see App. IV.

104 This is a typical division in high medieval commentaries. See for instance *The Commentary of Geoffrey of Vitry on Claudian "De Raptu Proserpinae*," ed. A. K. Clarke and P. M. Giles (Leiden: Brill, 1973), p. 24.

105 Consider the note at *uirum* (1.1). Servius writes "VIRUM quem non dicit, sed circumstantiis ostendit Aeneam." "Anselm" quotes this almost directly, and adds a brief narrative explanation: "VIRUM non dicit quem. sed circonstansciis eneam esse ostendit, qui patrem et deos penates ab incendio troiano liberauit." There is similar borrowing at *Troiae.* Servius: "TROIAE Troia regio est Asiae, Ilium ciuitas Troiae; plerumque tamen usurpant poetae et pro ciuitate uel regionem uel prouinciam ponunt, ut Iuuenalis 'et flammis Asiam ferroque cadentem'" (6.23–26). "Anselm": "TROIE. troia prouincia est asie. ilion uero est cyuitas. sed auctores sepe usurpant ponentes alterum pro altero." The suppression of Servius's specific literary example is typical. Instances could be multiplied indefinitely.

106 "ARMA VIRUMQUE CANO id est armatum et bellicosum uirum. et est endiadis. Endiadis est quedam figura scilicet sermonis improprietas. quando duo substantiua sub eadem. uel sub diuersa loqutione ponuntur. ita quod alterum sine translacione resoluitur in adiectiuum, utroque sub eadem casu remanente. Ut hic 'pateris libabit et auro' [cf. *Georgics* 2.192] id est aureis pateris id est aureis uasibus. uel altero in alium casum transeunte. Ut 'quas delicias' id est quas deliciosas. 'panniculus bombicinus urit' [Juvenal 6.260]. et est eadem figura quando ita duo sustantiua ponuntur. quod alterum per translacionem in alium casum resoluitur. Ut hic 'molem positos, et montes' [cf. *Aeneid* 1.61] id est molem montium. uel ita, pro 'bella,' 'arma' posuit. et est methonomia, cum id per quod agimus ponimus pro eo quod agimus. ut arma pro bello. quia per arma fiunt bella. quasi dicat cano bella et uirum id est errores uiri. et est hysteron proteron, peruersus ordo. aliter enim exequitur quam promittit. Nam primo de erroribus enee. post de bello dicit."

107 For example at 1.237: "POLLICITUS. ut discit priscianus participium potest poni sine uerbo ut hic, Sponte pollicemur, rogati promittimus. hec est proprietas." Cf. H. Keil, *Grammatici Latini*, 8 vols. (Leipzig: Teubner, 1855–1923), III, 305.6–14. Or at 1.323: "SUCCINCTAM PHARETRA ET TEGMINE MACULOSE LINCIS. hunc uersum adducit priscianus in exemplum. et dicit quod qualis casus precedit, talis debet subsequi" (cf. Keil, Ibid., III, 162.11–16). "Anselm" also himself adduces examples of proper grammar from Virgil, without citing sources, as at 1.683: "UNAM NOCTEM. per unam noctem. melius ponuntur nomina tempus significantia per acusatiuum quam per ablatiuum. et melius sine propositione quam cum propositione. et tamen subauditur propositio. melius est dicere 'uixi centum annos' quam 'uixi centum annis.' et melius 'centum annos' quam 'per centum annos.' (Cf. Keil, ibid., III, 327.12–13; 348.6–8; 363.6–8; but the formulation is "Anselm's" own.).

108 At 1.719, "insidat," for which a frequent medieval reading was "insidiat": "INSIDIAT. antiquum est. modo dicitur insidior, aris. uerbum est insidiantium."

109 For instance at 1.8: "Reciprocus uel retrogradus est uersus iste, MUSA MIHI CAUSAS MEMORA QUO NUMINE LESO. Item leso numine quo memora causas mihi musa. alium in sequentibus faciet ibi, scilicet [*Aen.* 7.634] 'aut ocreas leues lento ducunt argento.' Item argento ducunt lento leues ocreas." Cf. the *Ars Grammatica* of Marius Victorinus, Keil, ibid., VI, 113.26–34.

110 At 1.3 *littora*: "duo miliaria faciunt unam leugam, ergo, quattuor leuge erant a mari usque ad lauinum."

111 At 1.267: "Refert enim beatus augustinus excidium troie fuisse in illo tempore in quo moyses duxit israeliticum populum per rubrum mare."

112 The comparisons of situation can be far more simple, too, as at 1.700: "DISCUMBITUR. quia discumbentes comedebant. unde in euangelio 'facite homines discumbere' [cf. Luke 9:14]."

113 "ASPERA TUNC SIC POSITIS. augusto remanente fuit pax per uniuersum orbem, quam rem fabulose ascripserat augusto. sed fuit propter actorem pacis qui natus per ihesum christum scilicet CANA FIDES. cana dicitur fides uel quia in canibus inuenitur uel quia ei manu inuoluta albo panno sacrificabatur. per quod ost<endit> in fide debere esse secretum. VESTA dea est religionis. hoc est ignis sancti spiritus."

114 "uel FATIS. Quedam eueniunt ex libero hominum arbitrio. quedam ex fatorum necessitate, ut hominem nasci et mori. quedam ex numinum uoluntate ut honores attingere, officiis applicare. Enean uero ad ithaliam uenire, erat in numinum uoluntate." The note goes on to take "fatis" in terms of Juno's resentment against Pallas, who is not prevented by fate from harrassing the Greeks, in the following passage: "ex nimia indignacione dicit se a fatis prohiberi. uel alius est sensus latentior et subtilior. qui a comparacione sequenti sumptus est. quasi dicat pallas non est prohibita a fatis grecos uictores persequi. Ego uero troianis

exulibus et mersis nequeo nocere?" "In great indignation, she says that she is prevented by the fates. Or there is another sense, more hidden and subtle, which is adduced from the following comparison, as if [Juno] should say, 'Pallas is not prohibited by fate from persecuting the victorious Greeks. Am I indeed unable to harm the exiled and overwhelmed Trojans?'"

115 "O TERQUE QUATERQUE BEATI. finitum \numerum/ pro infinito posuit, id est multociens. uel quidam referunt ad corpus, et ad animam. \quater/ quantum ad corpus, quia constat ex quattuor elementis. ter ad animam, quia est irascibilis, concupiscibilis, rationalis."

116 At 6.13: "uel bene iuncta sunt eorum templa utpote quia apollo deus est sapientie, diana uero eloquentie, et alterum parum ualet sine altero. Unde oportet ut prius instruamur in gramatica que docet loqui, postea in dialetica que docet probare aliquid, postea in rethorica que docet ad recte uiuendum."

117 For instance, the note in Bern, Bürgerbibliothek 474, s. xii: "Item LATET ARBORE OPACA RAMUM. Nouimus pytagoram samium uitam humanam diuisisse in modum .y. littere, scilicet quod prima incerta sit etas, que adhuc se nec uiciis nec uirtutibus dedit; biuium uero a iuuentute incipere, quo tempore homines aut uicia, ad que facilis est uia id est partem sinistram, aut uirtutes ad quas ardua est uia, quod in figura notatur id est dextram partem, sequuntur. Per aureum ramum dextram partem rami intellige, qui significat sapientiam, innocentiam, et uirtutes ceteras que latent in siluis. Quia uirtus et integritas latent in huius uite confusione. Alii dicunt aureo ramo inferos peti, quia diuites facile mortales intereunt."

118 These figures appear in the longer versions of the note. The kinds of descent are discussed notably by "Bernard Silvestris," ed. Jones and Jones, p. 30.1–16. A related analysis of the descents is found in "Anselm" at 6.154, in BL Add. 33220, but not in Bern 474 or Berlin lat. fol. 34.

119 For example, Commentary II describes Aeolus's toadying speech to Juno in Book One as "liptota"; Commentary III adds "Litotes ubi minus dicit et plus ..." (Here we encounter, only for the first time, a note fallen victim to the binder's knife. A typical close would be "significat" or "intelliget"; see Hexter, pp. 116, 119, and 128 for examples.)

120 "Ibi erat quidam fluuius quem uocabant Simountem (sic) ut ita memoriam haberent simountis qui erat aput troiam."

121 "Explicat causa odii iunonis."

122 "Postquam socii enee ita torrebant fruges ad ignem eneas descendit de naui ad scopulum supradictum ut alicubi posset uidere socios suos pereuntes."

123 "Unum portentum."

124 "Ita uenus filio suo attulerat arma clipeum."

125 "Ad hoc quod aliquis posset dicere non esset bonum uictoriam dolo

adquirere." This filling in of an imagined dramatic situation is not unique or new with All Souls Commentator III. Hexter has found similar notes in twelfth-century Ovid commentaries; see pp. 57–60.

126 "Quia dido posset querere de isto polidoro ideo quia mentionem fecerat de ipso eneas ideo exequitur de ipso" (at 3.49).

127 Whatever the source of his Servius, the notes do suggest at one point that Commentator III had access to another manuscript of the *Aeneid*. For at 1.83, *perflant*, he offers a variant reading: *uel pulsant*. The correct reading is not found in Servius. This is, however, the only variant reading noted in the commentary.

128 As at 1.404 ("uestis defluxit"), where Commentary III reads, "Quia superius dixerat sinus collecta fluentes." The text of Servius here is "quia dixit supra sinus collecta fluentes." Examples need not be multiplied. It should be noted, though, that near-quotation and general dependence on Servius become more marked in the commentary on the later books of the *Aeneid*, where notes are far less frequent and the commentator appears to be hurrying over his material.

129 "topotesia id est ficta loci descriptio. topografia uera loci descriptio." Here Commentator III may be drawing his succinct formulation from "Anselm": "EST IN SECESSU. topothesia est ficta loci descriptio. topografia uera loci descriptio..." "Anselm" too omits much of the rest of Servius's note.

130 This suppression provides another instance of the medieval tradition moving away from Servius's verbal authority, his grammarian's firm control of usage, and retaining instead his rhetorical and substantive notes. See above, p. 52.

131 For instance, when Virgil says that a hill "loomed" over Carthage (1.420), the commentator identifies the figure: "Prosopopeia ut attribuit rei insensibile sensum." Compare "Anselm": "ASPECTAT. prosopopeia. rei insensibili dat sensum." Elsewhere, Commentator III identifies "locutio plenaria" (at 2.288), and "hendiadys" (at 7.142).

132 "Ducere uitam nobilium et fortunatorum est sed trahere uitam miserorum." "Anselm": "TRAHO. qui male uiuit uitam trahit, qui bene uiuit uitam ducit." For notes like these, which display no special information and have independent phrasing, some common third source is also possible. Later examples, though, will establish more conclusively Commentator III's direct use of Anselm.

133 For a discussion of the *ordines* in several Virgil commentaries, see Jerome E. Singerman, *Under Clouds of Poesy: Poetry and Truth in French and English Reworkings of the "Aeneid," 1160–1513* (New York: Garland, 1986), pp. 2–8.

134 "<S>equitur modo artificiali."

135 "Primum cecidit ilium. postea molitus est classem..."

136 "VIX E CONSPECTU. hic narrat. et artificiose agit. Primum enim cecidit ylion. postea molitus est eneas classem. postea fugam arripuit.

demum post multos labores in siciliam deuenit. ubi et patrem suum mortuum sepeleuit. Inde iterum uentis uela commisit. et ab hoc puncto incipit. Cetera modo usque ad thalamum didonis reseruantur. et est ordo artificialis qui in quodam artificio consistit, non naturalis."

137 "Transit auctor de historia ad figmentum."

138 At 1.132, Servius reads: "Astraeus enim unus de Titanibus, qui contra deos arma sumpserunt, cum Aurora concubuit, unde nati sunt uenti secundum Hesiodum. et hoc loco fiduciam pro confidentia posuit, cum fiducia in bonis rebus sit, confidentia in malis." Commentary III renders this more briefly: "de astreo qui cum titanibus pugnauit et aurora nati sunt uenti." This is independent of "Anselm" who however shows a comparable will to shorten and simplify: "GENERIS FIDUCIA nostri. astreus unus de tytanibus cum aurora concubuit. et inde nati sunt uenti, secundum hesiodum." Servius is quoted almost verbatim in explanation of the Harpies in Book Three (3.241), and again to explain "genium loci" at 7.136.

139 "Venus dicitur alma quia alit luxuriosos in luxuria sua." Earlier he had seemed less judgmental when explaining why leaving Aeneas, she was "joyful"(1.416): "Leta quia leticia semper comitatur diuinitatem."

140 "Proprium nomen nimphe que interpretatur serrenitas."

141 Jones and Jones, p. 8.17–18. My translation here differs from Schreiber and Maresca. No such line is found in "Anselm." Jones and Jones suggest no prior source for this treatment of the nymphs, though of course their identification with Juno as goddess of the air is ancient (see Servius *ad loc*).

142 Servius is cited to explain the history of the horses of Rhesus (at 1.469), the family of Ilioneus (at 1.520), the "true" history of Laocoon (at 2.201), the reference to Priam's request for the body of Hector (at 2.541), the genealogy of Helen (at 2.601), and the story of Dardanus and Iasius (at 3.167, in a compressed paraphrase).

143 Servius writes: "et ueritas quidem hoc habet: Troili amore Achillem ductum palumbes ei quibus ille delectebatur obiecisse: quas cum uellet tenere, captus ab Achille in eius amplexibus periit. sed hoc quasi indignum heroo carmine mutauit poeta." The All Souls commentator expands this: "Troilus tenere etatis erat cum habuit conflictum cum achille qui interfectus est ab eo. re uera troilus secundum seruius fuit filius priami qui fuit mire pulcritudinis et uacabat columbis nutriendis. achilles eum amauit et misit ei duas columbas quas cum reciperet ab achille amplexus eum et ita pro nimio amore erga se strinxit et eum suffocauit."

144 "Aliquis posset dicere unde cognoscis tam bene eneam. ad hoc respondet atque equidem...."

145 Vat. Myth. I.135, ed. G. H. Bode, *Scriptores rerum mythicarum* (Celle, 1839), p. 43. It is also found in Servius on *Georgics* 3.35.

146 "...anchises eneam eneas iulium cesarem."

147 The closest such note in "Anselm" occurs at 1.284: "CUM DOMUS
ASSARACI. familia troiana. assaracus genuit capin. Capis anchisem.
anchises eneam romane gentis auctorem per iulum."

148 "ORIENTIS uicto farnace metridatis filio qui in oriente rex fuit.
siquidem pompeius missus est et non potuit uincere. cesar missus et uicit
statim unde uictoriam uersus expressit ueni uidi uici."

149 "SPOLIIS ORIENTIS. uicto pharnace metridatis filio qui in oriente rex
fuit. in quem pompeius missus est, et non potuit deuincere. cesar missus
est et deuicit statim. unde uictoriam suam tribus uerbis expressit. 'ueni.
uidi. uici.'" "Anselm" in turn has obviously come across some
inaccurate history, however, since Pompey was in fact an earlier
conqueror of Pharnaces; it was Caesar's lieutenant Calvinus who at first
failed to quell the rebellion. *Oxford Classical Dictionary*, ed. N. G. L.
Hammond and H. H. Scullard (Oxford: Clarendon Press, 1970), p. 810.

150 "BELLI PORTE templum iam erat rome ubi erant arma publica que
[*sic*] in belli tempore aperiebatur, pace uero confecta claudebatur.
constat enim ipsum esse clausum numa pompilio regnante, 2° post
bellum punicum, 3° post bella actia que confecit augustus cesar quo
tempore pax est facta quantum ad exteras gentes. sed post bella
flagrauere ciuilia, ideo dicit FUROR IMPIUS INTUS." Here again,
Commentator III is clearly making use of the historical information
available to him through "Anselm," whom he quotes almost directly.
"BELLI PORTE. una dictio est. Siquidem templum iam erat rome ubi
erant arma publica. quod in belli tempore aperiebatur. Const<at>
autem ipsum ter esse clausum. primum numa pompilio regnante.
Secundo post bellum punicum. tercio post bella actia. que fecit augustus
cesar. quo tempore quidem pacis facto quantum ad extremas et
extraneas gentes. sed postea bella flagrauere ciuilia. unde inferius.
FUROR IMPIUS INTUS et cetera."

151 "Antiquitus erat consuetudo quod rex esset rex et summus pontifex unde
legitur de iulio cesare quod fuit summus pontifex quod erat maximus
honos." "Anselm": "REX ET SACERDOS maiorum enim hoc erat
consuetudo ut rex etiam esset sacerdos uel pontifex. unde legitur de iulio
cesare quod fuit summus pontifex quod erat maximus honor."

152 "LIBIE id est cartaginis, prouincia pro ciuitate."

153 "arabico. sabea est regie in oriente ubi thus habundat." This provides
another good example of a note, relatively close to "Anselm," which
may however have been taken independently from Servius. "Anselm's"
note reads: "SABEO. sabea regio est ubi thus habundat. et est in
oriente."

154 *P. Vergilii Maronis Aeneidos liber secundus* (Oxford: Clarendon Press, 1964),
p. 282.

155 At 2.312, "Sigean... straits," for example, Commentator III combines
information drawn from Servius, *ad loc* and at 6.505: "Incendii ostendit
magnitudinem. duo promontoria erant extra troiam, retheum et sigeum.

in altero fecit achilles asilum in altero aiax." This combination does not derive from "Anselm," who simply notes "SIGEA. a promontorio." Again, at 1.317, "the Hebrus," Commentator III writes: "Hebrus fluuius tracie qui alio nomine dicitur danubius." This comes directly from "Anselm": "HEBRUM hebrus fluuius est tracie, qui alio nomine dicitur danubius."

156 "Id est fallaci quia greci naturaliter fallaces sunt."

157 "ASIAM id est asianos. ambiciose dixit quia asia est tercia pars mundi. troia est regio asie. asia ponitur ponitur (sic) pro troia que est in asia."

158 "ASIAM id est asiaticos. ambiciose dixit. Nam asia tercia pars est mundi, troia regio asie, ylion ciuitas."

159 "Anselm": "DIVERSO INTEREA. hic innuit eneam non fuisse proditorem, sed propter remotionem domus et tarde cognouisse bella et facilius uitasse discrimen."

160 "Vates omnia nouit sed iuno non permittit dicere omnia scilicet mortem patris et tempestatem ab eolo amissam et didonis amorem. nam si sciret eneas se de affrica exiturum non facile consentiret amori didonis." The paraphrase is quite independent of "Anselm," who not surprisingly does include the same material.

161 For full description and discussion of the renaissance annotation of the manuscript, see Virginia Brown and Craig Kallendorf, "Two Humanist Annotators of Virgil: Coluccio Salutati and Giovanni Tortelli," in *Supplementum Festiuum: Studies in Honor of Paul Oskar Kristeller*, ed. James Hankins (Binghamton: MARTS, 1987), pp. 65–148.

162 Ibid., pp. 67–69.

163 Ibid., p. 69. The annotations added by Petrarch to his Virgil manuscript, only slightly if at all earlier, are discussed by W. Berschin, "Glossierte Virgil-Handschriften dreier *aetates Virgilianae*," in *The Role of the Book in Medieval Culture*, ed. Peter Ganz (Turnhout: Brepols, 1986), II, pp. 116–21.

164 Brown and Kallendorf, "Two Humanist Annotators," pp. 74, 76.

165 In this, AS82 also parallels the Basel manuscript. Brown and Kallendorf make no mention of the extent (if any) to which Salutati or Tortelli made use of previous annotation, as did Commentator III. But a survey of B in microfilm shows no places where they effaced earlier notes, as other humanist owners of medieval Virgils sometimes did.

166 Brown and Kallendorf, "Two Humanist Annotators," p. 77.

167 Ibid., pp. 72–74.

168 *From Humanism to the Humanities: Education and the Liberal Arts in Fifteenth- and Sixteenth-Century Europe* (London: Duckworth, 1986), pp. 10–15. For general observations on reading Latin classics in the school of Guarino, see Remigio Sabbadini, *Il Metodo degli humanisti* (Florence: Le Monnier, 1920), pp. 40–45.

169 Grafton and Jardine, *From Humanism to the Humanities*, p. 15.

170 See ibid., pp. 58–67. See also Grafton, "Renaissance Readers and

Ancient Texts: Comments on Some Commentaries," *Renaissance Quarterly* 38 (1985): 615–49.

171 "Renaissance Readers," p. 619.
172 Brown and Kallendorf, "Two Humanist Annotators," pp. 92, 96.
173 Ibid., pp. 99–115.
174 Ibid., p. 98.
175 For instance, he sometimes identifies Salutati's source by adding "Ser" (Servius) at the end of Salutati's notes. See ibid., p. 113.

3 SPIRITUAL ALLEGORY, PLATONIZING COSMOLOGY, AND THE BOETHIAN *AENEID* IN MEDIEVAL ENGLAND

1 The attribution of the twelfth-century allegorical commentary to Bernard Silvestris remains uncertain; by enclosing his name in quotation marks I acknowledge the commentary's widespread association with the Latin poet but try to remind my readers of its still debated status. See below, pp. 108–10.
2 The humanist Ciones de Magnali (Zono de Magnalis), for example, frequently echoes "Bernard" in his *Aeneid* commentary. Professor Mary Louise Lord is presently engaged in a study of Zono. For some preliminary results of her investigations, see "A Commentary on *Aeneid* 6: Ciones de Magnali, not Nicholas Trevet," *Medievalia et Humanistica*, n.s. 15 (1987): 147–60. Coluccio Salutati used "Bernard's" commentary in his *De Laboribus Herculis*; see Jones and Jones, pp. xviii–xix. Later, Cristoforo Landino also makes considerable use of "Bernard" in his "Platonist" Virgil commentary. See Phillip Russell Hardie's M. Phil. thesis, "Humanist Exegesis of Poetry in fifteenth-century Italy and the Medieval Tradition of Commentary" (University of London [Warburg Institute], 1976), ch. 3.
3 *Policraticus* VIII, 24, ed. C. J. Webb (Oxford: Clarendon Press, 1909), II, pp. 415–16.
4 The contents–list of a lost manuscript containing William's Virgil commentary is printed by Giorgio Padoan, "Tradizione e fortuna del commento all' 'Eneide' di Bernardo Silvestre," *Italia Medioevale e Umanistica* 3 (1960): 234. For William and Virgil generally, see *Enciclopedia* II, pp. 811–15. For Julian Jones's intriguing recent suggestion that Peterhouse 158 itself may contain a surviving fragment of this commentary, see below, note 85.
5 I print Peterhouse I and Peterhouse II as Appendices I and II of "Allegorization." Numbers in the translations that follow refer to sentence numbers in those appendices.
6 "Peterhouse II" is copied in a distinctively English hand of the late twelfth century; the manuscript with its allegorical exegesis was available to university readers at least as early as 1418, when it appears in the Peterhouse catalog of that date.

348   Notes to pages 86–91

7 P158 today contains the entire works of Virgil, but the *Aeneid* appears to have been copied before the *Eclogues* and *Georgics*, and it is not now clear when the two parts of the manuscript were joined together (though certainly by 1418, see note 6 above); my discussion below concerns only the *Aeneid* and its growing body of apparatus. For a fuller description, see Appendix I, no. 11.

8 For an excellent general discussion of "Academic prologues" such as these, see Alistair Minnis, *Medieval Theory of Authorship*, 2nd ed. (Philadelphia: University of Pennsylvania Press, 1988), ch. 1, esp. pp. 15–28. In P158, the *accessus* on fol. 42r conforms closely to the shorter version of "Type A" in Richard Hunt's schema (see Minnis, p. 17); it begins "Quatuor a doctissimis solent percunctari doctoribus: locus, tempus, persona, scribendique occasio," and responds to the four headings in that order. The second *accessus*, on fol. 42vb, is rather more confused; it uses some of the topics of Hunt's "Type B" (Minnis, pp. 15–16) but offers no preliminary list of headings, and it seems to conflate more than one earlier *accessus* (all, however, largely dependent on Servius and the *Vita Donatiana*), giving two different versions of Virgil's *intentio*. The second of the conflated fragments on fol. 42vb (inc. "Titulus huius libri talis est. Incipit liber eneidos. ex hac intitulatione habetur materia.") corresponds to part of the *accessus* appended at the end of London, BL Add. 32319A, which has other connections to P158 (see pp. 102–07). This latter *accessus* in Add. 32319A, however, has been rearranged in the format of Hunt's "Type C" prologue (see Minnis, Medieval Theory, pp. 19–28).

9 See p. 58 above.

10 For a discussion of terminology, see Nikolaus M. Häring, "Commentary and Hermeneutics," in *Renaissance and Renewal in the Twelfth Century*, ed. Robert L. Benson and Giles Constable (Cambridge, Mass.: Harvard University Press, 1982), pp. 173–200.

11 A single commentary, Abelard on Romans, is called *commentariorum liber*, *exposicio*, and *glose* in three different manuscripts. Häring, "Commentary and Hermeneutics," p. 175.

12 Ibid., p. 179.

13 The most frequent title given in the manuscripts for the Virgil commentaries of "Anselm" is *glosule*.

14 "Commentary and Hermeneutics," p. 180. See also Hexter, p. 42. Comparison can be drawn to the collected Virgilian *glosule* of "Anselm," which (as seen in ch. 2) is often very dependent on Servius and other notes already long traditional in the margins of Virgil manuscripts. For a detailed study of the progressive collection and organization of biblical exegesis from Anselm, through Gilbert of Poitiers and Peter Lombard, see de Hamel, *Glossed Books of the Bible*.

15 There do exist witnesses, however, to an equally independent *commentum*, that of "Bernard Silvestris," being redistributed (somewhat awkwardly) into the margins surrounding the *Aeneid*; see note 83 below.

16 Thilo-Hagen, II, p. 1: Totus quidem Vergilius scientia plenus est, in qua hic liber possidet principatum ... et dicuntur aliqua simpliciter, multa de historia, multa per altam scientiam philosophorum, theologorum, Aegyptiorum, adeo ut plerique de his singulis huius libri integras scripserint pragmatias.

17 "Maro omnium disciplinarum peritus...," *Ambrosii Theodosii Macrobii Saturnalia*, ed. Jacob Willis (Leipzig: Teubner, 1970), I.16.12. Translations are from *The Saturnalia*, trans. Percival V. Davies (New York: Columbia University Press, 1969). For the debated dating of this text, see Robert Kaster, "Macrobius and Servius," *Harvard Studies in Classical Philology* 84 (1980): 223–24. Kaster accepts Alan Cameron's date of sometime around 431 AD.

18 See especially Book Three; but also I.24 and V.2. Comparetti's discussion of Macrobius, pp. 63–69, while condescending, is still useful. See also *Enciclopedia* III, pp. 299–304.

19 *Saturnalia* V.1.18–20.

20 Alexander Neckam, for instance, makes this the justification and organizing principle for his treatise *De Naturis Rerum*: "Mundus ergo ipse, calamo Dei inscriptus, littera quaedam intelligenti repraesentans artificis potentiam cum sapientia eiusdem et benignitate. Sic autem totus mundus inscriptus est, ita totus littera est, sed intelligenti et naturas rerum investiganti, ad cognitionem et laudem Creatoris" (ed. Thomas Wright [London: Rolls Series, 1863], p. 125. Also cited by S. Viarre, "Le Commentaire ordonné du monde dans quelques sommes scientifiques des XIIe et XIIIe siècles," in R. R. Bolgar, ed., *Classical Influences on European Culture, A. D. 500–1500* (Cambridge University Press, 1971), p. 210. Viarre explores the application of this notion in a wide range of encyclopedic texts.

21 I am indebted here to the analyses developed by Robert Kaster, both in "Macrobius and Servius" and in *Guardians of Language*, ch. 5. While Kaster convincingly articulates the considerable differences between the Servius of the commentaries and the Servius depicted in the *Saturnalia*, the similarities between their senses of Virgil's hidden wisdom only better emphasize the widespread influence of such ideas in late antiquity.

22 See Robert A. Kaster, "The Grammarian's Authority," *Classical Philology* 75 (1980): 216–41, esp. pp. 223–24.

23 III.9.16, 10.1.

24 V.18.1–3. This is a typical throw-away line in Macrobius, who repeatedly gives the impression, as Kaster puts it, that "the grammarian's function was too important to be left to the grammarian" ("Macrobius and Servius," p. 221).

25 This idea of the text as a privileged, even sacred architectural space points forward to the kind of architecturalized book we will encounter in Chaucer's *House of Fame*.

26 I.24.13: "sed nos, quos crassa Minerva dedecet, non patiamur abstrusa esse adyta sacri poematis, sed arcanorum sensuum investigato aditu doctorum cultu celebranda praebeamus reclusa penetralia."

27 "Macrobius and Servius," p. 237.

28 The *Saturnalia* does admit the possibility of criticizing Virgil for his language or his dependence on Homer and earlier Latin poetry – a critical tradition also of great antiquity. But Macrobius puts almost all such attacks in the mouth of the obnoxious Evangelus, and has them triumphantly answered by the more polished and noble figures in the dialogue, such as Praetextatus, Symmachus, or the impeccably modest Servius.

29 Even in his appeals to obscure religious points, Macrobius tends to rely more on scholarly texts than on direct knowledge of practice; he appeals repeatedly, for example, to a *de religionibus* of Trebatius for details of belief and ritual.

30 For a comprehensive survey of this material, see J. W. Jones, Jr., "Allegorical Interpretation in Servius," *Classical Journal* 56 (1960–61): 217–26. I leave aside Jones's categories of euhemerist and historical allegory, not because they are unconvincing (indeed they make up Jones's most numerous subdivisions), but because, as exegetical responses, they dissipate mystery and difference rather than validating them. Euhemerism and historical allegory, important as they clearly were for Servius and in some of the "pedagogical" commentaries, are little pursued by the allegorizers I study in this chapter.

31 See Jones, "Allegorical Interpretation," pp. 219–20.

32 "nam inferi ... humanam continent vitam, hoc est animam in corpore constitutam." This is a persistent attitude, but it is widely attacked for its heretical, dualistic tendencies. Courcelle I, pp. 429–435.

33 "novimus Pythagoram Samium vitam humanam divississe in modum Y litterae, scilicet quod prima aetas incerta sit, quippe quae adhuc se nec vitiis nec virtutibus dedit: bivium autem Y litterae a iuventute incipere, quo tempore homines aut vitia, id est partem sinistram, aut virtutes, id est dexteram partem sequuntur..." (6.136).

34 See Pierre Courcelle, "Les Pères de l'église devant les enfers virgiliens," *Archives d'histoire doctrinale et littéraire du moyen âge* 30 (1955): 21–24; and Courcelle I, pp. 442–44. For high medieval insertions of the liberal arts into the progress of the soul back from its fallen state, see for instance the *De septem septenis*, for which the study of the arts is the first step in the seven–fold way of the soul to heaven (Patrologia Latina 199, col. 948). Adelard of Bath makes a similar argument in his *De eodem et diverso*, ed. H. Willner, *Beiträge zur Geschichte der Philosophie des Mittelalters* 4:1 (1906): 16–17. See also Robert Bultot, "*Grammatica, Ethica* et *Contemptus Mundi* aux XIIe et XIIIe siècles," *Arts Libéraux*, pp. 815–27; and Robert Darwin Crouse, "Honorius Augustodensis: The Arts as *Via ad Patriam*," *Arts Libéraux*, pp. 531–39.

35 Macrobius quotes Virgil to make a similar point about the dulled senses of the soul on earth, *In somnium Scipionis*, i.3.19.

36 "Allegorical Interpretation," p. 224.

37 Ed. Rudolph Helm, *Fabii Planciadis Fulgentii V. C. Opera*, rev. Jean Préaux (1898, repr. Stuttgart: Teubner, 1970), pp. 81–107; trans. Leslie G. Whitbread, *Fulgentius the Mythographer* (Columbus, Ohio: University of Ohio Press, 1971), pp. 105–53. For a survey of Fulgentius's work, with bibliography, and a good discussion of the continuing debate over his identity, see Ferruccio Bertini, "Fulgenzio," in *Enciclopedia* II, pp. 602–05.

38 Helm, *Fabii Planciadis Fulgentii*, p. 83.10–11.

39 Whitbread, *Fulgentius*, pp. 122, 125.

40 Ibid., pp. 128–29.

41 " 'Videris ipse quid te uera maiestas docuerit; nobis interim quid uisum sit edicamus,' " Helm, *Fabii Planciadi Fulgentii*, p. 87.11–12.

42 This reduction of the public epic to the private world of student and *grammaticus* is discussed by Seth Lerer, *Boethius and Dialogue: Literary Method in "The Consolation of Philosophy"* (Princeton University Press, 1985), pp. 56–69.

43 Whitbread, *Fulgentius*, p. 133.

44 Ibid., p. 107.

45 Ibid., pp. 105, 112–114.

46 *Commentarii in somnium Scipionis*, ed. Jacob Willis (Leipzig: Teubner, 1970), 1.2.7–13. Translations are from *Commentary on the Dream of Scipio*, trans. William Harris Stahl (New York: Columbia University Press, 1952). For a clear and useful schematization of Macrobius's divisions of fables, see Peter Dronke, *Fabula: Explorations into the Uses of Myth in Medieval Platonism*, Mittellateinische Studien und Texte 9 (Leiden: Brill, 1974), p. 26, note 1.

47 1.2.17–18.

48 Twelfth-century discussions of fables and their uses have been the object of a series of penetrating analyses in the past two decades, to which I am constantly indebted in what follows. Particularly important among these are Brian Stock, *Myth and Science in the Twelfth Century* (Princeton University Press, 1972), ch. 1, "Narratio Fabulosa," pp. 11–62; Winthrop Wetherbee, *Platonism and Poetry in the Twelfth Century: The Literary Influence of the School of Chartres* (Princeton University Press, 1972), pp. 36–48, 104–25; Peter Dronke, in a challenging series of articles which culminate in *Fabula*; and most recently Haijo Jan Westra, in the introduction to his edition of *The Commentary on Martianus Capella's De Nuptiis Philologiae et Mercurii Attributed to Bernardus Silvestris*, Studies and Texts 80 (Toronto: Pontifical Institute of Mediaeval Studies, 1986), pp. 23–33. These analyses converge in turn, to a very great extent, on texts uncovered and edited by Edouard Jeauneau, as the notes in each reveal. See his "Note sur l'école de Chartres." *Studi Medievali*, ser. 3, 5 (1964): 821–65.

49 *Fabula*, 13–67, with texts of important passages, pp. 68–78.

50 Ibid., esp. pp. 21–30.

51 Ibid., p. 28.

52 Again, Jeauneau's exploration of this term is fundamental to all later discussion; see "L'Usage de la notion d'Integumentum à travers les gloses de Guillaume de Conches," *Archives d'histoire doctrinale et littéraire du moyen âge* 24 (1957): 35–100. See also Stock's very fine analysis of *integumentum* in varying relation to *involucrum*, *Myth and Science*, pp. 49–59.

53 Dronke, *Fabula*, pp. 48, 75. William in his note thus reinforces Macrobius's knitting together of his idea (textual mystery) and its analogy (Nature's body).

54 Dronke's translation, *Fabula*, p. 49; text p. 75.

55 Ibid., p. 52; see also pp. 119–22. In terms of William's imagination, then, I do not agree with Westra's strictures on Dronke's argument; but, as I suggest in what follows, it may be fair to argue that "Bernard" by comparison does tend to maintain "an all-pervasive distinction between form and substance" (Westra, *Commentary*, p. 31).

56 Throughout his chapter on these notes, Dronke argues eloquently for William as a defender of the role of creative imagination in *fabulae*; I would extend this only to emphasize the potentially equal creative role of the exegete. Stock sees some of the ideas I discuss in the two paragraphs above already fully operating in Macrobius: "Most importantly, through neoplatonism two different sorts of activity become legitimized: first, the demythologization of ancient fables and myths to elicit their hidden meanings; secondly, the making of new myths, the actual creation of structures that seek to symbolize the true nature of reality" (p. 47).

57 Stock, *Myth and Science*, pp. 38–41, 48–49; Wetherbee, *Platonism and Poetry*, pp. 112–14, 267; Dronke, *Fabula*, pp. 119–22; Westra, *Commentary*, pp. 23–33.

58 Westra, *Commentary*, p. 45. I use Westra's translation, p. 24, inserting a few key Latin terms in parentheses. Westra's rendering of "genus doctrine," alone of those I have seen, rightly takes into account that this paragraph occupies roughly that part of the *accessus* usually pertaining to *pars philosophiae* (see Minnis, *Medieval Theory*, pp. 23–26). The final phrase in the penultimate sentence, "quod alias discutiendum erit," might better be taken to mean "[a profound hidden truth] which must be expounded elsewhere" (see Niermeyer "discutere," 6). This reading of the phrase would emphasize the critical role that the commentary itself, as a codicologically separate text, must occupy in an approach to the *auctor* like "Bernard's."

59 Westra, *Commentary*, pp. 45–46, p. 24.

60 In fact, Bernard does propose a number of theological interpretations in his Martianus commentary (see Wetherbee, *Platonism and Poetry*, pp. 114–16); but he was much more hesitant in this regard in his earlier Virgil commentary.

61 Ed. Westra, *Commentary*, pp. 46–47, p. 25.
62 See "Allegorization," pp. 184–88, 190–98.
63 The two texts of the opening sections are remarkably similar in P158 and Vat. lat. 1574 ("V1574"), particularly given the great tendency of masters and copyists to introduce variations in commentaries. The two versions cannot be fully compared, however; the notes at the very beginning of *Aeneid* 1 are missing from V1574, since here (as at beginning of the *Georgics*) a fourteenth-century hand has erased the first few lines of Virgil's text and entered them again, along with an elaborate pen–drawn initial. The first extant notes in V1574 correspond to sentence 7 in "Allegorization," App. I. The notes on fol. 42va in P158 end exactly where the marginal notes on fol. 32r in V1574 do. It does not appear, though, that one manuscript is the copy of the other, since later allegorizing notes will be absent in one or the other manuscript. Some of the notes in P158 and V1574 also appear in London, BL Add. 32319A (App. I, no. 14), which is probably English. A very few of these notes also appear in Cambridge, Pembroke College 260 (App. I, no. 10), also English, whose marginalia are otherwise almost entirely Servian. The commentary clearly circulated in England.
64 I have found no sign, however, that these notes are influenced by the commentary of "Anselm of Laon," though they share common interests. See above, chapter 2, pp. 63–68.
65 "Arma id est bella: metonomia, efficiens pro effecto. Vel arma et uirum id est armatum uirum: et est endiadys. Vel isteron proteron id est preposterus ordo. Vel etiam arma preponuntur quia deus Vulcanus fecerat illa. Vel continuate ad supradicta, arma martis id est digna ipso marte, quia omnia bona arma dicata sunt marti." The identical note appears in BL Add. 32319A.
66 "Hic Virgilius materiam suam in duo partitur: in errorem, et in laborem, quos passus est eneas terra et mari..." The same note again appears in BL Add. 32319A.
67 At 1.8: "NUMINE id est potestate iunonis, uel QUO NUMINE id est quo deo, uel neptuno, uel pallade, qui omnes uexabant troianos." BL Add. 32319A has a closely similar note.
68 At 1.8: "MEMORA deprecatiue, a minore ad maiorem; uocatiue, quando socius ad socium; imperatiue, quando maior ad minorem" (also in BL Add. 32319A). At 1.64: "nominat eum ut maior debet loqui a<d> minorem." Longer entries in much the same vein appear in BAV Vat. lat. 1574.
69 This is a tricky point, as so much widespread medieval mythography has Servius as a radical source. Usually the phrasing of these entries is distant enough from Servius to suggest an intermediate source.
70 "Neptuno assignatur tridens, quia mare a quibusdam dicitur tercia pars mundi, uel quia tria genera aquarum sunt – maris, fluminum, fluuiorum

– quibus preesse neptunus dicitur." The same note appears in Vat. lat. 1574, BL Add. 32319A, and Pembroke 260.

71 The rhetorical terminology is frequent and well informed: "afferesis" (1.35), "istrologia" (1.88), "eneletica oratio" (1.135), "antitesis" (1.254), "paradigma" (1.242), "anastrophe" (1.348), "perifrasis" (1.546), "anafora" (1.664), "ypallage" (1.707) are all found in Book One alone. This continues in the later books, though less frequently. A non–Servian explanation of Mercury is at 1.297, the "good" Juno at 1.734, the death of Hercules at 2.13, and Janus at 7.180.

72 For a more detailed discussion of these connections, see "Allegorization," pp. 190–98.

73 As we will see, "Bernard" allows for, though he does not pursue, ethical interpretation of the *Aeneid*. If this proposed sequence of developments is correct, the history of the allegorizing commentaries corresponds nicely to the progressive systematization of biblical commentary reported by Robert of Auxerre; see above p. 91.

74 See "Allegorization," pp. 195–97.

75 "Allegorization," p. 197.

76 "Allegorization," pp. 192–93.

77 For discussion of recently raised doubts about its English origin, see p. 134. Parallels between Vat. Myth. III and the Peterhouse fragment are discussed in "Allegorization," p. 198.

78 "Iste poeta proprietates multum obseruat, nam primum eneam utpote iuuenem et nondum aduersitatibus exercitatum timidum, et quasi extasi oppressum. Virtutem tamen quodammodo intuentem, inducit. Deinde tantam animi perfectionem ei exhibet ut ad infernum eum descendisse ostendat. Quod autem eum primum timidum, deinde aliquantulum confortatum dicit. Naturale est uirtuoso, nam inopinas aduersitates primum pauet, deinde uirtute roboratus resistit." The notes in Vat. lat. 1574 and BL Add. 32319A differ only in minor details.

79 "Dii uero dicebantur preesse unicuique elementorum. iupiter igni. iuno aeri. neptunus aque. pluto terre." Cf. Vat. lat. 1574 and BL Add. 32319A.

80 "deos id est bonas leges."

81 At 1.587: "Quod autor poetice scribens dicit eneam circumdatum a nube. Significat curas quas habebat in corde, que cure recedunt receptis sociis et adepta amicitia didonis." The note is longer and phrased rather differently in BL Add. 32319A and Vat. lat. 1574, but the content is similar.

82 At 6.406: "Ramus iste significat uirtutes quibus homines liberantur de inferno huius uite, et feruntur ad celum. Vel per ramum intelliguntur diuicie que multos precipitauerunt in infernum. In siluis dicitur latere, quia re uera in huius uite confusione et maiore parte uiciorum, uirtus et integritas latet." Cf. BL Add. 32319A. Part of the note is found in Vat. lat. 1574. It is also in Pembroke 260.

83 To the four manuscripts used by Jones and Jones we can add:.
    (1) Wolfenbüttel, Herzog-August Bibl., Guelf. 7.10 Gud. lat. 155 4°
    (4459), fols. 83v–95 (s. xiii–xiv).
    (2) Berkeley, University of California, Bancroft 2 (s. xiii, a fragmentary
    copy, containing the commentary through *Aeneid* 5.606). Edouard
    Jeauneau identified this manuscript; see "Berkeley, University of
    California, Bancroft Library MS. 2 (notes de lecture)," *Mediaeval Studies*
    50 (1988), 448–49.
    Discussing the question of authorship in that article, Jeauneau rightly
    notes (pp. 450–51) that I misrepresented him (in "Allegorization," p.
    210) as fully accepting Bernard Silvestris as the author; in fact, his
    position has been far more qualified, and I regret having oversimplified
    his earlier arguments. Jeauneau does insist, very justly, that "Si l'auteur
    du *Commentum* n'est pas Bernard Silvestre, c'est quelqu'un qui lui
    ressemblait beaucoup, quelqu'un qui avait lu les mêmes textes et les
    avait interprétés dans le même esprit" (p. 452).
    (3) Copenhagen, Kongelige Bibliotek, Gl. kgl. 2007, 4° (s. xii–xiii; in the
    margins of the Virgil text, a full version of "Bernard" on *Aeneid* 6,
    extending some forty lines past the point at which the commentary
    breaks off in other manuscripts.).
    Fragments and echoes of "Bernard's" commentary appear in the
    margins of many *Aeneid* MSS, for instance: Oxford, Bodleian Library,
    Auct. F.4.22 (s. xii ex., probably France); Copenhagen, Kongelige
    Bibliotek, Gl. kgl. 2006, 4° (s. xiii, extensive selections); Perugia, Bibl.
    Comunale Auguste C.57 (s. xiv).
84 "Allegorization," pp. 200–04.
85 "The So-Called Silvestris Commentary on the *Aeneid* and Two Other
    Interpretations," *Speculum* 64 (1989): 838–48. Along with Elizabeth
    Frances Jones, Prof. Jones has given us the distinguished recent edition of
    the *Aeneid* commentary of "Bernard"; his sense of departures in tone and
    detail between Peterhouse II and "Bernard" must be given the most
    serious consideration.
86 Ibid., pp. 839–42. Jones is certainly right to insist that, in distinguishing
    between one user and another of the vast shared body of interpretive
    commonplaces, we must pay particular attention to unusual or idiomatic
    details (p. 839).
87 This second argument seems less convincing than the first. Peterhouse II
    begins with *Aeneid* 6 and a discussion of the kinds of descent to the
    underworld, then asks why the descent occurs at Book Six, and circles
    back to a summary narration and interpretation of the first five books
    before returning again to Six. Because of this order, Jones feels that
    Peterhouse II's "absorption with *Aeneid* 6 was all but total" (p. 843). But
    Peterhouse's return to the first five books occupies thirty–eight notes
    (18–56), a little over a quarter of the surviving fragment; "Bernard" uses
    twenty-four pages in Jones's edition (pp. 4–28) to cover the first five

books, a slightly smaller proportion of the 115 pages of "Bernard's" text. The proportions of emphasis in what survives are roughly similar, though of course Peterhouse II breaks off much earlier than does "Bernard."

88 Ibid., pp. 843–46. Moreover, William did use the term *allegoria* for the interpretation of secular texts, as does Peterhouse II, whereas "Bernard" never does (pp. 839, 844); but see below, note 91.

89 See ibid., p. 839, note 22.

90 Jones seems to agree with me regarding these aspects of text's transmission, p. 847.

91 It thus seems inappropriate, for instance, to speak of Peterhouse II as having "*omitted* reference" (my emphasis) to "Bernard's" "fundamental notion that the creator may be recognized through his creation" (p. 840), when Peterhouse's whole discussion of the descents to the underworld was at some point written so hastily that it promises to describe four descents but only names three (as Jones registers elsewhere, p. 846, note 52), yet calls the last of these *quartum* (Peterhouse II, 7–15). The single incidence of the term *allegoria*, too, could have slipped in along the line of transmission; if it is authorial, we may well remind ourselves of Jeauneau's trenchant question: "pouvons nous refuser à un homme du XIIe siècle un droit auquel aucun de nous, pour son compte, ne voudrait renoncer, celui de changer d'opinion?" ("Bancroft 2," p. 451).

The interpretation of the golden bough in Peterhouse II is indeed unusual (Jones, p. 841), but nonetheless consonant with "Bernard's" sense of the importance of the teacher in spiritual development (for which see below).

92 Ibid., p. 846.

93 Ibid., p. 846.

94 Ibid., pp. 835–38. See also below, pp. 130–32.

95 I do pause to note, however, that while Jones has certainly problematized the first element of my arguments for significant English connections (by challenging whether "Peterhouse II" should be considered an early redaction of "Bernard"), he does not (given the focus of his article) address the second and, I think, rather stronger part of my claim. That is, not only in the Virgil commentary but also in the Martianus commentary, "Bernard" shows extensive and specific parallels with two texts for which there are only English witnesses: an *Ysagoge in theologiam* and the *Plato ad ostendendum* ("Allegorization," pp. 211–15).

96 For a survey of Bernard's life and work, and arguments that the *Aeneid* commentary is correctly attributed to him, see Peter Dronke, "Bernardo Silvestre," in *Enciclopedia* I, pp. 497–500.

97 Marilynn Desmond offers an intriguing and sensitive reading that complements much of what follows, approaching "Bernard's" commentary in terms of twelfth-century developments in attitudes toward the human body. See "Bernard Silvestris and the *Corpus* of the *Aeneid*," in *The*

human body. See "Bernard Silvestris and the *Corpus* of the *Aeneid*," in *The Classics in the Middle Ages*, ed. Aldo S. Bernardo and Saul Levin (Binghamton, N.Y.: MARTS, 1990), pp. 129–39.

98 For another discussion of "Bernard's" development of the Pythagorean Y, see Jane Chance, "The Origins and Development of Medieval Mythography from Homer to Dante," in *Mapping the Cosmos*, ed. Jane Chance and R. O. Wells, Jr. (Houston, Tex.: Rice University Press, 1985), pp. 61–62.

99 Whitbread, *Fulgentius*, pp. 128–29. "ramum ... aureum, id est doctrinae atque litterarum ... studium" (Helm, *Fabii Planciadis Fulgentii*, pp. 96–97).

100 Ibid., p. 98.

101 For the Virgil commentaries of "Anselm," see ch. 2, pp. 63–68.

102 "Alii dicunt ideo aureo ramo inferos peti, quia diuitiis facile mortales intereunt. Unde tiberianus ait: Aurum quo facile reseratur ianua ditis. Vel aliter, nouimus pitagoram samium, de samo insula, .y. litteram in modum humane uite inuenisse, que littera habet duos ramos. Per perticam inferiorem pueritia que incerta et tenuis est designatur, quia si aliquid peccant pueri etati imputatur. Per biuium uero adolescentia intelligitur, ubi homines aut sinistrum ramum id est uitia tenent, qui primitus latus est et amplus, in fine uero anxius et strictus, sicut uitia que prius delectant, postea uero pungunt. Et ramus iste sinister est aureus, quia aurum delectat, et ita per aurum dicuntur ad inferos descendere. Aut dexter id est uirtutes sequntur, qui prius est arduus et strictus, postea latus et amplus. Ardua enim est uia que ducit ad uitam, postea in eterna et ampla beatitudine. Ramus quoque multiplex in foliis multiplices ramos libidinis significat."

(BL Add. 33,220 is somewhat garbled at this note; I quote from Bern 411, whose content is identical.).

103 Cf. Isidore of Seville, *Etymologiarum sive originum libri XX*, ed. W. M. Lindsay (Oxford: Clarendon, 1911), I.iii.7.

104 Bern 474: "Per aureum ramum dextram partem rami intellige, que significat sapientiam, innocentiam, et uirtutes ceteras que latent in siluis." Wolfenbüttel 323 Gud. lat. 8°: "Per aureum uero ramum qui dextrum littere exprimit pitagorice [*sic*], nobis uirtutes insectandas esse ostendit, per quas ab inferis ad superos facile peruenitur."

105 At 6.406: "Ramus iste significat uirtutes quibus homines liberantur de inferno huius uite, et feruntur ad celum."

106 Peterhouse II, 92–94; see also Jones, "So-Called Silvestris Commentary," p. 841.

107 Jones and Jones, p. 58.6–7.

108 "AUREUS quia per aurum sapientia intelligitur..." (Jones and Jones, p. 58.14); cf. Peterhouse II (90): "...ramum id est sapientia terre."

109 Jones and Jones, p. 58.19–22.

110 Jones and Jones, p. 1.1–2.

111 Jones and Jones, p. 1.3–5. For the "modern" *accessus* widely popular in

the twelfth century, see Minnis, *Medieval Theory*, pp. 19–26. Bernard immediately restates his three questions as topics: "primo poete intentionem et modum agendi et cur agat breviter dicamus" (1.7); while this is a shortened list of subjects typical of the "modern" *accessus*, "Bernard" also addresses *ordo* (1.15) and *utilitas* (2.11,19).

112 Jones and Jones, pp. 2.11–3.3. The fictive level also has negative examples, such as Aeneas's uncontrolled desire for Dido.

113 Jones and Jones, p. 3.8–12. I differ somewhat from Schreiber and Maresca's translation here.

114 William of Conches, in his commentary on Macrobius, argues that an impossible fable calls for allegorizing: "But when *argumentum* is taken to mean a fictitious event which could not have happened, then it is what theologians call allegory, that is, alien discourse" (Dronke, *Fabula*, p. 19). This is just what "Bernard" has written for himself by selecting parts of the *Aeneid* in *ordo naturalis*.

115 For instance, Book One "Continentia Fabulosa"–"Evadit cum septem navibus. Cartaginem venit nube tectus. Videt socios neque alloquitur eos" (p. 4.2–3); "Expositio"–"Cum septem navibus evasit" (p. 11.12), "Tectus nube Carthaginem venit" (p. 12.8), "Socios videt nube tectus et non videtur ab eis nec alloquitur eos" (p. 13.1).

116 See Jones and Jones, p. 20.3–12.

117 Jones and Jones, p. 26.2–18. Summaries presented in several *accessus* linked to the pedagogical tradition have their own ways of rewriting Virgil, even more aggressively, to suit his narrative to imitable ethical norms. In particular they share a tendency to ignore Dido and simply say that the Trojans "delayed a while" in Carthage. I will examine several such instances, in connection with the *Roman d'Eneas'* imperial rewriting of the *Aeneid*, in ch. 5.

118 *Platonism and Poetry*, p. 8. For Wetherbee's discussion of the *Aeneid* commentary itself (to which I am much indebted), see pp. 104–11.

119 For another discussion of "Bernard's" exegetical program in the commentary, focussing on the Genius figure and modes of descent to the Underworld, see Jane Chance Nitzsche, *The Genius Figure in Antiquity and the Middle Ages* (New York and London: Columbia University Press, 1975), pp. 42–64. Chance Nitzsche presents convincing examples of "Bernard's" dependence on William of Conches.

120 Jones and Jones, pp. 20–21.

121 Jones and Jones, pp. 23–25.

122 "Quamvis enim non sit in creaturis, pater, scilicet creator, cognitione tamen creaturarum cognoscitur." Jones and Jones, p. 27.24–26. Schreiber and Maresca do not translate this sentence.

123 Schreiber and Maresca's translation, pp. xxviii–xxix.

124 "FAUCIBUS: nativitatibus" (Jones and Jones, p. 69.8). See also the argument for two lives and two deaths at 6.306 (Jones and Jones, p. 79.1–9).

125 Jones and Jones, pp. 58, 63–64.

126 Jones and Jones, pp. 90–91.

127 On the descent as a form of second birth, see Chance Nitzsche, *Genius Figure*, pp. 50–55. See also the Introduction to Schreiber and Maresca's translation, *Commentary on the First Six Books of Virgil's Aeneid*, pp. xxvii–xxix.

128 See also Desmond, "Bernard Silvestris," pp. 130, 136.

129 See for instance the interpretation of Euboa as knowledge, followed by discussion of the divisions of knowledge into four parts ("sapientia, eloquentia, poesis, mechania") and further subdivisions thereof (Jones and Jones, p. 32.10–20). Later, when the Trojans draw sparks from rocks, "Bernard" delivers a little lecture on the elements and humors (34.5–15). He also pauses to explain the various Muses and Sibyls (35.10–19).

130 Jones and Jones, pp. 31.17–19, 38.1–3, and 61.11; 43.17, 49.9–11; 58.15; 62.4; 64.16; 71.25–27; 110.4–9.

131 Jones and Jones, p. 10.3–8; and see above, p. 101. Larger clusters of ideas (like the grouping of wit, reason, and memory as the components of wisdom) are also invoked under multiple integuments.

132 Jones and Jones, p. 62.2–11. Note the use of natural science in this fable of the schoolroom. It would seem indeed that "Bernard's" note develops that in Peterhouse II, though it is not so daring; so I am not as certain as is Jones that the Peterhouse II note could not be by a writer like "Bernard"; see "The So-Called Silvestris Commentary," p. 841.

133 Jones and Jones, pp. 90.25–91.10.

134 See comments in my review of Westra's edition, *Speculum* 63 (1988): 734–35.

135 Jones and Jones, p. 36.20–26.

136 Jones and Jones, p. 38.21–22.

137 Jones and Jones, p. 9.9.

138 Jones and Jones, p. 62.4–5.

139 Jones and Jones, p. 53.16–22.

140 See *Enciclopedia* I, pp. 516–18.

141 Pierre Courcelle, *La Consolation de Philosophie dans la tradition littéraire* (Paris: Etudes Augustiniennes, 1967). For references see p. 430. *Boethii Philosophiae Consolatio*, ed. Ludwig Bieler, Corpus Christianorum, Series Latina 94 (Turnholt: Brepols, 1957), see references on pp. 120–21. Virgil is by far the most cited Latin poet in Bieler's table, approached in frequency only by Horace, whose sententiousness is more obviously relevant to the tone of the *Consolation*. Joachim Gruber, *Kommentar zu Boethius De Consolatione Philosophiae* (Berlin: De Gruyter, 1978), passim. See also Boethius, *Theological Tractates, Consolation of Philosophy* (Cambridge: Harvard University Press, 1973), trans. H. F. Stewart, E. K. Rand, and S. J. Tester. All quotations are taken from this edition.

142 Luigi Alfonsi explores a pattern of thematic and verbal dependence on

Virgil, especially the *Georgics*, in Boethius's references to a pastoral golden age. "Virgilio in Boezio," *Sileno: rivista di studi classici e cristiani* 5–6 (1979–80): 357–71.

143 This has been widely noted. For bibliography, see Suerbaum, pp. 33–34. A recent treatment is Sarah Spence, *Rhetorics of Reason and Desire: Vergil, Augustine, and the Troubadours* (Ithaca, N.Y.: Cornell University Press, 1988), pp. 55–60. Anna Crabbe offers a fine reading of the *Consolation* as a response to the *Confessions* and its mediated Virgilianism; see "Literary Design in the *De Consolatione Philosophiae*," in *Boethius*, ed. Gibson, pp. 251–63.

144 Quoted in the notes to *P. Vergili Maronis Aeneidos Liber Primus*, ed. R. G. Austin (Oxford: Clarendon Press, 1971), p. 25.

145 Virgil, *The Aeneid*, trans. W. F. Jackson Knight (Baltimore, Md.: Penguin, 1962), p. 27.

146 We may also be reminded here of Aeneas's tearful fascination with the images of his lost past, as presented on the walls of Juno's temple at Carthage. See also Alfonsi, "Virgilio in Boezio," p. 369.

147 When Philosophy speaks of the dangers attendant upon any attempt to lead a life both wise and publicly responsible, she repeats the metaphor: "So it is no wonder if we are buffeted by storms blustering round us on the sea of this life, since we are especially bound to anger the wicked" (I, pr. 3.37–39).

148 Lady Philosophy expresses this promise in language directly borrowed from Neptune's comforting speech to Venus. Philosophy tells Boethius: "Gaudia pelle, / Pelle timorem" (I, met. 7.25–28), which echoes Neptune's promise to see Aeneas safely to Italy despite the stormy wrath of Juno: "pelle timores. / tutus, quos optas, portus accedet Auerni" (*Aen.* 5.812–13). The two heroes are thus again linked in common pursuits, dangers, hopes.

149 *Fulgentius*, trans. Whitbread, p. 130.

150 "Nondum est ad unum omnes exosa fortuna nec tibi nimium valida tempestas incubuit, quando tenaces haerent ancorae quae nec praesentis solamen nec futuri spem temporis abesse patiantur." ("Fortune does not yet hate every single one of your family, nor has too violent a storm overwhelmed you, when those anchors still hold firm which ensure that neither present consolation nor future hope shall be wanting"; II, pr. 4.30–34.) This uses the image of the ship but specifically echoes Aeneas's prayer: "Iuppiter omnipotens, si nondum exosus ad unum / Troianos…" (*Aen.* 5.687–88). The passage also echoes Aeneas's final approach to his promised homeland, when in Book Six his ship at last arrives at Cumae and casts anchor: "tum dente tenaci / ancora fundabat navis…" (6.3–4).

151 This echoes *Aen.* 4.174 and 183.

152 *Fulgentius*, trans. Whitbread, p. 132.

153 *Fabii Planciadi Fulgentii*, ed. Helm, p. 98; *Fulgentius*, trans. Whitbread, p. 130.
154 Thilo–Hagen, II, p. 1.
155 In what follows, I am constantly indebted to Courcelle, *La Consolation.*
156 Courcelle, *La Consolation*, pp. 241–74. The two most important commentaries, by Remigius and William of Conches, remain unedited and available only in a few published fragments. What follows will of necessity be tentative and incomplete.
157 *Saeculi noni auctoris in Boetii consolationem philosophiae commentarius*, ed. E. T. Silk (Rome: Papers and Monographs of the American Academy in Rome 9, 1935). Silk's attribution of the commentary to John the Scot has been rejected by Courcelle, *La Consolation*, pp. 250–53.
158 Courcelle, *La Consolation*, p. 304.
159 See *Saeculi noni auctoris*, ed. Silk, pp. 62, 223, and 238; and Courcelle, *La Consolation*, p. 282.
160 On Bovo's learned and insightful commentary, see Courcelle, *La Consolation*, pp. 292–95. The text cited is in "Mittelalterlichen Kommentare zum O qui perpetua," ed. R. B. C. Huygens, *Sacris Erudiri* 6 (1954): 372–427.
161 "Mittelalterliche Kommentare," ed. Huygens, pp. 390–91, 396.
162 Courcelle, *La Consolation*, p. 301.
163 Ibid., pp. 302, 306–13.
164 William's comment on *Consolation* III, met. 9 is printed by Charles Jourdain, "Des Commentaires inédits de Guillaume de Conches et de Nicholas Triveth sur la *Consolation de la Philosophie* de Boèce," in *Excursions historiques et philosophiques à travers le Moyen Age* (Paris: Firmin–Didot, 1888), pp. 60–62.
165 Courcelle, *La Consolation*, pp. 305, 178–79.
166 Parallel passages are printed by Jeauneau, "Integumentum," pp. 39–40. This use of Fulgentius, though interesting, may not be of special significance. Fulgentius, like Servius, had encyclopedic uses beyond his capacity as a simple commentator. William could be approaching Fulgentius here, then, not as an *Aeneid*-commentator but as a mythographer.
167 See ch. 2, pp. 60–61.
168 *Commentary*, ed. Westra 2.114–120, p. 47.
169 Jones and Jones, p. 20.11–18.
170 See the secondary apparatus in Jones and Jones.
171 Jones and Jones, pp. 32.26–33.8.
172 This was first noticed by Jeauneau, "Integumentum," p. 42. Jones and Jones cite many other examples, for instance, pp. 41, 42, 46, 53, 71, 80. A really thorough review of intertextual parallels, not my purpose here, would have to take into account as well the several passages which are common to William on the *Consolation*, "Bernard's" *Aeneid*-commentary, and his commentary on Martianus Capella edited by Westra.

173 I discuss this in my analysis of the late fourteenth-century commentary on the *Aeneid* in London, BL Add. 27304; see ch. 4.

174 Trevet's commentary has not been printed; a working typescript edition was prepared by E. T. Silk. I am grateful to Mrs. Silk for generously providing me with a microfilm of her late husband's edition. Trevet does use the term *integumentum* in this commentary, but sparingly. For an excellent survey of Trevet's exegetical habits and terminology, see Mary Louise Lord, "Virgil's *Eclogues*, Nicholas Trevet, and the Harmony of the Spheres," *Mediaeval Studies* 54 (1992): 186–273.

175 For a study of John's allegorical approach to the *Aeneid*, see Seth Lerer, "John of Salisbury's Virgil," *Vivarium* 20 (1982): 24–39. Differences between John's summary allegorization and "Bernard's" are noted by Jones in "The So-Called Silvestris Commentary." For John and Virgil more generally, see *Enciclopedia* II, pp. 737–40.

176 "...qui suam volunt in omnibus implere voluntatem... Mundus itaque Epicureis plenus est": *Ioannis Saresberiensis Policraticus*, ed. Clement C. I. Webb (Oxford University Press, 1909), II, p. 412.

177 "...nimium cecus est": *Policraticus*, II, p. 414.

178 "Quae via fidelissima sit ad sequendum quod Epicurei appetunt vel pollicentur": *Policraticus*, II, p. 418.

179 Another popular work, Bernard Silvestris's *Cosmographia*, takes advantage of the intertextual relationship, thus possibly extending the idea to readers unacquainted with the Chartrian commentaries themselves. See the Introduction to Winthrop Wetherbee's translation, *The Cosmographia of Bernardus Silvestris* (New York and London: Columbia University Press, 1973), pp. 18–19, 26, 31.

180 Richard W. Southern, "The Place of England in the Twelfth Century Renaissance," *Medieval Humanism* (New York and Evanston: Harper and Row, 1970), pp. 158–180.

181 Ibid., p. 158.

182 Jeauneau's manuscript O in his edition of William of Conches's *Glosae in Platonem*, pp. 43–44, is an Oxford manuscript copied in 1423. Pierre Courcelle, *La Consolation*, p. 409, cites several manuscripts of William's *Consolation* commentary now in England. Peter Dronke bases his edition of the *Cosmographia* of Bernard Silvestris (Leiden: Brill, 1978) on Oxford, Bodleian Library, Laud. misc. 515, an early thirteenth century manuscript from Waltham in Essex; he lists fourteen other manuscripts now in England (pp. 64–66).

183 Margaret Gibson, *Lanfranc of Bec* (Oxford: Clarendon Press, 1978), pp. 175–77. Sir Richard Southern, *St. Anselm and his Biographer* (Cambridge University Press, 1963). The list of Becket's *eruditi* is edited in J. C. Robertson and J. B. Sheppard, eds., *Materials for the History of Archbishop Thomas Becket* (London: Rolls Series, 1875–83), III, pp. 362–3. We should not ignore, however, the important contribution of English masters to the early educational establishment in Paris; see Astrik L.

Gabriel, *Garlandia: Studies in the History of the Mediaeval University* (Notre Dame: The Mediaeval Institute, 1969), ch. 1, "English Masters and Students in Paris during the Twelfth Century," pp. 1–37.

184 "The Place of England," pp. 160–171.

185 Dorothée Metlitzki, *The Matter of Araby in Medieval England* (New Haven and London: Yale University Press, 1977), chs. 1–3.

186 Austin Lane Poole, *From Domesday Book to Magna Carta*, The Oxford History of England 3 (Oxford: Clarendon Press, 1955), p. 161. As we saw in ch. 2 (pp. 44–46), as well, he was taught by the Englishman Magister Aluredus, though just when that teaching occurred is not clear.

187 "England and the Twelfth-Century Renaissance," *Past and Present* 101 (1983): 3–21. The quotation is on p. 11.

188 Ibid., pp. 11–15. Thomson's recent study, *William of Malmesbury* (Woodbridge, Suffolk: The Boydell Press, 1987), focusses in great part on William's classical study. See especially pp. 11–38.

189 I do not think, however, that Jones and Jones take sufficient account of possible English influences on the scientific content in the commentary.

190 On Peter of Blois, see E. Jeauneau, "*Nani gigantum humeris insidentes*: Essai d'interprétation de Bernard de Chartres," *Lectio Philosophorum: Recherches sur l'Ecole de Chartres* (Amsterdam: Hakkert, 1973), pp. 65–67. For a far less flattering view of Peter, see Richard W. Southern, "Peter of Blois: A Twelfth Century Humanist?" *Medieval Humanism*, pp. 105–132.

191 *The Metalogicon of John of Salisbury*, trans. Daniel D. McGarry (Berkeley and Los Angeles: University of California Press, 1962), "Prologue," pp. 3–7.

192 *Saint Dunstan's Classbook from Glastonbury*, intro. R. W. Hunt, Umbrae codicum occidentalium 4 (Amsterdam: North Holland Publishing, 1961).

193 Discussed in App. I, no. 3.

194 See ch. 2, pp. 44–46.

195 See Beryl Smalley, *The Becket Conflict and the Schools* (Oxford: Basil Blackwell, 1973), pp. 51–58; and Dom A. Morey and C. N. L. Brooke, *Gilbert Foliot and his Letters* (Cambridge University Press, 1965), especially ch. 4.

196 See Metlitzki, *The Matter of Araby*, pp. 38–41.

197 *De naturis rerum*, ed. Thomas Wright (London: Rolls Series, 1863).

198 Discussed in Jeauneau, "Note," pp. 830–39.

199 *Les Oeuvres de Simund de Freine*, ed. John E. Matzke (Paris: SATF, 1909), pp. i–xi.

200 "in qua / proprius est trivii quadriviique locus": R. W. Hunt, "English Learning in the Twelfth Century," in *Essays in Medieval History*, ed. R. W. Southern (London: Macmillan and New York: St. Martins, 1968), p. 121, lines 33–34 (repr. from *Transactions of the Royal Historical Society*, ser. 4, 19 [1936]: 19–42). In Appendix I, pp. 121–22, Hunt prints important lines left out of the standard edition.

201 *Giraldi Cambrensis Opera*, ed. J. S. Brewer (London: Rolls Series, 1861), I, pp. 341–49.

202 Gerald: Instaurare solent solatia sera dolorem,
                     Et renovare magis quam removere malum.
    Aeneid 2.3–5: Infandum, regina, iubes renovare dolorem,
                     Troianas ut opes et lamentabile regnum.
                     eruerint Danai...

203 The commentator begins his discussion of one passage by mentioning other commentators with whom he disagrees: "Hunc locum quidam supersticiosi, quos in Gallia dudum vidi sub nomine astronomie indoctum vulgus magicam docentes, ad commodum sue cause valent detorquere." (*Commentary*, ed. Westra, 8.1067–69, p. 208); "Certain superstitious men whom I saw, formerly, in Gaul, teaching the ignorant rabble magic under the name of astronomy, are able to twist this passage to the advantage of their own faction." If the writer is in fact working in France, why should he say that he formerly saw such superstitious men "in Gallia"? Why does he not just say *hic*, or *apud nos*? It seems more reasonable that "in Gallia" points to a place where the writer is *not*. Further, the present tense of "valent" might mean, not that such superstitious men used to exist (here in France), but rather that they still exist, and that the writer, no longer in France, no longer sees them.

204 Kathleen O. Elliott and J. P. Elder, "A Critical Edition of the Vatican Mythographers," *Transactions and Proceedings of the American Philological Association* 78 (1947): 189–207.

205 Eleanor Rathbone, "Master Alberic of London, 'Mythographus Vaticanus Tertius'," *Mediaeval and Renaissance Studies* 1 (1941): 35–38.

206 *Scriptores rerum mythicarum*, ed. Bode, p. 167.4–17 (on Juno, Aeolus, and Deiopea, based on Fulgentius); pp. 170.19–171.7 (on Juno and her nymphs, deriving from Servius); pp. 180.34–181.19 (Palinurus, Dido, and the return of souls, deriving from Servius); pp. 183.41–184.32 (*Aeneid* 6 and the purgation of souls, deriving from Servius); pp. 185.26–186.18 (Virgil's nine circles of hell as the sins of the world, citing Fulgentius), pp. 230.13–231.34 (an astrological allegory of the events following the shipwreck on the coast of Libya, citing Fulgentius). Three of these come very close indeed to "Bernard," and at each of these three points Albericus uses and explicitly cites Fulgentius.

207 Even if the *Allegoriae Poeticae* in its present form was written by Albericus, Charles Burnett has shown that major portions of his text are of earlier and continental origin. "A Note on the Origins of the Third Vatican Mythographer," *Journal of the Warburg and Courtauld Institutes* 44 (1981): 160–66. Burnett shows the virtual identity between a long passage on the soul in Albericus and a passage in the *De mundi coelestis terrestrisque constitutione* (*DMC*), a text originating in southern Germany in the early twelfth century. Burnett suggests that *DMC* and Albericus must have had

a common source, Albericus perhaps supplying only a general redaction. Nonetheless, even if his work is derivative, Albericus does prove the existence of English interest in classical reading and mythological allegoresis.

4 MORAL ALLEGORY AND THE *AENEID* IN THE TIME OF CHAUCER

1 See Gordon Leff, *Paris and Oxford Universities in the Thirteenth and Fourteenth Centuries* (New York: Wiley, 1968), and J. A. Weisheipl, "The Curriculum of the Faculty of Arts at Oxford in the Early Fourteenth Century," *Mediaeval Studies* 26 (1964): 143–85.
2 Brother Bonaventura, "The Teaching of Latin in Later Medieval England," *Mediaeval Studies* 23 (1961): 1–20.
3 See *English Friars*. The literary implications of this importation of classical reference into Biblical exegesis are studied by Judson B. Allen, *The Friar as Critic* (Nashville, Tenn.: Vanderbilt University Press, 1971).
4 Until recently, no commentaries by "classicizing friars" on ancient epic or lyric texts were known. In 1984, a commentary on Virgil's *Eclogues* was published, attributed on rather slender evidence to Trevet, who did most of his writing in the early years of the fourteenth century. See Aires Augusto Nascimento and José Manuel Díaz de Bustamante, ed., *Nicolás Trivet Anglico, Comentario a las Bucólicas de Virgilio: Estudio y edición crítica*, Monografías de la Universidad de Santiago de Compostela 97 (Santiago de Compostela, 1984). In the past year, Mary Louise Lord has re-examined the attribution and offered complex but convincing arguments for Trevet's authorship, in "Virgil's *Eclogues*, Nicholas Trevet, and the Harmony of the Spheres," *Mediaeval Studies* 54 (1992): 186–273. This commentary apparently circulated only in Italy, where Trevet spent considerable time (see pp. 187–91), but shows occasional interesting analogies to the fourteenth-century marginalia in Add27304. A commentary on *Aeneid* 6, attributed to Trevet in its sole surviving manuscript, has been shown to be the work, in fact, of the Italian Zono de Magnalis; see Mary Louise Lord, "A Commentary on *Aeneid* 6: Ciones de Magnali, not Nicholas Trevet," *Medievalia et Humanistica*, n. s. 15 (1987): 147–60.
5 The best survey of these developments is by Paule Demats, *Fabula: Trois études de mythographie antique et médiévale*, (Geneva: Droz, 1973), pp. 61–177. See also Lester K. Born, "Ovid and Allegory," *Speculum* 9 (1934): 362–79.
6 *Ovide Moralisé*, ed. Cornelis de Boer, 5 vols. (Amsterdam: Koninklijke Akad. van Wetenshappen, 1915–38). Petrus Berchorius, *Reductorium morale, liber XV: Ovidius moralizatus, cap.* i, ed. J. Engels (Utrecht: Instituut voor Laat Latijn, 1966). The latter has been translated by William D. Reynolds, "The *Ovidius Moralizatus* of Petrus Berchorius: An Introduction and Translation" (Ph.D. Diss., University of Illinois at Champaign-

Urbana, 1971). For the Dido and Aeneas story in the *Ovide Moralisé*, see Leube, *Fortuna in Karthago* (see Introduction, note 29), pp. 41–45.

7 Demats, *Fabula*, pp. 61–65.

8 Ralph Hexter notes a similar appearance of student hands in German manuscripts of Ovid. Copying texts or parts of texts had its place in the process of monastic education. See Hexter, pp. 143–44, 151–54.

9 "Utitur ordine artificiali."

10 Alberic of Monte Cassino, *Flowers of Rhetoric*, trans. Joseph M. Miller, in *Readings in Medieval Rhetoric*, eds., J. M. Miller, M. H. Prosser, and T. W. Benson (Bloomington and London: Indiana University Press, 1973), p. 142.

11 In 5.422 the *–que* in "lacertosque" is in fact hypermetric but should elide with "exuit" beginning the following line; while in 5.432 "genua" has its *u* consonantalized.

12 At 1.305: "Ostendit qualiter uenus dissimulans se uenit ad eneam."

13 At 1.321: "Inquisitio ueneris."

14 "In hoc libro continetur bellum troianum."

15 "Ostende (*sic*) qualiter pastores inueniebant sinonem et eum ducebant qui eos postea tradidit."

16 "Describit traciam ad quam uenit ubi polidorus mortuus est. talis est fabula. Polinestor rex erat tracie qui celionem filiam priami duxit. Tempore uero belli priamus polidorum filium suum polinestori cum multa pecunia alendum. Destructa uero troia eum interfecit quia pecuniam habere uoluit"; cf. Servius *auctus*.

17 It will be recalled that Commentary II in All Souls 82, also from the thirteenth century, similarly limits itself to brief notes and appears only in Book 1. Again, the parallel between the early histories of the two manuscripts is striking.

18 "Verba auctoris ad musam."

19 "Verba sunt iunonis ad seipsam."

20 M. B. Parkes, *English Cursive Book Hands* 1250–1500 (London: Scolar Press, 1979), pp. xxii–xxiii.

21 See ibid., plate 1,ii. I am again grateful to the late Professor T. Julian Brown, who examined the manuscript and confirmed my dating.

22 "Fuit curua aqua sicud inter Norwycum et Iernemutam."

23 "Respectu troie sicud nunc flandria respectu anglie."

24 "Quia ibi frequens est populus ibi est crebra sedicio."

25 "Nota quomodo rustici et ignobiles et communitas insurgunt contra maiores."

26 "Hic ostendit quid facit talis populus quando insurgit. Iohannes latimer in Norwico. et horyn londoniis."

27 Dates are summarized by Percy Milligan, "Biographical Notices of the Donors," in *Inventory of Church Goods temp. Edward III*, ed. Aelred Watkin, Norfolk Record Society 19 (1947), p. 151. See also pp. 2, 23, and 25 for details of gifts to churches by Latimer and his wife. For further details on

Latimer, see Francis Blomefield, *History of Norwich*, vol. III of his *Essay Toward a Topographical History of the County of Norfolk* (Norwich: 1739–75, 5 vols.; 2nd ed., London: 1805–10, 11 vols.), pp. 100–01, 116–17; and vol. V, pp. 35 and 469 (Latimer's two manors); *The Records of the City of Norwich*, ed. Wm. Hudson and J. C. Tingey (Norwich: Jarrold and Sons, 1906), I, p. 264 (Latimer acts as surety for John Disse 1365), p. 269 (elected bailiff for Conisford), p. 381 (Leets Verdicts), pp. 391–92 (at head of twenty armed men for the Leet of Conisford), and II, p. 46 (taxation 1378–79), p. 50 (contribution for the wool staple 1390–91); Rev. Wm. Hudson, "Norwich Militia in the Fourteenth Century," *Norfolk Archaeology* 14 (1901): 273, 302; L. G. Bolingbroke, "St. John Maddermarket, Norwich," ibid. 20 (1921): 230 (Latimer's house); and M. A. Farrow, ed., *Wills Among the Norwich Enrolled Deeds 1298–1508*, Norfolk Record Society 16, pt. 3, p. 419 (Latimer's will 1392). I am grateful for a letter from Miss Jean M. Kennedy, County Archivist of Norfolk, confirming details of Latimer's life and activities, and providing information about his will.

28 Henry T. Riley, *Memorials of London and London Life 1276–1419* (London: Longmans, Green, and Co., 1868), pp. 244, 371, 373 note 3, 431. *Liber Custumarum*, in *Munimenta Gildhallae Londoniensis*, ed. H. T. Riley (London: Longmans, Green, and Co., 1860), II.i, pp. 239–40, 295.

29 R. B. Dobson, *The Peasants' Revolt of 1381* (London: Macmillan, 1970), pp. 214–17, 221–25.

30 Ibid., pp. 212–13; see also May McKisack, *The Fourteenth Century* (Oxford University Press, 1959), pp. 409–10.

31 Dobson, *The Peasants' Revolt*, p. 213.

32 Ibid., pp. 259–61. There are further and intriguing connections to Virgil and themes of aristocratic power in Norwich around the time of the Peasants' Revolt. This same Bishop Despenser himself owned a fourteenth-century copy of the *Roman d'Eneas*. See ch. 6, note 2.

33 As for instance at 5.230.

34 "Inquisitio ueneris."

35 "Ad instruendum homines loqui cum aliis in certis causis." He expands similarly at 2.7.

36 "TYRII id est carthaginenses."

37 1.196, "CICILIA, TRINACRIA, et SICULA idem sunt"; 1.235, "teucri, dardani, et troiani idem sunt et frigii"; 1.366, "cartaginenses, tirii, peni, libici, affricani, idem sunt"; 1.467, "GRAII id est greci, et argiui idem sunt et pelasgi."

38 "EXPLORARE LABOR quasi dicat cogites tu quicquid uolueris et dabo tibi."

39 "Cum ambabus manibus rogabat deos."

40 "Id est latus nauis inclinatur undis."

41 "Id est aqua maris intrabat."

42 "Hic iuno alloquitur deum uentorum ita dicendo."

43 "Conqueritur de enea et suis."
44 "Laudat mercedem quam promittit deum uentorum."
45 "Hic deus uentorum respondet iunoni, concedo peticionem, exprimendo causas."
46 This appears not to be an isolated habit. In Vatican, Ottob. lat. 1373 (App. I, no. 19) the thirteenth-century annotator also enters a list of words in the outermost margin. Some are glossed, some not; this could be a kind of finding-list, providing access to particular passages through significant vocabulary rather than plot summary. More likely, though, it shows the text of the *Aeneid* being prepared to contribute words or exemplary phrases to a lexicon or glossary, a form of reference tool that was on the rise in the thirteenth and fourteenth centuries. The rather erratic habits of the Norwich commentator would explain his failure to carry through on the project, just as in his inconsistent provision of topic headings.
47 "Per sincopam."
48 "SEVUS id est seuus magister achillis." Grammatically, Virgil's *saeuus* must refer to Hector who was killed by Achilles's spear.
49 "Are erant saxa in medio mari inter duo regna."
50 The commentator mistakes the Greek accusative plural for a feminine form. Such technical errors in an enthusiastic reader of the *Aeneid* are significant in relation to the redaction of Virgil in the *House of Fame*. Chaucer makes comparable errors (including an error of gender regarding Marsyas), which have led some critics to doubt whether and how well he knew ancient mythology or read the Latin *Aeneid*. See ch. 6, pp. 231–33 for further discussion of this point.
51 "Topotesia id est ficta loci descriptio. Topographia est uera loci descriptio. Hic utitur topotesia."
52 "Telurem pro terra posuit. Cum tellurem deam dicamus terram elementum. Ut uulcanum pro igne. Cererem pro frumento."
53 Servius, at 1.171: "tellurem autem pro terra posuit, cum Tellurem deam dicamus, terram elementum; ut plerumque ponimus Vulcanum pro igni, Cererem pro frumento, Liberum pro vino."
54 "SCENIS AGITATUS id est pulpitis theatralibus recitatus ad modum antiquorum qui solebant ibi recitare facta uaria aliis iuxta ludentibus conformiter carminibus."
55 "Docet modum antiquum sepelendi."
56 On a few occasions, though, he does cite Servius as the source of a note. At 4.462: "bubo cantans malum. tacens uero bonum significant secundum seruium." Compare Servius at 4.462: "cantus autem eius aut fletum imitatur, aut gemitum: tacens autem ostendit felicitatem." Servius is again cited at 6.484, "nota quod sunt alii quam quos liber statim nominat sicud uult Seruius," and again at 7.637.
57 "Nota fabula in theodolo et bernardo sil."
58 Dr. Joannes Osternacher, ed., *Theoduli eclogam* (Urfahr: Verlag des

bischoflichen Privatgymnasiums am Kollegium Petrinim, 1902), p. 38, lines 125–28. The Norwich commentator could be recalling a very loose parallel between the story of Hippolytus (once dead, but restored by intercession of Diana) the father of Virbius, and Bernard Silvestris's poem about a father fated to die by the hand of his son, Patricida (who is thought to be dead, but is in fact "restored" to public life by an odd fluke). See *Le Mathematicus de Bernard Silvestre et la Passio Sanctae Agnetis de Pierre Riga*, ed. B. Hauréau (Paris: Klincksieck, 1895).

59 *Bernard d'Utrecht, Commentum in Theodulum (1076–1099)*, ed. R. B. C. Huygens (Spoleto: Biblioteca degli "Studi medievali," 1977).

60 See above, pp. 108–10.

61 Augustine's *De civitate Dei* enjoyed a revival of interest among the classicizing friars; Trevet wrote the first full commentary on the work, and citations of Augustine appear in many of his classical commentaries, including his *Eclogues* commentary. See Lord, "Nicholas Trevet," pp. 235–38, 246.

62 These references are entered in an ink much paler than most of the commentary, but in the Norwich commentator's distinctive hand.

63 At 6.809 ("3° de c d. c. 14. de numa pompilio"), 6.814 ("de ci dei. li 3 c. 15"), 6.820 ("3 de c d. c. 15"), and 6.849 ("Aug(ustin)us de ci li").

64 "3° de ci. d. c. 13." It is not clear to me what passage the commentator refers to in his final such note, at 7.601: "Mos et c'. 3. de. ci. d. c 15 in p(r)in(cipi)o." This chapter makes no reference to the gates of war or the battles between the Trojans and Latins.

65 Nonetheless, this combination of reading further associates the Norwich commentator with the interests of the "classicizing friars," who produced the earliest commentaries on the *City of God*; see *English Friars*, pp. 58–65 (Nicholas Trevet), pp. 88–94 (Thomas Waleys), pp. 121–32 (John Ridevall).

66 "Describit modum agendi consolatoris."

67 "Ostendit qualis mulier debet dari uiro."

68 At 1.375: "Ecce quam conuenienter respondet et ad propositionem homines debent respondere ad quesita."

69 "Hic docet quomodo homines debent ire ad mensam" (at 1.697). "Nota quod primus nos debemus (......) deo uel benedicere potum antequam attingamus ore" (at 1.736). "Nota pro pace optinenda preces sunt porrigende" (at 3.261). "Nota qualia uerba recedentes debent permanentibus" (at 3.492). "Nota quando primo uiderunt italiam et quo lumine et modum loquendi ad patrias quando homines ueniunt de longinquo" (at 3.52). "Nota modum ueniendi hominis ad inimicum suum in ultima necessitate" (at 3.598). "Hic quomodo homo debet intrare ad amicum suum nota" (at 8.143).

70 "Nota hic quomodo homines non debent loqui contra seipsos nisi ubi non possunt aliter euadere ullo modo" (at 3.609). "Allicire homines per precia est bonum" (at 5.291). "Cogitare debet homo quomodo potest se

proprium adiuuare et pericula euadere" (at 8.21). "Unus bonus et ualens potest impedire multa mala" (at 8.570). "Qualiter debemus celebrare festa sanctorum" (at 8.281).

71 At 8.460: "ad modum quo Wallentis utitur clamide." A note like this ostentatiously moves the epic's terms of reference to local place and present time, yet it is not without subtlety. The strangeness of Welsh dress might, to a sophisticated Norwich cleric, parallel the difference of classical dress; moreover, the rusticity of medieval Wales nicely matches the tone in which Virgil describes Evander's Rome.

72 The later medieval approach to literary exegesis as an aspect of ethics is central to Judson B. Allen's *The Ethical Poetic of the Later Middle Ages: A Decorum of Convenient Distinction* (University of Toronto Press, 1982). See especially ch. 1, "Ethical poetry, poetic ethics, and the sentence of poetry."

73 J.–Th. Welter, *L'Exemplum dans la Littérature Religieuse et Didactique du Moyen Age* (Paris: Guitard, 1927), pp. 335–75. See also Beryl Smalley's comments on Vincent of Beauvais, John of Wales, and Nicholas Trevet as sources of classical citation for the later classicizing friars, in *English Friars*, pp. 47–61.

74 "Nota eneas fugit didonem ad preceptum mercurii et iouis. et homo non fugit peccatum ad preceptum dei et predicatoris" (at 4.287).

75 "Nota quid fecit eneas et quod impleuit iussa deorum" (at 4.331).

76 "Respondet eneas didoni opponens ei exemplum de se ipsa quomodo fatis deorum fugit de phenesia ad cartaginem quam dilexit et quod sic oportuit eum ire ad italiam a (*sic*: for *et*?) allegabat causas plures."

77 At 4.441: "Exemplum bonum pro constancia uiri seruanda et pro humilitate et c'."

78 "Nota de auaricia."

79 "Bonum uerbum pro auaricia."

80 At 4.86: "Nota quod luxoria (*sic*) impedit multa bona."

81 At 4.612: "A multo forciori timenda est excommunicacio."

82 A few notes do indeed suggest some inherited knowledge of platonizing approaches to the epic, but they are infrequent. The kind of physical allegory of the gods much loved by the Chartrians, but still practiced in the fourteenth century by Bersuire among others, is seen in the notes on Phaeton at 5.105: "pheton fuit filius solis id est lux. equi dicuntur eius esse scilicet calor splendor etc." Anchises's cosmological speech (6.724 ff.) is headed "de anima mundi," but this note is followed by some biblical parallels, not any platonic exegesis except for the rather vague "hic ponit quod omnes anime aliorum erant producte de anima mundi" (at 6.728). In the commentator's only direct reference to Plato, he explains Anchises's "longa dies" (6.745) as being "de magno anno platonis."

83 E.g., "Nereus est deus maris et accipitur pro mari" (at 2.419). Fama is later said by Virgil to grow "inter nubila" (4.176), and the Norwich commentator says this is "quia ascendit usque ad magnanimos."

84 At 2.419: "Accipitur pro mari."
85 "Nota quod multi perierunt propter unum. Nota de primo parente et inuentoribus malorum."
86 At 1.295: "De ligatione satane."
87 "In nostro ydiomate deus faciat nos letos quia ab ipso est omnis leticia."
88 "Dura est uia in celum."
89 At 6.531: "Hic querit deiphebus ab enea quomodo uenit ad inferos et potest applicari ad cristum." Such open Christological interpretation, a genuine rarity among English *Aeneid* commentaries I know, nonetheless has widespread precedents in comments and commentaries on Virgil's Fourth Eclogue. It is especially persistent in Trevet's commentary on that Eclogue; see Lord, "Nicholas Trevet," pp. 244–47. While that commentary (as noted above) circulates only in Italian manuscripts, it nonetheless reflects widespread (if contested) exegetical habits.
90 Ovid, (*Met.* xiv.101–53); *Ovide Moralisé*, ed. de Boer, xiv.790–896.
91 See also Demats, *Fabula*, p. 111.
92 At 6.724: " 'In principio fecit deus celum et terram' [cf. Genesis 1:1] et c'. Nota concordiam. 'Spiritus domini ferebatur super aquas' " [Genesis 1:2].
93 "Applica historiam enee cristo."
94 "Applica ad mariam omnia bona de uenere."
95 "Applica historiam ueneris beate marie uirginis."
96 At 8.190: "Nota de loco caci et applica inferno, cristum herculi, boues detentis in limbo."
97 "Hic nota quomodo hercules pastor fuit."
98 At 8.257: "Saltare, et nota de cristo quomodo interfecit dyabolum. iuxta (......) O mors ero mors tua."
99 See *Ovide Moralisé*, ed. de Boer, viii. 1681–1951. The story is also told briefly by Bersuire in the *Ovidius Moralizatus* (trans. Reynolds, p. 336). But Bersuire allegorizes Hercules as Christ only in passing, instead emphasizing him as a figure of the good prelate who recovers souls from the grip of the devil.
100 Of course, *divisio* was an integral preliminary part of most later medieval exegesis, biblical or secular. See Allen, *The Ethical Poetic*, where he notes, in regard to Bersuire, "the result of his analysis is a set of discrete parts of a narrative plot, which exist as more or less independent events, each having its meaning" (p. 139). See also pp. 138–42.
101 *English Friars* and Allen, *The Friar as Critic*.
102 *English Friars*, pp. 28–44. For specific instances of friars' interest in Virgil, see pp. 130–31, 152, 171, 231–38.
103 As the funeral games begin in Book Five, the commentator writes, in large letters (fo. 44r, upper right corner), "primus ludus agonalis in mari." The numbered list continues, always in large letters and usually underlined, through the five games. When Aeneas moves through the circles of hell, the commentator begins by numbering them (6.426, "in primo introitu inferni sunt infantes"; 6.430, "proximi sed inferius sine

crimine dampnati"; 6.434, "tercii sed inferius sunt illi qui maluerunt interimere se ipsos quam uiuere in egestate"; 6.440, "quarti qui propter amorem interficiunt seipsos ut dido"; 6.477, "quinto loco ponuntur qui bello interficiuntur"). But he soon runs out of steam and reverts to his less systematic habit of underlined topic headings (6.581, "de gigantibus et factis eorum"; 6.638, "de paradiso"; etc.) The catalog of champions who gather around Turnus is also numbered, from Mezentius (7.647, "primus dux cum populo suo Mezencius") to Camilla (7.803, "loco 13^i ducis venit Vulsca camilla bellatrix").

104 Only two survive, "capitulum 2^m" at 1.34 and "capitulum 4^m" at 1.92. Here as with many other projects, the Norwich commentator starts on an idea but quickly drops it. The brief sequence of allusions to Virgilian citation in Augustine's *De civitate Dei* is a similar case. See above, p. 150.

105 *English Friars*, pp. 151–52. The *Eclogues* commentary now solidly attributed to Nicholas Trevet (see Lord, "Nicholas Trevet") suggests one kind of medium by which later classicizing friars might have gained access to (sporadically) allegorized texts of classical poetry. It should be recalled that this particular commentary, though by an Englishman, had no English circulation; yet its analogies with the Norwich *Aeneid* commentary may suggest more widely spread classical allegoresis in their common English background.

106 Ibid., p. 2.

107 Ibid., pp. 211–14.

108 *Schools and Scholars in Fourteenth-Century England* (Princeton University Press, 1987), p. 107.

109 Ibid., pp. 110–11.

110 David Knowles and R. N. Hadcock, *Medieval Religious Houses, England and Wales* (New York: St. Martin's Press, 1972), pp. 218, 227. Theological teaching in the Franciscan school at Norwich "was of university standard," and foreign students were sometimes sent there: A. G. Little, *Franciscan Papers, Lists, and Documents* (Manchester University Press, 1943), p. 227. There is the possibility of a direct link between the classicizers and the Norwich Franciscan school, in the person of John de Walsham. John was lector of the Franciscans at Cambridge, *c.* 1353. Smalley has shown that the classicizing friar Thomas Ringstead was probably lecturing there between 1347/8 and 1353 (*English Friars*, p. 215). If John de Walsham studied at Cambridge before becoming lector, he might have heard the classicizer Thomas Hopeman, Regent 1344–45 (ibid., p. 209). See John R. H. Moorman, *The Grey Friars in Cambridge 1225–1538* (Cambridge University Press, 1952), p. 220; Little, *Franciscan Papers*, p. 227. For the Franciscan studium at Norwich, see also Norman P. Tanner, *The Church in Late Medieval Norwich, 1370–1532* (Toronto: Pontifical Institute of Mediaeval Studies, 1984), pp. 32–35.

111 This should not minimize, however, the potential of some of his modes

of annotation for creating a Virgil manuscript available for new uses without the need for a sustained reading of Virgil.

112 Judson Allen has attempted to make just such a connection, moving from a study of the literary analysis of the classicizing friars to critical applications regarding vernacular literature, in *The Friar as Critic*. Allen however never addresses himself to the *limitations* of the friars' response to classical literature.

113 At 1.738: "signum boni uini."

114 We will encounter an analogous interest in this episode when we turn to the much earlier *Roman d'Eneas* in the next chapter.

115 "Signa futurorum."

116 "Socius non debet dimittere socium in periculo solum" (at 9.199).

117 "Quare socius non accipit socium suum semper in periculo sed quandoque dimittit" (at 9.207).

118 "Amicus debet ponere se in periculo pro amico" (at 9.207).

119 "Quare homines optant (........) et amicos uiuere post mortem eorum" (at 9.212).

120 "Celebret exequias" (at 9.215).

121 "Mater hominis quid facit pro eo" (at 9.217).

122 "Requies post laborem" (at 9.224).

123 "Nota de Niso et eurialo" (at 9.239).

124 "Homo debet primo explorare locum insidiarum. Sic dyabolus facit" (at 9.237).

125 "Signa amoris. Ita nos debemus memorari de passione cristi. tenere brachia et lacrimari" (at 9.250).

126 "Amor filii ad parentem" (at 9.261).

127 "Id est magna gracia debetur sibi propter talem partum. A multo fortiori marie propter cristum filium suum" (at 9.298).

128 "Contra superbiam" (at 9.373).

129 "Homo non debet errare ab amico suo et dimittere eum in periculo. Nec debet separari ab eo quia nos separabit a caritate cristi" (at 9.389).

130 "Nota quid amicus debet facere pro amico suo existente in periculo et quid fecit nisus pro euriali" (at 9.397).

131 "Homo in periculo debet orare sanctos pro adiutorio et maxime in bello" (at 9.403).

132 "Nota quid amicus fecit pro amico" (at 9.427).

133 "Nota quod Nisus occidit uolcentem. sic cristus dyabolum pro homine occiso" (at 9.439).

134 *The Ethical Poetic*, p. 34.

135 Minnis, *Medieval Theory of Authorship*; see especially ch. 3, "Authorial Roles in the 'Literal Sense'," pp. 73–117.

136 Allen, *The Friar as Critic*, pp. 39–40, 63–69. Demats, *Fabula*, pp. 150, 165, and *passim*.

137 As Allen puts it, "the dominant feature is the reduction of organic

narrative to a series of essentially substantive bits" (*The Friar as Critic*, p. 73).

138 "bonum uerbum pro"

5 THE ROMANCE *AENEID*

1 A full discussion of date and provenance, with references to earlier arguments, is by Giovanna Angeli, *L' "Eneas" e i primi romanzi volgari* (Milan and Naples: Riccardo Ricciardi, 1971). Angeli argues for a *terminus a quo* of about 1155, and for an author working in the immediate context of the Norman court; see pp. viii, 100, 141.

2 *Eneas: Roman du XIIe siècle*, ed. J.-J. Salverda de Grave, 2 vols. (Paris: CFMA, 1925–29; repr. 1973); trans. John A. Yunck, *Eneas: A Twelfth-Century French Romance*, Records of Civilization 93 (New York: Columbia University Press, 1974). All further citations are from this edition, and from Yunck's translation with occasional minor alterations. In this passage, the French "l'autre part" may refer specifically to the other side of the leaf Lavine has been reading: "turn your page, make me look at the other side."

3 On the "bookishness" of the *roman antique*, and the self–conscious readerliness (*clergie*) of its redactor, see the excellent article by Renate Blumenfeld-Kosinski, "Old French Narrative Genres: Towards the Definition of the *Roman Antique*," *Romance Philology* 34 (1980): 143–59. See also the recent and important observations of Barbara Nolan, *Chaucer and the Tradition of the* Roman Antique (Cambridge University Press, 1992), pp. 15–23 (hereafter cited as "Nolan").

4 See Nolan, "Lavine's transformation of Ovidian *fole amor*," pp. 90–92.

5 See Edmond Faral, *Recherches sur les sources latines des contes et romans courtois du moyen âge* (Paris: Champion, 1913), pp. 150–54. The parallels adduced by Faral are most convincing, but the darker associations of these echoes – infanticide (through Medea) and incest (through Myrrha and Byblis) – remain unexplored.

6 See Hexter, pp. 21–23. Faral, *Recherches*, p. 146, note 1, suggests that the figure of Amor as master may result from a misreading of the Latin in the *Remedia amoris*, lines 39 ff. This seems the more possible since the reading would have been from a fairly unpunctuated manuscript.

7 Marie–Luce Chênerie has shown that the system of gift–giving in the *Eneas* also emphasizes, even more strongly than in Virgil, the dominance of patriarchal reign and its extension through matrimony. See "Le Motif des présents dans le *Roman d'Énéas*," in *Relire le "Roman d'Eneas*," ed. Jean Dufournet (Paris: Honoré Champion, 1985), pp. 43–61.

8 Royal learned ladies were not, however, unknown among the Normans; the first wife of Henry I, Mathilda of Scotland, had studied "literatoriam artem," thus presumably in Latin, at Romsey, according to Orderic Vitalis. See Walter F. Schirmer and Ulrich Broich, *Studien zum literarischen*

Patronat im England des 12. Jahrhunderts (Cologne and Opladen: Westdeutscher Verlag, 1962), p. 12. On the other hand, Henry I's second wife, Adeliza, is associated only with patronage of vernacular writers (pp. 13–14), as is Henry II's queen, Eleanor of Aquitaine (p. 19).

9　For discussion of the context of literacy this implies, especially in regard to the audience for romance, see Raymond J. Cormier, *One Heart One Mind: The Rebirth of Virgil's Hero in Medieval French Romance* (University, Miss.: Romance Monographs, 1973), pp. 229–41. Cormier's study provided the fundamental impetus for serious critical treatment of the poem in the past two decades.

10　In *Le Roman médiéval* (Paris: Presses universitaires de France, 1984), Jean-Charles Huchet concentrates on the poem's depiction of the sexual subconscious of the twelfth-century world. Three central patterns emerge from Huchet's discussion of the *Eneas*, all of them having to do with escape and restoration. First, the hero escapes from incestuous desire (for the mother or for himself as a figure of the father) and achieves instead a legitimizing relation with the father and the father's word; from this stems the hero's establishment of legitimate exogamous marriage and political power. Second, the race escapes from cycles of destruction stemming from rape (such as Helen's) or from patricidal or infanticidal violence (such as Oedipus's and his sons'), and creates a new nation. And third, the *roman* itself escapes from its Virgilian forebear and discovers a new and radically different form. While Huchet's psycho-analytic perspective is far different from my approach here, our conclusions are at certains points interestingly similar, as I will note below. For hesitations about Huchet's argument, see my review essay, "Medieval Readers and Ancient Texts: The Inference of the Past," *Envoi: A Review Journal of Medieval Literature* 1 (1988): 1–22, esp. 9–16.

11　Diana B. Tyson, "Patronage of French Vernacular History Writers in the Twelfth and Thirteenth Centuries," *Romania* 100 (1975): 185–86, 190–95, 219–20. Following M. D. Legge, Tyson notes the English dominance in the encouragement of vernacular history. See also Schirmer and Broich, *Studien*, pp. 15, 199.

12　Cf. Blumenfeld–Kosinski: "The revival of learning accorded new dignity to the clerk since only he could serve as mediator between ancient material and his contemporary audience" ("Old French Narrative Genres," p. 147).

13　*Inescapable Romance: Studies in the Poetics of a Mode* (Princeton University Press, 1979), p. 4.

14　Ibid., p. 5.

15　Huchet also sees the poem as fundamentally structured by delay in finding and acknowledging a legitimating father: "Et le roman n'est que le retard, subtilement organisé par la fiction, apporté à la mise en actes de cette parole paternelle..." (*Le Roman médiéval*, p. 26). Huchet goes farther yet, to see a structure of renounced incestuous desire at work in all the *romans antiques*. They are, he writes, "la mise en fiction d'une structure élémentaire qui transforme le mariage en un don d'une femme par un homme à un autre homme, par un père cédant sur son désir incestueux" (p. 26); see also p. 144. As I argue below, I see a pattern rather of alteration between epic linearity and romance delay, at both structural and thematic levels, in the poem.

16 The principal study of the interplay of the (transformed) mythical and the political in the poem is Daniel Poirion's "De l''Énéide' l''Eneas': mythologie et moralisation," *Cahiers de civilisation médiévale* 19 (1976): 213–29. For a fine study of courtly love themes in the poem, see Helen C. R. Laurie, "'Eneas' and the Doctrine of Courtly Love," *Modern Language Review* 64 (1969): 283–94. Angeli, *L' "Eneas,"* pp. 107–14, however, argues that the eroticism of the poem is rather more Ovidian than courtly. For an important discussion, see Nolan's chapter, "The poetics of *fine amor* in the French *romans antiques*," pp. 75–118.

17 Lee Patterson, in an important essay to which I will return, speaks of the *Eneas* as suppressing most of the darker complexities of Trojan history it found in Virgil. Yet he also acknowledges that "the *Eneas* is not immune to a counterawareness ... of the human cost of the historical life," seen especially in the marvellous; see "Virgil and the Historical Consciousness of the Twelfth Century: The *Roman d'Eneas* and *Erec et Enide*," in *Negotiating the Past: The Historical Understanding of Medieval Literature* (Madison: University of Wisconsin Press, 1987), pp. 170–83, esp. p. 181. In what follows I will try to show that the pattern of romance suspensions in the poem shows a more pervasive such "counterawareness," more complexly articulated, than Patterson explores.

18 This would require a full study of its own, and is being pursued by Professor Raymond Cormier, whose results will have much to add to what I outline here. For some preliminary findings, see "An Example of Twelfth Century *Adaptatio*: The *Roman d'Eneas* Author's Use of Glossed *Aeneid* Manuscripts," *Revue d'Histoire des Textes* 19 (1989): 277–89; most of the examples there derive from Servius. A cursory survey of influences from Servius and other late antique commentaries is offered by Francine Mora, "Sources de l'Énéas: la tradition exégétique et le modèle épique latin," in *Relire le "Roman d'Eneas,"* ed. Dufournet, pp. 83–104, esp. 86–92.

19 Huchet also sees glossing, with its production of an excess of meaning, "un 'surplus' de sens," as fundamental to the structuring of the poem (*Le Roman médiéval*, pp. 10–11 and *passim*).

20 See discussion of such interlinear or brief marginal notes in All Souls 82, in ch. 2, pp. 54–8.

21 See for instance Yunck, p. 10. I do not agree with Yunck, though, that the poet is "clearly embarrassed by Vergil's gods." For a very good discussion of the gods in the poem, including the sort of glossed explanation mentioned above, see Marilynn R. Desmond, "I wol now singen, yif I kan: The 'Aeneid' in Medieval French and English

Narrative," Ph.D. diss. (University of California, Berkeley, 1985), pp. 67–80.

22 Poirion notes the redactor's detached, non-judgmental interest in the pagan gods ("De l''Énéide,'" p. 215).

23 For just one example, see Peterhouse 158 at *Aen.* 1.8: "dii uero dicebantur preesse elementis. iupiter igni. Iuno aeri. Neptunus aque. pluto terre." This kind of basic information can extend to human character as well, of course. Eneas has to carry his father from Troy, it is explained, because Anchises "molt vialz hom ere" (line 56). This detail is clear from context in the *Aeneid* itself, but the information is also articulated in Servius at 2.639 and 3.103.

24 Servius at 5.735: "elysium est ubi piorum animae habitant..." and at 6.404: "ad Elysium non nisi purgati perveniunt..." "Anselm" at 6.426: "In octauo [circulo] uero sunt anime eorum que ita sunt purgate quod ad incorporandum possunt redire. In nono autem sunt anime que ita sunt purgatissime quod semper manent in eterna beatitudine scilicet elissi ubi erat anchises unde infra PAUCI LETA ARVA TENEMUS."

25 See lines 99–182 and 4353–84.

26 "The Judgment of Paris in the *Roman d'Eneas*: A New Look At Sources and Significance," *The Classical Bulletin* 56 (1980): 52–56. Nolan's conclusions in that article are now elegantly contextualized in the section of her recent book, "The *Roman d'Eneas* and the question of *fole amor*," pp. 78–96, where she also considers the impact of *Heroides* commentaries on the redactor.

27 See ch. 3, pp. 102–03, and ch. 2, p. 65.

28 See also Aimé Petit, "L'Anachronisme dans les romans antiques, et plus particulièrement dans le Roman d'Eneas," in *Relire le "Roman d'Eneas*," ed. Dufournet, pp. 120–22.

29 Lines 1040–41: "desus lo chief me mistrent sel, / vin et oille, farine et cendre." Cf. Servius at 2.133: "SALSAE FRUGES sal et far, quod dicitur mola salsa, qua et frons victimae et foci aspergebantur et cultri."

30 See for example lines 6045 ff., 6077 ff., 6090, 6092, 6377 (the burial of Pallas). The particular reference to national differences in burial practice (line 7363, "a la costume del païs") would appear to derive from Servius's long note at 11.186: "quia apud varias gentes diversa fuerunt genera sepulturae..." Guy Raynaud de Lage claims that "l'auteur de l'*Enéas* est d'ailleurs de tous nos romanciers celui qui connait le plus précisément les choses de l'Antiquité, ce qui n'implique pas fatalement qu'il en soit toujours scrupuleux": "Les Romans antiques et la représentation de l'antiquité," in *Les Premiers romans français* (Geneva: Droz, 1976), p. 138.

31 "deos id est bonas leges."

32 Edinburgh, National Library of Scotland, Advocates' 18.4.13. fo. 1r: "Intencio autoris est materiam suam metrice describere. causa suscepti operis est captatio beneuolentie augusti cesaris. Utilitas est ut perlecto libro sciamus bella prudenter gerere uel penitus euitare."

33 London, BL Add. 32319A (Appendix I, no. 14) has a typical note around 1.12: "duo ordines sunt narrandi. artificialis et naturalis. Naturalis quando res gesta certo ordine narratur. Artificialis quando rapit auditorem in medio."

34 Ostendit enim quod ipse eneas post destructionem troie, cum aliquot nauibus scilicet uiginti, monitus ab apolline ut materna peteret ubera, anchisse (sic) patre eiusdem enee verba interpretante, per traciam cretam uenit, dicens tamquam uetustatis non inscius teucrum inde uenisse. Sed orta ibidem maxima pestilencia coacti sunt recedere, et tercium ingressi naues suas, per siciliam ubi anchises mortuus est, et cartaginem ubi aliquando diu commorati sunt, in italiam uenerunt unde dardanus uenerat. Eoque tempore quo eneas italiam uenit, latinus ibidem regnauit. Audito autem aduentu enee, statim latinus ei natam suam despondit, quam mater sua prius turno spoponderat uxorem. Unde ortum bellum inter turnum et eneam. Tandem turnus uictus est. Mater uero ipsius non ausa remanere, aufugit in flandriam ibidemque ciuitatem unam a nomine filii sui dictam tornacum condidit. Hec de materia breuiter dicenda sunt (BL Add. 32319A, fo. 149v).

35 In his accessus to the Aeneid, "Anselm of Laon" similarly expunges Dido from his summary of events; see Appendix IV.

36 Consider this passage, remarkably similar to the summary above: "et ce li comandent li dé / que il aut la contree querre / dunt Dardanus vint an la terre, / qui fonda de Troie les murs" (lines 38–41). See also lines 342 ff.

37 See Servius at Aeneid 1.380 and 3.104. A typical simplification is in the early marginalia of Additional 27304 (still probably later than the Eneas), at 3.102: "teucer uenit a creta, dardanus ab italia. anchises putans febum dixisse de teucro fecit eos ire ad cretam. et ita decepti fuerunt." "Anselm" gives a fuller version at 1.235: "REVOCATO SANGUINE. non enim ad teucrum, sed ad dardanum reuocabantur. dardanus enim de ithalia profectus est. et uenit ad loca illa ubi troia fuit. et fecit quasdam paruas domos. Teucer autem de creta et post ad eadem loca uenit et augmentauit." Often the marginal material also supplies the generations between Dardanus and Aeneas, as in Add. 32319A at 1.245: "iupiter dardanum dardanus erictonium erictonius troeam troes asaracum asaracus capin capis anchisen."

38 Additional 27304, at 1.235: "teucer et dardanus fuerunt primi pater [sic] enee. Unde eneas in responsis accepit petite primum patrem."

39 An overview and preliminary bibliography of these poems and verse summaries can be found in the incipit lists in Hans Walther, Initia carminum ac versuum medii aevi posterioris Latinorum (Göttingen: Vandenhoeck und Ruprecht, 1969), nos. 61, 580, 748, 1258, 1473, 2117, 4645, 4946, 6254, 6549, 7266a, 8218, 8673, 8683, 8857, 9517, 9948, 9580, 10901, 11665, 11856, 12513, 12579, 13985, 14338, 14655, 14661, 14663, 14710, 15252, 15622, 15897, 18895, 19183, 19346, 19457–61, 19568,

19703, 19715, 19746, 20005, 20582. I am grateful to Prof. Ralph Hexter for sharing his lists of medieval Troy poems.

40 Walter, no. 20582. P. Leyser, *Historia poetarum et poematum medii aevi* (Halle, 1721) pp. 404–08, and following him PL 171, col. 1451–53, print it as an uninterrupted continuation of a Troy poem of Simon Aurea Capra. Edélestand du Méril, *Poésies populaires latines antérieures au XIIe siècle* (Paris, 1843), pp. 400–05, prints it as an independent work; I quote from this text. No editor, however, makes use of more than three of the numerous manuscripts of this poem (Walther lists fifteen), and du Méril's many suggested emendations give a good sense of its troubled text. A modern edition is needed. In just the first line, for instance, I read "data Troja" with Oxford, Bodleian Library, Bodl. 851, not "clara Troja" with Leyser and du Méril.

41 Quoted in Edmond Faral, "Le Manuscrit 511 du 'Hunterian Museum' de Glasgow," *Studi Medievali*, n.s. 9 (1936): 47. See also Schirmer and Broich, *Studien*, p. 29.

42 Manuscripts range from the twelfth to the fifteenth century. The poem clearly had a considerable English tradition, with at least nine surviving manuscripts: Cambridge, CCC 450 (s. xiv), p. 194; London, BL Royal 12.D.III (s. xv), fo. 155; Royal 13.A.IV (s. xiii), fo. 23v; Oxford, Bodleian Library: Add. A.365 (s. xv), fo. 6, Bodley 851 (s. xiv ex.), fo. 89vb–90rb, Bodl. Misc. Laud. D 15, Digby 65 (s. xiii), Laud. lat. 86 (s. xii or xiii), fo. 47v, and Rawl. G. 109 (s. xii/xiii), p. 104 (not 33 as in Walther). An overview of shorter Latin Troy poems in English manuscripts can be gleaned from A. G. Rigg, "Medieval Latin Poetic Anthologies," parts I–IV, *Mediaeval Studies* 39 (1977): 281–330, 40 (1978): 387–407, 41 (1979): 468–505, and 43 (1981): 472–97. For links between "Viribus" and several other Troy poems, see André Boutemy, "Le poème *Pergama flere uolo* ... et ses imitateurs du XIIe siècle," *Latomus* 5 (1946): 233–44.

43 "talibus heu! talis femina causa malis": du Méril, *Poésies populaires*, p. 403. A very similar moralizing rancor toward Helen is also found in earlier and contemporary mythography; see Christopher C. Baswell and Paul Beekman Taylor, "The *Faire Queene Eleyne* in Chaucer's *Troilus*," *Speculum* 63 (1988): 293–311, esp. 295–97.

44 "Ne quis amet temere docet obruta Troja cavere, / quae Paridis scelere fit nihil...": du Méril, *Poésies populaires*, p. 402.

45 "sic gens Romulea surgit ab Hectorea": ibid., p. 405.

46 "te servat pietas, ut nova regna petas": ibid., p. 404. In the *Ilias Latina* of Simon Aurea Capra, these ideals are even further exaggerated; see "La Version Parisienne du poème de Simon Chèvre d'Or sur la guerre de Troie," ed. André Boutemy and others, *Scriptorium* 1 (1946–47): 267–88. I quote from a fragmentary alternate version, ed. Hermann Hagen, *Jahrbucher für class. philo.* 111 (1875): 696–700:

> Si gestus quaeras, elegans, si verba, disertus,
> Si mores, mitis, si genus, altus erat.

> Si proba gesta probas, probus est in Marte probatus,
> Si pia facta, pius traxit ab igne patrem.
> Si laudem laudes, laus eius splendet ubique,
> Ut breviter laudem, nil sibi laude carens.
> (7–12).

[If it's bearing you seek, his was elegant; if it's words, he was eloquent; if manners, his were gentle; if race, he was noble. If you approve noble deeds, his nobility was proven in war; if pious acts, this pious man dragged his father out of the fire. If it's praise that you praise, his praise shines forth everywhere. To praise him in brief: he lacks nothing but praise.]

47 Du Méril, *Poésies populaires*, p. 405. It is interesting to speculate on a pedagogical context and the frequent use of second-person address to Aeneas in the poem, as seen here. To what extent might the second-person be simultaneously addressed to a princely student? Achates, the faithful companion of Aeneas upon his arrivals both in Libya and Latium, is interpreted by "Bernard Silvestris" as a symbol of study in the liberal arts (Jones and Jones, 31.17–26). Does Pierre thus cast himself in his program for imperial imitation?.

48 This excursus may once again reflect the Latin commentary tradition. The redactor's wish to tell his story "asez briemant" (line 4354) is rather like "Anselm's" repeated statement that he will relate some piece of mythology "summatim." Drawing from Servius's explanation of the story of Daedalus and Pasiphae (6.14), "Anselm" comments: "tangenda summatim fabula. Siquidem uulgato martis et ueneris adulterio a sole. et factis subtillissimis catenulis a uulcano et illis ibi simul captis unde postea odium in prolem solis uindicauit." Indeed the French redactor's "roi soltil" ("a fine net," 4361) is rather closer to "Anselm's" "subtillissimis catenulis" than it is to Servius's "minutissimis catenis" or Ovid's "graciles ... catenas" (*Met.* 4.176), although more of the Ovidian narrative is told in the *Eneas* than I have yet found in a manuscript of "Anselm."

49 For the *Eneas*'s version in the context of its ancient and medieval analogues, see Margaret J. Ehrhart, *The Judgment of the Trojan Prince Paris in Medieval Literature* (Philadelphia: University of Pennsylvania Press, 1987), esp. pp. 37–39.

50 See also Huchet, *Le Roman médiéval*, p. 191.

51 The *Eneas* redactor himself identifies Pallas as goddess of that male work, battle: "Pallas, / qui est deesse de bataille..." (lines 146–47).

52 Patterson too points out that the poem's Ovidian allusions "are meaningful solely with reference to a timeless world that stands apart from, and at times even in opposition to, a specifiable and singular historicity" (*Negotiating the Past*, p. 173). Patterson sees this as part of an almost systematic "suppression of historicity" in the *Eneas*. While I agree with him that references like these are largely "relevant at the level of

theme" (p. 172), I do not think that their lack of historical connection deprives them of impact in the imagination of their reader. Rather, like other instances of suppressed challenge discussed below, their incomplete disconnection from history ensures that they can never be fully left behind. Eneas sheds his past, as Patterson shows, but the poem recalls in forms more permanent than his memory the violences he caused in that past. See also Huchet, *Le Roman médiéval*, pp. 58–59, who sees in these mythological "microrécits en abyme" a resistance to chronology. I find Huchet's specific interpretation of the Arachne tale, pp. 204–07, largely unconvincing.

53 My discussion of several Dido laments in this section is indebted to the survey of Latin and vernacular examples by Peter Dronke, "Dido's Lament: From Medieval Latin Lyric to Chaucer," in *Kontinuität und Wandel: Lateinische Poesie von Naevius bis Baudelaire*, eds. U. J. Stache, W. Maaz, and F. Wagner (Hildesheim: Weidmann, 1986), pp. 364–90.

54 This is perhaps most overtly registered in the much–noted word plays on "l'amor" and "la mort," for instance at lines 1302, 1527–28 and 1972. See further David Shirt, "The Dido Episode in the *Enéas*: The Reshaping of Tragedy and its Stylistic Consequences," *Medium Aevum* 51 (1982): 3–17. Shirt makes excellent comments on Dido's "passion which is *death*": "Thoughts of love inevitably lead to thoughts of death as far as Dido is concerned" (pp. 6–7). See also Nolan, pp. 84–90, for a fine discussion of Dido and *fole amor*.

55 Penelope awaiting Ulysses (1), Phyllis married then abandoned by Demophon on his return from the war (2), Briseis separated from Achilles (3), Oenone left behind by Paris (5), Dido (7), Hermione separated from Orestes and betrothed to Pyrrhus in exchange for his aid at Troy (8), Laodamia mourning the departure of Protesilaus for Troy (13), the letter of Helen to Paris (17). For the role of Troy and Virgil in the *Ars Amatoria*, see E. D. Blodgett, "The Well Wrought Void: Reflections on the *Ars Amatoria*," *Classical Journal* 68 (1973): 322–33.

56 Dronke, "Dido's Lament," p. 370.

57 This connection is by no means limited to the *Eneas*. In poem 100 of the *Carmina Burana*, probably only slightly later than the *Eneas*, Dido overtly calls Lavinia an *altera Dido*: "...et thalamos Lavinie / Troianus hospes sequitur! / quid agam misera? / Dido regnat altera!" (4a, lines 7–10; ed. Carl Fischer [Zurich: Artemis, 1974].)

58 "Anna Soror" appears in Oxford, Bodleian Library, Add. A 44, the so–called "Florilège Mixte de Thomas Bekynton," described by Dom A. Wilmart in *Mediaeval and Renaissance Studies* 1 (1941): 41–84 and 4 (1958): 35–90. It is printed by Wilmart, *Mediaeval and Renaissance Studies* 4 (1958), 35–37. It is also edited, with discussion, by Otto Schumann, "Eine mittelalterliche Klage der Dido," in *Liber Floridus: Mittelalterliche Studien Paul Lehmann*, ed. Bernhard Bischoff and Suso Bechter (St. Ottilien: Eos Verlag, 1950), pp. 319–28. Dronke, "Dido's Lament," discusses it

briefly, pp. 370–71. According to Walther, *Initia*, the poem (no. 61) also occurs in Vienna, ONB 208 (s. xv). Dronke, "Dido's Lament" pp. 364–69 and 372–73, offers an eloquent reading of the related Dido poem from the *Carmina Burana*. In it, he finds none of the anger characteristic of Virgil's Dido, but rather an unchanging erotic enslavement: "Dido's only purpose at the moment of dying is to be reunited with Aeneas in the otherworld" (p. 370).

59 "Hospes, abi! / quid elabi, / furtive fugam rapere / quid laboras? / Dido moras / nullas festinat nectere; / sub rume tamen sidere / uult parcere / tibi prolique tenere / nec tradere / uos Nerei tormentis" (strophe 2b). Schumann ("Eine mittelalterliche Klage der Dido," p. 322) mentions further parallels to *Aeneid* 4.51 and 4.305–09.

60 "neque te teneo neque dicta refello:/ i, sequere Italiam uentis, pete regna per undas."

61 "An expectem destrui,/ que statui,/ urbis noue menia?" (4a, 1–3); cf. *Aen.* 4.320–30. Schumann, "Eine mittelalterliche Klage der Dido," pp. 321–22, cites yet further parallels with Virgil.

62 Cf. *Her.* 7.119–28 and 73–75.

63 "Dido's Lament," p. 371.

64 Poirion, "De l'*Énéide*," pp. 224–29, explores the close links between erotics and death in the *Eneas*; here we see the same theme operating, in even more intense form, elsewhere in the tradition.

65 "molt grant tresor, / pailes et dras, argent et or," 389–90.

66 As in other instances studied above, pp. 175–76, the commentary tradition had of course begun clearing this space as early as Servius, who provides the reader with the story Virgil leaves out (1.367): "adpulsa ad Libyam Dido cum ab Hiarba pelleretur, petit callide, ut emeret tantum terrae, quantum posset corium bovis tenere. itaque corium in fila propemodum sectum tetendit occupavitque stadia viginti duo: quam rem leviter tangit Vergilius..." Servius's information is often repeated in the margins of later manuscripts. See Cormier, "Twelfth Century *Adaptatio*," pp. 279–80.

67 In a stylistic note after the quote in the footnote above, Servius points out that Vergil does not use the verb *tegere* (cover), but rather *circumdare* (surround, enclose).

68 It was in medieval Latin that *byrsa* (a proper name in Virgil, *Aen.* 1.367, and explained by Servius as the Greek for "hide") took on the widespread sense of a leather purse and the money from it (see Niermeyer, "byrsa"). Huchet, *Le Roman médiéval*, pp. 116–18, has very good comments on Dido's ruse, though in terms of her producing a verbal, not a mercantile, surplus.

69 Daniel Poirion identifies the golden apple of Paris's judgment as "le symbole d'une sexualité coupable," in *Résurgences: Mythe et littérature à l'âge du symbole* (*XIIe siècle*) (Paris: Presses universitaires de France, 1986), p. 69. It is not surprising that the triad of Paris's rewards – wealth, bravery,

feminine beauty – is echoed in Dido's triad of attributes, with beauty alone changed to *angin*. For the connections between Paris and Dido around these terms, see also Nolan, pp. 86–90.

70 "jingnor... / qui batoient l'or e l'argent" (4403–04).

71 "diues opum studiisque asperrima belli" (1.14).

72 It is worth noting, too, that the Dido of the *Eneas* will repeat none of the Virgilian Dido's threats to call out her troops against the departing Trojans.

73 It should be remembered that Juno, Dido's tutelary goddess, is herself linked to multiples of seven in the *Aeneid*: "sunt mihi bis septem praestanti corpore Nymphae" (1.71). Macrobius, in a long numerological explication that connects seven with a variety of themes, pays particular attention to the development of the fetus in the womb in stages of seven days. See *Commentary on the Dream of Scipio*, trans. William Harris Stahl (New York: Columbia University Press, 1952), pp. 100–17, esp. 112–13.

74 *Scriptores rerum mythicarum*, ed. Bode, cap. 4 (p. 76); see also cap. 4.3 (p. 166).

75 See Angeli's good comments on measure as a theme in the poem, *L'"Eneas,"* pp. 120–21.

76 See Lester K. Little, *Religious Poverty and the Profit Economy in Medieval Europe* (Ithaca: Cornell University Press, 1978), chs. 1 and 2, esp. pp. 38–41.

77 Ibid., p. 35.

78 Erich Auerbach sees in the fantasizing of courtly romance a related aristocratic discomfort at the growing power of trade; see *Mimesis: The Representation of Reality in Western Literature*, trans. Willard R. Trask (Princeton University Press, 1953), p. 138. Alfred Adler explores the links between Carthaginian mercantile *angin* and the tired, elderly passion of Eneas and Dido. "Eneas and Lavine: *Puer et Puella Senes*," *Romanische Forschungen* 71 (1959): 73–91, esp. 80–82. Adler's essay remains, despite its cozy homophobia, one of the most insightful interpretations of the *Eneas*.

79 This section is quite faithful to the *Aeneid* (4.74–79).

80 Cf. *Aen.* 4.134–39.

81 "et li chevals fu aprestez, / d'or et de pierres tot covert," (1492–93); cf. the *porpres* and *pierres* of the Carthage market.

82 Shirt, "The Dido Episode," p. 10.

83 See also Angeli, *L'"Eneas,"* pp. 109–10, on the symbolic role of Dido's oath in this episode; for the repeated references to the breaking of her vow, see p. 116.

84 The spread of male hostility in the *Eneas* can be compared to that in "Anna soror," 4a–4b, where Dido imagines the wrath of her brother, Iarbas, and the murmurs of her own Tyrians.

85 For further discussion, see Nolan, p. 88.

86 The word continues primarily to indicate a weight of money, a pound, in

medieval Latin, but Niermeyer (q.v.) does list the sense of "inclination, desire" as early as the eleventh century. Conversely, in Old French the term is used largely in the sense of "desire," but in a technical discussion it still indicates a weight of gold; see Adolf Tobler and Erhard Lommatzsch, *Altfranzösisches Wörterbuch* (Wiesbaden: Steiner, 1915–), X, col. 59–61.

87 Viewing her sister's corpse, Anna says "or voi ge bien que m'enginastes" (2092, "now I see well that you tricked me").

88 This seems to look forward to the controlled and less threatening erotics of Lavine, whose relation to *amors*, as we have seen, will be one of servant and humble student rather than abandoned patron. The context there will change from feudal obligation to the clerical schoolroom, Lavine being educated in obedience to a Love who in that case serves the already fixed intentions of gods, father, and conqueror. For further discussion of Dido's sequence of laments, see Dronke, "Dido's Lament," pp. 374–77.

89 Raymond Cormier's approach to the term in a context of private feeling is not inconsistent with my emphasis. See "*Comunalement* and *Soltaine* in the *Eneas,*" *Romance Notes* 14 (1972): 1–6.

90 Dido goes on to refer to her broken faith twice again in the next six lines.

91 See Yunck's note 47, *Eneas*, p. 97.

92 For the role of tombs and sepulchres in the romances of antiquity, see Nolan, pp. 25–28.

93 This combination of civic power and excessive love is also to be found in Latin poems like Simon Aurea Capra's *Ilias Latina* (see above, note 40). The Dido of the *Ilias Latina* is even more superhuman, and more explicitly manly in her virtues, than that of the *Eneas*:

> Ut breviter doceam dotes Didonis: eidem
> Posse mori demas, nil vetat esse deam.
> Et genus et regnum sibi nobile, sed cor utroque.
> Nobilius vera nobilitate viget.
> Iustitia, sensu, studiis animoque virilis.
> Praeter amare nimis nil mulieris habens.
> (lines 54–59).

[Let me briefly teach you Dido's qualities: except that she could die, nothing kept her from being a goddess. Both her race and her realm were noble, but her heart was nobler than both, flourishing in true nobility. Manly in justice, in understanding, in study, and in spirit, she had nothing womanly except that she loved too much.].

94 Nolan approaches Dido's epitaph in terms of the poem's ethical structure of foolish and wise love; see pp. 84–87.

95 A recent and important corrective is Patterson's essay cited above. While Patterson sees an emphasis on linear, imperial history as the central gesture of the *Eneas* (in contradistinction to Virgil's ambivalence toward Augustan empire), I think the redaction stands in an unresolved, even

obsessive conflict with forces of anti-historical dilation, figured largely through feminine eroticism such as Dido's but also, as I show below, by homoeroticism and the archaic values of Turnus. Moreover, as Patterson himself notes (p. 181), the episode of Silvia's stag (3525–3782), whose beauty is exaggerated from Virgil as is the violence of its death, further presents a desirable (and possibly Celtic) pastoralism that too stands in opposition to the kind of development promised by Eneas's heir. Another fine essay, exploring the *Eneas* as a poem of dynastic foundation, is Christiane Marchello-Nizia's "De l'*Énéide* à l'*Eneas*: les attributs du fondateur," in *Lectures*, pp. 251–66.

96 For excellent and more extensive comments on this episode, contextualized both in terms of gender theory and of male friendship in the *chansons de geste*, see now Simon Gaunt, "From Epic to Romance: Gender and Sexuality in the *Roman d'Enéas*," *Romanic Review* 83 (1992): 1–27, esp. 6–7, 20–25.

97 A tripartite division of the poem, as proposed by Cormier, centers similarly on the struggle with Turnus and demonstrates the expanded role of *Aeneid* 7–12 in the French redaction; see *One Heart One Mind*, esp. pp. 108–10.

98 Adler sees in the episode an emerging model of Ciceronian friendship that points toward Eneas's divestiture of his earlier cupidinous desires ("Eneas and Lavine," pp. 86–87). It will be recalled that the element of sacrifice in the episode is exactly what will catch the attention of the "Norwich commentator" more than two centuries later, and lead him to allegorize the story in terms of Christ; see ch. 4, pp. 160–63. Gaunt sees it as part of a "marginalization of what might be called a monologic construction of masculinity,... based on the mythic unity of males with no significant engagement with femininity" ("From Epic to Romance," p. 7; see also p. 24). The neatness of closure in the episode supports Gaunt's point; I would suggest, though, that like the tombs discussed below, the episode and its model of exclusively male virtue repeatedly threaten to escape their marginalized status by means of echoes and parallels in other loves, other deaths.

99 See pp. 178–80, above.

100 The manuscript setting of the *Roman d'Eneas* sometimes pushes this process even further by making the poem only one in a sequence of ancient narratives. See ch. 1, p. 20. See also the comments on how the poem is inserted, in its manuscripts, into a "cycle recounting the rise of the west": Singerman, *Under Clouds of Poesy*, pp. 119–36.

101 Consider, just for one example, the great care with which the redactor describes the siting of Eneas's first defensive fortress in Latium, lines 3145–65.

102 *Etymologies and Genealogies: A Literary Anthropology of the French Middle Ages* (Chicago and London: University of Chicago Press, 1983), pp. 66–79.

103 See for instance lines 2819–20, which closely translate *Aen.* 6.681–82;

the redactor follows Virgil where he emphasizes lineage and number. Again at 2879–82 lineage is emphasized by explicit terms (cf. *Aen.* 6.716–18). And finally at 2933–68 Anchises sketches the Roman imperial line. Patterson, pp. 174–76, makes a telling argument for the suppression of a dangerous past in so neatly linear a genealogy. Marchello-Nizia also emphasizes genealogical themes in the poem, especially in the context of its elaborate tombs; see "De l'*Énéide* à l'*Eneas*," pp. 254–56.

104 Nolan's book now provides a rich context for this discussion. See her chapter, "*Plaits*, debates, and judgments in the *Roman de Thèbes*, the *Roman de Troie*, and the *Roman d'Eneas*," pp. 48–74.

105 The links between beauty and death in both these characters is explored by Poirion ("De l'*Énéide*," pp. 219–22). Gaunt also emphasizes their status as doubles, "From Epic to Romance," p. 12.

106 Poirion, "De l'*Énéide*," pp. 221–22, discusses the two tombs as a temporal resistance to death.

107 I do not suggest that Eneas's own affection for Pallas, and his lament over Pallas's death, necessarily imply an erotic bond. But that possibility is overtly raised by Amata's later accusations of Eneas's homosexuality (8567–611) and its impact on reproduction (8596–98), and by Lavine's brief acquiescence (9130–70). A much more developed discussion of the issue is Gaunt, "From Epic to Romance." For the erotic implications of an androgyne Camille and a homosexually desired Pallas, see Poirion, *Résurgences*, pp. 72–75.

108 The quilt, "quatre esmaus ot as quatre cors" (6120); the helmet, "sus el pomel ot quatre esmaus" (4437).

109 See Marchello–Nizia, "De l'*Énéide* à l'*Eneas*," pp. 254–55.

110 Dido: "Malvese foi ont Troïan!" (1700). Pallas's mother: "lor male foiz vos ont mostree" (6326), "Malveise foi vos demostrerent" (6332).

111 The temple of Juno at Carthage: "molt estoit riche a desmesure" (517). Pallas's tomb: "molt fu riche a desmesure" (6412).

112 Carthage: "Li mur sont fait a pastorals, / a pilerez et a merals, / a bisches, oisiaus, a flors; / o le marbre de cent colors / sont painturé defors li mur, / sanz vermeillon et sanz azur" (427–32). Pallas's tomb: "li quarrel sont de cent colors, / tailliez o bisches et o flors" (6427–28).

113 Poirion ("De l'*Énéide*," p. 224) has explored the linkage of love and death in the *Eneas* through his examination of the "marvelous" tombs of Pallas and Camilla. He sees in this linkage a superposition of Virgilian myth and Ovidian eroticism. "L'amour derrière la mort, la mort derrière l'amour: le lecteur du moyen âge a pu découvrir cet échange dans l'*Eneas* qui double l'épopée virgilienne d'un art d'aimer ovidien."

114 Yunck, *Eneas*, p. 183, note 114.

115 For an extended treatment, focusing on her extended portrait, see Aimé Petit, "La reine Camille dans le *Roman d'Énéas*," *Les Lettres romanes* 36 (1982): 5–40. I discuss the illustrations in ch. 1, pp. 25–28.

116 "Laissiez ester desmesurance..." (7081). Camille's potential for excess is even seen in her appearance; her hair flows out the cape of her hauberk, down her back and over her whole body to the horse's back (6929–34). See also Huchet, *Le Roman médiéval*, pp. 74–76.

117 This helmet is so described as also to recall the death of Eurialus at the poem's exclusively male center. In Virgil, Euryalus weights himself down with practically a whole set of plundered arms (9.359–66), but in the *Eneas*, he takes only a glittering helmet (5086–89); this more closely aligns his fall with that of Camille who exposes herself to the spear of Arranz in her pursuit of the helmet (7169–206).

118 These numbers may further help configure the common thematic threats to patriarchy we have seen explored in Dido, Pallas's death, and Camille. While Dido's Carthage was made up of sevens, tens, and their multiples – numbers thus, in the Macrobian scheme, both earthly and heavenly, human and divine, elemental and mathematical – these numbers split off from one another in their later association with Pallas and Camille. Pallas's tomb is associated with the square of ten (6427), the divine and perfect number, whereas Camille (*via* the helmet) is linked to the worldly, elemental, generative number seven. But note that seven is also associated with Athena and virginity (Macrobius, trans. Stahl, p. 102), and thus on its own very appropriate to Camille.

119 Parallels and contrasts among Camille, Pallas, and Dido are discussed by Petit, "La Reine Camille," pp. 21–25 and 39.

120 The tomb is assembled, we hear repeatedly, "mestrement" (7541) and "par mestrie" (7546).

121 In "Romance and Tragedy in the Knight's Tale: Chaucer's Dark Statius," delivered at the 1987 meeting of the New Chaucer Society, Winthrop Wetherbee argues for an even more resonant though indirect echo of Dido's passion in this moment, which recalls the tethered bird of the funeral games in *Aeneid* 5, and thence the release of Dido's spirit by Iris in Book Four.

122 Arguing from a psychoanalytic perspective, Jean-Charles Huchet argues for an even tighter pairing of Camille and Pallas as inverted reflections of one another; see "L'Énéas: un roman spéculaire" in *Relire le "Roman d'Eneas,"* pp. 63–81.

123 Adler discusses Turnus's commitment to an aging feudal system ("Eneas and Lavine," pp. 82–83). See also the good comments on the archaism of Turnus's social assumptions by Cormier (*One Heart One Mind*, pp. 187–95).

124 For a discussion of the theme of lineage as a way of suppressing the more uncomfortable aspects of Eneas's history, see Patterson, *Negotiating the Past*, pp. 173–77.

125 Occasional details in the pedagogical tradition, it will be recalled, also practice this move from *antiquam ... matrem* to a specifically patriarchal destiny for the Trojans. See above, pp. 176–77.

126 Latinus's soothsayer sees in Aeneas an *externum . . . uirum* (7.68–69), and
     the oracle of Faunus calls the Trojans *externi . . . generi* (7.98).

127 There is striking congruence between versions of Ilioneus's speech to
     Latinus in Virgil (7.213–48) and the *Eneas* (3177–222), but in the latter
     the justification of lineage and divinity is even more emphatic: "Nostre
     ancestre fu nez de ci, / qui funda Troie et lo donjon; / bien sai que
     Dardanus ot nom; / par les deus somes revertu / ça dont nostre linnages
     fu" (3202–06). Later Eneas will justify himself to Evander in exactly
     similar terms: "Quant la cité destruistrent Gré, / si me comanderent li
     dé / que o tote ma compaigne / m'an revenisse an Lonbardie, / la dont
     nostre ancestre fu nez, / qui Dardanus fu apelez, / qui funda Troie la
     cité" (4711–17).

128 Bloch, *Etymologies*, p. 69.

129 See also Huchet, *Le Roman médiéval*, pp. 93–94.

130 Poirion, too, notes how the redactor retains largely those pagan gods
     who work to Eneas's benefit ("De l'*Énéide*," p. 215).

131 Ironically but understandably, Amata's messenger characterizes Lati-
     nus's action with a term until now associated with feminity and fatality:
     "desmesurance" (3447).

132 R. Howard Bloch, *Medieval French Literature and Law* (Berkeley: University
     of California Press, 1977), p. 64; see also p. 66.

133 Turnus's later speech to Latinus will be even more replete with
     terminology of feudal possession and obligation; see especially lines
     3847–68. For Turnus's orations, see also Nolan, pp. 71–72.

134 See for instance Latinus's speech to his barons during the first truce in
     the war, especially lines 6545–68 where he appeals both to *linnage* and,
     repeatedly, to *li deu*; and see Eneas's similar argument of lineage and
     divine guidance before he engages in single combat with Turnus, lines
     9351–66.

135 Bloch, *Literature and Law*, pp. 16–21, 64–66, 108–20.

136 This language of *mesure* and legal process will reappear in the affair of
     Eneas and Lavine; see below, pp. 215–19.

137 *Literature and Law*, p. 9.

138 Ibid., pp. 112, 120.

139 For the love of Dido and Eneas, and particularly the role of dialogue
     therein, see also Nolan, pp. 92–95.

140 Huchet, *Le Roman médiéval*, pp. 25–26, discusses the inadequacy of simple
     mutuality to legitimate marriage; the consent of a third, the voice of the
     father, is needed. In the disastrous mutual affair of Dido and Eneas, of
     course, no such third party sanctions the match.

141 See Gaunt, "From Epic to Romance," p. 18.

142 For the discourse of love in the Lavine episode, particularly as figured in
     the description of Amors, see Huchet's fine chapter, "La naissance de
     l'amour," in *Le Roman médiéval*, pp. 151–74.

143 Further, Dido carried one hundred arrows of gold (1477), and within

three lines (8057–59) Lavine is struck by Cupid's dart and changes color one hundred times.

144 Moreover, as Poirion points out (*Résurgences*, p. 71), the dominant deity in this affair is no longer Venus but rather her son Cupid, "principe d'un amour viril et conquérant qu'incarnera Lavine."

145 For fuller discussion of this passage and Dido's analogous inability to name Eneas, see Gaunt, "From Epic to Romance," pp. 16–18.

146 See also Poirion, "De l'*Énéide*," p. 225, and his further comments in *Résurgences*, p. 75.

147 The poem's connection of woman, realm, and land, particularly through rhymes, is explored by Marchello-Nizia, "De l'*Énéide* à l'*Eneas*," pp. 252–54; and from a psychoanalytic perspective by Huchet, *Le Roman médiéval*, *passim*, but see esp. pp. 30–31.

148 For discussion of this dialogue, see Cormier, *One Heart One Mind*, pp. 241–46.

149 Cormier, *One Heart One Mind*, discusses this passage in terms of a community of mind between Eneas and Lavine, and its implications for the state; see pp. 275–85.

6 WRITING THE READING OF VIRGIL.

1 See App. I, nos. 8, 9, 10, 12, 13, 15, 18, 19 for manuscripts annotated in the fourteenth century; and nos. 23, 24, 25 for manuscripts copied then.

2 This is manuscript "C," London, BL Add. 34114. See the edition of J.-J. Salverda de Grave, *Eneas* (Paris: CFMA, 1973), I, p. iv. For a fuller description, see Paul Meyer, "Récit de la Première Croisade," *Romania* 5 (1876): 2–4.

3 For a broad survey of the multiple states of classical tradition by Chaucer's time, see (in addition to the chapters above) John P. McCall, *Chaucer Among the Gods: The Poetics of Classical Myth* (University Park: Pennsylvania State University Press, 1979), and Alastair J. Minnis, *Chaucer and Pagan Antiquity* (Cambridge: Brewer, 1982).

4 Chaucer's capacity to absorb the authoritative voice of ancient Latin poetry is eloquently argued by Winthrop Wetherbee in *Chaucer and the Poets: An Essay on "Troilus and Criseyde"* (Ithaca and London: Cornell University Press, 1984). Yet Wetherbee's own readings are profoundest, perhaps, when he explores Chaucer reading the ancients through a medieval optic, as in "Thebes and Troy: Statius and Dante's Statius," pp. 111–44.

5 For discussion of dates, see *The Riverside Chaucer*, gen. ed. Larry D. Benson (Boston: Houghton Mifflin, 1987) pp. 978 and 1059. All Chaucer quotations will be taken from this edition.

6 *Canterbury Tales* VII, 3141–50 (Andromache's dream and the death of Hector), 3228–29 (Sinon), 3355–59 (the Trojan women and the death of

Priam). For the date of the tale, see Susan Cavanaugh's notes in *The Riverside Chaucer*, pp. 935–36.

7 Barbara Nolan's recent treatment of the *Troilus* in terms of the *roman antique* supersedes all previous discussion of this poem and the literary reception of Troy and Thebes. Her chapter offers an important complement to my focus on Chaucer's more specifically Virgilian inheritance in the *House of Fame* and *Legend of Good Women*. See her ch. 6, "Saving the poetry: authors, translators, texts, and readers in Chaucer's *Book of Troilus and Criseyde*," pp. 198–246.

8 Robert W. Frank provides a lucid analysis of Chaucer's growth as a narrative technician between the two versions; see *Chaucer and The Legend of Good Women* (Cambridge: Harvard University Press, 1972), pp. 57–78.

9 *Legend of Good Women*, line 725.

10 The narrator is not named until line 729, and then quite casually by the golden eagle who soars aloft carrying the terrified Geffrey in his talons.

In *Chaucer and the Fictions of Gender* (Berkeley: University of California Press, 1992), Elaine Tuttle Hansen proposes a telling linkage between the narrator's at best unstable masculinity and Dido's insistently typical femininity: "it is actually impossible for the figure of the poet as represented here to leave Woman behind him completely, in part because femininity as Dido represents it is so obviously integral to his own nature and experience" (p. 98). The contradiction between my proposal of Aeneas and Tuttle Hansen's proposal of Dido as narratorial models is more apparent than real. Aeneas, of course, cannot leave Dido behind either: there she is in the Underworld, and in the whole aetiology of the Punic Wars. More important, Aeneas himself is explicitly feminized in Troy; Dido protects him and Iarbas scorns him along with the whole "semiuiro comitatu" (*Aen.* 4.215) of Trojans. Further, the parallels I adduce below feature Aeneas at moments of nearly passive aesthetic response, as open to visual influence as is Dido herself in the presence of Aeneas's body.

11 William Joyner has also identified a "carefully worked–out parallel relationship ... between the summary version of Aeneas's voyage to Carthage and Italy and the dreamer's account of his own journey to the halls of Fame and Rumor" (p. 3). See "Parallel Journeys in Chaucer's *House of Fame*," *Papers on Language and Literature* 12 (1976): 3–19. Joyner finds these parallels largely in elements of plot (see p. 4); many are quite convincing, while others seem too strained or too much the common stuff of any quest narrative to work as "parallels." The connection I will try to make operates rather less through narrative links than through a convergence of the settings in which Aeneas and Geffrey find themselves, taking "settings" both in the sense of physical place and of exegetical reception.

12 Joseph Dane, in "Chaucer's *House of Fame* and the *Rota Virgilii*," *Classical and Modern Literature* 1 (1980): 57–75, makes an intriguing proposal that

the three books of the *House of Fame* employ, in reverse order, the three levels of style (and content) that were associated with the works of Virgil in medieval rhetorical analysis: "humilis, mediocris, grandiloquus," as Geoffrey of Vinsauf put it (p. 59). Dane also thinks that Chaucer's Book Three reprises all three styles, starting after line 1307. Dane's claims about didactic "middle" style in Book Two seem very apt, while his argument for an "epic" high style in Book One works less well. It seems important that Chaucer turns the traditional order of the styles on its head; many of Dane's points become more convincing if we think of Chaucer as parodying or deconstructing these aspects of Virgilian style. For the *rota* and its general diffusion, see also *Enciclopedia* IV, pp. 586–87.

13 Structural and verbal echoes of Virgil, Ovid, Dante, French dream poets, and Boccaccio in the poem are well established. W. O. Sypherd, *Studies in Chaucer's House of Fame* (London: Chaucer Society, 1907), part 1 (French dream poets); Edgar F. Shannon, *Chaucer and the Roman Poets* (1929; repr. New York: Russell and Russell, 1964), pp. 48–119 (still the fundamental survey for echoes of Ovid and Virgil); McCall, *Chaucer Among the Gods*, pp. 48–58 (use of classical mythology); John Fyler, *Chaucer and Ovid* (New Haven: Yale University Press, 1979), chs. 1 and 2 (Fyler's study is especially helpful in pointing out how Ovid contests, even subverts, the authority of Virgil, pp. 3–17); Piero Boitani, *Chaucer and the Imaginary World of Fame* (Woodbridge, Suffolk: D. S. Brewer, 1984), chs. 3 and 4; David Wallace, *Chaucer and the Early Writings of Boccaccio* (Woodbridge, Suffolk: D. S. Brewer, 1985), ch. 1; and references to earlier literature in each. The most elaborate effort to link the poem systematically with the *Divine Comedy* is by B. G. Koonce, *Chaucer and the Tradition of Fame* (Princeton University Press, 1966); Koonce outlines his strategy pp. 73–88. More convincing is Piero Boitani's discussion in "What Dante Meant to Chaucer," in *Chaucer and the Italian Trecento*, ed. Boitani (Cambridge University Press, 1983). Boitani traces Chaucer's meditation on Dantean poetics in *The House of Fame*, pp. 117–25, but also sees there a "counterpoint to Dante" (p. 122) by which Chaucer sets out his own poetic limits and ambitions: "Between the Proem to Book II and the Invocation in Book III ... Chaucer thus comes to understand the limits of his 'vertu' and his 'art', measuring them against Dante's achievements" (p. 124).

14 *Chaucer's House of Fame: The Poetics of Skeptical Fideism* (University of Chicago Press, 1972), p. 1.

15 Most recently, J. M. Gellrich, *The Idea of The Book in the Middle Ages* (Ithaca: Cornell University Press, 1985), ch. 5; and Robert M. Jordan, *Chaucer's Poetics and the Modern Reader* (Berkeley: University of California Press, 1987), ch. 2.

16 An approach from a quite distinct perspective that nonetheless converges with many of my conclusions is offered by Penelope Reed Doob, in *The Idea of the Labyrinth from Classical Antiquity through the Middle Ages* (Ithaca and

London: Cornell University Press, 1990), pp. 307–39. Doob uses the persistent presence of labyrinths, both literal and metaphoric, in the poem to explore its themes of literary authority, textual reception, and poetic creation: "Given its available sources, poetry ... must necessarily be a labyrinth, however 'wonderlych ywroughte' in imitation of Daedalus. Its validity is dubious, its meaning ambiguous, its reception unpredictable. For a poem that discusses these issues, what more appropriate controlling image could there be than the labyrinth, on one hand the most elaborate of artistic creations, on the other a prison of error for anyone trapped within and deprived of philosophical wings?" (pp. 335–36). The labyrinth is both a thematic motif and an image of the narrator's quest, and Doob deploys it in the richest and most unified reading I know. Most important, perhaps, the traditional view of the labyrinth as a triumph of human artifice allows Doob to identify the poem's paradoxical optimism: "Believing all this, some men might despair, but that response would never occur to Geoffrey, whose dream, after all, is wonderful: if these be labyrinths, they are enchanting ones, as full of delight as of frustration" (p. 337).

17 For comment on this passage as a kind of interlingual play on "kan" and "cano," see Joseph A. Dane, "Yif I 'arma uirumque' kan: Note on Chaucer's *House of Fame*, Line 143," *American Notes and Queries* 19 (1981): 134–36.

18 This much has been widely noted. Shannon, *Chaucer and the Roman Poets*, pp. 104–06. John M. Steadman, "Chaucer's 'Desert of Libye,' Venus, and Jove (*The House of Fame*, 486–87)," *Modern Language Notes* 76 (1961): 196–201. C. P. R. Tisdale, "The *House of Fame*: Virgilian Reason and Boethian Wisdom," *Comparative Literature* 25 (1973): 247–61, esp. 248 and 254. More recently, see David L. Jeffrey, "Sacred and Secular Scripture: Authority and Interpretation in *The House of Fame*," *Chaucer and Scriptural Tradition*, ed. Jeffrey (University of Ottawa Press, 1984), pp. 209–13, where Jeffrey links the similarity of situations to the problem of readership. Nolan's recent book has a brilliant section on the use of visual perspective as a narrative device in the *roman antique*, which powerfully complements my remarks here. See "Inner and outer perspectives in the *Roman de Troie*," pp. 28–44, and especially the discussion of *Durchsehung*, pp. 29–30.

19 Virgil here uses *aënus* to describe the metal used in the temple. Mandelbaum's translation is not quite accurate; brass was little known in the ancient world (see C. T. Lewis and C. Short, *A Latin Dictionary* [Oxford: Clarendon, 1975], "aes"). But brass was known in Chaucer's time and it was with "brass" and "brassyn," a century later, that Gavin Douglas translated Virgil's terms: *Virgil's "Aeneid" Translated into Scottish Verse by Gavin Douglas*, ed. David F. C. Coldwell, II (Edinburgh and London: Wm. Blackwood for the Scottish Text Society, 1957), Book

One, ch. 7, lines 55–57, p. 48. And there is a nice appropriateness to engraving the hero's story on a "table" whose metal recalls his name.

20 Beryl Rowland, "Bishop Bradwardine, the Artificial Memory, and the House of Fame," *Chaucer at Albany*, ed. R. H. Robbins (New York: Burt Franklin, 1975), pp. 41–62.

21 Renate Blumenfeld–Kosinski points out that the temple at Thebes "bears a singular resemblance to a precious medieval book" ("The Gods as Metaphor in the *Roman de Thèbes*," *Modern Philology* 83 (1985): 7).

22 For a related discussion of Aeneas's double poetic voices, "participatory" or "authorial," and their connection to moments of activity or more static observation, see the fine essay by Charles Segal, "Art and the Hero: Participation, Detachment, and Narrative Point of View in *Aeneid* 1," *Arethusa* 14 (1981): 67–83.

23 This aspect of the epic is not just the product of modern preoccupation with signs, visions, and interpretation. In his *Policraticus* (ed. C. C. I. Webb [Oxford University Press, 1909], I, Book Two, ch. 15), John of Salisbury treats the *Aeneid* almost as a dream book. John's discussion of dreams derives closely from Macrobius, though he treats them in a different order. More interestingly, he adds a number of examples to Macrobius, most of them from Virgil. Nightmare (*insomnium*) is discussed in terms of Dido's dreams of Aeneas (as in Macrobius). But the enigmatic dream (*somnium*) brings to John's mind the example of the Sibyl, and the frequency of nightmares in autumn reminds him of the leaves of the elm tree, filled with empty dreams, in the vestibule of Virgil's Underworld. And again, John's examples of *oraculum* from the *gentilium libris* focus on Aeneas and his visits from Anchises, Jupiter, Apollo and others.

24 See the very rich entry on this word in the *Middle English Dictionary*, particularly sections 3 and 4. See also the *Oxford English Dictionary* sections II9 and II12. Chaucer was using "figure" in its technical, hermeneutic sense as early as *c.* 1366, in the A.B.C. As we will see, even the strictly typological sense of "figure" is relevant to Chaucer's use of the word in the *House of Fame*.

25 The situation is complicated still further, John Fyler reminds us, by Virgil's own reputation among some medieval readers (like Alanus de Insulis) as "half historian, half liar" (*Chaucer and Ovid*, pp. 30–31).

26 See A. C. Friend, "Chaucer's Version of the *Aeneid*," *Speculum* 28 (1953): 317–23; L. B. Hall, "Chaucer and the Dido-and-Aeneas Story," *Medieval Studies* 25 (1963): 148–59; also J. A. W. Bennett, *Chaucer's Book of Fame* (Oxford: Clarendon Press, 1968), pp. 24–46. Bennett's suggestions about Geffrey's "Ovidian" reading of Virgil are especially useful. Of course, an Ovidianized Troy story is a major aspect of the "romance" versions of Virgil like the *Eneas*. A fourteenth-century version of the French *Histoire ancienne jusqu'à César* inserts letters from the *Heroides* into a narrative otherwise largely taken from Virgil and prose historians. See Clem C. Williams, "A Case of Mistaken Identity: Still Another Trojan Narrative

in Old French Prose," *Medium Aevum* 53 (1984): 59–72, and further references there.

27 See Fyler, *Chaucer and Ovid*, pp. 33–34.

28 See ch. 5, pp. 176–78, for a look at one of these summaries and other historical material from the pedagogical tradition. As I note there, further, these summaries often suppress Dido's story and concentrate instead on Aeneas's imperial fate; this too may have parallels with the diminution of overtly "pedagogical" details when Dido enters Geffrey's narrative.

29 The discussion above (pp. 223–30), by contrast, assumes a quite sophisticated level of response to Virgil's depiction of Aeneas, his role as a reader and viewer, and the place of ecphrasis in *Aeneid* Books One and Six. We should not, however, confuse Chaucer's clever construction of a narrative voice with Chaucer's own complete reaction to the text his narrator is now summarizing.

30 See pp. 54–58. In a related argument, William S. Wilson has shown that much of the simplified and hurried tone of Book One reflects practices of teaching lower level grammar in the period; see "Exegetical Grammar in the *House of Fame*," *English Language Notes* 1 (1964): 244–48.

31 For the classicizing friars, as explored in Beryl Smalley's groundbreaking studies, see above, ch. 4, pp. 138, 158–59. Smalley documents the friars' impressive command of Latin prose history. The increasing use of parallel and background texts, ancient and medieval, by readers of the *Aeneid* is nicely illustrated by the scribal glosses in Oxford, Ashmole 54 (Appendix I, no. 26), of the fifteenth century. The glossator there cites Guido delle Colonne, Ovid's *Metamorphoses*, "Ebrardus" (presumably Eberhard of Bethune), and others.

32 Elsewhere, Geffrey speaks of "Cresus, that was king of Lyde, / That high upon a gebet dyde" (105–06) and of "Demophon, duk of Athenys" (388).

33 There are, however, occasional telling parallels. At *Aen.* 1.52 "rex Aeolus," several glossators explain briefly that Aeolus is king of the winds. (Add27304, earliest layer of notes: "Eolus fuit rex uentorum et habuit dominium super omnes tempestates." Add27304's later fourteenth-century notes are even closer to Chaucer at 1.76, calling Aeolus "deus uentorum." London, BL Add. 32319A [App. I, no. 14], earliest notes: "Poete fingunt hunc esse regem uentorum." Oxford, Bodleian Library, Auct. F.1.17 [App. I, no. 23, s. xiv], even more simply: "scilicet uentorum.") Add27304 calls Juno "illa dea" (at 1.36). Virgil himself is almost self-glossing when he regularly calls Aeneas's first wife "coniunx Creusa" (2.597, 651, and 738).

34 E. K. Rand, "Chaucer in Error," *Speculum* 1 (1926): 222–25. Alfred David, "How Marcia Lost Her Skin: A Note on Chaucer's Mythology," in *The Learned and the Lewed*, ed. L. D. Benson (Cambridge: Harvard University Press, 1974), pp. 19–29. Francis X. Newman, " 'Partriches

Wynges': A Note on *Hous of Fame*, 1391–92," *Mediaevalia* 6 (1980): 231–38.

35 Virgil does switch freely between the two names for Aeneas's one son by Creusa, and has Mercury use both names in one line when he warns Aeneas to flee Carthage (4.274–75): "Ascanium surgentem et spes heredis Iuli / respice." Rand, however, points out that Livy was uncertain about the number and maternity of Aeneas's sons, and that Servius repeats some of Livy's doubt (223); so the confusion is not certainly unique or original to Chaucer. It is certain that Chaucer had gained a clearer command of the narrative by the time he retold it in the "Legend of Dido"; see below.

36 See Shannon, *Chaucer and the Roman Poets*, pp. 88–89. David has argued that this error could stem from an interpolated version of the myth found in some manuscripts of the *Roman de la Rose*, in which the satyr is feminine ("How Marcia Lost Her Skin," p. 26). Like the confusion about Iulus and Ascanius, though, it may well be a straightforward mistake.

37 This could result, it has been proposed, from a transcription error in a Virgil manuscript, reading "perdicibus" (partridges') for Virgil's "pernicibus alis," 4.180. The idea is plausible, though I have yet to encounter this error in a manuscript. Of course, it would only take one. Newman, " 'Partriches Wynges'," suggests that the Ovidian myth of Perdix, transformed into a partridge, has dark connotations appropriate to Chaucer's concept of Fame.

38 I would not dismiss the possibility, though, that these errors could be intentionally constructed as part of Geffrey's inadequate pedantry, showing the reverse side to the pompous glossing examined just above. They are not especially obscure mistakes; to many readers they would have been laughably obvious, and could have contributed to the impression of a narrator still wandering among the most basic of exegetical modes, even as he will later wander with equally uncomprehending enthusiasm among far more sophisticated interpretive settings.

39 See ch. 4, pp. 148–49.

40 Sanford Brown Meech long ago showed that Chaucer had indeed used a translation to aid his access to Ovid. See "Chaucer and an Italian Translation of the *Heroides*," *Publications of the Modern Language Association of America* 45 (1930): 110–28. A fairly loose, fourteenth-century Italian translation of the *Aeneid* by Andrea Lancia may also have been available to Chaucer; see Hall, "Chaucer and the Dido-and-Aeneas Story," p. 148.

41 Hall in particular points out the similarities of narrative organization between Chaucer and other vernacular versions of the Troy story ("Chaucer and the Dido-and-Aeneas Story"). Dane, however, points out that Chaucer seems to hesitate between the two orders ("Rota," pp. 63–64).

42 Possible relations between architectural structures in the *House of Fame*

and medieval memory books have been studied by Rowland, "Bishop Bradwardine."

43 This shift may further reflect Geffrey's re-enactment of Aeneas at the temple of Juno. For the report of Aeneas too moves, though rather more subtly, from him seeing pictures ("uidet ... uidebat ... agnoscit," 1.456–70) to perceiving distraught women rather more directly ("interea ad templum non aequae Palladis ibant ... Iliades," 1.479–80), and back to seeing a picture of himself ("se quoque ... agnouit," 1.488).

44 This move away from and return to ecphrasis has been widely noted, for instance by Boitani, *World of Fame*, p. 10.

45 A. C. Friend, "Chaucer's Version of the *Aeneid*," has pointed out several telling parallels between Chaucer's Trojan narrative and the organization and certain details of the same narrative in the mid-twelfth century *Ilias* of Simon Aurea Capra (ed. André Boutemy and others, "La Version Parisienne du poème de Simon Chèvre d'Or sur la guerre de Troie," *Scriptorium* 1 [1946–47]: 267–88). The most convincing of these is the detail, in Simon (411) and Chaucer (182) but absent from Virgil, that Creusa was lost along a byway (p. 318). As notes below will show, I think that Simon had a rather more substantial impact on the later "Legend of Dido."

46 A telling piece of Dido's erotic prehistory, her oath to remain loyal to her dead husband Sychaeus (*Aen.* 4.24–29), is suppressed both here and in the *Legend of Good Women*. In each case, the absence of erotic commitment removes any courtly blame Dido might bear for infidelity. In the "Legend of Dido," though, it also increases the sense of Dido's initial regal independence.

47 In perhaps its most striking similarity to the *House of Fame*, the *Ilias* of Simon Aurea Capra (ed. Boutemy) also virtually omits the central events of the affair: the hunt, storm, cave scene, and aftermath in Carthage. Simon too moves straight from Aeneas's erotic delay to his sudden preparations to depart (ed. Boutemy, 601–06); see Friend, "Chaucer's Version of the *Aeneid*," pp. 320–21. But Simon's general focus is on the imperial story of Troy and Rome, and his tone is quite unlike Chaucer's. Simon is clear that Aeneas is properly following the urgings of the paternal spirits, the gods, and the fates ("Quem patrii manes, quem dii, quem fata perurgent," 605); and while (like Geffrey) he addresses Dido directly, Simon does so only to assure her that she has no strength against the gods and fates ("Non facis ut retrahas quem sua fata trahunt," 634).

48 See lines 364–74. The reader, instead, is referred to Virgil or Ovid for the full story: "Whoso to knowe it hath purpos, / Rede Virgile in Eneydos / Or the Epistle of Ovyde" (377–79).

49 This displacement of Dido's erotic suffering from narrative time should be compared to quite similar effects in some of the Latin laments of Dido examined in ch. 5, pp. 187–89. Of course, it is just to this tradition that Chaucer is moving in these passages.

50 *Chaucer and Ovid*, p. 37.
51 Götz Schmitz, *The Fall of Women in Early English Narrative Verse* (Cambridge University Press, 1990) notes the almost exclusively Ovidian tone of the episode, and the absence of even the typically indirect Ovidian irony in Dido's speeches and Geffrey's responses here (pp. 34–36); "there are few Virgilian echoes in the episode, and there is none of the Ovidian innuendo. Chaucer's Dido is a guileless girl..." (p. 34).
52 Geffrey's insertion of alternate examples of male treachery tends to reduce the pathos of Dido to nothing *more* than an example. This move into reductionist moralizing has real parallels in the somewhat unreflective quest for *exempla* seen in the late fourteenth-century notes in Add27304.
53 On the "jarring return" to Virgilian authority at this point, see also Fyler, *Chaucer and Ovid*, p. 39.
54 "Chaucer's 'Desert of Libye,' " pp. 199–200; see also Tisdale, "Virgilian Reason and Boethian Wisdom," pp. 254–55. Shannon pointed out another parallel to Virgil and the story of Ganymede carried off by an eagle, which Juno broods on at the beginning of *Aeneid* 1; see *Chaucer and the Roman Poets*, pp. 106–13.
55 See also Joyner, "Parallel Journeys," pp. 6–7.
56 Tisdale also posits a move from Virgilian to Boethian themes in Book Two ("Virgilian Reason and Boethian Wisdom," pp. 256–61). He is unaware of the earlier linkage between the two authors in the commentaries, however; and he sees Boethian ascent as a final resolution to the poem. "The eagle, the feathers of Philosophy, translates [the narrator's] mind beyond the clouds of mortality to a clear understanding of truth" (p. 260). To find such a resolution, Tisdale must almost ignore the descent with which the poem closes: see below.
57 The best treatment of the eagle, and particularly his humor, is by John Leyerle, "Chaucer's Windy Eagle," *University of Toronto Quarterly* 40 (1971): 247–265.
58 The literalized imagery of Book Two also brings to mind aspects of the "pedagogical" approach. Here I would scarcely argue for a programmatic exploitation of a mode of Virgilian reading. But the pedagogical exegesis of Virgil was most actively pursued in the basic education of the lower schools, the setting of *grammatica*, whose thematics as Martin Irvine has shown also take a central place in the *House of Fame* Book Two; see "Medieval Grammatical Theory and Chaucer's *House of Fame*," *Speculum* 60 (1985): 850–76. As Irvine notes, Virgil was a centrally cited author in the fundamental texts of grammar, such as Priscian's *Institutiones*; see pp. 854–55. Indeed, in the central texts of *grammatica*, Virgil is the primary source of normative examples, and in the process of extracting illustrative passages from the *Aeneid*, the grammarians atomize Virgil almost as fully as the eagle does Boethius. On the didactic tone of the book, see Dane, "Rota," pp. 65–68. The historical interests of the

pedagogical approach, with its careful attempts to distinguish fact from poetic invention, are also reflected by the battling pillar dwellers of Book Three.

59 Virgil's description of Fama had become a commonplace, quoted by Isidore and many other widely consulted writers, as Boitani, *World of Fame*, points out (p. 41). For the general relevance here of Aeneas as "almost a personification of fame," see Boitani, *World of Fame*, p. 167. See also Bennett, *Chaucer's Book of Fame*, pp. 129–32 on the intermingled Virgilian and Boethian echoes in Fame.

60 On tensions within medieval reports of the Troy story, see also Fyler, *Chaucer and Ovid*, pp. 30–32.

61 See Jones and Jones, p. 30.7–10.

62 Joyner, "Parallel Journeys," p. 11, sees in this figure a parallel to Mercury at Carthage, urging Aeneas to continue his journey. The analogy seems distant at first glance, yet other elements also press us to see this passage as a re-emergence of the *Aeneid* narrative.

63 In its synthesis of these linked texts, then, the House of Twigs works similarly to the Temple of Venus and House of Fame earlier in the poem.

64 For a superb discussion of the House of Rumor as itself a labyrinth, see Doob, *The Idea of the Labyrinth*, pp. 326–31.

65 See also Boitani, *World of Fame*, p. 210, and Doob, *The Idea of the Labyrinth*, p. 330.

66 Consider: "werres" – bellum (6.279), "reste" – consanguineus Leti Sopor (6.278), "labor" – labos (6.277), "deeth" – Letumque (6.277), "stryf" – Discordia (6.281), "seknesse"–Morbi (6.275), "drede" – Metus (6.276), "famyne" – malesuada Fames (6.276), "ruine" – turpis Egestas (6.276).

67 Who is the "man of gret auctorite"? Every exegete is allowed one guess: for this reader's imagination, he is Virgil's Aeneas, the double whom Geffrey has been so inadequately mimicking for two thousand lines. The imagistic links between the House of Twigs and the Virgilian Under-world are patent, and the crowd around this man replicates the crowd of souls around Aeneas, *Aen.* 6.486. Like many dreams, this one evaporates as the dreamer finally encounters his doppelgänger.

68 Piero Boitani, *World of Fame*, has very useful things to say about structural and imagistic repetition in the poem. Doob, *The Idea of the Labyrinth*, approaches these places as ever more challenging versions of labyrinth.

69 In this context, we should recall that Geffrey himself seemed able only to react, to gloss, and unable to report when he arrived in Book One at the pathetic climax of Dido's seduction and abandonment by Eneas; see above pp. 234–35.

70 See Sarah Spence, *Rhetorics of Reason and Desire: Vergil, Augustine, and the Troubadours* (Ithaca: Cornell University Press, 1988), p. 28 and further references there.

71 Boitani, *World of Fame*, pp. 193–94.

72 Tuttle Hansen sees a parallel process, in which Geffrey tries to extricate himself from a destabilizing and exclusively feminine identification with Dido. "In Book III, in particular, as the dreamer displays a more openly iconoclastic, less submissive attitude toward authority, his difference from Dido becomes even more overt and even more enabling, for the ambiguity that proves fatal for Dido is comprehended by the narrator's claim to artful, creative evasion and subjectivity" (*Chaucer and the Fictions of Gender*, p. 104). See also note 10 above.

73 *Manuscript Bodley 638: A Facsimile*, The Facsimile Series of the Works of Geoffrey Chaucer, Introduction to vol. II by Pamela Robinson (Norman, Okla.: Pilgrim Books, 1982). *Bodleian Library MS Fairfax 16*, Introduction by John Norton–Smith (London: Scolar, 1979). In Bodley 638, there are two Latin citations in the *Legend of Good Women*, fifteen in the *House of Fame* (taking "cavete...," line 305, and "Palinurus," line 430, not to be citations), and no others; see Robinson, pp. xxvi–xxvii. In Fairfax 16, Lydgate's *Reason and Sensualitee* (fols. 202r–300r) is provided with a far more extensive Latin gloss than either of the Chaucer poems. The aims of the Lydgate glosses are quite different, however; these provide explanations and topic headings, whereas the notes to the *House of Fame* are almost entirely citations of ancient Latin sources.

74 E.g. London, BL Add. 16166; Oxford, Bodleian Library, Ashmole 54; and Oxford, Bodleian Library, Auct. F.1.17 (App. I, nos. 24, 26, 23).

75 "Latin and Vernacular in the Northern European Tradition of the *De Consolatione Philosophiae*," in *Boethius: His Life, Thought and Influence*, ed. Margaret Gibson (Oxford: Basil Blackwell, 1981), pp. 365–71.

76 See the fine essay by John Ahern, "Binding the Book: Hermeneutics and Manuscript Production in *Paradiso* 33," *Publications of the Modern Language Association of America* 97 (1982): 800–09.

77 *The Idea of the Labyrinth*, p. 312.

78 At least for some later medieval readers, it should be noted, the "Legend of Dido" could indeed be read as a "free-standing" poem. In the late fifteenth-century Oxford, Bodleian Library, Rawl. C.86, fols. 113r–119v, the "Legend of Dido" has been copied without the Prologue or any of the other Legends. See *The Riverside Chaucer*, ed. Benson, p. 1178.

79 This Prologue was first written in the later 1380's in apparent reaction to criticisms of the *Troilus*. It was later revised, probably after the death of Anne of Bohemia in 1394, and thus at the summit of Chaucer's poetic maturity. These dates represent a general but not unchallenged consensus. While I focus on the G Prologue, my argument does not depend on the specific period, or the posteriority, of its composition. For the dates and backgrounds to the F and G Prologues, see the notes by M. C. E. Shaner and A. S. G. Edwards in *The Riverside Chaucer*, ed. Benson, pp. 1059–61.

80 Lisa J. Kiser approaches Cupid as "an incompetent literary critic,"

Telling Classical Tales: Chaucer and the "Legend of Good Women" (Ithaca and London: Cornell University Press, 1983), p. 71 and ff. Peter Allen discusses the God of Love as a wilfull misreader in "Reading Chaucer's Good Women," *Chaucer Review* 21 (1987): 419, 422–23.

81 Kiser offers a fine reading of Alceste's defense of the dreamer, and her superior command of literary theory (ibid., pp. 84–89; see also pp. 132–35).

82 V. A. Kolve shows how very small was Alceste's mythographic and iconographic presence in the Middle Ages; for Chaucer, this would make Alceste an attractive figure on whom to inscribe his own mythographic imagination; see "From Cleopatra to Alceste: An Iconographic Study of *The Legend of Good Women*," in *Signs and Symbols in Chaucer's Poetry*, ed. John P. Hermann and John J. Burks (University: University of Alabama Press, 1981), pp. 153, 171–74. For probable French background to Chaucer's mythographic invention, see Fyler, *Chaucer and Ovid*, pp. 116–19.

83 The difference between the F and G versions is interesting here, and symptomatic of G's relative shift of focus from love to textual authority. F makes it explicitly "ye lovers" (F 69, recalled with the pronoun "ye" F 73) who have reaped the fruit of language; in G, poets are generalized to "folk" (G 61).

84 Marilynn Desmond uses this passage as a starting point for a consideration of intertextuality in the Prologue and the "Legend of Dido"; see "Chaucer's *Aeneid*: 'The Naked Text in English,' " *Pacific Coast Philology* 19 (1984): 62–67. Desmond claims that ultimately "Virgil's text has overwhelmed [the narrator's] sensibility and his skill" (66), driving the narrator to turn to Ovid as an ally in subversive reading; I will try to show how the narrator achieves a voice and position independent of either source.

85 Cleopatre jumps naked into Antony's grave (696); Tisbe drops her wimple while fleeing the lioness (813). More immediately relevant to male gaze and violence, Tarquin's sword is put to Lucrece's heart (1795), and she later tries to cover herself as she dies (1856–59).

86 For the late antique articulation of these notions, and their twelfth-century developments in William of Conches and "Bernard Silvestris," see ch. 3, pp. 93–101. Carolyn Dinshaw explores these tropes of reading and writing from the perspective of gender, especially male violence, in the opening chapter of *Chaucer's Sexual Poetics* (Madison: University of Wisconsin Press, 1989), esp. pp. 17–25. Dinshaw's is the subtlest analysis of these themes that I have encountered, and my discussion throughout this section is widely indebted to her insights.

87 She may even carry an echo of the Prologue's themes of textual and hermeneutic veiling and unveiling. As told by Euripides, and invoked by Milton, Alcestis returns from the Underworld veiled and initially unrecognized by her husband. I find no medieval mythography, however, that records this detail of her story, nor is it present in either of

the two illustrations of her story uncovered by Kolve, "From Cleopatra to Alceste," p. 173 and figs. 29 and 30.

88 Elaine Tuttle Hansen explores a related and equally unresolved stress in the narrator, between a denigration of women and his own sense of feminization through the defense he receives from Alceste, *Chaucer and the Fictions of Gender*, pp. 3–10. Tuttle Hansen convincingly extends this tension to the position of all men in the legends, at once attracted (even obsessed) by women and unnerved (sometimes even unsexed) by the challenge these same women pose to masculine identity.

89 A more complete discussion of Alceste would have to explore the parallels between her myth and that of Christ, her iconographic and symbolic links to wisdom figures like the Virgin Mary and the Pearl Maiden in *Pearl*, and her echoes of late medieval notions of Christ himself as mother. These connections make Alceste's typological position much more complex than I suggest here; she stands between pagan and Christian myths of fallen and salvific woman. An approach to Alceste through Christian typology has already been eloquently sketched by Kolve: "The movement of the poem ... implies a clear progress from *topos* to *typos*, from a commonplace nineteen times rediscovered to a typological adumbration of transcendence... [Alceste] alone among this vast company points toward Christ" ("From Cleopatra to Alceste," p. 174). Kiser also approaches Alceste as a figure mediating between pagan and Christian divinities, Venus and Mary, *Telling Classical Tales*, pp. 24, 47.

90 George Sanderlin, "Chaucer's *Legend of Dido* – A Feminist Exemplum," *The Chaucer Review* 20 (1986): 331–40, opens with a useful survey of earlier critical response to the poem. In what follows, I will argue against Sanderlin's position that Chaucer proceeds by "stripping the love story of its ... political trappings" (337).

91 Virgilian and Ovidian borrowings in the "Legend" are helpfully surveyed by Shannon, *Chaucer and the Roman Poets*, pp. 196–208.

92 *The Fall of Women*, p. 37.

93 Elsewhere in the Legends, the narrator will establish the independence of his voice by emphasizing disagreement among his sources, as in the "Legend of Hypsipyle," 1462–68. For the narrator's contest with his double source, see also Fyler (*Chaucer and Ovid*, pp. 111–15), and Desmond, "Chaucer's *Aeneid*."

94 For those in the audience who might recognize an echo of Dante, the narrator borrows here a further tone of post-classical supervenience. His wish to follow the lantern of Virgil recalls the position of Dante in *Purgatorio* 1.43, led there by Virgil but soon to leave his guide behind. Chaucer thus summons up, if only very much in passing, the claims to wisdom of any post-pagan perspective. This corresponds (though quietly and briefly) to the suggestions of a realized post-pagan type in the Prologue's depiction of Alceste/Anne.

95 For a discussion of *Heroides* 7 and its influence on medieval Dido lyrics, see pp. 185–87.

96 The Trojans buffeted by storms at sea, *Her.* 7.53–54, 88–89; the rescue of Ascanius, Achates, and the Penates from the flames of Troy, 77–80; the death of Creusa, 83–85. The "Legend"'s scene of Eneas in "the mayster temple" (1016) gazing at the history of Troy painted on the wall there, 1025–35, is not in *Heroides* 7.

97 The seduction scene in the cave is mentioned in *Her.* 7.92–96; the murder of Sychaeus, Dido's flight from Pygmalion and foundation of Carthage appear at 7.111–20.

98 *Aen.* 1.321–24: "ac prior 'heus,' inquit, 'iuuenes, monstrate, mearum / uidistis si quam hic errantem forte sororum / succinctam pharetra et maculosae tegmine lyncis, / aut spumantis apri cursum clamore prementem.'" "Legend of Dido" 978–82: "'Saw ye,' quod she, 'as ye han walked wyde, / Any of my sustren walke yow besyde / With any wilde bor or other best, / That they han hunted to, in this forest, / Ytukked up, with arwes in hire cas?'"

99 See Elaine Tuttle Hansen's excellent demonstration of how men are systematically feminized in the Legends, *Chaucer and the Fictions of Gender*, pp. 3–10.

100 See also Kiser, *Telling Classical Tales*, pp. 126–27.

101 Fyler sees some of these silences as part of the narrator's evasion of embarrassing details in his sources, "a wonderfully comic exercise in censorship and distorted emphasis" (*Chaucer and Ovid*, p. 99).

102 The narrator can also use Virgil as a way to refuse details, as when he will not say whether any attendants accompanied Dido and Eneas to the cave in the storm scene, since "The autour maketh of it no mencioun" (1228). For many of these narratorial strategies toward Virgil, Chaucer had a model in the *Ilias* of Simon Aurea Capra. By means of echo and overt comparison ("Ipsius [Eneas's] immensas complecti carmine laudes / Nec Maro preualuit, nec Symon ipse potest," ed. Boutemy, 435–36), Simon links himself with Virgil; but like Chaucer, he explicitly summarizes and suppresses in the interest of brevity, and also like Chaucer he occasionally rejects parts of the Virgilian narrative (such as Juno begging for Aeolus's help, 507–08, or the metamorphosis of Eneas's ships into nymphs, 745–46).

103 For discussion of these plaints of Dido and their connection to the *Roman d'Eneas*, see above pp. 187–89.

104 See lines 1004, 1009, 1035, 1053, 1057, 1061, 1109, 1126, 1143, 1146, 1150, 1164, 1189, 1191, 1210, 1222, 1243, 1283, 1306, 1308.

105 *Aen.* 1.340, 1.446, 1.613, 1.670, 6.450, 9.266, 11.74. Virgil also often calls Dido "infelix" (1.749, 4.68, 4.450, 4.596, 6.456), which may be the term from which Chaucer derives the epithet "sely" at the end of the "Legend" (1237, 1336); the term could derive, though, from Ovid's "miseram" (*Her.* 7.7).

106 In the *House of Fame*, similarly, Dido is only once called "quene" (241), and is otherwise "woful" (318, cf. *Her.* 7.7) and "wrechched" (335).

107 Alceste is explicitly like a flower, the daisy (G Prologue 156) that the narrator had seen open to the sun; and Cupid too is either crowned with the sun (F Prologue 230) or has a face of solar brightness (G Prologue 162–65).

108 This redirects a Virgilian image in a way typical of Chaucer's sense of his own authority in the "Legend." In *Aeneid* 4, Dido herself burns with her passion for Aeneas; here it is her queenly beauty that sets royal men on fire.

109 The *Ilias* of Simon Aurea Capra again offers striking precedent for several of these details. His Dido would make a proper queen for Apollo or Jove ("Regia regine Phebo satis aut Ioue digna / Talis erat, qualis nec fuit ante nec est," ed. Boutemy, 561–62); except for her mortality, nothing keeps her from being a goddess (583–84); and she is the sum of manly virtues, but that she loves too much (587–88).

110 Under Dido's protection, Eneas will later feel he "is come to paradys / Out of the swolow of helle" (1103–04); this too may echo, however much in passing, the association of Dido with divinity.

111 Janet Cowen speaks of the "Legend"'s "leisurely and elegant extension in terms of its own courtly ethos" (427), "Chaucer's *Legend of Good Women*: Structure and Tone," *Studies in Philology* 82 (1985): 416–36.

112 As with other details of the "Legend," though, Chaucer had a model in Simon's *Ilias*. Simon's Eneas is wise, eloquent, handsome, nobly (even divinely) born, and everywhere praised (ed. Boutemy, 423–34).

113 Peter Allen sees a related narratorial aggressiveness: "When we compare Chaucer's versions of the stories with Ovid's... we find that the Chaucerian narrator is tying women up in his verbiage, his imposed morality, and his limitations on their speech" ("Reading Chaucer's Good Women," p. 434, note 21).

114 The rhetorically elaborate double negative of this catalog is virtually a grammatical figure for the "Legend"'s themes of plenitude and negation; I am grateful to Prof. Sandra Prior for bringing this to my attention.

115 Dido's move from political power to erotic servitude is underlined by another Chaucerian narrative invention, when Anne briefly resists Dido's attraction to Eneas, 1182–87.

116 Frank, *Chaucer and The Legend*, p. 69.

117 As seen above, Dido sent Eneas a "courser wel ybrydeled" (1114) and "large palfrey" (1116), "jewel" (1117), "gold" (1118), and "ruby" (1119), the last of which may be echoed in the red of her saddle.

118 And of course, horses were among her gifts to Eneas. Frank suggests Dido should be viewed even as a prey: "In fact, she becomes almost immediately the quarry" (69). Sheila Delany, "The Logic of Obscenity in Chaucer's *Legend of Good Women*" (*Florilegium* 7 [1985]: 189–205) argues

convincingly that Chaucer employs a whole pattern of obscene word play in the legends, punning with "prick" and the foamy bridle in this passage (194). I do not agree with Delany's suggestion (199) that the epithet "queen" so often used of Dido attracts to it the secondary sense of "loose woman."

119 Richard Firth Green suggests the hostility of Chaucer's attitude toward erotic (and especially Ovidian) "craft" in "Chaucer's Victimized Women, *Studies in the Age of Chaucer* 10 (1988), 11–12.

120 This particular characterization of Eneas will later rouse the nervous anger of Gavin Douglas; Green points out that "traitor" is "a heavily loaded term in the feudal vocabulary" (ibid., p. 15), and discusses Douglas's reaction (ibid., pp. 17–18).

121 Cf. *Aen.* 4.651–53: "dulces exuuiae, dum fata deusque sinebat, / accipite hanc animam meque his exsoluite curis. / uixi et quem dederat cursum Fortuna peregi..." In a detail not found in Virgil or Ovid, Dido kisses the cloth, 1336; this may come from Chaucer's memory of vernacular versions like the *Roman d'Eneas*, where Dido does kiss Eneas's garment, lines 2065–68. Earlier in the "Legend," there is another detail perhaps from the *Eneas* or a redaction like it, when Dido accompanies Eneas to his bedchamber, 1109; this does not occur in the *Aeneid*, but does in the *Eneas*, line 1211.

122 The linkage of the martial sword and sexual violence is explicit in the *Ilias* of Simon, whose apparent influence on Chaucer has been noted above. During the sack of Troy, "Ajax rages not only with his sword but with his genitals, wreaking foul compulsion on holy maidens" ("Aiax non solum gladio, sed in inguine seuit, / Virginibus fedam uim faciendo sacris," ed. Boutemy, 391–92).

CONCLUSION ENVOI, TO THE RENAISSANCE

1 For these and earlier retellings of the Troy story, see ch. 1, pp. 18–21; also C. David Benson, *The History of Troy in Middle English Literature* (Cambridge: D. S. Brewer; Totawa, New Jersey: Rowman and Littlefield, 1980), and Leube, *Fortuna in Karthago*, esp. pp. 65–75, on fifteenth-century France.

2 Guy Raynaud de Lage, "Les 'romans antiques' dans l'Histoire ancienne jusqu'à César," *Le Moyen Age* 63 (1957): 297–305. Virgil's text, though, remains very much the dominant source in this section of the *Histoire*.

3 For a survey and further references, see Jacques Monfrin, "Humanisme et traductions au moyen âge," *Journal des savants* 148 (1963): 161–90, and "Les Traducteurs et leur public en France au moyen âge," *Journal des savants* 149 (1964): 5–20.

4 *Caxton's Eneydos*, ed. W. T. Culley and F. J. Furnivall (London: Early English Text Society, 1890). The book is surveyed and compared to

earlier Troy texts by Louis Brewer Hall, "Caxton's 'Eneydos' and the Redactions of Virgil," *Mediaeval Studies* 22 (1960): 136–47.

5 Jacques Monfrin discusses the *Livre des Eneydes* and shows its dependence on the *Histoire ancienne jusqu'à César*, on Boccaccio's *De casibus*, and on a French Dido text that survives only in a fragment; see "Les translations vernaculaires de Virgile au Moyen Age," *Lectures*, pp. 211–20. See also Leube, *Fortuna in Karthago*, pp. 65–75, on the theme of Fortune in the book; Monfrin clarifies some confusions in Leube's account of its textual affiliations.

6 Culley and Furnivall: "Caxton very often translates the French idiom literally ... and he frequently uses the French words without rendering them into English at all" (vi).

7 *Eneydos*, p. 22. I regularize spelling and punctuate lightly. Further page references to this edition will be given in parentheses in the text.

8 This does no more than exaggerate tendencies, often encountered above, to incorporate marginal information into the master narrative. Consider for instance the insertion of originally marginal narratives into the *Roman d'Eneas*, or Chaucer's auto-glossation in *House of Fame*, Book One.

9 So Virgil's brief comparisons of Dido to Pentheus and Orestes (*Aen.* 4.469, 471) are emphasized in Caxton by expansive explanatory narratives (pp. 81–82, 83).

10 P. 73. Cf. *Heroides* 7.65–70.

11 Pp. 27–31. These two tales occur in the section of the work borrowed from Boccaccio.

12 Yarbas has already delivered a blustering, revisionary summary of Dido's history that denigrates Carthage ("a cyte of lityl pryce"), emphasizes his mastery and control as a generous provider of land "by curtoysie ..., & lawes for to governe her peple," and suppresses the story of the bull's hide (p. 60).

13 *Virgil's "Aeneid" Translated into Scottish Verse by Gavin Douglas*, ed. David F. C. Coldwell, Scottish Text Society 25, 27, 28, 30 (Edinburgh and London: Scottish Text Society [STS], 1957–64; repr. New York and London: Johnson Reprint Corporation, 1972).

14 In these brief comments, I do not deal with the genuine and still engaging mastery of Douglas's translation. For full discussion of his techniques as a translator, see Charles Blyth, *The Knychtlyke Stile: A Study of Gavin Douglas' "Aeneid"* (New York: Garland, 1987). See also Priscilla Bawcutt, *Gavin Douglas: A Critical Study* (Edinburgh University Press, 1976), ch. 6.

15 Prologue I.267–70.

16 Prologue IX.21, 31, 44.

17 "Direction," line 87 (STS 28, p. 190).

18 Prologue I.138–45. For Douglas's much more respectful chiding of Chaucer, see Prologue I.405–49.

19 Priscilla Bawcutt has demonstrated, quite convincingly, that Douglas used the printed commentary of Badius Ascensius, in the Paris edition of 1500–01, "Gavin Douglas and the Text of Virgil," *Edinburgh Bibliographical Society Transactions* 4 (1966–68): 213–31. This edition itself (like most classical incunabula) mimics the format of manuscripts; a writer of Douglas's station would have had access to manuscripts as well, possibly a quite grand illustrated Virgil linked to the Scottish crown and now in Edinburgh (App. I, no. 34). Further, Douglas clearly thinks of his own work as appearing in a decorated manuscript, as we see in the close of the twelfth Prologue: "The lusty crafty preambill, 'perle of May' / I the entitil, crownyt quhil domysday, / And al with gold, in syng of stait ryall / Most beyn illumnyt thy letteris capital" (Prologue XII.307–10).

20 Not surprisingly, the physical format of Douglas's translation mimics that of late-medieval Virgil manuscripts. This extends even to numbered subsections within each book, provided with brief plot summaries. (Douglas's summaries, in the form of rhymed couplets, may provide a model for Spenser's in the *Faerie Queene*.)

21 Douglas's newly restrictive respect for Virgilian Latin narrative never expunges awareness of the multiple medieval redactions, or other sources of vernacular classicism. His own self-glossing, in an often elaborate system of prose marginalia, still makes place for these alternate traditions, if only to reject them. In the prologues and marginalia, Douglas interestingly uses medieval material like Boccaccio and Raoul Lefevre's "Recolles of Troye" as authorities about subjects like the gods and the underworld. And he repeatedly rebuts the backbiters who criticize the very project of translating a profane author; see, for example, Prologue III.19–27, and the "Direction," lines 20–60 (STS 28, p. 188).

22 Douglas explores a more literal juncture of poetry and knighthood in his lovely and somewhat expanded translation of the death of the poet Cretheus at the hands of Turnus (*Aen.* 9.774–77; *Eneados* IX.xii.110–18).

23 Eneas will record the "lamentabill realm of Troy," a story sure to draw "mony a teir" (Book One, ch. xii, lines 8, 14); Douglas's Prologue looks toward "The drery fait with terys lamentabill / Of Troys sege..." (Prologue II.8–9).

24 Prologue III.37–39. Douglas returns to the trope, and again links himself to Aeneas as a mariner, in the "Exclamation" with which he closes the entire translation: "Now throw the deip fast to the port I mark" ("Exclamation," line 1 [STS 28, p. 192]).

25 Prologue VI.7–8.

26 Prologue I.83–86. The connection between Virgil and Augustus, and its analogies with Douglas and Sinclair, is raised again in Prologue IX.53–68, 87–96.

27 "Conclusio," lines 11–15 (STS 28, p. 187).

28 Prologue I.325.

29 Prologue I.410–16. Douglas pursues the same point in his prose note at I.v.28; he answers Guido delle Colonne's claim that Aeneas betrayed Troy with Livy's comment that Aeneas only sought peace: "Now I beseik ʒow, curtess redaris, ... wey the excellent awtorite of Virgill and Tytus Lyuius wyth ʒour pevach [mischievous] and corrupt Gwido." See also Douglas's note at I.iiii.41.

30 See IV.v.76–83, 157–64.

31 I.viii.1, X.iii.95, 60. This is a very widespread pattern. It results in part from the inevitable padding in the move from Virgil's iambic pentameter to Douglas's heroic couplets, but the choice of padding is nonetheless revealing.

32 "Direction," lines 128–34 (STS 28 p. 191).

33 Prologue I.163–72.

34 Prologue IV.264.

35 Prologue IV.5–7.

36 Prologue IV.228.

37 For Christine's sources, and her use of Dido in other works, see Leube, *Fortuna in Karthago*, pp. 54–65.

38 "Here begynneth the boke of the Cyte of Ladyes"; the printer was Henry Pepwell. On Christine's links to England, see P. G. C. Campbell, "Christine de Pisan en Angleterre," *Revue de littérature comparée* 5 (1925): 659–70. Modern English translation *The Book of the City of Ladies*, trans. Earl Jeffrey Richards (New York: Persea, 1982).

39 Book One, ch. 46.

40 Book One, ch. 46.

41 Book Two, ch. 53 (ch. 54 in Jeffrey's translation).

42 Quotations are from *The Faerie Queene*, ed. Thomas P. Roche and C. Patrick O'Donnell, Jr. (New York: Penguin, 1979). For a survey of Virgilianism in Spenser, with bibliography, see *Enciclopedia* IV, pp. 983–90.

43 *Faerie Queene*, III.iii.4, 22–24, and 49–50.

44 *Faerie Queene*, III.ix.32–37.

45 *Faerie Queene*, III.ix.38–40.

APPENDIX III

1 All but the last lines of this note were considerably trimmed by an early binder. I indicate the approximate number of missing letters in each line with points (. . . .). Hypothetical replacements of lost letters or words are marked at left by an angle bracket. Slash marks (/) at the right indicate line endings.

2 Compare the unpublished commentary in Glasgow, Hunterian U.5.19: "Mixtum uero in ipsis planetis potest intelligi, nam finito cursu redeunt ad idem." I am grateful to Dr. Diane K. Bolton for allowing me to consult her transcription of portions of this commentary.

3   Cf. Hunterian U.5.19: "Eodem modo est in hominibus. Nam idem consideratur in sanctis uiris, qui semper uolunt bonum."

4   Cf. Hunterian U.5.19: "Mixtum consideratur in illis qui modo hoc id est bonum modo illud id est malum uolunt.

APPENDIX IV

1   I base this text on London, BL Add. 16380, a twelfth-century manuscript that circulated in the environs of Canterbury and Rochester at least by *c.* 1210. The accessus appears on folio 2 *recto*, column A. My transcriptions were made from the manuscript, but I have also profited from transcriptions made from microfilm by Professor Mary Louise Lord, whose generosity I wish to acknowledge. To illustrate the fluidity of such commentary texts, variants from an earlier copy (Berlin, Staatsbibliothek Preussischer Kulturbesitz, lat. fol. 34, folio 43 *recto*, col. A) and a somewhat later copy (London, BL Add. 33220, folio 30 *verso*, col. A) are recorded in the notes below. Variant spelling is not recorded. I have punctuated lightly.

2   augustum ce(sarem) 33220.

3   parentibus suis 33220.

4   hoc facit 34, 33220.

5   describenda 34.

6   nauigio deuenerit 34, 33220.

7   composuit 33220.

8   figmenta quedam 34.

9   apposuit 33220.

10   numitio fluuio 33220.

11   interiit 33220.

12   enea et hercule 33220.

13   Satire XI.63.

14   Si enim ueritatem 34; Si tantummodo ueritatem 332200.

15   tantummodo sequeretur 34.

16   diceretur 33220.

17   est hoc 33220.

18   Venerem cum 34.

19   missum 33220.

20   mercurium ad didonem 34.

21   fictum et appositum 33220.

22   34, 33220 omit "uel deperderetur".

23   adderet 33220.

24   superflua queque 34.

25   delerent 34, demeret 33220.

26   etiam 34.

27   inueniemus 34.

28   semiplenos inuenimus 33220.

29 *Aen.* 1.534.
30 uero omnino 34.
31 considerantes carminis 34.
32 principii detraxerunt 33220.
33 subtracti. 34.
34 uirgilii maronis 33220.
35 sequitur secundus 34.
36 Publia fuit 34, 33220.
37 nisi 34, 33220.
38 astris celum 34, 33220.
39 34, 33220 omit this sentence.
40 est nomen 34.
41 et 33220.
42 et narrat 34.
43 *Aen.* 1.1.
44 *Aen.* 1.8.
45 ut ibi 34, 33220.
46 *Aen.* 1.34.

Select Bibliography

MANUSCRIPTS CITED

(Figures in square brackets refer to manuscripts listed in Appendices I and II.)

Basel, Öffentliche Bibliothek der Universität F II 23
Berkeley, University of California, Bancroft 2
Berlin, Staatsbibl., Germ. in–fol. 282
    lat. fol. 34
Bern, Bürgerbibliothek 411
    474
Brussels, Bibliothèque Royale 10014–10017
Cambridge
 Corpus Christi College 71
    450
    binding fragment from printed book EP–O–6 [I 4d]
 Jesus College 33 [I 12]
 Pembroke College 260 [I 10]
 Peterhouse College 158 [I 11]
    159 [I 36]
 Queens' College K.17.5, three pastedown fragments [I 27]
 St. John's College 54 [I 28]
    205 [I 33]
 Trinity College 457 [I 29]
    623 [I 13]
 University Library Ff.3.5
Cambridge MA, Harvard University, Richardson 38
Copenhagen
 Kongelige Bibliotek, Gl. kgl. 2006, 4°
    Gl. kgl. 2007, 4°
Kettering, Northamptonshire, Deene Park Library, binding fragment [I 4a]
Dijon, Bibliothèque municipale 493
Edinburgh
 National Library, Adv. 18.4.13 [I 8]
    18.5.12 [I 17]
 University Library 195 [I 34]
Ghent, Cathedral Library 9

Glasgow, Hunterian Museum U.5.19
The Hague, Rijksmuseum, 76 E 21
Heidelberg, Universitätsbibliothek, palat. germ. 403
Hereford Cathedral O.2.iv
Klosterneuberg, Stiftsbibliothek 742
Leiden, Bibliotheek der Rijksuniversitat B.P.L. 92A
Leningrad, Academy of Sciences Q.443 [II 4]
London
  BL Additional
    11959 [I 30]
    16166 [I 24]
    16380
    27304 [I 18]
    32319A [I 14]
    33220
    34114
  Burney
    257
    269 [I 20]
    273 [II 5]
    277, fol. 73 [I 35]
  Harley 4967 [I 22]
  Royal 8.F.XIV, fols. 3–4 [I 5]
    12.D.III
    13.A.IV
    15.B.VI [I 21]
  Sloane 1044, fol. 60, binding fragment [I 4b]
  College of Arms, Arundel 30 [I 2]
  Lambeth Palace 471 [I 15]
  Society of Antiquaries 44 [I 31]
Naples, Biblioteca Nazionale, Vindob. lat. 6
Oxford
  All Souls College
    19
    37
    82 [I 9]
    330, nos. 60 and 61 [I 1]
  Bodleian Library,
    Add. A.44
      A.208
      A.365
    Ashmole 54 [I 26]
    Auct. F.1.17 [I 23]
      F.2.7 [I 32]
      F.4.22

Bodley 638
     851
Digby 65
Canon. class. lat. 52
Fairfax 16
Lat. class. C.2, fol. 18, binding fragment [I 4c]
Laud. lat. 86
Laud. misc. D 15
Laud. misc. 515
Rawl. C.86
    C.552
    D.1230
    G.109
Wood 106, wrapper [I 6]
Jesus College 26
Lincoln College 58
Merton College 248
New College 271 [I 25]
Paris
  Bibliothèque de l'Arsenal
    3340
    5077
  Bibliothèque nationale,
    fr. 60
    fr. 301
    fr. 784
    fr. 9682
    fr. 9685
    fr. 20125
    lat. 7936
Parma, Biblioteca Palatina 2662 [I 16]
Perugia, Biblioteca Comunale Auguste C.57
Shrewsbury School IV (Mus.III.40) [I 37]
Vatican, Biblioteca Apostolica Vaticana,
  Ottob. lat.
    1373 [I 19]
    1410 [I 7]
  Reg. lat. 1671 [I 3]
  Vat. lat.
    1574
Wolfenbüttel, Herzog–August Bibliothek, Guelf. 7.10 (Gud. lat. 155 4°)

PRIMARY SOURCES

Baehrens, Emil, ed. *Poetae Latini Minores*. 5 vols. Leipzig, 1879–83. IV.

Bayer, Karl, ed. "Vitae Vergilianae." *Vergil Landleben*. Eds. Johannes and Maria Götte. Munich: Heimeran, 1977. 211–421, 654–764.

Benoît de Ste. Maure. *Le Roman de Troie*. Ed. Leopold Constans. 6 vols. Société des Anciens Textes Français. Paris: Firmin Didot, 1904–12.

Bernard of Utrecht. *Commentum in Theodulum (1076–1099)*. Ed. R. B. C. Huygens. Spoleto: Biblioteca degli "Studi medievali," 1977.

Bode, Georg Heinrich, ed. *Scriptores rerum mythicarum Latini tres Romae nuper reperti*. Celle, 1834.

Bodleian Library MS Fairfax 16. Intro. John Norton-Smith. London: Scolar, 1979.

Boethius. *Boethii Philosophiae Consolatio*. Ed. Ludwig Bieler. Corpus Christianorum, Series Latina XCIV. Turnholt: Brepols, 1957.

Theological Tractates, Consolation of Philosophy. Trans. H. F. Stewart, E. K. Rand, and S. J. Tester. Cambridge, Mass.: Harvard University Press, 1973.

Boutemy, André. "Le poème *Pergama flere uolo* . . . et ses imitateurs du XIIe siècle." *Latomus* 5 (1946): 233–44.

Brummer, Iacobus, ed. *Vitae Vergilianae*. Leipzig: Teubner, 1912.

Buechler, Francis and Alexander Riese, eds. *Anthologia Latina*. Leipzig: Teubner, 1894, 1906. Amsterdam: Hakkert, 1964. Part I, fasc. 1–2.

Caxton, William. *Caxton's Eneydos*. Eds. W. T. Culley and F. J. Furnivall. Early English Text Society e.s. 57. London: Early English Text Society, 1890.

Chaucer, Geoffrey. *The Riverside Chaucer*. Gen. ed. Larry D. Benson. Boston, Mass.: Houghton Mifflin, 1987.

Christine de Pisan. "Here begynneth the boke of the Cyte of Ladyes." Trans. Bryan Anslay. London, 1521.

The Book of the City of Ladies. Trans. Earl Jeffrey Richards. New York: Persea, 1982.

Dares Phrygius. *De Excidio Troiae Historiae*. Ed. Ferdinand Meister. Leipzig, 1873.

Dictys Cretensis. *Ephemeridos Belli Troiani Libri*. Ed. Werner Eisenhut. Leipzig: Teubner, 1973.

Douglas, Gavin. *Virgil's "Aeneid" Translated into Scottish Verse by Gavin Douglas*. Ed. David F. C. Coldwell. Scottish Text Society 25, 27, 28, 30. Edinburgh and London: Scottish Text Society, 1957–64. Repr. New York and London: Johnson Reprint Corporation, 1972.

du Méril, Edélestand. *Poésies populaires latines antérieures au XIIe siècle*. Paris, 1843.

Eneas: Roman du XIIe siècle. Ed. J.-J. Salverda de Grave. 2 vols. Paris: CFMA, 1925–29; repr. 1973.

Eneas: A Twelfth-Century French Romance. Trans. John A. Yunck. Records of Civilization 93. New York: Columbia University Press, 1974.

Excidium Troiae. Ed. Alan Keith Bate. Frankfurt and Bern: Peter Lang, 1986.

Faral, Edmond. "Le Manuscrit 511 du 'Hunterian Museum' de Glasgow." *Studi Medievali* n.s. 9 (1936): 18–121.

Frazer, R. M., trans. *The Trojan War: The Chronicles of Dictys of Crete and Dares the Phrygian.* Bloomington, Ind. and London: Indiana University Press, 1966.

Fulgentius, Fabius Planciades (Fulgentius Mythographus). *Fabii Planciadi Fulgentii V. C. Opera.* Ed. Rudolph Helm. Rev. ed. Jean Préaux. Stuttgart: Teubner, 1970.

Fulgentius the Mythographer. Trans. Leslie G. Whitbread. Columbus, Ohio: University of Ohio Press, 1971.

Guido de Columnis (Guido delle Colonne). *Historia destructionis Troiae.* Ed. Nathaniel E. Griffin. Cambridge, Mass.: Medieval Academy of America, 1936.

Historia destructionis Troiae. Trans. Mary E. Meek. Bloomington, Ind.: Indiana University Press, 1974.

John of Salisbury. *Ioannis Saresberiensis Policraticus.* Ed. Clement C. I. Webb. 2 vols. Oxford University Press, 1909.

Jones, Julian Ward, and Elizabeth Frances Jones, eds. *The Commentary on the First Six Books of the "Aeneid" Commonly Attributed to Bernard Silvestris.* Lincoln, Nebr.: University of Nebraska Press, 1977.

Macrobius. *Commentary on the Dream of Scipio.* Trans. William Harris Stahl. New York: Columbia University Press, 1952.

The Saturnalia. Trans. Percival V. Davies. New York: Columbia University Press, 1969.

Ambrosii Theodosii Macrobii Saturnalia. Ed. Jacob Willis. Leipzig: Teubner, 1970.

Commentarii in somnium Scipionis. Ed. Jacob Willis. Leipzig: Teubner, 1970.

Manuscript Bodley 638: A Facsimile. Intro. Pamela Robinson. The Facsimile Series of the Works of Geoffrey Chaucer 2. Norman, Okla.: Pilgrim Books, 1982.

Nicholas Trevet. *Nicolás Trivet Anglico, Comentario a las Bucólicas de Virgilio: Estudio y edición crítica.* Eds. Aires Augusto Nascimento and José Manuel Díaz de Bustamante. Monografias de la Universidad de Santiago de Compostela 97. Santiago de Compostela, 1984.

Ovide Moralisé. Ed. Cornelis de Boer. 5 vols. Amsterdam: Koninklijke Akad. van Wetenshappen, 1915–38.

Petrus Berchorius (Pierre Bersuire). *Reductorium morale, liber XV: Ovidius moralizatus, cap. i.* Ed. J. Engels. Utrecht: Instituut voor Laat Latijn, 1966.

"The *Ovidius Moralizatus* of Petrus Berchorius: an Introduction and Translation." Trans. William D. Reynolds. Diss. Ph. D. University of Illinois at Champaign-Urbana, 1971.

Schumann, Otto. "Eine mittelalterliche Klage der Dido." *Liber Floridus: Mittelalterliche Studien Paul Lehmann.* Eds. Bernhard Bischoff and Suso Bechter. St. Ottilien: Eos Verlag, 1950. 319–28.

Servii Grammatici qui feruntur in Vergilii carmina commentarii. Eds. Georg Thilo and

Hermann Hagen. 3 vols. Leipzig: Teubner, 1881–84. Repr. Hildesheim: Georg Olms, 1961.

Simon Aurea Capra. "La Version Parisienne du poème de Simon Chèvre d'Or sur la guerre de Troie." [=*Ilias Latina.*] Ed. André Boutemy *et al. Scriptorium* 1 (1946–47): 267–88.

Spenser, Edmund. *The Faerie Queene.* Ed. Thomas P. Roche and C. Patrick O'Donnell, Jr. New York: Penguin, 1979.

Virgil. *P. Vergili Maronis Opera.* Ed. R. A. B. Mynors. Oxford: Clarendon, 1969.

Wilmart, Dom A. "Florilège Mixte de Thomas Bekynton." *Mediaeval and Renaissance Studies* 1 (1941): 41–84 and 4 (1958): 35–90.

SECONDARY SOURCES

Adler, Alfred. "Eneas and Lavine: *Puer et Puella Senes.*" *Romanische Forschungen* 71 (1959): 73–91.

Allen, Don Cameron. "Marlowe's *Dido* and the Tradition." *Essays on Shakespeare and Elizabethan Drama in Honour of Hardin Craig.* Ed. Richard Hosley. London: Routledge and Kegan Paul, 1963. 55–68.

Allen, Judson B. *The Friar as Critic.* Nashville, Tenn.: Vanderbilt University Press, 1971.

The Ethical Poetic of the Later Middle Ages: A Decorum of Convenient Distinction. University of Toronto Press, 1982.

Angeli, Giovanna. *L'"Eneas" e i primi romanzi volgari.* Milan and Naples: Riccardo Ricciardi, 1971.

Avril, François. "Un manuscrit d'auteurs classiques et ses illustrations." *The Year 1200: A Symposium.* New York: Metropolitan Museum of Art, 1975. 261–82.

Baswell, Christopher. "A High Medieval Commentary on the *Aeneid.*" *Sixty Bokes Olde and Newe.* Ed. David Anderson. Knoxville, Tenn.: New Chaucer Society, 1985. 60–63.

"The Medieval Allegorization of the 'Aeneid': MS Cambridge, Peterhouse 158." *Traditio* 41 (1985): 181–237.

"Medieval Readers and Ancient Texts: The Inference of the Past." *Envoi: A Review Journal of Medieval Literature* 1 (1988): 1–22.

"Talking Back to the Text: Marginal Voices in Medieval Secular Literature." *The Uses of Manuscripts in Literary Studies: Essays in Memory of Judson Boyce Allen.* Eds. Charlotte Morse, Penelope Reed Doob, and Marjorie Curry Woods. Kalamazoo, Mich.: Medieval Institute, 1992. 121–60.

Baswell, Christopher and Paul Beekman Taylor. "The *Faire Queene Eleyne* in Chaucer's *Troilus.*" *Speculum* 63 (1988): 293–311.

Bawcutt, Priscilla. *Gavin Douglas: A Critical Study.* Edinburgh University Press, 1976.

Bennett, J. A. W. *Chaucer's Book of Fame.* Oxford: Clarendon Press, 1968.

Benson, C. David. *The History of Troy in Middle English Literature.* Cambridge: D. S. Brewer; Totawa, N.J.: Rowman and Littlefield, 1980.

Bishop, T. A. M. *English Caroline Minuscule.* Oxford: Clarendon, 1971.

Bloch, R. Howard. *Medieval French Literature and Law.* Berkeley, Calif.: University of California Press, 1977.

 Etymologies and Genealogies: A Literary Anthropology of the French Middle Ages. Chicago and London: University of Chicago Press, 1983.

Blumenfeld-Kosinski, Renate. "Old French Narrative Genres: Towards the Definition of the *Roman Antique.*" *Romance Philology* 34 (1980): 143–59.

Blyth, Charles. *The Knychtlyke Stile: A Study of Gavin Douglas' "Aeneid."* New York: Garland, 1987.

Boitani, Piero. *Chaucer and the Imaginary World of Fame.* Woodbridge, Suffolk: D. S. Brewer, 1984.

Bolgar, R. R. *The Classical Heritage and its Beneficiaries.* Cambridge University Press, 1958.

Born, Lester K. "Ovid and Allegory." *Speculum* 9 (1934): 362–79.

Brown, T. Julian. "An Historical Introduction to the Use of Classical Latin Authors in the British Isles from the Fifth to the Eleventh Century." *La cultura antica nell'occidente latino dal VII all'XI secolo.* Settimane di studio del centro italiano di studi sull'alto medioevo 22. Spoleto: Presso la sede del Centro, 1975. 237–99.

Brown, Virginia. "A Twelfth-Century Virgilian Miscellany-Commentary of German Origin (Vatican MS. Pal. Lat. 1695)." *Scire litteras: Forschungen zum mittelalterlichen Geistesleben.* Ed. Sigrid Krämer and Michael Bernhard. Munich: Bayerischen Akademie, 1988. 73–86.

Brown, Virginia and Craig Kallendorf. "Two Humanist Annotators of Virgil: Coluccio Salutati and Giovanni Tortelli." *Supplementum Festivum: Studies in Honor of Paul Oskar Kristeller.* Ed. James Hankins. Binghamton: Medieval and Renaissance Texts and Studies, 1987. 65–148.

Buchthal, Hugo. *Historia Troiana: Studies in the History of Medieval Secular Illustration.* Studies of the Warburg Institute 32. London: The Warburg Institute; Leiden: E. J. Brill, 1971.

Bultot, Robert. "*Grammatica, Ethica* et *Contemptus Mundi* aux XIIe et XIIIe siècles." *Arts Libéraux et philosophie au Moyen Age.* Congrès international de philosophie médiévale 4. Montréal: Institut d'études médiévales and Paris: Vrin, 1969. 815–27.

Campbell, P. G. C. "Christine de Pisan en Angleterre." *Revue de littérature comparée* 5 (1925): 659–70.

Comparetti, Domenico. *Vergil in the Middle Ages.* Trans. E. F. M. Benecke. London: Swan Sonnenschein, 1895.

 Rev. Giorgio Pasquali. *Virgilio nel Medio Evo.* 2 vols. Florence: La Nuova Italia, 1937–41.

Cormier, Raymond J. *One Heart One Mind: The Rebirth of Virgil's Hero in Medieval French Romance.* University, Miss.: Romance Monographs, 1973.

Courcelle, Pierre. *La Consolation de Philosophie dans la tradition littéraire*. Paris: Etudes Augustiniennes, 1967.

Courcelle, Pierre and Jeanne Courcelle, *Lecteurs païens et lecteurs chrétiens de l'Énéide*. I: *Les témoignages littéraires*. II: *Les manuscrits illustrés de l'Énéide du Xe au XVe siècle*. Mémoires de l'Académie des inscriptions et belles–lettres, Nouvelle série IV. Paris: Institut de France, 1984.

Crouse, Robert Darwin. "Honorius Augustodensis: The Arts as *Via ad Patriam*." *Arts Libéraux et philosophie au Moyen Age*. Congrès international de philosophie médiévale 4. Montréal: Institut d'études médiévales and Paris: Vrin, 1969. 531–39.

Dane, Joseph A. "Chaucer's *House of Fame* and the *Rota Virgilii*." *Classical and Modern Literature* 1 (1980): 57–75.

"Yif I 'arma uirumque' kan: Note on Chaucer's *House of Fame*, Line 143." *American Notes and Queries* 19 (1981): 134–36.

David, Alfred. "How Marcia Lost Her Skin: A Note on Chaucer's Mythology." *The Learned and the Lewed*. Ed. L. D. Benson. Cambridge, Mass: Harvard University Press, 1974. 19–29.

de Hamel, Christopher F. R. *Glossed Books of the Bible and the Origins of the Paris Book Trade*. Woodbridge, Suffolk: D. S. Brewer, 1984.

Delany, Sheila. *Chaucer's House of Fame: The Poetics of Skeptical Fideism*. University of Chicago Press, 1972.

Demats, Paule. *Fabula: Trois études de mythographie antique et médiévale*. Geneva: Droz, 1973.

Desmond, Marilynn R.. "Chaucer's *Aeneid*: 'The Naked Text in English.'" *Pacific Coast Philology* 19 (1984): 62–67.

"I wol now singen, yif I kan: The 'Aeneid' in Medieval French and English Narrative." Diss. Ph. D., University of California, Berkeley, 1985.

Dinshaw, Carolyn. *Chaucer's Sexual Poetics*. Madison: University of Wisconsin Press, 1989.

Doob, Penelope Reed. *The Idea of the Labyrinth from Classical Antiquity through the Middle Ages*. Ithaca, N.Y. and London: Cornell University Press, 1990.

Dronke, Peter. *Fabula: Explorations into the Uses of Myth in Medieval Platonism*. Mittellateinische Studien und Texte IX. Leiden: Brill, 1974.

"Dido's Lament: From Medieval Latin Lyric to Chaucer." *Kontinuität und Wandel: Lateinische Poesie von Naevius bis Baudelaire*. Eds. U. J. Stache, W. Maaz, and F. Wagner. Hildesheim: Weidmann, 1986. 364–90.

Dronke, Peter, ed. *A History of Twelfth-Century Philosophy*. Cambridge: Cambridge University Press, 1988.

Dufournet, Jean, ed. *Relire le "Roman d'Eneas."* Paris: Honoré Champion, 1985.

Edden, Valerie. "Early Manuscripts of Virgiliana." *The Library* ser. 5, 28 (1973): 14–25.

Eisenhut, Werner. "Spätantike Troja-Erzählungen – mit einem Ausblick auf die mittelalterliche Troja-Literatur." *Mittellateinisches Jahrbuch* 18 (1983): 1–28.

Emden, A. B. *A Biographical Register of the University of Oxford to A.D. 1500.* 3 vols. Oxford University Press, 1957–59.

A Biographical Register of the University of Cambridge to 1500. Cambridge University Press, 1963.

Enciclopedia Virgiliana. General ed. Francesco della Corte. 5 vols. Rome: Istituto della Enciclopedia Virgiliana, 1984–91.

Erhart, Margaret J. *The Judgment of the Trojan Prince Paris in Medieval Literature.* Philadelphia, Pa.: University of Pennsylvania Press, 1987.

Faral, Edmond. *Recherches sur les sources latines des contes et romans courtois du moyen âge.* Paris, 1913.

Frank, Robert W. *Chaucer and The Legend of Good Women.* Cambridge, Mass.: Harvard University Press, 1972.

Friend, A. C. "Chaucer's Version of the *Aeneid*." *Speculum* 28 (1953): 317–23.

Fyler, John. *Chaucer and Ovid.* New Haven, Conn.: Yale University Press, 1979.

Galinsky, G. Karl. *Aeneas, Sicily, and Rome.* Princeton University Press, 1969.

Gaunt, Simon. "From Epic to Romance: Gender and Sexuality in the *Roman d'Enéas*." *Romanic Review* 83 (1992): 1–27.

Gibson, Margaret, ed. *Boethius: His Life, Thought and Influence.* Oxford: Blackwell, 1981.

Goold, George P. "Servius and the Helen Episode." *Harvard Studies in Classical Philology* 74 (1970): 101–68.

Grafton, Anthony and Lisa Jardine. *From Humanism to the Humanities: Education and the Liberal Arts in Fifteenth- and Sixteenth-Century Europe.* London: Duckworth, 1986.

Hall, Lewis Brewer. "Caxton's 'Eneydos' and the Redactions of Virgil," *Mediaeval Studies* 22 (1960): 136–147

"Chaucer and the Dido-and-Aeneas Story." *Mediaeval Studies* 25 (1963): 148–159.

Hansen, Elaine Tuttle. *Chaucer and the Fictions of Gender.* Berkeley, Calif.: University of California Press, 1992.

Hardie, Phillip Russell. "Humanist Exegesis of Poetry in Fifteenth-Century Italy and the Medieval Tradition of Commentary." Diss. M. Phil., University of London (Warburg Institute), 1976.

Häring, Nikolaus M. "Commentary and Hermeneutics." *Renaissance and Renewal in the Twelfth Century.* Eds. Robert L. Benson and Giles Constable. Cambridge, Mass.: Harvard University Press, 1982. 173–200.

Hexter, Ralph J. *Ovid and Medieval Schooling. Studies in Medieval School Commentaries on Ovid's "Ars Amatoria," "Epistulae ex Ponto," and "Epistulae Heroidum."* Münchener Beitrage zur Mediävistik und Renaissance–Forschung 38. Munich: Arbeo-Gesellschaft, 1986.

Huchet, Jean-Charles. *Le Roman médiéval.* Paris: Presses universitaires de France, 1984.

Hunt, Richard W. "English Learning in the Late Twelfth Century." *Transactions of the Royal Historical Society*, 4th series, 19 (1936): 19–42.

Repr. in *Essays in Medieval History*. Ed. R. W. Southern. London: Macmillan and New York: St. Martin's, 1968. 106–28.

Irvine, Martin. "Medieval Grammatical Theory and Chaucer's *House of Fame*." *Speculum* 60 (1985): 850–76.

Jeauneau, Edouard. "L'Usage de la notion d'Integumentum à travers les gloses de Guillaume de Conches." *Archives d'histoire doctrinale et littéraire du moyen âge* 24 (1957): 35–100.

"Note sur l'école de Chartres." *Studi Medievali*, ser. 3, 5 (1964): 821–65.

"Berkeley, University of California, Bancroft Library MS. 2 (notes de lecture)." *Mediaeval Studies* 50 (1988): 438–56.

Jeffrey, David L. "Sacred and Secular Scripture: Authority and Interpretation in *The House of Fame*." *Chaucer and Scriptural Tradition*. Ed. Jeffrey. University of Ottawa Press, 1984. 209–13.

Jones, J. W., Jr. "Allegorical Interpretation in Servius." *Classical Journal* 56 (1960–61): 217–26.

"Vergil as Magister in Fulgentius." In *Classical, Mediaeval, and Renaissance Studies in Honor of B. L. Ullman*. Ed. C. Henderson, Jr. 2 vols. Rome: Edizioni di Storia e Letteratura, 1964. I, 273–75.

"The So–Called Silvestris Commentary on the *Aeneid* and Two Other Interpretations." *Speculum* 64 (1989): 838–48.

Joyner, William. "Parallel Journeys in Chaucer's *House of Fame*." *Papers on Language and Literature* 12 (1976): 3–19.

Kaster, Robert. *Guardians of Language: The Grammarian and Society in Late Antiquity*. Berkeley, Calif.: University of California Press, 1988.

Ker, Neil R. *Medieval Libraries of Great Britain*. London: Royal Historical Society, 1964.

Kiser, Lisa J. *Telling Classical Tales: Chaucer and the "Legend of Good Women."* Ithaca, N.Y. and London: Cornell University Press, 1983.

Knowles, Dom David, *et al. The Heads of Religious Houses, England and Wales, 940–1216*. Cambridge University Press, 1972.

Kolve, V. A. "From Cleopatra to Alceste: An Iconographic Study of *The Legend of Good Women*." *Signs and Symbols in Chaucer's Poetry*. Eds. John P. Hermann and John J. Burks. University, Ala.: University of Alabama Press, 1981. 153–74.

Lectures médiévales de Virgile. Collection de l'école française de Rome 80. Rome: Ecole française de Rome, 1985.

Leube, Eberhard. *Fortuna in Karthago: Die Aeneas–Dido–Mythe Vergils in den romanischen Literaturen vom 14. bis zum 16. Jahrhundert*. Heidelberg: Carl Winter, 1969.

Lord, Mary Louise. "Dido as an Example of Chastity: the Influence of Example Literature." *Harvard Library Bulletin* 17 (1969): 22–44 and 216–232.

"A Commentary on *Aeneid* 6: Ciones de Magnali, not Nicholas Trevet." *Medievalia et Humanistica*, New Series 15 (1987): 147–60.

"Virgil's *Eclogues*, Nicholas Trevet, and the Harmony of the Spheres." *Mediaeval Studies* 54 (1992): 186–273.

MacDougall, Hugh A. *Racial Myth in English History: Trojans, Teutons, and Anglo-Saxons*. Montreal: Harvest House; Hanover, N.H.: University Press of New England, 1982.

Marchello-Nizia, Christiane. "De l'*Énéide* à l'*Eneas*: les attributs du fondateur." *Lectures*. 251–66.

McCall, John P. *Chaucer Among the Gods: The Poetics of Classical Myth*. University Park, Penn.: Pennsylvania State University Press, 1979.

Meech, Sanford Brown. "Chaucer and an Italian Translation of the *Heroides*." *Proceedings of the Modern Language Association of America* 45 (1930): 110–28.

Minnis, Alistair J. *Chaucer and Pagan Antiquity*. Cambridge: D. S. Brewer and Totowa, N.J.: Rowman and Littlefield, 1982.

Medieval Theory of Authorship. 2nd ed. Philadelphia: University of Pennsylvania Press, 1988.

Monfrin, Jacques. "Humanisme et traductions au moyen âge." *Journal des savants* 148 (1963): 161–90.

"Les Traducteurs et leur public en France au moyen âge." *Journal des savants* 149 (1964): 5–20.

"Les Translations vernaculaires de Virgile au Moyen Age." *Lectures*. 211–20.

Munk Olsen, Birger. "Les Classiques latins dans les florilèges médiévaux antérieurs au XIIIe siècle." *Revue d'histoire des textes* 9 (1979): 47–121, and 10 (1980): 115–64.

L'Étude des auteurs classiques latins aux XIe et XIIe siècles. 3 vols. Paris: Éditions du CNRS, 1982–89.

Murgia, Charles. *Prolegomena to Servius 5: The Manuscripts*. Berkeley, Calif.: University of California Press, 1975.

Newman, Francis X. "'Partriches Wynges': A Note on *Hous of Fame*, 1391-92." *Mediaevalia* 6 (1980): 231–38.

Nitchie, Elizabeth. *Virgil and the English Poets*. New York: Columbia University Press, 1919.

Nitzsche, Jane Chance. *The Genius Figure in Antiquity and the Middle Ages*. New York and London: Columbia University Press, 1975.

Nolan, Barbara. "The Judgment of Paris in the *Roman d'Eneas*: A New Look At Sources and Significance." *The Classical Bulletin* 56 (1980): 52–56.

Chaucer and the Tradition of the Roman Antique (Cambridge University Press, 1992).

Oxford Classical Dictionary. Eds. N. G. L. Hammond and H. H. Scullard. Oxford: Clarendon Press, 1970.

Padoan, Giorgio. "Tradizione e fortuna del commento all' 'Eneide' di Bernardo Silvestre." *Italia Medioevale e Umanistica* 3 (1960): 227–40.

Paré, G., A. Brunet, and P. Tremblay. *La Renaissance du XIIe siècle: les écoles et l'enseignement*. Paris: Vrin, and Ottawa: Institut d'Études Médiévales, 1933.

Parker, Patricia. *Inescapable Romance: Studies in the Poetics of a Mode*. Princeton University Press, 1979.

Patterson, Lee W. *Negotiating the Past: The Historical Understanding of Medieval Literature*. Madison: University of Wisconsin Press, 1987.

Pattie, T. S. "Latin Manuscripts of Virgil in the British Library." R. D. Williams and T. S. Pattie. *Virgil: His Poetry through the Ages*. London: British Library, 1982. 125–38.

Pellegrin, Elisabeth, Jeaninne Fohlen, et al. *Les manuscrits classiques latins de la Bibliothèque Vaticane*. 2 vols. Paris: Éditions du CNRS, 1975–82.

Poirion, Daniel. "De l'Énéide' à l'Eneas': mythologie et moralisation." *Cahiers de civilisation médiévale* 19 (1976): 213–29.

Résurgences: Mythe et littérature à l'âge du symbole (XIIe siècle). Paris: Presses universitaires de France, 1986.

Présence de Virgile: Actes du Colloque des 9, 11, et 12 Décembre 1976. Ed. R. Chevallier. *Caesarodunum* XIII bis, Numéro spécial. Paris: Les Belles lettres, 1978.

Rand, E. K. "Chaucer in Error." *Speculum* 1 (1926): 222–25.

Reinhold, Meyer. "The Unhero Aeneas." *Classica et Mediaevalia* 27 (1966): 195–207.

Reynolds, L. D., ed. *Texts and Transmission: A Survey of the Latin Classics*. Oxford: Clarendon, 1983.

Riché, Pierre. *Ecoles et enseignement dans le Haut Moyen Age*. Paris: Aubier, 1979.

Rouse, Richard. "Florilegia and Latin Classical Authors in Twelfth- and Thirteenth-Century Orleans." *Viator* 10 (1979): 131–60.

Sanford, Eva M. "The Use of Classical Latin Authors in the Libri Manuales." *Transactions and Proceedings of the American Philological Association* 55 (1924): 190–248.

Scherer, Margaret R. *The Legends of Troy in Art and Literature*. New York and London: Phaidon Press for the Metropolitan Museum of Art, 1963.

Schirmer, Walter F. and Ulrich Broich. *Studien zum literarischen Patronat im England des 12. Jahrhunderts*. Cologne and Opladen: Westdeutscher Verlag, 1962.

Schmitz, Götz. *The Fall of Women in Early English Narrative Verse*. Cambridge University Press, 1990.

Segal, Charles. "Art and the Hero: Participation, Detachment, and Narrative Point of View in *Aeneid* 1." *Arethusa* 14 (1981): 67–83.

Seznec, Jean. *The Survival of the Pagan Gods*. Trans. Barbara F. Sessions. New York: Harper, 1953.

Shannon, Edgar F. *Chaucer and the Roman Poets*. 1929; repr. New York: Russell and Russell, 1964.

Shirt, David. "The Dido Episode in the *Enéas*: The Reshaping of Tragedy and its Stylistic Consequences." *Medium Aevum* 51 (1982): 3–17.

Singerman, Jerome E. *Under Clouds of Poesy: Poetry and Truth in French and English Reworkings of the "Aeneid," 1160–1513*. New York: Garland, 1986.

Smalley, Beryl. *English Friars and Antiquity in the Early Fourteenth Century*. Oxford: Basil Blackwell, 1960.

The Study of the Bible in the Middle Ages. Oxford: Blackwell, 1952. Notre Dame: University of Notre Dame Press, 1978.

Southern, Richard W. "The Place of England in the Twelfth Century Renaissance." *Medieval Humanism*. New York and Evanston: Harper and Row, 1970. 158–80.

Spargo, John Wells. *Virgil the Necromancer: Studies in Virgilian Legends*. Cambridge, Mass.: Harvard University Press, 1934.

Spence, Sarah. *Rhetorics of Reason and Desire: Vergil, Augustine, and the Troubadours*. Ithaca, N.Y.: Cornell University Press, 1988.

Steadman, John M. "Chaucer's 'Desert of Libye,' Venus, and Jove (*The Hous of Fame*, 486–87)." *Modern Language Notes* 76 (1961):196–201.

Stock, Brian. *Myth and Science in the Twelfth Century*. Princeton University Press, 1972.

Suerbaum, Werner. "Hundert-Jahre Vergil-Forschung: Eine systematische Arbeits-bibliographie mit besonderer Berüchsichtigung der Aeneis." Section F, "Nachleben und Nachwirkung." *Aufstieg und Niedergang der Römischen Welt*. Part 2. Gen. eds. H. Temporini and W. Haase. Vol. XXXII:1. Ed. W. Haase. Berlin and New York: De Gruyter, 1981. 284–358.

Thomson, Rodney M. "England and the Twelfth-Century Renaissance." *Past and Present* 101 (1983): 3–21.

Tisdale, C. P. R. "The *House of Fame*: Virgilian Reason and Boethian Wisdom." *Comparative Literature* 25 (1973): 247–61.

Ussani, Vicenzo. "Enea traditore." *Studi italiani di filologia classica*, n. s. 22 (1947): 109–23.

Wallace, David. *Chaucer and the Early Writings of Boccaccio*. Woodbridge, Suffolk: D. S. Brewer, 1985.

Walther, Hans. *Initia carminum ac versuum mediiaevi posterioris latinorum. Alphabetische Verzeichnis der Versanfänge mittellateinischer Dichtungen*. 2nd ed. Göttingen: Vandenhoeck and Ruprecht, 1969.

Wetherbee, Winthrop. *Chaucer and the Poets: An Essay on "Troilus and Criseyde."* Ithaca, N.Y.: Cornell University Press, 1984.

Platonism and Poetry in the Twelfth Century: The Literary Influence of the School of Chartres. Princeton University Press, 1972.

Woledge, Brian. *Bibliographie des romans et nouvelles en prose française antérieurs à 1500*. Geneva: Droz, 1954.

Zabughin, Vladimiro. *Virgilio nel rinascimento italiano*. 2 vols. Bologna: Zanichelli, 1921–23.

Index of manuscripts

BASEL
Öffentliche Bibliothek der Universität, F II 23:
80–82, 346 n. 165
BERKELEY
University of California, Bancroft 2: 355 n. 83,
356 n. 91
BERLIN
Staatsbibliothek, Germ. in-fol. 282: 23, 29,
322 n. 26
lat. fol. 34: 340 n. 101, 342 n. 118, 408 n. 1
BERN
Bürgerbibliothek, 411: 357 n. 102
474: 340 n. 101, 342 n. 117
CAMBRIDGE, England
Corpus Christi College 71: 338 n. 88
450: 288, 379 n. 42
Jesus College 33: 47, 294–95, 316 n. 19, 333
n. 29
Pembroke College 260: 135, 291–92, 353
n. 63, 354 nn. 70 and 82
Peterhouse 158: 69, 84–135, 136, 138–39,
153–54, 164, 168, 174–76, 238, 292–94,
296, 309, 347 n. 4, 377 n. 23
159: 308
Queens' College K.17.5, three pastedown
fragments: 304
St. John's College 54: 304–05
205: 306–07
Trinity College 457: 305
623: 295
University Library, Ff.3.5: 338 n. 88
CAMBRIDGE, Massachusetts
Harvard University, Richardson 38: 323 n. 37
COPENHAGEN
Kongelige Bibliotek, Gl. kgl. 2006, 4°: 355 n. 83
Gl. kgl. 2007, 4°: 355 n. 83
DIJON
Bibliothèque municipale, 493: 323 n. 37
EDINBURGH
National Library, Adv. 18.4.13: 290, 377 n. 32
Adv. 18.5.12: 297–98

University Library, 195: 307, 406 n. 19
GHENT
Cathedral Library, 9: 323 n. 37
GLASGOW
Hunterian Museum U.5.19: 60, 338 n. 91, 407
n. 2
THE HAGUE
Rijksmuseum 76 E 21: 323 n. 37
HEIDELBERG
Universitätsbibliothek, palat. germ. 403: 322
n. 29
HEREFORD
Hereford Cathedral O.2.iv: 44, 291, 330 nn. 8
and 9
KETTERING, Northamptonshire
Deene Park Library, binding fragment:
287–88
KLOSTERNEUBERG
Stiftsbibliothek, 742: 23, 25–26, 28–29, 323
n. 42
LENINGRAD
Academy of Sciences Q.443: 309–10
LONDON
British Library, Additional
11959: 305–06
16166: 302–03, 399 n. 74
16380: 39, 339 n. 100, 340 n. 101, 408 n. 1
27304: 69–71, 129, 136-67, 174, 177,'220,
232, 298, 330 n. 3, 362 n. 173, 365 n. 4,
378 n. 37, 378 n. 38, 394 n. 33, 397 n. 52
32319A: 107, 135, 176–77, 292, 295–96, 348
n. 8, 353 n. 63, 353 nn. 65–68, 354
nn. 70 and 78–82, 378 nn. 33–34 and 37,
394 n. 33
33220: 339 n. 98, 339 n. 100, 340 n. 101, 342
n. 118, 408 n. 1
34114: 389 n. 2
Burney 257: 35
269: 141, 299–300
273: 310
277, fol. 73: 307–08

Harley 4967: 300–01
Royal 8.F.XIV, fols. 3–4: 288–89
    12.D.III: 379 n. 42
    13.A.IV: 379 n. 42
    15.B.VI: 300
Sloane 1044, fol. 60, binding fragment: 287
College of Arms, Arundel 30: 286–87
Lambeth Palace, 471: 22, 296–97
Society of Antiquaries, 44: 306
NAPLES
Biblioteca Nazionale, Vindob. lat. 6: 322 n. 24
OXFORD
All Souls College 19: 46
    37: 46
    82: 41–84, 87, 90, 94, 102,
    118, 121, 132, 136, 139,
    141–43, 146–48, 163–64,
    168, 173–74, 176, 178, 220,
    232, 290–92, 311–12, 366
    n. 17, 376 n. 20
    330, nos. 60 and 61: 286
Bodleian Library,
    Add. A.44: 381 n. 58
    A.208: 327 n. 89
    A.365: 379 n. 42
    Ashmole 54: 303–04, 399 n. 74
    Auct. F.1.17: 301-02, 394 n. 33, 399 n. 74
    F.2.7: 306
    F.4.22: 355 n. 83
    Bodley 638: 399 n. 73
    851: 379 nn. 40 and. 42
    Canon. class. lat. 52: 24–25
    Digby 65: 327 n. 89, 379 n. 42
    Fairfax 16: 399 n. 73
    Lat. class. C.2, fol. 18, binding fragment:
    287–88
    Laud. lat. 86: 379 n. 42
    Laud. misc. D 15: 379 n. 42

Laud. misc. 515: 362 n. 182
Rawl. C.86: 399 n. 78
    C.552: 35
    D.1230: 35
    G.109: 379 n. 42
Wood 106, wrapper: plate 6, 283–84, 289
Jesus College 26: 44, 291
Lincoln College 58: 327 n. 89
Merton College 248: 327 n. 89, 327 n. 90
New College 271: 303
PARIS
Bibliothèque de l'Arsenal, 3340: 322 n. 25
    5077: 28, 322 n. 30
Bibliothèque Nationale,
    fr. 60: plate 1, 24, 26, 323 n. 36
    fr. 301: 28 fr.
    784: 26
    fr. 9682: 323 n. 50
    fr. 9685: 323 n. 51
    fr. 20125: 323 n. 50
    lat. 7936: 23-26, 28
PARMA
Biblioteca Palatina, 2662: 297
PERUGIA
Biblioteca Comunale Auguste, C.57: 355 n. 83
SHREWSBURY
Shrewsbury School IV (Mus.III.40): 308
VATICAN
Biblioteca Apostolica Vaticana,
    Ottob. lat. 1373: 298–99, 326 n. 75, 368
    n. 46
    1410: 289–90
    Reg. lat. 1671: 287, 326 n. 76
    Vat. lat. 1574: 102–03, 107, 353 nn. 63 and
    68, 354 nn. 70 and 78–82
WOLFENBÜTTEL
Herzog-August Bibliothek, Guelf. 7.10 (Gud.
    lat. 155 4°): 355 n. 83

General index

access to Virgil, in England, 36–40, 130–35, 220–21; varieties and vectors, 5–16; vernacular, 6–7, 10–14, 20–21, 168–284; *via* illustrations, 21–29; *via* Latin redactions, 17–21; *via* Latin texts, 30–31, 164–67, and *passim*; *via* selections and quotations, 31–36; *see also* counter-tradition

accessus (academic prologues), 34, 64, 301, 316 n. 18, 348 n. 8, 352 n. 58
  of "Anselm of Laon," 64, 313–14, 339 n. 101
  of "Bernard Silvestris," 113–14, 357 n. 111
  of Servius, 306
  to Virgil, general, 6, 85–87, 173, 176–78, 231, 277, 285, 293, 300, 309, 358 n. 117

Achaemenides, 74
Achates, 94, 118, 179, 257–58, 380, 402
Adelard of Bath, 46, 131, 134, 350 n. 34
Adler, Alfred, 383 n. 78, 385 n. 98, 387 n. 123
adolescence, in allegorical commentaries, 10, 68, 96, 116
Adso of Montier-en-Der, 325 n. 71
Aeneas, in *accessus*, 176–77; ancestor of Augustus, 6; of Julius Caesar, 76; compared to Christ, 154–57, 164; compared to Moses, 66; in counter-tradition, 18–21; as *exemplum* of proper behavior, 151–53, 167; figure of Everyman, 10, 39, 67, 92–130; and Hector, 3; as hermeneutic hero, 223–29; ideal prince, 20, 78–79, 153, 178; as liminal figure, 248; in medieval illustration, 23–29; as model for Douglas's translating, 277–78; in Ovid's *Heroides*, 7, 186, 268; and *pietas*, 51; as traitor, 78; *see also* Eneas
Aeneas-and-Dido story, 19, 21, 36, 39, 220, 233, 318 n. 30
Aeolus, 74–75, 79, 106, 134, 147–48, 175, 325 n. 70, 342 n. 119, 364 n. 206, 394 n. 33, 402 n. 102

ages of man, in allegorical exegesis, 85–86, 96–97, 106–07, 110–12, 115–19, 130; *see also* adolescence, infancy, youth
Agrippa, 56
Alan of Lille, 35, 224; *Liber parabolarum*, 301
Albericus of London, the "Third Vatican Mythographer," 106, 130, 134, 238
Alcestis, Alceste, 249–56, 260–63, 266, 268, 271
Alcuin of York, 31, 37–38
Aldhelm, 37–38
Aletes, 161
Alexander of Villedieu, *Doctrinale*, 34
Alfonsi, Luigi, 359 n. 142, 360 n. 146
Alfred, king of England, 38
Alfred of Sareschal, 332 n. 25
Allan, George, 306
Allecto, 150, 207
allegory, Virgilian, 10, 12–13, 47–49, 55, 220–21
  in late antiquity, 91–98
  moralizing, 136–39; Norwich commentator, 151–67
  spiritual and scientific, 62, 84–86, 99, 101, 136–39, 223, 236–44; influence of Boethius and his commentators, 61, 86, 120–30, 225; influence of Martianus Capella and his commentators, 100–01; Peterhouse commentator I, 101–07; Peterhouse commentator II, 108–20
  see also Bernard Silvestris, Fulgentius, *bivium, cuniculus, integumentum, multivocatio*, neoplatonic, Pythagoras, veil
Allen, Judson B., 158, 163, 165–66, 318 n. 29, 365 n. 3, 370 n. 72, 373 n. 112
Allen, Peter, 399 n. 80, 403 n. 113
Aluredus (Alfred), Magister, 44–46, 61–62, 133, 291, 363 n. 186
Amata, 26, 150, 201, 207, 212, 214, 386, 388
Ambrose of Milan, 32
anachronism, in Christianizing allegory 157; in

Li Fet des Romains, 319 n. 1; in *Roman d'Eneas*, 173, 200, 204

Anchises, 51, 60, 76, 84, 96, 101, 115–17, 119, 120–21, 125, 127–29, 150, 156, 176, 219, 228, 234, 257, 266, 370 n. 82, 377 n. 23, 385 n. 103

ancient mother (*antiquam . . . matrem, Aen.* 3.96), 115–16, 124, 128, 177, 206, 228

Andrew of St. Victor, 46, 48–49

Angeli, Giovanna, 374 n. 1, 376 n. 16, 383 n. 75

Angevin court and empire, 11, 16, 45, 62, 168, 177, 180, 210; *see also* Anglo-Norman, Henry II

Anglo-Norman, 1, 11, 13, 15, 57, 174, 206, 208, 210, 321 n. 18

Anna, 55, 193, 196, 214, 234, 259, 264, 383 n. 84

"Anna soror" (Latin sequence), 187–89, 198–200

Anne of Bohemia, 399

"Anselm of Laon," *Aeneid* commentary, 39, 49, 63–68, 72, 111–12, 136, 148–49, 175, 299, 313–14, 315 n. 8, 334 n. 50, 337 n. 77, 353 n. 64, 378 nn. 35 and 37, 380 n. 48; allegorical aspects, 66–68; Bible commentary, 91; source for later commentators, 69–70, 73–74, 76–80

Antenor, 18, 51, 65, 152

Apollo, 19, 59, 67, 96, 116, 120, 128, 176, 226–28, 245–46, 393 n. 23, 403 n. 109

Arachne, 180–84, 191, 198, 380 n. 52

aristocrat, as character or theme in Troy narratives, 151, 181, 193, 202, 206–09, 270, 274; as reader or patron of Troy narratives, 2, 15, 168, 177, 206–07, 220, 276–79

arms of Aeneas, 181–84, 193, 195

Arnulf of Orléans, Ovid commentator, 10

Arthur, king of the Britons, 40

Ascanius, 25, 51, 66, 161–62, 234, 257, 259, 395 n. 35, 402 n. 96

Asia, 51, 78

Astraeus, 74, 344 n. 138

Athena (Pallas), 75, 155, 174, 180–83, 195, 341 n. 114, 380 n. 51, 387 n. 118

auctor (*auctour, autour*), 6, 11, 15–16, 32, 37, 58, 86–87, 91, 99, 101, 115, 224, 233–34, 247, 256, 259–60, 265, 313, 319, 339, 344, 352 n. 58

auctores, respected Latin authors, 3, 7–8, 35, 53, 116, 118–19, 222, 245, 250–52, 268

audience of Virgilian and Troy narratives, 65, 67, 86, 137–39, 245–46; Latin-educated, 46, 130, 172, 174, 178; levels of learning,

8, 98, 118, 149, 163, 167, 247; urban, 275; variety of, 2, 220–21, 270, 274; vernacular-reading, 137, 168–69, 176, 201, 273; *see also* aristocrat

Augustine, St., 32, 66, 122, 279, 341 n. 111; *City of God*, 33, 150–51; *Confessions*, 33, 360 n. 43

Augustus Caesar, emperor, 1, 6, 19, 56, 64, 66–68, 77, 80, 113, 155, 180, 278, 305, 313, 319 n. 1, 345 n. 150, 384 n. 95

Aulne, Belgium, 3

Aurora, 74

Austin, R. G., 50, 78, 330 n. 5, 360 n. 144

authorial intention (*intentio scribentis*), 5–6, 64, 80, 100, 103, 113–14, 165, 232, 246, 316 n. 18, 348 n. 8

authority (*auctoritee*), 17–18, 51, 60, 65, 144, 146, 150, 249, 253, 255, 267, 270–74, 277, 398 n. 67; Chaucerian, 221–22, 256, 260, 262–63, 266, 271, 399 n. 72; Ovidian, 240; Virgilian, 2, 11, 17–21, 30, 92, 128, 163, 166–68, 171, 221, 236, 244, 271, 273–74, 282, 319 n. 6, 397 n. 53

Avernus, 120–21, 243

Avianus, 301

Avril, Franƈois, 23, 322 nn. 32 and 33

Babcock, Robert, 339 n. 99

Bagford, John, 287

Barker-Benfield, Bruce, 288–89

Barlow, Thomas, 297

Barrow, Julia, 330 n. 7

Baswell, Christopher, 294, 316 n. 14, 339 n. 100, 379 n. 43

Bawcutt, Priscilla, 405 n. 14, 406 n. 19

Beaumont, Jacqueline, 338 n. 91

Bede, 38, 329 n. 106

Beer, Jeanette M., 319 n. 1

Beeson, Charles H., 328 n. 97

Bekynton, Thomas, 381 n. 58

Bennett, Adelaide, 310

Bennett, J. A. W., 393 n. 26, 398 n. 59

Benoît de Ste. Maure, *Roman de Troie*, 19–20, 22, 271, 320 n. 9, 321 n. 16, 322 n. 25, 386 n. 104, 392 n. 18

Bernard of Utrecht, commentary on *Ecloga* of Theodulus, 369 n. 59

Bernard Silvestris, 150; *Aeneid* commentary attributed to, 10, 19, 48–49, 61, 67, 75, 79, 85–86, 93–130, 136, 138, 153–57, 160, 164, 166, 168, 227, 238, 241, 245–46, 293, 355 n. 83; Martianus Capella commentary attributed to, 100, 108, 119, 127–28, 131–34, 351 n. 48, 352 n. 60, 356 n. 95, 361 n. 172;

Cosmographia, 332 n. 19, 362 nn. 179 and 182

Bersuire, Pierre (Petrus Berchorius), *Ovidius Moralizatus*, 10, 138, 370 n. 82, 371 n. 99

Bible, 4; as analogy to episodes in *Aeneid*, 154, 156, 370 n. 82; history in, 66; illustration of, 22–24; medieval study of, 12, 137, 158–59, 165; and secular eloquence, 52; twelfth-century exegesis of, 44, 46, 48, 59, 100–01, 348 n. 14, 354 n. 73

Bitias, 160

bivium, image of moral choice, 95, 110–12, 114, 116, 325 n. 71; *see also* Pythagoras

Bloch, R. Howard, 202, 206, 210

Blumenfeld-Kosinski, Renate, 374 n. 3, 375 n. 12, 393 n. 21

Blyth, Charles, 405 n. 14

Boccaccio, Giovanni, 223–24, 272–73, 275, 391 n. 13, 406 n. 21

Boethius, *Consolation of Philosophy*, in Anglo-Saxon England, 38; echoes of *Aeneid*, 121–33, 359 n. 141; influence on Virgil commentary, 59–61, 84, 87, 91, 108, 121–33, 156, 238; references by Chaucer, 224, 237–40, 242, 244–48

Boitani, Piero, 246, 391 n. 13, 396 n. 44, 398 n. 59

Bolgar, R. R., 334 n. 46, 349 n. 20

Bolton, Diane K., 338 n. 91, 407 n. 2

Bovo of Corvey, 60, 122, 127, 361 n. 160

Brandt, Sebastian, 29

Brevis Expositio, 37

Brown, T. Julian, 288; 328 n. 97, 103, 105; 329 n. 106, 335 n. 57, 366 n. 21

Brown, Virginia, 63, 317 n. 27, 339 n. 100, 346 nn. 161–67, 347 nn. 172–75

Brut, 11, 20, 177

Brutus, 40

Brygon, William, 303

Buchthal, Hugo, 21–22, 29, 322 nn. 22 and 25

burghers, as audience, 270, 274

Burnett, Charles, 316 n. 16, 364 n. 207

Bury St. Edmunds, 287, 295, 338 n. 88

Cacus, 138, 157

Caesar, Julius, 76–77, 156, 319 n. 1

Camilla (Camille), 25–26, 28, 157, 174, 184, 198, 202–06, 211–212, 371 n. 103

canons and canons' schools, 42, 61, 330 n. 7, 332 n. 24; Augustinian (Austin) canons, 44–46, 331 n. 15; *see also* Haughmond

Canterbury, 31, 38–39, 339 n. 100, 408 n. 1; St. Augustine's monastery, 288, 300

capitula, as numbered subheadings, 158

Carmina Burana, 170, 187, 381 nn. 57 and 58

Carolingian period, 8; and manuscript format, 42, 52; and Virgilian commentary, 63; Virgil manuscripts of, 286–88

Carthage and Carthaginians, 75, 77, 141, 147, 149, 153, 172, 176, 178, 184–86, 197–98, 202, 225, 234, 242, 248, 257, 275, 279, 280, 282; in allegoresis, 104, 106–07, 116, 128; in *exempla*, 154; in manuscript illustration, 25–26, 29; mercantile wealth of, 189–95, 203, 205–06

Cassandra, 155, 228

catalogs of manuscripts, modern, 9; medieval, 31

Caucasus, 273

Caxton, William, 14, 167; *Eneydos*, 272–79, 281, 318 n. 30; rejected by Gavin Douglas, 279

cento, centones, 17–18

Cervini, Cardinal, 289, 290, 299

Chance, Jane (Jane Chance Nitzsche), 357 n. 98, 358 n. 119, 359 n. 127

Chaucer, Geoffrey
and Troy traditions, 17, 19, 20
and Virgil illustrations, 23
and Virgilian reading, 7–8, 13–14, 30, 39–40, 69, 130, 137, 167, 220–21, 270–71, 276–77
Boece, 6, 239, 244, 316 n. 13
Book of the Duchess, 221
Canterbury Tales, 221, 249, 389 n. 6
House of Fame, 14, 20, 23, 84, 119, 120, 128, 136, 167, 221–48, 250, 255–58, 266, 268, 270; Dido-and-Aeneas story in, 231–36; figure of eagle, 226, 237–41, 243; House of Twigs, 227, 242–47; marginal Latin annotation, 247, 399 n. 73; palace of Fame, 240–42; theme of artifice and craft, 223, 227, 229, 233, 245, 391 n. 16; theme of textual authority, 222–24, 235–37, 240–41, 244–49
Legend of Good Women, Prologue, 249–55; "Legend of Dido," 255–69; theme of autocanonization, 250–51, 268; of craft, 252, 266, 269, 404 n. 119; of governance and reading, 249–50
Parliament of Fowls, 221, 250
Troilus and Criseyde, 222–23, 249–50

Chênerie, Marie-Luise, 374 n. 7

Chichele, Archbishop, 46, 143, 291

Christ, figured by Aeneas, 96, 155–57, 164; by Augustus Caesar, 66, 155; by Nisus and Euryalus, 161–63, 385 n. 98; by other classical characters, 138, 154–55, 325 n. 70

Christianizing uses and interpretations of

Virgil, 17, 66–67, 95, 152–63, 318 n. 29;
their comparative infrequency, 333 n. 43;
of Boethius, 127
Christine de Pizan, 14, 271–72; *Book of the City
of Ladies*, trans. Bryan Anslay, 279–82
Cicero, M. Tullius, 51, 65, 309, 337 n. 79
Cirencester, and ownership of Virgil
manuscript, 44–46, 133, 291
classical Latin, and medieval readers, 9, 12,
44–46, 317 n. 20, 328 n. 97; and
Chaucer, 221, 256; mixed with later
materials, 272
Claudian, 35, 224, 340 n. 104
Cleopatra, in *Legend of Good Women*, 254, 400
n. 85
Cloreus, 205
codex, as site of classical reception, 5–7, 69,
175, 224, 238; and commentary, 52,
86
Colville, John, 307
commentum, term for extended commentary, 58,
86–91
Comparetti, Domenico, 315 n. 4, 318 n. 28,
319 n. 6, 349 n. 18
contest in margins of Virgil text, 1–2, 7, 26, 29,
277; between mortals and gods, 180–83
Cormier, Raymond, 375 n. 9, 376 n. 18, 382
n. 66, 384 n. 89, 385 n. 97, 387 n. 123,
389 n. 149
cosmological themes, 60–61, 84–85, 119, 121,
123, 133, 136, 164
counter-tradition (challenges to Virgilian
authority in Troy tradition; non-Virgilian
Troy narratives), 2, 5, 13–14, 17–21, 30,
79, 137, 153, 185, 270, 283
Courcelle, Pierre and Jeanne, 21, 32, 122, 318
n. 28, 319 n. 5, 322–24, 325 n. 69, 350
n. 34, 359 n. 141, 361–62
Courtenay, William 159
Cowen, Janet, 403 n. 111
Crabbe, Anna, 360 n. 143
Creusa, 186, 228, 232–34, 257–58, 396 n. 45,
402 n. 96
cuniculus, figure of textual mystery, 99–100
Curteys, Willelmus, 295

Daedalus (Didalus), 120, 241, 244–45, 325
n. 71, 380 n. 48; as artisan, 226–27, 242,
245–46, 391 n. 16; Domus Dedaly, 224,
227, 242–45
Dane, Joseph, 390 n. 12, 392 n. 17, 395 n. 41,
397 n. 58
Dante Alighieri, 34, 119, 223–24, 248, 317
n. 20, 401 n. 94; *Divine Comedy*, 8, 84, 391
n. 13

Dares the Phrygian, *De Excidio Troiae Historia*,
18–20, 320 n. 9
de Hamel, Christopher, 330 nn. 8 and 11, 331
n. 18, 348 n. 14
De septem septenis, 350 n. 34
Despenser, Bishop Henry, 220, 367 n. 32
Deiopea, 75, 364
Delany, Sheila, 224, 403 n. 118
Demats, Paule, 165–66, 365 n. 5
descent to the Underworld, 4, 10, 20, 25, 67,
92, 108, 110, 117, 125, 128, 156–57,
200, 226, 228, 234, 238, 241–45, 358
n. 119
Desmond, Marilynn, xii, 356 n. 97, 359
n. 128, 376 n. 21, 400 n. 84, 401 n. 93
Diana, 56, 67, 162, 368 n. 58
Dictys Cretensis, *Ephemeridos Belli Troiani Libri*,
18–19, 320 nn. 9 and 11
Dido, *altera Dido*, 186, 214, 381; in Anselm of
Laon, 64; in Bernard Silvestris 114, 116;
in Caxton's *Eneydos*, 272–75; in Christine
de Pizan, 279–81; in commentaries 72,
75, 79, 107; in Fulgentius, 96; in Gavin
Douglas, 276, 279; illustrations, 24–28,
36; in medieval Latin lyrics, 187–89, 201;
in Norwich commentary, 151, 153–55,
160; in Ovid's *Heroides*, 20, 185–87,
257–58; in Renaissance Troy redactions,
270; in romance vision, 137; in Servius,
51, 94; in Spenser's *Faerie Queene*, 281–83;
non-Virgilian versions 11, 19, 21; see also
Roman d'Eneas; Chaucer, *House of Fame* and
"Legend of Dido"
difference of Virgilian world, production and
erasure in commentaries, 11–12, 23,
28–29, 41, 49, 51, 53, 60, 66, 68–69, 72,
79–81, 83, 138, 150, 163–64, 176
dilatio and delay, as themes of romance,
172–73, 183–85, 189–90, 198–200, 202,
205, 211, 214, 217, 384 n. 95
Dinshaw, Carolyn, 400 n. 86
Dirae, 301
divisio, as stage of exegesis, 165–66, 371 n. 100
domestication of Trojan world in commentary
and redaction, 10–11, 13, 23, 41, 55, 62,
68, 87, 152, 154, 156, 165, 176
Donatus, Aelius, 37; *Ars Grammatica* 33–34
Doob, Penelope Reed, 248, 391 n. 16, 398
nn. 64 and 65
Douglas, Gavin, *Eneados*, 7, 13–14, 19, 40,
167, 276–79, 281, 392 n. 19, 404 n. 120
Drances, 209
dream and dream vision, 125, 224–25,
228–29, 231, 233, 236, 249–50, 254–55,
257, 277, 391 n. 13, 393 n. 23

Dronke, Peter, 98–99, 189, 351–52, 356 n. 96, 358 n. 114, 381–82, 384 n. 88
Dunstan, St., 38, 132

Eberhard of Bethune, *Graecismus*, 34, 304, 394 n. 31
ecphrasis, 181, 230–33, 235–36
"Edwardus G.," 292
Eisenhut, Werner, 320 n. 9
Eleanor of Aquitaine, 374 n. 8
element theory, 133; in Virgil commentary, 67, 94, 104–07, 149, 342 n. 115, 354 n. 79, 359 n. 129, 377 n. 23
eloquence, classical *vs.* biblical, 52; model of Virgil, 2, 4, 12–13, 49, 67, 116; quality of Aeneas, 19, 118, 120
Eneas, allegorized in *Ovide Moralisé*, 156; in Caxton's *Eneydos*, 272–76; in Gavin Douglas, 278–79; in *House of Fame*, 232, 234–36; in illustration, 24; in "Legend of Dido," 256–68; in Pierre de Saintes' "Viribus, arte, minis...," 178–79; in *Roman d'Eneas*, 169–219; son of Humphrey de Bohun 40; *see also* Aeneas
Euboean cave, 242
Euridice, 68
Euryalus (Eurialus), 24, 138, 157, 160–63, 201, 387 n. 117; *see also* Nisus
Eusebian model of history, 66, 92, 98
Evander, 152, 156, 180, 203–04, 370 n. 71
Everyman, figured by Aeneas in allegorical tradition, 20, 97, 115, 138, 156, 164, 227
exegesis, biblical, 12, 46, 48, 59; and classical myth, 138; conflicting, 220–21, 272; and etymology, 94; in *House of Fame*, 224, 227, 229, 246; interlinear, marginal, independent, 86–91; multiple layers, 85; numerological, 67; *see also* allegory, gloss, margins, pedagogical exegesis
exempla, in classical florilegia, 35; derived from *Aeneid*, 137–38, 152–55, 157–58, 160, 279; in *House of Fame*, 236, 397 n. 52

fable (*fabula*), 19, 85, 91, 97–101, 108, 110, 114–16, 119, 120, 160, 165, 241, 244, 380 n. 48
Fame (Fama), 125, 196, 224, 226–30, 232, 235, 237, 240–41, 245, 266, 395 n. 37
Faral, Edmond, 374 nn. 5 and 6, 379 n. 41
Farrow, James, 320 n. 11
fides, 66, 341 n. 113
figural, in play with literal in *Roman d'Eneas*, 212–14, 216, 229
figure (*figura*), of eroticism, 25, 186, 190, 212, 384 n. 95; of grammar master, 171; in

House of Fame, 225–27, 229, 237, 248, 393 n. 24; in *Legend of Good Women*, 254, 265–66; of poetry as holy place, 93–94; as hidden place, 98; of rhetoric in *Aeneid* exegesis, 33, 68, 73, 81; *see also* allegory, rhetoric
Filargyrian scholia, 37
fire (*ignis*, "fyr"), 3, 25–26, 54, 66, 71, 104–05, 107, 149, 186, 189, 206, 239, 264–65, 311, 341 n. 113, 342 n. 122, 354 n. 79, 368 nn. 52 and 53, 377 n. 23, 379 n. 46, 403 n. 109
"flattening," simplifying impact of glosses, 55–56, 61–62, 164, 231
Flemmyng, Robert, 304–05
florilegia, classical texts in, 15, 35–36, 152
fragmentation of text in moral allegoresis, 10, 138–39
Frank, Robert W., 390 n. 8, 403 nn. 116 and 118
Freud, Sigmund, instance of extra-textual reception, 16, 31
friars, and classical study, 39, 137–38, 158–59, 163, 166, 232, 289–90, 299, 305, 369 n. 61, 370 n. 73, 394 n. 31
Friend, A. C., 393 n. 26, 396 nn. 45 and 47
Fulgentius, Fabius Planciadis, *Expositio Vergilianae Continentiae*, 10, 17, 48, 85, 94–97, 103, 106–07, 110–11, 116, 122–27, 134, 137, 315 n. 3, 351 n. 37
Fyler, John, 234, 391 n. 13, 393 n. 25, 397 n. 53, 398 n. 60, 400 n. 82, 401 n. 93, 402 n. 101

Ganz, David, 288
Gaunt, Simon, 385 nn. 96 and 98, 386 nn. 105 and 107, 388 n. 141, 389 n. 145
genealogy, 170, 173, 177–78, 181, 201, 206–07, 273, 281, 303, 307; Angevin and English links with Trojan, 7, 40, 168, 172, 179, 202, 282; and epic, 1, 7; in Virgil commentaries, 149, 219
Geoffrey of Monmouth, 329 n. 116
Geoffrey of Vinsauf, *Poetria Nova*, 35, 301, 309–10, 390 n. 12
geography in Virgilian commentary, 11–12, 22, 29, 41, 48–52, 54–57, 64–65, 68, 73, 75–79, 81, 84, 141–43, 146, 148, 152, 163, 231, 296
Gerald of Wales, 133, 338 n. 88, 364 n. 202
Gerbert of Reims, 63
Gervase of Melkley, *Ars Poetica*, 4, 315 nn. 5 and 6
Gilbert of Poitiers, commentary on Pauline Epistles, 44–45, 91, 291

Gilbert Foliot, 133

Gildas, 36, 38

Glauche, Günter, 324 n. 65

gleaning, image for poetic creation, 251–52

gloss (*glosa*), *see* chs. 2–4; vs. *commentum*, 58, 86–91; in *House of Fame*, 234–35; incorporated in translations, 6, 173–76; interlinear, 53; in "Legend of Dido," 266; and scripts, 53–54; simplifying primary text, 54–56, 62, 231–32; vernacular, 63, 147; *see also* exegesis, margins

glossaries, 33, 57

glosule, collected annotations, 58, 87, 91, 348 n. 13

Gneuss, Helmut, 287–88

golden bough (*aureus. . .ramus, Aen.* 6.137), 36, 67, 95–96, 107, 110–12, 116–18, 120, 125, 143, 156, 342 n. 117, 354 n. 82, 356 n. 91, 357 nn. 99 and 102–05, 358 n. 108

Goldstoy, Laurens, 300

Goold, George, 328 nn. 97, 100 and 102; 334 n. 45

Grafton, Antony, 81–82, 346 nn. 168–70

grammar, focus in Virgil exegesis, 12, 46, 49–50, 52–54, 57, 61–62, 65, 67, 84, 141–42, 148, 165, 173, 290, 295–96, 299, 300–01, 305; in gloss *vs.* in commentary, 87–91; schools 137, 159, 171; in translation, 231; Virgil citations in texts, 33–34, 36–37, 39; *see also* exegesis, pedagogical, liberal arts

grammatica, 33, 56, 248, 335 n. 56, 341 n. 109, 397 n. 58

Gratian, *Decretum*, 44–45

Gray, Sir Thomas, *Scalacronica*, 4–5

Greek, etymology, 57, 94; grammar, 368 ·n. 50; Macrobius and, 93, 337 n. 77; Servius and, 50–51, 382 n. 68

Guarino da Verona, 47, 81–82, 294, 316 n. 19, 346 n. 168

Guenée, Bernard, 319 n. 33

Guido delle Colonne (Guido de Columins), *Historia Destructionis Troiae*, 18–20, 22, 29, 271, 304, 320 n. 9, 394 n. 31, 407 n. 29

Gullick, Michael, 330 n. 8

Gunthorpe, John, 47, 294, 333 n. 29

Hagendahl, H., 32

Hall, Lewis Brewer, 318 n. 30, 393 n. 26, 395 nn. 40 and 41, 404 n. 4

Harpies, 58, 228, 344 n. 138

Haughmond, Augustinian abbey, 45, 331 nn. 14 and 16–17; *see also* canons and canons' schools

Häring, Nikolaus M., 91, 348 n. 10

heaven (*caelum, celum*), 59, 107, 112, 156, 226, 240, 307, 314, 316 n. 10, 322 n. 33, 325 n. 70, 350 n. 34, 354 n. 82, 357 n. 105, 371 nn. 88 and 92, 387 n. 118

Hector, 3, 18, 76, 178, 186, 228, 344 n. 142, 368 n. 48, 389 n. 6

Helen of Troy, 18, 178, 214, 283, 344 n. 142, 375 n. 10, 379 n. 43, 381 n. 55

Helenus, 75, 79, 228, 242–43

hell (the Underworld), 3–4, 10, 20, 24, 68, 95, 106–07, 111, 117, 134, 155–57, 200, 224, 243–45, 364 n. 206, 371 n. 103

Henry I, 374 n. 8

Henry II, 1, 42, 44–46, 62, 131, 133, 168, 178–80, 201, 210, 374–75

Henry of Huntingdon, 32–33, 325 n. 68

Hercules, 68, 118, 138, 152, 157, 336 n. 72, 354 n. 71, 371 nn. 96–99

Hereford, 40, 44, 132–34, 291, 330 nn. 8–10

hermeneutic dialogue, 254–55, 268

hero, heroism, 5, 15, 18, 20–23, 26, 28, 79, 92, 115, 137, 173, 181, 211, 221, 244, 246, 258, 278, 282; and Boethian journey, 122–29; male, 25, 262; model for contemporary moral action, 151–54, 164–65; as poet, 242, 248, 271, 277–78; as reader, 14, 222–36; as student, 115–19; *see also* Aeneas, Eneas, Nisus and Euryalus

heroine, 26, 191, 200, 222, 254–55, 257, 261; *see also* Dido, Camilla, Lavinia

Hexter, Ralph, 33, 316 n. 18, 326 n. 74, 333 n. 43, 336 n. 64, 342 nn. 119 and 125, 348 n. 14, 366 n. 8, 374 n. 6, 378 n. 39

Hippolytus, 150, 368 n. 58

Histoire ancienne jusqu'à César, 11, 20–22, 25, 28, 271–72, 321 n. 19, 393 n. 26, 404 n. 2, 405 n. 5

Holcot, Robert, 39

Holtz, Louis, 328 n. 103, 335 n. 53

homeland, Boethian quest, 124–25, 244, 360 n. 150

Homer, 19, 113, 334 n. 46, 350 n. 28

homosexuality, male friendship, homosociality, 3, 160–63, 201, 203, 385 nn. 96 and 98, 386 n. 107

Honorius of Autun, 193

Horace, 33, 35, 39, 332 n. 20, 359 n. 141

Hornsen, Johannes, 304

hortatory tone in moral allegory, 152, 154, 158, 163

Huchet, Jean-Charles, 375 nn. 10 and 15; 376 n. 19; 380 nn. 50 and 52; 382 n. 68; 387 nn. 116 and 122; 388 nn. 129, 140 and 142; 389 n. 147

Hugh of St. Victor, 48, 58, 60, 315 n. 6
Humphrey de Bohun, 40
Hunt, Richard W., 286, 291, 300, 303, 331
nn. 12 and 15, 348 n. 8, 363 nn. 192 and
200
Hunt, Tony, 339 n. 96

Iarbas (Yarbas), 196, 266, 275, 383 n. 84, 390
n. 10, 405 n. 12
ideology, articulated in commentary, 152, 165,
334 n. 46; see also Servius
Ilium, 51, 74, 186, 340 n. 105, 343 n. 135
illustrations of Virgil texts and vernacular
versions, 8, 10, 13, 15–16, 21–30, 204,
220–21, 231, 322
imitation of Virgil and Aeneid, 5, 7, 11, 17, 49,
51, 62, 78, 127–28, 172, 179, 223, 255,
338 n. 94, 380 n. 47; in spiritual allegory,
112, 116, 128; by Virgil of harmony of
nature, 92; by Virgil of Homer, 113, 313
Imtheachta Æniasa, 39, 329 n. 112; see also Irish
integumentum, 99–100, 105, 352 n. 52, 361
nn. 166 and 172, 362 n. 174
interpenetration of approaches to Virgil, 13; of
Virgil with Boethius, 121, 127–29, 238; of
Virgil with Ovid, 170
intertextuality, 127–30, 361 n. 172, 362
n. 179, 400 n. 84
Irish, tradition of Servius, 37, 328 nn. 101 and
102, 335 n. 53; Virgilianism, 37–39; see
also Imtheachta Æniasa
Irvine, Martin, 334 n. 46, 397 n. 58
Isidore of Seville, 57, 204, 337 n. 77, 357
n. 103, 398 n. 59
Italy, Aeneas in, 11, 51, 64–65, 67, 104, 153,
176, 188, 228, 234, 258, 290, 313, 360
n. 148, 378 n. 37, 390 n. 11;
allegorization of, 116, 128, 155; humanist
exegesis in, 41, 80–82, 85, 137;
illustration of Troy narratives in, 22,
24–26, 322 n. 22; influence of vernacular
on Chaucer, 221, 391 n. 13; on Christine
de Pizan, 272; manuscripts of Virgil in,
30, 40, 47, 294, 296, 303–04, 309–10;
reading of Virgil in, 8–9, 347 n. 2, 395
n. 40; see also Latium
Ivo of Chartres, 44, 291

Jardine, Lisa, 81–82
Jean de Meun, 34
Jeauneau, Edouard, 351 n. 48, 352 n. 52, 355
n. 83, 356 n. 91, 361 nn. 166 and 172,
362 n. 182, 363 nn. 190 and 198
Jerome, St., 21, 32, 250, 325 n. 68
John Free, 47, 294–95, 316 n. 19

John of Garland, 34
John of Salisbury, Metalogicon, 132; Policraticus,
85, 110, 130, 238, 321 n. 15, 338 n. 88,
347 n. 3, 362 n. 174, 363 n. 191, 393
n. 23
John of Westphalia, 308
Jonah, 24
Jones, Julian W., 95, 108–10, 112, 294, 315
n. 3, 334 n. 47, 350 n. 30, 359 n. 132; and
Elizabeth Frances, 132, 134, 316 n. 16,
333 nn. 31 and 42, 347 n. 2
Joseph of Exeter (Josephus Iscanus), Daretis
Yliados libri sex, 62, 338 n. 94
Joyner, William, 390 n. 11, 397 n. 55, 398
n. 62
judicial duel (judicium Dei) in Roman d'Eneas,
208–11
judicial rhetoric and procedure in Roman
d'Eneas, 202, 250
Juno, 36, 71, 74–75, 79, 94, 101, 103–04,
106–07, 119, 128, 134, 142, 148, 150,
155, 174, 179, 192, 207, 209, 225–26,
232, 234, 237, 241, 245–46, 258
Jupiter, 24, 59, 66, 94, 101, 107, 119, 125,
128, 153, 155, 196, 238, 325 n. 70, 393
n. 23
Justin, Epitome of Trogus, 21
Justinian, Emperor, 20, 300
Juvenal, 33, 308, 340 n. 106

Kallendorf, Craig, 80, 346 nn. 161–66, 347
nn. 172–75
Kaster, Robert, 51, 53, 93, 319 n. 2, 349
nn. 21–22 and 24
Ker, Neil R., 44, 289–91, 295, 297–301, 304,
306, 330 n. 9, 332 nn. 22 and 28
kingship, 177, 205, 211, 251, 255
Kirkstede, Henry de, 288
Kiser, Lisa J., 399 n. 80, 400 n. 81, 401 n. 89,
402 n. 100
Kolve, V. A., 400 nn. 82 and 87, 401 n. 89

labyrinth (laboryntus), 227, 242–45, 391 n. 16,
398 nn. 64–65 and 68, 399 n. 77
Lactantius Placidus, 32, 95, 110, 325 n. 71
Lady Philosophy, 121, 123–26, 128, 130,
238–40, 244, 360 nn. 147 and 148; see also
Boethius, Consolation of Philosophy
laments, of Dido, 185, 187–89; for death of
Pallas, 203, 234–35, 381 nn. 53 and 58,
384 n. 88, 396 n. 49
Landino, Cristoforo, 82, 137, 347 n. 2
Laocoon, 344 n. 142
Lapidge, Michael, 36, 324 nn. 63 and 65, 327
nn. 93 and 94, 328 n. 99

late antiquity, and reverence for Virgil, 2, 32–34, 36, 40–41, 50–51, 53, 66, 92, 95–96, 123, 221, 349 n. 21; *see also* Boethius; Fulgentius; Kaster, Robert; Macrobius; Servius
Latimer, John, 144–46, 366 nn. 26 and 27
Latinity and access to Virgil, 2, 11, 23, 30–36, 68, 171, 180
Latium, Aeneas in, 107, 110, 155, 176, 179, 200, 202, 325 n. 71, 380 n. 47, 385 n. 101; imperial destiny in, 180, 183, 206–07, 282; *see also* Italy
Latona, 56, 118
Lavinia (Lavina, Lavine), 24, 26, 97, 148–49, 168–74, 177, 181, 185–86, 195, 200–03, 207–08, 210–17, 234, 281
law, Dido and, 261; in *Roman d'Eneas*, 172, 175–76, 180, 200–02, 208–10, 213, 216; texts, 44–45, 300; Virgil as authority in, 50, 92–93; in Virgilian *accessus*, 176; in Virgilian allegory, 107
Leclercq, Dom Jean, 3, 315 nn. 1–3
Lefevre, Raoul, *Recolles of Troye*, 271, 406 n. 21
Leff, Gordon, 326 n. 80, 365 n. 1
legends, 16, 75, 271; of Virgil, 15–16, 319 n. 6
lemmata, 44, 115, 247, 294
Lerer, Seth, 351 n. 42, 362 n. 174
Lerna, 57
Leube, Eberhard, 318 n. 29, 321 n. 19, 365 n. 6, 404 n. 1, 405 n. 5, 407 n. 37
Li Fet des Romains, 319 n. 1
Liber Prometheus, 300
liberal arts (*artes*), 3, 10, 86, 92, 108, 110, 115–20, 132, 175, 301, 350 n. 34, 380 n. 47; *quadrivium*, 117, 133; *trivium*, 33, 44, 46, 51, 56, 73, 117–18, 133; *see also grammatica*
libraries, medieval, and Virgil texts, 8, 31, 38, 44, 69, 289
Libya, 73, 77, 134, 184, 225, 237, 257, 325 n. 70, 364 n. 206, 380 n. 47
Lincoln College, 304–05, 327 n. 89
littera, and exegesis, 58, 87, 90, 102, 117; and the writing of God, 349 n. 20
Little, Lester K., 193, 383 n. 76
Livre des Eneydes, 11, 272, 405 n. 5
Lord, Mary Louise, 322 n. 20, 339 n. 100, 347 n. 2, 362 n. 174, 365 n. 4, 369 n. 61, 371 n. 89, 372 n. 105, 408 n. 1
Lucan, 33
Lucrece, 253–54, 400 n. 85
Lydgate, John, 320 n. 9, 399 n. 73

Macrobius, 19, 49, 59–61, 92–101, 105, 113, 123, 136; *Commentary on the Dream of Scipio*, 94, 97, 383 n. 73; *Saturnalia*, 59–60, 75, 84, 92–94, 97–99, 123, 136, 338 n. 88, 349 nn. 17 and 21, 350 n. 28; notion of elite readership, 93–94, 98; figure of Praetextatus, 60, 93, 98
magister, 86, 114–15, 118, 330 n. 7, 368 n. 48; Anselmus, 339 n. 98; Virgil as, 96, 315 n. 3
manuscripts, format of and commentary, 14, 42, 44, 57, 86–91, 139, 141, 247, 406 nn. 19 and 20
margin, annotation of, 2; damaged by use, 69–70; format of, 44, 52–53; *vs.* interlinear space, 58; and move to center of page, 6, 173, 271, 273, 316 n. 12, 405 n. 8; record of multiple reading, 8, 13, 30, 42, 84, 166; *vs.* separate commentaries, 91, 102, 355 n. 83; site of contest, 1–2, 5–7, 183, 253, 277; site of readership, 247–48; voices in, 86, 316 n. 14; *see also* exegesis, gloss
marginality, of Chaucerian narrator, 250; of Dido, 198; of feminine power, 200, 211, 385 n. 98; of grammarian, 51–52; of Latin, 247
Manitius, Max, 324 n. 65, 339 n. 98
Mapheus Vegius, 303, 306–07
Marchello-Nizia, Christiane, 384 n. 95, 385 n. 103, 386 n. 109, 389 n. 147
Mars, 59, 95, 123, 175, 180–81, 183
Marsyas, 232, 368 n. 50
martial themes, 26, 137, 160, 181, 183, 227, 404 n. 122
Martial, 35, 289, 291
Martianus Capella, 224; commentary by Alexander Neckam, 133; *see also* Bernard Silvestris
Martyn, Parcyuall, 304
marvels, omission of, 20; in *Roman d'Eneas*, 184, 192–93
Mary, Virgin, 138, 156–57, 162, 280, 401 n. 89
Mathilda of Scotland, 374 n. 8
Matthew of Vendôme, 35; *Tobias*, 301
Matthew of Westminster, *Flores historiarum*, 46
McCall, John P., 389 n. 3, 391 n. 13
Medea, 254, 374 n. 5
Meech, Sanford Brown, 395 n. 40
Mercury, 95–96, 116, 119, 128, 153, 196, 228, 237, 239, 266, 275, 322 n. 33, 354 n. 71, 395 n. 35, 398 n. 62
Mezentius (Mesencius), 208–09
metonymy, 51, 102, 210–11, 214
metrical annotation and commentary, 33, 35,

37–38, 65, 141–42, 298, 301, 326 n. 77,
336 n. 73, 366 n. 11
Meyer, Paul, 321 n. 19, 389 n. 2
Minnis, Alistair J., 165, 300, 317 n. 20, 318
n. 29, 340 n. 102, 348 n. 8, 352 n. 58, 357
n. 111, 373 n. 135, 389 n. 3
Minos, 58, 337 n. 85
Misenus, 96, 150
mistice, term for allegorical reading, 87
modus agendi, category in *accessus*, 113–14
monasteries, and education, 137; and texts of
Virgil, 3, 37, 39, 41, 52, 285, 289
Monfrin, Jacques, 316 n. 12, 319 n. 31, 321
nn. 18 and 19, 322 n. 21, 323 n. 44, 404
n. 3, 405 n. 5
Mountford, James F., 326 n. 75
multivocatio, multiple meanings in allegorical
exegesis, 118
Munk Olsen, Birger, 9, 30, 39, 320 n. 10, 324
nn. 59 and 60, 326 n. 84, 327 nn. 85 and
87–89
Murgia, Charles, 49, 290, 317 n. 21, 328
n. 101, 333 nn. 40 and 41
Muses, 124, 142, 359 n. 129
musical notation, 324 n. 59
mystery, of Virgilian text, 11, 75, 94, 99, 350
n. 30, 352 n. 53
Mythographers, Three Vatican, 76, 85, 106,
130–31, 134, 175, 192, 238, 303–04, 364
n. 204; *see also* Fulgentius; Servius
mythography, 65, 75, 102–03, 105, 175,
220–21, 231, 289, 317 n. 20, 318 n. 29,
353 n. 69, 357 n. 98, 365 n. 5, 379 n. 43,
400 n. 82

naked text, 252, 256, 268, 400
narratio fabulosa, 97, 99, 351 n. 48
Neckam, Alexander, commentary on
Martianus Capella, 133; *De Naturis Rerum*,
349 n. 20
Neoplatonic influence on allegorical exegesis,
92, 95, 111, 352 n. 56
Neptune, 59, 74, 102, 104, 107, 144, 182, 325
n. 70, 360 n. 148
Nereids, 56
New Philology, 316 n. 11
Nigel Whiteacre, *Brunellus*, 46, 72
Nisus, 24, 138, 157, 160–63, 201; *see also*
Euryalus
Nitchie, Elizabeth, 318 n. 28
Nitzsche, Jane Chance, see Chance, Jane
Nolan, Barbara, xii, 175, 316 n. 12, 374 nn. 3
and 4, 376 n. 16, 377 n. 26, 381 n. 54,
382 n. 69, 383 n. 85, 384 nn. 92 and 94,

386 n. 104, 388 nn. 133 and 139, 390
n. 7, 392 n. 18
Norman, cultural milieu, 3, 22, 39, 171–73,
210; political claims, 206, 208, 321 n. 18,
374 nn. 1 and 8; vernacular, 168; *see also*
Angevin; Anglo-Norman
Norwich, 143–67; moral exemplum and moral
allegory in Norwich commentator,
151–67; *see also* allegory, moralizing
notularis, handwriting and annotation, 53, 58,
69, 141, 336 n. 75
number symbolism, 67, 115, 192, 205, 383
n. 73, 387 n. 118
Nykke, Richard, 307

Oceanus, 56
Octavien, 271
Oenotri, 57, 78, 337 n. 77
Orcus, 117
ordines, 64, 74, 96, 114, 343 n. 133, 357 n. 111,
378 n. 33, 395 n. 41; *ordo artificialis*
(narration out of chronological order), 74,
114, 141, 176, 186, 224, 343 n. 136, 366
n. 9; *ordo naturalis* (narration in
chronological order), 74, 114, 176, 233,
318 n. 30, 358 n. 114
Orestes, 111, 149, 381 n. 51, 405 n. 9
Origo troianorum, 306–07
Orléans, and classical studies, 10, 34–35, 135,
326 n. 84
Orpheus, 68, 100, 244
Osbert of Clare, 332 n. 20
Ovid, 16, 19, 33, 35, 152, 160, 165–66, 170,
179, 185, 197, 223–24, 247, 249, 301,
304; *aetas Ovidiana*, 39; *Ars amatoria*, 170,
381; *Heroides*, 17, 20, 185–89, 213–14,
218, 233–35, 256–62, 264, 266–68, 275,
377, 393, 395, 402, 405; *Metamorphoses*,
10, 39, 138, 156, 166, 181–85, 227,
231, 240, 242, 394; *see also* Petrus
Berchorius
Ovide Moralisé, 10, 138, 156–57, 365 n. 6, 371
nn. 90 and 99
Oxford, classical studies at, 39, 158; Virgil in
medieval, 143

Paetow, Louis John, 34, 326 n. 80
Palinurus, 23–24, 156, 234, 323 n. 42, 364
n. 206, 399 n. 73
Palladium, 75
Pallas, 24, 29, 202–07, 210–11, 377 n. 30, 386
nn. 107 and 110, 387 n. 118
Palmer, Nigel, 247
para-narrative in allegorical exegesis, 87
Paris, prince of Troy, 6, 18, 175, 178–79, 191,

207, 218, 282–83, 316 n. 12, 377 n. 26, 380 n. 49, 381 n. 55, 382 n. 69

Paris, France, English students at, 362 n. 183

Parker, Patrica, 172

Pasquali, Giorgio, 318 n. 28

passion, 96, 116, 144, 161, 221, 268; of Christ, 161, 373 n. 125; of Dido, 234, 261, 264, 269, 282, 381 n. 54, 383 n. 78, 387 n. 121, 403 n. 108; in allegorical exegesis 125, 128

patriarchy, 195–96; and empire, 170–71, 174, 180–81, 200, 203, 205, 282, 374 n. 7, 387 n. 125; and divine justice, 182–84

Patterson, Lee W., 376 n. 17, 380 n. 52, 384 n. 95, 385 n. 103, 387 n. 124

Pearl, 6, 401 n. 89

Peasants' Revolt, 143–46, 151–52, 367 nn. 29–32

pedagogical exegesis, 8, 9, 12, 13, 28, 41–42, 47–49, 50–53, 61, 64–65, 68, 72, 78–84, 94, 102–03, 106–07, 113, 118, 135–37, 139, 141, 143, 146–55, 159, 163–65, 167–69, 173–75, 179, 202, 212, 219, 231–32, 236–37, 290

Penwortham, Henry, 44, 46–47, 72, 143, 291, 332 n. 28

Persius, 301, 308

Peter Damian, 193

Peter Lombard, 45, 193

Peter of Blois, 132, 363 n. 190

Peterhouse commentator I, 101–07; Peterhouse commentator II, 108–20; *see also* allegory, spiritual and scientific

Petrarch, 32, 346 n. 163

Petrus Berchorius (Pierre Bersuire), *Ovidius moralizatus*, 10, 138, 365 n. 6, 370 n. 82, 371 nn. 99 and 100

Pharnaces, 77, 345 n. 149

Philoctetes, 336 n. 72

Phrygians, 78, 147

Pierre de Saintes, poet and tutor of Henry II, 46, 184, 187; "Viribus, arte, minis," 178, 201, 379 n. 43

pietas, 19, 51, 146, 379 n. 46

pilgrimage, in allegorical exegesis, 84, 86, 115, 119, 121, 155, 164, 325 n. 71; theme in *House of Fame*, 242, 248

Pisan, Christine de, *Book of the City of Ladies*, 14, 271–72, 279–82, 407 nn. 37 and 38

plaint, of Dido, 173, 185, 187–88, 197–98, 264; *see also* laments

Plato, *Timaeus*, 105, 109

Plato ad ostendendum, 356 n. 95

platonic tradition, 60–61, 84, 91–92, 94–95, 105, 111, 121, 127, 130–33, 136–39, 154, 164, 221, 352 n. 56, 370 n. 82

Plautus, 33

Poirion, Daniel, 11, 376 n. 16, 377 n. 22, 382 nn. 64 and 69, 386 nn. 105–07 and 113, 388 n. 130, 389 nn. 144 and 146

Polydorus, 72, 142, 154

Polyxena, 76, 185

Pompey, 77

pre-Carolingian Virgil exegesis, 31, 335 n. 53

pregnancy, Dido's, 95, 186, 188, 261, 267

Priam, 18, 76, 344 nn. 142 and 143, 366 n. 16, 389 n. 6

Priscian, *Institutionum Grammaticarum Libri XVIII*, 33–34, 65, 326 n. 77, 339 n. 98, 341 n. 107, 397 n. 58

Prise, Sir John, 291, 330 nn. 9 and 10, 332 n. 22

private war, 206–10

Proba, *cento* of, 18, 301, 309, 319 n. 7

prophet, Virgil as, 16–17, 20

Proserpine, 111, 183

Prudentius, 35, 302, 306, 325 n. 70

pseudo-Ovid, 42, 251, 309

Pygmalion, brother of Dido, 190, 402 n. 97

Pythagoras, 68, 92, 95, 110–12, 121, 201, 350 n. 33, 357 n. 98; *see also bivium*.

quaestio, in Virgil exegesis, 59–60, 338 n. 89

queenship, 205, 264, 267–68

Quintilian, 52

Quirinus, 56

Rabon, William, 302

Rand, E. K., 34, 359 n. 141, 394 n. 34, 395 n. 35

Raynaud de Lage, Guy, 321 n. 19, 377 n. 30, 404 n. 2

Raynoldes, John, 305

referential landscape, 55, 223–24, 238

reification, in *House of Fame*, 237–38, 240

Remigius of Auxerre, 63, 126–27, 361 n. 156

revestiture, in *Legend of Good Women*, 253, 255

rhetoric, in Anselm of Laon, 65–68; in biblical exegesis, 165; in *House of Fame*, 235; in Macrobius, 92; in *Roman d'Eneas*, 175, 201–02, 217; in Servius, 50–53; study of, 4, 33–34, 36, 46, 61, 160; in Virgil exegesis, 12, 49, 56, 71, 73–74, 79–81, 102–03, 141, 148, 165, 295–301, 304–05, 307; Virgilian, 19; see also pedagogical exegesis

rhetorical figures cited: afferesis, 354 n. 71; anafora, 354 n. 71; anastrophe, 354 n. 71; antitesis, 354 n. 71; antonomasia, 4; eneletica oratio, 354 n. 71; exclamatio, eneletica oratio, 354 n. 71; exclamatio, 336 n. 70; hendiadys (endiadis), 65, 102, 343 n. 131; hiperbole, 336 n. 70; hysteron proteron, 65, 102; istrologia, 354 n. 71; litotes, 73, 342 n. 119; locutio plenaria, 343 n. 131; methonomia, 51, 340 n. 106; paradigma, 354 n. 71; perifrasis, 354 n. 71; prosopopeia, 343 n. 131; syncope, 148; tapinosis, 142; temesis, 336 n. 70; topographia, 73, 149, 343 n. 129, 368; topothesia, 73, 149, 343 n. 129, 368 n. 51; ypallage, 354 n. 71

Richard of Poitiers, 178

Ringstead, Thomas, 159, 372 n. 110

ritual, antique, in Virgil exegesis, 24–25, 50, 59–60, 136, 175–76, 350 n. 29

Robert de Saint Victor, 290

Robert of Auxerre, 354 n. 73

Roman and sub-Roman Britain, learning and Virgilianism, 36, 327 nn. 91–93

roman antique, 11, 227, 321 n. 19, 374 n. 3, 375 n. 15, 376 n. 16, 377 n. 30, 392 n. 18

Roman d'Eneas, 11, 13, 28, 62; *Amors*, 169–73, 197, 212, 214–15; *angin*, 190–92, 197–98, 216; arming of Eneas, 172, 180, 184; *Arranz*, 205, 387 n. 117; containment as theme, 169–71, 181, 190, 198–200, 204, 210–11; debate in, 202, 211–16; Dido, esp. 190–200; *desmesure* (excess), 192–93, 199–200, 203–05, 211, 215; *fole amor*, 169, 216–17, 377 n. 26, 381 n. 54; illustrations of, 24, 26; manuscripts of, 20, 321 n. 18; *mesure*, 208–09, 215–17, 388 n. 136; *proëce*, 190–91, 198; *richece*, 190–92, 192, 198; trade, 168, 190–95, 205, 383 n. 78; transgression, 215, 255, 260, 264, 267; unbinding, 246, 248, 267–68; *volente*, 195, 215–16; *see also* Camilla; Eneas; Nisus; and Euryalus

Roman de Thèbes, 20, 386 n. 104, 393 n. 21

romance vision of Virgil, 8–11, 13, 15–16, 136–37, 153–54, 167–219, 224, 231, 233, 235–36, 262, 283

Romulus, 56, 177–78, 336 n. 73

Rouse, Richard, 35, 288, 326 n. 84, 327 n. 86; Richard and Mary, 326 n. 84

Rudd, John, 298

Rumor, 235, 238, 240, 390 n. 11, 398 n. 64; *see also* Fame

Russell, John, 303

Rutilians, 64

Sabaea, 77

Salutati, Coluccio, as Virgil annotator, 80–82, 346 nn. 161–67, 347 nn. 172–75

Salverda de Grave, J.-J., 321 n. 18, 374 n. 2, 389 n. 2

Sanford, Eva M., 302, 326 n. 84

Schmitz, Götz, 256, 397 n. 50

Scholia Bernensia, 37

Schreiber, Earl G., and Thomas E. Maresca, 116, 316 n. 16, 344 n. 141, 358 n. 113, 358 n. 122, 359 n. 127

scientia, Virgil's, 17, 52, 92, 321 n. 15, 349 n. 16; and grammatical education, 335 n. 56

scientific content of Virgil tradition, 11, 13, 16, 98, 103, 106–07, 115, 117, 170, 172, 363 n. 189; learning at Hereford, 133–34; *see also* allegory, spiritual and scientific

Scipio Africanus, 94, 97, 351 nn. 35 and 46, 383 n. 73

Segal, Charles, 393 n. 22

sententia, as aspect of exegesis, 58, 60, 87, 90–91, 102

Serranus, 57

Servius, 8, 12, 41, 47–53, 56, 61, 93–95, 110, 123, 126; allegory in, 50–51, 94–95; in Anselm of Laon, 63–68; in England, 31, 37; as source for medieval commentaries, 12, 53, 56–58, 63, 68–70, 72–81, 84, 102, 105, 107, 111, 136, 142–43, 149–50, 155, 164, 167, 175, 287–306, 309; as source for *Roman d'Eneas*, 175–77

Servius *auctus*, 37, 50, 142, 328, 366

Seznec, Jean, 318 n. 29

Shakespeare, William, example of extra-textual access, 16, 31

ship and shipwreck, image of, 10, 26, 36, 56, 71, 94, 96, 106, 116, 124, 128–29, 134, 147–48, 179, 237, 257, 260, 277, 325 n. 71, 360 n. 150, 364 n. 206, 402 n. 102

Shirt, David, 195, 381 n. 54, 383 n. 82

Shuttleworth, Richard, 298

Sibyl, 4, 24, 75, 110, 117–18, 120, 128, 150, 226–28, 242–43, 246, 248, 359 n. 129, 393 n. 23

Silk, Edmund T., 126, 361 nn. 157 and 159, 362 n. 174

Silvia, 25, 208, 384 n. 95

Simois, 71

Simon Aurea Capra, *Ilias Latina*, 379 n. 46, 384 n. 93; as source of *House of Fame*, 396 nn. 45 and 47; as source of *Legend of Dido*, 402 n. 102, 403 nn. 109 and 112, 404 n. 122

Singerman, Jerome, 321 nn. 16 and 19, 343 n. 133, 385 n. 100

Sinon, 78, 142, 176, 366 n. 15, 389 n. 6

338 n. 89, 363 n. 195, 370 n. 73, 372 n. 110, 394 n. 31

Southern, Sir Richard W., 131, 331 n. 15, 362 nn. 180 and 183, 363 nn. 190 and 200

Spargo, John Wells, 319 n. 6

Spence, Sarah, 360 n. 143, 398 n. 70

Spenser, *Faerie Queene*, 14, 270, 281–83, 406 n. 20

stage production, medieval view of classical, 149

Stanyhurst, Richard, translator of *Aeneid*, 283–84, 289

Statius, *Thebaid*, 33, 298, 317 n. 20, 387 n. 121, 389 n. 4

Steadman, John M., 237, 392 n. 18

Stock, Brian, 351 n. 48, 352 nn. 52 and 56–57

Styx, 95

Suerbaum, Werner, 32, 317 n. 23, 318 n. 28, 319 nn. 2 and 7, 320 n. 9, 324 n. 59, 325 n. 66, 360 n. 143

suicide, 25, 26, 28, 197, 203, 205, 234, 259–60, 267

summaries of *Aeneid*, 8, 20, 35–36, 378 n. 39, 406 n. 20; in *accessus*, 176–77, 187, 231, 358 n. 117; in allegorical commentaries, 108, 114–15, 117; in marginal commentaries, 71, 74, 81, 142, 146, 148; pseudo-Ovidian verses, 42, 277, 285–308; *see also* topic headings

Sychaeus (Sicheüs), 151, 186, 190, 193, 195–97, 396 n. 46, 402 n. 97

Symmachus, in Macrobius, *Saturnalia*, 93, 350 n. 28

syntactic exegesis, 50, 54, 58, 68, 73, 297, 305

Syrtes, 56

technological imagery, 181, 184, 190, 192–93, 205, 275

Terence, 33, 322 n. 23

Tertullian, 21, 32

Teucer, 76, 176–77, 378 n. 37

textuality, 5, 6, 15, 231, 233, 272

Theodulus, *Ecloga*, 150, 368 n. 58; commentary of Bernard of Utrecht, 369 n. 59

Theseus, 68

Thomson, Rodney M., 131, 363 n. 188

Tiber, 78, 143, 277

Tilliette, Jean-Yves, 338 n. 94

Tiptoft, John, 309

Tisdale, C. P. R., 392 n. 18, 397 nn. 54 and 56

Tityus, 118

tomb, 189, 199, 203–06, 211, 214, 384 n. 92, 385 nn. 98 and 103, 386 nn. 106 and 111–13, 387 nn. 118 and 120

topic headings in Virgil exegesis, 71, 81, 292, 304, 307, 368 n. 46, 371 n. 103

Tortelli, Giovanni, 80–82, 346 nn. 161 and 165

Toulouse, as site of classical studies, 34

Tournai, foundation myth, 177

translatio imperii, 46

Trevet, Nicholas, classical citations, 370 n. 73; commentary on *Consolation of Philosophy*, 129, 318 n. 29, 362 n. 174; on *Aeneid*, wrongly attributed, 347 n. 2, 365 n. 4; on *Eclogues*, 138, 362 n. 174, 365 n. 4, 371 n. 89, 372 n. 105; on Augustine's *City of God*, 369 nn. 61 and 65

Trésor des hystoires, 23, 324 n. 53

Troilus, 76, 344 n. 143

Troy, 1–4, 51, 71, 77; in Bernard Silvestris, 113–14, 116; and dynastic genealogy, 40, 76, 156, 177, 202–03, 273, 282; fall of, 18–20, 64, 66, 75, 133, 178, 185, 234, 257–58, 277, 282; matter of, 18–22, 40, 78, 137, 168, 174, 177–80, 187, 220–22, 258, 270–71, 274; names of, 78, 147; women of, 185–86

Turnus, 24–26, 175, 177, 179–80, 183, 202–03, 206–12, 214, 216, 218, 234, 371 n. 103, 378 n. 34, 384 n. 95, 385 n. 97, 387 n. 123, 388 nn. 133 and 134, 406 n. 22

Tuttle Hansen, Elaine, 390 n. 10, 399 n. 72, 401 n. 88, 402 n. 99

tyranny and readership in *Legend of Good Women*, 249, 251–55, 266

Tyrians, 147, 188, 383 n. 84

Ullmann, B. L., 327 n. 87

Ulysses, 68, 178, 381 n. 55

underworld, 24–25, 67, 92, 94–95, 108, 110, 116–18, 124–25, 128, 156–57, 201–02, 226, 228, 234, 241–46, 248, 254, 277

utilitas, topic in *accessus*, 113–14, 176, 357 n. 111, 377 n. 32

veil (*velamen*), image for allegorical exegesis, 97, 100–01, 104–05, 254, 256

Venus, 55, 59, 71, 74–75, 94, 95, 104, 134, 142, 147, 151, 157, 174–75, 180–86, 188, 193, 206, 225–27, 229, 231, 233–34, 236–38, 240, 243, 246, 257–61, 263, 279

vernacular and Troy tradition, 1–2, 5, 8, 10–11, 13–16, 20–24, 26, 28–29, 34, 39, 55, 62–63, 137, 159, 168–71, 173, 175, 180, 185, 187, 211, 220–21, 223, 247, 271–72, 274, 277

Vesta, 55–56, 66, 149, 335 n. 62, 341 n. 113

Virgil (P. Virgilius Maro)
Aeneid, passages cited or annotated
Book 1: 1 (26, 51, 64–65, 102, 314,
340 nn. 105 and 106, 392 n. 17), 1–4 (36,
103), 2 (65), 3 (341 n. 110), 5 (335 n. 58),
6 (107, 176), 8 (314, 341 n. 109, 353
nn. 67 and 68, 377 n. 23), 11 (335 n. 58),
12 (71, 378 n. 33), 14 (191), 14–18 (104),
15 (106), 16 (55), 20 (335 n. 58), 22 (77),
32 (67), 34 (74, 314, 372 n. 104), 35 (354
n. 71), 36 (394 n. 33), 41 (155), 47 (94), 52
(75, 394 n. 33), 61 (340 n. 106), 64 (353
n. 68), 71 (94, 383 n. 73), 72 (75), 73 (335
n. 58), 76 (394 n. 33), 76–80 (342 n. 119),
77 (62, 73), 78 (94), 81 (106), 83 (343
n. 127), 88 (354 n. 71), 92 (372 n. 104), 94
(67), 94–101 (175), 100 (55), 107 (54), 111
(336 n. 67), 113 (55), 124 (74), 132 (74),
135 (354 n. 71), 138 (102), 159 (73), 171
(155), 177 (335 n. 61), 180 (71), 183 (55),
198 ff. (36), 204–06 (155, 325 n. 71), 208
(151), 213 (63), 223 (94), 235 (378 nn. 37
and 38), 237 (341 n. 107), 242 (152, 354
n. 71), 245 (378 n. 37), 254 (354 n. 71),
265–71 (66), 275 (336 n. 73), 284 (344
n. 147), 285 (76), 286 (76), 289 (76), 291
ff. (66), 292 (55, 56), 294 (77), 295 (155),
297 (354 n. 71), 312 (94), 317 (346
n. 155), 323 (341 n. 107), 340 (402
n. 105), 345 (151), 348 (354 n. 71), 349
(190), 367 (382 nn. 66 and 68), 367–68
(190), 380 (378 n. 37), 393–400 (238), 403
(55), 404 (343 n. 128), 416 (77, 344
n. 139), 420 (343 n. 131), 441 ff. (75), 443
(75), 446 (402 n. 105), 447 (245), 448–49
(226), 455–64 (225), 456–70 (396 n. 43),
463 (226), 464 (128), 468 (78), 469 (344
n. 142), 474 (76), 479–80 (396 n. 43), 488
(396 n. 43), 498 (55), 500 (55), 502 (56),
520 (344 n. 142), 532 (57), 534 (313), 535
(55), 546 (354 n. 71), 587 (107), 613 (402
n. 105), 618 (75), 619 (76), 630 ff. (36),
637–42 (226), 664 (354 n. 71), 670 (402
n. 105), 672 (336 n. 76), 683 (341 n. 107),
697 (151), 700 (341 n. 112), 707 (354
n. 71), 719 (341 n. 108), 726–27 (226),
732 (155), 734 (354 n. 71), 736 ff. (151,
335 n. 59), 738 (160), 741 (55), 749 (402
n. 105)
Book 2: 1 (336 n. 74), 3–5 (133), 13
(354 n. 71), 16 (336 n. 73), 133 (377
n. 29), 152 (78), 166 (75), 193 (78), 201
(344 n. 102), 234 (186), 268–97 (3),
274–86 (324 n. 59), 288 (343 n. 131), 293
(228), 298 (79), 310–11 (54), 312 (345

n. 155), 316 (337 n. 84), 352 (59), 355
(152), 369 (325 n. 68), 379 (152), 390 (72,
166), 419 (370 n. 83), 541 (344 n. 142),
597 (394 n. 33), 601 (344 n. 142), 604–06
(228), 632 (59, 157), 639 (377 n. 23), 651
(394 n. 33), 738 (394 n. 33), 781–82 (78)
Book 3: 21 (59), 24 (74), 26 (59), 44
(154), 49 (72), 56–57 (154), 74 (5), 80 (77),
96 (115–16, 124, 128, 177, 206, 228), 102
(378 n. 37), 103 (377 n. 23), 104 (37
n. 37), 111 (74), 119 (59), 147–71 (228),
165 (78), 167 (344 n. 142), 167–68 (206),
211 (58), 241 (344 n. 138), 261 (151), 302
(71), 374–462 (228), 379 (79), 402 (336
n. 72), 423 (336 n. 70), 444 (75), 444–47
(243), 468 (337 n. 82), 484 (335 n. 59),
492 (151), 511 (337 n. 76), 522 (151), 598
(151), 609 (152), 646–47 (74), 689 (77)
Book 4: 9 (188), 24–29 (396 n. 46), 31
(55), 51 (382 n. 59), 52 (336 n. 63), 68
(402 n. 105), 74–79 (383 n. 79), 86 (370
n. 80), 86–89 (186), 134–39 (383 n. 80),
173–90 (240), 174–77 (36, 125, 327
n. 89), 176 (370 n. 83), 180 (395 n. 37),
183 (360 n. 151), 193 (196), 215 (390
n. 10), 274–75 (395 n. 35), 287 (153),
305–09 (382 n. 59), 320–30 (382 n. 61),
331 (153), 347 (153), 365–70 (188),
380–81 (188), 412 (336 n. 70), 441–49
(154), 450 (402
n. 105), 460–68 (186), 468 (267), 596 (402
n. 105), 612 (370 n. 81), 621–29 (200),
651–53 (404 n. 121), 655–60 (186)
Book 5: 24 (336 n. 72), 104 (371
n. 103), 105 (370 n. 82), 291 (152),
687–88 (360 n. 150), 735 (377 n. 24), 751
(335 n. 59), 812–13 (360 n. 148)
Book 6: 1 ff. (92), 2 (359 n. 129), 3–4
(128–29, 360 n. 150), 6–7 (359 n. 129),
13–14 (120), 14 (380 n. 48), 32–33
(245–46), 34 (227), 35 (120), 37 (226),
42–81 (243), 49 (118), 62 (336 n. 70), 118
(120–21), 136–37 (67, 95, 110–12), 154
(342
n. 118), 165 (335 n. 61), 170 (257), 179
(120), 204–11 (118), 273 (117), 274–76
(125), 276–81 (398 n. 66), 286 (95), 305 ff.
(243), 306 (358 n. 124), 312 (257), 314–41
(257), 364 (156, 261), 404 (377 n. 24), 406
(107, 357 n. 105), 424 (118), 426 (95, 371
n. 103, 377 n. 24), 430 (371 n. 103), 432
(58), 434 (372 n. 103), 439 (95), 440 (372
n. 103), 450 (402 n. 105), 455–66 (202),
456 (402 n. 105), 459–60 (258), 477 (94,
372 n. 103), 486 (398 n. 67), 496 (261),

505 (345 n. 155), 531 (156), 540 (325 n. 71), 565 (337 n. 76), 576 (336 n. 63), 581 (372 n. 103), 613 (67), 617–18 (257), 636 (120), 638 (372 n. 103), 657–94 (259), 679 (120), 681–82 (385 n. 103), 686 (261), 699 (124), 703–51 (119), 705 (95), 714 (95), 716–18 (386 n. 103), 719 (311–12), 724 ff. (60, 121, 127, 129, 156, 370 n. 82), 728 (370 n. 82), 743 (337 n. 76), 745 (370 n. 82), 781 (156), 783 (337 n. 82), 793 (156), 803 (57), 844 (57), 893–99 (229)

Book 7: 59 (71), 68–69 (388 n. 126), 84 (337 n. 82), 98 (388 n. 126), 136 (34, n. 138), 142 (343 n. 131), 180 (354 n. 71), 206 (337 n. 82), 213–48 (388 n. 127), 302 (56), 315 (75), 535 (157), 634 (341 n.109), 647 (372 n. 103), 803 (157, 372 n. 103)

Book 8: 12 (335 n. 60), 21 (152), 97–101 (180), 143 (151), 190 (157), 203 (157), 257 (157), 281 (152), 337–61 (180), 460 (370 n. 71), 511–12 (157), 532 (157), 570 (152), 626–731 (180)

Book 9: 1 (71), 176–250 (161), 176–502 (201), 261–439 (162), 266 (402 n. 105), 359–66 (387 nn. 117), 504 (160), 774–77 (406 n. 22)

Book 11: 74 (402 n. 105), 165 (203), 180 (203), 186 (377 n. 30), 227 (335 n. 60), 774–75 (205), 803 (205)

attributed and spurious works

Copa, 301, 308

Culex, 287, 301, 310

De pulice, 309

De rosis nascentibus, 301

"Epitaphium uirgilii," 294

"Exprobacio in uetulam," 291

"Ille ego…" (spurious opening lines of *Aeneid*), 42, 287, 290–91, 295, 301, 303–04, 306, 313

"Mantua me genuit" (epitaph), 291, 301, 306

Moretum, 301, 308

Vir bonus, 301

Eclogues, 5, 22, 35, 37, 40, 44, 64, 96, 123, 138, 285, 287, 289, 290–92, 295–96, 298, 300–09, 315 n. 9, 319 n. 7, 348 n. 7

Georgics, 5, 31, 35, 37, 44, 56, 96, 285,

287, 289–92, 295–96, 298, 301–09, 315 n. 9, 348 n. 7, 359 n. 142

Vita Virgiliana, 277, 285, 295–96, 305, 309, 334 n. 46, 348 n. 8; Bernensis, 289, 293; Donatiana, 123, 293, 348 n. 8; Noricensis, 293

Volscens, 162

von Veldeke, Heinrich, *Eneit*, 22–23, 25, 29, 322 n. 26

Vulcan, 54, 149, 180–82, 184, 191

Walden, Wylelmus, 302

Walsyngham, John, 305

Walter of Châtillon, 62; *Alexandreis*, 296

Warner, Thomas, 302

wealth, 111, 190–99, 203, 264, 270, 275, 282–83

West Country, 38, 44–45, 330 n. 9

Westhaugh, Thomas, 292

Wetherbee, Winthrop, 115, 317 n. 20, 332 n. 119, 338 n. 93, 351 n. 48, 352 nn. 57 and 60, 358 n. 118, 362 n. 179, 387 n. 121, 389 n. 4

Whitbread, Leslie G., 97, 319 n. 4, 351 n. 37, 357 n. 99, 360 nn. 149 and 152, 361 n. 153

William of Conches, 60, 352 n. 52, 358 nn. 114 and 119, 361 nn. 156 and 164, 362 n. 182, 400 n. 186

William of Malmesbury, 38, 131, 363 n. 188

William of Poitiers, 325 n. 68

William the Conqueror, 210, 325 n. 68

Wilson, William S., 394 n. 30

Wood, Thomas, 294

Worcester, and classical reading, 31, 38, 132, 287, 301

Yarker, Luke, 298

Yarmouth, 143

youth, in allegorical exegesis, 95, 96, 106, 110, 111, 116

Ysagoge in theologiam, 356 n. 95

Yunck, John A., 192, 196–97, 204, 374 n. 2, 376 n. 21, 384 n. 91, 386 n. 114

Zabughin, Vladimiro, 317 n. 22